The 5th Battalion of the 60th (Royal American) Regiment was the first rifle battalion in the regular British Army. Raised in 1797, it marked a significant step in the development of British light infantry and rifle corps. Lieutenant Colonel Francis de Rottenburg, the battalion's commander for almost 10 years, formulated the first British Army light infantry manual.

After serving in Ireland during the 1798 Rebellion, in the West Indies, and in the Americas, the battalion rose to fame during the Peninsular War. It was one of only three battalions to be present from the initial landings in Portugal through to the invasion of France and victory six years later. Divided between the brigades of Wellington's army to provide specialist rifle and skirmishing capability, the riflemen often formed advance or rear guards, patrols, and outposts. Frequently praised by Wellington and his divisional commanders, the battalion won 16 battle honours.

Drawing on official records, memoirs, court martial transcripts, inspection reports, and unpublished letters, *Riflemen* recounts not only the campaigns in which the battalion fought, but also many personal stories of the soldiers who served with it. *Riflemen* includes tales of murder, promotion from the ranks, desertion, prisoners of war, and small actions that are often overlooked. As the first history of the battalion written in almost 100 years, it sheds new light on a vital component of Wellington's army and its important place in the history of the British Army.

Ever since he picked up the first of Bernard Cornwell's Sharpe books as a teenager, Robert Griffith has been passionately interested in the Napoleonic period. As the author of several historical fiction novels set during the long wars against the French, and an ardent Napoleonic re-enactor, he has long strived to bring alive the stories of the men who fought for Britain against the armies of Napoleon. Having now turned to writing history he exhaustively researches his subjects to draw out previously overlooked details of both the campaigns and the everyday life of Napoleonic soldiers.

Riflemen

The History of the 5th Battalion 60th (Royal American) Regiment, 1797-1818

Robert Griffith

Helion & Company

Helion & Company Limited
Unit 8 Amherst Business Centre
Budbrooke Road
Warwick
CV34 5WE
England
Tel. 01926 499619
Email: info@helion.co.uk
Website: www.helion.co.uk
Twitter: @helionbooks
Visit our blog at http://blog.helion.co.uk/

Published by Helion & Company 2019. Reprinted in paperback 2021
Designed and typeset by Mach 3 Solutions Ltd (www.mach3solutions.co.uk)
Cover designed by Paul Hewitt, Battlefield Design (www.battlefield-design.co.uk)

ISBN 978-1-914059-63-6

British Library Cataloguing-in-Publication Data.
A catalogue record for this book is available from the British Library.

Contents

List of Plates

List of Colour Plates

List of Maps

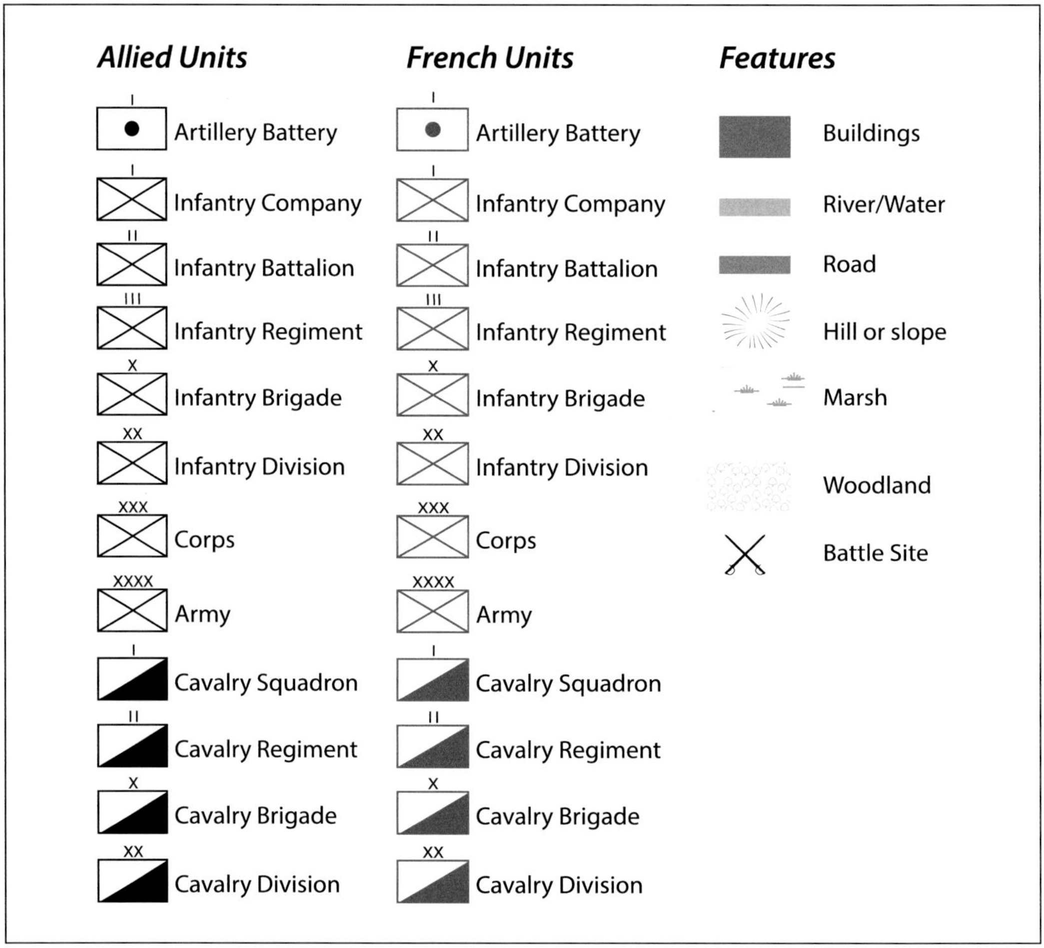

Key to Map Symbols.

Preface

The 5th Battalion of the 60th (Royal American) Regiment was the first rifle battalion in the British Army. One of its commanders wrote the regulations for light and rifle-armed infantry, and it was one of only three battalions to be present for the whole of the Peninsular War from 1808 to 1814, during which it won 16 battle honours and was praised in Wellington's dispatches many times.

The 5th Battalion was split into detached companies and fought with five of the eight Anglo-Portuguese divisions that Wellington eventually fielded. They often provided the advance and rear guards, and manned the pickets or outposts of the army close to the enemy. In battle they were usually the first troops to fire as the French columns approached the allies' positions, and were ruthlessly efficient in picking off French officers and NCOs.

However, despite the 5th Battalion's distinguished record, the popular perception of a Napoleonic rifleman begins and ends with the much more famous 95th. There are several reasons for this. Firstly, around a dozen memoirs came from the 95th in the years following the wars, whereas not one came from the 5th Battalion. The second reason is Richard Sharpe, fictitious rifleman of the 95th and protagonist in Bernard Cornwell's series of books and the subsequent popular television series. Sharpe has coloured the public's perception of Wellington's army now for decades.

Perhaps the most important reason for the 5th Battalion being overlooked is that the riflemen, and many of the officers, were mostly Germans and not British. Formed from specialist foreign regiments of riflemen, the 5th Battalion recruited exclusively from Europe, and also from prisoners of war. Britain and Ireland could not provide enough volunteers for the Army so foreign recruitment was vital to the war effort. The 5th Battalion was eventually made up of men from almost every country in Europe, except France.

Two previous histories of the battalion have been written, one in the 19th century and one in the early 20th. Both give a good outline of the services of the battalion but, in common with many regimental histories of the time, they focus on the officers, rarely mentioning the ordinary soldiers. Using the original regimental returns and pay lists, I have tried to tease out as many stories of the rank and file as I can. I have also found courts martial records to be a rare source of reading the riflemen's own words. The cases I have found cover everything from a murder, to desertions, accusations of cowardice, and petty squabbles between the officers. I have also found two previously unpublished series of letters from officers who served with the battalion. With no memoirs written by the riflemen themselves I have also turned to the many mentions of the battalion in the memoirs of the men they served beside.

With so many nationalities represented in the records, deciphering the names on the documents has been a challenge. The spellings can vary widely and most of the first names are often anglicised. I have generally favoured consistency and chosen the most often used form of an individual's name, even if initially they often used a slightly different form. As far as place names are concerned they also vary widely in the original documents and where necessary I have prioritised enabling the reader to find the place on a modern map rather than using the contemporary spelling.

The 5th Battalion deserves a far more prominent place in the history of the British Army than it currently holds, and also in the history of the Peninsular War. I shall leave the last word of this preface to Sir Arthur Wellesley, the future Duke of Wellington, who replied to a report from one of his brigade commanders in 1809 with: 'I am delighted with your account of the 5th battalion 60th regiment. Indeed every thing that I have seen and known of that excellent corps has borne the same stamp'.

Acknowledgements

Riflemen is my first work of military history and it would not have been possible without the encouragement and assistance of many individuals and institutions. The foremost amongst these is Steve Davies, founder of the 5/60th Living History Society. Steve welcomed me into the group, introduced me to the rich history of the battalion, and, crucially, bowed out when approached by Helion to write this book and offered them my name instead. Since then he has been a constant source of support, as have the rest of the group who have put up with my increasingly large fund of anecdotes around many camp fires. Next on the list is my editor, Dr. Andrew Bamford; an experienced military historian and author himself, he has been extremely patient with my many questions and constantly supportive. My wife Natalie has also been there for me and taken the strain when the project began to take more and more of my time.

Adrienne Hopf, Dr. Andrew Cormack, and Marc Middleton were very generous with their time and translated the letters of John Galiffe for me. I also could not have written this book without the wonderful staff at The National Archives, the National Army Museum, Royal Green Jackets Museum, Hampshire Record Office, Warwickshire County Record Office, the Albany Institute of History & Art, and the War Heritage Institute in Brussels. I would also like to thank the University of Southampton for permission to quote from MS61, The Duke of Wellington's papers. Jan Starnes at auctioneers Dix Noonan Webb was also incredibly helpful when I sought permission to use images of two lots they had sold relating to the 5th Battalion. Eamonn O'Keeffe, Zack White, Ian Soulsby, Paul Demet, Jonathan Rogers, and Ben Townsend have also very kindly shared their knowledge and opinions with me when I needed them.

Lastly, and in many ways most importantly, I would like to thank the descendants of the riflemen of the 5th Battalion whom I have made contact with and who have shared their family histories; Rodney Galiffe, Alan Brown, Michael Cayley, and Julia Love have all helped to remind me that I was writing about real people, and not just faded names on old forms.

1

Formation

When France declared war on Britain on 1 February 1793 the British Army was ill prepared for a conflict that would last, with one brief respite, for over 20 years. It was too small, poorly trained, badly organised and many of its commanders clung to outmoded tactics and doctrines. Long term public and parliamentary distrust of a standing army dating back to the English Civil War, the Glorious Revolution, and the sometimes heavy-handed use of the army to suppress dissent, meant that Parliament kept the establishment and the budget of the army dangerously low. The total strength of the Army was 38,945, but only 10,993 soldiers were actually in Britain (along with a further 8,450 county militia). There were 9,644 in Ireland, and 18,308 spread between the West Indies, North America, India, and other colonies.[1] As well as its role in national defence, the Army in Britain and Ireland had a policing role; supporting local magistrates, combatting smugglers and coping with the recent phenomenon of industrial unrest. This required the Army to be spread thinly around the country in small units, so it was difficult to gather sufficient troops for commanders to gain experience in manoeuvring large bodies of men. The use of the Army in the suppression of disorder made soldiering an unpopular career, limiting both the number and quality of recruits. The Army also answered to three masters with the home secretary, foreign secretary, and colonial secretary all competing for troops.[2] It was not until 1794 that the position of secretary of state for war was created, but even then they still had to negotiate with the home secretary for resources.

The Army needed men, and it needed them quickly, if it was going to be able to adequately defend the country, let alone field a force capable of aiding Britain's allies on the continent against France's army of 550,000.[3] The British Army was made up solely of volunteers with forced conscription being politically unthinkable, and so the fastest method of expanding the army was to hire soldiers from other countries. By July 1794 nearly 20,000 troops had been hired from the Germans states of Hannover, Hesse Cassel, Hesse Darmstadt and Baden.[4] Such transnational recruitment was commonplace and Britain had relied on regiments hired from the rulers of the plethora of small German duchies and electorates

1 Return of the Effective Men in the British Army 1793-1806, The National Archives (TNA), WO 1/903, p.33.

2 D. Gates, *The British Light Infantry Arm c. 1790-1815* (London: Batsford, 1987), p.37.

3 F. C. Schneid, *European Armies of the French Revolution 1789-1802* (Norman: University of Oklahoma Press, 2015), p.21.

4 P. Demet, *We Are Accustomed to do Our Duty* (Warwick: Helion & Company, 2018), p.223.

throughout the wars of the 18th century. Hiring out such regiments was very lucrative for small nations with few other resources; their merchants would profit from outfitting the regiments, and the ruler could maintain a larger army and hence play a greater role on the European stage. During the American War of Independence between a third and a half of the British forces in the field were German.[5] It was not only Britain that used foreign troops; both France and Spain had long traditions of regiments composed of Swiss, German, and even Irish recruits. Such regiments existed for historical or religious reasons, or to provide a state with specialist soldiers that would be difficult to recruit from within its own borders. Soldiers from one country that enlisted in another country's army were not mercenaries, and are still not counted as such today. Mercenaries are soldiers hired separately to a regular army, usually at different rates of pay and terms of service.

The British Army and the German auxiliary units were soon in action on the continent. The small force sent to the Netherlands in the spring of 1793 under the Duke of York is remembered more for the nursery rhyme than for any great victories. British troops fought alongside Hanoverians, Dutch, Austrians, and others. The duke, second son of George III, did have some successes but overall the campaign served to underline the failings of the Army's organisation, tactics and training, and also Britain's lack of certain types of troops. It cost men the Army could not afford to lose, as did the campaign amongst the valuable colonies of the West Indies, where disease consumed men in far greater numbers than enemy action. In 1795 France signed a series of peace treaties with the German states, the terms of which included clauses that prevented the hiring out of their armies.[6] Another source of recruits had to be found.

The Enlistment Act of 1794 enabled the creation of regiments of foreign recruits and many were formed from French émigrés who had fled from the chaos and terror of the Revolution. Some were created from entire émigré regiments that had been in the service of countries defeated by France, while others were formed by foreign noblemen or British officers. The contracts governing these units were called capitulations and they set out the size of the corps, its arms, and the fees to be paid. Mostly these foreign corps were raised for principled reasons by royalists and others who wanted to overthrow the Revolutionary regime, or at least halt its spread, but some were raised for profit by their colonel-proprietors who aimed to pocket the difference between the fees paid by the government and those paid to the troops. Similarly the recruits themselves enlisted for a variety of reasons, from anti-Revolutionary fervour, to those seeking plunder, those escaping debts or poverty, or those looking to just take the bounty and then desert.[7] By 1795 the émigré corps numbered 14,832 infantry and 5,057 cavalry, or over 15 percent of the British Army's infantry and over 33 percent of its cavalry.[8]

5 M. Wishon, *German Forces and the British Army; Interactions and Perceptions 1742-1815* (Basingstoke: Palgrave Macmillan, 2013), p.15.

6 P. Demet, *Our Duty*, p.111.

7 C.T. Atkinson, 'Foreign Regiments in the British Army 1793-1802 – Part 1', *Journal of the Society of Army Historical Research*, Vol. XXI, p.175.

8 N. Arielli & B. Collins, (eds.), *Transnational Soldiers – Foreign Military Enlistment in the Modern Era* (Basingstoke: Palgrave Macmillan, 2013), p.54.

The quality of these myriad of regiments was highly variable. For example, the Loyal Emigrants were known for their bravery, hard fighting and discipline.[9] However, many other units failed to reach their establishment and were quickly disbanded; some found it difficult to replenish their ranks and were forced to recruit from French prisoners of war, lowering the quality of what may have begun as a good regiment. The foreign corps ended up containing recruits from almost every part of Europe, but German recruits were particularly sought after. There was a perception that Germans made good soldiers; obedient, steadfast, sober and professional.[10] The British monarchy had strong links to Germany, as the first three Georges were head of state in Hannover as well as Britain, and, historically, British and German interests seldom clashed. German soldiers also had a strong reputation as being very good light infantry, a type of soldier that Britain desperately needed.

A lack of light infantry was one of the shortcomings that had been highlighted by the Duke of York's campaign in the Low Countries and one that he sought to address once he became commander-in-chief of the Army in 1795. Most infantry at the time fought in tightly packed ranks, manoeuvring as solid blocks of troops and delivering rapid volleys of musket fire. Regimentation, precision of drill, discipline, and speed of reloading were more important than accuracy when thousands of troops were firing at each other at short range. Light infantry on the other hand operated in smaller units, often well ahead of the main army, fighting what was called at the time *le petit guerre*. They provided advance and rear guards, outposts and patrols, and formed screens of skirmishers that protected the main force from the enemy's light infantry. They needed to be able to think for themselves, and were taught to aim for individual targets. The line infantry were armed with smooth-bore muskets that were quick to load but wildly inaccurate beyond 100 yards. Many German light infantry units on the continent were armed with rifled muskets, or shorter carbines, which could hit a man at 200 or even 300 yards, but they were slower to load. There was a tradition of hunting and shooting with rifled guns in Germany that meant that German *jägers* were very much sought after, and were recruited by many of Europe's armies. The terms for light infantry, such as *jägers* or *chasseurs*, derived from the words for hunters in German and French.

The early campaigns of the war had seen the French using large numbers of poorly trained troops as makeshift light infantry because there had not been the time to train the raw recruits in the intricacies of line infantry drill. The French army had also historically recognised the importance of light infantry skills, with many specialist regiments and good training across the army. Such hordes of skirmishers proved difficult for the British Army to counter because they had too few light infantry troops of their own. The French would take cover or retreat as the British line infantry manoeuvred to deliver their volleys, returning again when it was safe. The British had learned similar hard lessons in both the Seven Years War and American War of Independence. During both conflicts innovative officers had come to recognise the need for well-trained light infantry to counter skirmishers and irregular troops, but such units that had been formed or hired had been allowed to lapse at the end of the wars and light infantry skills continued to be neglected and institutionally

9 C.T. Atkinson, 'Foreign Regiments in the British Army 1793-1802 – Part 2', *Journal of the Society of Army Historical Research*, Vol. XXII, p.3.

10 Wishon, *German Forces*, p.27.

resisted. There was a feeling amongst some British officers that the independence required of light troops undermined discipline and cohesion when fighting in line.[11]

Many of the foreign corps formed in 1795 and afterwards were light infantry units, often armed at least partially with rifles and recruited predominantly from Germany. Prince Charles of Lowenstein-Wertheim, from the small German state of that name, raised a regiment of chasseurs armed with rifles in May 1794. By August they were in the service of the Dutch Republic. Composed of mainly Swiss and Alsatian soldiers, along with Prussians and even Russians, they were noted for their enthusiasm, courage, and the 'ability to use the advantage of the terrain, the quality of their carbines, the extraordinary habit they had to shoot and be constantly exposed to fire'.[12] The chasseurs retreated into Hannover in the spring of the following year and were taken into British service in January 1795. Beginning as one battalion of eight companies, the Lowenstein Chasseurs grew to 12 companies across two battalions and were very well regarded.[13]

The Chasseurs, commanded by Lieutenant Colonel Frederick von Schlammersdorf, sailed for Britain in November 1795. One of the transports was wrecked off Calais but fortunately all 150 men on board were rescued. Sailing to a posting in the West Indies in January 1796 the Chasseurs were caught in a severe storm and forced back, with another of their transports sinking, but once more the men were rescued. When they sailed again a month later yet another ship sank, this time with 100 men being lost. They did eventually reach the West Indies and took part in the attack on St Lucia under Sir Ralph Abercromby. They were the only foreign corps about which he was complimentary. Both the first and second battalions of the Chasseurs took part in other actions around the Caribbean through 1796 and 1797, but it was disease more than the French that thinned their ranks. They arrived in the West Indies with 1,063 men and by the end of 1797 this had been slashed to 573.[14]

Lowenstein also formed another regiment, Lowenstein's Fusiliers, at the Isle of Wight in early 1796. A fusil was a term for a lighter musket often carried by light infantry, and in German states light infantry units were often were called fusiliers. However, in France and Britain fusiliers were usually ordinary line infantry. The Fusiliers capitulation specified that they were also to be partially armed with rifles. They were commanded by Lieutenant Colonel Baron Lancelot Lindenbaum, and by the autumn of 1796 they were up to strength, but when inspected by Abercromby, who had returned briefly from the West Indies, he found them to be inferior to the Chasseurs.[15] The Fusiliers were sent to the Caribbean at the start of 1797 and took part in Abercromby's unsuccessful attack on Puerto Rico where they recorded a loss of 100 men, up to 70 of whom may have deserted. Arriving in the West Indies with a strength of 967, the Fusiliers mustered 809 by the end of the year.[16]

11 Gates, *British Light Infantry*, p.23.

12 R. Grouvel, *Les Corps de Troupe L'Émigration Française (1789-1815)* (Paris: Les Édtions de la Sabretache, 1857), p.260 (translated).

13 C.T. Atkinson, 'Foreign Regiments in the British Army 1793-1802 – Part 6', *Journal of the Society of Army Historical Research,* Vol. XXII, p.248.

14 Atkinson, 'Foreign Regiments – Part 6', p.248.

15 Atkinson, 'Foreign Regiments – Part 6', p.249.

16 Atkinson, 'Foreign Regiments – Part 6', p.250.

At the same time as Lowenstein's Fusiliers were forming on the Isle of Wight another unit of German troops was also being raised. Baron Charles Hompesch had already successfully raised a regiment of light cavalry, Hompesch's Hussars, and his younger brother Ferdinand followed suit by forming Hompesch's Light Infantry. By October 1796 the unit had a strength of 460 chasseurs and 690 fusiliers, commanded by Lieutenant Colonel Baron Francis de Rottenburg. The fusiliers were armed with long rifled muskets and the chasseurs armed with shorter rifled carbines.[17]

Colonel Nesbitt, inspector general of foreign corps, found the Hompesch Light Infantry to be excellent with a good standard of equipment and men.[18] The bulk of the Hompesch Light Infantry, 933 officers and men, sailed for the West Indies at the start of 1797 and were present at the attack on Trinidad where they subsequently stayed for most of the year.[19] The government had agreed to an augmentation of Hompesch's regiment by adding *chasseurs à cheval*, who were to be mounted riflemen and attached to the infantry, and also further companies of chasseurs. These new companies remained at the Isle of Wight, with de Rottenburg, because they had not yet fully recruited or received all of their equipment.[20] A return of the Hompesch regimental depot, dated 10 May 1797 shows three companies of *chasseurs à cheval* and one of *chasseurs à pied* with a total strength of 468 men, with 17 wives and five children.[21]

However, all was not well with the foreign corps. In February Nesbitt had found the Hompesch Chasseurs to be lacking clothing, arms, and equipment. The men of Lowenstein's Fusiliers on duty at Sandown Fort had had to borrow equipment and forage caps, and the York Rangers and Royal Foreigners only had great coats to wear. He went on to comment further on the foreign corps' clothing and infestations of lice:

> I think it a pity to be sending away men in this way, they should be at least covered with Slop clothing, & if possible an officer with each corps' depot to go with 50 or so at a time. A number of the men arrived lately from the Continent are Itched. They complain much of the filth and nastiness on board of the Hulk at Cuxhaven. They ought to have a separate place for those who want Butter & Brimston; & where it ought to be used and that not sparingly. The disorder has now got so much into the bedding at E. Cowes, that it ought all to be changed, and a new plan adopted for curing the men as they arrive here.[22]

Plans were already afoot to reduce the number of foreign corps. In an undated note Nesbitt listed the foreign corps as: Prince of Wales' Hussars, Duke of York's Hussars, Lowenstein's Chasseurs, Hompesch's Light Infantry, Lowenstein's Fusiliers, the York Rangers, Royal Foreigners, Waldstein's, and Wittgenstein's. He estimated their total strength to be 1,600

17 Atkinson, 'Foreign Regiments – Part 6', pp.240-1.

18 C.T. Atkinson, 'Foreign Regiments in the British Army 1793-1802 – Part 4', *Journal of the Society of Army Historical Research*, Vol. XXII, p.114.

19 Atkinson, 'Foreign Regiments – Part 6', pp.240-1.

20 Nesbit to Horse Guards, 19 April 1797, TNA, WO 1/900, pp.99-101.

21 Return for depot of Regiment de Hompesch 10 May 1797, TNA, WO 1/900, p.117.

22 Memorandum 3 February 1797, TNA, WO 1/900, p.13.

cavalry, 1,300 chasseurs, 2,500 light infantry, and 4,000 line infantry. He also noted that 'Hompesch's corps has at present 3 companies of riflemen & three companies of mounted riflemen. Both being a kind of troop we never can possess by any other means it would perhaps be advisable to keep up.' He listed Rohan's Cavalry, the Loyal Emigrants, and the Legion of Domingo as 'to be reduced'.[23]

Part of the problem with the foreign corps was that so many had been devastated by disease in the West Indies that they were no longer effective. Also, French successes on the continent meant that it was becoming much harder to find new recruits, with the attitude of many German rulers changing and recruiters having to pay higher bounties.[24] Sustaining so many small units was getting to be uneconomic. The cost of the 11,773 soldiers of the foreign corps was £412,638 for 1797; £31,000 more than sum authorised by Parliament.[25] Something had to change but the army still desperately needed men. The costs of the war in general had risen at a much higher rate than revenue from the new taxes introduced to finance it, despite a thriving economy, and the government was seeking savings wherever it could.

Henry Dundas, Secretary of State for War, wrote to the Duke of York on 25 October 1797:

> Among the various arrangements which I have lately had the Honor of discussing with your Royal Highness with a view on the one hand to simplify, and as much as possible to place upon a footing of uniformity His Majesty's Land Forces, and on the other, to reduce within the narrowest Limits the amount of the Army Expenditure for the ensuing year, some suggestions appeared to me sufficiently matured to be submitted to His Majesty, who in consequence, has been graciously pleased to signify His Commands.
>
> 1st) That instead of continuing an Establishment of Foreign Troops in the West Indies distinct from the general Establishment of the Army, it is proposed that the several Regiments of this Description should be incorporated into the four Battalions of the 60th or Royal American, and that a 5th Battalion should be added to that Regiment in order to complete it to the number of Foreign Forces it is His Majesty's Intention to retain in British Pay for Service in America and in the West Indies.
>
> If upon a communication with these Corps any of them or any part of them should refuse to accede to this Arrangement they must be reduced and disbanded in the manner specified by their Capitulation, but the advantages of it both for the officers and men are so obvious, that this unpleasant contingency is by so means unlikely to occur for carrying it into effect. However, many Points of detail which it is unnecessary for me to observe upon, will require your Royal Highness' particular attention, for the present I shall confine myself to state generally that His Majesty's Intention that each Battalion of the 60th should consist when complete of 1000 Rank & File that some effectual means of recruiting adequate to the probable consumption of Men in the West Indies, should be established, so as to prevent any

23 Undated note but archived between April and May 1797 letters, TNA, WO 1/900, p.103.

24 Atkinson, 'Foreign Regiments – Part 2', p.12.

25 Foreign Corps Estimate 1797, TNA, WO 25/3213, p.5.

material or permanent diminution in the effective Force of the Battalions. That the 5th Battalion should be formed by incorporating the two Battalions of Lowenstein's into one, to the Command of which, if it should not appear inconvenient to your Royal Highness, I beg leave to suggest the propriety of appointing the Reigning Prince of Lowenstein, as the most likely means of obtaining his Consent to the measure, and of incurring the continuance of his Exertions in procuring Recruits for his own and the other Battalions of the Regiment. It is further His Majesty's intention that no difference should be established between this Battalion and the other four, except in what may arise from the manner of arming them with Rifle instead of common Musquets.

As I understand that the Corps of Chasseurs raised by Colonel Hompesch and now at the Isle of Wight, cannot be included in this general Arrangement, and that it will be very difficult to obtain his consent to the drafting his Battalion of Infantry, unless this Corps shall be retained in the British Service, it is His Majesty's pleasure, that your Royal Highness should authorize Colonel Nesbitt to stipulate with the Colonel for its remaining on the British Establishment for any term, not exceeding, [blank] years, on condition of his receiving no other compensation for the loss he may sustain by the reduction of his Battalion of Infantry. With respect to the compensation to be granted to the Colonels of the other Battalions reduced and drafted into the 60th as Colonel Nesbitt is the best judge of their claims & merits in this respect, it may be right for your Royal Highness to authorize him to settle the amount of it with them upon the best terms that can be made for the Public. All the other officers of the reduced Regiments who cannot in the first instance be provided for in the Battalion of the 60th should for the present be seconded upon them until vacancies corresponding to their respective Ranks shall occur in the Battalion to which they may be attached. It being intended to recruit these Battalions entirely from Germany, it does not appear right to admit Officers from other Nations on the Continent, and it is therefore His Majesty's pleasure that the French Officers, if any, in the Battalion to be drafted should receive the usual allowance granted to Foreign Officers who have served in the West Indies on their reduction instead of being attached to the 60th Regt.

Having now stated the outlines of the plan with respect to all the German troops in his Majesty's pay I shall not dwell longer on the subject, as I am persuaded your Royal Highness' judgement will best supply the details and overcome any difficulties which may attend the carrying it into execution.[26]

Dundas continued with other proposed economies for the army. This letter marks the conception of the 5th Battalion of the 60th (Royal American) Regiment, the first all-rifle regular battalion in the British Army.

The 60th was a natural home for the men of the foreign corps being reduced. The regiment had been formed in 1755 after the British Army had suffered defeats fighting French and Native American irregulars in the forests of the American colonies. It had been the idea

26 Dundas to Duke of York, 25 October 1797, TNA, WO 6/131, pp.152-9.

of a Swiss-born army agent and recruiter of somewhat dubious reputation called Jacques Prevost, who had found it expedient to leave Europe for the American colonies. He recruited several experienced Swiss officers, including Colonel Henri Bouquet who would go on to mould the 1st Battalion into an excellent light infantry unit.[27] Prevost also found space for two of his brothers in the regiment and the Prevost family would continue a close association with the 60th for many generations including, eventually, the 5th Battalion.

Initially numbered the 62nd and consisting of four battalions, it was soon re-designated the 60th following the disbandment of two regiments captured by the French. It was hoped that recruits could be found amongst Swiss and German settlers in the colonies, who were used to hunting and fighting in the forests, but recruits also came directly from Germany and even other British and Irish regiments.[28] It served through the rest of the Seven Years War with distinction, and subsequently in the American War of Independence. Its terms of service limited it to serving in North America but that definition was expanded to include the West Indies. Over the years the 3rd and 4th battalions were reduced during times of peace but then raised again when required in wartime. By 1793 the 60th was back up to four battalions and was recruited mostly from Germany, but with significant numbers of Britons and Irishmen who had been sentenced to service in the colonies. Some of the officers were also foreign, but most were British or Irish. During the subsequent two decades the 60th would grow further to eight battalions and become by far the largest regiment in the British Army.[29] The pay and conditions of the 60th were the same as for any other regiment, the one exception being that the foreign soldiers could enlist for a limited time period, usually seven years, rather than for life. Many of the men of the Lowenstein's and Hompesch regiments had enlisted for five years and their service was continued in the 60th. It was not until 1806 that limited service was introduced throughout the Army.

In December at Martinique the adjutant general to the commander-in-chief in the West Indies made arrangements for the formation of the 5th Battalion:

> Instructions for Brigadier General Cameron relative to the forming of the 5th Battalion 60th Regt.
>
> His Majesty's commands having been communicated by Field Marshall H.R.H the Duke of York to his Excellency the Commander in Chief for forming a 5th Battalion of the 60th, or Royal America Regiment of Foot according to the Establishment herewith annexed you are required to proceed to Barbados where you will give the necessary directions and make the requisite arrangements for incorporating the Regiments of Lowenstein Chasseurs and Fusiliers into the said additional Battalion of the 60th Regiment; for your further guidance on this occasion I transcribe so much of a letter from His Royal Highness the Duke of York to the Commander in Chief as relates to the business in question.

27 Gates, *Light Infantry*, p.12.

28 L. Butler, *The Annals of the King's Royal Rifle Corps* (London: Smith, Elder & Co., 1913) Vol. I, p.2.

29 R. Burnham & R. McGuigan, *The British Army against Napoleon, Facts, Lists, and Trivia 1805-1815* (Barnsley: Frontline Books, 2010), p.88.

'Sir
I have to acquaint you with His Majesty's pleasure, that the two Corps of Lowenstein's Chasseurs & Fusileers are to form a 5th Battalion of the 60th Regiment.

The 5th Battalion when formed is to be on the same footing in every respect as the other four, and for the present are to retain the Arms the Soldiers that are to be incorporated into it, are furnished with.

The different Companies of Artillery and Officers of Engineers belonging to the Foreign Corps, are until a further arrangement can take place with regard to them, to be collected and remain attached to the 5th Battalion, or if they cannot all be assembled in one spot, are notwithstanding to be borne on its strength, and to be considered belonging to it.

The Colonel of the 5th Battalion is to be a British Officer and lest any doubts should arise among the men of the corps to be incorporated relative to their present Colonels, you will assure them that they are perfectly satisfied with the arrangement proposed.'

As soon as the 5th Battalion is formed you will be pleased to transmit to my Office for the information of the Commander in Chief an exact return thereof and a List of Officers with the dates of their respective commissions.

I have the honor to be etc etc
R M Dicken
Adj General.

P.S. There will probably be found on inspection a number of men who are not fit for service which together with about twenty French and Spaniards to be Discharged at the request of Lieutenant Colonel Schlammersdorf must remain at Barbados till further orders, and not to be borne on the strength of the Regiment.[30]

The first muster roll of the 5th Battalion was dated from 25 December 1797, five days before Parliament passed the act authorising the raising of the 5th Battalion. The Act of Parliament, which amended the original act raising the 60th, stated:

I. WHEREAS it is judged expedient for the better defence of His Majesty's Colonies in America, to augment His Majesty's Sixtieth Regiment of Infantry, now consisting of four battalions of one thousand men each, by the addition of a Fifth Battalion in *America*, any of the Foreign Troops now in His Majesty's Pay, or other Foreigners who shall voluntarily enter themselves to serve in the said Fifth Battalion in *America*, and such Foreigners cannot be so well disciplined, without the assistance of some Officers who are acquainted with their manners and language: And whereas it is expedient, in the present juncture of affairs, to facilitate the speedy raising of such Fifth Battalion, and to enable a certain number of Foreign Officers to serve and receive pay as Officers in such Fifth Battalion: Be it enacted by the King's most Excellent Majesty, his heirs and successors, to augment the said Sixtieth Regiment

30 Dicken to Cameron, 28 December 1797, TNA, WO 40/11.

> of Infantry, by the addition of a Fifth Battalion, to consist of one thousand men, and to enlist as soldiers to serve in such battalion, any such Foreign troops now in His Majesty's Pay, or other Foreigners who shall voluntarily enter themselves to serve as soldiers therein in *America*.[31]

The act went on to limit the number of foreign officers in the 60th to 50, allow them half-pay when they ceased to serve with the regiment, and limited their service to America.

On a return dated 1 January 1798 the battalion numbered 1,072 officers and men.[32] Lieutenant Colonel von Schlammersdorf was placed in command and the troops drawn from the two Lowenstein regiments on Barbados. Prince Lowenstein had either not accepted the colonelcy of the battalion, or not been offered it, as the colonel-commandant of the new battalion was Major General William Morshead. Those Lowenstein Fusiliers left over, and other foreign corps, were incorporated into other battalions of the 60th. The men of the Hompesch Light Infantry in the West Indies were incorporated into the 2nd Battalion in May 1798.[33]

In January, Dicken wrote to Schlammersdorf to say:

> The Commander in Chief desires to express the entire satisfaction which he has received from the appearance of the 5th Battn. of the 60th Regt. and will make a favourable report thereof to the King. His Excellency requests Lieut. Colonel Schlammersdorf to accept his best thanks, & to communicate the same to the officers and men of the battalion under his command.[34]

Back in England, Colonel Nesbitt had been negotiating with Baron Ferdinand Hompesch about the fate of his chasseurs. Article 15 of the capitulation for Hompesch's corps prohibited any merger of the regiment without his consent.[35] In April 1797 Baron Charles Hompesch had written a long and passionate letter protesting at the proposed reduction of his regiment of hussars.[36] This protest seems to have failed; the hussars were so decimated by disease that the few survivors were returned to England in the autumn and the unit ceased to exist.[37] Dundas may have been anticipating similar resistance from Ferdinand. However Nesbitt's negotiations were successful as in January 1798 the decision was made to form the *chasseurs à cheval* on the Isle of Wight into Hompesch's Mounted Riflemen.[38] Furthermore, the *chasseurs à pied* on the Isle of Wight would, after all, join the new 5th Battalion.

Three full companies and one recruiting company totalling 372 officers and men mustered on 25 February 1798 at the recently built Albany Barracks, just outside of Cowes.[39] At the end of March the Duke of York, colonel-in-chief of the 60th, was showing off the men who

31 Augmentation of 60th Regiment Act 1797, Hampshire Record Office (HRO), 170A12W/D/0661.
32 January 1798 Return, TNA, WO 17/2489.
33 Atkinson, 'Foreign Regiments – Part 6', p.241.
34 Dicken to Schlammersdorf, 22 January 1798, TNA, WO 40/11.
35 Capitulation of Hompesch's Light Infantry, TNA, WO 24/1112, pp.255.
36 C. Hompesch to Dundas, 16 April 1797, TNA, WO 1/1100, pp.335 313.
37 Atkinson, 'Foreign Regiments – Part 6', p 242.
38 Atkinson, 'Foreign Regiments – Part 6', p.242.
39 March 1798 Pay List, TNA, WO 12/7066.

were to be added to his new battalion to his father, King George III, with the newspapers reporting:

> The Duke of York, on the King's return from court yesterday, brought with him two Hungarian soldiers, who are to serve in the 60th regiment of foot, for his Majesty's inspection. They were dressed in the regimentals of the country, which consisted of an olive-green jacket, blue pantaloons, black gaiters striped with red, and wore on their heads hussar caps with a green feather; they were accoutred with rifle-barrel guns, and went through their exercise with astonishing celerity, which their method of ramming down and drawing the charge greatly contributes to, they returning the rod into its place after it is thrown up with only one motion, instead of twirling it between the fingers as practiced by our troops; his Royal Highness has for his regiment several more of these men, who are also to be viewed by his Majesty for his approbation.[40]

The uniform of the 5th Battalion was to be based on that of the Hompesch chasseurs rather than conforming to the red jacket and white breeches of the other battalions of the 60th, or being based on the blue-grey uniforms of the Lowenstein Chasseurs. In January the king approved the proposed uniform: green coats with scarlet facings, collar, and cuffs, blue breeches with scarlet piping, and a black Hungarian style shako cap with a green plume.[41] Green was the traditional colour of German *jägers* and had been used before by smaller and volunteer rifle units but the 5th Battalion was the first regular battalion to wear the famous green jacket that was to become the hallmark of British riflemen.

40 *Northampton Mercury*, Saturday 31 March 1798.
41 Fawcett to Fauquier, 19 January 1798, TNA, WO 7/31 p.48.

2

Barons and *Jägers*

The establishment of the new 5th Battalion of the 60th was set as follows: one colonel commandant, two lieutenant colonels, two majors, seven captains, one captain lieutenant, 21 lieutenants, eight ensigns, one adjutant, one quartermaster, one surgeon, two assistant surgeons, one paymaster, one paymaster-sergeant, 52 sergeants, 50 corporals, 20 drummers, two fifers and 950 privates.[1] The drummers and fifers were used in line battalions but light infantry and rifle units used buglers. The riflemen were organised into 10 companies of 100 rank and file each, plus a recruiting company. Rank and file refers to both corporals and privates. Buglers and sergeants, who stood outside the ranks and files of the companies when they formed up, were counted separately.

Secretary of War Henry Dundas had predicted that the incorporation of the various foreign corps into the 60th could leave them over-manned in the short term, and this was certainly the case with the 5th Battalion. The merging of Lowenstein's Chasseurs and many of the officers and men of Lowenstein's Fusiliers meant that the battalion was considerably over establishment in many ranks, even before the addition of the companies of the Hompesch chasseurs on the Isle of Wight.

The first colonel-commandant of the battalion was Major General William Morshead. Most regiments had a colonel who was the titular and administrative head of the regiment but who did not actually serve with them, and whom they probably rarely saw. The 60th, being a large regiment with multiple battalions, had a colonel-in-chief, the Duke of York, and then each battalion had a colonel-commandant. Morshead was a former Coldstream Guards officer and former aide-de-camp to the king. One of the duties of the colonel was to arrange the supply of uniforms for the battalion. Morshead seems to have been diligent in this duty as he was soon claiming for uniforms supplied over and above the establishment.[2]

The establishment called for two lieutenant colonels but the battalion had three; Frederick von Schlammersdorf, Baron Francis de Rottenburg, and Henry Couper. Couper, formerly of the York Hussars and Royal Foreigners Regiment, was the junior. He served on the inspector general of foreign corps' staff on the Isle of Wight until his death in 1802.[3]

1 Windham to Duke of York, 12 January 1798, TNA, WO 4/170, pp.292-3.
2 Entry in General Administrative Out-Letters Index, 60th Foot, 1798, TNA, WO 2/2, p.108.
3 Foreign Corps Officer Lists, Inspector General's Department, TNA, WO 65/167, p.46.

Frederick von Schlammersdorf has rather unfairly been written out of the chronicles of the 5th Battalion. The first history of the unit, *Celer et Audax* written by Major General Gibbes Rigaud in 1879, does not mention him at all and has the battalion first forming on the Isle of Wight and not on Barbados.[4] The second volume of *The Annals of the Kings Royal Rifle Corps* by Lieutenant Colonel Lewis Butler, published in 1923, does mention von Schlammersdorf but claims that the formation of the 5th Battalion on Barbados and the subsequent formation on the Isle of Wight were separate units that, through some clerical error, had the same designation and only merged once the Isle of Wight companies eventually arrived in the West Indies. Butler continues:

> Thus it happened that two separate formations of the 60th, each termed the 5th Battalion, were being organised in different hemispheres; but whether it was inadvertence that the nucleus of two separate battalions received the same numeral, or whether it was from the outset the intention of the Commander-in-Chief to amalgamate them at a future date, cannot at this distance be positively ascertained.[5]

Both Rigaud and Butler give the honour of the first commander of the battalion to Baron Francis de Rottenburg. However, Vicomte Grouvel in *Les Corps de Troupe L'Émigration Française*, written in 1857, states that von Schlammersdorf was the commanding officer of the new battalion and that the Hompesch chasseurs were added later.[6] Dundas' letter to the Duke of York clearly indicates that the intention was to form the 5th Battalion from the two Lowenstein regiments and that the decision to include the Hompesch chasseurs came later. The formation on Barbados predates that on the Isle of Wight by two months. Von Schlammersdorf's commission was dated 24 April 1795, whereas de Rottenburg's was dated 25 July 1796 so Schlammersdorf was the senior and would have been given command of the battalion.[7] Various letters survive addressed to von Schlammersdorf as commander of the battalion,[8] and the companies on the Isle of Wight are referred to as a detachment in other surviving records.[9] It is also true that in other records de Rottenburg signed as commander of the battalion, and so there is some justification for the confusion, but he was on leave from April until July and left Major de Verna commanding the four companies even after they were deployed to Ireland.[10] The sheer distance between the two parts of the battalion, and the capture or sinking of packets carrying dispatches, would have also lead to delays in communication and it is not until July 1798 that the returns of the battalion in the West Indies begin to mention the former Hompesch officers as being absent in Europe.[11] The battalion is listed as being at the Leeward Islands in the general returns for the army dated April 1798, although curiously an entry was started under the section for infantry in

4 G. Riguad, *Celer et Audax* (Oxford: Hall & Stacy, 1879), p.3.
5 Butler, *Annals*, Vol. II, pp.7-11.
6 Grouvel, *Les Corps de Troupe L'Émigration Française*, pp.63 & 262.
7 Foreign Corps Officer Lists, Lowenstein's Chasseurs and Hompesch Light Infantry, TNA, WO 65/167 pp.36 & 59.
8 Dicken to Schlammersdorf 18 April 1798, & Dicken to Schlammersdorf 19 April 1798, TNA, WO 40/11.
9 Entry in General Administrative Out-Letters Index, 60th Foot, 1798, TNA, WO 2/2, p.108.
10 April to July 1798 Pay Lists, TNA, WO 12/7066.
11 July 1798 Return, TNA, WO 17/2489.

Britain and then deleted.[12] The reason that von Schlammersdorf has been side-lined so effectively and easily is that he died on 28 September 1798, most likely from a fever,[13] but he had also been wounded in the unsuccessful attack on Puerto Rico the previous year. In 1799 Lieutenant Colonel Couper was asked to obtain an account of the 'late Commanding Officer' von Schlammersdorf's effects and a death certificate.[14]

Baron Francis de Rottenburg, commander of 5/60th and author of the first British Army manual for rifles and light infantry. (The Royal Green Jackets (Rifles) Museum)

Whilst Baron Francis de Rottenburg may have been the second commanding officer of the battalion rather than the first it is still the case that the battalion owed much of its later success and character to him. De Rottenburg was born 4 November 1757 at Gdansk in the Polish-Lithunanian Commonwealth. In 1782, at the relatively late age of 24, he was commissioned as a *sous-lieutenant* in the Regiment de la Marck, a German regiment in French service. In 1787 he was aide-de-camp to General Baron de Salis Marcelius when he was seconded to the Kingdom of the Two Sicilies to assist in the re-organisation of their army, later marrying the general's daughter. He left French service in 1791 during the Revolution and returned home. In 1794 he commanded a regiment of Polish infantry during Tadeusz Kościuszko's unsuccessful uprising against Russian rule, and was wounded at the final Battle of Praga. A year later he was commissioned as a major in the Hompesch Hussars in British service. Many of his former comrades from the Regiment de la Marck had already entered British service. When the Hompesch Light Infantry was raised de Rottenburg was promoted to lieutenant colonel, but did not sail with the unit to the West Indies and remained at the Isle of Wight. By the time he joined the 5th Battalion he was 40 years old and an experienced soldier.[15] When von Schlammersdorf died, command of the battalion transferred to de Rottenburg, but it is likely that he did not learn of this until late in 1798, given the length of time it took for a packet to sail from the West Indies.

In the summer of 1798 the Duke of York, keen to increase the skills of British light infantry, authorised the publication of *Regulations for the Exercise of Riflemen and Light Infantry* written by de Rottenburg and translated from German by the adjutant general,

12 April 1798 Return, TNA, WO 17/1160.

13 Muster Roll of 5/60th, 25 December 1797 to 24 June 1798, TNA, WO 12/7065.

14 Entry in General Administrative Out-Letters Index, 60th Foot, 1799, TNA, WO 2/3, p.121.

15 Butler, *Annals*, Vol. II, p.2.

William Fawcett.[16] It is unclear when de Rottenburg wrote the text, which drew heavily on Johann von Ewald's *A Treatise Upon the Duties of Light Troops*, but it may have been that he was working on it during his prolonged leave in the spring and summer of 1798, or he may have already written it for his unit prior to its incorporation into the 60th. De Rottenburg's manual became the standard text for light infantry training and was one of the library of books each battalion of infantry was required to have.[17]

The absence, for one reason or another, of the lieutenant colonels meant that the majors of the battalion were soon to bear the burden of temporary command and share much of the credit for turning an amalgamation of three units into a very effective and efficient battalion. In the West Indies there were three majors; Adam von Dörsner, Lewis von Mosheim, and Wilhelm von Crezielsky.[18] The battalion was quickly called upon to provide detachments for other islands and was split up, as it was to be for much of its existence. Von Mosheim had started his military career in the Württemberg Regiment of Foot Guards and joined Lowenstein's Chasseurs when it was formed. He was with the company at Trinidad that had probably been there since before the battalion was formed.[19] In March orders came to send three companies to Martinique under von Dörsner. Von Schlammersdorf obviously had concerns about the division of his battalion and requested that it be re-united as soon as possible.[20] The headquarters and remaining companies left Barbados for Grenada in April, leaving von Crezielsky behind on leave. [21] He re-joined the battalion in August, just before von Schlammersdorf joined the detachment in Martinique and later died.

Adding to the excess of majors was George Lewis de Verna, serving with the companies on the Isle of Wight. With him as lieutenants were his two sons; William and George. De Verna, from Münden in Saxony, signed himself as such on the first muster roll of the companies at the Isle of Wight but his two sons wrote 'v' (short for von) Verna. 'Von' and 'de', meaning 'of' in German and French respectively, seem to have been used interchangeably and this, combined with the inconsistent Anglicisation of first names, poor spelling and clarity of the handwriting, can make it hard to keep track of individuals across the various records.

The Vernas were not the only family in the battalion; Privates William Schmidt junior and senior were on the Isle of Wight, along with several sets of what could have been brothers. On Barbados were brothers Captain Joseph de Wend (sometimes written as Wend, Wendt or de Wendt) and Lieutenant Michael de Wend, and again several other sets of possible brothers.[22] The de Wends had joined Lowenstein's Chasseurs in April 1795.[23]

The establishment of the battalion called for 10 companies. Seven were to be commanded by one of seven captains, one by a captain-lieutenant (who commanded a company on behalf of the absent colonel-commandant, and which rank was soon to be abolished), one

16 Gates, *British Light Infantry*, p.63.
17 Butler, *Annals*, Vol. II, p.13.
18 Muster Roll of 5/60th 25 December 1797 to 24 June 1798, TNA, WO 12/7065.
19 January 1798 Return TNA, WO 17/2489,
20 Dickens to von Schlammersdorf 5 March & 18 April 1798, TNA, WO 40/11.
21 January to May 1798 Returns, TNA, WO 17/2489.
22 Muster Roll of 5/60th 25 December 1797 to 24 June 1798 , TNA, WO 12/7065, & March 1798 Pay List, TNA, WO 12/7066.
23 Foreign Corps Officers Lists, Lowenstein's Chasseurs, TNA, WO 65/168, p.10

Silhouette of Captain Ladislaus de Villers Masburgh, who was wounded in Ireland in 1798 and retired on half-pay soon afterwards. (Collections Musée Royal de l'Armée – Brussels, Inv. nr. 400716. Photographer Luc van de Weghe, 2018)

by one of the majors, and one by one of the lieutenant colonels. There were 10 captains and one captain-lieutenant on Barbados, additionally Captain Gandt was a prisoner of war on Puerto Rico.[24] A further three captains who appear on the Barbados muster roll were actually on the Isle of Wight. The Barbados pay list is not completed on the standard form used at the time, stretches for an unusually long period from 25 December 1797 to 24 June 1798, and has suffered some damage.[25] Some, but not all, of the officers on the Isle of Wight are listed, but often with poor spellings of their names. The Isle of Wight pay list shows four captains, including the three also mentioned on the Barbados muster, making a total of 15 in all.[26]

Not all the officers were happy with their regiments being subsumed by the 60th. Captain Guillaume de Lasalle de Louisenthal appears on the first muster in the West Indies but exchanged into the Hompesch Mounted Riflemen in September 1798.[27] Louisenthal was born in 1768 near the town of Saarlouis on the northern border of France. In 1781, at the age of 13, he became a *sous-lieutenant* in the Alsace Regiment of the French army. His regiment was caught up in the chaos and in-fighting of the Revolution and he decided to leave France in December 1791. He served with the Régiment de Royal-Allemand cavalry, which had deserted to the royalist armies *en masse*, and saw action in the campaigns of 1793 against the Revolutionary army. He then joined the Lowenstein Chasseurs in May 1794 and fought with them in the United Provinces and Germany. When the Chasseurs transferred to British service Louisenthal came with them. He led his company in the attack on St Lucia and was hit by two musket balls in his thigh. He was recovering in Martinique when he caught yellow fever. During his long convalescence and absence from the Chasseurs he captained a 14-gun brig privateer, named *Ryfleman*, and attacked Spanish shipping and colonies. He re-joined his regiment in time for the unsuccessful assault on Puerto Rico. When the Lowenstein regiments were merged with the 60th he thought the British were being ungrateful for their service. He married Mademoiselle Augier, who had looked after

24 January 1798 Return, TNA, 17/2489.

25 Muster Roll of 5/60th 25 December 1797 to 24 June 1798 , TNA, WO 12/7065.

26 March & April 1798 Pay Lists, TNA, WO 12/7066,

27 *London Gazette*, 18 September 1798, Issue 15061, p.876.

him while he was wounded and ill and who was the daughter of a rich plantation owner.[28] He would not have been able to stay with the battalion for long in any case, because in 1800 all French-born officers were removed from the 60th.[29]

Most of the officers, though, stayed with the new battalion. There were 21 lieutenants and 13 ensigns, although Ensigns Ammon, Henkledy, and Zerzen were soon promoted to lieutenant. Four of the officers, including de Rottenburg, used the title of baron. This can be either an honorific denoting a landowner from a noble family, or a junior rank of nobility, depending on which European state the holder is from, so this does not mean that the battalion was aristocratic. Many may have had little access to any wealth back in Europe, if indeed such wealth had survived the turmoil of the Revolution. Some of the officers would have come from humbler origins; Ensign Henry Hugon had only recently been promoted from sergeant major. Promotion from the ranks was not common but as many as one in 20 British Army officers came from the ranks at the time.[30] Almost every sergeant major the 5th Battalion had during its 20 year history was commissioned, with one eventually rising to be a lieutenant colonel. Even many of the most junior of the officers of the new battalion had considerable military experience. Ensign George Henry Zühleke had joined the Hesse Cassel Guards in 1794 and served in Prussian and then British service in Germany and the Low Countries.[31]

There were two main routes to promotion; purchase or seniority. When a vacancy arose it would be offered for purchase to the senior officer in the rank below, calculated on the date of their commission. If they could not afford the several hundred pounds involved it would be offered to the next most senior officer and so on. Vacancies could also be filled by officers exchanging from other regiments and in multiple-battalion regiments, like the 60th, officers often moved from one battalion to another as they stepped up the promotion ladder. Vacancies occurring due to the death of an officer were usually filled without purchase, on seniority alone, making active service or unhealthy postings attractive to the ambitious. The various steps up in ranks cost many times an officer's annual salary and so all too often only those additional wealth or income could afford to purchase their advancement. Prices did vary between regiments though, although efforts were made to impose stricter regulation and pricing. Political influence and patronage could also be used to secure commissions or promotions.

For much of the two decades that the battalion existed the demand for officers, caused by expansion of the army and attrition, outstripped the supply of those able or willing to buy commissions, and so most new commissions or promotions did not involve purchase.[32] However, the battalion being significantly over establishment in majors and captains would have lowered any prospects of promotion and advancement for the junior officers. With the 60th being restricted to duty in the Americas, and especially the West Indies, it would have made the commissions slightly cheaper than more desirable or famous regiments but still

28 H. Contamine, *La Vie Aventureuse d'un Émigré Lorrain: Guillaume de Lasalle de Louisenthal* (Metz: Académie Nationale de Metz, 1930), pp.289-328.

29 Copy of order from Colonel Brownrigg, 13 August 1800, HRO, 170A12W/D/1183.

30 Haythornthwaite, *Armies*, p.28.

31 Butler, *Annals*, Vol. II, p.105.

32 Haythornthwaite, *Armies*, p.22.

there was risk of impoverished officers losing out to those who could afford to purchase. The other battalions of the 60th had mostly British or Irish officers and it was not long before some joined the 5th Battalion. The first was Lieutenant Thomas Kavanagh in the summer of 1799,[33] and he was quickly followed by Ensign Bysshe Molesworth. Like many other British officers appointed to the battalion, Molesworth quickly moved on, in his case to the 15th Foot. Molesworth chose to transfer between regiments to gain advancement and he went from the 15th to the 62nd, before settling on the 47th where he reached the rank of major in 1813.[34]

John Galiffe, pictured towards the end of his life in the 1840s. His General Service Medal, right, with 11 clasps for actions in the Peninsular War was only issued after his death in 1847 and must have been added later. (Image courtesy of Mr Rodney Galiffe)

With the 5th Battalion being so far over establishment in so many ranks there was no need to promote anyone as deaths from disease, retirements, and exchanges led to officers leaving. Around one fifth of the officers present on formation were still with the battalion 10 years later, of those only Charles Henkledy had progressed by more than one rank, rising from ensign to captain, six had received just one promotion and three were still in the same rank. Significantly, both majors of the battalion in 1808 were British officers who joined much later. However, the long service and experience of the battalion's captains would serve it well in a unit that was expected to be split into detachments in order to spread the benefit of rifle-armed troops more widely.

One officer who would remain with the battalion from formation almost to disbandment was Jean Pierre, or more often John, Galiffe. Born in Geneva in 1767, he was commissioned into the Regiment de Chateauvieux, one of several Swiss regiments in French service, at the age of 17. In 1792, following the massacre of the Swiss Guard and the deposing of King Louis XVI, the regiment left its barracks and joined the Royalist armies in Germany. Galiffe returned to Geneva to help defend it against the French, serving as a captain. He then subsequently joined the Red Hussars regiment in Dutch service as a volunteer and then captain, and was an aide de camp to the Prince of Orange. He fought in the campaigns of 1794 and 1795 before entering British service with the York Rangers in 1796, and then the 5th Battalion when it was formed a year later.[35] The Revolution had robbed him of a good position with good prospects and returning to soldiering under a different flag was, for him, the only alternative. His father

33 November 1799 Pay List, TNA, WO 12/7066.

34 *London Gazette*, Issues. 15225, 15540, 15733, 16783.

35 Booklet on services of J.P. Galiffe, HRO, 170A12W/D/0066/12.

did not have the money to set him up in an alternative profession and Galiffe in any case felt himself unsuited to commerce.[36] However, one can get some idea of the frustrations of life as an officer without an additional income or wealth from a letter Galiffe wrote to a friend during the brief Peace of Amiens, four years after the battalion was formed:

> I believe that you are still of the same opinion regarding the subject of my situation and, to calm your worries, let me tell you that I am starting to get settled but, believe me, there are still many things that whilst appearing agreeable or, at least, bearable, actually leave lots of scars for those that manage them.
>
> On the bright side, it is evident that I have a good position that allows me to live a comfortable life and to be introduced everywhere which, for the poor devil of an émigré Swiss officer that you were kind enough to help, is most agreeable. It was like winning the big prize in a lottery where I had not bought a ticket. However, one is only as happy as one's social state improves, I would have quickly appreciated my advancement if I had not had served previously. That is the core of all my aversions but now, seeing that it is without any solution, I've resigned myself to my lot and would be foolish and mad to do otherwise. Besides, I've quickly climbed the list of captains in the 60th Regiment and, before long, I will find myself at the top and there will be Hell to pay if, by chance, I am not any further advanced in a year or two. That said, I must not be so bold as in times of peace, there will be so many officers on half-pay to replace that this situation may last longer than I expect.
>
> In several of my letters, I had mentioned that I absolutely needed my Royal letter, that states that I joined the army on 13th October 1796 with the York Rangers. This is even more important now as I have only received a temporary letter from General Abercromby, despite having been on the army lists since 1796, which can be contested for any reason since I do not have my letter proving my status. This can have huge consequences on my advancement, especially when it will be my turn to be Brevet-Major. In fact, this situation has already prevented me from being put in front of all the captains in my battalion since Lt-Colonel de Rottenberg continues not to recognise the legality of my claim by my letter's absence. Unable to back my claim I had, as a consequence, not been put at the back of the captains' list but as good as. Now there is only one fellow in front of me but that is just not acceptable: Once the captains of 96 become Brevet-Majors, there will be many obstacles and I will most certainly not be nominated. Again, I wish to remind you of the absolute necessity to have my Royal letter.[37]

He goes on to insist that his friend does not give his commission to de Rottenburg, who was in London at the time, as he might have destroyed it. Galiffe would not get to be a brevet major (acting as a major but still a captain) until 1808 and not be substantively promoted to major until 1810.[38]

36 J. Galiffe to his mother, 3 September 1793, Bibliotheque de Geneve (BG), ms fr 2751c pl22 f008-9.

37 J. Galiffe to Sir Francis D'Ivernois, 24 June 1802, BG, ms fr 2751c pl22 f0004-5 (translated).

38 N. Willoughby Wallace, A *Regimental Chronicle & List of Officers of the 60th, or the King's Royal Rifle Corps* (London: Harrison, 1879), p.161.

The officers' commissions for the Hompesch and Lowenstein regiments had been signed by the Duke of York. Those for the 60th were signed by the King. All the commissions for those officers joining the new battalion on formation were dated 30 December 1797. The *London Gazette*, the official newspaper of record, published details of the first appointments that included Lieutenant Colonels von Schlammersdorf, de Rottenburg, and Couper, as well as Major de Verna and his sons, Captain Lambert Lewis de Weise, and Surgeon Reiser and two of his assistants.[39] Further appointments were announced on 17 April and contained the rest of the officers from the Isle of Wight as well as Lieutenant Adolphus Munsthal from Lowenstein's Fusiliers who was in Germany on leave.[40] The following week's *Gazette* published the rest of the Lowenstein officers' commissions, the list having presumably arrived from Barbados.[41] The final appointments were published in September; Ensigns Muller, Jockell, and Winkler, with Adjutant Amon and Quartermaster Kemmeter.[42]

An often unsung element of a battalion were the administrative roles of paymaster, quartermaster, and adjutant. The battalions first paymaster, Frederic Pohl, would have had to pay a large surety to the Army for his position and provide several references. He remained paymaster for seven years. James Kemmeter, an ensign and the quartermaster in charge of the battalion's billets, clothing, ammunition, and other supplies, served with the battalion in that post until 1813. The adjutant was usually one of the lieutenants who kept the records, oversaw the training of junior officers, and also carried out a myriad of other administrative tasks to keep the battalion running smoothly. Both parts of the battalion managed to get through two adjutants in the first few months of the unit's existence. The posts of quartermaster and adjutant were often filled by those promoted from the ranks.

Attempting to keep the battalion healthy were the medical staff of a surgeon and two assistants. The first surgeon of the battalion was Franz Reiser, initially with four assistants in Barbados, as well as Joche Fockens on the Isle of Wight, but this was soon trimmed down to the number set in the establishment. Reiser was not a surgeon in the modern sense but his role spanned those we would now call surgeon, doctor, and pharmacist. A surgeon's training, skills and knowledge varied but assistant surgeons were often appointed with very little medical knowledge whatsoever. Fortunately for Reiser, German recruits proved to be healthier, on average, than their British counterparts.[43] Whilst contemporary sources attribute this to greater sobriety on the part of the Germans it is more likely that foreign regiments had a smaller percentage of raw recruits.

Not many recruiting records survive for the 60th but some do exist for the years 1795 to 1802 and cover the Hompesch and Lowenstein units as well, but they do not state which battalion of the 60th recruits joined.[44] The vast majority of recruits list previous military service, most for the various German states but also for Denmark, Austria, and Poland amongst others. The records also list their age, height, origin, occupation and physical description. The average age was 26 making them slightly older than average British recruits.

39 *London Gazette*, 23 January 1798, issue 14084, p.62.
40 *London Gazette*, 17 April 1798, issue 15007, p.313.
41 *London Gazette*, 21 April 1798, issue 15008. p.321.
42 *London Gazette*, 25 September 1798, issue 15063 pp.899-900.
43 Wishon, *German Forces*, p.150.
44 Foreign Corps Description & Succession Book 1795-1802, TNA, WO 25/668 pp.90-3, 118-27, 136-7, 162-4, 202-226.

Heights are recorded in columns for French *pieds*, *pouces* and *lignes* and if they are the units that were used rather than British feet and inches (a *ligne* was one twelfth of a *pouce*) it makes the average height of the recruits an unlikely six feet. If, however, British units were used the average height of five foot seven inches still makes them slightly taller than the average British recruit.[45]

There was, of course, considerable variation around those averages. Christoph Reisleke – blond, blue eyes, round faced, a shoemaker from the Hague in Holland – joined the 60th aged 18, was five foot five inches (assuming British units), and had already spent three years in Dutch service. Johann Hofke – black hair, long faced, blue eyed – a 31 year old tailor from Danzig was the same height but had served for 10 years with the Mecklenburg army. Jacob Reinkel, 24, from Amsterdam, a blond haired and blue eyed tailor with a long face, was only five foot one and had served two years with the French royalist Armée de Condé. A surprising number of the recruits were in their forties. Joseph Pomerath of Switzerland enlisted aged 46, having already served 10 years in a Swiss regiment. Ferdinand Schulth was 40, and served 10 years in the Prussian army but was originally a merchant from Libau in what is now Latvia. Urban Matheiss was the eldest recruit listed at 64, with 16 years Austrian service already behind him. When an occupation is listed they range from simply soldier, to bakers, masons, carpenters, tailors, shoemakers, gunsmiths, and sailors.

A ready supply of foreign recruits could be obtained from the thousands of prisoners of war in prisons and prison hulks around Britain. Many of these men were not French, or came from areas only recently incorporated into France. The Royal Navy's victory against the Dutch at the Battle of Camperdown in October 1797 resulted in thousands of sailors and soldiers of various nationalities being captured. In December 1797 the Transport Board, who oversaw prisoners of war, wrote to the commander of the prison camp at Norman Cross to authorise their recruitment:

> Such persons as Colonel Nesbit may appoint are to be permitted to enlist into the 60th regiment such Natives of Germany as were taken on board the Dutch Fleet and are willing to enter into that Corps and you will accordingly cause the 84 men that have already agreed to enter to be immediately released for that purpose.[46]

The registers for both Norman Cross and Portchester prisons show consistent evidence of recruitment of prisoners into the 60th, many of whom could have ended up in the 5th Battalion.[47]

The primary source of information on the officers, NCOs, and soldiers of the battalion are the monthly, or later quarterly, pay lists. These record the name, rank, and pay, but also have a 'remarks' section that can reveal a little more of the internal life of the battalion. The first pay list for Barbados for December 1797 to June 1798 records 219 deaths, 12 desertions, 51 Frenchmen removed, and 26 recruits (one of whom, Joseph Posen, managed only 20

45 Haythorntwiate, *Armies*, pp.49-50.

46 Transport Board to Captain Woodriff, TNA, ADM 98/233, p.183.

47 Registers of Prisoners of War, TNA, ADM 103/250 & ADM 103/316.

days with the battalion before he died).[48] The battalion saw no action during that period so almost all the deaths would have been from disease.

The first pay list for the Isle of Wight, from 25 February to 24 March, is on the correct forms and gives much more detail. To the heading for drummers was added 'or horns' reflecting that bugles and not drums were used to relay orders. Sergeant Joshua Baring was employed as a clerk for a major general. Captain d'Erp's company was on detachment, possibly at Sandown Fort, which was often garrisoned by foreign corps. Private Heinrich Dam was in the general hospital, as were 10 others. Private Henry Bartholoman had joined from La Chatre's Corps of Emigrés. Private George Weischuhlz was under arrest on the cutter at Cowes, and Private Anton Faber was also under arrest but due to be discharged. Two deserters were listed; Privates Adrian Van Der Velden and Wilhelm Kuttman. Sergeant Andreas Schneider and Corporal Michael Lesser were recruiting in Germany.

The following month's pay list shows nine soldiers with French surnames as transferred to La Chatre's Corps of Emigrés, presumably continuing the effort to make the unit all-German, which definition at the time seems to have included the Dutch, Swiss, Austrians, Poles and many others, except the French. Four additional recruits enlisted and Private David Kremke decided he had had enough of the army life and deserted.[49] Desertions were not uncommon at the time, especially for units destined to be sent to the West Indies when the inherent risk of death from disease led many to take the risk. However, the four companies on the Isle of Wight would not sail to join the rest of the battalion for many months, and would see battle before they did.

48 Muster Roll of 5/60th, 25 December 1797 to 24 June 1798 , TNA, WO 12/7065.

49 March & April 1798 Pay Lists, TNA, WO 12/7066.

3

The Infantry Rifle

The standard infantry weapon of the Revolutionary and Napoleonic Wars was the smoothbore musket, a weapon essentially unchanged in design and performance for over 100 years. There were slight variations in quality, reliability and design between the various nations of Europe, but essentially the vast majority of line infantry on all sides were armed with very similar weapons.

A musket fired a soft lead ball of around an ounce in weight that could inflict horrendous injuries, if one was unlucky enough to be hit. The Prussian Army conducted tests with a platoon of ordinary infantrymen firing at a target representing a squadron of cavalry and found that only 40 percent of 1000 shots hit the target at 100 paces, and this fell to less than 20 percent at 200 paces.[1]

Many muskets did not even have sights to assist in aiming. Soldiers were drilled to just point the guns forwards, fire when ordered to, and then reload as quickly as possible in a series of tightly proscribed movements. When firing in close order it would have been very difficult to aim with any care, even if the troops had been required or trained to. With muskets packed so closely every soldier's face would have been stung by sparks and gunpowder, and the noise of so many muskets being fired would have been deafening. After the first volley, smoke would have obscured the enemy from view even if the soldiers had wanted to aim at individual targets. After the Battle of Vittoria one of the British supply officers calculated that there may have been as many 3,607,500 musket rounds fired at the enemy. The French suffered 8,000 killed or wounded, out of an army of 90,000, and so he calculated that only one shot out of every 459 hit an enemy, not accounting for the 7,000 rounds the British artillery fired at the battle, which in all likelihood accounted for a good proportion of the French killed and wounded.[2]

At the outbreak of war in 1793 there were two patterns of musket in service with the British Army; the Long Land Service Pattern with a 46-inch barrel, and the Short Land Service New Pattern with a 42-inch barrel. Both had a 0.75-inch calibre. The sudden rise in demand proved difficult for British gunmakers to supply, and even though many were

1 G. Scharnorst, *Handbuch für Officiere, in den anwendbaren Theilen der Krieges-Wissenschaften: Von der Tactik : worin von den Waffen, der Stellung und den Bewegungen der Cavalerie und Infanterie, von dem Verhalten derselben in Actionen* (Hannover: Helwing, 1790), p.273.

2 Gates, *British Light Infantry*, p.140.

ordered from abroad the government had to buy 30,000 weapons from the stores of the East India Company. From 1797 the 39-inch barrelled India Pattern became the standard weapon because, even though it was inferior in quality to the other patterns, it was cheaper and easier to manufacture.[3]

The common musket was technologically incapable of accuracy at anything but short range. In order for them to be quick to load, the diameter of the ball had to be slightly smaller than the diameter of the barrel. The gap between the ball and sides of the barrel, known as windage, meant not only that the ball would bounce from side to side as it was fired and then continue in whatever slightly deviant direction it was heading when it emerged, but also that some of the explosive force of the powder would escape around the ball resulting in low muzzle velocity and a consequent fall of up to five feet over 120 yards.[4] Also, the balls were not perfectly spherical and any imperfections in the surface could lead to unequal air resistance and increase the unpredictability of the direction of flight. In 1808 Colonel George Hanger, a noted expert marksman and proponent of more accurate rifled weapons, wrote:

> A soldier's musket, if not exceeding badly bored, and very crooked, as many are, will strike the figure of a man at 80 yards, it may even at 100 yards; but a soldier must be very unfortunate indeed who shall be wounded by a common musket at 150 yards, PROVIDED HIS ANTAGONIST AIMS AT HIM; and as to firing at a man at 200 yards with a common musket, you may just as well fire at the moon, and have the same hopes of hitting your object.[5]

The solution to the problem of smooth-bore musket accuracy had been found as early as the 16th century when rifled weapons were first developed. Using grooves inside the barrel to spin the ball meant that any imperfection in the shape or surface of the ball would be negated, while the tight fit required would eliminate windage and provide a higher muzzle velocity.[6] The British Army began to use rifles in very small numbers as early as 1746. In 1757 Colonel Jacques Prevost of the 60th purchased 300 German rifled carbines for his regiment and some of these were issued to the 60th during the Seven Years War.[7] Rifles were also used during the American War of Independence with the first British manufactured rifle, the 1776 Pattern, being used as well as imported German models. In 1776 Major Patrick Ferguson, demonstrating his innovative breech-loading design and firing at a target 200 yards distant, managed to fire four rounds in the first minute and six in the second, only missing three times.[8] Unfortunately, Ferguson's innovation proved short-lived because manufacturing techniques and tolerances were not yet up to meeting the requirements of the design.

The rifle's advantage in accuracy was well proven by 1793, but still at the outbreak of war the Board of Ordnance, which controlled and provided the Army's weapons, had no rifles

3 Haythornthwaite, *Weapons & Equipment of the Napoleonic Wars*, p.21.
4 Gates, *British Light Infantry*, p.139.
5 G. Hanger, *A Letter to Lord Castlereagh* (London: Ridgway, 1808), p.78.
6 H. Beaufoy, *Scioppetaria* (London: Egerton, 1808), p.29.
7 D. W. Bailey, *British Military Flintlock Rifles 1740-1840* (Lincoln: Andrew Mowbary, 2002), p.11.
8 Butler, *Annals*, Vol II, p.3.

in their stores.[9] The rifle had three major disadvantages compared to the standard smoothbore musket that stopped it being more widely adopted by the British Army. Firstly, they were much more difficult and expensive to manufacture. Secondly, they were difficult to maintain, with the rifle grooves becoming clogged with powder and innovations such as Ferguson's breech loading proving unreliable in the field. Thirdly, they were much slower to load. It was estimated that if a musket-armed enemy closed to within 250 yards of a body of riflemen then the doubled or trebled rate of fire from the muskets would drive the riflemen back.[10] To many military thinkers it was not clear how a few hundred rifle-armed troops could have a major impact on a battle involving tens of thousands.

The continued reluctance of the British military establishment to embrace light infantry tactics meant that there was simply no requirement for a weapon capable of aimed fire. It was only when this thinking was proved so erroneous in the campaigns of 1793 that the British Army quickly recruited foreign light infantry and turned to Germany, not only for riflemen but also for rifles. The capitulation of the Lowenstein Fusiliers stated that they be armed with rifles like the Prussian '*Schutzen*' and that of the Hompesch Light Infantry that most of the men be similarly armed, but 10 men per company were to have a new type of rifled carbine.[11] The capitulation of the Lowenstein's Chasseurs was lost in the first of their many shipwrecks but it is likely that they too had rifled carbines.[12] The Prussian Model 1787 *Fusilier-Schützengewehr* had a 41-inch barrel and 0.68-inch calibre, so it was approximately the same size as standard musket.[13] Its length would have made it difficult to load in anything other than a standing position. Shorter rifled carbines were developments of the traditional German hunting rifles designed to have sufficient accuracy and stopping power to kill a wild boar. Their short length made them easier to handle in dense woodland and meant that they could be loaded kneeling, or lying prone. However, being shorter they needed a longer bayonet to have the same reach as a bayonet on the end of a musket, and so riflemen with carbines were often issued swords that could be attached to their rifles.

The arms that Lowenstein's and Hompesch's units actually used may have changed over time as the initial batch of weapons provided to them were replaced. It is possible that they were issued with some of the 6,000 Prussian rifles, based on the 1787 *Fusilier-Schützengewehr*, that the Board of Ordnance ordered in 1797.[14] By the time they were merged into the 5th Battalion it is likely that they were carrying an assortment of different rifles of differing designs, and that they would have continued using what they had to hand for some time.

In late 1799 the Board of Ordnance finally began to seek to source a British-made rifle. In early 1800 seven different rifled barrels of varying length with differing numbers and twists of rifling grooves were tested by fixing them to a mortar bed and firing at a target at 300 yards. The barrels came from a variety of British and foreign manufactures. The barrel made by London gunsmith Ezekiel Baker was selected. Baker tried several designs with

9 Bailey, *Flintlock Rifles*, p.93.

10 Beaufoy, *Scioppetaria*, p.192.

11 Capitulation Book, Capitulations for Lowenstein's Fusiliers and Hompesch Light Infantry , TNA, WO 24/1112, p.246 & pp.252-3.

12 Bailey, *Flintlock Rifles*, p.98.

13 Bailey, *Flintlock Rifles*, p.94.

14 Bailey, *Flintlock Rifles*, p.94.

differing barrel lengths and calibres until he came up with a design that was acceptable. The finished rifle was submitted and the 1800 Pattern Infantry Rifle went into manufacture, only becoming referred to as 'the Baker rifle' much later when it was replaced in the Victorian era.[15]

Baker's design was essentially a copy of a typical German *jäger* rifled carbine. It featured a 30 and 3/8-inch barrel of 0.625 inch calibre with seven rifling grooves twisting by a quarter turn along the barrel length. The calibre was the same as the cavalry's carbines, easing possible supply problems in the field and helping to reduce the recoil that occurred with musket calibre rifles. The overall length was 46 and 1/4-inches.[16] It weighed just under 9 pounds. The stock was made of walnut, with brass fittings including a butt box for holding tools and ball patches, although this was sometimes omitted. It had a fore sight and a folding rear sight that could be raised for aiming at more distant targets, and a shaped trigger guard for a firmer grip. A simpler and cheaper version was created in 1801 designed specifically for units serving in the West Indies where the climate often led to the corrosion of more intricate metal parts, with half of those produced omitting the sword bayonet fitting and butt box. In 1805 the pattern was revised with minor improvements to increase reliability, with the barrel lengthening by a quarter of an inch but the overall length of the weapon dropping by half an inch.

Sword cutler Henry Osborn designed the sword-bayonet for the infantry rifle. The original version was 27 inches in length with a square knuckle guard with a slot and sprung release for attaching to the rifle. An amended version in 1801 was slightly longer with a 'D' shaped knuckle guard.[17] The sword-bayonet was an unhappy compromise. It provided the necessary reach but made the rifle heavy and unbalanced, so they were seldom used for much more than chopping food or clearing undergrowth.[18] The rifles were produced by a large number of manufacturers, each providing different parts and performing various finishing tasks, with the main bottleneck being the very few gunsmiths who could perform the rifling to the standard required. In 1800, for a fully finished rifle with sword bayonet and all the tools, Baker charged the Board of Ordnance 97 shillings,[19] substantially more than the 15 shilling cost of the Long Land Pattern musket or the 33 shilling cost of the Prussian rifles.[20]

The first regiment to get the new rifle was the recently formed Rifle Corps. This unit had evolved from the Experimental Corps of Riflemen formed in early 1800 to train British soldiers from a number of regiments in the use of the rifle, with the plan to return them to their units so they could train others. However, the experiment was so successful that they were eventually retained as a permanent corps and were numbered as the 95th Foot in 1803. The first evidence of the 5th Battalion receiving the new rifle comes from a receipt dated May 1803:

15 Bailey, *Flintlock Rifles*, p.105.
16 Bailey, *Flintlock Rifles*, p.205.
17 Bailey, *Flintlock Rifles*, pp.108 & 141.
18 P. J. Haythorntwiate, *British Rifleman 1797-1815* (Oxford: Osprey, 2002), p.17.
19 Bailey, *Flintlock Rifles*, p.108.
20 Cusick, *Wellington's Rifles*, p.104.

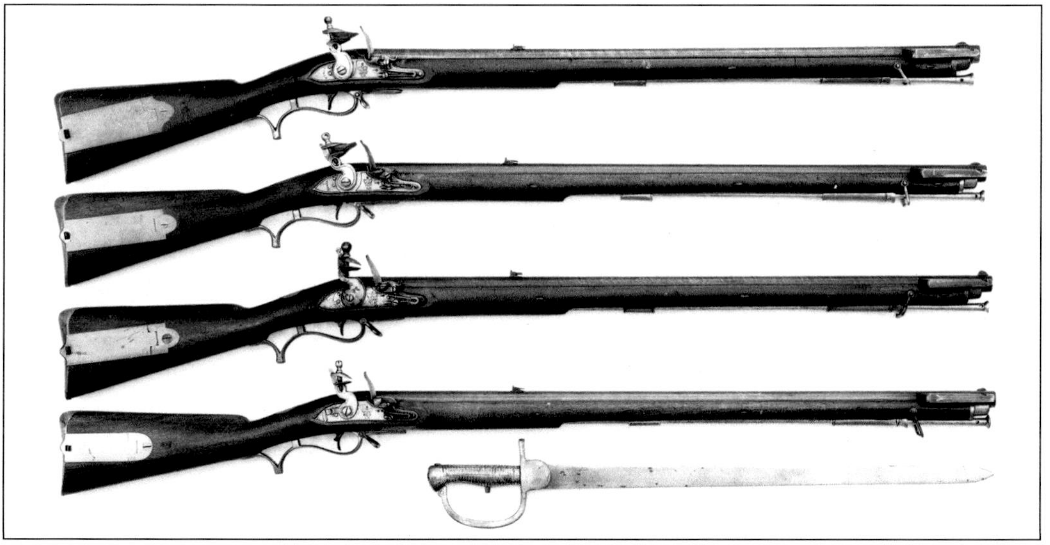

Various examples of the Infantry Rifle from around 1808 (top), two examples from around 1812 (middle) and 1825 (bottom). Also the 1801 sword bayonet. (Royal Armouries)

> Delivered out of His Majesty's Stores at the *Tower* to Mr Clarke, Carrier, the undermentioned Arms to be by him conveyed to Portsmouth and there delivered to William Spencer esq. Ordnance Store Keeper who is to apply to Admiral Gambier to forward them to Nova Scotia, being for Service of the 5th Battalion of the 60th Regiment of *Foot*:
>
> Rifle Musquets with Sword Bayonets, Scabbards, Boxes, Ball Drawers, Wiping Eyes & Levers – 350
> Rifle Musquets without ditto. – 350[21]

By 1815 the 5th Battalion had received 1,481 infantry rifles of all patterns.[22]

Despite the formation of the 5th Battalion of the 60th and the 95th, the adoption of the rifle by the British army still met with resistance. When more light infantry units were created from 1803 onwards they were armed with a slightly improved version of the smooth-bore musket. One officer would later recall a rifle company and a musket-armed light infantry company going to the ranges on the same day and the rifles almost destroying their target at 200 yards whilst the light infantry inflicted far less damage to theirs at 90 yards.[23] Two types of ammunition were issued for the infantry rifle; loose powder and ball, and prepared cartridges. For aimed fire it was envisaged that loose powder, poured from a powder horn or flask, be used, with the ball being wrapped in a leather, or cloth, patch to help it fit tightly in the rifling. Loading with loose powder and patched ball was a slow process, perhaps

21 Sent from Tower 30 May 1803, received at Portsmouth 6 June, HRO, 170A12W/D/0665/
22 Bailey, *Flintlock Rifles*, p.157.
23 'Vanguard', Distribution of Light Cavalry and Infantry in the Field, *The United Service Journal*, 1831 Part II, p.208.

Two riflemen of 5/60th firing and loading their infantry rifles. (Anne S.K. Brown Military Collection)

taking a full minute or more, but it did ensure the greatest accuracy. Lieutenant Colonel de Rottenburg in his manual set out the procedure training recruits to load with cartridges:

The words of command for firing and loading are as follows:

1. *The Company will Prime and Load.*

2. *Attention.*
   At which the flugelman steps in front.

3. *Prepare to Load.*
   For which the flugelman gives the time in two motions,-
   1st. Is the same as the first motion in the present.
   2nd. The soldier half faces to the right, and in the motion brings down the rifle to an horizontal position just above the right hip, the left hand supports it at the swell of the stock, the elbow resting against the side, the right thumb against the hammer, the knuckles upwards, and elbow pressing against the butt, the lock inclining a little to the body to prevent the powder from falling out. The officer now warns the men in going through the loading motions.

   To wait for the words of Command.
   At which caution the flugelman falls in.

At the word, *One*,
The pan is pushed open by the right thumb, the right hand then seizes the cartridge with the three first fingers.

Two,
The cartridge is brought to the mouth, and placed between the two first right double teeth, the end twisted off and brought close to the pan.

Three,
The priming is shaken into the pan; in doing which, to see that the powder is properly lodged, the head must be bent; the pan is shut by the third and little finger, the right hand then slides behind the cock, and holds the small part of the stock between the third and little finger and ball of the hand.

Four,
The soldier half faces to the left; the rifle is brought to the ground with the barrel outwards, by sliding it with care through the left hand, which then seizes it near the muzzle, the thumb stretched along the stock, the butt is placed between the heels, the barrel between the knees, which must be bent for that purpose; the cartridge is put into the barrel and the ramrod seized with the fore finger and thumb of the right hand.

Rod,
The ramrod is drawn quite out by the right hand, the left quits the rifle and grasps the ramrod the breadth of a hand from the bottom, which is sunk one inch into the barrel.

Home,
The cartridge will be forced down with both hands, the left then seizes the rifle about six inches from the muzzle, the soldier stands upright again, draws out the ramrod with the right hand, and puts the end into the pipe.

Return,
The ramrod will be returned by the right hand, which then seizes the rifle below the left.

Shoulder,
The right hand brings the rifle to the right shoulder; turning the guard outwards, the left seizes it above the hammer-spring till the right has its proper hold round the small of the stock, when the left is drawn quickly to the left thigh.[24]

24 F. de Rottenburg, *Regulations for the Exercise of Riflemen and Light Infantry and Instructions for their Conduct in the Field* (London: Egerton, 1803), pp.6-9.

A flugleman was a soldier who demonstrated or controlled the timing of a drill movement. When the recruits had perfected the procedure they would be expected to carry it out with just three commands; attention, prepare to load, and load. De Rottenburg carried on to state:

> The above regulations for firing with cartridges, will only be applicable when a corps of riflemen is required to act in close order, an instance which will very seldom occur, provided this arm is put to its proper use, and officers will observe in all cases, where riflemen act as such, and whenever it is practicable, their men are to load with the powder measure and loose ball; the principal instructions therefore for recruits, will be how to load with the loose ball and to fire at the target; the loading with cartridge is a secondary object.[25]

During the Peninsular War, loading with cartridges became the norm but when the expedition sailed to the Iberian Peninsula in 1808 the transports carried 30,000 rifle ball cartridges at 22 to the pound, 260,410 at 30 to the pound, and 300,000 rifle balls at 20 to the pound, which shows an approximately even split between the two types of ammunition.[26]

Loading with cartridges was quicker, but riflemen could still probably not match the speed of reloading of the line infantry because of the need to use considerable force to ram the ball down the grooves. Modern experiments with a replica 1800 pattern infantry rifle resulted in a time of one minute 55 seconds for firing three shots using separate patched balls and loose powder. Using an un-patched ball in a cartridge reduced this to 1 minute and 10 seconds but at a large cost in accuracy. Using a patched ball in the cartridge gave a time of 1 minute and 26 seconds, with a smaller, but still noticeable, reduction in accuracy over loose powder and ball.[27]

The regulations of 1811 allowed line infantry 30 rounds of live cartridges per year for shooting practice, with a further 60 of blanks. Light infantry units were allowed 50 rounds and rifle corps 60 rounds per year.[28] A key skill for marksmen, and one that many thought German *jägers* were naturally good at, was judging distance. Hanger wrote; 'Jägers from their natural servitude, and great practice, are in no want of being taught distances; the knowledge and precision of judging different distances comes to them naturally from practice, from their early youth.'[29]

Not all the 5th Battalion's recruits would have had such experience though, and de Rottenburg outlined the procedure for training recruits to shoot in his manual, slowly building up their confidence and skills:

> In firing at a mark, it is to be observed, that the target should be at least five feet in diameter; for if it were smaller, the unpractised recruit would be apt to miss so often as to despair of hitting it; and to become expert, a man should find encouragement,

25 Rottenburg, *Regulations,* p.12.

26 Bailey, *Flintlock Rifles*, p.153, and Return of Ordnance and Ammunition dated 9 July 1808, TNA WO 1/228.

27 YouTube.com; britishmuzzleloaders, https://youtu.be/n2YldCG9iBo (accessed 7 September 2018).

28 H. Calvert, *General Regulations and Orders for the Army* (London: W. Clowes, 1811), p71.

29 Hanger, *A Letter to Lord Castlereagh*, p.68.

RIFLEMAN PRESENTING.
I.—Prone Position.
From E. Baker's "Remarks on Rifle Guns."

The advantage of a shorter carbine-style rifle was that it could be fired and loaded in a range of positions. (Anne S.K. Brown Military Collection)

> and even amusement in this practice. Another disadvantage in its being too small would be, that the rifleman could not become acquainted with his rifle, as in missing the target altogether, he could not ascertain whether he had shot too much to the right, or too much to the left; whereas a target of a proper size, and painted in circles, being easily hit, the rifleman sees at once the fault he has made, and learns to correct it. The rifle recruit must at first be taught to fire at the target without a rest, for if he accustoms himself to make use of a support, he will rarely fire true without one; but as this method will at first be found difficult, and only rendered easy by practice, he should begin by firing at the distance of fifty yards, and increase it by degrees to three hundred.[30]

Riflemen were taught to have pride in their craft, and the various units held competitions, awarded medals, and divided their men into different classes of shots to encourage them to improve.[31] A reasonable level of proficiency at hitting targets at 200 yards was expected, with the best shots competent to 300 yards. Recruits would graduate from the round targets to man-shaped targets at various distances, sometimes even mounted on moving carriages, and firing from a range of positions in different types of terrain. Of course not all recruits would have reached the expected levels, and shooting in battle would have been very different to shooting at targets that did not return fire.

It seems as though the Board of Ordnance and the army took some time to become familiar with the special requirements of a rifle battalion. In 1804 de Rottenburg was having to ask to be repaid his expenses for two moulds for casting balls, and in 1806 he again had to request reimbursement for linen and tallow used in patching the balls that had been provided by the Ordnance Board in Nova Scotia but which were not forthcoming in Portsmouth. He also

30 De Rottenburg, *Regulations*, p.13.
31 Gates, *British Light Infantry*, p.144.

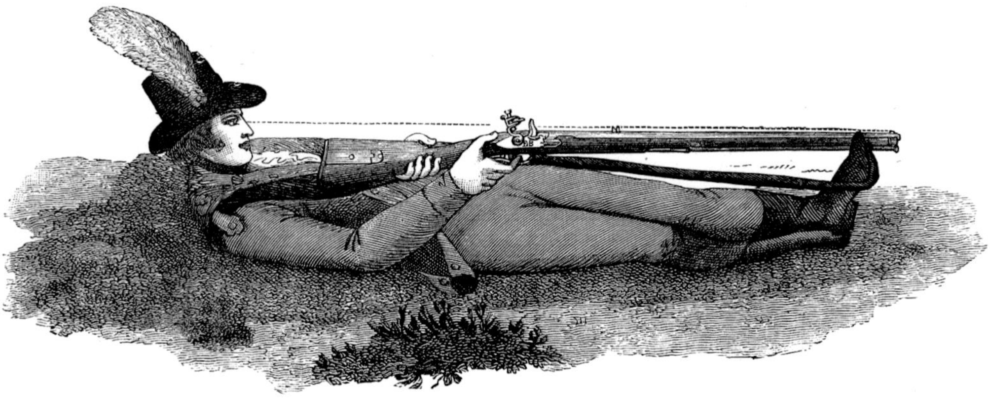

RIFLEMAN PRESENTING.

II.—Back Position.

From E. Baker's "Remarks on Rifle Guns."

This unlikely looking firing position was also advocated by Ezekiel Baker. (Anne S.K. Brown Military Collection)

had to lobby for the same allowances and articles for rifle repair that were allowed for the 95th.[32] In 1813, after five years in the field, repairs and maintenance to the 5th Battalion's rifles were costing over £500 per year.[33]

In 1808, just prior to the battalion sailing for Portugal Major William Davy, who had recently taken over command of the battalion, still had to request items he considered essential. He wrote:

> The 5th Battalion, 60th regiment, never having been provided with small wooden mallets for the purpose of driving the forced rifle-balls into the barrel, and this instrument being absolutely necessary in the field, I feel it my duty to represent that one mallet for every two men should, if possible, be furnished. They should be made of hard wood with a handle about six inches long, pierced with a hole at the extremity of the handle for fastening a string to it.[34]

In 1809, whilst on campaign, Davy wrote to the adjutant general informing him of problems with the powder horns issued to the 5th Battalion:

> I beg leave to state to you, for the information of his Royal Highness the Commander-in-Chief, that the powder-horns with which the 5th Battalion 60th regiment is supplied, have, by experience, been found to be ill-adapted to the service, and by their construction have not only occasioned much loss of powder, and subjected the

32 Entry in Index to Out-letters, Foreign Troops, 5/60th, TNA, WO 2/54, pp.33 & 36.

33 Particulars of the yearly extra allowances to captains of companies for the repair of rifles, TNA, WO 12/7075.

34 Davy to AAG, Cork, 11 June 1808, quoted in Rigaud, *Celer et Audax*, p.24.

> colonel to great expenses in repairs, but have proved after all to be entirely useless, being too large and having no measure fitted to them.
>
> They have been furnished by Messrs. Beseley and Reise of Parliament Street, London, after patterns delivered to them, but experience having now shown their inutility, I beg leave to suggest the propriety of providing the battalion with powder-flasks of the same description as those in possession of the 95th regiment, large enough to contain forty rounds of fine-grain powder at five drachms each round, including the priming, with proper measures adapted to them for different distances.[35]

However, the Peninsular War was not the first opportunity that the 5th Battalion would have to prove their skills and their equipment. Only weeks after they had been incorporated into the battalion in 1798 the plan for the Isle of Wight companies to join the others in the West Indies had to be postponed. They were instead to be sent to Ireland where rebellion had broken out and French invasion threatened.

35 Davy to AG, 14 June 1809, quoted in Rigaud, *Celer et Audax*, p.25.

4

Rebellion

As Revolution embroiled France in deepening chaos, many in Ireland viewed the prospect of similar turmoil spreading to their country with increasing fear, but for others the French example was one to be emulated and a reason for hope. Deep divisions were already all too evident in Irish society. The mostly Protestant ruling class struggled to maintain control over a largely Catholic population but the conflict was not as strictly sectarian as it was to become during the 19th and 20th centuries. The United Irish Society was formed in 1791, largely by Anglican and Presbyterian liberals seeking moderate political reforms such as an extension to the voting franchise. Some concessions were made, but the society was banned in 1794, turning it into an underground movement that spread from parish to parish, and county to county. One of the leaders, Wolfe Tone, called for all-out revolution and an alliance with France. In 1796 14,000 French troops sailed for Ireland and were only stopped by bad weather.[1]

The government raised local yeomanry and militia units to counter the threats of rebellion and invasion. Many of these troops turned out to be ill-disciplined and prone to inflame opposition by their brutality. Some of the population, who were loyal to the crown, also formed their own society called the Orange Order, to defend the Protestant ascendency. Tensions remained high in 1797 and into early 1798; magistrates were murdered by United Irishmen and a sometimes brutal programme of arms searches by the Army resulted in 129,583 guns, swords, pikes, and other weapons being seized or surrendered.[2] Spies confirmed the government's worst fears; Wolfe Tone had petitioned the French government for support and French troops were being gathered in readiness for an invasion. Ireland was a powder keg with a fuse rapidly burning towards it. In March the Privy Council declared that the country was in a state of rebellion. The government arrested much of the Untied Irish Society leadership and began to urgently reinforce the Irish garrisons.[3] It was not going to be a conventional conflict and light troops, with their skirmishing and patrolling skills, would be especially useful.

1 E.H.S. Jones, *An Invasion that Failed* (Oxford: Blackwell, 1950), p.108.

2 Anon., *The Report from the Secret Committee of the House of Commons* (Dublin: James King, 1798), Appendix XXXIX, p.334.

3 T. Pakenham, *The Year of Liberty: The Great Irish Rebellion of 1798* (New York: Times Books, 1998), pp.10-34.

The men of 5th Battalion from the Isle of Wight disembarked from the *Medusa* transport ship at Cobh on 20 April. Sailing with them in the *Medusa,* and also on the *Ulysses*, were their former comrades of the Hompesch Mounted Riflemen. Lieutenant Colonel de Rottenburg was still on leave so Major de Verna was in command of the 5th Battalion's detachment. Captains Gerhardy, d'Erp, and Schneider led companies of just over 100 men each, with Captain de Weise's being a cadre of less than 30. The total strength of the detachment was 361.[4] Earlier in April the home secretary, the Duke of Portland, had relayed a letter from Lord Castlereagh, acting chief secretary for Ireland, to the secretary at war, William Windham, voicing his concerns about the employment of the 60th in Ireland.[5] Many captured United Irishmen had been forced to enlist in the other battalions of the 60th and sent to the West Indies. An inspection of the 1/60th from 1797 shows that 80 of the men were Irish.[6] Enquiries were requested to be made to ensure that no United Irishmen were included in the troops being sent to Ireland, but with the 5th Battalion being newly formed from exclusively foreign troops the fears were unfounded.

Major de Verna marched his men first to Cork and then south west to Bandon, where they were placed under the command of Brigadier General John Moore. Moore would later win fame and an early grave in the Spain but even in 1798 he was recognised as a capable and experienced officer, having seen action during the American War of Independence, in the Mediterranean, and the West Indies. He would go on play a large part in the creation of more light infantry units in the British Army. An order had been given for all arms to be surrendered by the populace and Moore set about enforcing it in his district:

> My orders were to treat the people with as much harshness as possible, as far as words and manner went, and to supply themselves with whatever provisions were necessary to enable them to live well. My wish was to excite terror, and by that means obtain our end speedily. I thought this better than to act more mildly, and be obliged to continue for any time the real oppression; and, as I was present everywhere myself, I had no doubt of being able to prevent any great abuses by the troops.[7]

Moore was one of the more liberal commanders and did his best to stop his men committing atrocities.[8] In May the remaining leaders of the United Irishmen, frustrated with delays and prevarication from the French and knowing that the disarmament campaign was weakening them, decided to go ahead with a full scale rebellion. The chosen date was 23 May but the government's spies gave them sufficient warning so that most of the Dublin leadership were arrested before they had chance to act, and the Army was on the streets to quash the revolt in the capital before it caught hold. This left the rest of the United Irishmen around the country without any central direction and rather than one explosive eruption of dissent the rebellion fizzled and spluttered sporadically as the leadership in each county decided to take action.

4 Disembarkation Return 20 April 1798, TNA, HO 100/73, p.143.

5 M. Lewis to W. Windham, 15 April 1798, TNA, WO 40/10.

6 Inspection of 1/60th, TNA, WO 27/80,

7 J.F. Maurice, *The Diary of Sir John Moore* (London: Arnold, 1904), Vol. I, p.289.

8 C.H. Teeling, *Sequel to Personal Narrative of the Irish Rebellion of 1798* (Belfast: John Hodgson, 1830), p.126.

The 5th Battalion's campaign in and around Wexford, 1798.

The organisation of the United Irishmen was based on the existing political boundaries. Each parish was expected to raise a company of approximately 30 men with an elected captain. Each barony (a collection of parishes) formed a battalion headed by a colonel. Generals commanded groups of battalions. Most of the leaders were liberal Protestant land owners or merchants, but there were also many Catholic landowners, tradesmen, tenant farmers, and a surprising number of Catholic priests. The rank and file were drawn from the predominantly Catholic lower classes, apart from in Ulster where they were largely Presbyterian. The level of military experience, radicalism, commitment, and brutality varied greatly, adding to the sporadic and patchy nature of the rebellion. For most companies and battalions the first priority was arming themselves, and many of the locations where seized arms had been stored were their early targets. Whenever any soldiers were killed they were quickly stripped of their muskets, cartridge boxes, swords, or pistols.[9] Most rebels though, were armed with pikes or anything else they could lay their hands on. In many areas where the rebels were initially successful the rebellion stalled because the local leaders, with no central direction, did not know what to do next.

The Army's response was equally sporadic in the early stages. With communication to Dublin often cut by the uprising, local commanders had to decide what action to take themselves. Only 19,000 of the 77,000 troops in the country were from regular battalions, with the rest being made of less experienced and often ill-disciplined yeomanry, militia and volunteer units.[10] Many of these chose to stay in their barracks, some withdrew to safer areas, but a few commanders responded with a level of savagery that inflamed the situation further. As reports reached him from around the country, Lieutenant General Gerard Lake, newly appointed Commander-in-Chief for Ireland, began to make his dispositions and order his troops to deploy where they were needed most. One of those areas was County Wexford, where the rebels had effectively taken control of large areas of the county.

Captain Schneider's company was detached to join Major General Henry Johnson's brigade at New Ross in early June. Captain Weise's understrength recruiting company remained in Bandon, whilst Moore, with a battalion of light companies drawn from various units and the remaining two full strength companies from the 5th Battalion, was, after some indecision, ordered north to Fermoy, in the direction of Wexford. Leaving on 13 June Moore's men arrived in Fermoy two days later, and two days after that they reached Waterford before carrying on for New Ross and joining with Johnson. The total distance of the march was approximately 120 miles, meaning that the troops would have had to cover an average of 20 miles a day. They would start marching before dawn, but Moore still described the heat and the dust as intolerable.[11]

The rebels were camped on nearby Lacken Hill and Johnson planned an attack for the morning of 19 June. Moore wrote:

> The march was ordered for 2 A.M., but from rain it was necessarily postponed till 6 A.M. I had the 60th Yagers, 900 Light Infantry, 50 Hompesch Cavalry, and six pieces of artillery. The rebels were posted on a hill about a mile and a half from Ross. We saw them plainly drawn up, I thought with the intention of fighting us. The road I marched by led directly on the left of their position; they allowed me to come within cannon shot, and then retreated. General Johnstone, with the centre, was moving at the same moment to attack them in front. The Yagers in the pursuit killed sixty or seventy of them.[12]

The heavy rain had led to many of the rebels coming down off the hill to seek shelter. As the sun rose, mist in the valley prevented them from seeing the approach of three British

9 D. Gahan, *The People's Rising* (Dublin: Gill & Macmillan, 1995), p.16.
10 Butler, *Annals*, Vol. II, p.20.
11 Maurice, *Moore*, p.295.
12 Maurice, *Moore*, p.297.

columns. They quickly formed a rearguard of pikemen and retreated, leaving behind significant quantities of their supplies and arms.

Johnson's brigade took possession of the hill and then returned to New Ross. They marched north-east towards Enniscorthy the following day. Moore was ordered south-west to Foulksmills where he was to meet Lieutenant Colonel Lord Dalhousie, who was landing with troops on the coast, before advancing to Taghmon near Wexford. Lake's plan to encircle the rebels with columns coming from multiple directions was progressing well, preventing the rebels from advancing to Dublin or moving west. The rebels could have dispersed and awaited the arrival of the French but many wanted to defend their home and families, so they gradually concentrated around their camp on Vinegar Hill.

Moore's brigade reached the vicinity of Foulksmills just before noon on 20 June. There was no sign of Dalhousie so they made camp for the night. The following morning there was still no sign of the reinforcements, patrols were sent out and came back without having found Dalhousie, and by mid-afternoon Moore's patience was exhausted and he ordered his men to march. Just as they began to move off, the dust of an approaching force was spotted across the shallow valley of the Corock River. Moore wrote in his diary:

> We had not marched above a mile when a cloud of dust was seen moving towards us. This we immediately perceived to be a large party of rebels. I knew something of the ground from having reconnoitred it in the morning. I immediately ordered the Yagers to advance and skirmish, whilst I formed part of the Light Infantry on the right and left of the road, and then ran forward the guns to a commanding situation at the crossing of two roads.[13]

Moore deployed his troops either side the crossroads, about a quarter mile from Goff's Bridge. The rebels were not expecting to encounter any British troops but their commander, a priest named Roche, arranged his troops on the opposite side of the valley and sent several hundred armed men to take the bridge. Moore's force of around 1,000 was outnumbered by more than five to one. There was a steady exchange of shots between the 5th Battalion and the armed rebels. The accurate and sustained fire of the rifles inflicted heavy casualties on the rebels. Roche sent his pikemen around to outflank the troops. Moore ordered the light infantry to counter the move, in his report to Lake he stated:

> The 60th regiment, finding no further opposition in front, had, of themselves, inclined to their left to engage the body which was attempting to turn us – and the action here was for a short time pretty sharp, as the rebels were in great numbers, and armed with both muskets and pikes.[14]

There was fierce fighting amongst the dense woods and in the fields. The superior numbers of the rebels began to push the army back. Moore had to personally steady his men:

13 Maurice, *Moore*, p.296.

14 Quoted in W.H. Maxwell, *History of the Irish Rebellion in 1798* (London: George Cruikshank, 1871), p.141.

> I met the Light Infantry, the Yagers, and some Dragoons all in the woods mixed and retreating. The enemy was following close, and firing. I succeeded in stopping some immediately, and got them to jump out of the road and make a front on each side of it. I then encouraged the rest first to halt, then to advance, and, when I saw them ready for it, I took off my hat, put my horse into a trot, gave a huzza, and got them to make a push. The tide immediately turned; we drove the rebels before us, and killed a great many. They attempted two or three times afterwards to make a stand, but failed.[15]

Roche sent more pikemen to attack the centre and they fought with bravery and determination but the cannon, rifle and musket fire defeated them and they could not break through. In the early evening, after four hours of battle the rebels began to withdraw. Moore let them go. Dalhousie arrived just as the last of the rebels left the field. Rebel casualties were heavy and they may have left 300 dead on the battlefield. Moore's force lost 10 killed and 48 wounded.[16] Privates Ernst Klitzman and Gerhard Osting from Captain Gerhardy's company were the first members of the 5th Battalion to fall in battle.[17] Captain Ladislaus de Villers Masburgh was slightly wounded.

With Moore delayed, the rest of Lake's columns got into position for what he hoped would be a decisive battle. Miles Byrne, one of the rebels, described their position and their predicament:

> How could our generals for an instant think that Vinegar Hill was a military position susceptible of defence for any time without provisions, military stores, or great guns? It stands high, no doubt, over the river Slaney and the town of Enniscorthy, which it commands but on the other side, both artillery and cavalry, as well as infantry, can march to the top of the hill with the greatest ease. But the die of war was cast. Our little Irish army must be drawn up and assembled on this hill en masse, and there wait the arrival of the English army, now moving after us from all directions, with vast parks of artillery, well supplied with everything necessary for battle, whilst we had with us but two six-pounders, and a small mortar or howitzer, with scarcely a round of ammunition for these cannons.[18]

Captain Schneider's company, with the rest of Johnson's brigade, arrived at the edge of Enniscorthy on the evening of 20 June. The troops were in the process of making camp when a large force of rebels advanced from the town in several columns protected by skirmishers. Johnson replied with heavy cannon fire and the rebels fell back to a nearby ridge. The rebels on Vinegar Hill were now aware they were effectively surrounded. Byrne wrote:

> It was a dark night, but the thousands of little fires to be seen in the fields and plain all round the hill, where our people were preparing to get something to eat and to

15 Maurice, *Moore*. pp.297.

16 E. Ó Cathaoir, 'German Mercenaries in Ireland 1798-1807', *The Irish Sword No. 90 Vol. XXII*. p.413.

17 June 1798 Pay List, TNA, WO 12/7066.

18 M. Byrne, *The Memoirs of Miles Byrne* (Dublin: Maunsel & Co, 1907), p.122.

The rebels' camp on Vinegar Hill. (Taken from W.H. Maxwell, *The History of the Irish Rebellion in 1798*)

> pass the night, afforded plenty of light, and presented at the same time the appearance of a vast camp, or rather the bivouac of a regular French army.[19]

Just before dawn, at around 5:00 a.m., Johnson ordered his cannon to open fire at the rebels blocking his path to Enniscorthy. The artillery and rapid volleys drove the rebels off the ridge and back into the town but the rebels' sharpshooters made good use of the hedges, ditches, and other cover to inflict numerous casualties on the army as they advanced. Johnson paused for an hour whilst the main attack on Vinegar Hill began. Lake's columns also used the ground to their advantage and the rebels, with little cover and less firepower, were enfiladed by cannon, howitzer and musket fire from all sides. As the soldiers marched forwards they could see the rebel flag and a tree of liberty attached to the old windmill at the top of the hill. Lake's three columns quickly reached the summit, capturing 13 artillery pieces,[20] but many of the rebels manage to retreat, Miles Byrne amongst them:

> Our retreat from Vinegar Hill was not so disastrous as might have been expected, from the powerful force of regular troops well supplied with artillery, which

19 Byrne, *Memoirs*, p.123.
20 Return of Ordnance taken from the Rebels on Vinegar Hill 21 June 1798, TNA, HO 100/77 p.190.

The defeat of the rebels on Vinegar Hill. (Taken from W.H. Maxwell, *The History of the Irish Rebellion in 1798*)

> General Lake had at his disposition to send after us. No doubt, the cruel slaughter of all those unarmed and helpless people who were overtaken in the environs of Enniscorthy, and for a mile from the hill, was beyond all description. Mercy at this moment was out of the question; there was no instance of a single person being made prisoner on this occasion, all were barbarously butchered.[21]

Meanwhile Johnson had pushed his troops, including Captain Schneider's company, into the town, reaching Duffry Gate, and so began the fiercest fighting of the day. The rebel pikemen contested every street, those with muskets fired from windows and doorways, but the soldiers drove them steadily back to the market square where the army's advance was stalled for an hour. A 6-pounder was brought forward but then stormed by the rebels. It was rapidly retaken and the rebels driven back towards the vital bridge over the wide river Slaney. If Johnson's men could take the bridge they would be able to attack the rebels retreating from Vinegar Hill in the flank. The rebels left many wounded men in the court house, which was soon set on fire by the troops, killing those trapped inside.[22]

21 Byrne, *Memoirs*, p.133.
22 Gahan, *Rising*, p.210.

Rebels occupied one side of the bridge and the army the other. Each side made repeated charges along the narrow, five-arch length. The rebels were tenacious. Johnson eventually managed to take the western end, but it was too late. Rebel reinforcements arrived and acted as a rearguard, giving time for many of the rebels to flee. Archibald McLaren, a sergeant in the Dumbartonshire Militia, who took part in the attack, wrote:

> As soon as the Light Brigade had gained the summit of the hill a general foot-race commenced among the Croppies, and happy was the man who could sit down some miles hence and thank his legs for carrying him so far out the reach of danger. When the enemy retreated the cavalry pursued and made great havock among them, though some of them had the impudence (when they got on the inside of a ditch) to turn about and fire upon their pursuers.[23]

McLaren also recalled what happened in the aftermath of the battle:

> At Owlart there lived a woman who had three daughters, she had a son also who was wounded at Vinegar-hill, he returned to his mother's house to be cured, but the soldiers dragged him out and shot him in a potatoe garden where he was afterwards buried. Two Militia Soldiers watching their opportunity, caught one of the dumb girls and her mother whom they ravished. The father coming to their assistance was used with the utmost brutality. The mother and daughter came to the Camp and by the General's permission pointed out the ravishers, who were condemned to receive a severe flogging.[24]

During the morning Moore's brigade advanced to Taghmon as ordered, but received two emissaries from the rebels in Wexford offering the town's surrender. Moore sent word to Lake for instructions but receiving no reply moved to occupy high ground near Wexford, driving off a few rebels in the process. Unfortunately Moore's movement opened up a gap in Lake's trap sufficient for 4,000 to 5,000 rebels to escape. From the hills Moore could see people fleeing from Wexford and also noticed fires starting. Fearing for the safety of the population, he sent a small force to occupy the town, wary of exceeding his orders and knowing that Lake planned to occupy the town himself.

George Weale, of the 29th Foot, who had arrived with Lord Dalhousie and seen the aftermath of Foulkesmills, now entered Wexford:

> ...to a young soldier, the scene was appalling and revolting. War, even among the most illuminated and Christian powers, is dreadful and disastrous; but here it raged in all the horrors of cool, malevolent, and murderous destruction;– and language itself must shrink from an attempt at the description of the fell and ruthless cruelties practised by those rebels on their loyal fellow subjects and countrymen.

23 A. McLaren, *A Minute Description of the Battles of Gorey, Arklow, & Vinegar-Hill* (Publisher Unknown, 1798), p.29.
24 McLaren, *Battles*, p.32.

The rebels executing their prisoners on the bridge at Wexford. (Taken from W.H. Maxwell, *The History of the Irish Rebellion in 1798*)

> The spacious bridge of Wexford, built over the river Slaney, was made of wood. On this the unfortunate loyalists, who had fallen into the hands of the rebels, were brought, and in humanly and barbarously piked to death, and thrown into the river. This bloody operation was performed by a number of rebels thrusting their pikes in front and rear of those miserable victims and then poising them up by main strength, and precipitating them into the river. With reluctance I add, that these atrocities were sanctioned by a man, the duties of whose office required him to use every means to suppress them; and such was the quantity of human blood that was thus shed on the bridge, that it had all the appearance of a slaughter house.[25]

The 5th Battalion's casualties on 21 June mostly came, unsurprisingly, from Captain Schneider's company: Sergeant Frederick Degenhardt was killed; Privates Gatz, Koch, Schwab, and Walzer, were wounded, as was their commander Lewis Schneider. Corporal Christian Wolbold was also wounded: subsequently promoted to sergeant to replace Degenhardt, he was invalided from the regiment before the end of the year. Private Christian Bick went missing from the companies with Moore and does not appear on the muster again.[26]

25 G. Weale, *An Interesting Memoir of George Weale* (Leamington: G. Weale, 1838), p.9.
26 June 1798 Pay List, TNA, WO 12/7066.

Of the rebels that escaped from Vinegar Hill as many as half deserted the night after the battle and went back to their homes.[27] Those that remained headed for the Wicklow mountains, hoping that they could bide their time there and await the promised French invasion. Lake occupied Wexford and began the first of many trials, hanging two rebels from the bridge. Johnson returned to his original base at Mallow. Moore marched his brigade to Taghmon, was promoted to major general, and tasked to hunt down the rebels in the mountains. He was reinforced with another battalion of light infantry to give him a total force of between 1,600 and 1,700.[28]

The rebels were rumoured to be in the area of Glenmalure in the Wicklow Mountains, Lake joined Moore and an attack was planned. Again four columns were to try and surround the enemy. Moore's brigade advanced up a steep hill overlooking the valley. Sergeant McLaren, who had joined the brigade and referring to the 5th Battalion as Hessians wrote: 'We marched, or rather climbed up a large hill, while a flanking party of the Hessians kept on our left among a number of rocks which we would imagine to be inaccessable to any creatures but goats.'[29] At the summit the 5th Battalion took three prisoners, and the riflemen were allowed bread and whiskey before they descended into the valley. There was no further sign of the rebels. Arriving at a hamlet at dusk, and without rations, the men were allowed to butcher some cows from a nearby field. McLaren then recalls:

> A poor country man having complained that his cabin had been destroyed, the Colonel gave orders that no body should give him any further molestation, but a little after this a Hessian came and offered to pull down some sticks from the hut; the centinel told him it was against orders 'I don't care damn for order, I must have stick, boil cow' said the Hessian, and seemed mightily offended at the interruption; for, he looked upon a liberty to plunder, as his undoubted priviledge.[30]

The following day Moore's brigade retraced their steps and the 5th Battalion fired upon some rebels shadowing the brigade, driving them off. That night it rained heavily and the men spent an uncomfortable night under blankets, huddling around turf fires. McLaren then wrote: 'Two Hessians who ventured too far upon a marauding scheme were Piked by the Rebels; but as their conduct was quite contrary to repeated orders, the loss was not much lamented.'[31] Several men of the 5th Battalion went missing or were killed during July. From Captain Schneider's company, which had re-joined the others, Private John Lohmann was killed on 6 July at Taghmon, Privates John Asper and Adrian Heiges are marked as 'missing 12th July, suspected to be killed', and Private William Batallion is listed as 'missed 17th July, suspected to be killed' and was later confirmed dead. Two other soldiers are marked as having died that month as well but the cause is not given. Privates John Pollenstein and Henry Todges from Captain Gerhardy's company are also listed as missing from 17 July,

27 Gahan, *Rising*, p.222.
28 Maurice, *Moore*, p.301.
29 McLaren, *Battles*, p.35.
30 McLlaren, *Battles*, p.36.
31 McLaren, *Battles*, p.37.

suspected killed. Private Anton Horwarth went missing on 19 July but was recorded as in the hospital at Dublin on the next pay list.[32]

It is not clear from the dates which two 'Hessians' were the ones that were not lamented, but there is an account of two members of the 5th Battalion falling into the hands of the rebels:

> As soon as they were made prisoners, one of them perceived a rebel named Harry Flood to be without shoes. Instantly taking off his own shoes, he said to Flood, "You have no shoes; try will these fit you". Flood put them on, and when the poor fellows' examination had ended, and they were condemned to death – horrible to think of it Flood was the first man to pike him. The Hessian seized the pike, though fast through his body, pulled it out and wrested it from the unmanly Flood, and would have killed him but was knocked down, and both men were killed…'[33]

Lieutenant Colonel de Rottenburg returned from leave on 20 July. Moore continued to try and find the elusive rebels, harassing them, engaging in several small actions and patrolling the mountains. As August progressed there were a spate of 10 desertions from the 5th Battalion; even the recruiting party in Germany was listed as having deserted in September. On the night of 21 August the brigade was in the Glen of Imaal and the rebels were suspected to be very close. Private George Pallas was placed on picket duty at 11:00 p.m. Corporal Buntz arrived with his relief at 2:00 a.m. but Pallas was not at his post. Buntz and the relief searched for him but without success and reported Pallas to Sergeant Schille, who ordered another search. Nothing being found of Pallas, or his rifle and equipment, de Rottenburg was informed.[34]

On 22 August the French invasion finally came, too late to help most of the rebels, and too little to have any real hope of successfully taking Ireland. *Général de Brigade* Humbert landed with just over 1,000 men at Killala, County Mayo, in the north-west. Humbert succeeded in defeating British troops at Castlebar, giving new hope to the rebels, but as British forces gathered it became obvious that the French, and the few rebels who had joined them, were heavily outnumbered. Moore's brigade, with the 5th Battalion, was ordered to Athlone and travelled part of the way by canal. British columns, including Moore's, harried and pursued Humbert's troops eventually confronting them at Ballinamuck on 8 September. After a brief battle Humbert surrendered. The rebellion was over.

The 5th Battalion was quartered at Carrick-on-Shannon for a short time before returning to Cork. In the meantime an advert was placed in *The Dublin Journal* newspaper on 11 September:

> Deserted. From the 5th Batt. of the 60th Regt., George Pallas, Rifleman, native of Hungary, aged 19 years; 5 feet 2 inches high; brown eyes, black hair, small face, speaks no English, wears green uniform with red facing, his regimental sword with black belt and cartridge box, brown leather knapsack, and his rifle gun.[35]

32 July 1798 Pay List, TNA, WO 12/7066.
33 Quoted in Ó Cathaoir, 'German Mercenaries', p.414.
34 The Trial of George Pallas, TNA, WO 71/181.
35 Butler, *Annals*, Vol. II, p.16.

George Pallas was subsequently arrested at Naas by Lieutenant Timan of the Hompesch Mounted Rifles. On 7 November his court martial was convened in Cork's council chamber.[36] Lieutenant Colonel Thomas of the 41st Foot was president, with the court made up of 11 officers from various regiments including the recovered Captain Schneider and Lieutenant Münsthal of the 5th Battalion. Schneider and Sergeant Michel acted as interpreters for some of the witnesses and the defendant. Corporal Buntz, Sergeant Schille, and Lieutenant de Gilse all testified. Particular attention was placed on the facts that the rebels were thought to be close to the camp and that Pallas had taken his rifle and equipment with him. Then it was Pallas' turn to defend himself:

> The prosecution being closed and the Prisoner put on his defence, says he was exceedingly in liquor when he quitted his post and that on getting about a mile from it, he fell asleep, and on awakening he feared returning to the camp, but having heard that a soldier who had given himself up, had been pardoned, he was taking the road to Dublin, for the same purpose, in hopes of obtaining his pardon, when he was apprehended by Lieutenant Timan of Hompesch Dragoons, with his arms accoutrements & ammunition, and absolutely denies any intention of joining the Enemy, and further submits to the mercy of the court.[37]

The facts of the case being clear, the court passed sentence:

> The court having taken into consideration, the prosecution and what the prisoner had to offer in his defence, do find the Prisoner George Pallas private of the 60th Regiment Guilty of the crimes with which he is charged, being in breach of the 1st Article, of the 6th Section, and the 10th Article of the 14th Section, of the Articles of War, and do thereby adjudge him to suffer Death.[38]

The first article of war, the rules that governed the Army and Royal Navy, which Pallas contravened, dealt with desertion, and the second with leaving his post. Pallas was shot in a field by a firing squad, probably made up of men from the 5th Battalion, on 24 November.[39] Several other deserters were returned to the battalion before the end of the year and they received much more lenient punishments, with many being sent to Duncannon for transfer to other battalions of the 60th. Pallas' crime seems to have been deemed more severe because he had deserted his post in the face of the enemy, and also taken his weapon. There were fears at the time that many deserters were joining the United Irishmen. One of the captured rebel leaders did claim that three 'Hessians' were amongst 126 deserters in his ranks.[40]

Many of the histories of the rebellion, folk songs, and memoirs single out the behaviour of the 'Hessians', a term applied both to the 5th Battalion and the Hompesch Mounted Rifles,

36 The Trial of George Pallas, TNA, WO 71/181.

37 The Trial of George Pallas, TNA, WO 71/181.

38 The Trial of George Pallas, TNA, WO 71/181.

39 November 1798 Pay List, TNA, WO 12/7066; F. H. Tuckey, *The County & City Remembrancer* (Cork: Osborne, Savage & Son, 1837), p.352.

40 Ó Cathaoir, 'German Mercenaries', p.415.

as being more brutal and savage than other soldiers. The Reverend James Gordon wrote in 1803:

> The Hessians exceeded the other troops in the business of depredation and many loyalists who had escaped from the rebels, were put to death by these foreigners. — To send such troops into the country in such at state of affairs, was, in my humble opinion, a wrong step in government, who cannot be supposed indifferent to the lives of loyal subjects.[41]

Charles Hamilton Teeling, a rebel, also singled out the Hompesch Mounted Rifles in particular:

> This body of German mercenaries, selected by the British Minister as admirable auxiliaries in his war of extermination on the Irish people, had, by the perpetration of outrages hitherto unexampled, rendered themselves peculiarly obnoxious. Their acts of pillage, and of yet greater atrocities, were not always confined to any particular party: and the grossness of their insults to unprotected females, rendered their name detested and accursed. "Kill a Hessian," became a proverbial term and men, infuriated by their presence, have been known to break from their ranks, regardless of consequences, even should they perish in the attempt, to deal out their full meed of vengeance on the ruffian despoiler.[42]

Some of the claims were made long after the rebellion and became part of the mythology of the uprising. The very term 'Hessian' harked back to the Germans employed during the American War of Independence and who were similarly vilified; largely unjustly and for political reasons. Whilst there are many general claims about the behaviour of the 5th Battalion and the Hompesch Mounted Rifles there are no incidences of them being admonished by senior officers or being punished for excessive brutality, unlike many yeomanry and militia units. However, there is also no reason to think they would have behaved any better than other units. To some extent it may have been that their uniform and appearance meant they were easily identifiable, and with many speaking no English they may have found it difficult to distinguish the innocent from the rebels.[43]

At the end of 1798 and the start of 1799, de Rottenburg began to make preparations to leave Ireland for the West Indies to join with the rest of the 5th Battalion. He had likely heard of von Schlammersdorf's death and knew he was now in command of the battalion. Nine soldiers, including former deserters, were transferred to other battalions, 15 were invalided out of the regiment, several were left in hospitals, and 27 Hompesch Mounted Riflemen were transferred into the battalion.[44] However, the 5th Battalion was not quite finished with the United Irishmen.

41 J. Gordon, *History of the Rebellion in Ireland in the year 1798* (London: Dewick, 1803), p.239.

42 C.H. Teeling, *Sequel to Personal Narrative of the Irish Rebellion of 1798* (Belfast: John Hodgson, 1830), p.131.

43 Ó Cathaoir, 'German Mercenaries', pp.406-8.

44 January & February 1799 Pay Lists TNA, WO 12/7066.

At 6:00 a.m. on the morning of 26 February 1799 the men of the 5th Battalion and several hundred other troops, including artillery, marched nearly four hundred United Irishmen from New Geneva Barracks in Cork to a ship waiting in the harbour.[45] These men had been sentenced to forced enlistment in the army and service overseas. The ship was the *Admiral de Vries*, a former 68-gun ship-of-the-line captured from the Dutch at the Battle of Camperdown in 1797 which had been put back into service as a troop transport. It would not only take the prisoners to Martinique, but also carry the four companies of the 5th Battalion who would act as guards for the voyage. There were even fears of mutiny aboard the *Admiral de Vries*. Several men who had taken part in the naval mutinies in 1797 were removed from the crew and de Rottenburg requested that there be no United Irishmen in the crew, something that apparently could not be guaranteed.[46]

The embarkation return lists one lieutenant colonel, one major, five captains, seven lieutenants, three ensigns, one adjutant (one of the lieutenants), one paymaster, one assistant surgeon, 18 sergeants, 20 corporals, nine buglers, 292 privates, two officers' servants, 23 women, and nine children. Five sick were left back on the Isle of Wight. Captain de Villers Masburgh, wounded at Foulksmills, was on leave. The *Admiral de Vries* finally set sail 9 March, as the sun went down behind the Wicklow Mountains. Far more of the 5th Battalion who sailed that day would die of fever in the Caribbean than had died in action during the fighting in Ireland.

45 M. Durey, *Andrew Bryson's Ordeal* (Cork: Cork University Press, 1998), p.67.

46 M. Durey, 'White Slaves: Irish Rebel Prisoners and the British Army in the West Indies 1799-1804', *Journal of the Society of Army Historical Research*, Vol. LXXX, p.308.

5

The Windward and Leeward Islands

Whilst the companies formed on the Isle of Wight fought the Irish rebels the rest of the 5th Battalion remained in the West Indies. The Windward and Leeward Islands are two groups of islands that form a long arc from Puerto Rico, eastwards and southwards, down to the northern coast of South America. Some were French colonies, some British, but there were also Spanish, Dutch, Danish and Swedish islands amongst them. The region was vitally important to both the British and French economies. Goods flowed from Britain to West Africa where they were traded for slaves, who were then shipped to work on the sugar, coffee, and other plantations of the Caribbean. The taxes and duties raised either directly or indirectly from this trade were crucial to Britain affording to continue the war against France. Defending the scattered islands and attempting to deny the French the profits from their own colonies was a substantial drain on the Army's manpower, but strategically vital to Britain's war effort.

Despite its importance, the West Indies was not a popular posting for either the French or British armies. British regiments would frequently protest, or even riot, when told they were to be sent there. Officers would often seek to transfer to other regiments.[1] The reason for this fear was disease, particularly yellow fever, which could claim up to half or three quarters of a battalion's strength in a single year.[2] However, since the 60th was limited to service in North America and the West Indies most of its battalions served there for many years. Writing to Lieutenant General Trigge, commander-in-chief of the Windward and Leeward Islands in July, 1799, Henry Dundas, Secretary of War, stated that he considered 'the 60th Regiment as an institution highly beneficial and almost absolutely necessary' for maintaining a European force in the Leeward Islands.[3] Dundas carried on to sing the regiment's praises, but did admit they sometime needed diligent attention from their officers.

George Bent, of the 6/60th, had a very clear opinion on why foreign troops were well suited to service in the West Indies:

> Let two regiments of an equal strength embark at Portsmouth for the West Indies, the one composed entirely of Britons, the other of Foreigners; let them arrive together and be stationed in the same quarters, and, at the expiration of two years,

1 M.R. Howard, *Death Before Glory* (Barnsley: Pen & Sword, 2015), p.138.

2 Howard, *Death Before Glory*, p.199.

3 Dundas to Trigge 15 July 1799, TNA, WO 1/87, p.227.

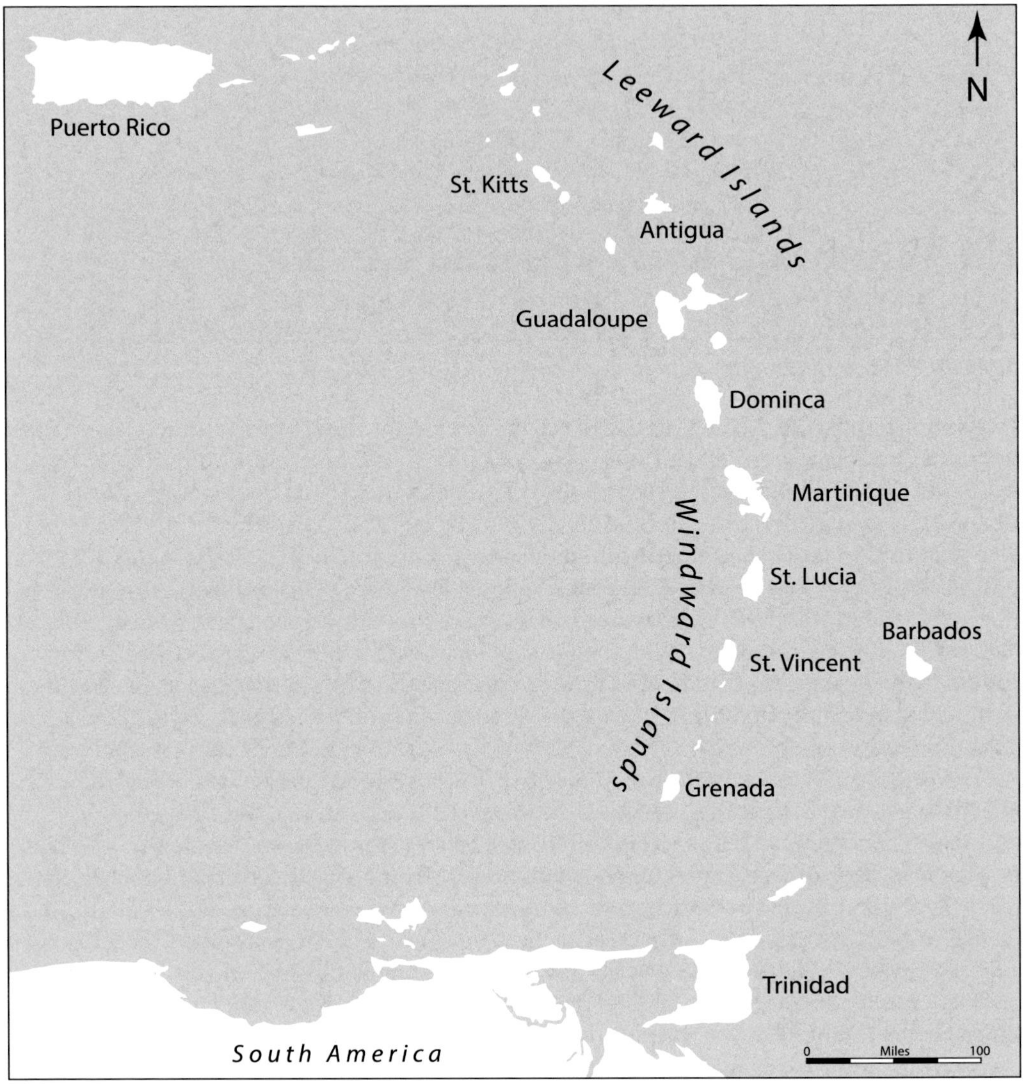

The Windward & Leeward Islands

it is found that the latter regiment musters double the effectives of the former, and it is the liquor that must account for it. The cheapness, and great plenty of intoxicants is too great a temptation to the British soldier, who, when weakened by a state of continued inebriation, falls an easy victim to the Island fevers. The foreigner on the contrary, being more naturally inclined to sobriety, and subject also to severer discipline, does not so readily collapse.[4]

4 M. Bent, 'A Royal American', *Journal of the Society of Army Historical Research*, Vol. I, p.98.

Drunkenness was a major problem in the West Indies garrisons, and was exacerbated by long periods of inactivity combined with the ready availability of cheap rum. Foreign troops' increased sobriety, it was thought, led to fewer succumbing to disease.[5] Light infantry skills were also much in demand as the fighting in the region often took place amongst the forests and mountains of the islands' interiors against locally raised militias, or involved quelling slave revolts. Cavalry often could not be used due to the terrain and conventional line infantry tactics were not effective against irregular troops.[6] In 1794 Lieutenant General Sir Charles Grey had established a light infantry school to improve the skills of the troops under his command.[7]

As 1798 progressed the 5th Battalion was split into several detachments. One was on Martinique, a French island that had been in British hands for four years. A smaller detachment was on Trinidad, a Spanish colony that the Lowenstein Chasseurs had helped to capture the year before. The rest of the 5th Battalion moved from Barbados, the oldest British colony in the region, to Grenada which had changed hands several times between the French and British during the 18th century but had been British since 1783. A French inspired and supported slave revolt on Grenada during 1795 and 1796 had only been narrowly defeated.

St. Ann's Garrison in Bridgetown, Barbados. The first home of the 5th Battalion. (Taken from *The History of Barbados*, published 1848)

5 Wishon, *German Forces*, p.150.

6 Howard, *Death Before Glory*, p.179.

7 J.F.C. Fuller, 'Sir John Moore's Light Infantry Instructions of 1798-1799', *Journal of the Society of Army Historical Research*, Vol. XXX, p.68.

All the companies would have garrisoned forts, barracks or batteries around the islands, often rotating between locations. The routine that the soldiers faced was designed to minimise exposure to the heat of the Caribbean day. They would wake, dress, and parade before the sun was up. A couple of hours of drill would be followed by breakfast at dawn. The men would stay in their barracks until their second meal just after noon, be back in their barracks by two o'clock, have another parade at five, then have more drill and return to their barracks as night fell. Those on guard or other duties would have to suffer the heat, humidity, and frequent heavy rain. Field training gave a break from the routine, but was often limited by the weather.[8] Rum was a predictable solution to boredom, and the army licensed slave women as prostitutes as a further diversion. Larger towns would also have unlicensed brothels and officers often took black mistresses.[9]

Lieutenant James Prevost, who would later join the 5th Battalion. (The Royal Green Jackets (Rifles) Museum)

Lieutenant James Prevost, grandson of Major General Augustine Prevost, who was one of the three Prevost brothers who joined the 60th on its formation during the Seven Years War, served with the 11th Foot in the West Indies before joining the 5th Battalion in 1807. The Prevost family had continued to serve the British crown despite being on the losing side in the American War of Independence and still living in New York State. James' father had been a major with the 60th, and he had three brothers in the British Army, as well as two uncles who were generals and one who was an admiral. James' letters back to his father were often rushed as he sought to ensure his letter was on a departing packet ship. Officers too had to find ways to alleviate the boredom. In May 1804 he wrote:

> I get on very well here, our Dress is rather expensive, we are allowed to wear no other Pantaloons excepting white Jaine which is certainly a little cheaper than in America but everything else is enormous high. I read a great deal now in the morning & more particularly military Books our Colonel is a very sensible & Good Officer he is rather strict with officers as well as Privates. He is very much hurt at present to see some of his Young Officers immediately after breakfast sit down at a Gameing table & nothing is so common as Grog drinking so early in a morning. Thank God I have never had a wish for that Drink in my life.[10]

8 Howard, *Death Before Glory*, p.159.

9 Howard, *Death Before Glory*, p.174.

10 J. Prevost to A. Prevost, 16 May 1804, The Albany Institute of History & Art (AI), Prevost Papers, CR549/II/1dd.

Many of James' letters to his family contain reassurances about his health. In another letter in May 1804 he says: 'I have had a slight attack of the fever only a couple of days confined but am as well as if I was in America.[11]' However, like everyone else at the time he had no understanding of the causes of the fevers that so ravaged the islands and in another letter he wrote:

> Some of the Islands are very unhealthy at present especially to new Comers, a Young man come out in the same vessel with me has had a violent attack of the fever. We left him at Barbados he caught it by getting tipsy and staying out in the Night air – but I am as well as ever I was.[12]

Those soldiers who fell sick were treated either in the regimental hospital by the surgeon and his assistants, or in larger general hospitals. James Anderson, former surgeon of the 3rd and 4th Battalions of the 60th, published *A Few Facts and Observations on the Yellow Fever of the West Indies* in 1798. He described the symptoms at length and in graphic detail:

> The disease generally commences with universal lassitude and debility; and in some cases the patient suddenly falls down insensible, and remains so for several minutes; pains in the back and loins, and over all the limbs, but particularly in the calves of the legs; violent headach, with pain, especially over the orbits, and affecting the eye-balls; a most uneasy sensation at stomach, attended with pain on pressure, with nausea, and inclination to vomit. If vomiting ensues, what is first brought up is generally nothing more than what had been drank, mixed with phlegm, and a thick, ropy, whitish matter, unless where an emetic had been exhibited; and in that case, great quantities of bile was forced through the pyloris, in the action of vomiting.
>
> The face appears remarkably flushed, with inflamed eyes, which at the same time have a watery appearance, and are unable to bear the light.
>
> The thirst is generally considerable, yet the tongue is tolerably moist, but white and tremulous.
>
> The breathing is short, hurried, and oppressed; with insupportable anxiety, sighing, and depression of spirits, the patient every now and then tossing, and throwing himself from one side of the bed to the other.
>
> The pulse is quick, generally full, and soft, often unequal.
>
> The skin gives a hot burning sensation, when the finger is applied, although it be not unusually dry or parched.
>
> The belly is generally costive.
>
> Delirium is an almost constant attendant on this disease; and after the second day, a comatose state often supervenes; sometimes earlier.

11 J. Prevost to A. Prevost, 9 May 1804, AI, Prevost Papers, CR549/II/1cc.

12 J. Prevost to A. Prevost, 9 January 1804, AI, Prevost Papers, CR549/II/1aa.

> The urine is always voided in small quantities, and of a high colour; accompanied with a sense of burning along the urethra. After twenty-four hours, or from that to forty-eight, many of the symptoms change their appearances.
>
> The pulse continues quick, but weaker, tremulous, generally irregular, and sometimes intermitting.
>
> The countenance acquires a yellowish appearance; the tunica conjunctiva has now changed from a red to a yellow, and the upper part of the breast and neck are deeply tinged of a yellow colour.
>
> Vomiting now becomes very frequent; and what is brought up is extremely acrid, excoriating the throat and fauces as it passes, consisting mostly of a thick ropy stuff, of a blackish colour; and at last, there is a free and copious discharge of a fluid, greatly resembling the grounds of coffee. This has got the name of Black vomiting. From this stage of the disease I never saw one recover.[13]

Anderson believed that there were two types of fever; one caused by marsh miasma, and one a contagion. The bad marsh air variety progressed more slowly than the contagion but the symptoms were similar.[14] Mosquito borne yellow fever and malaria were probably what he was identifying as caused by marsh miasma, and the contagion could have been typhoid, or some other bacterial disease.

The treatments that surgeons used to combat fever may well have hindered rather than helped any possible recovery. Anderson recommended purgatives such as calomel (mercurous chloride) and James' Powders, which were a blend of the metal antimony and calcium phosphate, both of which were toxic.[15] He also wrote: 'In the latter stages of the disease, and after free evacuations downwards, wine will be of service; particularly good Madeira, to the extent of a pint in the twenty-four hours but I have never seen good effects from a larger quantity'.[16]

The mortality rate for yellow fever at the time was around 70 percent, but even those that survived often found their health permanently broken and had to be invalided back to Britain. Malaria, especially, could affect health for many years and was referred to as intermittent or remittent fever. Younger soldiers seemed to be more prone to severe fevers than their older comrades, and the rank and file were hit proportionally more than officers. However, fevers were not the only cause of illness or death amongst the troops. Dysentery was common, bites and cuts became easily infected, alcoholism was rife, and even the rum that the troops drank was contaminated with lead from vessels used during its production.[17]

Attempts were made to improve the health of troops in the West Indies but the Army and its medical staff were hindered by their lack of understanding of the true causes of the illnesses that the men suffered. Anderson recommended more fresh food for the troops, which could well have been beneficial, but he also advocated calico shirts which he said

13 J. Anderson, *A Few Facts & Observations on the Yellow Fever of the West Indies* (Edinburgh: Mudie, 1798), pp.3-7.
14 Anderson, *Yellow Fever*, p.12.
15 Anderson, *Yellow Fever*, p.20.
16 Anderson, *Yellow Fever*, p.40.
17 Howard, *Death Before Glory*, pp.199-206.

absorbed perspiration better.[18] Changes to the thick woollen uniforms were proposed and some regiments were issued with thinner, looser trousers, flannel waistcoats, and white felt wide-brimmed hats, but supplies were short and many units had to make do with uniforms designed for colder European climates. Local exotic fruits, vegetables, and meats were often included in rations and would have done something to alleviate the monotony, as well reduce sickness rates.

In the 15 months from formation until May 1799, when the companies from Ireland arrived, the 5th Battalion in the West Indies lost 210 men to fevers and other illnesses; approximately 20 percent of its strength. In some months there were only a handful of deaths, but there were four months with over 20 deaths, and the most deadly month was May 1798 when 53 died. The returns also show that the number of sick men varied from 93 in January 1798 to only 22 in October of the same year, but that there were normally over 30 riflemen sick, either in the regimental hospital or the various general hospitals across the islands.[19]

Sickness often first appeared in the cramped conditions of troop transports bringing the troops to the West Indies. For the four companies of the 5th Battalion sailing from Ireland aboard the *Admiral de Vries* the first death came early in the voyage. Private Peter Bruelleisen died on 17 March, just eight days after leaving Ireland. Private William Clercke died on 23 March, Private Christian Barth on 24 March, and then on 26 March there were three deaths: Privates John Gellerman, Conradt Stegman, and Ferdinand Wickman.[20] Bacterial infections such as typhus often thrived in the cramped conditions of troop ships.

An account has survived of the voyage on the *Admiral de Vries*. Andrew Bryson was a colonel of the United Irishmen in County Down and later wrote a long letter to his sister about his experiences after the rebellion. He seems to have taken little part in the actual fighting but he was arrested for treason, pleaded guilty, and was sentenced to enlist in a regiment of the British Army for a set period, but this sentence was increased to service overseas for life.[21] He paints a vivid picture of life aboard the ship, and the illnesses that the crew, soldiers and prisoners suffered starting with sea sickness: '...the decks were as dirty as anything possibly could be & 3 out of every 4 Vomiting till their hearts were like to come up.[22]

As they crossed the Bay of Biscay a gale damaged two of the masts. Whenever the lookouts spotted a strange sail the ship would beat to quarters and prepare for battle. On one of these occasions the sea was very rough:

> It was blowing pretty hard & the Old Vessel Tumbled about So confoundedly as to break the lashing of one of the Guns which, running back, broke a poor hessian's leg & in a few minutes A Sea Struck her with Such Violence that every man on deck who had not hold of a rope fell on the deck & the Balls being laid out on the Qtr. Deck, one of the hessians fell with his Cheek on them & Smashed it all to pieces.[23]

18 Anderson, *Yellow Fever*, p.44.
19 Monthly Returns, Windward & Leeward Islands 1798 & 1799, TNA, WO 17/2489 & 2490.
20 May 1799 Pay List, TNA, WO 12/7066.
21 Durey, *Bryson*, p.9.
22 Durey, *Brsyon*, p.70.
23 Durey, *Brsyon*, p.71.

It is possible that some of the deaths in the 5th Battalion were the result of these or other injuries, but Bryson also writes that the ship's surgeon did have to partition off part of the ship as a hospital to deal with an outbreak of a fever, and that two prisoners, three 'Hessians', and two of the 5th Battalion's wives were amongst the victims who had to be buried at sea:

> '... & The next morning one of our men was found dead. After prayers was read over him He was Sewed up in His Hammock and a 30lb. shot put at his head & feet, then laid on one part of the main Hatch & lowered into the water with the Greatest decorum. Just as the hatch was drawn up one of the Hessians came running up & told us not to take away the tackles, for they were wanting. "For whom?", said I. "For mine Frow," Said the German. "O very well," Said I, "bring her here & we will ease you of her at once." I thought he was funning us, which was the reason I answered him So Merrily & ordered the Tackles to be unhooked & Hatch laid on, which was Just done when he came back carrying the Corps[e] of his Frau on his Shoulder. And on Seeing the Hatch was gone he Gave a kick with his Shoulder & pushed her overboard without any Shot. Nor did She Sink as long as were in Sight. As Soon as he lost Sight of her he Set up a most lamentable Cry, which Set all the people about a-laughing, upon which I left him & them.[24]

When the ship crossed over the line of the Tropic of Cancer the crew, soldiers, wives and prisoners took part in the traditional line crossing ceremony in front of King and Queen Neptune:

> As soon as the Vessel was hove to, the Curtain drew & he issued forth with his Lady in a triumphal Car drawn by 8 noted men, whose bodies were painted in a fantastical manner. As Soon as the Capt. & Officers of the Vessel had paid their Respects to Mr. & Mrs. Neptune, They asked them how they dared pass through their dominion without their Liberty.[25]

A tub of dirty water was put on deck to dunk those that were deemed to have offended Neptune. The treatment of the 'offenders' was very brutal with the ship's barber roughly shaving them after lathering them from a bucket of tar, often drawing blood. Colonel de Rottenburg and the other officers of the 5th Battalion escaped with just a few cans of water being thrown over them, but one of the other officers on board had been singled out by the prisoners. Forewarned, he had hidden himself and it took the sailors an hour to find him. He drew his sword to defend himself but it was smashed from his hands and Neptune then whipped him. He offered Neptune a guinea but he was tied up, placed in the tub, water thrown over him and the barber covered his face with lather and thrust his brush into his mouth and then shaved him roughly. Bryson comments that the poor officer's only uniform was ruined in the process. Queen Neptune then took the throne and ordered three of the sailors' wives who had not crossed the line before to be ducked, then two of the 5th

24 Durey, *Brsyon*, p.75.
25 Durey, *Brsyon*, p.72.

Battalion's officers' wives had water thrown over them and were also 'shaved' by the barber. The ceremony finished with the whole crew throwing water over all the officers.[26]

On 7 April the *Admiral de Vries* anchored in the harbour at Fort Royal, Martinique. Bryson with 34 others enlisted in the 43rd Foot and were shipped around the island to St. Pierre, still guarded by men of the 5th Battalion:

> The Beauty of the Prospect as we passed from Fort Royal to St. Pierres far exceeded anything I had either Seen or had any Idea of. In every little Val[le]y, of which there are a prodigious number, there was a plantation [at] the Bottom of the Vale planted with Plantain Trees, the leaves of which were 6 feet long & 2 broad and on each Side of the Banks the Negro huts [were] arranged in straight lines. At the base of each [were] a number of Fruit Trees Such as Oranges, Limes, Saursap, Gave, Sugar Apple, Mungos, Mammy Apples, Alligator Pears, Cocoa Nut & Cabbage Trees, all of which they arrange in Such order that they run above each other as Regularly as the hills does, except the two last which tower far above the rest & are So much similar that you would not know the difference for Sometime.'[27]

Bryson continues to note with disgust that in contrast to the beauty of the island the treatment of the black slaves was unremittingly brutal. He joined his regiment and within 48 hours had caught a fever that put him into hospital, but he survived and later deserted, eventually making his way to New York. At Fort Royal the *Admiral de Vries* embarked the 1st Battalion of the 60th, and a detachment of 4th Battalion, then sailed for Jamaica. Sixty of the Irish prisoners also went to Jamaica, with the rest being distributed amongst the regiments at Martinique.[28]

The four companies of the 5th Battalion from Europe maintained their own pay lists until the end of May, which record 10 deaths in the first few weeks after arrival, including the drowning of Private Frederich Bunds on 30 April. De Rottenburg took command of the companies already in Martinique under Major Dörsner. The 5th Battalion now had a total strength of 992; 580 of which were 'on command' on other islands.[29] The first pay list for the battalion as a whole is June's and contains the following note: 'N.B. The four companies from Ireland are from this date incorporated with those found already formed in the West Indies, and that were already formed into ten companies, but a fresh formation took place.'[30]

The companies on Martinique were the colonel's company (the headquarters of the battalion), Major Adam von Dörsner's, Captain Frederic Gerhardy's, Captain Joseph de Wend's, and Captain Christian Monmartin's. The companies on Grenada, commanded by Major William Crezielsky, were the lieutenant colonel's, Captain Ladislaus de Villers Masburgh's and Captain Carl Emmenhausen's. The companies on Trinidad, commanded by Major Lewis von Mosheim, were Captain Charles Hurdt's and Captain John Galiffe's. With the former Lowenstein captains' commissions having dates prior to those of most of the former Hompesch captains, Gerhardy was the only one from the Isle of Wight formation to

26 Durey, *Brsyon* pp.71-75.
27 Durey, Bryson, p.82.
28 Trigge to Dundas 24 April 1799, TNA, WO 1/87, pp.197-8, & 201.
29 May 1799 Return, TNA, WO 17/2490.
30 June 1799 Pay List, TNA, WO 12/7066.

retain his company; the others were attached with the rest of the supernumerary officers to the colonel's company. Captain Ladislaus de Villers Masburgh, a former Hompesch officer, was also senior enough to warrant a company even though he had not had a company at the Isle of Wight and was on leave back in England.

With yet another major having arrived from Ireland it was time for one of them to leave the battalion. Lewis von Mosheim was ordered to join the new 6th Battalion of the 60th, and left the West Indies after four years there in November 1799. Unfortunately his ship was captured by a French privateer and he was taken to Bordeaux as a prisoner of war. He was allowed back to Britain under parole where he was formally exchanged with a French prisoner of equivalent rank and allowed to actively serve again in April 1800. He joined his battalion on the Isle of Wight and by the winter was back in the West Indies, this time on Jamaica. He was in command of the 6th Battalion from 1801 until July 1805, when he was allowed to return to Europe for the sake of his health. He had been promoted to lieutenant colonel in 1804. He served on the staff of Lord Cathcart's expedition to Hannover in 1806, and then was put in charge of the foreign recruiting depots in various towns in northern Germany before again serving on Lord Cathcart's staff during the campaign to attack Copenhagen. He also served on the staff of the Walcheren expedition in 1809. Then in 1810 he was give the command of the army's Foreign Depot and promoted to colonel, and then later major general.[31] He died a lieutenant general in 1830. Mosheim's tenure as commandant of the Foreign Depot would be of considerable benefit to the 5th Battalion during Peninsular Campaign as he became instrumental in maintaining the quality of its recruits.

For the rest of the 5th Battalion the 1799 muster records show that the deaths from disease continued, with 24 dying during June and July, including Assistant Surgeon Schiller. Eleven men were invalided, their health too broken to continue serving, and two soldiers deserted. When the companies on Martinique mustered on 25 July, 13 men were 'at work as taylor'[32] implying perhaps that a shipment of new uniforms had arrived or other repair or alteration work was required to the battalion's uniforms. Captain Galiffe's company, and the soon-to-depart Major von Mosheim, remained at Trinidad but on 28 July the companies from Grenada arrived at Martinique, leaving behind only a small detachment of 40 men.

Lieutenant General Thomas Trigge, commander-in-chief of the Windward and Leeward Islands, was gathering troops for an invasion of the well defended Dutch colony of Surinam, on the South American coast. The expedition totalled 1,277 officers and men, including 28 staff officers, 68 men from the Royal Artillery, 17 from the Royal Artificers, 901 from the 5th Battalion, 105 from the 87th Foot, and 158 from the 9th West India Regiment.[33] They sailed from Martinique on 31 July in a squadron under the command of Vice Admiral Lord Hugh Seymour, consisting of two ships of the line, five frigates, one sloop and a hired brig, plus several smaller vessels carrying stores and supplies. The brig, which was carrying the artillery and artificers, collided with a stores vessel soon after leaving port and had to return. Fighting strong currents, the expedition arrived off the coast of Surinam on 11 August and prepared to seize the lucrative colony.[34]

31 *The Royal Military Calendar* (London: Egerton, 1820), 3rd ed. Vol. III. p.358.
32 July 1799 Pay List, TNA, WO 12/7066.
33 Embarkation Return July 1799, TNA, WO 1/87, p.355.
34 Trigge to Dundas, 23 August 1799, TNA, WO 1/87, pp.371-381.

6

Surinam

Surinam was one of four Dutch colonies along the north coast of South America. To the west were Essequibo, Berbice, and Demerara which had all been captured by the British in 1796: after changing hands a few more times they would eventually become British Guyana, and then much later the independent state of Guyana. To the east was the French colony of Cayenne, and to the south stretched the Amazon rainforest and the Portuguese colony of Brazil. Surinam was named after the river which wound its way through savannah and jungle to the sea. Prussian traveller Baron Albert von Sack described his arrival in Surinam in 1805:

> The weather was very serene and refreshed by the eastern breeze, but the sails filled so moderately, that we glided almost imperceptibly along the coast of the fine river of Surinam, and gave us full time to view the handsome country houses, intermixed with a great number of fine growing trees, amongst which the different species of the palm are particularly pleasing to the eye.
>
> About eleven miles from the entrance of the river we passed Fort Leiden, which lies at the entrance of the Commewyne into the river Surinam: on the opposite side of the Commewyne is Fort Amsterdam; and opposite, on the west shore of the river Surinam, are the batteries of Red Pamerend, all which are extremely well placed for the defence of the colony, and some of the passengers said they were of considerable strength. After advancing about seven miles more up the river, we came to Fort Zelandia, to which the town of Paramaribo is adjacent. This town has a very inviting aspect from the river, which favourable impression, so far from being attended with disappointment, is greatly increased upon landing; the streets are wide and regular, planted on both sides with orange trees, which blossom and yield fruit twice a year; whilst in Italy, which is styled the garden of Europe, the orange trees produce fruit only once a year. The place where we landed is called Government Square, as facing it stands the Government House, a fine building of two stories high, but seemingly out of repair. Very nearly opposite, to the left, and close to the river, is Fort Zelandia, in which are the arsenal, several large magazines and barracks, all built of brick.[1]

1 A. von Sack, *A Narrative of a Voyage to Surinam* (London: G & W Nicol, 1810), pp.39-40.

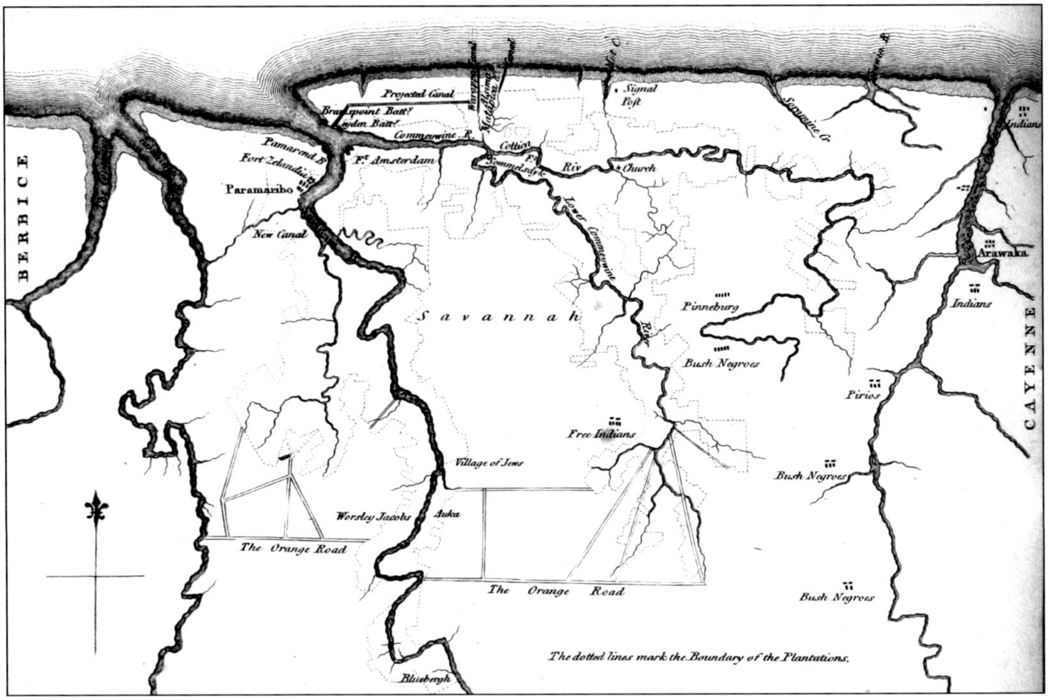

Map of Surninam. (From Albert von Sack, *A Narrative of a Voyage to Surinam*)

Any invading force would have first come up against the battery at Brams Point with its seven 18-pounder cannon covering the 2,500 yard width of the river. Then at the confluence of the Surinam and Commewijne Rivers any ships would be caught in a crossfire between: Fort Leyden's ten 24-pounders and two 18-pounders; Frederici Battery's twelve 24-pounders; Purmurent Redoubt's four 24-pounders and two 18-pounders; and Fort New Amsterdam's twenty-one 24-pounders, fourteen 18-pounders, plus many more smaller cannon and mortars. If the ships made it as far as the capital, Paramaribo, they would still face the 19 smaller guns of Fort Zelandia.[2] Fort New Amsterdam was a star shaped fortress a thousand yards across with an outer glacis, a moat, and then an thick inner wall enclosing barracks, officers' quarters, stores, magazines and workshops.[3]

During the voyage to Surinam Seymour and Trigge had received detailed intelligence on the defences of the colony from the captain of an American brig, *Resistance*, which had recently sailed from there. In addition to the batteries, redoubts and forts there was a schooner at Brams Point, a French 20-gun ship and a dismasted Dutch frigate used for signals at Fort New Amsterdam, and a further Dutch frigate of 44 guns was anchored below Paramaribo. The frigate HMS *Amphitrite* was sent ahead of the squadron with Lieutenant Colonel Shiply of the Royal Engineers to reconnoitre the coast and the entrance to the river.[4]

2 Map of Surinam defences, TNA, CO 700/BritishGuiana5.
3 Plan of Fort New Amsterdam, TNA, MR 1/1080.
4 Admiral Seymour's dispatch on the taking of Surinam, Warwickshire County Record Office (WCRO), CR114A/332.

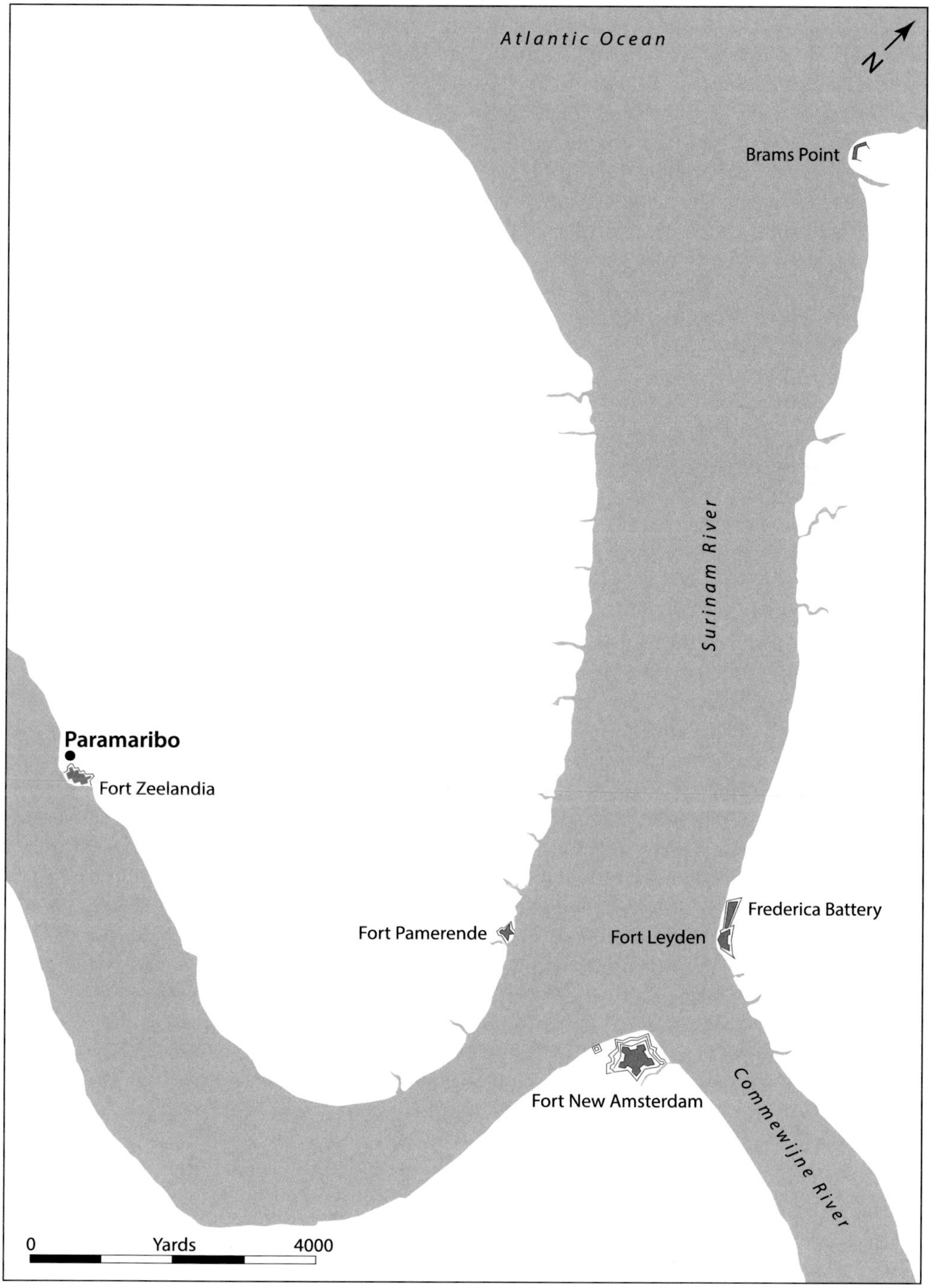

The Forts & Batteries of the Surinam River.
Source: TNA, MR 1/1080/6 Plan of the River Surinam and its Defences, 1799.

On 14 August an attempt was made to capture the battery at Brams Point but the boats were swept down the coast by strong currents.[5] On the evening of 16 August Lieutenant Colonel de Rottenburg and Captain William Cayley from HMS *Invincible* were sent up the river to Paramaribo under a flag of truce to offer terms to Governor-General Juriaan François Frederici. The governor asked for 48 hours to consider his position. Trigge and Seymour received a deputation of officials, merchants, and Dutch officers on 18 August with the governor's reply; he would surrender the colony to the British. Negotiations for the final terms of the articles of capitulation commenced and the capitulation was received on 20 August. The following morning the troops were transferred from the ships of the line to smaller vessels that could sail up the shallow river. A detachment of the 5th Battalion landed at Brams Point, this time without incident, and took possession of the battery. The Dutch troops had already left.[6] The British were on the brink of gaining one of the richest colonies in the region without firing a shot, but it was an outcome that was never in doubt. The entire invasion was a sham.

In March 1799, the British representative in Hamburg, Sir James Craufurd, had written to the government that he had received a proposal from a French royalist, Antoine Omer Talon, acting on behalf of Governor-General Frederici and several other individuals.[7] Talon was well known to the Alien Office, the British spy agency co-ordinating counter-Revolutionary activities within France. He had also been the middleman involved with the selling of French grain to Britain, despite the two countries being at war. In 1800 he took up a post in the French secret police whilst still reporting to London, before being arrested after another failed coup attempt in 1803.[8]

Talon pointed out that if the British gained Surinam it would threaten the French colony of Cayenne, protect Portuguese Brazil, and threaten Spanish possessions in the area. However, he also outlined the strong defensive position of the colony, with its formidable batteries and narrow, difficult to navigate river. He listed the troops present as 800 European troops, being the remains of three different units and mostly Swiss or German rather than Dutch, a Dutch artillery company, and 600 free black soldiers. He also warned that Spain had sent two frigates with reinforcements from the Walloon Guards regiment. Frederici and the principal proprietors of the colony, he claimed, were willing to surrender the colony because the war was restricting their trade. Talon listed the contents of the warehouses in Surinam as 70,000 barrels of sugar, 20 million pounds of coffee, 20 million pounds of cocoa and three million pounds of cotton. He also said that there was a good labour force of black slaves. Seven people would expect pecuniary recompense for the delivery the colony, including Frederici, the commander of the garrison, and others. Talon even demanded a deposit in advance as the Dutch were wary of trusting the British. He was also very clear that the colony would defend itself if attacked prior to a deal being struck. Upon agreement three of the conspirators, including Talon, would travel to Surinam with the British fleet to finalise the arrangements.[9]

5 Trigge to Dundas, 24 August 1799, TNA, WO 1/87, p.423.
6 Trigge to Dundas, 23 August 1799, TNA WO 1/87, pp.371-381.
7 Copy of letter from James Craufurd, 19 March 1799, TNA, WO 1/88 pp.378-408.
8 E. Sparrow, *Secret Service, British Agents in France 1792-1815* (Woodbridge: The Boydell Press, 1999), p.217.
9 Copy of letter from James Craufurd, 19 March 1799, TNA, WO 1/88, pp.378-408.

Negotiations went ahead and a price agreed. Frederici and his colleagues would get £100,000 for delivering the colony to the British.[10] Talon added another £70,000 for his expenses.[11] Secretary of War Henry Dundas wrote to Trigge in June to inform him of the agreement and specifically requested that a battalion, or detachment, of the 60th be used in the operation.[12] Seymour was instructed to embark three officers of the 60th to the West Indies.[13] These were almost certainly Talon, the lieutenant-governor of Surinam Colonel de Cohoin, and another of the conspirators travelling incognito. Trigge's orders from Dundas began:

> A secret convention having been entered into between certain persons now in Europe acting in concert with Mr Frederici Governor of Surinam and authorised by him, by which it is agreed that he shall place that valuable colony under his majesty's protection and deliver it over into the possession of the King's forces. I am now in the most secret and confidential manner to signify to you His Majesty's command for the execution of this important service.[14]

Dundas also stressed the need for a convincing show of force to allow the Dutch to surrender without raising suspicions. When Seymour's squadron arrived in the Caribbean Talon and his colleagues were sent on to Surinam, ostensibly under a flag of truce to arrange an exchange of prisoners of war.[15] They reported back that Frederici was fearful and willing to proceed with the surrender, but was also proud and advised that in any negotiation the British should exaggerate their strength.[16]

Following the receipt of the governor's acceptance of the terms a flotilla of small ships sailed up the Surinam River to take possession of the colony. Four hundred men of the 5th Battalion, commanded by Major Dörsner, landed to take Fort New Amsterdam. At first the Walloon Guards refused to march out of the fort and surrender their arms but Dorsner and the acting adjutant general of the expedition, Major Thomas, managed to persuade them and the garrison surrendered. The Walloons were kept in the fort as prisoners of war but the Dutch troops were allowed to keep their arms and were sent to Paramaribo. The British took possession of the town and other fortifications on the following day with no resistance from the inhabitants or troops.[17]

The return of the Dutch and Spanish troops listed 113 artillerymen, 687 in the Dutch battalion, 443 Walloon Guards, 110 White Chasseurs and 316 Black Chasseurs (made up of freed black slaves), totalling 1,669 and outnumbering the invading force.[18] The articles of capitulation gave these troops the option of enlisting into British service rather than becoming prisoners of war. Roughly half of the Dutch garrison volunteered and were

10 Dundas to Trigge, 14 June 1799, TNA, WO 1/87 p.257 & unsigned letter from Downing Street to Trigge, 6 November 1799, WO 1/87, p.581.
11 Sparrow, *Secret Service*, p.271.
12 Unsigned letter from Downing Street to Trigge, 14 June 1799, TNA, WO 1/87 pp.257-70.
13 Order marked Downing Street, June 1799, WCRO, CR114A/332.
14 Dundas to Trigge, 14 June 1799, WCRO, CR114A/332.
15 Seymour to Dundas, 20 July 1799, TNA, WO 1/87 pp.331-2.
16 Report from the colony, WCRO, CR114A/332.
17 Trigge to Dundas, 23 August 1799, TNA, WO 1/87 pp.371-81.
18 Return of Dutch & Spanish troops at Surinam 20 August 1799, TNA, WO 1/87 p.469.

formed into the Royal Dutch Artillery and Royal Dutch Infantry and were retained in the colony although Trigge was not complimentary about their quality. Dundas had suggested to Trigge that the Dutch troops should join the 60th but Trigge reported that this 'could not have been adopted without attracting disgust; both in officers and men.'[19] Three quarters of the White Chasseurs and almost all the Black Chasseurs opted to serve the new regime and were also incorporated into the British garrison.[20] Such changes of loyalty were considered perfectly normal and acceptable. The 5th Battalion would become increasingly reliant on Germans and others already in the service of France, often conscripts from conquered territory, choosing to serve King George rather than remain in a prisoner of war camp or hulk.

Historically, the Walloon Guards had been recruited from Spanish territory in what is now Belgium, but the men in Surinam were mostly German or Hungarian prisoners of war who had been handed over to Spain by the French.[21] So, whilst they may have been opting to serve a third country they were at least back on the same side of the war that they had started on. A total of 133 were recruited by the 5th Battalion, with 56 being distributed into the companies and 77 being retained in a depot company under Captain Schneider, which was then used to replenish the companies as the inevitable wastage from disease continued. One recruit, Private Francis Ballestrat, changed his mind very quickly and deserted on 8 September.[22] Those who did not wish to enter British service were shipped back to Spain on the condition that they did not serve again against the British until formally exchanged for British prisoners. On 18 September Trigge wrote to Dundas:

> I have the satisfaction to add that the 5th Battalion of the 60th which I have left at Surinam, is a remarkably fine Body of Men, well Disciplined and in every point of view a most efficient Corps; and I am extremely happy in being inabled to assure You, that nothing can exceed the good Conduct of both Officers and Men on all occasions.
>
> I hope I shall not be disappointed in the expectation I have formed, that the Men (being one hundred and thirty five in number) which enlisted in this Battalion from the Walloon Guards, and who are all Germans, will turn out remarkably well, as hitherto they have Conducted themselves with great propriety and much to the satisfaction of the Officers of the Regiment.[23]

All Dutch government property was inventoried and valued and the list included four ships; a prison ship (£2,469 19s), frigate (£2,098), schooner (£1,032 10s 2d) and brig (£1,698 3s).[24] The more than 300 guns of various calibres captured were estimated to be worth £14,771 11s with the hundreds of barrels of powder, cartridges, balls, muskets and 31 rifles worth another £10,167 11s 10d.[25] The inventory for the engineer's department included £4,954

19 Trigge to Dundas, 29 August 1799, TNA, WO 1/87 pp.465-8.

20 State of His Majesty's Forces in the Colony of Surinam, 31 August 1799, TNA, WO 1/87 p.473.

21 Atkinson, 'Foreign Regiments – Part 4', p.115.

22 September 1799 Pay List, TNA, WO 12/7066.

23 Trigge to Dundas, 18 September 1799, TNA, WO 1/87, pp.544-5.

24 Observations on colony enclosed with letter from Trigge, TNA, WO 1/87 pp.505-8; Seymour to Dundas 11 September 1799, *ibid.*, pp.497-504.

25 Inventory of Ordnance, WCRO, CR114A/332.

12s worth of stores, boats worth £831 16s, and slaves valued at £18,585 4d. The slaves, it was noted, were 'absolutely necessary to conducting the different works of the Military Establishment' and were presumably retained under British ownership.[26] The total value of all the items listed amounted to £86,828. This was not just an idle accounting exercise. It was established practice that the value of shipping, guns, and stores be distributed amongst the soldiers and sailors involved in their capture. Shares of prize money were allocated on the basis of rank. Seymour and Trigge submitted the following proposal to the government:

> Proposed Distribution of the Booty taken on the Expedition under the Command of Lieutenant General Trigge, and The Right Honble: Lord Hugh Seymour humbly submitted for the approbation of His Majesty.
>
> Two Commanders in Chief, equally 8/64ths
> Brigadier Generals – 4/64ths
> Colonels, Lieutenant Colonels and Majors, Post Captains and Commanders – 15/64ths
> Captains of the Army and Marines and Lieutenants of the Navy – 7/64ths
> Subaltern Officers of the Army and Marines, and Warrant Officers of the Navy – 7/64ths
> Petty Officers of the Navy, and Serjeants of the Army and Marines – 7/64ths
> Soldiers, Seamen and Marines – 16/64ths[27]

Had the government accepted the proposal then Trigge and Seymour would have pocketed over £5,000 each, and de Rottenburg around £2,000. It is difficult to be sure of the individual shares of the lower ranks as the ships' companies are not listed on the returns, but after making some assumptions about the typical ships complements a soldier of the 5th Battalion may have received approximately £7, which was more than their annual pay, net of deductions. However, having already paid £170,000 to the conspirators for the colony the government were unwilling to be so generous with prize money. After a protracted series of letters back and forth Dundas wrote to Trigge in December 1800 that because of the manner of the colony's capture only those provisions useable by the garrison were to be considered booty, cutting the value down to just £21,388 1s 10d, which would have reduced the value of the shares to around a quarter of what was initially proposed.[28]

The capital of the colony, Paramaribo, had a population of around 20,000, of which around 11,000 were slaves.[29] The buildings were largely white painted wood with coloured shutters. Most windows used gauze rather than glass to keep the interiors as cool as possible. The worst of the day's heat began to abate around 3:00 p.m. and the sun set around 6:00 p.m. The squares were lined with orange or tamarind trees. Hedges made of lime trees separated the houses on the edge of the town. Paramaribo was prosperous and well ordered, but savannah and patches of forest were only a short stroll away. The waterfront was busy with fishermen

26 Observations, TNA WO 1/87, p.506.
27 Trigge & Seymour to Dundas 25 August 1799, TNA, WO 1/87, p.429, proposed distribution of booty.
28 Dundas to Trigge, December 1800, TNA, WO 1/89 p.577.
29 Sack, *Voyage to Surinam*, pp.40.

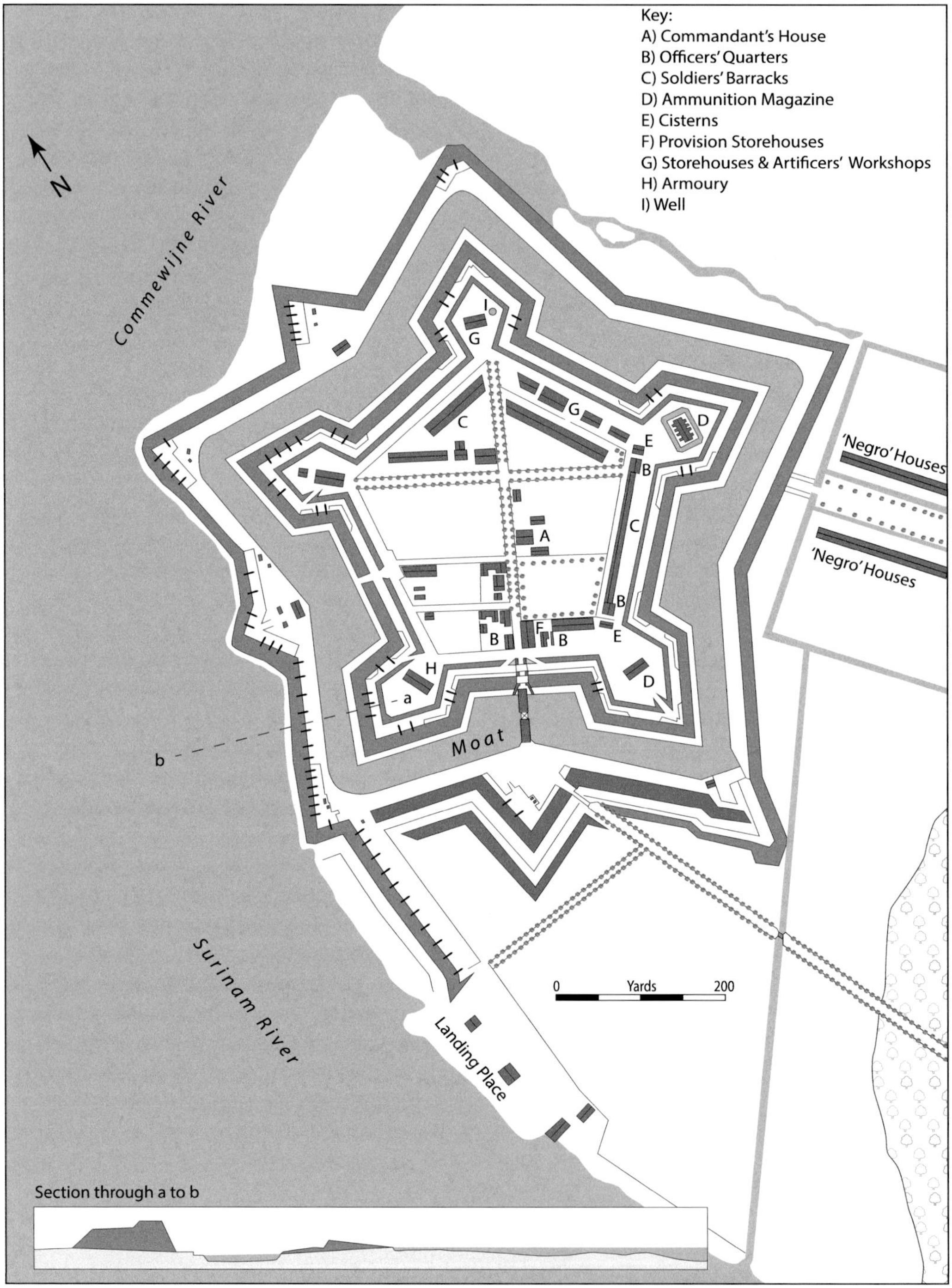

Fort New Amsterdam.
Source: TNA, MR 1/1080/5 Fort Amsterdam upon the River Surinam, 1799.

and ships being loaded. A shipping return for November 1799 shows that 852 hogsheads of sugar, 190,868 pounds of coffee, 425 bales of cotton, 13,200 pounds of cocoa and 571 hogsheads of molasses were shipped from the colony, presumably enriching both the merchants and providing the new rulers with export duties. [30]

The 5th Battalion was headquartered at Fort New Amsterdam but companies were detached to Bramms Point, Fort Leiden, and Fort Zeelandia in Paramaribo, and regularly rotated between them. Captain Galiffe's company remained in Trinidad and in November two companies were transferred back to Martinique, along with the men of the 87th and West India Regiments, to reinforce the garrison there.[31] The troops in Surinam were primarily there to defend against any Dutch or French attempt to retake the colony, but also to guard against any unrest from the slave population, or from the indigenous peoples further up the rivers. Trigge recorded a long list of gifts he sent to the local chiefs including: 12 walking canes and medals decorated with King George's crest; 12 scarlet coats and gold trimmed hats; bales of cloth; powder, flints and shot for fowling pieces; 500 each of axes, cutlasses (for chopping wood), parcels of needles, scissors, razors, and 1,000 pounds of various coloured beads.[32]

De Rottenburg later described Fort New Amsterdam as being surrounded by jungles infested by tigers, by which he probably meant jaguars. He also claimed that the men of the battalion were so miserable that he had to cope with a spate of suicides,[33] but the surviving records do not have any deaths noted as being self-inflicted, although they do for other stations later. As with every post in the Caribbean region the men were in far more danger from sickness and disease than any potential French action, slave revolt, or even their own depression. The death rate from disease did decline slightly from their time on the various islands, with an average of seven deaths per month during their long stay in the colony. The sickness rate, however, did markedly increase to an average of 79 men sick and with many months well over 100.[34] A convalescent hospital was established in early 1800 to house the men recovering from fever. Most of the sick returned to duty, but a handful each month were invalided out of the battalion.[35]

Some of the officers of the battalion took lodgings in Paramaribo and settled into colonial society. On the evening of 8 February Captain and Mrs de Weise entertained four of their new acquaintances for dinner; three were local planters or merchants and one, Ensign Bachoffenen, was an officer in the White Chasseurs.[36] After dinner Louis de Weise proposed a game of dice, with bets of two guilders per round. Mr Brumeren declined and left, Mr Van der Hoop said he would play for half an hour, and Mr Schmeidle said he would stay for a while but not play. There were soon several hundred guilders and 30 or 40 Spanish dollars on the table. De Weise began to lose and had to ask his wife for more money, who then retired to bed. De Weise and Bachoffenen were left alone.

30 Report of Goods Shipped, TNA, WO 1/88, p.673; a hogshead was a barrel size holding around 200-250 litres.

31 Trigge to Dundas, 13 November 1799, TNA, WO 1/87 p.593.

32 Memorandum of Gifts Given, TNA, WO 1/87 p.531.

33 Rigaud, *Celer et Audax*, p.9.

34 Monthly returns, Windward & Leeward Islands 1798-1802, TNA, WO 17/2489-2493.

35 Pay lists 5/60th, 1798-9, TNA, WO 12/7066.

36 Transcript of the Court Martial of Captain de Weise, TNA, WO 71/187. The following section is based upon the evidence given during the trial.

Private Andreas Buchovsky, de Weise's servant, had also gone to bed but sometime after 10:00 p.m. he heard a commotion downstairs and went back down. He entered the parlour to see de Weise standing with his sabre drawn about to strike. Mrs de Weise, who had also come down, asked her husband to lower his sword and he handed it to her. Bachoffenen was still standing and ran out of the house, towards 'the necessary' in the back yard. De Weise ran after him, grabbed him by the hair and dragged him to the floor and punched him six or seven times. Bachoffenen did not defend himself.

Three soldiers were passing in the street and heard the scuffle. Privates Bianco and Rossi of the White Chasseurs went to investigate but Private du Paul of the 5th Battalion, who was with them, knew it was his captain's house and decided that whatever was happening was none of his business. Bianco and Rossi entered through door into back yard after the beating had finished. De Weise was picking Bachoffenen up by his arms. To the soldiers the ensign did not appear to be wounded. Mrs de Weise told the soldiers it was nothing. De Weise repeated it and ordered them to leave. They did, supposing that the noise they had heard was someone flogging a slave.

De Weise, his wife and Buchovsky carried the now bleeding Bachoffenen into the house. De Weise ordered Buchovsky to go and get the battalion's surgeon but Buchovsky said he did not know his address, so de Weise sent a slave boy for Surgeon Reiser, and his friend Mr Schmeidle. Surgeon Reiser hurried to de Weise's house and found Bachoffenen, close to death, on a sofa. On examining him he found a deep two-inch wide wound between the sixth and seventh ribs, Reiser tried to revive him by holding smelling salts under his nose. Mr Schmeidle and de Weise came into the room and the surgeon asked what had caused the wound. De Weise replied that Bachoffenen had fallen on a fruit knife that he had been using to peel a shaddock fruit.[37] Reiser looked around and saw neither knife nor fruit. De Weise, clearly drunk and very agitated, claimed such an accident could have happened to anyone and should anyone implicate him in the death 'he would make his Soul Dance on the point of his Sword'. Reiser told them that the wounded man would likely die that night, but should be undressed and put to bed.

Buchovsky and a slave carried Bachoffenen on a bedstead to his own lodgings, accompanied by Surgeon Reiser. After only 15 paces one of the men fell and dropped Bachoffenen, and then after a few more paces he was dropped again. Reiser checked his patient and thought that he was still alive, but by the time they arrived at his lodgings Bachoffenen was dead.

De Weise stayed up until the early hours at Mr Schmeidle's house, still drinking. Major Tobin, of the Royal Dutch Infantry, arrived and de Weise calmly told him that Bachoffenen must have accidentally stabbed himself with a dessert knife. By the morning the fiscal, the local official in charge of law and order, had begun to question witnesses. De Weise changed his story and said that Bachoffenen may have fallen on broken glass rather than stabbed himself. The 5th Battalion's adjutant, Lieutenant Ammon, called on de Weise and took away his sabre. De Weise asked Schmeidle and another friend, Mr Schweike, to help him leave the colony. They went away and offered 500 guilders to a man to help their friend escape but he refused. The next day de Weise, in civilian clothes, arrived at the house of another friend, Mr Lobo, and asked him to send for Schmeidle and Schweike as he needed to talk to them.

37 A large citrus fruit.

June and 24 December, 34 men deserted from the 5th Battalion, the highest number of any unit in the Windward and Leeward Islands command in the period, but not by much as the 1st Foot lost 33 to desertion in the same period. Major Crezielsky, the only remaining field officer, was on leave in Barbados by September, leaving Captain Joseph de Wend in command.[51]

Lieutenant General William Grinfield replied to Cambell's letter in September, having taken over the command of the region from Trigge. He agreed that it would be expedient to remove the garrison as soon as possible but lacked the transport ships to do so, and suggested that the ships bringing the Dutch garrison be hired to embark the British troops. He also informed Cambell that the 5th Battalion would be sent to Halifax, Nova Scotia, for their next posting.[52] In November the Dutch were still expected to arrive at any time, and had reoccupied the neighbouring colony of Demerara. Finally on 2 December 1802 the Dutch reclaimed their colony and the 5th Battalion left Surinam. They had dwindled to only three captains, 14 lieutenants, four staff, 51 sergeants, 22 buglers and 697 rank and file.[53] In the five years from formation to when the battalion finally left the West Indies at least 520 men of the battalion died.[54]

The Peace of Amiens ended when Britain declared war on France again in May 1803. A year later another British expedition arrived off the coast of Surinam, including the 2nd Battalion of the 60th. This time Governor Frederici, still in post, did not surrender without a fight. Seven British troops were killed and 21 wounded retaking the colony,[55] which was then once more returned to the Dutch in 1814. The colony gained its independence in 1975.

The 5th Battalion sailed to Barbados to await onward transport to Nova Scotia. However, that journey would be delayed as events on board HMS *Thalia*, one of the ships transporting the men away from Surinam, would result in a series of courts martial involving almost half the officers of the battalion.

51 Half -Yearly return, June to December 1802, TNA, WO 17/2493.

52 Grinfield to Campbell 6 September 1802, TNA, CO 318/20, p.81.

53 Strength of the Troops 1 December 1802, TNA, CO 318/20, p.359.

54 Calculated from the Windward & Leeward Island returns TNA, WO 17/2489-93. There are some months missing.

55 Howard, *Death Before Glory*, pp.120-2

7

Disagreements, Discharges and Drafts

By Christmas Eve 1802 the 5th Battalion had been aboard their transports for three weeks, sailing from Surniam to Barbados. For most of that time Lieutenant Lewis Ellert, aboard the 36-gun frigate HMS *Thalia*, had been chronically sea sick. He did, however, feel well enough to indulge in some Christmas cheer and had a convivial drink with some of the other officers in the wardroom. It may have been an empty stomach or simple over-indulgence, but Ellert quickly became drunk, noisily so. He sang Rule Britannia, banged his fists on the table, threw his glass into the corner, and used vulgar expressions in his native German. The target for some of his vitriol was Captain Lieutenant Ambrose Hillerich, the senior officer of the battalion on board. Hillerich and Ellert had previously had a minor disagreement over a small gambling debt during the voyage.[1]

When Hillerich asked Ellert to be quieter he reacted belligerently, claiming that since he was not on duty he did not have to do anything that Hillerich asked, saying that Hillerich 'did not have a turd of command over him'. Hillerich replied that Ellert was conducting himself not like officer but like drunken grenadier. Ellert called Hillerich a rascal and a coward. Other officers urged Ellert to be quiet but without success. In the end it was decided to let Ellert tire himself out and eventually he went to his hammock to sleep it off.

The next morning Hillerich summoned all of the 5th Battalion officers on board, with the exception of Ellert, to discuss the events of the night before. It was agreed that Ellert would be 'sent to Coventry' – ostracised – for the remainder of the voyage and that on arrival at Barbados Hillerich would report Ellert to Captain de Wend, the officer commanding the 5th Battalion, so that he could be reprimanded. Hillerich gave his word that he would not speak of the matter to anyone else and that the reprimand would suffice for punishment. The *Thalia,* which was often used as a troop transport, reached Barbados on New Years Eve. Captain de Wend called a meeting of all officers to settle the matter on 3 January. Ellert failed to attend. On 4 January Lieutenant Charles Koch knocked on Hillerich's door and on Ellert's behalf issued a challenge to a duel, asking Hillerich to name a place and time. Hillerich replied that Ellert was not in a position to fight him, being a junior officer, and that he had no particular quarrel with him. Koch grew angry that Hillerich would not fight.

1 Proceedings of the court martial of Lt. Ellert, TNA, WO 71/195. All the details of Ellert's and Hillerich's disagreement and the events that followed are taken from witness testimony in the subsequent courts martial.

Hillerich went directly to Captain de Wend and reported the challenge. De Wend responded that Hillerich should have put Ellert in arrest, and summoned Ellert and Koch. He also took the precaution of sending for his brother, Lieutenant Michael de Wend, and Lieutenant Adam Krein to witness the meeting. Hillerich went to find Ellert and found him in the officers' mess. Hillerich informed Ellert he was under arrest. Ellert was again belligerent and denied that Hillerich had the authority to arrest him but he did go to Captain de Wend's room. Koch and Ellert denied the challenge. De Wend informed Ellert that he was under arrest. Ellert took off his sword and threw it down onto a table.

Matters were not at all calmed by Ellert's arrest. Koch's objection to Hillerich not accepting Ellert's challenge was either sufficiently insulting or he caused some other offence because Hillerich issued his own challenge to Koch and the two fought a duel on 6 January. Duelling was expressly forbidden by the Articles of War. The details of the duel are not recorded but both lived to face the consequences. Other officers thought that Hillerich had broken his word that Ellert would only face a reprimand for his drunken behaviour and sought to send Hillerich to Coventry, confronting him in the mess.

On 11 January a court martial convened at Charles Fort, part of the St Ann's garrison, in Bridgetown, Barbados. It was the first of four courts martial that were to involve almost half the officers with the 5th Battalion at the time. The president of the court was Lieutenant Colonel Maclean of the 2/60th. The members of the court were drawn from the officers of that battalion, and from the Royal Artillery, the 64th and the 68th Foot, and the West India regiments. The prosecutor was Captain de Wend. Once again the court had to appoint a translator for those defendants and witnesses who required it, and several times during the trials the level of understanding of the English language by officers of the battalion was mentioned or questioned.

Captain Hillerich was the first to be tried, for the crime of challenging and fighting Lieutenant Koch. No evidence was offered in support of the charge and he was acquitted. All those involved obviously kept quiet. Next Lieutenants Michael de Wend, Adam Krein, and John Gardiner Herbert were tried for acting as seconds in the duel between Hillerich and Koch. Captain Hillerich was called as a witness in support of the charge but it was argued that since he had just been acquitted of a related crime he should not be admitted as a witness. There being no other evidence that trial too was quickly dispensed with and all the defendants were acquitted.

On 15 January the court turned its attention to Lieutenant Ellert, who was charged with getting drunk and making a disturbance, being disrespectful to Hillerich, using intimidating language intended to provoke a challenge, for sending a challenge via Koch, for refusing to go into arrest, and behaving in a disrespectful and unofficer-like manner to Captain de Wend. Ellert pleaded not guilty and this time witnesses were called and began to testify. The first witness was Captain Lieutenant Hillerich, who proceeded to lay out the events as he saw them. A further nine witnesses were called over seven days and set out the sequence of events as described above. The commander-in-chief, Lieutenant General Grinfield, became increasingly exasperated with the slow pace of the trial and frequent adjournments. In his defence Ellert outlined his 22 years of good service; 15 in his native country and seven for the British. He claimed that there was no independent evidence of the challenge, that Hillerich had not had sufficient authority to order him into arrest and that only his commanding officer, Captain de Wend, could do so, and that he had not been disrespectful to de Wend. He also ascribed his drunkenness on 24 December to his sea sickness and not being used to strong liquor, and said that he would have apologised if he had been asked to. The court agreed with him regarding the challenge but found him guilty of the other three charges and sentenced him to be cashiered from the army.

On 25 January the court reconvened. On trial this time were Lieutenants Koch, John Gardiner Herbert, George Zühleke, William Yates Johnson, and Alexander Mackenzie. The charge was conspiring to cause dissensions within the battalion by attempting to exclude Hillerich from the mess until the Ellert affair had been settled. Captain de Wend was the first to testify, with Hillerich and seven others following over four further days in court, including two privates of the 5th Battalion who had been acting as mess waiters. It was said that all five defendants had approached Captain de Wend and argued that Hillerich should not be allowed in the mess, but that de Wend refused their request. At dinner that day, whilst Hillerich, as mess president, was serving the soup the five requested that the waiters set another table and Koch stated loudly that he would not dine with a '*schluhter kerl*' – German for a man of bad character.

Koch was singled out during the trial as the ringleader. His defence was that he considered that Hillerich had broken his word by taking things with Ellert further than a reprimand and attempting to arrest him, and he also claimed that Hillerich had brought up another previous affair involving Ellert that had long been considered settled. The court found that the charge of conspiring to cause dissension had not been proven and acquitted all five, but did go on to say that their behaviour had been prejudicial to good order and military discipline. Koch's behaviour was highlighted as being more aggravated than the others and the court sentenced him to six months suspension from rank and pay, and forced him to apologise to Hillerich in front of all the officers and to be reprimanded at the head of the whole battalion; the other four defendants were to be reprimanded only in front of the other officers.

During the final trial Grinfield continued to send letters to the court complaining about the procedures and the pace of the trials. A letter from the judge advocate general's office dated 4 May 1803 upheld many of Grinfield's complaints and criticised the court for proceeding on some charges and not others, the many adjournments, and not proceeding against the other defendants at the same time as Ellert.

The trials were over but Koch remained under arrest since the charge of his having relayed Ellert's challenge had not been considered due to lack of evidence. Koch was only released from arrest in September, the same month that Ellert's sentence was confirmed and he was dismissed from the 5th Battalion.

When reading the transcripts of the trial it is difficult not to get the impression that Ellert and Koch were hot-headed, and that Hillerich had not handled the situation as well as he might have done. It is, however, clear that Ellert's arrest, in Hillerich's mind, resulted from his behaviour after arriving on Barbados and not from the initial incident. None of the defendants emerge with any credit and one wonders at the atmosphere in the mess after the trials. Hillerich went on leave in November 1804 and did not return; he retired from the Army in December 1805. Joseph de Wend sold his commission and had left the Army by May 1803.[2]

2 December 1805 Return TNA, WO 17/180 (misfiled with the 1810 returns); May 1803 Pay List, TNA, 12/7070.

The court papers mention Grinfield's concern that that proceedings were delaying the 5th Battalion's onward journey to Halifax but in a letter to the war office in January he blamed the delay on it being late in the season. The harbour at Halifax would have been frozen over, and a lack of transports meant there were no ships available to take them anyway.[3]

In January 1803 445 men were discharged due to their time of service expiring, leaving less than 300 rank and file with the battalion.[4] 59 men are marked in the muster books as having re-enlisted, mostly for a further five years but some for ten years, for which they received bounties of £5 8s or £10 5d respectively.[5] On 1 April 139 officers and riflemen under the command of Captain Galiffe embarked on the frigate HMS *Andromache* for Halifax. On 2 May the remainder of the battalion, only 181 officers and men, boarded another ageing frigate, HMS *Boston*, and followed the *Andromache* north.[6] Whilst their colleagues sailed for Nova Scotia the discharged men sailed back to Britain. In March deputy adjutant general William Wynyard wrote to Major General Hewett, the inspector general of the recruiting service:

> I have rec'd. Directions to acquaint you that a Number of Invalided Men are arrived at Portsmouth from the West Indies, and with them a considerable number of Men of the 5th Batt'n of the 60th, who have been discharged, having served out the time they were engaged for, and that the whole of the men above alluded to will be ordered to the Army Depot, for the purpose of having their discharges confirmed. The Com'dr in Chief concludes that many of the Detachment of the 5th Batt'n of the 60th are still fit for service & under such persuasion HRH wishes you to use your Endeavours to engage all such as you wonder eligible for the British Service.[7]

And he added in a postscript:

> Baron de Rottenburg Lt. Colonel of the 60th will endeavour to be in the I. of Wight in the hope of prevailing on some of the men of the 5th battn. to re-inlist, as he does not embark for Halifax till further orders, he being prevented by an order from HRH.

De Rottenburg was still on leave and due to return to the battalion with a draft of 100 men. The discharged men were at the Foreign Depot in Lymington and despite the best efforts of Lieutenant Colonel Howard, commandant of the depot, de Rottenbrug, and Ensign Starck none of the men could be induced to re-enlist, even after offers of shorter enlistment periods, raised bounties and assurances they would go to North America rather than the West Indies. The discharged men returned to Germany and the draft for the 5th Battalion was instead made up from recruits originally intended for other battalions of the 60th. De Rottenburg sailed with the draft in June, with orders to stop at Newfoundland before

3 Grinfield to Foreign Office 6 January 1803, TNA, CO 318/21 p.10.
4 February 1803 Return, TNA, WO 17/2494.
5 January 1803 Pay List, TNA, WO 12/7070.
6 May 1803 Return, TNA, WO 17/2494.
7 Wynyard to Hewett, 24 March 1803, TNA, WO 3/35, p.478.

carrying on to Halifax. Howard was ordered by Horse Guards to send all foreign recruits arriving at the depot to the 5th Battalion for the time being.[8]

Other measures had been put in place as early as the summer of 1802 to bolster the 5th Battalion's numbers. In 1800 Prince Lowenstein had raised another foreign corps to fight the French. Formed in Bavaria, Lowenstein's Light Infantry, usually called Lowenstein's Jägers, fought with Britain's Austrian and Bavarian allies around Nuremberg in November and December. The capitulation, negotiated by Captain Gomer of the 5th Battalion who was in Europe recruiting, called for eight companies of fusiliers, and two of chasseurs armed with carbines. The rank and file were mainly Polish, with German and Walloon NCOs, and German or French officers. The contract also stated that the officers and men would be incorporated into the 60th if the unit was disbanded.[9] Lieutenant Colonel Charles Schoedde was appointed to command the Jägers. Schoedde had joined the 60th as an ensign in 1776,[10] slowly working his way up to major by 1799. Lieutenant Colonel Henry Couper, deputy inspector of foreign corps, referred to Schoedde in a letter about his appointment: 'He is a very old officer, and understands his profession most perfectly, indeed he is the most proper person I know of for the purpose of superintending the levy & disciplining of this corps'.[11]

Once he had taken up his post and joined the Jägers, who were still with the Austrian army, Schoedde reported the progress of recruitment to William Wickham, a British diplomat and spy who was also in the area, and added:

> I flatter myself that a regiment of riflemen, thus formed on service, will be a most useful corps, particularly calculated for the defence of the West Indies, where even in times of peace, good wood and marksmen are necessary to overawe the negroes and check the depredations of the maroons.[12]

One of the officers of the Jägers was Major Guillaume de Lasalle de Louisenthal, formerly of Lowenstein's Chasseurs, who had left the 5th Battalion soon after formation. He had exchanged into the Hompesch Mounted Riflemen and served with them in Ireland, but returned to the continent before being asked to join Prince Lowenstein's new regiment. His service with the Jägers was to be his last campaign. He left the regiment at the end of 1800 and travelled to look after his estates in the West Indies before settling back in France, although he did offer to raise a regiment for Bavarian service for his former commander in the Alsace Regiment during the 100 days in 1815.[13]

Once Britain's allies had signed the Treaty of Lunéville with France in early 1801 the Jägers, along with the Chasseurs Britanniques and de Watteville's Regiment who were also raised from the remnants of the armies that had fought the French, embarked at Trieste in May

8 C-in-C's office to Howard, 31 May 1803, C-in-C's office to Howard, 2 June 1803, C-in-C's office to de Rottenburg, 9 June 1803, & C-in-C's office to de Rottenburg, 14 June 1803, TNA, WO 3/591, pp.127-8, pp.130-1, pp.157-8, & pp.173-4.

9 Capitulation of Lowenstein's Light Infantry, TNA, WO 1/900, pp.249-255; Grouvel, *Les Corps de Troupe L'Émigration Française*, p.265.

10 Wallace, *Regimental Chronicle*, p.99.

11 Couper to unknown, 10 April 1800, TNA, WO 1/900, p.257.

12 Papers relating to Lowenstein Regiment, HRO, 38M49/3/2.

13 Contamine, *Guillaume de Lasalle de Louisenthal*, pp.331-338.

for passage to Malta. From there they were sent to reinforce Lieutenant General Sir Ralph Abercromby's Egyptian expedition, where they saw action at the siege of Alexandria. In 1802 the 450 men of the Jägers were sent to Isle of Wight, where the regiment was disbanded in May.[14] Two-thirds of the regiment were enlisted in the 5th Battalion, and 75 in other battalions of the 60th. In August Lieutenant Colonel Schoedde, Major Austen, Lieutenant Hinckeldy who had been on the staff on the Isle of Wight, Schoedde's son Lieutenant James Schoedde, Lieutenant Francis Holmes, two sergeants, 12 corporals, four drummers, and 240 privates embarked on the *Devon* transport for Halifax to join the 5th Battalion, arriving before the men from the West Indies.[15]

In September 1803 de Rottenburg arrived in Halifax with the draft of 109 men, and also 40 men from the Foreign Depot on Newfoundland, along with Captain John Welsford. A further draft of 144 men from Lymington arrived soon after.[16] Welsford had already requested an exchange out of the battalion as he felt himself self 'unequal to the duties required in a rifle corps'.[17] However, he was still with the battalion year later, but then went on leave until he exchanged into the 8th Garrison Battalion in 1806.[18]

Retention of those men whose service was expiring continued to be a concern. In November Horse Guards wrote to Lieutenant General Henry Bowyer, commanding at Halifax:

> Your letter of the 21st Sept. with its enclosure having been laid before the com'r in chief, and by HRH's command referred to the right honorable the Sect. at War, I have directions to inform you that the measure of offering a bounty to such of the men of the 60th Regt. who are now serving under a limitation of time, to Inlist for Life, has been approved upon the following stipulations, viz. those men who have one or two years to serve, will, upon being attested without limitation in regard to time or Place of service, be entitled to a Bounty of Nine Guineas; those, whose present Engagements have a period of more than two years unexpired, will be entitled to the bounty of Five Guineas; the bounty in either case liable to such deductions as may be pointed out in the General Recruiting Regulations. The men whose time of service expires this year may receive the same bounty as is allowed to recruits (vis. ten guineas).
>
> HRH desires you will be pleased to make the foregoing known to the Officer Commanding the 5th Bttn. of the 60th Rgt, now serving under your command.[19]

The proportion of those re-enlisting compared to those discharged did improve during 1803, but the numbers grew very slowly and the battalion was still well under its establishment strength, and many officers were still absent.

14 Atkinson, 'Foreign Regiments – Part 6', p.250.
15 August 1802 Pay List, TNA, WO 12/7069.
16 May, June, & September 1803 Pay Lists, TNA, WO 12/7070.
17 C-in-C's office to de Rottenburg, 7 June 1803, TNA, WO 3/591, pp.147-8
18 Army List 1806, TNA, WO 65/56, p.227.
19 Calvert to Bowyer, 10 November 1803, TNA, WO 3/36 p.353.

8

Uniforms and Equipment

The 5th Battalion inherited the uniform of the chasseur companies of Hompesch Light Infantry, but there is some confusion as to the exact details of that uniform. This is partly because there is uncertainty over the clothing of the Hompesch Light Infantry as the chasseurs and fusiliers each had a slightly different uniform,[1] but also it is unclear if any changes were made prior to its adoption by the 5th Battalion. One contemporary description is from the presentation at court of two soldiers in late March 1798, whose uniform; 'consisted of an olive-green jacket, blue pantaloons, black gaiters striped with red, and wore on their heads hussar caps with a green feather'[2]. Captain Ladislaus de Villers Masburgh described the initial officer's uniform as 'pretty and elegant, green with a silver trim, short coat, sky blue pantaloons, a black shako with a green feather forward'.[3]

All the units raised by the Hompesch brothers wore scarlet and green. It was a common colour combination amongst European armies, but not in the British Army. The rest of the 60th Foot wore red coats and white breeches, the same as other line infantry regiments. Due to the 60th being a royal regiment (the Royal American) the facings (cuffs, collar, and lapels) on the coat were blue. Had the 5th Battalion followed convention then the facings on their green coats should have been changed to blue, but whether for reasons of economy or aesthetics they retained the scarlet facings of the Hompesch units.

The tight-fitting pantaloons were sky blue with scarlet feathering, and the coats had scarlet edging, epaulettes, collar, pointed cuffs, and lapels. The coat was probably turned back to show the white waistcoat beneath.[4] The 5th Battalion was one of the first units in the British Army to wear the black, cylindrical, lacquered felt and leather, Hungarian hussar style csákó regimental cap, later referred to as a shako.[5] Prior to the introduction of this style of regimental cap the infantry had generally worn a tricorne hat. It is likely that all that the companies on the Isle of Wight had to do was to change their buttons to reflect their new regiment, and also exchange the brass plate on their cap for a white-metal light infantry bugle horn. Regulations insisted that the men's hair be bound in a queue, but the

1 Atkinson, 'Foreign Regiments – Part 6', p.240.

2 *Northampton Mercury*, Saturday 31 March 1798.

3 Grouvel, *Les Corps de Troupe L'Émigration Française*, p.65.

4 R. Chartrand, *Émigré and Foreign Troops in British Service (1)* (Oxford: Osprey, 1999), p.17.

5 B. Fosten & G. Gibbs, *The British Infantry Shako 1800-1897* (Chelsea: The Military Historical Society, 2008), p.4.

An original shoulder-belt plate of the 5th Battalion. (Dix Noonan Webb Ltd)

5th Battalion were unique in having moustaches.[6] It is probable that the rest of the battalion in Barbados had to wait several months to get their new uniform, which was only approved by the King almost a month after they first mustered.[7]

The officer's uniform also showed the fashion for Hungarian hussar styles which was then influencing many European armies. The officers of the 5th Battalion wore a short green dolman jacket with scarlet collar and cuffs, silver lace, and three rows of buttons. Around the waist was a crimson sash. Their pantaloons were either green for full dress or blue for general wear. On their heads they wore a black Tarleton style helmet with a bear fur crest, green feather, and silver bugle horn, but this would have most likely been replaced by a tall, round, mirliton cap for day-to-day wear. The leather work for both officers and men was black. The officers wore a pouch-belt over the left shoulder, with a silver whistle and chain. The curved sabre hung from waist-belt in a black leather scabbard. The men wore cross-belts carrying their sword-bayonet and cartridge pouch with an oval plate engraved with '60' and a bugle horn.[8] Later, after the battalion changed to shoulder-belts rather than cross-belts, the oval plate was changed to a bugle horn with the roman numerals LX, 'RIFLE-MEN' across the top and '5th BATTN' across the bottom. They also wore leather stocks around their necks, in common with the rest of the infantry.[9]

To carry all their spare clothing, cleaning equipment, and everything else they owned, the soldiers had a brown knapsack. In 1805 a new black lacquered knapsack began to be introduced. The men would also have had a wooden canteen to carry water and a linen haversack for rations. It is likely that some changes to the 5th Battalion's uniform were made in November 1798 as a new pattern jacket and pantaloons were approved by the Duke of York.[10] With their unusual colour uniforms, novel cap, and fearsome facial hair the men of the 5th Battalion would have appeared very foreign compared to other British units, but the uniform slowly changed as other rifle corps were formed and some consistency between the units was imposed.

6 S. Milne & A. Terry, *The Annals of the KRRC, Appendix Dealing with Uniform, Armament & Equipment* (London: Murray, 1913), p.16.
7 Fawcett to Fauquier, 19 January 1798, TNA, WO 7/31 p.48.
8 Milne & Terry, *Appendix,* pp.14-15.
9 Howard to de Rottenburg, 7 September 1806, TNA, WO 7/77 p.15.
10 Fawcett to Fauquier, 28 November 1798, TNA, WO 7/31, p.150.

The first image we have of the 5th Battalion's uniform formed part of a series of sketches and paintings by army officer and artist Charles Hamilton Smith made between 1797 and 1802.[11] The image of the 5th Battalion mostly likely reflects changes made in the 1800 clothing regulations:

> Clothing established for the new regulations 1800 for 5th Battn. 60th Regt.
> Private Green Coat, no lapels – 15s
> Serge Waistcoat – 3s 2d
> Blue Pantaloons – 8s
> Hat Cap – 4s 3d
> 2 Pair Shoes – 11s
> £2 1s 5d
>
> Deduct so much to be stopped from the soldier – 2s
> to be charged to the colonel – £1 19s 5d
>
> The Colonel paying 4/6 per pair the soldier paying the difference of 1s which is saved to him in the price of the gaiters, as he wears short instead of long gaiters.[12]

Most of the uniform was provided for the soldiers by the regiment; however, the cost of items such as shirts, gaiters, the black leather stock they wore around their necks, and many others, was deducted from their pay. Soldiers' uniforms were produced by government contractors but officers had to buy their own uniforms from a number of specialist tailors. The cost could often be substantial with one account giving an average cost for clothing a new officer as £9 13s, around one-tenth of an ensign's annual salary.[13]

The Hamilton Smith painting shows a private of the 5th Battalion in a green coat, without turnbacks or lapels, but with short tails edged in scarlet. Scarlet collar and pointed cuffs, scarlet and green tufted wings on the shoulders, and a single row of nine white metal buttons. The pantaloons have scarlet piping, the black gaiters are also edged in scarlet. Black cross belts are still worn with an oval brass regimental plate. The cap has a leather peak, silver bugle horn, green trim near the top, a red cockade and green plume.[14]

In 1802 it was decided that all rifle units, such as the recently formed 95th, would share the same pattern of clothing, with only facings and buttons changing:

> It is his majesties pleasure, that all companies, corps, battalions or regiments of Rifle Men in his service, should be clothed, in one and the same kind of uniform jacket, without any further variation than the distinction of facing and button.
>
> I herewith transmit to you, by the Com. in Chief's order a Pattern Jacket for the general use of Rifle Corps, which his majesty has approved, and which by HRH's

11 See colour section.
12 Clothing Established for 5/60th, TNA, WO 7/32, p.169.
13 Burnham & McGuigan, *British Army Against Napoleon*, p.141.
14 Milne & Terry, *Appendix*, p.15 and plate I.

> command, is to be lodged in the office of the comptroller of the army accounts, to be had recourse to, as circumstances may require.
>
> I beg you will be so good as to direct any patterns of Rifle jackets, now in your office, to be returned, as being of no further use.[15]

Also the 1802 regulations stated that:

> In the 5th Battalion of the 60th Regiment and the 95th Regiment of foot, or Rifle Corps, each Sergeant shall have for clothing
>
> Annually
> A jacket the sleeves unlined
> A waistcoat with serge sleeves
> A pair of pantaloons, and
> A pair of military shoes, and
> Once in every two years;
> A cap as above
>
> Each Corporal, Drummer and Private man shall have for clothing
> Annually
> A jacket lined, but not laced, with sleeves unlined
> A kersey waistcoat with serge sleeves
> A pair of blue pantaloons made of cloth of the same quality as the jacket and
> A pair of military shoes, and
> Once in every two years;
> A cap as above[16]

The officer's undress uniform changed to a shorter dolman jacket with black lace and the regulations also stated that officers of rifle corps should carry a small pistol in their pouch, and that the armourer sergeant's coats be grey and not green.[17]

It is often assumed that green was chosen as the colour for rifle corps because it afforded better camouflage than the traditional infantry red coat, but experiments at the time proved that it was not necessarily the best choice. The often bright and easily visible uniforms of the Napoleonic period were perfectly logical for line infantry, and even for heavy cavalry. A commander needed to be able to easily tell which units were friend or foe on a smoke-shrouded battlefield. However, for light infantry, riflemen, and light cavalry engaged in skirmishing, patrolling, and outpost duty, being easily seen was a distinct disadvantage. In 1800 on the Isle of Wight, Charles Hamilton Smith, who was serving with the 6/60th at the time, conducted a series of experiments to find which colour was most effective for assisting soldiers from being hit by aimed rifle and musket fire. Using men from the battalion's rifle

15 Calvert to Fauquier 13 July 1802, WO 3/35 p.108.

16 Sergeants' Clothing 5/60th & 95th, WO 26/39 p.153-4.

17 W.Y. Carman, 'Infantry Clothing Regulations, 1802', *Journal of the Society of Army Historical Research*, Vol. XIX, pp.206, 210 & 220-1.

company he first ascertained that a white target was, not surprisingly, more easily hit than a black one but he then went on to evaluate red, green, and grey. He does not say how large the targets were but the standard target at the time was a circle five feet in diameter:

> From this company were selected the six best marksmen, all educated jager, and each was supplied with six bullets. The red target, placed on the open heath, was distant 125 yards from the stand: the time selected was seven in the morning, with weather sufficiently moderate not to have perceptible influence on the direction of the shot; the men were to load as to them seemed best, and to fire at leisure. After each had fired six shots, the party returned home. On the next day, when the weather was equally favourable, and the sun at the same angle of elevation, the same number of shots were delivered by the same men, and under the same conditions, at the green target; and on the third, at the grey.
>
> On the third day of the second series of trials, the men immediately observed that they were now so familiar with the distance, that their fire would be more effective than in the first. But it was this time the grey target that was to be aimed at, and the result turned out by no means commensurate with the expectation of the marksmen. In this manner the second series of experiments was conducted, even with more care, if possible, to maintain the conditions perfectly similar: each day the targets had the shot-holes stopped, and the surface repainted; but now the red target was already so much damaged, that fearing it would not hold together for the day's trial, the distance for the third and last series of rounds was increased to 150 yards, and not withstanding the changes resulting therefrom, it fell to pieces before the last shot was delivered, and, being bound together by withies, was brought home in a bundle. The green also was so much battered in the fiery ordeal as to be unfit for repairing; but the grey remained sound, and was afterwards used again. There had been fired 108 shots at each, 72 of which at 125, and the last 36 at 150 yards.[18]

Hamilton Smith estimated that the red target received double the number of hits compared to the grey, with the green being between the two. The findings were reported to Sir Robert Brownrigg, quartermaster general, but the Army continued to use green for the rifle corps and when new light infantry units were created later they still wore red. In 1806 the pantaloons of the 5th Battalion were changed from light blue to dark blue, which may have helped to make them less conspicuous.[19]

A critique of rifle corps uniforms and equipment published anonymously in 1808 advocated making the clothing looser and easier to move in, having the stock worn around the neck made of something more flexible than thick leather, extending the tails of the coat so it covered more of the back and legs when bending, sitting, or lying down, the addition of elbow and knee pads to make various firing positions more comfortable, and that the cap should be smaller and without a tuft. Over all the author recommended that the clothing be designed ergonomically and that the amount the rifleman had to carry be reduced:

18 C. Hamilton Smith, 'Experiments on the Comparative Effect of Rifle and Musketry Fire on Different Colours', *Aide-Mémoire to the Military Sciences*, 1853, pp.257-9.

19 Wynyard to Fauquier, 16 April 1806, TNA, WO 7/33, p.438.

> In proposing the above plan of clothing the light troops, we have had nothing but utility in view, bearing constantly in mind the impossibility of a man's doing light duty when loaded with the present quantity of belts, accoutrements, arms, canteen, haversack, knapsack, great coat, blanket, &c. &c...
>
> ...We conceive that with a very little trouble, besides arms, and accoutrements, a canteen, haversack and a blanket, (so contrived as that it may occasionally be used as a cloak at night when on sentry) may be made to comprise all the requisite incumbrances of a light corps.[20]

Criticism of the rifle corps' uniform and equipment was evidently justified as in 1811 the commandant of the Foreign Depot, Colonel Mosheim, replied to suggestions made by Lieutenant Colonel Williams, then in command of the 5th Battalion:

> I have the honor in acknowledging the receipt of your letter dated Alicentra 6th Inst. To acquaint you in reply, that I perfectly conclude in your opinion that proper and suitable equipments should be made, for the men of 5th Battn. 60th Regt. under your Command, and would evince every readiness to comply with your Suggestions as to their packs &c if it came within my province. The packs for all Recruits all furnished by a Contractor appointed by the Commissary in Chief, and the Clothing as received from the Clothiers is duly issued to the Men. I have given directions to keep the Pantaloons as wide as possible.[21]

The heavy wool clothing of the period kept the soldiers warm in cold weather, and offered some resistance to moderate rain, but could be uncomfortable in summer or tropical heat. After prolonged campaigning uniforms would have to be patched or otherwise repaired, caps suffered in the rain, and boots fell apart. Their 'regimentals' were not the only set of clothes that the men of the 5th Battalion had. They were also issued with waistcoats of white kersey with serge sleeves, and white duck (a type of canvas-like cloth) trousers, which was their undress uniform that they would wear most of the time in barracks or camp. The men were meant to be issued clothing at the end of each year, but some years this failed to happen on time, or at all, when a unit was on service abroad.

The uniforms did not always stand up well to the rigours of campaigning. In 1809 Major Davy ordered:

> On halting-days the officers commanding companies will inspect their men at eleven o'clock roll-call, and they will pay particular attention to the state of the arms, ammunition, and accoutrements. The blue pantaloons which have been torn upon the march are immediately to be repaired, and those men who are under the absolute necessity of wearing their white drawers must appear with them well washed and cleaned.

20 Beaufoy, *Scioppetaria*, p.242.

21 Mosheim to Williams 26 July 1811, TNA, WO 7/83, pp.206-7.

> The stocks are to be worn, and the rosettes and bugles which have been torn out of the caps are to be replaced, etc.[22]

Things got so bad that Davy allowed them men to cut away the tails of their jackets to patch the rest.[23]

In March 1809 Davy had asked for Lieutenant General Craddock, commander of the forces in Portugal at the time, for his assistance in getting replacement clothing:

> The clothing of the men having suffered much from the nature of the service in which the battalion has constantly been employed, and his Excellency having been pleased to say that he would afford us his assistance to have the clothing for the present year forwarded, permit me to request the influence of his Excellency to get it expedited to this country with as little delay as possible. The battalion having been on the Irish establishment, the clothing will come from thence through Messrs. Armit and Borough, Army Agents, Dublin.[24]

However, in October of the same year Wellesley wrote to the secretary at war:

> I have the honour to submit for your consideration an application which I have received from the 5th Battalion 60th regiment for a remuneration to the men for the extraordinary expense they have been at in repairing their clothing, in consequence of the unusual delay which has occurred in sending out clothing which has been due to them for a long while. I have, therefore, to request your decision upon this claim.[25]

In 1812 the officers changed from the Tarleton helmet in favour of a similar style cap to the other ranks, and also a hussar-style heavily laced pelisse was added, often worn over one shoulder. The pantaloons for the men were also changed from blue to green,[26] which met with some resistance from the riflemen, but later in the same year troops serving in Spain and Portugal were ordered to wear grey trousers and short gaiters. The then colonel-commandant received the following letter from the regimental agents, Greenwood, Cox & Co.:

> We have the honour to transmit herewith, for your information, the copy of a letter which we have received from the Adjutant General, authorizing grey pantaloons, and short gaiters, to be worn, in lieu of breeches and long gaiters, by all regiments serving in Spain and Portugal: a copy has also been forwarded to the Officer Commanding the 5th Battn. 60th Regiment of Foot, and directions given to the

22 Battalion Order, quoted in Rigaud, *Celer et Audax*, pp.85-6.

23 Rigaud, *Celer et Audax*, p.86.

24 Davy to military secretary to Craddock, 20 March 1809, quoted in Rigaud, *Celer et Audax*, p.67.

25 Duke of Wellington (2nd), *Supplementary Despatches, Correspondence and Memoranda of Field Marshal Arthur Duke of Wellington, K.G.* (London: Murray, 1860), Vol. VI, p.416.

26 Milne & Terry, *Appendix*, p.17.

> regimental Clothiers to furnish pantaloons accordingly, with the clothing for the year 1812, but as the gaiters are to be paid for by the men, and as they are probably already in possession of those articles, no orders are intended to be given by us respecting them, unless we hear from the Commanding Officer on the subject.[27]

The warrant of July 1812 stated that sergeants were issued with the following accoutrements; sword and belt, pouch, sling, sword-knot, whistle, lock cover, powder-horn, copper flask and bullet bag. The rank and file received; Pouch, sling, lock cover, powder-horn, copper flask, waist belt with sliding carriage and bullet bag, with buglers also getting a sword.[28] Buglers' uniforms were also slightly different to the rank and file, with green and scarlet wings and decorated with twisted scarlet and green cord. It is not known if the battalion band had a specific uniform but it was usual for musicians to have very colourful uniforms, often with the jackets reversing the facing and base colours; so that for the 5th Battalion they may have been scarlet with green collars and cuffs.

In 1813 7th and 8th Battalions of the 60th were formed and also clothed in green with scarlet facings. These battalions were mostly light infantry with two rifle companies each, although there is no evidence the 8th Battalion ever received any rifles. From 1815 the 1st, 2nd, 3rd, 4th, and 6th Battalions also swapped to wearing green and were styled as light infantry.[29] The rifle companies of these battalions had worn green since their inception from around 1799, but of a slightly different design and with white pantaloons.[30]

The regimental cap underwent a number of changes and was changed from lacquered to plain felt in 1806. The 1806 pattern was found not to survive the rigours of campaign and was replaced with a better design in 1812 that featured a raised front and stouter felt. The 1812 pattern was itself replaced in 1816 by a design with a wider top.[31] A year earlier the number of the regiment had been added beneath the bugle-horn on the caps of all rifle and light infantry regiments.[32]

Whatever the regulations stated it is likely that the appearance of the battalion during the long Peninsular campaign varied considerably from the ideal. The uniforms would have been ragged and patched, and items often replaced either with their undress equivalent or whatever was to hand. In 1814, Major General Stopford commented that the company of the 5th Battalion attached to his brigade: '...appears in great want of Cloathing, not having had any since the year before last – Their arms and accoutrements are in good order'.[33]

27 Library and Archives of Canada (LAC), Sir George Prevost, Record Group 8 I, Vol. 30, p.77.

28 Milne & Terry, *Appendix*, p.18.

29 Calvert to Clothing Board, 29 May 1815, TNA WO 7/36, p.10.

30 Milne & Terry, *Appendix*, p.18.

31 Fosten & Gibbs, *British Infantry Shako*, pp.9-23.

32 *Saunders's Newsletter,* 18 January 1815.

33 Confidential Report of 5/60th company attached to 2nd Brigade of Guards, 8 May, 1814, TNA, WO 27/172.

9

Nova Scotia

If the West Indies was one of the worst postings for soldiers in the early 19th century then Halifax, Nova Scotia, was held to be one of the best. The town had been founded in 1749 and was the Royal Navy's principal base on the North American coast. The 13 square miles of natural harbour make it one of the largest in the world. Deep and well sheltered, it was used by fishermen, merchants, and privateers, as well as the Royal Navy. The town had a population of around 9,000 but the personnel at the naval dockyard, the sailors on the ships, and the garrison to protect them could number up to a further 6,000, depending on the time of year. With cheap rum from the Caribbean, close to a hundred drinking establishments, and little disease, it was a favourite with both soldiers and sailors. When the 5th Battalion arrived in 1803 the garrison was in the midst of a renovation and building program started by the Duke of Kent during his tenure as commander in British North America.[1]

George Weale, serving in Halifax with the 29th Foot at the same time that the 5th Battalion was there described the locale:

> The town of Halifax is built chiefly of wood, on a gentle declivity, rising from the sea. The entrance of the harbour is defended by the batteries of Camperdown and York redoubt, and further up towards town by George's Island, in the middle of the channel, on the Halifax side, by Point Pleasant, the grand battery, and the citadel; and on the opposite side by Fort Clarence. The environs of Halifax, about two miles from the town, are one continued range of wood and rock.[2]

Spring came in April with a sudden thaw. The local population would go hunting, fishing, and picnicking in the forests or besides the many lakes. Mid-summer was usually hot, but September was often very pleasant with sharp frosts in the morning and clear, warm days. Fogs were common, and autumn was brief and colourful before the uniform whiteness of winter came with the first snows in October. The snow would deepen and remain until April. The contrast with the unchanging heat, humidity and rain of the Caribbean could not have been greater for the 5th Battalion.

1 D.E. Graves, *Fix Bayonets!* (Stroud: Spellmount, 2007), pp.114-116.

2 Weale, *Interesting Memoir*, p.16.

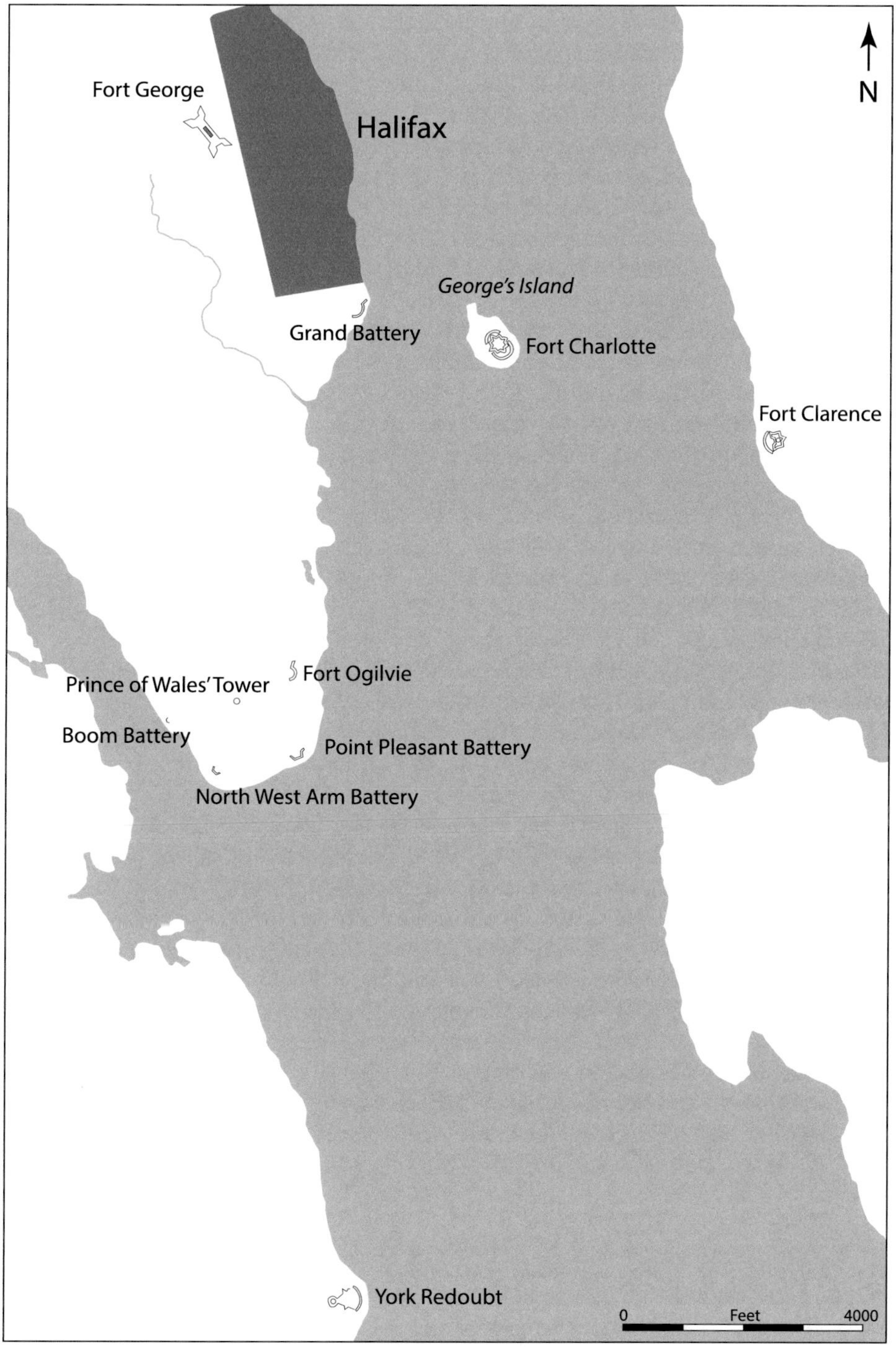

Plan of the defences around Halifax harbour.
Source: TNA, MPH 1/799/6, Outline of the Harbour of Halifax, shewing the several Forts & Batterys for its defence.

Winter halted most activities, including military exercises, and so for the officers there was a constant round of balls, parties and sleigh rides. The wooden houses were designed well for the climate, although they did have tendency to catch fire and the garrison were often roused to help with fire-fighting. The ice-bound navy ships would be brought alongside the wharves and wooden sheds built on top of their decks, heated by stoves. Plays would be performed in them and parties held.

Nova Scotian mothers were frequently very keen for their daughters to meet eligible army officers, and the officers equally keen to make their acquaintance. Charles Leslie, who was stationed in Halifax in 1816 with the 2/60th, noted:

> Halifax may justly pride itself on the beauty of its daughters. They have fine complexions, lit up by soft blue eyes. Their peculiar charms of countenance have been attributed to the humidity of the climate, which is liable to frequent fogs during summer; and it certainly would appear that this dampness of atmosphere does impart a softness and clearness of complexion to the female features...[3]

At least two of the 5th Battalion's officers fell for local girls. George Zühleke married Crithiana Campbell in Sydney, Cape Breton, in March of 1805 and the happy couple had their first child, rather rapidly, in June.[4] Michael de Wend married Sarah Douglas, a Scot living on Prince Edward Island, in August 1804.[5] Sergeant Charles Recknoy, who had arrived with Lowenstein's Jägers, married at Halifax in December 1802. According to his record of service he was already 55 years old and had lost an eye during the Egyptian campaign. He would go on to serve another 16 years with the battalion.[6]

However, one officer of the 5th Battalion was not so keen on the new posting. In May 1804, after a year in Halifax, Captain John Galiffe wrote to his brother:

> The recent garrison changes, especially the transfer from Antigua to Halifax, and our change of uniform, have cost me dearly. This garrison is the worse of all in times of war. It is very expensive but we are not given the allowances attributed to officers in times of war and, therefore, have to get by with our pay only which, as you know, is not much. In fact, they only cover a quarter of what I was earning in the Caribbean. I hope that my half-pay from the York Rangers will be enough to help you and it would really be bad luck if we did not shortly find a way out of this tight spot.
>
> My own position is starting to improve. I have been the senior captain of the battalion for two years now and one of the most senior of the regiment. It is certain that had I remained in England when war was declared, I would have been appointed

3 C. Leslie, *Military Journal of Colonel Leslie* (Aberdeen: Aberdeen University Press, 1887), p.288.

4 The dates for the marriage differ between 1804 in the army records and 1805 in the Nova Scotian records, perhaps to disguise the date of conception of their son. TNA, WO 25/779/40 & Nova Scotia Marriages, 1711-1909, database, (via familysearch.org, accessed 7 September 2018), George Henry Zuhlikie and Crithiana Campbell, 12 Mar 1805; citing Saint George, Sydney, Cape Breton, Nova Scotia; FHL microfilm 814,172.

5 TNA, WO 42/49/85 & de Wend-Fenton family records courtesy of Michael Cayley.

6 Recknoy Record of Service, TNA, WO 25/772/92.

> major without too much help. But I was too precious for the regiment here, having been for a long time the only captain present, that I could not go back to England in time and now, it is too late. But my turn, with a little help, will come soon.[7]

After discussing family business, including his sister's wedding, he continued:

> Even though I might have been tempted to allow myself to be shackled in holy matrimony, I would have always made sure that I was independent and useful to my family, but I have never managed to jump that hurdle and have so many times backed out when I was on the point of jumping it that I am now tired of it all and I doubt I ever will. That said, after finding out about Louise's wedding, I do not think that I am too old 'to drink from the fountain' from time to time.
>
> Whilst we are on the subject, you must give me more details about your liaison with the Rodney family. I would have never thought that the first news of it all would have been given to me in Halifax by a stranger to us both! So I now expect full details about this family in general and your connection to it in particular. With regards to myself, I do not have much to say expect that I live day-to-day and each day brings its equal share of boredom.
>
> This garrison is not much fun and offers few pleasures. I am not much respected by the people here, who are very gloomy. If you want to meet people here, you must become a slave of society as you are condemned to endless official visits, which I cannot bear. I am too old for that sort of thing and value my freedom too much to suffer it being impeded.
>
> Lady Wentworth has been kind enough to invite me to visit her on a number of occasions and holds me in great affection but, as I have told you, I am no courtesan and I am sure that she complains that I am not more assiduous towards her. Sir John W is an excellent man that I am quite fond of and his wife is pleasant. Finally, they have everything they need to make their home most pleasing, except at Halifax, and I would happily visit more if it were not for this damn country. We really do wish to go back to the Caribbean where advancement is less difficult and where we can make some money. We have to hope that the god of war continues to spare me. It really would be the happiest thing to happen to us.

Galiffe's view of Halifax is at odds with most memoirs from the period. He ended the letter with:

> If you find a good moment to do so, please send me a family seal as I have none and I need it for some documents that I want to send to you just in case because, whilst I am well, I am not immortal.

The uniform change that Galiffe alludes to was the change made in the 1802 warrants to make all rifle corps, including the 5th Battalion and the recently formed 95th, have the

7 John to Jacques Galiffe, 14 May 1804, BG, ms fr 2751c pl23 f003 (translated).

View of Halifax from Fort Needham, 1801 by George Isham Parkyns. (Toronto Public Library)

same pattern of uniform. Galiffe's brother, Jaques Augustin Galiffe, was a diplomat and knew many of the members of the British government, and others in the establishment. The Rodney family he mentions was possibly that of the late Admiral Rodney, and Galiffe's's interest in his brother's connections may have been more about seeking influential patrons rather than his social life. As far as his own friendships were concerned, Lady Wentworth was the wife of the Lieutenant-Governor of Nova Scotia, Sir John Wentworth; she was known for her beauty and in 1804 she was 58, compared to Galiffe's 37.

The 5th Battalion was once again split between various batteries and forts, they also provided detachments for Prince Edward Island and Cape Breton further up the coast. In the continued absence of Lieutenant Colonel de Rottenburg, Lieutenant Colonel Schoedde was in command.[8] The principal fortress was Fort George, often referred to as The Citadel, on a hill overlooking the town. It had been completed in 1800 and was oblong in shape, approximately 800 feet by 400 feet, with triangular bastions on each corner. Inside the walls were powder magazines, accommodation, mortar platforms, and a guardhouse. Nearby was the headquarters and further barracks. A total of 105 guns were spread over 10 batteries and towers around the harbour, including Fort Charlotte on George's Island.[9] Winter may have meant a packed social calendar for the officers but the men would have spent long hours in their quarters, punctuated by freezing guard or other duties, with little to spend their pay on but drink.

The peace following the Treaty of Amiens collapsed in the spring of 1803. The treaty had not addressed the underlying tensions in Europe and the British balked at fulfilling some of the terms such as evacuating Malta, and France continued to attempt to dominate Europe, taking over territory in Switzerland and Northern Italy. Britain declared war again in May, not wanting to give France any further respite and time to prepare for hostilities to recommence. The garrison in Halifax received the news in June. Halifax might have gotten busier

8 Various Pay Lists, TNA, WO 12/7070, WO 12/7071.

9 Plan of Halifax Harbour Defences TNA, MPH 1/799/6.

with the resumption of war, but the day to day life of the battalion probably changed very little. In September de Rottenburg finally returned to the battalion and resumed command. In October Captain William Gabriel Davy joined the battalion after exchanging with Captain Gomer, who had long been in Germany recruiting. In November Sergeant Major Charles Sawatsky was promoted to ensign. Even though Nova Scotia must have been a more pleasant posting than Surinam Private John Muller shot himself on 26 July, but no reason is recorded in the pay list. September saw five men desert, two of whom, Sergeant Francis Reiss and Corporal John Gleisch, were caught and sentenced to life in the Army.[10]

In January 1804 the Duke of York had decided that Quartermaster and Lieutenant John Kemmeter should be asked to resign one of his two commissions. He opted to remain as quartermaster. In September the 5th Battalion was inspected by Lieutenant General Henry Bowyer, commander of the garrison at Halifax. Every battalion was meant to be regularly inspected but the inspections were not always carried out, or the reports have not survived, and the level of detail varied. The 1804 inspection is the first inspection in The National Archives for the 5th Battalion and it gives a very detailed picture of the unit at that time.[11] In his covering letter to the adjutant general, Bowyer wrote:

> I have the Honour to transmit to you the Review Returns of the 5th Battalion of the Royal American Regiment with my Report on the occasion, which I beg you will lay before His Royal Highness the Commander in Chief.
>
> Lt. Col. De Rottenburg has requested me to say how gratifying it would be to him if His Royal Highness would be pleas'd to order the 5th Battalion to be completed & I hope I shall be excused in adding that Soldiers cannot be taken better care of or brought quicker to perfection than when under the Command of that Excellent Officer.

Bowyer's report was very favourable. He wrote that the officers 'March & Salute well. Were dress'd & arm'd agreably to His Majesty's Orders & Regulations respecting this Battalion'. The non-commissioned officers were 'Creditable in their appearance & perfect in their Field Exercises & Duty,' and the rank and file were 'A very serviceable Body of Men; some low & old among them, but in the whole are active, alert & in the highest discipline & order'.

The information in the return of the officers gives a great deal of insight into the battalion and how it had changed since formation: 11 of the officers present were English, Scottish, or Irish with 17 still being foreigners, compared to being all foreigners in 1798. Fifteen were still absent and noted as never having joined, being on leave, or having overstayed their leaves. One company was vacant after Captain Cartwright had died the previous month. Of those marked as having not joined seven were probably British, judging by their surnames, and three foreign. Two officers appointed to the battalion four years previously had still not deigned to make an appearance but both had reasonable excuses that came to light later; Lieutenant Anthony Suasso was serving with the 1st Battalion in Quebec and Lieutenant George Schneider had drowned in 1801.[12]

10 June to September 1803 Pay Lists, TNA, WO 12/7070.

11 Inspection of 5/60th, TNA, WO 27/88.

12 Schneider was included in a list of deceased officers in the 1801 Windward & Leeward returns, WO 17/2492, and Suasso is listed as being with 1/60th on the November 1804 return WO 17/178.

The officers' age varied from 19 to 50 with an average of 29 for the commissioned officers and 36 for the staff. Their length of service ranged from 29 years for Lieutenant Colonel Schoedde to just a few months for Ensign Rauch and Assistant Surgeon Dumoulin. Some of the officers had started their careers very young. Charles Hinckeldy received his ensign's commission aged 11, Alexander Mackenzie at 14, and James Schoedde at 15. Also notable is the rapidity of some of the officer's progression through the ranks, illustrating the inequities of the purchase system. Major Thomas Austen went from ensign to captain in just five months, a progression that took Charles Schoedde 18 years. William Yates Johnson spent just 20 days as an ensign. John Galiffe was the senior captain but William Davy would beat him to a majority. However, Ensigns Starck and Sawatsky had both been promoted from the ranks and so the social background and wealth of the officers did vary considerably. Major Austen was to continue his rapid rise through the ranks by his promotion to lieutenant colonel in the 2nd Battalion soon after the inspection.

The return for the NCOs, buglers and privates of the battalion recorded that 585 were foreign, and one Irish. The lone Irishman was possibly Daniel Yearly, judging by the surnames in the relevant company. Yearly exchanged into the Nova Scotia Regiment in November.[13] Each of the ten companies had between 54 and 62 men. The battalion was 232 men short of its establishment. The age of the men was broken down into five year intervals and most were between 25 and 35. There were just two 18 or under, but 89 in the 40 to 55 brackets. The height was recorded mostly in half inch increments with three at the maximum six foot two inches but the largest number, 221, recorded as five foot five inches or under. Two men were recorded as having 15 years of service behind them, implying they had enlisted around 1789 and so must have come from another battalion of the 60th, or another regiment. Only 40 men are listed as having served for ten years, implying that they had originally joined the Hompesch or Lowenstein units when they formed in 1790s. The majority of the 218 with four years of service probably came with Schoedde from Lowenstein's Jägers. Only 33 were new recruits with one year or less of service. Fourteen sergeants, six buglemen, and 211 rank and file were noted as having re-enlisted for life rather than the more limited terms common for foreign troops.

Table 1: Age

Age	Number
55	5
50	8
45	24
40	52
35	111
30	166
25	149
20	69
18 and under	2

Source: 5th Battalion 60th Foot 1804 Inspection. TNA, WO 27/88.

13 September & November 1804 Pay Lists for Captain Galiffe's Company, TNA, WO 12/7071.

Table 2: Height

Height (feet & inches)	Number
6' 2"	3
6' 1"	2
6 ½"	3
6'	8
5' 11½"	5
5' 11"	8
5' 10½"	10
5' 10"	20
5' 9½"	26
5' 9"	23
5' 8½"	21
5' 8"	40
5' 7½"	33
5' 7"	62
5' 6½"	25
5' 6"	76
Under 5' 5"	221

Source: 5th Battalion 60th Foot 1804 Inspection. TNA, WO 27/88.

Table 3: Length of Service

Years of Service	Number
15	2
10	40
8	60
7	65
6	25
5	94
4	218
3	24
2	25
1 and under	33

Source: 5th Battalion 60th Foot 1804 Inspection. TNA, WO 27/88.

At the time of the inspection Captain Davy was shown as being on duty as aide de camp to Lieutenant General Bowyer; Captain Galiffe and 22 men were on Prince Edward Island; Lieutenant Zühleke with 22 men at Cape Breton; Lieutenant Herbert and 22 men at Fort Sackville; and Lieutenant Mackenzie and 35 men at York Redoubt. 11 men were on guard and a further nine men at three other posts. Fifty-three officers and men were sick, either in their quarters or the hospital. Three privates were under arrest in the garrison prison and one sergeant under regimental arrest. One sergeant was noted as being in Europe; Sergeant Francis Verdet was at the Foreign Depot; four men were still in the West Indies – of these, two were sick, one had been invalided, and one was in gaol for debts. Twenty-one men were listed as musicians, implying that the battalion had formed its own band.[14]

It was not only the officers and men that were inspected. Bowyer also reported on the arms and accoutrements; 351 rifles and swords were 'good' and 432 'bad'. Bowyer noted that of the 432 bad rifles 351 were new ones without swords and hence unserviceable. The 351 good and 351 bad without swords were undoubtedly the ones that had been recently shipped from Portsmouth.[15] Bowyer noted that de Rottenburg had been promised by the Board of Ordnance that 200 new swords would be sent to the battalion. Also listed are 10 good bugles and 12 bad, along with 22 good buglers' swords. Pouches with shoulder belts, sword belts, slings, powder horns, bugle sword belts, and breast plates were all good, with some still in store at Barbados and Antigua. New sets of coats, waistcoats, pantaloons, shoes, and caps had been delivered to the battalion that year and were well fitted.

The battalion's manoeuvres were 'well chosen, well performed and well calculated for light troops'. The regimental records and accounts were well kept. There were no complaints but Bowyer did comment that the number of sick was quite high and blamed this on the change of climate from the West Indies. Bowyer concluded with his general remarks: 'The present high State & Order of this Battalion is owing to the Solicitude & unremitting attention of its Lt. Colonel, Baron de Rottenburg, who has brought it to a principle of discipline suitable to the Services for which it was rais'd & may be required'.

Soon after the inspection Lieutenant Colonel Schoedde is marked in the musters as 'sick in the country.[16]' He then returned to Europe on leave but resigned his commission in December. He died in early 1805. He had served for 28 years. In his will he left £2,000 to his son James, for the purchase of a captaincy.[17] Major Edward Drummond purchased Schoedde's lieutenant colonelcy.[18]

In October 1804 Private Michael Ranst was discharged and became the surgeon's mate on HMS *Amsterdam*, a former Dutch frigate captured that year at the retaking of Surinam. He left 10 guineas to pay for another man to enlist in his place. While some were still choosing to leave, more than 60 soldiers opted to enlist for life before the year's end.[19] In November Captain George Grau was court martialled for 'behaving in a scandalous and infamous manner, such as is unbecoming the Character of an Officer and a Gentleman, by grossly abusing and ill treating Lieutenant Charles Henckelday' [sic].[20] Grau and Hinckeldy had an argument in the mess and then a petty disagreement over an

14 September 1804 Pay List, TNA, WO 12/7071.
15 See Chapter 3.
16 September 1804 Pay List, TNA, WO 12/7071.
17 Will of Lt. Col. Schoedde, TNA, PROB 11/1421/91.
18 June 1805 Return (misfiled with 1810 returns), TNA WO 17/180.
19 October to December 1804 pay lists, TNA, WO 12/7071.
20 Trial of Captain Grau, TNA, WO 71/199.

View of Halifax from George's Island, 1801 by George Isham Parkyns. (Toronto Public Library)

invitation to breakfast. Grau was found not guilty of both charges. Lieutenant Michael de Wend was promoted to captain in December,[21] and the establishment of the battalion was raised by 50 to 800 rank and file.[22]

In March 1805 George Menschel was granted 12 months leave in Europe, an exceptional mark of trust in a private soldier.[23] Others were clearly less worthy of such trust. In May 42s was paid to a Mr James Thomson for the apprehension of two deserters; Joseph Hubert and John Richter. They were tried by court martial and sentenced to be transferred to Britain as felons and then transported to Australia for life. Also in May, Privates John Engstrom and Frederic Jurgens shot themselves; no further details are given. The following month at the end of the pay list and records of allowances is a sheet headed 'Remarks'.

> Private Anton Jaeger of the 3rd Vacant Company discharged 11th June, by sentence of a Regimental Court Martial, approved of by the Lieutenant General; Commanding in British North America. The following is a Copy of the Sentence, and of the approval.
>
> Sentence
> The Court having duly considered the Evidence against the Prisoner, together with what he brought in his defence; is of Opinion that he is Guilty of the crime laid to his Charge (viz an attempt to commit the crime of sodomy) in

21 Willoughby Wallace, *Regimental Chronicle*, p.151.
22 TNA, WO 380/1, p.167.
23 March 1805 Pay List, TNA, WO 12/7072.

> breach of the Articles of War and knowing that he is an Invalid and unable to bear Corporal Punishment; and also taking into consideration the Infamy and disgrace attending the shameful crime he is found Guilty of. Sentence the said prisoner Private Anton Jaeger to be drummed out of the Battalion; with a rope round his neck at such time and in such a manner as the Lt. Colonel commanding shall think proper.
>
> Alex Andrews, Capt.
> 5th Battn, 60th Reg. President.[24]

At the bottom of the sheet de Rottenburg noted his own approval, and included a copy of the approval of Lieutenant General Bowyer. As late as the 1990s a soldier could still be dismissed from the British Army for homosexuality, albeit in a less brutal manner.

As the battalion's time in Halifax approached its end some soldiers decided they wanted to remain. Private John Liedgens transferred to the Nova Scotia Fencibles, and Privates Gotlieb Stierlein, Anton Krasny, and John Haneman were accepted into the Royal Military Artificers at Halifax; a corps of skilled artisans used to perform carpentry and building work. Some soldiers took their desire to stay in North America into their own hands and there was a flurry of 11 desertions in the last two months of the year. The battalion also had two men still listed as sick in Trinidad and, having no news of them, de Rottenburg arranged for their transfer to the 98th Foot, presumably because that regiment was in Trinidad.[25] Davy remained in Halifax as Bowyer's aide-de-camp.

The leading inhabitants of Halifax delivered an address on 6 November to de Rottenburg:

> Sir, While the Inhabitants reflect with pleasure on the Harmony that has subsisted between them and the excellent Regiment under your Command since it has been in this Country, it is with unfeigned regret they contemplate its departure.
>
> They consider it their duty publicly to bear testimony of the Soldier-like and regular deportment both of the Officers and Men. And while the high state of Military perfection and order which the Battalion has attained, reflects on you Sir the most distinguished professional reputation your own correct and amiable manner have intitled you to universal esteem.
>
> We will thank you to communicate to the Officers and Men the high estimation in which they are held in the Community, and the lively interest we shall take in their future Glory and Reputation.
>
> To you Sir and your most amiable Lady we wish a pleasant and agreeable passage, and that reception from Our Most Glorious Sovereign to which your merit is eminently intitles you.[26]

The return of 1 November 1805 put the strength of the battalion at one lieutenant colonel, two majors, four captains, 12 lieutenants, five ensigns, one quartermaster, one surgeon, one assistant surgeon, 30 sergeants, 17 buglers and 522 rank and file; 225 men below

24 June 1805 Pay List, TNA, WO 12/7072.
25 October to December 1805 Pay List, TNA, WO 12/7072.
26 Address to de Rottenburg, LAC, MG 24 F 78, R4156-0-4-E.

establishment. Later that month a detachment of the battalion consisting of Captain Andrews, Lieutenant White, six sergeants, four buglemen and 90 rank and file embarked on the 98-gun HMS *St George* to serve as marines on the passage back to Britain; de Rottenburg went with them. The remainder of the battalion followed aboard various transports.[27] The 5th Battalion of the 60th (Royal American) Regiment would not serve on its eponymous continent again.

27 November 1804 and January 1806 returns TNA, WO 17/178.

10

Prisoners and Preparations

Whilst the 5th Battalion had been in the Americas, Napoleon Bonaparte had risen to the pinnacle of his power. In 1804 he had crowned himself Emperor of France. The following year he had defeated the armies of Russia and Austria at Ulm and Austerlitz. Prussia would suffer humiliating defeats in 1806 at Jena and Auerstädt, and by 1807 Napoleon's empire would stretch from the Baltic to the Mediterranean. However, Nelson's destruction of the combined French and Spanish fleets at Trafalgar in October 1805 had thwarted any plans Napoleon had to invade Britain. The French no longer had the ships to challenge the Royal Navy at sea, but likewise Britain did not have a large enough army to challenge Napoleon on the continent, and was quickly running out of significant allies to subsidise.

The 5th Battalion arrived back in Britain in early December 1805. They did not head for the Isle of Wight, which had for many years been the home of the foreign corps, but instead they landed at Portsmouth. Necessity and changes in the law had finally allowed foreign troops to be quartered on the mainland, and not just the Channel Islands and the Isle of Wight. The battalion marched first for Hilsea Barracks, just north of Portsmouth, and then in February they moved to Haslar Barracks, near Gosport, which was adjacent to a large Royal Navy hospital.

The battalion's proximity to the recently-moved Foreign Depot at Lymington, on the edge of the New Forest, meant that it was soon receiving batches of new recruits. Some of the older or more infirm men of the battalion transferred to veteran or garrison battalions and some were discharged as their service had expired. The strength of the battalion rose from 481 rank and file in February to 560 in July.[1] James Schoedde used his father's bequest and purchased his captaincy.[2] Peter Blassiere achieved the same promotion without purchase by exchanging into the 66th Regiment and then back to the 60th.[3] Captain Charles de Salaberry exchanged into the 5th Battalion from the 4/60th. De Salaberry was a Canadian who had joined the 44th Regiment as a volunteer aged 14. He was commissioned into the 60th in 1793 and saw action in the West Indies, rising to captain by 1799. Whilst in the Caribbean

1 February to July 1806 Returns, TNA, WO 17/178.

2 January 1806 Pay List, TNA, 12/7072.

3 *London Gazette*, 10 December 1805, Issue 15870, p.1537.

he also killed a fellow officer in a duel.[4] His Royal Highness the Duke of Kent recommended de Salaberry for a company in the 5th Battalion and wrote to him in May 1806:

> I am delighted to find you met with so kind a reception from that excellent officer and worthy man, Lieut.-Colonel Baron de Rothenburg; but it was not more than I expected, as I know there was every disposition on his part to show attentions to anyone that comes recommended from me…
>
> I hope that you will… perfect yourself in all the scientific details of the manoeuvres of a rifle corps for which he is master unquestionably in our service.[5]

On 1 July Major General Sir George Prevost, Lieutenant-Governor of Portsmouth and General Officer Commanding South-West District, inspected the battalion. It had been two years since the previous inspection carried out in Halifax. Sir George was the son of Major General Augustine Prevost, one of the founding officers of the 60th. Sir George's notes are brief and to the point. He described the battalion's general appearance as 'Soldierlike, uniform & steady' and the arms as 'fit for service'. He was also satisfied with the drill, and accounts. He thought the officers and NCOs were 'active & intelligent' and the words of command 'loud and distinct'. His only criticisms were that; 'Several of the Sergeants Books of Rules & Regulations were wanting' and the hospital dresses were worn out. He also wrote that a German translation of the regulation books would be useful, 'as in their present state they are not understood'.

Lieutenant General Sir George Prevost, Bart. 1818, by Samuel William Reynolds (Anne S.K. Brown Military Collection)

Far fewer of the officers were absent this time but the battalion was still more than 200 men understrength. There were 131 men aged between 16 and 25, 428 from 25 to 40, and 67 from 40 to 50 and upwards. The way the ages were tallied differs from 1804 but the data shows slightly more younger men and slightly fewer in the oldest category. The heights were also recorded differently but seem broadly in line with the previous inspection with 278 being five foot six inches and under, 259 between five foot six and half inches and

4 Butler, *Annals*, Vol. II, p.276.

5 Butler, *Annals*, Vol. II, p.15.

five foot nine inches, and 89 taller than that.[6] A separate statement completed on 24 June listed the periods of service of the men of the battalion. Thirty-one corporals and privates had served 14 years or more, 190 between seven and 14 years and 337 less than seven years.[7] The delineation at seven and 14 years was important as those with seven years' service were now paid 1d more per day, and those who had served 14 years got an extra 2d over the standard 1s.

On 6 August Sir George was back with the battalion, this time with the Commander-in-Chief of the British Army and Colonel-in-Chief of the 60th Regiment, His Royal Highness the Duke of York who, accompanied by his brothers the Dukes of Cumberland and Cambridge, was on an inspection tour of the south coast. Lieutenant Colonel de Rottenburg had by this time been given command of a brigade consisting of 31st Foot, 1st Garrison Battalion, and the Bedford Militia, as well as his own battalion. The troops paraded near Fort Monckton and were inspected by the dukes. It was noted that; 'Military men particularly admired the 5th Battalion of the 60th; they are a rifle corps dressed in green; the extreme exactness and precision of their movements were really admirable'.[8]

The battalion may have been receiving high praise but de Rottenburg still had the usual disciplinary issues to address. Even at a benign posting some soldiers chose to desert and the courts martial of eight men are illustrative of the range of reasons for such a decision. The court convened at Haslar Barracks on 6 August. De Rottenburg was the president of the court. Captains de Salaberry and de Wend, and Lieutenant Hinckeldy from the 5th Battalion were members of the court, along with eight officers from the King's German Legion (KGL) and one for the 31st Foot.[9] The first three trials involved three men who had absconded together on 26 April 1806. Bugleman John Angebrand, and Privates Thomas Kroschinsky and Sebastian Frietz, all of Captain Galiffe's company, were persuaded by Bugleman Schoenbach to leave Haslar Barracks and to go to a nearby village to drink, which was perfectly permissible. However, the four men got drunk, strayed further than was allowed and woke up in the middle of the night. Sergeant Joseph Bucks, pay sergeant of Captain Galiffe's company, had noted the men's absence at evening tattoo and roll call and informed Sergeant Major Fürst and the adjutant, Lieutenant Starck. Schoenbach, according to the others, said that as they would be punished for missing roll call they might as well quit the regiment entirely. Schoenbach was not caught but on 5 May a party of the 39th Foot from the Isle of Wight returned Angebrand and Kroschinsky. Frietz had separated himself from the others but three days after running he had repented and surrendered himself to a justice of the peace in Guildford. He was handed over to the care of a battalion of the KGL there and returned to Haslar on 8 May.

In the testimony of all three trials, as well as the details of the prisoner's absences, witnesses also stated which items of their uniform were missing when they returned, as these items would have to be paid for by the men. All the men pleaded not guilty but had very little to say in their own defence. They did call upon their officers to attest to their previous good character. Captain Galiffe called Angebrand one of the best soldiers in his

6 1806 Inspection of 5/60th TNA, WO 27/90.

7 Statement of the Periods of Service, 5/60th, 24 June 1806, TNA, WO 25/1008.

8 *The Morning Post* – Wednesday 6 August 1806.

9 Proceedings of 5/60th Courts Martial TNA, WO 71/208.

company. Captain Schoedde, who had served in Lowenstein's Jägers with Kroschinsky, vouched for his previous good behaviour. Galiffe also said that he had previously been very satisfied with Frietz.

Despite their previous good conduct all three were clearly guilty and the court quickly passed sentences on them all. Angebrand was sentenced to 'six hundred Lashes on his bare back with a Cat o nine tails' and stoppage of 6d for his missing regimental breast plate. The prisoner would be bound and then flogged in front of the battalion. Kroschinsky was sentenced to 700 lashes and stoppages of 4s for his missing gaiters and breast plate. His regimental jacket, which also did not return with him, had been issued December 1804 and so was considered expended and he did not have to pay for it. Frietz was sentenced to 600 lashes and stoppages of £1 2s for his missing kit, but because he had given himself up the court added that they 'most humbly beg leave to recommend the Prisoner as a fit object of His Majesty's Royal Clemency, for the remission of the Corporal Punishment'. Frietz was pardoned by the king, but the other sentences were carried out.[10]

Such large numbers of lashes were by no means unusual for the time. A surgeon would attend to the prisoner during the punishment and stop it if there was a danger of the prisoner dying, and sometimes the commanding officer would halt a flogging if he considered the man contrite, or that he had endured enough.[11] In his history of the 5th Battalion, Gibbes Rigaud maintains that de Rottenburg never flogged any man in the 5th Battalion.[12] Rigaud mentions that he had been in communication with de Rottenburg's son, who also rose to become a colonel, and it seems likely that this was the source of this information. However, these sentences would seem to refute the claim and de Rottenburg was the president of the court that awarded them.

The next trial was that of Private John Langeneckhard, of Captain Blassiere's company. He been found absent on 29 April. Blassiere had been sent to the KGL barracks in Winchester to enquire if they had had any recruits recently. Langeneckhard was brought forward, he had joined the KGL under a false name and received his bounty of three guineas. In his defence Langeneckhard told of how when he had enlisted in the 60th in London the recruiting sergeant had told him the attestation he was signing was for a limited term of seven years. However, when he had joined the battalion he was told that he had enlisted for life. Bugleman John Rolle and Private Francis Schalch, who had joined at the same time, testified that the same fraud had been committed against them. They could not read English and so did not know what they were signing. Blassiere stated that Langeneckhard was an excellent soldier and one of the best behaved in regiment. Langeneckhard was sentenced to 800 lashes, but this was subsequently reduced to 500.[13]

Private Ernst Mellin also absconded from the battalion on 29 April but was back in early May. In his defence he said that a Private Richards, who had deserted at the same time but was not caught, had promised him employment as a sugar baker in a London shop where Richards' wife was employed. Mellin was caught by some 'country people' near Winchester and handed over to the KGL. Mellin had only been enlisted for three months and said he

10 Register of General Courts Martial, TNA, WO 92/1, p.5.

11 Haythornthwaite, *Armies*, pp.68-69.

12 Rigaud, *Celer et Audax*, p.5.

13 Register of General Courts Martial, TNA, WO 92/1, p.5.

was very young and inexperienced, and he asked for mercy from the court. He was given 700 lashes and 14s 9d stoppages for missing uniform.

The tale of Private John Müntzler, from Captain de Salaberry's company, was slightly more involved, and Bugleman Schoenbach again seemed to be at the centre of it. On 23 April a dispute had arisen over a watch that Müntzler had sold, he said on behalf of a recruit who was sick in the regimental hospital. Müntzler had lent half the proceeds of the sale to Schoenbach, who refused to give it back when the owner of the watch protested. Lieutenant Starck confined Müntzler to his quarters and the following day sent him in the charge of Sergeant Charles Schultz to retrieve the watch. Müntzler, fearing he would be in trouble over the debt, escaped his escort and ran. He was returned to the battalion on 5 May by the 39th Foot after being caught on the Isle of Wight. Lieutenant Zühleke, commanding the company in de Salaberry's absence, gave him a good character reference but he was sentenced to be transported to Australia as a felon for seven years.

Bugleman Michael Greth deserted on 20 June, but was brought back 14 July by a party of the North York Militia from Hilsea Barracks, where he had been sent from the Savoy military prison in London. When Greth was brought into the guardhouse at Haslar Lieutenant Starck asked him why he had deserted. Greth gave no excuse but said that as soon as he was free from his handcuffs he would do it again. In court he claimed in his defence that he could not get liberty to go into town without a pass, nor to quit barracks after evening parade. He stated that he did not like the 5th Battalion and wanted to be transferred to another. The court sentenced him to be transported for life.

Brought back at the same time as Greth, Private John Whiting had deserted on 28 June. He had only been a soldier for six months and offered no excuse for his behaviour except drunkenness, youth, and inexperience. His company commander, Captain Andrews, said that Whiting was a very good soldier and would not have deserted except due to bad advice from others. Whiting was sentenced to 600 lashes.

The men sentenced to flogging returned to duty with the battalion but the severity of the punishments was not deterrent enough for two of them. Kroschinsky and Langeneckhard both deserted again in August 1807 and were not retaken. Private Mellin was transferred to the 2nd Garrison Battalion in January 1807.

Sir George Prevost took over as colonel-commandant of the 5th Battalion in September 1806.[14] He had recently returned from the West Indies where his nephew in the 11th Foot, Lieutenant James Prevost, had become his aide-de-camp. In a note, added to a letter in April 1805 from James to his father, Sir George had informed his brother:

> It is my intention (if I can obtain leave of absence for him) to take him to England with me next month. I have desired he would relate more intimately his first campaign. His conduct has hitherto given me satisfaction & I shall indeed be disappointed should it ever be otherwise. His heart I believe Excellent & likely to incline him to follow good example It shall be my endeavour to stow his mind with a feast of the information he requires. And as his abilities give hopes of success I shall stimulate him to incessant application so that he may neither be dunce or a

14 Willoughby Wallace, *Regimental Chronicle*, p.153.

> drudge in his profession but be fitted for the higher walks. In short my dear friend whilst James' conduct is correct I shall be a friend to him & when he evinces talents seconded by prudence & modest merit he will find that which you have been to him in.[15]

James did get to Britain and in May 1806 had written again to his father back in New York state:

> I have received yours and Mamas letters of the 10th February and would have answered them sooner but was in hopes by delaying it a few days I should be able to have told you something new about myself, but I find I have that pleasure still to come. I am yet in London and situated as you have already been informed by Brother Augustin in his last letter – Sir George Prevost expects me at Portsmouth in a few days where, I do not think it likely I shall long remain as I have no appointment there, and he being already provided with an Aid de Camp, I think my time is better employed where I am at present though I do not yet know what his instructions are. He was in London last week & gave me a letter to the Duke of Yorks secretary respecting a Company and I have received an answer quite satisfactory – a copy of which I have sent to Brother Augustin – I must not however be too sanguine in my expectations for if I do succeed I must consider myself particularly fortunate as I am only a Lieutenant of 1803.[16]

James then went on to relate news about his younger brother starting at the new Royal Military College at Marlow, and his elder brother Augustin's hopes for a lieutenant colonelcy before ending with:

> I think when I last wrote to you I mentioned the probability of Troops from this, going to the Continent on Service, but by the suden Peace between Austria & France, that was of course droped – if they had gone General P would certainly have gone.
>
> I had hopes of accompanying him but at present things are quiet here – there has been a great deal said concerning a difference between this Government and America but I hope it will soon terminate amicably – I have this instant heard from Brother Augustin who says he has got letters from Louisa & Susan from New York I am glad to hear they are well, but should liked better to have received letters from themselves – I expect my Regiment from the West Indies daily as I have heard of their being embarked at St Kitts & I am only afraid of their being sent to Ireland to recruit but until they do arrive I shall be my own master – Adieu my dearest father say everything that is kind for me to Mama – and Marianne & Frederick & the little ones – and believe to remain your most affectionate and dutiful son.

15 Note added to J. Prevost to A. Prevost, 8 April 1805, AI, Prevost Papers, CR549/II/2a.

16 J. Prevost to A. Prevost, 15 May 1806, AI, Prevost Papers, CR549/II/2m.

As an American James was particularly concerned with any danger of war between Britain and his homeland. By February 1807 James was able to tell his father that:

> Sir George has said something to me about getting into his own Regiment (the 5th Battn. of the 60th your old Regt.) the only reason I should like it is their being a Rifle Corps & likely to be soon employed on active service & a Capt. in those Corps have more frequent opportunities of being distinguished as they are generally Detached & have a small Command. I only hope they will not be sent to the West Indies for sometime.
>
> In my next letter I hope to be able to tell with certainty – in the course three weeks I will have exchanged.[17]

James' commission for a captaincy was dated 26 February 1807, and he joined the battalion soon after.[18] However, Sir George was not only trying to use his position for his family's advantage and the proximity and position of their colonel-commandant seems to have worked in the battalion's favour. Several recruits are noted as having come via Sir George, including at least one prisoner of war.

Prisoners of war featured strongly in the duties of the battalion during 1806 and would prove to be a good source of recruits for them. They had already absorbed some of the Walloon Guards whilst in Surinam and with foreign service seeming imminent they needed more recruits than the slow trickle that came from the Foreign Depot at Lymington, or from the efforts of Captain Kenzinger, who was recruiting in Germany.

There were many prisoner of war camps on the south coast, as well as prison hulks in the estuaries, and the battalion found itself escorting prisoners of war from Portsmouth to camps further afield. For example, on 11 January 1806 a detachment of seven men from the battalion and members of the East Devon Militia escorted prisoners to Guildford, and then in May and June over 30 men escorted more prisoners with the North York Militia to Reading on two occasions. An unspecified number of men also visited the large prisoner of war camp at Portchester Castle in January. The reason is not recorded but it could well have been in an effort to recruit from the prisoners.[19] However, the returns of the battalion only show small numbers of recruits for the first half of the year,[20] but that was about to change when an unexpected windfall of potential recruits became available in the autumn.

On 2 September Napoleon wrote to *Vice Amiral* Denis Decrés that he was ordering the minister of war to make available 2,000 men to reinforce the French garrisons in the West Indies, in order to facilitate an attack on Martinique. The admiral was to embark them on frigates and arrange their departure. Two companies of 300 men would be drawn from the 82e and 26e Régiments de Ligne and one company each from the 66e Ligne and the Bataillon Colonial de l'Ile de Ré – a penal unit.[21]

17 J. Prevost to A. Prevost, 4 February 1807, AI, Prevost Papers, CR549/II/2s
18 Willoughby Wallace, *Regimental Chronicle,* p.159.
19 Multiple Pay Lists TNA, WO 12/7072.
20 January to June 1806 Returns, TNA, WO 17/178.
21 H. Plon & J. Dumaine, *Correspondance de Napoléon 1er* (Paris: Imprimeur de l'Empereur, 1863), Vol III, pp.124-5.

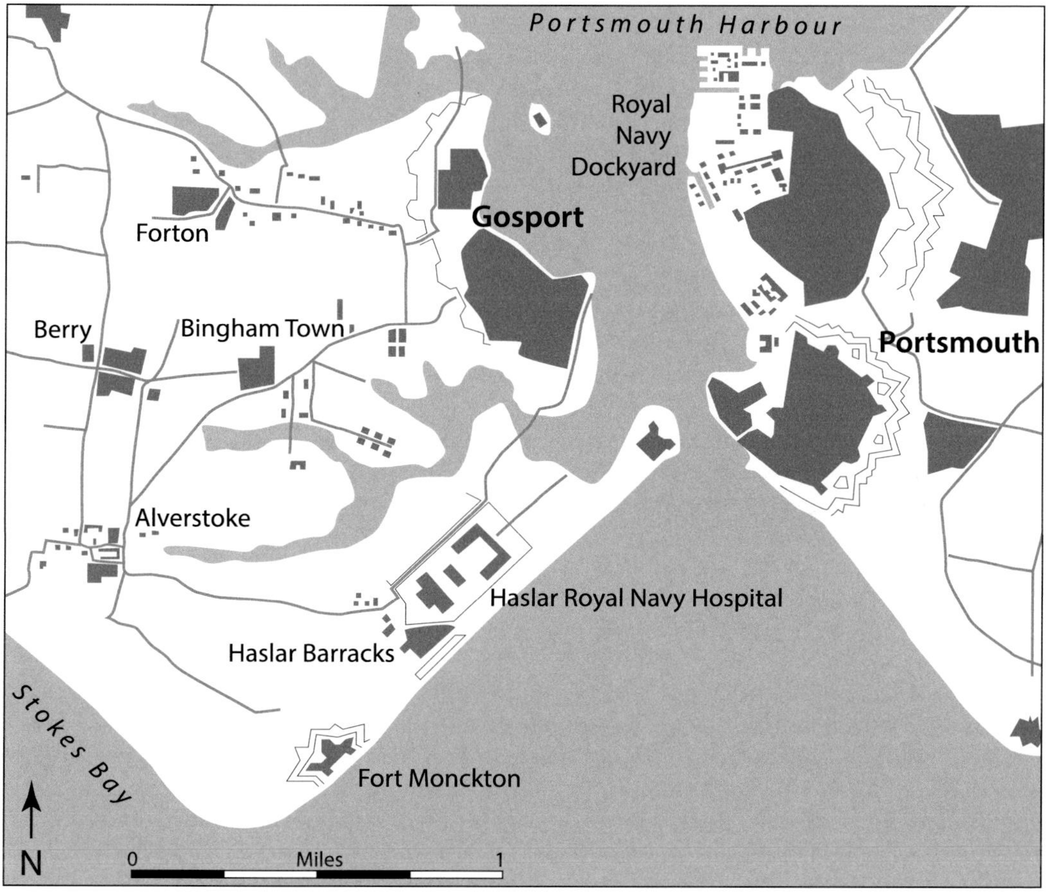

Gosport and Surrounding Area. Source: Ordnance Survey First Series, 1810.

Five frigates and two smaller corvettes packed with stores and men duly sailed from Rochefort. On the night of 25 September the Royal Navy squadron blockading that section of coast, commanded by Commodore Samuel Hood, spotted them and gave chase. At dawn the British ships closed with them and opened fire. The French ships split up and Hood directed his squadron to pursue. One frigate and the two corvettes managed to escape but the other four frigates surrendered after a long and bloody battle, in which Hood was wounded –subsequently having to have an arm amputated. In his dispatch Hood noted that 'those Ships of the Enemy made an obstinate Resistance, but the Result was, as may well be supposed, attended with much Slaughter, being crowded with Troops, out of Rochefort the Evening before'. British losses were nine killed and 32 wounded.[22]

The four captured frigates were *La Gloire*, *L'Infatigable*, *La Minerve* and *L'Armide*. They were sailed to Britain as prizes and the seamen and soldiers distributed to various prisons

22 *London Gazette*, 4 October 1806, Issue 15562, p.1306.

in the south and south-west. The 26e Ligne had many conscripts from the banks of the Rhine around the city of Mainz, an area only recently incorporated into France. As German speakers they were ideal recruits for the battalion. Similarly the 66e had recruits from territories in what is now Belgium, and that had also recently been subsumed into France. Speaking Flemish, with presumably few ties of loyalty to France, many of these men would also have been prime targets for recruitment.[23]

The 5th Battalion were authorised to recruit 100 of the prisoners from the frigates and did so in early October.[24] Further prisoners were then recruited later from nearby Forton Prison, from Mill Prison at Plymouth, and Stapleton Prison near Bristol. In total, 213 men enlisted on various dates in October and November, with an additional 58 men coming from the Foreign Depot at Lymington. In December, possibly because of the plentiful supply of recruits, 36 men were transferred to the 3/60th, including five of the recent additions.[25] With both the 3rd and 5th Battalions being up to strength some of the prisoners recorded in the prison records as joining the 60th were sent to the foreign depot for the 2nd Battalion. Colonel Howard of the foreign corps staff was requested to inspect the recruits and choose those to be sent to the other battalions.[26]

The 60th were not the only unit recruiting from the prisons and the men of the ill-fated convoy. General Merck, an émigré, had been authorised to raise a regiment of 1,000 Swiss and Germans from prisoners of war,[27] and a recruiting party went into Mill Prison soon after that of the 60th. Early in 1807 both the 5th and 87th Foot also recruited small numbers from the prisons.[28]

Most of the new recruits seemed to have taken their change of employer well, and settled into the 5th Battalion without any remarks being made against them in the pay lists. Ten would be made buglemen or promoted to corporal in the next 18 months, but six would desert, or attempt to. Some had existing light infantry skills, such as Pierre Beeker, Jean Guttelmann and Pierre Keisser; all *voltigeurs* of the 26e Ligne taken from the frigate *La Gloire*.[29] Beeker came from Kirchheimbolanden near Mainz, as did Geoffrey Uhl and Guillaume Schneider. Others also came from around Mainz; Conrad Burkay, Daniel Braun, Jean Stark and Henry Froster. All were recent recruits who had joined the 26e in January that year.[30] They had been conscripted into what for them could have seemed like an occupying army. They were all born in 1784 or 1785 in what was then an independent German state. During the Revolutionary Wars the territory was taken by the French, then the Prussians, before being made part of France in 1800. Cornelius Vanophen and John

23 Whilst many recruits can be traced back to the 26e or 66e regiments no recruit from the 82e has been identified by the author. The 82e seemed to have recruited from the traditional regions of France.

24 Lists of Recruits December 1806, TNA, WO 2/54 p.22, & WO 12/7072.

25 December 1806 Pay List, TNA, WO 12/7072.

26 Lists of Recruits December 1806, TNA, WO 2/54 p.22.

27 Index to Out-letters, Foreign Troops, Letter 'M', TNA, WO 2/54.

28 Register of Prisoners of War, Plymouth, TNA, ADM 103/286.

29 Prize court papers of *La Gloire*, TNA, HCA 32/1040/2497.

30 26e régiment d'infanterie de ligne. An XII-1815. SHD/GR 21 YC 239 26e régiment d'infanterie de ligne, 16 germinal an XII [6 avril 1804]-19 janvier 1806 (matricules 1 à 3 096) at http://www.memoiredeshommes.sga.defense.gouv.fr (accessed 7 September 2018).

Jansens both came from Brussels and had been similarly enlisted in the 66e Ligne only a few months previously.[31]

After the trauma of a battle at sea and the prospect of years in grim prison camps, or, worse, the hulks, enlisting in the 5th Battalion with their smart green and red uniforms must have been very tempting, especially if they would still be serving alongside friends that they may have known from their home towns and villages. Of course, some would have been enlisting to take the bounty and then desert at the first opportunity, like John Lohman who ran as early as 6 November. Others made the battalion their home, such as George Koester from the village of Guntersblum, near Mainz. He had left Rochefort as part of the 26e but enlisted in the 60th at Mill Prison Plymouth on 23 October.[32] He joined Captain Michael de Wend's company, taking his £8 8s bounty, and would remain in the 60th for more than 18 years.[33]

Many of the recruits who came to the battalion that autumn were only in the prisoner of war camps for a few weeks, but it would have been long enough to appreciate how hard life was for the inmates. Mill Prison near Plymouth had housed prisoners both in the Seven Years War and the American War of Independence, but had been extensively rebuilt in 1799. Corruption between suppliers to the prison and the guards meant that the quality of provisions was very poor and many prisoners were near starvation. The prisoners were ruled over by the strongest, with fighting, duelling, and gambling rife. Some of those prisoners from the Rochefort convoy who chose not to take the King's shilling may well have been involved in an escape attempt in 1807 when the prisoners dug a 500 yard long tunnel, disposing of the spoil in the latrines. The plan was for all the inmates to escape but they were betrayed by an informant and the first men out of the tunnel were met by a detachment of a Scots regiment. The informant was subsequently brutally murdered.[34]

Stapleton was little better. It had been expanded in 1805 to house up to 5,000 men. In 1801, the commander Lieutenant Ormsby, wrote to the Transport Board:

> Numbers of prisoners are as naked as they were previous to the clothing being issued. At first the superintendants were attentive and denounced many of the purchasers of the clothing, but they gradually got careless. We are still losing as many weekly as in the depth of winter. The hospital is crowded, and many are forced to remain outside who ought to be in.[35]

However, some prisons were better. In 1811 an officer of the 26e who had been taken prisoner at the Battle of Fuentes de Oñoro visited Forton Prison, just a short distance from Haslar Barracks, and found it cheerful, quite comfortable, and had a very nice meal there.[36]

31 An XIII-1815. SHD/GR 21 YC 551 66e régiment d'infanterie de ligne, 3 brumaire an XIII [25 octobre 1804]-7 mai 1808 (matricules 1 à 3 000) at http://www.memoiredeshommes.sga.defense.gouv.fr 66e régiment d'infanterie de ligne (accessed 7 September 2018).

32 Prisoner No. 13446, TNA, ADM 103/286.

33 December 1806 Pay List, TNA, WO 12/7072.

34 F. Abell, *Prisoners of War in Britain 1756 to 1815* (Oxford: Oxford University Press, 1914), pp.228-230.

35 Quoted in Abell, *Prisoners*, p.210.

36 Abell, *Prisoners*, p.218.

On at least one occasion officers from the 5th Battalion did duty at Forton and by the end of 1806 the battalion was also providing two companies for nearby Fort Monckton, which protected Portsmouth harbour.[37]

By the end of 1806 the battalion was finally up to strength with 842 rank and file, 21 buglers, and 43 sergeants; in fact, it was slightly over its establishment of 800 rank and file.[38] One major and two ensigns needed to be appointed, there were six officers absent, including the only major, and three on recruiting service.[39] With a quarter of the rank and file being new recruits the officers and NCOs must have had their work cut out training and integrating the men over the winter and into the spring. Another two men shot themselves early in 1807; Private Michael Gorsky in January and Private Lorenz Lucka in March.[40] Both were recent recruits.

In May 1807 newspapers reported that the battalion was on the move: 'The fine Rifle Battalion of the 60th regiment, composed entirely of Germans, will march on Monday from Haslar, for the Kentish Coast, there to be embarked with the German Legion for the Continent'.[41]

On 4 May 1807 the bulk of the battalion, along with three wagons, began their march from Haslar to the barracks at Brabourne Lees in Kent. Smaller detachments followed on over the next two days, each with a further three wagons for the battalion's baggage. Their route took them through Chichester, Arundel, Shoreham, Lewes, Hailsham, Battle, Rye, and Romney, covering an average of 15 miles per day, arriving on 13 May. Private John Borr died on the march but the cause is not recorded; he had only joined the battalion in June 1806.[42]

The battalion was to be included in Lord Cathcart's expedition to Denmark, and it was reported in the newspapers that de Rottenburg, having been appointed brevet-colonel, was to command a brigade.[43] Denmark was a neutral country but the British government suspected that it was about to be invaded by the French. Whilst Napoleon had managed to defeat his enemies on the continent in battle he realised that Britain could best be tackled by threatening its commercial and colonial interests. In Berlin he declared an embargo on all trade with Britain from both his own territories and those of his allies. The weak points of this continental system were two neutral countries; Denmark and Portugal. Both also had large fleets which Napoleon could use the threaten Britain's colonies. Having intelligence of Napoleon's plans the British government ordered a pre-emptive expedition to Denmark to make them surrender their fleet.

However, whilst the rest of the troops allocated would sail to attack Copenhagen, bombard the city, and force the Danes into submission, the 5th Battalion only got as far as Ramsgate before their orders were countermanded.[44] The 5th Battalion would have to wait another year for its first campaign on the continent. The battalion did eventually embark at Ramsgate at the end of August, but sailed for Cork, Ireland. *The Kentish Gazette* reported their departure:

37 November 1806 Return, TNA WO 17/178.

38 Regimental Records, 60th Foot, TNA, WO 380/1 p.167.

39 December 1806 Return, TNA, WO 17/178.

40 January & March 1807 pay lists, TNA, WO 12/7073.

41 *Bury & Norwich Post,* Wednesday 6 May 1807.

42 May 1807 Pay List, TNA, WO 12/7073.

43 *Public Ledger and Daily Advertiser,* Monday 25 May 1807.

44 *Kentish Weekly Post or Canterbury Journal,* Tuesday 28 July 1807.

> *Ramsgate, Aug 28.* Five companies of the fifth bat. of the 60th came in yesterday, and after taking refreshments in the barracks embarked in the transports 52 and 6. The pier was crowded till a late hour at night with fashionable company, which the music and chorusses of the troops had highly delighted.[45]

The battalion arrived in Ireland in September and were based at New Barracks, Cork. In the same month a draft of a further 214 men left the foreign depot to join the battalion.[46] The establishment of the battalion had been increased again from 800 to 1,000 rank and file in July and the men brought it up to the new strength.[47]

At the beginning of 1808 de Rottenburg was appointed brigadier general, and left the battalion he had led for ten years. He briefly trained four battalions of light infantry at the Camp of Instruction on the Curragh plain in County Kidlaire, and then left Ireland.[48] He was to take up a command in North America, but he first went back to Brabourne Lees to train a brigade of light infantry, comprised of the 68th, 71st, and 85th Regiments. Private John Green described his reception:

> About the 13th July, General Baron Derottenburgh arrived, and took the command of the light brigade. As soon as he came into the camp, the whole of our regiment and that of the 85th turned out of their tents, and received the venerable baron with three times cheers: he beckoned for us to cease, but our respect for him was too great so to do; besides we had no other way of testifying our approbation but by cheering him. He was an able general, and, in every respect, a good officer.[49]

De Rottenburg and his brigade, with two companies of the 95th attached, took part in the ill-fated expedition to Walcheren in 1809 and it was not until 1810 that he reached Quebec and took command as a major general.[50]

De Rottenburg's imminent departure caused something of a problem for the battalion as one majority was vacant and one major was serving with another battalion, making Captain Galiffe the next most senior officer. With foreign service still expected the lack of majors had to be addressed. Unfortunately for Galiffe two former captains of the battalion who had purchased majorities in other battalions of the 60th returned. Major William Woodgate was appointed first but seems to have taken his time arriving, much to the frustration of de Rottenburg who in the 1 February return wrote against Woodgate's name under absent officers: 'Without leave. Repeatedly ordered to join & unknown to the Commanding Officer what is become of him since the 4th Jan. On which day he reported that he would set off from London the 9th of the same month'.[51]

45 *The Kentish Gazette,* 1 September 1807.

46 September 1807 Pay List, TNA, WO 12/7073.

47 TNA, WO 380/1, p.167.

48 J. Phillipart (ed.), *The Royal Military Calendar* (London: Egerton, 1820), Vol. III, 1820. p.15.

49 J. Green, *The Vicissitudes of a Soldier's Life* (Louth: J & J Jackson, 1827), p.25.

50 Butler, *Annals*, Vol II, p.36.

51 February 1808 Return, TNA, WO 17/179.

Woodgate arrived three days after de Rottenburg wrote his testy note and was briefly in command of the battalion until the more senior Major William Davy arrived in March. Born in 1780 at Holm, near Gloucester, Davy had joined the 61st Foot from Eton at 17, before joining the 5th Battalion in 1802 as a captain. He purchased his majority in February 1807, over the heads of 13 more senior captains.[52] He was ADC to Bowyer whilst the 5th Battalion was in Halifax, and remained with him there after they left. He then went with Bowyer when he took a command in the West Indies.

Other absent officers were asked to re-join and some vacancies were filled but by April there were still eight lieutenants and one ensign that needed to be appointed. Captain James Prevost left the battalion to re-join his uncle, Sir George Prevost, as ADC, travelling with him to North America, Captain John Galiffe finally got his brevet as major, after more than six years of, perhaps impatient, waiting.[53] Galiffe's lodgings in Cork were in the household of the married sister of Lieutenant Francis Holmes, and he and the eldest daughter began to form an attachment.[54]

Lieutenant Starck, promoted from the ranks at Halifax, left to become a captain in the Royal African Corps, a regiment mostly of condemned prisoners. One half of the Royal African Corps was renamed the Royal York Rangers in 1808 and Starck became a major and then lieutenant colonel, commanding the regiment at the capture of Guadeloupe in August 1815, the final battle of the Napoleonic Wars.[55]

Some of those officers filling vacancies or re-joining the battalion would have been doing so with the hope of the more rapid promotion that was likely on foreign service. John Joyce had been commissioned in the 60th as an ensign in July 1807[56] and he wrote to the Duke of York in March 1808 from Cork requesting a lieutenancy, the common form of such a letter was termed a memorial, and it outlined his previous service and why he deserved the promotion:

> The Memorial of Ensign John Joyce of the 5th Battn. 60th Regiment.
>
> Humbly sheweth
> That your Royal Highnesses Memorialist has served 15 years in the Army and was never absent from any Duty which the corps of Royal Irish Artillery to which he had the honor to belong was ever called or sent upon, he served with that corps as a Protestant Volunteer under your Royal Highnesses own command on the continent in the years 1794 and 1795 and for his diligence he was then promised rank and promotion by General Straton but before that Promise was realised after having served eight years and upwards the Union took place and the Corps was disbanded. Your Royal Highnesses Memorialist having thus lost all hopes of the rank and promotion promised he volunteered his service to England and was employed by the Ordnance and for 6 years he acted as Qr. Master to a Troop of

52 Butler, *Annals*, Vol. II, p.37.

53 April 1808 Return, TNA, WO 17/179.

54 J. Galiffe to J. Galiffe, 7 January 1816, BG, ms fr 2751c pl23 f018-9.

55 *London Gazette*, 18 September 1815, Issue 17062, pp.1909-12.

56 Willoughby Wallace, *Regimental Chronicle*, p160.

> Horse in that department and served under General Lord Cathcart in the late Expedition to Hanover where he was entrusted with the Principal Management of all the Ordnance Horses then on that service the difficult duties of which he discharged to the perfect satisfaction of the Officers in Command and for all of which he was recommended particularly to the Earl of Moira who again promised him Promotion but before that second promise could be realised a change of Administration again deprived him of the patronage he had so long and dearly earned by his Lordship going out of Office. He was afterwards recommended by General Douglas and Colonel de Rottenburg for an Ensigncy and had the good fortune through your Royal Highnesses Munificence to obtain the same in the 60th Regiment and under all those circumstances your Memorialist prays and humbly hopes in consideration of his long devoted voluntary and faithful services in the late Troubles and actions in Ireland and several of the most desperate Engagements on the continent where he was wounded at the siege of Nimiengen that your Royal Highness will be graciously pleased to permit him to succeed to any vacant Lieutenancy in the Army to which you may think proper to appoint him and as in duty bound he will never cease to pray.[57]

John Joyce was promoted to Lieutenant, without purchase, in October 1809.[58]

In June the recently promoted Lieutenant General Sir Arthur Wellesley took command of the 9,000 men assembled around Cork and finalised plans to support Venezuelan rebels in their rising against Spain. The pay lists of the 5th Battalion for March to June show the sort of housekeeping typical of a unit preparing for overseas service. Five men were transferred to garrison battalions, 10 were invalided, and one was discharged. Others took matters into their own hands, again; three successfully deserted including Sergeant Eberhard Baumstarck, senior sergeant of Prevost's company; six ran and were recaptured, and Private Marten Posanach ran in March, was caught and then ran again in April. He was caught a second time and transferred for foreign service for life, as was one other soldier. There were also six deaths in the three months, not including Private John Zenzen noted as having died by accident. Privates John Klasgy and Jacob Fritz escaped the coming rigours of campaigning by being servants to Sir George Prevost and de Rottenburg respectively.[59] In May the battalion provided one officer and 32 men to do duty at the Ballincollig Royal Gunpowder Mills, probably either as guards or escorts to shipments out of the mills. A sergeant and 12 men were stationed at the small village of Monckstown on the shore of Cork harbour, possibly overseeing the loading of the battalion's baggage.[60] With a limited number of places available on board the transports for wives and children some of the men would have been faced with the prospect of leaving their loved ones behind and this may have accounted for some of the desertions.

Major Davy did not have long to get used to his new command. Departure for South America was imminent and there was still a shortage of officers. Besides Captain Prevost

57 Memorial of Ensign Joyce, HRO, 170A12W/D/1183.

58 *London Gazette*, Issue 16306 14/10/1809, p.1634

59 June 1808 Pay List, TNA, WO 12/7073.

60 May 1808 return TNA, WO 17/179.

there were other officers doing duty elsewhere: Lieutenant Frederick Schneider was with the 6th Battalion, and Lieutenant Duchesnay was absent, without leave, in Quebec. Ensign William Morgenthal was serving as deputy assistant quartermaster general on Lieutenant General Sir John Moore's staff. Captain Kenzinger and Lieutenant Hoffman were still in Germany recruiting.

On 7 June Davy felt compelled to write to the military secretary:

> As the 5th Battalion 60th Foot is under orders for embarkation, I feel it my duty to enclose to you a state of the absent officers, and vacant commissions, by which you will perceive that at the present moment there are two captains, three lieutenants, and one ensign, employed upon the staff and recruiting service; and that eight lieutenants are wanting to complete the battalion to its proper establishment.
>
> I must also beg leave to represent that of the subalterns doing duty with this regiment at least four (from youth and inexperience in the profession) are unfit to be trusted with the command of detachments, should the service require them to be made, and which from the nature of that for which this regiment is particularly appointed there is every reason to suppose may be the case.
>
> Under these circumstances I trust I may be allowed to request, that, should H.R.H. be pleased to make any further appointments to this battalion, the officers to whom they may apply may be ordered without delay to follow the regiment to the place of its destination.[61]

One appointment was made soon after Davy's letter. Sergeant Major Matthew Fürst was promoted to ensign 23 June 1808.[62] Originally a labourer from the port of Kiel, which at that time belonged to Denmark, Fürst joined the Lowenstein Jägers in 1800 and transferred to the 5th Battalion in 1802 when they were disbanded.[63] He had been recommended for promotion by de Rottenburg in early 1807.[64] Promotion of an experienced NCO would mean that Davy could fill one of his officer vacancies without having an inexperienced ensign who knew little of the role of a rifle corps, especially as the battalion was about to sail to face an enemy for the first time in nearly a decade.

However, the enemy the battalion would face was about to change. It would not be the Spanish, but the French. In the autumn of 1807 Napoleon had looked southwards to another weak point in his trade embargo against Britain; Portugal. The Treaty of Fontainebleau with Spain secured the co-operation of his Spanish ally, and the refusal of Portugal to stop trading with Britain gave him the pretext for invasion. In November *Général de Divison* Andoche Junot led 25,000 French troops to Lisbon, with Spanish support. However, the Portuguese regent and his court had already fled to Brazil on the Portuguese fleet, with the assistance of the Royal Navy. Portugal became the latest addition to Napoleon's empire but he had not achieved all his aims, and the terrain, weather, and resentful population exacted a high cost from the invasion force.

61 Davy to military secretary, 7 June 1808, quoted in Rigaud, *Celer et Audax*, p.27.

62 Willoughby Wallace, *Regimental Chronicle* p.160.

63 TNA, WO 25/1008.

64 Howard to de Rottenburg, 9 February 1807, TNA, WO 7/77, p.374.

All was not well with his Spanish ally either. Riven by court intrigues, financial and political problems, Spain was not the reliable partner he needed. Exploiting the unpopularity of the Spanish prime minister, Godoy, and the ambitions of the heir to the throne, Prince Ferdinand, Napoleon used troops already in Spain to take control and place his own brother, Joseph, on the throne. In May 1808, Spain rose in revolt against the French and in June a delegation arrived in Britain for asking help. With a supportive population, and the roads and terrain making for poor French communications back to the border, the Iberian Peninsula was the ideal location for Britain to commit her small army to a campaign on the continent. With Spain now an ally, not an enemy, the decision was taken to send the troops already assembled for the Venezuela expedition to the Peninsula instead. Had the Spanish uprising happened just a couple of weeks later the troops would have already sailed for South America and the history of both the 5th Battalion and Arthur Wellesley may have been very different.

The 5th Battalion embarked at Monckstown on to the transports *Juliana*, *Atlas*, and *Malabar* on 14 June 1808, however they would remain in Cork harbour for nearly a month, waiting for favourable winds. On 27 June Davy put pen to paper and outlined how he wanted his officers and men to conduct themselves on campaign:

> Regimental Orders.
> Cork Harbour, on board the Malabar,
> June 27th, 1808.
>
> As there is every reason to imagine that the battalion will shortly be honoured with an opportunity of distinguishing itself in the field, the Commanding Officer feels it his duty to recall the attention of the younger part of the officers to the absolute necessity of making themselves acquainted with the several duties of the outposts, that they may be enabled to lead and instruct the men entrusted to their care. He also expects they will seriously consider that any neglect on their part before the enemy may cause the most fatal consequences, (from the particular service allotted to the battalion) not only to themselves, but to the whole army.
>
> He doubts not their own good sense will point out to them the necessity of impressing upon their minds that vigilance and activity are the first duties required from an officer on an outpost, and hopes they will not lose the opportunity of profiting by the advice which may be given to them by such of their brother officers who have had the advantage of acquiring experience upon actual service.
>
> The men are to understand that by the maintenance of order and discipline we can alone look forward to a successful opposition to the designs of an enemy; they must on every occasion conform with alacrity to the orders of their officers, and as great fatigue is often connected with the duties of light troops, they must cheerfully submit, and bear like men the hardships attending a soldier's life. He feels convinced of their bravery, and is satisfied that they will never yield in that respect to any troops in his Majesty's service.
>
> The true 'Rifleman' will never fire without being sure of his man, he should if possible make use of forced balls, and only load with cartridges in case of necessity, as when a brisk fire is to be kept up. And he will recollect that a few well-directed

> shots, that tell, will occasion greater confusion than thousands fired at random and without effect, which will only make the enemy despise our fire, and inspire him with confidence in proportion as he finds us deficient in skill and enterprise.
>
> It is particularly recommended to the men, and will be strictly enforced, to behave with humanity to the people in an enemy's country, and not to plunder or destroy their houses, or attempt their lives, without the most urgent necessity, or an order to that effect. Interest and humanity both require the maintenance of a strict discipline, as the only way to conciliate the minds of the people, and to make them our friends. A contrary conduct, besides all other disadvantages attending, will certainly reflect strongly on the credit of the Corps.
>
> It is the duty of every officer carefully to provide for the wants of his men. This, he may be assured, will give him their confidence and esteem, and on some particular occasion the maxim may be adopted that, "necessity knows no laws;" but it must never be forgotten, that the "laws" are again in force the moment that necessity ceases, and the officers will recollect that the wants of their men are not to be provided for by allowing individuals to plunder or maraud.
>
> The officers should endeavour to learn the capacities and characters of their men that they may employ them to the best advantage; this may be easily done by conversing with them, and hearing their opinion and sentiments on different subjects.
>
> The Commanding Officer will feel sincere pleasure in recommending and rewarding all such non-commissioned officers and men as may distinguish themselves by their good conduct in the field; but if, on the contrary, any man should be guilty of cowardice, desertion, or any other such infamous crime as may reflect on the credit of the Corps, he will show no mercy to such an offender, but use every exertion to bring him to the punishment he deserves.[65]

On board the three transports were 33 officers and staff, 52 sergeants, 48 corporals, 21 buglemen, and 883 privates; a total of 1,055.[66] The battalion was short of its establishment by 69 men. Sixty wives and 50 children were also aboard.[67] With only six wives allowed per company many would have been left behind. Officers were allowed to bring their wives with them, if they chose. Captain Michael de Wend left his young wife, Sarah, six months pregnant. The child, a boy, was born in October but died the next summer.[68]

Eight sick men were left in Cork, and one was still sick back in Kent.[69] The battalion had also lost another company commander; de Salaberry had opted to return to North America as de Rottenburg's ADC. Whilst they waited to sail Davy allowed some men ashore and on 6 July received a note from a Mr J. Floyd asking him to forgive the late return of two soldiers:

65 Rigaud, *Celer et Audax*. p.19

66 July 1808 Return, TNA, WO 17/179.

67 Rigaud, *Celer et Audax*, p.284.

68 De Wend-Fenton family records, courtesy of Michael Cayley.

69 June 1808 Pay List, TNA WO 12/7073.

> for any command. When he has fired, the right hand quits its hold in facing to the right about, the left swings the rifle round into an horizontal position with the barrel downwards; the rifleman resumes his post in the platoon, in fronting to the left about, brings his rifle into the position to prime and load, half cocks, and proceeds to load, going through the motions as above without further words of command.[6]

This method of files going to forward, firing, falling back in, and the next file going forward in rotation ensured constant fire from the company, while keeping most of the men loaded. Once the recruits were used to single files going forward to fire, two files would then go forward together and words of command would be replaced by bugle calls. Officers and NCOs also had whistles, with which they could issue commands that could be heard at a greater distance than shouted orders.

Riflemen would have not have operated in close order very often. They would spend most of the time in the field in extended order:

> When the company is formed at close order, and is required to extend from the right.
>
> The words of command will be given as follows:
>
> *To the Left extend.*
> At this word of command the company, except the right hand file, faces to the left, moves on in quicktime, casting the eyes over the right shoulder, so that each file when at two paces distant from his right hand file may halt, front, and dress by the right. The rear rank steps to the right, in order, if necessary, to march or fire without impediment through the intervals of the front rank. This is the usual distance between files, at which light troops when ordered to extend will form; but in particular cases, when they are required to cover the front of a corps, or mask a manoeuvre, the commanding officer will signify at what distance the files are to form from each other, before he gives the order for them to extend themselves.[7]

The line could be extended to the right or from the centre as well, and the command would normally be given by bugle. The purpose of extending was to cover a greater frontage and to make it harder for the enemy to inflict casualties by cannon or musket fire because of the decreased density of the formation. When extended each file of two men would work as a team, making sure that one of them was always loaded and ready to defend them both:

> When riflemen or light corps are to fire from the spot in extended order, the bayonets of the latter must be first unfixed, the commanding officer then orders the horner to give the signal to commence firing. At this signal the front rank makes

6 Rottenburg, *Regulations*, pp.10-11.
7 Rottenburg, *Regulations*, p.15.

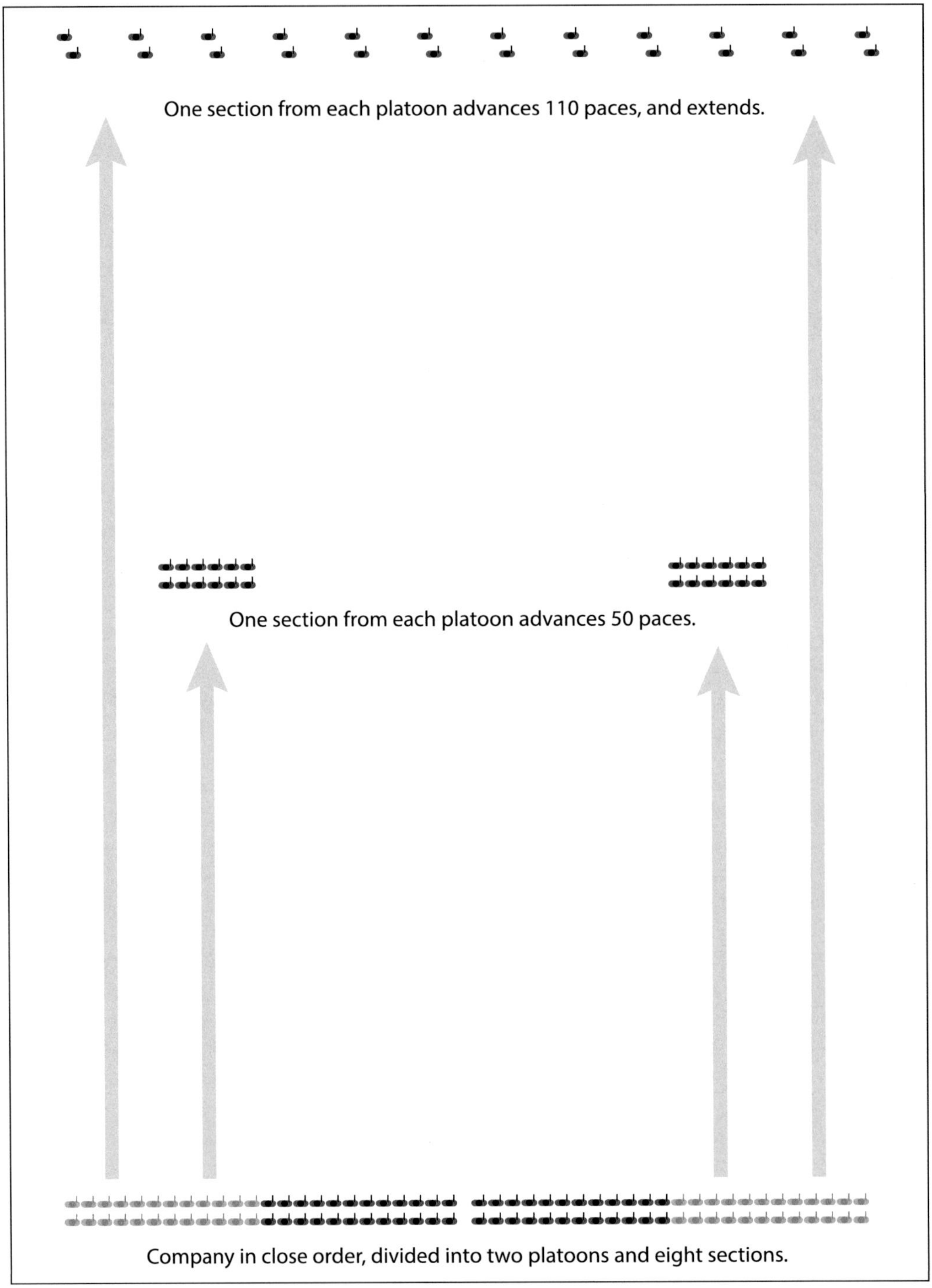

The disposition of a company deployed for skirmishing, taken from F. de Rottenburg, *Regulations for the Exercise of Riflemen and Light Infantry and Instructions for their Conduct in the Field*. Plate 3. Not to scale.

> ready, presents (each man selecting his particular object), and fires: as soon as the rear rank man sees his file leader put the ball into his piece, he makes ready, and fires through the intervals of the front rank; and when the rear rank men have got their balls into their pieces, each man gives notice to his file leader to fire. In this manner the fire is continued on the spot, til the signal is given to cease firing.[8]

As well as firing on the spot, the manual also detailed procedures for firing whilst advancing or retiring. When advancing the rear rank man would advance six paces in front of the front rank man, passing him on his the right, and then fire and begin to reload. As soon as the sergeant saw that the rear rank had fired he would order the front rank to advance six paces in front of the rear rank and fire, by a blast on his whistle. In this manner the unit could leapfrog forwards with each rank taking careful aim and hopefully driving the enemy backwards. The procedure for firing and retiring was similar, with whichever rank was in front marching rearwards by 12 paces and then firing and reloading. The next rank then did the same, and so the unit would retire in good order, with each rank supporting the other.

De Rottenburg also stressed in the manual that never more than half of the available riflemen should be sent forwards to skirmish, usually by 50 paces. The remainder should be kept back as a reserve. If the whole unit had to advance then the reserve should keep their distance behind the skirmish line, but if the rifle unit was operating with the support of either line infantry or musket-armed light infantry then all the riflemen could go forward to skirmish, with the other troops providing the reserve. Riflemen and light infantry soldiers were trained to act independently and were used in many situations other than actual battles. They would form the advance guard of an army advancing, and the rear guard of an army retreating, especially where the terrain was not suitable to the deployment of light cavalry. They could also be used to cover wide areas of ground:

> The object of this branch of the duty of Light troops is to scour a tract of country by means of numerous and detached bodies, clearing the woods and inclosures of the enemy's posts, and in a word, to establish a complete chain of your own troops, by occupying, as far as circumstances will permit, every advantageous spot; taking particular care, however, that your own posts are so stationed as to have easy communication, and the power of mutually supporting each other.[9]

Again when forming this chain of troops de Rottenburg recommended that the reserve be kept 50 paces behind the foremost troops. When ordered to form the chain, pairs of files –four men – would extend to 10 paces from each other. The chain could then advance, with the reserve keeping their distance so that they could help any part of the chain that came under attack. If the command to fire was given then the front right hand man of each four-man section would step forward three paces, fire, and then go back to his place whilst his rear rank man stepped forward and so on, so that the chain could keep up a continuous rate of fire.

8 Rottenburg, *Regulations*, p.18.
9 Rottenburg, *Regulations*, p.24.

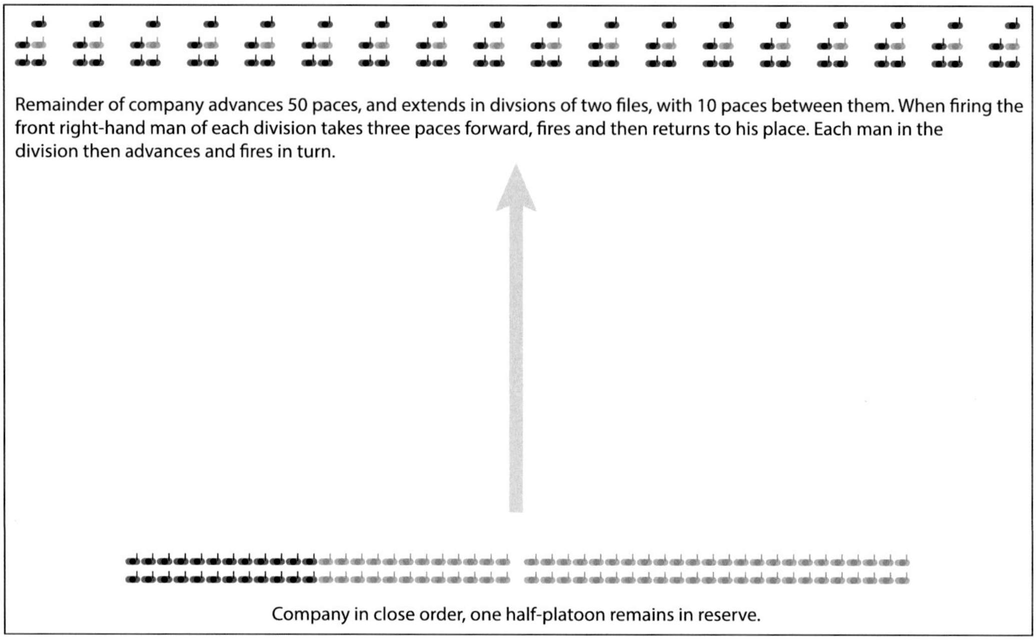

Forming the chain, taken from F. de Rottenburg, *Regulations for the Exercise of Riflemen and Light Infantry and Instructions for their Conduct in the Field.* Plate 5. Not to scale.

De Rottenburg was also very explicit about the dispositions of troops forming an advance guard at the head of any portion of an army on the march. A company would be split into four half platoons. The first half platoon would be 500 paces ahead of the main force. The second half platoon would be 200 paces in front of the first, with a sergeant and six men detached 100 paces further still. The third and fourth half platoons were to be positioned 300 paces to the left and right of the first half platoon, with a sergeant and six men 100 paces ahead and further out from the line of march. The whole company would form an arrowhead that scoured the terrain ahead and to the flanks, searching for any sign of the enemy. Of course, the distances between the half platoons and the spacing of the men within them would vary as the terrain, and even the weather, changed so that each section could maintain contact with the next. The one golden rule was not to let anything impassable, such as a lake, get between one portion of the advance guard and another. If the advance guard came across any person they were to be stopped and taken to the main body for questioning. Rear guards were to be formed in a similar manner to advance guards, but in reverse so that the main body of the guard was to the front and the smaller sections to the rear.

A similar pattern would be used for a patrol, which was another duty of riflemen and light troops. Patrols usually consisted of a sergeant and 12 men. A corporal and two men would be sent forward, and two sent to each flank with the distances adjusting as fitted the terrain and the conditions. If a building or anything else of interest was found one man would investigate while his file partner stayed back ready to provide support. If the enemy was located the men would conceal themselves, if possible, and report back to the sergeant, who could then decide to attack or retire, depending on the strength of the enemy. Any hill

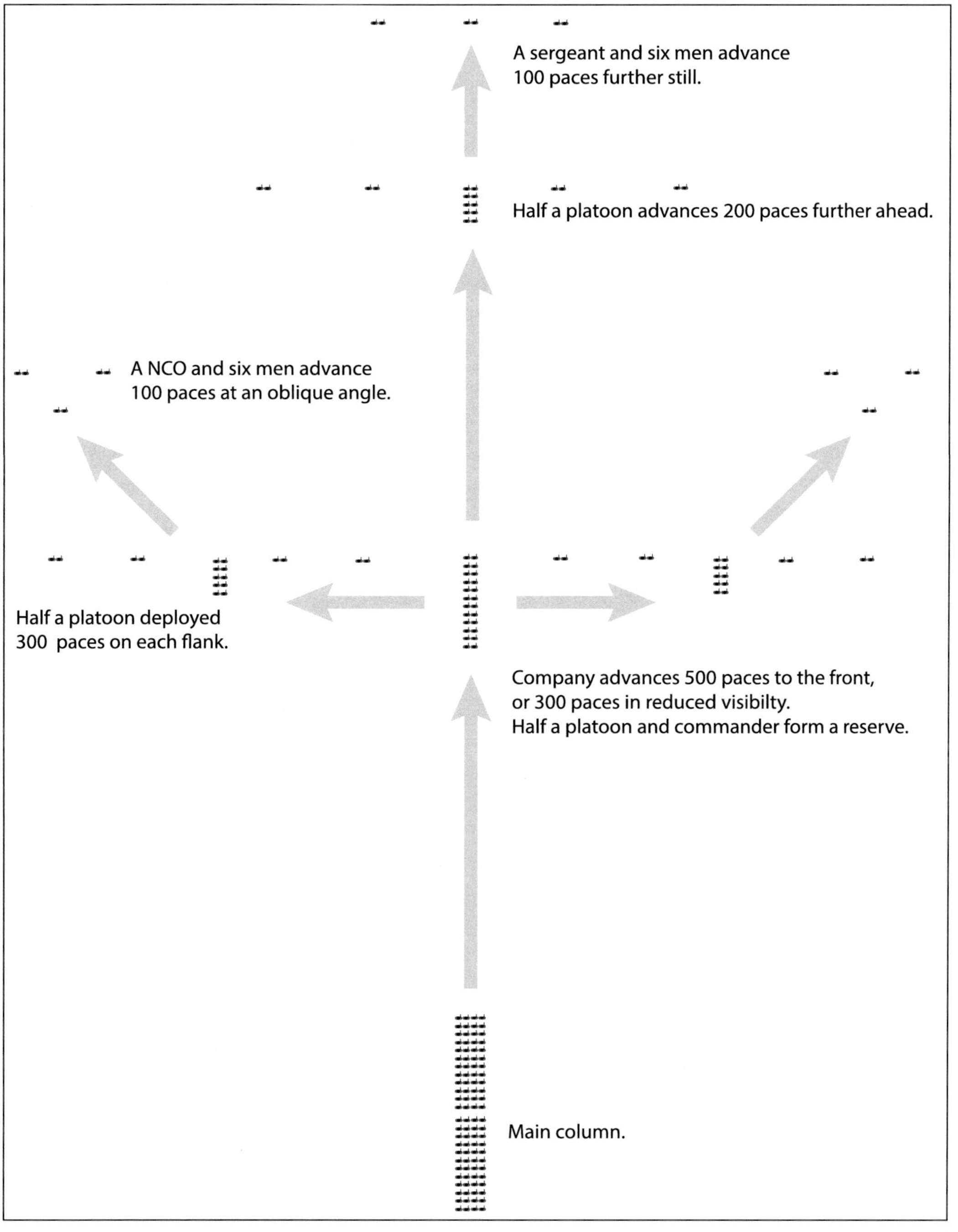

The disposition of a company forming an advance guard, taken from F. de Rottenburg, *Regulations for the Exercise of Riflemen and Light Infantry and Instructions for their Conduct in the Field*. Plate 5. Not to scale.

should be investigated and the manual even suggested that trees be climbed to help reconnoitre an area.

De Rottenburg then provided instructions for a patrol, or advance guard, encountering woods, defiles, and other features, before tackling what should happen if they should come across a village:

> Whether the patrole is a strong one or not, it must halt at a few hundred paces from the village, assemble all the skirmishers, and lie concealed; a few men must then be sent towards the village, and must endeavour to seize one of the inhabitants, and conduct him to the officer commanding the patrole, in order that he may be examined respecting the presence of the enemy. If upon diligent inquiry it is found that the enemy are in the village, the patrole must make its retreat: the deposition of one person should not, however, be depended upon; the men who have been sent to the village must endeavour, if possible, to take another person, who must be separately examined, to see whether his report coincides with the former one.[10]

If the unfortunate villagers claimed no enemy were present then a portion of the patrol was to enter the village, make contact with the mayor, and make thorough search to be certain. At night the procedure was slightly different:

> When a patrole is to reconnoitre a village by night, the whole must assemble at some distance in front of it, as in patroling by day, and the environs must be examined; but the men who are sent into the village must, in this instance, be directed to creep gently along the fronts of the houses, and particularly along those of the public houses, looking at the same time in at the windows, and endeavouring to distinguish whether any of the enemy are within.[11]

It was made clear that the purpose of patrolling was to gather intelligence and not to engage the enemy. However, should a patrol unexpectedly be confronted by an equal or inferior number of the enemy then they could attack, after the commander of the patrol had sent back word to the main force. If the patrol was outnumbered then they could scatter and the men make their way back to the main force individually. De Rottenburg stressed the need to fully brief the men of the patrol as to what was expected of them and any contingencies that might occur.

As well as patrolling, and advance or rear guards, the other duty that often fell upon light troops was providing pickets around a camp:

> The strength of the pickets must in a great measure depend on the ground it is intended they should occupy, the distance or proximity of the enemy, and the importance that may be attached to the post to which they are intended to give security. Before the pickets are posted, as exact a knowledge as possible should be

10 Rottenburg, *Regulations*, p.35.
11 Rottenburg, *Regulations*, p.36.

> acquired of the country, in which particular care should be taken to ascertain all the approaches from defiles, villages, or from woods. No picket should be posted so as to be seen from a distance by the enemy, but behind a small wood, or elevated ground, or hedge, or in an hollow; and it is well posted, provided its operations are not impeded by any of the above objects. The number of sentries required should in general regulate the force of pickets, which should be calculated to furnish three reliefs; but when the enemy is near at hand, it is usual to reinforce them, either that more sentries may be posted, or, that in case of attack, they may be able to make a greater resistance.[12]

Advice was then given for posting pickets in different weather conditions, at night, and in different terrain. Procedures for challenging anyone who approaches were also explained, as were changes to the picket once night fell:

> A picket would derive great security, and avoid being easily surprized, by detaching at night small parties from two to three hundred paces to the right and left, which in case of attack of the main body, would be most advantageously posted for its protection, and for galling the enemy by their fire on his flanks. Pickets, as well as advanced sentries, should remove at night from the spot they occupy during the day; so that if the enemy, from the observations he may have made of the post, should attempt to surprize the may him self be led into an error. In cold weather, when fires are requisite, it is adviseable that the position of the picket be frequently changed, and the fires left burning. If the enemy means to attack, he naturally directs his march on the fires, and when he arrives there, finding the post abandoned, he may reasonably suppose the picket has retired: should he loiter on the spot, or be at all off his guard, he may himself be attacked with every advantage.[13]

De Rottenburg recommended that any officer in charge of a picket share the privations with his men and not take shelter. Small patrols should also be sent out from the picket to reduce the risk of the camp being surprised, and also to go from sentry to sentry to ensure that all was in order. By far the largest portion of de Rottenburg's manual concerned patrolling, advance guards, and pickets. Only a few pages were concerned with full blown battles. The expectation was that rifle and light infantry units would spend far more of their time in small sections using their field craft and their marksmanship to protect or shield the main body of the army.

In 1803 the Duke of York ordered a supplementary manual for light infantry to be published. General François Jarry was commandant of the Royal Military College and had served in both the Prussian and the French armies. His *Instructions Concerning the Duties of Light Infantry in the Field* was written when there was still a real risk of the French invading Britain:

12 Rottenburg, *Regulations*, p.51.

13 Rottenburg, *Regulations*, p.61.

> Their army will be constantly covered by sharp-shooters, concealed behind inclosures, hedges, trees, bushes, walls, houses, in equalities of the ground; they must be dislodged by a chain of English sharp-shooters, advancing under the same sort of cover, and driven behind their line.
>
> The knowledge which we have of the country, must give us a great superiority over the enemy. The present Treatise contains lessons, and may create ideas which will enable the officers of light infantry to adapt their movements to the varieties of the ground.[14]

Jarry stressed the requirement for light infantry to be the army's eyes and ears in terrain where light cavalry could not operate. He also advocated that light infantry officers should know the individual strengths and weaknesses of their men so as to better allocate tasks, and lead them rather than bully them. Jarry did not mention drill or specific formations but went into even greater detail on forming pickets, patrolling, and reconnoitring. For example, when an officer was calling in a picket that was being attacked:

> Before recalling his sentries, he will place all the riflemen belonging to his piquet in every favourable situation, and in front of his rear-guard. When those riflemen have fired, they retire upon the rear-guard. Such of the riflemen as have loaded their pieces will take post again in favourable positions, in front of the rear-guard; that is to say, the riflemen will serve as a rear-guard to the rear-guard.[15]

Light troops would also often be called upon to escort a staff officer for the purpose of discovering the location and strength of the enemy and Jarry also outlined other forms of intelligence gathering:

> At certain moments, in certain circumstances, when from want of spies information cannot be procured of what is passing in the enemy's camp, it is customary to send at the same time, and to different quarters, small detachments, for the purpose of making prisoners.
>
> Those prisoners, coming from different places, and belonging to different corps, will report what is going on, where they were individually; and by comparing their different accounts, more or less light will be thrown upon the situation and projects of the enemy.[16]

He went so far as to suggest ruses such as dressing a soldier up as a peasant with food to trade and having them approach an enemy picket, or by the men pretending to be deserters.

Jarry did not get to covering light infantry duties in battle until page 195 out of 219. He then stated that in an attacking army, before a battle, light infantry should cover the deployment of the main force, countering the enemies skirmishers by occupying any cover or strategic points. Then, when the battle commences they can cover the flanks or attempt to

14 F. Jarry, *Instructions Concerning the Duties of Light Infantry in the Field* (London: Dulau & Co., 1803), p.vii.

15 Jarry, *Instructions*, p.94.

16 Jarry, *Instructions*, p.181.

turn the enemies flank and attack them in the rear. In defence, light infantry should occupy the same type of strategic posts and hold them at all costs to give the commander time to deploy their forces to counter the enemy's attack. If the battle is won then the light infantry can be used to pursue then enemy. Should it be lost then the light infantry must form the rear guard, slowing and harassing the enemy to let the main army withdraw.

Jarry's work complemented de Rottenburg's but both of them put the major emphasis on the role of riflemen and light infantry in *le petit guerre*; the war of pickets, patrols, and advance guards. In these kind of small actions a lot of reliance would be placed on the individual soldiers, NCOs, and junior officers. Teamwork, skills, initiative, trust, and *esprit de corps* were vital to make de Rottenburg's tactical system work. German troops did have a good reputation for skirmishing and it would be one that the 5th Battalion would enhance, amongst other German units, in the Peninsular Campaign. Moyle Sherer, of the 34th Foot, who served in a brigade with a company of the 5th Battalion wrote:

> The English do not skirmish so well as the Germans or the French; and it really is hard work to make them preserve their proper extended order, cover themselves, and not throw away their fire; and in the performance of this duty, an officer is, I think, far more exposed than in line-fighting.[17]

The memoirs, journals and letters that survive from the Peninsular Campaign rarely detail the specifics of the formations used in battle, or the minutiae of everyday tasks such as posting pickets or forming advance guards, but whilst the letter of de Rottenburg's or Jarry's manuals may have not always been followed their principles would have been. As the 5th Battalion sailed to war Major Davy knew that his men would have to put their training to the test against French troops that had probably far more combat experience, and that *le petit guerre* of outposts and patrols might be a small war but was not going to be an easy one.

17 M. Sherer, *Recollections of the Peninsula* (London: Longman, Rees, Orme, Brown, & Green, 1827), p.325.

12

Roliça and Vimeiro

The fleet carrying the 5th Battalion and the rest of Sir Arthur Wellesley's expedition arrived at Mondego Bay on the Portuguese coast on 30 July. Wellesley had sailed ahead of the troopships and met with commanders of the Spanish Army at Corunna on Spain's northern coast. The Spanish were distrustful of the British after centuries of rivalry and conflict. Only three years before the British had decimated the Spanish fleet at Trafalgar. They were happy to accept British cash and arms, but not troops. Wellesley, who had been given considerable latitude by the government as to where he chose to land, sailed on to Oporto in Portugal.

Portugal was one of Britain's oldest allies and Wellesley received a much warmer welcome from the Bishop of Oporto, who was the head of the junta – the provisional government. The occupation by the French had stifled Portugal's trade, just as Napoleon had intended. However, this had led to widespread economic hardship and political discontent. Portugal had followed Spain's example and revolted against French rule. The Portuguese rebellion was more sporadic and lacked both trained soldiers and weapons, but it still had forced Junot, the French commander, to concentrate his forces around the easily-defended capital of Lisbon. Some of the Spanish troops who had been allied to the French during the invasion also turned on their former allies and had helped the Portuguese take the city of Oporto. The Portuguese rebels controlled most the country but did not have the means to take Lisbon from the French. British troops would help to tip the balance.[1]

Wellesley did not get all the cooperation he wanted from the Portuguese generals but they did agree to lend him 5,000 more troops including some much-needed cavalry, and to march their main army to protect the British flank. The Portuguese also advised Wellesley where to land his troops. There were possibilities close to Lisbon but they risked early French counter-attacks. Figueira da Foz, 120 miles from the capital, was chosen because the students of Coimbra University had taken Santa Catarina Fort and it was already garrisoned by 300 Royal Marines.[2]

The town of Figueira da Foz stands near the north end of the long stretch of wind-swept sand that is Mondego Bay beach. The disembarkation began on 1 August, and the men of the 5th Battalion, and four companies of the 2/95th, were the first ashore. The strong swell

1 C. Esdaile, *The Peninsular War* (London: Allen Lane, 2002), pp.90-95.

2 C. Oman, *A History of the Peninsular War* (Oxford: Clarendon Press, 1902), Vol. I, p.229.

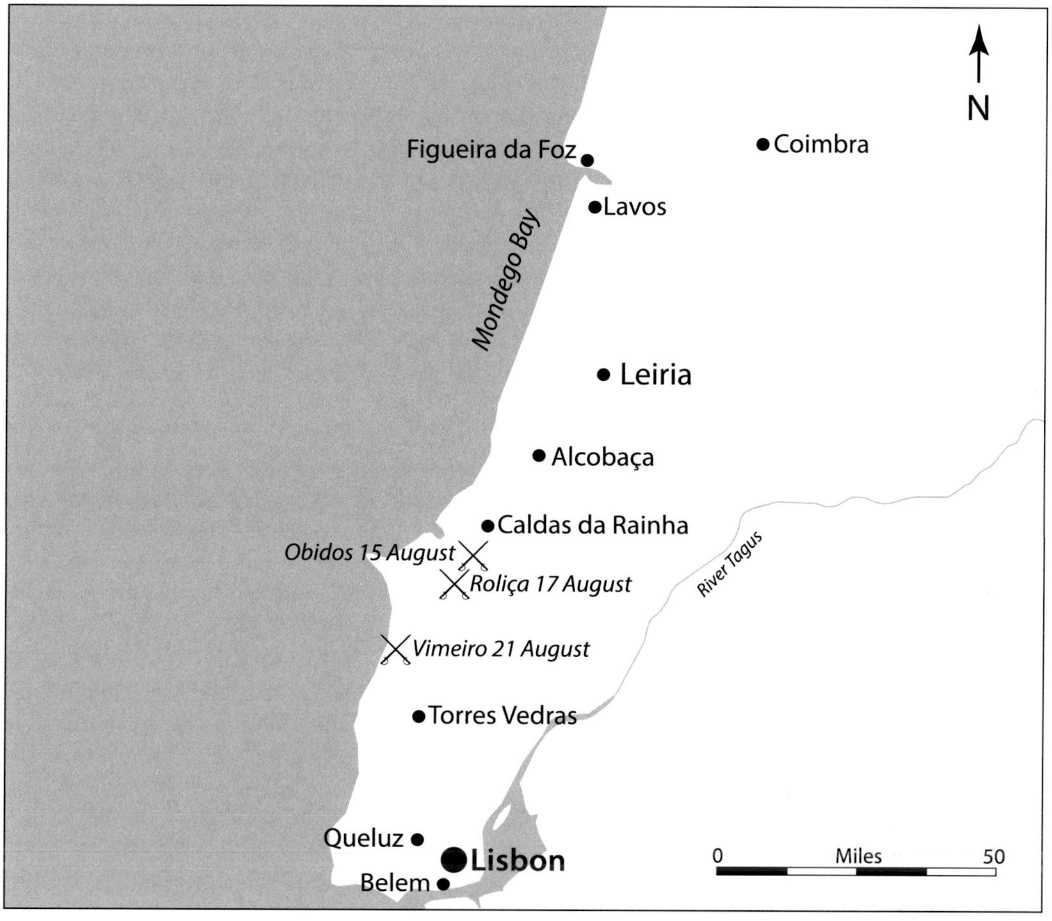

The Liberation of Portugal, August to September 1808.

made it difficult and dangerous to enter the boats, and then heavy surf made landings on the beach very hazardous. Several boats were swamped or capsized, and Portuguese fishermen were eventually hired to help get troops ashore.[3] Once on land the riflemen found trudging through the sand in the heat of an Iberian summer difficult after weeks spent on board ship. The 5th Battalion and the 95th advanced six miles southwards to cover the landing of the rest of the troops, and to give ample warning should the French appear. Jonathan Leach of the 95th recalled his landing at Mondego Bay:

> Whilst we were drawing up our men near the landing-place, and waiting for further orders, we were beset with a host of padres, friars, and monks, of all ages, each carrying a huge umbrella of the most gaudy colour imaginable; intended, no

3 Leslie, *Military Journal*, p.31.

doubt, to protect their complexions, which vied with those of chimney sweeps. These gentry welcomed us with vivas, and protested that, with our assistance, every Frenchman in Portugal should speedily be annihilated. Our visitors were not confined to the male sex; for some olive beauties, with sparkling eyes and jet black hair, were induced to take a peep at us; and, before we parted, some of the more favoured of us were presented with flowers and fruit from the hands of these damsels.

Keeping our right towards the sea, we marched several miles over an uninterrupted plain of white sand, hot enough almost to have dressed a beef steak, into which we sunk ankle deep at every step. The troops having been on board ship so many weeks, were much fatigued with this their first day's march. We encamped near the village of Lavaos, where the whole of the army assembled as soon as the disembarkation was effected.[4]

The landing all of Wellesley's troops took until 5 August, the same day that Major General Brent Spencer arrived with an additional 5,100 men from garrisons in the Mediterranean, the landing of which took another three days. Spencer would become Wellesley's second-in-command. Wellesley had also discovered that since his departure from Britain the government had learned that French forces in Portugal were more numerous than at first thought, and so had gathered another 4,800 men under Brigadier Generals Robert Anstruther and Wroth Acland, some of whom had been set to raid the French coast. Also on his way was Lieutenant General Sir John Moore with another 10,000 men from an abandoned expedition to the Baltic.[5] With the army potentially growing much larger than initially anticipated Wellesley was now too junior to lead it and orders arrived informing him that he was to be superseded.

Sir Arthur Wellesley, an unsigned portrait c.1810 (Anne S.K. Brown Military Collection)

Sir Arthur Wellesley had risen through the ranks quickly by both purchase and political influence. He had won fame fighting in India but had little experience of campaigning in Europe and was not popular with the government. Lieutenant General Sir Hew Dalrymple

4 J. Leach, *Rough Sketches of the Life of an Old Soldier* (London: Longman, Rees, Orme, Brown, & Green, 1831), p.42.
5 Oman, *Peninsular War*, Vol. I, p.224.

was given command with Lieutenant General Sir Harry Burrard as his deputy. Neither had much experience of actually fighting the French but Dalrymple was, at least, familiar with the Peninsula. Moore was also senior to Wellesley, but fortunately for the ambitious young general all of his seniors were days or weeks away and in the meantime he retained command of the army.

Wellesley's main problem was that due to the expedition being scraped together from various sources it was severely lacking in cavalry, artillery, transport, and especially horses. He spent several days gathering horses, mules, and carts from the surrounding area but still could not get enough mounts for all the cavalry, or to pull all the guns.[6]

Wellesley divided his army into six brigades, with two or three battalions of infantry in each. Some artillery was also attached to each brigade:

1st Brigade – Major General Hill
 1/5th, 1/9th & 1/38th.
2nd Brigade – Major General Ferguson
 36th, 1/40th, & 1/71st.
3rd Brigade – Brigadier General Nightingall
 29th & 1/82nd.
4th Brigade – Brigadier General Bowes
 1/6th & 1/32nd.
5th Brigade – Brigadier General Craufurd
 1/45th, 1/50th & 91st.
6th, or Light, Brigade – Brigadier General Fane
 5/60th & 4 companies 2/95th.[7]

On 3 August, in a general order prescribing formations of the army, Wellesley wrote:

> When the army shall move from its left, the 95th and 5th Battalion 60th will lead the column in the ordinary course. When the army shall move from its right, the 95th and 5th Battalion 60th must form the advanced guard, and lead the column from the right of the two corps with the howitzer and 6-pounders attached to General Fane's brigade.[8]

The riflemen of Fane's 6th Brigade would be the vanguard of the army. Whilst Wellesley continued to search for enough horses and transport before the army could begin its march, a few of the 5th Battalion decided that they would rather make their own travel arrangements. On 7 August five men deserted, three from Captain Wolff's company and two from de Wend's. All but one had joined the battalion relatively recently, including at least one who was a former French prisoner of war. The two from Captain de Wend's company, Privates Francis Marschefsky and Christoph Lemke, were retaken on the 13th. Marschefsky and Lemke, along with Private George Guentes who had not deserted, were court martialled

6 Esdalie, *Peninsular*, p.97.
7 Wellington, *Supplementary Despatches*, Vol. VI, p.101.
8 Wellington, *Supplementary Despatches*, Vol. VI, p.96.

for murder at Lavos on 8 August, according to the register of general courts martial. The actual trial papers have not survived but the register states that Guentes was acquitted, but Marschefsky and Lemke were both found guilty and sentenced to hang. Marschefsky had served with the 5th Battalion since August 1799 and was one of the Walloon Guards who had opted to enter British service in Surinam.[9]

At 3:00 a.m. on 9 August the 6th Brigade, along with some of the 20th Light Dragoons, marched from the army's camp near the village of Lavos, leaving the rest of the army behind them to follow on later that day. The orders given to Brigadier General Fane's were:

> I am directed by Lieut.-General Sir Arthur Wellesley to desire that you will be pleased to march to-morrow morning, at three o'clock, towards Leyria, and take post in front of Giao. Captain Douglas, Assistant Quartermaster-General, will point out the ground.
>
> Captain Gomm will attend the column from the camp, to show the road. In the evening you will be pleased to push forwards some dragoons, with a detachment of 200 infantry, as far as you may judge expedient; and should you receive intelligence that the enemy are not at Leyria, or in the neighbourhood, you will cause the town of Leyria to be occupied by this detachment either to-morrow evening or on Wednesday morning.
>
> Should you find that the enemy are in any force at or in the neighbourhood of Leyria, you will withdraw the detachment, and remain in front of Giao, until you receive orders from Sir Arthur Wellesley, to whom you will transmit the earliest intelligence you may obtain. You will be pleased to cause a detachment to remain in camp, to deliver over the camp equipage of the 60th and 95th Regiments to the storekeeper, who will be on the ground at three o'clock A.M. to receive it.
>
> The tents are to be packed up in bales ready for embarkation, with the number in each bale marked on the outside, and they are to be packed on the waggons by the detachments of the regiments.
>
> An Assistant Commissary will attend the brigade to supply provisions, and he will also make every inquiry respecting the resources the enemy may be likely to find at and near Leyria, and you will be pleased to give him any assistance he may require to execute this duty.[10]

Captain Landmann of the Royal Engineers was attached to the brigade and left a detailed account of the march in his memoir. The brigade stopped for breakfast at 8:00 a.m. and then continued on, pausing for an hour or so at intervals to let the troops rest. At dusk, Landmann and the rest of the staff were startled by a shot. The advance guard of the 20th Light Dragoons galloped back down the road, forcing the rest of the brigade, and even the general, into the ditches at the side of the track. Fane reformed his brigade across the road and then questioned the dragoons, who claimed to have seen one of the enemy's vedettes – a mounted sentry or picket – and had fired on him before falling back. Fane led the column

9 September 1799 pay list, TNA, WO 2/7066; September 1808 pay list, WO 12/7073; Register of General Courts Martial Abroad WO 90/1 p.67.

10 E. Sidney, *The Life of Lord Hill* (London: John Murray, 1845), pp.79-80.

back to the spot only to find a corporal of the 20th Light Dragoons sitting on the grass next to his horse with a wounded arm. The corporal told the general he had ridden away from the rest of his party to look over a small bank and returned to the road slightly ahead of the rest of the dragoons, who then spotted him and in the fading light mistook him for one of the enemy. Landmann claims this episode as the first British shot of the Peninsular War.[11]

The brigade marched on until past midnight, stopping, 22 hours after they had started that morning, at a village called Cham-de-Ruaes. The next morning they continued on, cautiously, expecting to meet the French. They reached Leiria early in the day and waited there for the rest of the army. Wellesley's troops would remain at Leiria for two days whilst logistical issues were addressed. On 12 August 6,000 Portuguese commanded by *Marechal de Campo* Freire arrived. Disagreements between Freire and Wellesley over rations and the planned route to Lisbon lead to Freire refusing to join with the British army, but he did reluctantly agree to provide some cavalry and 1,000 infantry.

The various brigades camped amongst the olive groves around the town, making temporary shelters from branches and whatever else they could find. The tents had been left behind due to lack of transport. Just before disembarking Wellesley had outlined what rations were to be issued:

> Until further orders the troops will receive rations from the Commissary. The rations will consist for each day of 1Ib. of bread or biscuit, and 1Ib. Of meat, salt or fresh. If the soldiers should have fresh meat, they are not entitled to spirits or wine; if they should have salt meat, and upon all occasions when it can be got for them, they shall have each one quarter of a pint of spirits, or a pint of wine. The troops are also entitled in camp to 3Ibs. of wood each man.
>
> The women, that is to say, six for each company of 100 men, will receive half a ration per diem, and the children a quarter; but no spirits or wine will be issued to women or children.[12]

Those with money could supplement their rations with the produce offered by the locals who came into camp with such exotic delicacies as oranges, grapes, figs, and melons.[13]

The army continued its march southwards on the 13th, the men suffering from the heat, sunburn, and dried, swollen lips. Very fine dust that coated everything and even made it difficult to breathe.[14] They reached Alcobaça on the 14th. Landmann recalled marching straight through the town and past the monastery:

> We, the light brigade, took up our position at a mile or thereabouts beyond the top of the hill, in order to protect the remainder of the army, whilst they took up their night's lodging in and about the town; and we deeply regretted that the nature of our position in the army did not permit our accepting an invitation which the whole of the staff of the army had received to dine with the monks of Alcobaça.

11 G. Landmann, *Recollections of My Military Life* (London: Hurst & Blackett, 1854), Vol. II, pp.93-100.

12 Wellington, *Supplementary Despatches*, Vol.VI, p.92.

13 B. Harris, *The Recollections of Rifleman Harris* (London: Century Publishing, 1985), p.12.

14 Landmann, *Military Life*, Vol. II, pp.114-5.

> Our inability to dine at the convent having been communicated to the Abbot, a messenger was, in consequence, sent to General Fane, with orders to express the deep regret of the whole of that community at being deprived of the General's company; and, at the same time, to inquire for what number of persons the General might wish to be supplied with a dinner, which should be sent to him with the least possible delay from the convent kitchen.
>
> It is necessary I should here state, that the General's orderly was a German, named Schwalbach, a private in the 5th Battalion of the 60th Regiment, a Rifle battalion; and in order to augment the importance of his office, he pretended to be conversant with the Portuguese language, but of which he had a very imperfect knowledge. Now, as the General had invited Captain Geary, of the Artillery, and Lieutenant Stanway, of the Engineers, and myself, to dine with him on this occasion, the party, including the General and his staff, would amount to six; he, therefore, directed his orderly, in compliance with the messenger's communication, to state that he should require dinner for that number. Schwalbach was not a man that would miss a good opportunity, such as the present; so mustering up his best Portuguese, he contrived to explain that dinner for six would be sufficient, but added with extraordinary gravity, and in a tone of voice truly German, "Mit wine fur twelf;" which, after many gestures, and more swearing by Schwalbach, the messenger appeared to comprehend; and he immediately departed at the utmost speed of his mule.
>
> In the short space of little more than an hour, eight men, all well mounted, on splendid mules, arrived at the ground occupied by the General and his staff; each of them carrying a large and apparently a heavy basket. With magical expedition the cloth was spread, and covered with innumerable dishes of the most delicate viands, superlatively well cooked, and without any garlic, which, we feared, would have formed a prominent ingredient. The dinner for six would have been sufficient to satiate six times as many; for amongst the variety now placed before us, I observed a roasted turkey, two boiled fowls with rice, two roasted ducks, a ham weighing twenty pounds at least, two tongues, stews, fricasees, ragouts, vegetables in profusion; and a superb dessert of melons of every sort, grapes, pomegranates, green almonds, peaches, &c.; and, to the extraordinary delight of, and greatly surpassing his expectations and intentions, Schwalbach now had the gratification of beholding an ammunition box, which served as a sideboard, covered with twenty-four bottles of the most excellent red and white wines, being a general assortment of Colhares, Hock, Champaign, Port, Madeira, Lisbon, &c.[15]

The excess food was packed away, with Schwalbach being allowed a share in return for his translation skills. John Schwalbach had enlisted in May 1806 and had been promoted to corporal in September 1807.[16] Landmann must have misremembered his rank.

15 Landmann, *Military Life*, Vol. II, pp.109-11.

16 May 1806 Pay List, TNA, WO 12/7072; September 1807 Pay List, TNA, WO 12/7073.

On the 15th the 6th Brigade marched on, aware that they were only just behind the French. The heat was still oppressive and the army reached the spa town of Caldas da Rainha that afternoon. Landmann describes the scene as they marched through the streets:

> At the time when we marched through, there were a great number of elegantly dressed promenaders in a sort of public garden on our left; and as we proceeded through the streets, from every balcony flowers were showered upon us in the greatest profusion, accompanied with an incessant shouting of '*Viva-oz-Ingleses!*' a compliment we had not before received; and then the people also shouted '*Viva Portugal*' upon which some of the soldiers, in a merry humour, would echo, 'That's right, I say, viva the Purty Gals!' supposing the Portuguese to have thus attempted to speak English.[17]

The brigade continued through the town and halted about a mile further on. Wellesley wanted the town of Obidos taken, four miles further south, and Fane sent four companies of the 5th Battalion and four companies of the 95th forwards in the late afternoon.[18] A handful of dragoons also accompanied the riflemen. The medieval walled town of Obidos, dominated by a Moorish castle, stood on a steep triangular shaped hill rising abruptly from a plain. To the south a two-mile-long 16th century aqueduct towered over orchards and olive groves.

The eight companies were commanded by Major Robert Travers of the 95th. Travers sent one company of the 95th and three of the 5th Battalion ahead, holding the other four companies in reserve. As they neared Obidos the advance guard encountered a French picket and began to take fire from a windmill on a small hill and from the walls of the town. Lieutenant Ralph Bunbury of the 95th was killed by a shot to the head. The riflemen drove the French back across the plain and carried on the pursuit towards the aqueduct. More French opened fired from the cover of the arches but then slowly withdrew, firing all the time. The riflemen continued to skirmish forwards, with the other four companies having come forward in support. Travers had led his men a considerable distance from the rest of the army and they suddenly met a full French battalion of infantry plus some cavalry. The riflemen were in danger of being surrounded. Travers began a fighting withdrawal and fortunately Major General Spencer, who had heard the firing, brought a brigade forward and extricated Travers and his men from their predicament. The riflemen occupied a small hill and waited there, under arms, for the rest of the night.

Private Baptiste Debass, of the 5th Battalion, was the only other fatal casualty of the skirmish. He had joined the battalion in May 1806 and served in Captain Hammes' company. The return of casualties for the action states that five of the 5th Battalion were wounded and 17 were missing.[19] The September pay list does not mention any men specifically wounded on the 15th but seven men entered the army's general hospital that day, with two subsequently

17 Landmann, *Military Life*, Vol. II, p.120

18 The account of the subsequent skirmish is drawn from Landmann, *Military Life,* Vol. II, pp.121-4; Leach, *Rough Sketches*, p.80; Harris, *Recollections*, p.19; W. Verner, *The History & Campaigns of the Rifle Brigade* (London: John Bale, 1912), Vol. I, pp.145-148.

19 Return of Killed, Wounded & Missing, 15August 1808, TNA, WO 1/228, p.219.

dying; one on 19 August and one on 12 September. All came from Hammes', Wolff's, or de Wend's companies, so it would be logical to assume that they were the three companies sent forward. Only seven men are listed as missing on the pay lists, from the same three companies, indicating, perhaps, that 10 men managed to make their way back some time after the action.[20] Men could go missing if they used the confusion of battle to desert, were killed or wounded but not found, or chose to slip off after the battle to search the dead and wounded for loot and then took a day or two to return. If they were taken prisoner by the French it could also take some time before the British were informed. The 95th, in addition to the death of Lieutenant Bunbury, had one officer wounded and four men missing.

In his dispatch to Lord Castlereagh the next day, Wellesley wrote:

> The enemy, about 4000 in number, were posted about ten miles from hence at Roliça; and they occupied Obidos, about three miles from hence, with their advanced posts. As the possession of this last village was important to our future operations, I determined to occupy it, and as soon as the British infantry arrived upon the ground I directed that it might be occupied by a detachment consisting of four companies of riflemen of the 60th and 95th regiments.
>
> The enemy, consisting of a small picquet of infantry and a few cavalry, made a trifling resistance and retired; but they were followed by a detachment of our riflemen to the distance of three miles from Obidos. The riflemen were there attacked by a superior body of the enemy, who attempted to cut them off from the main body of the detachment to which they belonged, which had now advanced to their support; larger bodies of the enemy appeared on both the flanks of the detachments; and it was with difficulty that Major General Spencer, who had gone out to Obidos when he heard that the riflemen had advanced in pursuit of the enemy, was enabled to effect their retreat to that village. They have since remained in possession of it, and the enemy have retired entirely from the neighbourhood.
>
> In this little affair of the advanced post, which was occasioned solely by the eagerness of the troops in pursuit of the enemy, I am concerned to add that Lieut. Bunbury, of the 2nd batt. 95th regiment, was killed, and the Honorable Captain Pakenham wounded, but slightly; and we have lost some men, of whose numbers I have not received the returns.[21]

In a letter to the Duke of Richmond the same day he was slightly more critical:

> We had yesterday evening a little affair of advanced posts, foolishly brought on by the over-eagerness of the riflemen in the pursuit of an enemy's piquet, in which we lost Lieutenant Bunbury of the 95th, killed, and Pakenham, slightly wounded, and some men of the 95th and 60th. The troops behaved remarkably well, but not with great prudence.[22]

20 September 1808 Pay List, TNA, WO 12/7073; Periods of Service 5/60th, June 1806, WO 25/1008.

21 J. Gurwood, *The Dispatches of Field Marshall the Duke of Wellington* (London: John Murray, 1835), Vol.IV, p.79.

22 Wellington, *Supplementary Despatches*, Vol. VI, p.115.

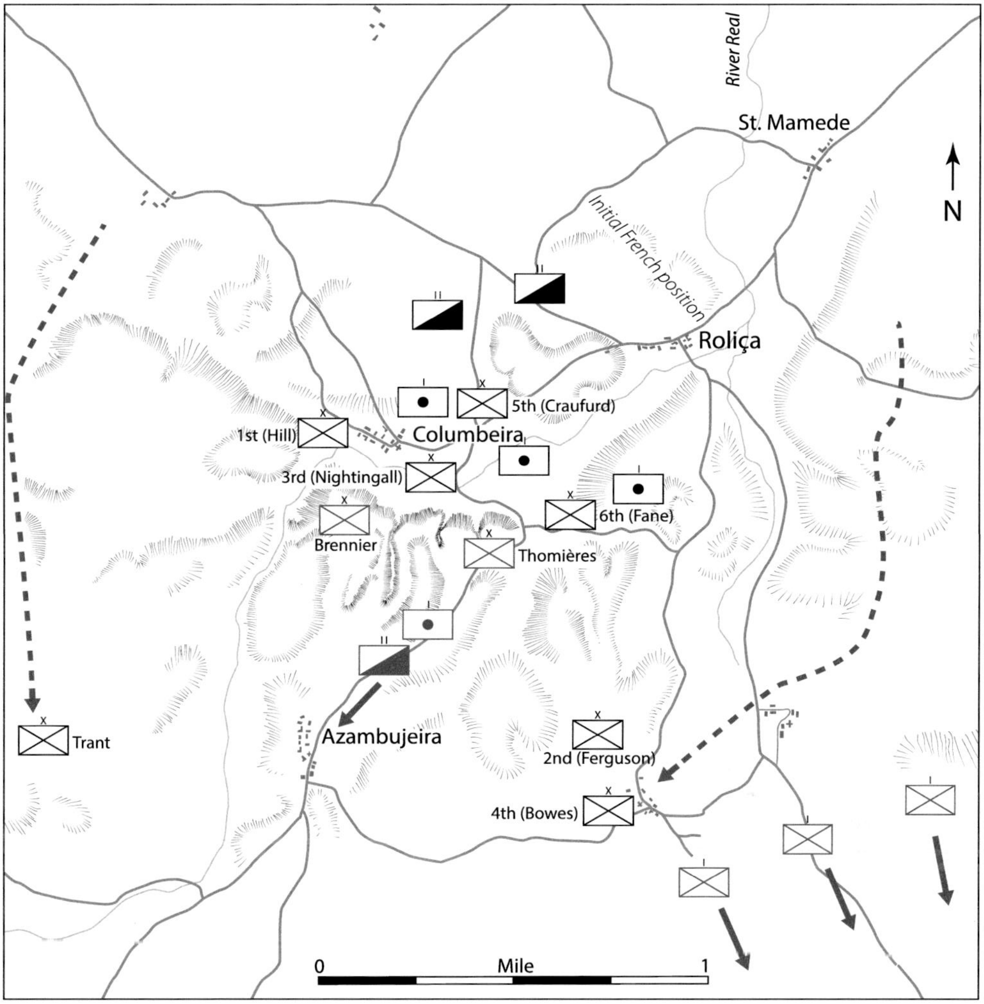

Battle of Roliça, 17 August 1808.
Sources: N. Lipscombe, *The Peninsular War Atlas* & J. Wyld, *Maps & Plans, Showing the Principal Movements, Battles & Sieges in which the British Army was Engaged During the War from 1808 10 1814 in the Spanish Peninsula and the South of France.* (London: Wyld, 1841)

The commander of the approximately 4,000 French troops closest to the British was *Général de Division* Henri François Delaborde, who knew that he had to delay Wellesley's advance until Junot could concentrate the rest of his forces to face them. Delaborde had two battalions of light infantry, two of line infantry, two companies of the 4e Régiment Suisse, the 26e Chasseurs à Cheval, and five field guns with which to slow down the much more numerous British.[23] After the skirmish at Obidos, Delaborde picked his ground carefully and deployed

23 Oman, *Peninsular War*, Vol.I, p.235.

his men around the small town of Roliça on a low hill, thick with scrub, at a point where the valley narrowed to less than a mile.

Wellesley studied the French position from the top of a high tower on the edge of Obidos.[24] He waited a day for the rest of the army to catch up, and then made his move on the morning of 17 August. He split his army into three. Ferguson would advance through the hills on the left with the 2nd and 4th Brigades, Three companies of the 5th Battalion were attached to Ferguson's column. *Coronel* Trant, an Irish officer in Portuguese service, would take three battalions of Portuguese infantry and some cavalry along the base of the hills on the right. Each would attack the French in the flanks whilst Wellesley deployed the rest of the army in a long line across the valley and advanced directly at the French.[25]

As soon as the advance started, the rifles of the 6th Brigade were detached to the hills on the left to maintain contact between the centre and left wing and protect the centre's flank. Jonathan Leach of the 95th recalled the challenges of the terrain:

> We were very soon warmly engaged with the French light troops, who contested the rough and mountainous ground in which we attacked them, with great obstinacy; and it was not without many severe struggles and a considerable loss, that we succeeded in dislodging and driving them from mountain to mountain, and in rooting them out from amongst the thick brush wood and high heath, from which they kept up an invisible and destructive fire as we advanced.[26]

Delaborde let Wellesley make his dispositions, which took some time, and then as the riflemen engaged his own skirmishers and Ferguson and Trant appeared on his flanks, he calmly withdrew a mile, to a line of hills and a much stronger position. Delaborde's withdrawal was covered by a thick screen of skirmishers who were harassed by the rifles of the 6th Brigade as they went. The new position on the heights of Azambujeira, behind the village of Columbeira, was much more formidable. The hills surrounded the valley on three sides. They were steep, and covered in woods and thick scrub. Four narrow, winding, and heavily eroded gullies ran up the slope in the centre.

The British artillery was placed on a hill, near a windmill, and began to bombard the French line. Wellesley was forced to waste more time redeploying his troops to assault the new position but he kept to the same plan; Trant and Ferguson would sweep around Delaborde's flanks and the rest of the army would, once the flanking attacks commenced, make a frontal assault up the gullies. That was the plan, but Ferguson turned too early and attacked the front of the French right and had to withdraw before getting into the correct position. The 29th Foot attacked up its assigned gully before the flanking attacks got under way. In places the gully was only two or three men wide and the redcoats soon found themselves being fired on from three sides and taking heavy losses.

Leach commented the tenacity of the defenders as they withdrew to the heights:

24 Landmann, *Military Life*, Vol.II, p.135.

25 The account of the subsequent battle is drawn from Butler, *Annals*, Vol II, pp.49-52, Riguad, *Celer et Audax*, pp.36-9, D. Buttery *Wellington Against Junot* (Barnsley: Pen & Sword, 2011), pp.93-101, & Oman, *Peninsular War*, Vol. I, pp.236-40.

26 Leach, *Rough Sketches*, p.46.

> The 60th and ourselves attacked the enemy's right, and threw in so destructive a fire on their column, such as we could get within shot of, as to make them retreat in great disorder. You cannot conceive, nor can anyone who was not present on that day, the situation of ourselves and the 60th. We had to ascend first one mountain so covered with brushwood that our legs were ready to sink under us; the enemy on top of it lying down in the heath keeping up a hot and constant fire in our face, and the men falling around us. Before we could gain the summit the French had retired to the next hill where they again lay concealed and kept up a running galling fire on us as we ascended. Having beaten them off the second hill and taken possession of it, the enemy retreated to a wood, there being a valley between us and it, and commenced a most tremendous fire, having received a reinforcement.[27]

The three companies of the 5th Battalion with Ferguson were also facing stiff opposition from the French. As they reached the top of the hills the French would charge them and drive them back down into the woods. It was perhaps at this point in the battle that Captain Keating Bradford, deputy assistant adjutant general, was killed when steadying a company of the 5th Battalion. In a letter dated March 1809 to the Patriotic Fund seeking support for Bradford's family Wellesley wrote:

> This officer, who was Assistant-Adjutant-General to the army lately under my command in Portugal, and aide-de-camp to General Spencer, was killed at a most interesting and critical moment of the battle of the 17th of August, in the performance of a most important service on which he had been employed by me. He was sent to ascertain the exact situation of a detachment of riflemen, who, I imagined, had pushed themselves into the enemy's rear, and to form a judgment in what manner they could be supported. When he reached them they were about to give way, pressed by superior numbers, and he succeeded in rallying them before he received the wound of which he died.[28]

After repeated attempts Ferguson's column began to make headway, as did the frontal assaults. Delaborde started an orderly fighting withdrawal, using the 26e Chasseurs à Cheval to cover his retreat. As they repeatedly made partial charges to discourage the British pursuit the rifles of the 5th Battalion and the 95th took many of them down, including their commanding officer.

Delaborde, outnumbered four to one, had done exactly what he planned to do: slow the British down. French casualties were around 600 and British 474.[29] The return made after the battle states that 5th Battalion lost eight privates killed, two lieutenants, one staff, five sergeants, and 34 privates wounded. Sixteen men were missing after the battle.[30] Lieutenant Frederick Steitz, Ensign J. R. d'Arcy, and Adjutant Frederick de Gilse were the wounded

27 Quoted in Butler, *Annals*, Vol. II, p.52.

28 Wellington, *Supplementary Despatches*, Vol.VI, p.201.

29 Oman, *Peninsular War*, Vol. I, pp.239-41

30 Neale, *Spain & Portugal*, Appendix XVI, p.38.

'The attack on the French Corps, commanded by General Laborde, on the 17th of August. 1808', by Henri Leveque. (Anne S.K. Brown Military Collection)

officers and staff.[31] Steitz had returned to his company at the height of the action as soon as his wound had been dressed.[32]

However, the pay list marks only seven men killed, including one, Private Jacob Billetter, whose remark is corrected to 'died by accident on the 16th'. The six killed in action included Privates Frederick Glicker, Christoph Reckow, and Caspar Spaling, who had all joined the battalion within the previous two years. Glicker, though, must have served in another regiment before he joined from the Foreign Depot as he was marked as having more than seven years' service. Spaling was a former French prisoner of war. Privates Jacob Neiss and Constatine Rissman had both joined the battalion after the disbandment of Lowenstein's Jägers in 1802. Private Conrad Zengerie was the longest serving to be killed having joined in Surinam in 1799 from the Walloon Guards. Four men are marked specifically as having been wounded on the 17th, including Sergeant Daniel Koch who died on the 22nd. Koch had been with the battalion for five years. A further 24 are marked as having entered the general hospital on the 17th, of whom two died before the end of August and one was invalided out of the battalion before the end of September. The pay list also has just six men listed as missing that day, indicating again that 10 men had returned to the battalion after the official casualty list was compiled.[33]

Captain Landmann encountered one member of the 5th Battalion on the battlefield the day after the fighting:

31 Butler, *Annals*, Vol. II, p.52.

32 Trial of Lieutenant Steitz November 1809, TNA, WO 17/2464, p.22.

33 September 1808 Pay List, TNA, WO 12/7073; multiple Pay Lists WO 12/7072; Periods of Service 5/60th, June 1806, WO 25/1008.

I saw a woman, one of the British nation too, with a large stone in her hand levelling a finishing blow at a poor fellow of the 9th or 45th Regiment, I do not now recollect to which he belonged.

This wretch was at the man's back, as he sat on the ground, having had one of his legs broken on the preceding day by a musket shot, and was, therefore, quite helpless. My sudden appearance for a moment suspended the course of this infernal creature, and she remained with her hand raised, grasping a stone as big as both her fists, pausing no doubt, to consider how far my presence ought to check her murderous views; and during this momentary hesitation, from the opposite side, out of the thicket, a man stepped forth, whom I immediately perceived was a private soldier in the 5th Battalion of the 60th Regiment.

His occupation was not doubtful; plunder had induced him to straggle from his corps and remain in the rear, and I sincerely hope, his cupidity was confined to the property of the dead. This man was a German, and he also, as well as myself, had seen the diabolical intent of the woman before us. My hand was still strongly grasping the hilt of my sword, which I had half drawn, with a determination of stopping by force the further progress of this fiend; but the German lost no time in considering, he ran up, his rifle half up to his shoulder, and without any parley or ceremony, merely muttering as he sprang upon her, 'You be no fouman, py Got! you be de tifle!' he put his rifle close to her ear, and before I had had time to form any clear conjecture as to his views, the upper half of her head vanished, and was dispersed into atoms amongst the bushes, and her body in falling almost extended to the wounded soldier.

Under any other circumstances, such a sight would have filled me with horror; I, nevertheless, here shouted loudly 'Bravo!' with the most ample satisfaction; and whilst I was engaged in giving the unfortunate man a drink of wine out of my canteen, who informed me that the woman had already struck him one desperate blow on the shoulder with the stone, because he would not submit peacefully to be plundered of every stitch he had on, my German was engaged in very deliberately reloading his rifle, and then having carefully untied the woman's apron, which was richly filled with watches, rings, and valuables of all kinds, he darted from the spot, and disappeared amongst the bushes, casting at me a ferocious glance.[34]

Wellesley wanted to pursue the French but word had reached him that British reinforcements were arriving imminently, so he decided instead to head to the village of Vimeiro in order to cover their landing at Maceira Bay. On 18 August Wellesley wrote in a general order to the army:

The Lieutenant-General was perfectly satisfied with the conduct of the troops in the action of yesterday, particularly with the gallantry displayed by the 5th, 9th, 29th, 60th, and 95th, to whose lot it principally fell to engage the enemy.[35]

34 Landmann, *Military Life*, Vol.II, pp.174-6.

35 Wellington, *Supplementary Despatches*, Vol. VI, p.121.

Before the army left for the coast Wellesley made some adjustments to his brigading of the army, in order that all the brigades had some rifle armed troops:

> The following new distribution of brigades to take place on leaving this ground:
>
> The 6th, or light brigade, to consist of the 50th Regiment, four companies of the 95th, and five companies of the 60th.
> One company of the 60th to be attached to each of the following brigades: the 1st, 2nd, 3rd, 4th, and 5th; and to join them as soon as possible.[36]

The 5th Battalion was to split into detached companies for almost all of the rest of the peninsular campaign. Riflemen were specialist troops with both training and a weapon that the rest of the army lacked. It made sense to deploy them in small numbers with conventionally armed and trained redcoats to make the best use of them, rather than to concentrate them. However, when larger numbers of the 95th arrived in the Peninsula later in the campaign they were generally kept together in the Light Division.

The army made its way towards the sea and reached Vimeiro on the 19th. On the same day 2,700 men under Brigadier General Robert Anstruther managed to disembark through the rough surf, and on the 20th 1,300 men commanded by Brigadier General Wroth Acland landed at the mouth of the Maceira River. The two new brigades were to be numbered the 7th and 8th respectively.[37] Acland brought with him two companies of the 1/95th. Also with the reinforcements came Lieutenant General Burrard. Wellesley reported to his new superior on board the sloop HMS *Brazen* and outlined his plans to advance and find the French. Burrard thought it too risky and argued that the new brigades would need more time to recover from being cooped up on the transports. He was also inclined to wait a few more days for Sir John Moore's convoy to arrive before making any move. Burrard decided to spend one more night on board ship and disembark the next day, 21 August. The reinforcements brought the British and Portuguese army up to just over 18,000 men.[38]

Wellesley had picked his ground for covering the landings every bit as well as Delaborde had at Roliça. He placed his brigades along a line of hills that stretched from north to southwest. In the centre, where the river Maceira cut through in a narrow gorge, was the village of Vimeiro. The southern-most hills nearest the sea were the steepest, with the northern ones being lower and more rolling with a road running along the top and a ravine in front. Before Vimeiro stood a low hill, partly covered by thick scrub and vineyards, on which Wellesley placed Fane's 6th Brigade, including five companies of the 5th Battalion, and Anstruther's 7th Brigade and six cannon. Ferguson's 2nd Brigade, and what little cavalry was available, was placed near the river with Trant's Portuguese infantry ready to support Fane and Anstruther on the hill. Wellesley put eight more cannon on a hill covering the village.[39]

36 Wellington, *Supplementary Despatches*, Vol. XIII, p.294.

37 Oman, *Peninsular War*, Vol.I, p.248.

38 Oman, *Peninsular War*, Vol.I, pp.250-1.

39 Buttery, *Junot*, pp.105-6.

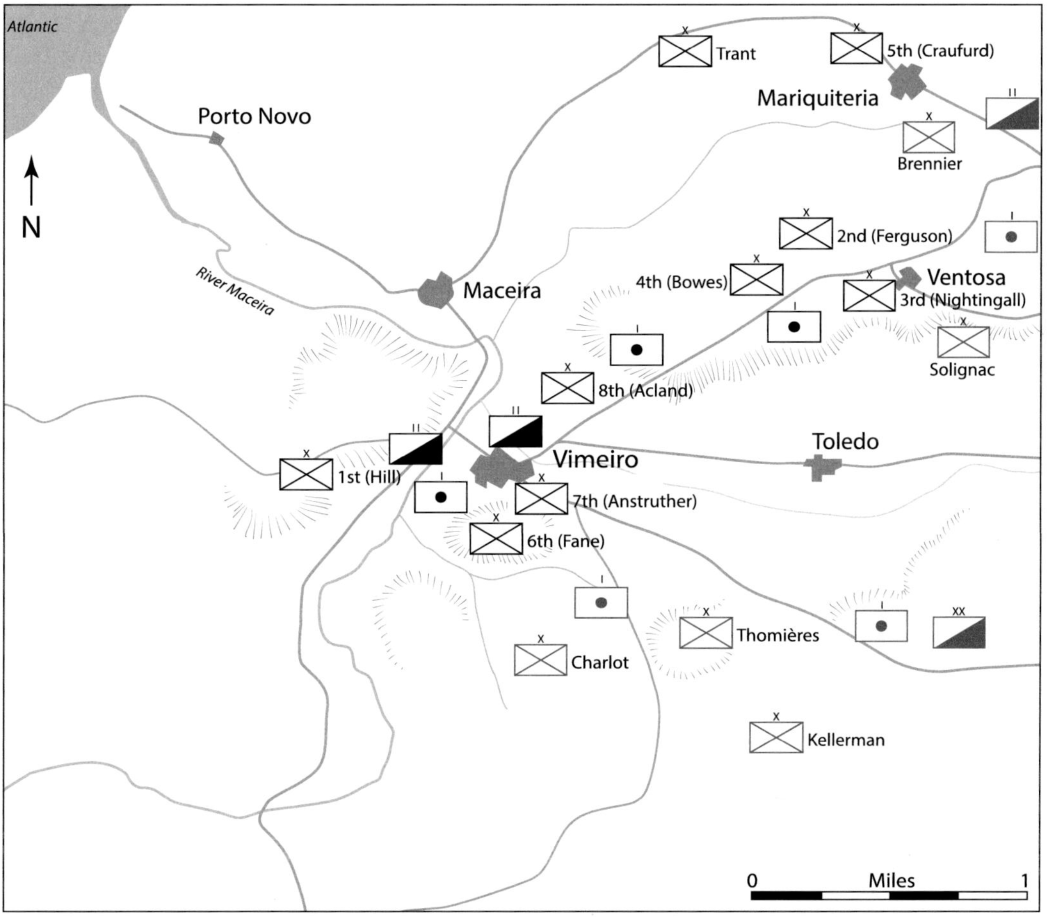

Battle of Vimeiro, 21 August 1808.
Sources: Lipscombe, *Atlas* & Oman, *History of the Peninsular War.*

Wellesley had also ensured he had posted cavalry vedettes on the likely approaches and a strong picket of 200 riflemen of the 95th and 5th Battalion in the wooded hills on the northern bank of the river. At around midnight on the 20th Sergeant Norbertus Landsheit of the 20th Light Dragoons, formerly of the Hompesch Hussars, galloped into the British camp with the news that the French were approaching.[40] Wellesley ordered his troops to be under arms and in position an hour before dawn. Acland's 8th Brigade marched into the British camp at around 6:00 a.m., after spending the night on the beach.

Junot had gathered between 13,000 and 14,000 men and, hearing that the British were at Vimeiro, thought that he had a chance to drive them into the sea. He was not aware that Wellesley had received reinforcements and now outnumbered him. Junot marched his men

40 G. Gleig, *The Hussar* (London: Henry Colburn, 1837), Vol.I, p.264.

through the night, and after a short rest continued to advance and by 7:00 a.m. they could be seen from the British lines. Due the heat they were not wearing their usual blue coats but long white linen ones and white cap covers, both stained with dust. At about eight o'clock French skirmishers supported by line infantry entered the woods in front of the British position. Jonathan Leach of the 95th recalled:

> The night before the battle I belonged to a picket of about two hundred riflemen, of our own regiment and the 60th, under the command of Major Hill, of the 50th regiment. We were posted in a large pine wood, to the right and front of General Fane's brigade. About eight or nine o'clock in the morning of the 21st, a cloud of light troops, supported by a heavy column of infantry, entered the wood, and assailing the pickets with great impetuosity, obliged us to fall back for support on the 97th regiment.[41]

Reports of French movements had led Wellesley to think that the French would attack the right of his army but after a hasty look at the battlefield Junot decided on a frontal attack on the British centre and a flanking manoeuvre by *Général de Brigade* Brenier's brigade around their left. It was serious misreading of the strength of Wellesley's position in the centre. The hill on which Fane's 6th and Anstruther's 7th Brigades were posted offered good cover for the defenders, and was well supported by reserves. Wellesley moved two brigades and the Portuguese infantry north to counter the flanking move, and placed three brigades behind the village of Vimeiro.[42]

Junot, seeing Wellesley's counter moves, reinforced Brenier with three more battalions at the cost of reducing the men available for his main assault. Junot did not appreciate that the ravine in front of the hills would force the flanking move to march so far before they could turn and attack. In the centre the remaining battalions of Delaborde's and *Général de Division* Loison's divisions formed into columns of around 1,500 men, and sent a screen of light infantry forward. Fane had sent most of the rifle companies to the base of the hill. Behind them on the crest were the 50th and some more rifles. Anstruther had placed his four battalions well, deploying most of his men behind the crest, with two formed in column ready to act as a reserve. The rifles on the slope fired as they retired toward the British line. The French were confident but most would not have encountered the accurate long-range fire of the infantry rifle before. One French officer later recalled:

> I met the English. Oh, that morning was one of the most happy of my life! My men to a man had the same feeling. I was sent out to skirmish against some of those in green-grasshoppers I call them; you call them Rifle Men. They were behind every bush and stone, and soon made sad havoc amongst my men, killing all the officers

41 Leach, *Rough Sketches*, p.50.

42 The account of the subsequent battle is drawn from Butler, *Annals*, Vol. II, pp.55-62; Riguad, *Celer et Audax*, pp.41-6; Buttery *Junot*, pp.105-22; R. Chartrand *Vimeiro 1808* (Oxford: Osprey, 2001); pp.64-80; Oman, *Peninsular War*, Vol. I, pp.242-62.

> of my company, and wounding myself without being able to do them any injury. This drove me nearly to distraction.[43]

Charles Leslie, with the 29th Foot, also recalled the 5th Battalion's predilection for targeting French officers:

> In this battle the 60th Riflemen, who were all Germans, showed great tact in taking advantage of the ground and dexterity in the use of their arms. General Fane, who commanded the light troops, observing one of these men successfully hit one or two French officers who were gallantly exposing themselves in front leading on their men, exclaimed in the excitement of the moment, 'Well done, my fine fellow! I will give you half a doubloon for every other one you bring down.' The man coolly loaded again, fired, and hit another, then looking at the General, he said gravely, 'By Got, I vill make my vortune'.[44]

As the two French columns marched up the hill, 400 yards apart, the riflemen continued to fire on them and on the light infantry screen trying to protect them. Moving from cover to cover the riflemen would often have to pause for the smoke to clear before they could see a target. The densely packed columns were each around 76 men wide and offered a large target for the British artillery which soon opened fire. Round shot ploughed through the French ranks but did not stop the columns. The long lines of the redcoat battalions only opened fire once the French were close enough and there was no danger of them hitting the riflemen. As the French columns approached the redcoats shifted their positions slightly to meet them and then were given the order to fire. The massed volleys at last made the French columns falter. The 97th advanced with fixed bayonets and charged the front of a French column whilst the 2/52nd did the same in its flank. The Frenchmen broke and ran back down the hill. The 50th and the rifles that had held the top of the hill then did the same to another column. Two of the French generals leading the columns were injured. Junot sent two battalions of grenadiers to repeat the assault, support by eight guns which attempted to subdue the British defenders. The Royal Artillery gunners responded with Henry Shrapnel's spherical case shot that exploded over the heads of the French and showered the columns with musket balls and metal shards. The grenadiers' attack faltered then failed as they too met the withering fire of the British rifles and muskets.

At about this point in the battle Captain Landmann, who had left the 6th Brigade to serve Wellesley as the senior Royal Engineer, was trying to find Brigadier General Anstruther:

> On returning to the place where I had left Anstruther, I could see nothing of him, but I was informed that he had gone off towards the left. Accordingly I went away in that direction, and unwilling to waste much more time in vainly hunting about for him, and falling in with Fane's Light Infantry, who were actively engaged in driving back the enemy's Voltigeurs, I joined my old friends, and in a very few

43 Quoted in G. Simmons, *A British Rifle Man* (London: A & C Black, 1899), p.102. Simmons is quoting a conversation the Englishwoman nursing the officer in question had with him, not one he had himself.

44 Leslie, *Military Journal*, p.53.

minutes I observed a Frenchman amongst the bushes, not more than sixty to eighty yards distant; shifting about from one concealing place to another, and at length I perceived him taking up a convenient position for giving me a proof of his abilities as a marksman. At the same moment I perceived just under my horse's nose a man of the 5th Battalion of the 60th Regiment, belonging to Fane's brigade, and whose German countenance I recognized. Upon this, I called to him, 'Do you not see that rascal taking his aim at me? Fire at him quickly, if you do not, he will hit me to a certainty.'

A mounted officer amidst a parcel of riflemen stands but a bad chance of escaping, for he alone is visible, and seems to be put up as a target for the enemy to shoot at, whilst the privates or riflemen are all creeping about with so much industry in trying to conceal themselves, particularly the foreigners; and it has been observed that a German or a Prussian *jäger* will make himself quite comfortable behind a cabbage, a pumpkin, or even a large turnip, and there remain for hours, if he have the opportunity, dogging his prey, and that, too, without the least chance of being seen.

My friend of the 60th, however, had other views of greater interest to him than my life; for after repeatedly pressing and then ordering him to knock off the Voltigeur, who was taking so much pains to prevent me from becoming grey-headed in the service, he pettishly and half turning round, said, 'Silence! ton't tisturp me; I want de officeer.'

'Why do you want to kill the officer,' cried I, 'you rascal?' with as much vexation as he had manifested.

'Pecaus ter pe more plunder,' muttered the wretch, keeping his eyes fixed on the object of his ambition.

It now immediately occurred to my mind, that, as we were rapidly driving back the enemy, this worthy had calculated on permitting the Voltigeur to pick me off, whilst he should return the compliment on the French officer; and thus secure the advantage of plundering me first, trusting to the almost certainty of getting up to the enemy before the French officer's carcase should be stripped by his friends, whose life he was unwilling to endanger.[45]

Landmann then saw a French artillery crew trying to gallop from the battlefield with their cannon and gave chase, passing Fane with two of his staff and his orderly, Corporal Schwalbach, he called upon them to assist and the party raced after the gun and captured it after Fane shot one of the horses with his pistol.[46]

Junot then committed his final reserve, two more battalions of grenadiers, led by *Général de Division* Kellerman. After seeing the failure of the first two attacks Kellerman decided to try another route and to try and outflank the British position. Anstruther saw what Kellerman was trying to do and sent the 2/43rd Light Infantry into the village. The 43rd took cover behind the high wall of the churchyard and fired from buildings on the other

45 Landmann, *Military Life*, Vol.II, pp.219-22.
46 Landmann, *Military Life*, Vol.II, pp.222-23.

side of the road to catch the grenadiers in a lethal crossfire. Acland also deployed the two 1/95th companies and the light companies of his two line battalions to attack the grenadiers in the flank. British guns fired into the ranks of the grenadiers inflicting many casualties. The French attempted a charge through the village but were met with a counter-charge by the 50th and 43rd and a desperate hand-to-hand and point-blank struggle finally stopped the grenadiers and drove them back. The British centre had held. Wellesley sent his cavalry forward to attack the retreating French; they charged too far and were counter-charged by two French dragoon regiments but most managed to survive.

Meanwhile Brenier was moving around the British flank but he and *Général de Brigade* Solignac, who was leading the battalions Junot had sent to reinforce him, took different routes so that Solignac arrived in position, near a farm named Ventosa, before Brenier. Solginac advanced towards a thin line of British skirmishers on top of a hill, not knowing that three British brigades were deployed in two lines, lying down, out of sight on the reverse slope of the hill. The French voltigeurs drove the British light infantry and rifles back but the French, in a line of three battalion sized columns, then saw the much longer British lines rise up and prepare to fire. As the French closed the first British line let loose a devastating volley, wounding Solignac. The redcoats reloaded and then marched silently forward. The French broke and ran, pursued by the British. As the British took prisoners and captured some of the French guns Brenier finally arrived and charged into the flank of the 71st and 82nd with four battalions of infantry, and his cavalry. The surprise of the attack caused the British to retire quickly but they then rallied. The companies of the 5th Battalion present positioned themselves on the flanks of the French and carried on firing relentlessly. Reinforced by the 29th the redcoats formed line and began volley fire at the French, who broke and fled, harried by the fire of the British artillery. Brenier was wounded, unhorsed and then captured. After two and a half hours both Junot's attacks had utterly failed. Wellesley had won his first major battle on European soil.

Much of Wellesley's army were still fresh and had hardly been engaged. He wanted to advance on the retreating French and cut them off from Lisbon to complete the victory but Burrard, who had come ashore that morning, ordered the army to stay where it was. Wellesley and his subordinates made their cases vociferously but the cautious commander would not be swayed and the French were allowed to escape.

The battlefield was littered with the dead and wounded, piles of which marked the limit of each advance like a dreadful tide line. Abandoned muskets, knapsacks, canteens, guns, wagons, and dead horses lay all around. It began to rain. One of the French wounded fired at Benjamin Harris of the 95th. Harris fired back and killed him and then went to search the body:

> Whilst I turned him about in the endeavour at finding the booty I felt pretty certain he had gathered from the slain, an officer of the 60th approached, and accosted me.
>
> 'What! looking for money, my lad,' said he, 'eh?'
>
> 'I am, sir,' I answered; 'but I cannot discover where this fellow has hid his hoard.'
>
> 'You knocked him over, my man,' he said, 'in good style, and deserve something for the shot. Here', he continued, stooping down and feeling in the lining of the Frenchman's coat, 'this is the place where these rascals generally carry their coin. Rip up the lining of his coat, and then search in his stock. I know them better than you seem to do.'

Battle of Vimiero, by Henri Leveque. (Anne S.K. Brown Military Collection)

> Thanking the officer for his courtesy, I proceeded to cut open the lining of his jacket with my sword-bayonet, and was quickly rewarded for my labour by finding a yellow silk purse wrapped up in an old silk handkerchief. The purse contained several doubloons, three or four Napoleons and a few dollars. Whilst I was counting the money, the value of which, except the dollars, I did not then know, I heard the bugle of the rifles sound out the assembly, so I touched my cap to the officer, and returned towards them.[47]

The French suffered more than 2,000 casualties. The British and Portuguese lost 135 killed, 534 wounded, and 49 missing. Most of the casualties came from the 2nd, 6th, and 7th Brigades. Three brigades had no casualties at all.[48] The few prisoners came from the pickets of the 2/95th and the 5th Battalion taken at the start of the battle, and from the cavalry after they charged too far in pursuit of the French.

Fourteen riflemen of the 5th Battalion were killed, and Lieutenants Koch and Ritter, one sergeant, and 22 men were wounded; one man was reported missing.[49] The casualties were spread over seven of the 10 companies. The 14 men killed included several that had served with the 5th Battalion for many years: Private Sebastian Traumüller was one of the original members of the battalion, having joined the Lowenstein Chasseurs in 1795; Private Christian Muller, a tailor from Fischen in Bavaria, had been with the Hompesch chasseurs before they were incorporated into the 5th Battalion in February 1798; Private Adam Langsdorf joined the companies on the Isle of Wight shortly afterwards in April;

47 Harris, *Recollections*, p.39.
48 Oman, *Peninsular War*, Vol.I, p.261.
49 Butler, *Annals*, Vol.II, p.60.

Private Jacob Laturnus joined in August 1801, whilst the battalion was in Surinam; Privates Martin Bechenbaur, Christian Hoffert, Wenzel Lachman, Christian Martin, and Christian Muller had all joined from Lowenstein's Jägers in 1802, Martin was a labourer from Rötha in Saxony, and Muller was a butcher from Cologne; Private Lewis Henniger had served two years with the Hompesch Mounted Rifles before joining at the same time as the jägers; Private John Herbach had served four years in the 4/60th before joining the 5th Battalion in 1803; Privates Niclas Engman, John Jugler, and Baptiste Kessler were former French prisoners of war who had joined in the autumn of 1806.[50]

The 5th Battalion was one of the units that Wellesley singled out for praise in his general order following the battle, and in which he also ordered that a company of the battalion be attached to each of the brigades that had recently arrived:

> Lieutenant-General Sir A. Wellesley congratulates the army on the signal victory they have this day obtained over the enemy, and returns them his warmest thanks for their resolute and heroic conduct. He experienced the sincerest pleasure in witnessing various instances of the gallantry of the corps, and has, in particular, to notice the distinguished behaviour of the Royal artillery, 20th light dragoons, the 36th, 40th, 43rd, 50th, 52nd, 60th, 71st, 82nd, 95th, and 97th regiments.
>
> It will afford the Lieutenant-General the greatest pleasure to report to the Commander-in-Chief the bravery displayed by all the troops, and the high sense he entertains of their meritorious and excellent conduct throughout the day.
>
> The brigade under the orders of Brigadier-General Acland is denominated the 8th brigade. The two companies of the 95th, attached to it, will join those with the 6th brigade; and one rifle company of the 60th will be transferred immediately from the 6th to the 7th brigade, and another from the 6th to the 8th brigade.[51]

Sir Hew Dalrymple arrived 22 August and took over command from Burrard. On the same day Kellerman turned up in the British camp with an offer of a truce from Junot and authority to negotiate the surrender of French forces in Portugal. Kellerman had been chosen by Junot for his diplomatic skills and presented a list of terms that was the best that the French could hope for. Dalrymple agreed to almost all of them. The French army was to be repatriated to France in British ships and allowed to take their personal property with them, the definition of which was loose enough to allow any loot taken from the Portuguese. Dalrymple was conscious of the fact that attempting to drive the French from the fortifications around Lisbon would have been very costly in terms of men and time. British troops could be better used assisting the Spanish rather than dealing with an already-defeated French army in Portugal. However, Dalrymple excluded both his Portuguese allies and Wellesley from the negotiations and agreed to terms that were too much in favour of the French. There was no article to prohibit the repatriated French army from serving in the Peninsula again, as was often stipulated in such agreements, nor was there an article requiring the French to leave behind their much-needed horses for the British to use.

50 September 1808 pay list, TNA, WO 12/7073; December 1806 pay list, WO 12/7072; Periods of Service 5/60th, June 1806, WO 25/1008.

51 Wellington, *Supplementary Despatches*, Vol.VI, p.121.

When the final agreement was signed and the terms made public there was outrage from the Portuguese at the leniency of them. Wellesley also had severe misgivings, even though he felt obliged to sign the treaty. Wellesley left Portugal in September to return to Ireland. Burrard and Dalrymple were subsequently recalled for an enquiry into what became known as the Convention of Cintra. All three generals were exonerated by the enquiry but Dalrymple's refusal to accept responsibility, and attempt to blame Wellesley, did not reflect well on him and Wellesley was the only one to emerge with his reputation intact. By mid-September most of the French troops had left Portugal.

At Vimeiro the weather worsened in the days after the battle with strong winds, lightning and hail as big as musket balls. On 26 August Dalrymple reviewed the entire army, including the Portuguese army under Freire. The 30,000 men were arrayed in a line six miles long.[52] On 27 August the army marched towards Torres Vedras.

Once the army was camped around the town of Torres Vedras, Landmann was invited to dine with Fane; the general's orderly, Corporal Schwalbach, was dispatched to buy some wine:

> The dinner had been ready during some time, but our purveyor was not in sight. I was sitting on the brow of the hill by the side of a windmill on the left of the road, as it enters the valley from the North, and with my telescope straining my sight to catch the first glimpse of friend Schwalbach on his return, when, after puzzling my head to find out the cause of his long delay, I, at length, caught sight of something advancing like a rifleman; but he had, as I then thought, a large Chinese hat on his head, instead of his military cap.
>
> 'This fellow,' thought I, 'greatly resembles Schwalbach in all matters excepting the strange covering of his head.'
>
> I called the General to look at him, who was equally unable to make out the cause of so novel a head-dress; Bringhurst and Mac Lean were as much perplexed, and we all continued to keep this man in sight until he actually came so near as to be sure he was in reality friend Schwalbach, who, instead of being the bearer of a keg, a stone bottle, a jar, a pot, a pitcher, or a basket of bottles, had on his head a brown earthenware deep dish, a yard wide or more, and, of course, only about half-full.
>
> We were greatly diverted, and laughed most heartily as Schwalbach deposited on the ground this immense dish, whilst he was perspiring most violently, and declaring that he had never in his life been so fatigued by carrying any weight. He said, that to keep the dish level on his head and the wine from splashing out, had strained his movements so much, that nothing could equal it. The wine was most excellent, in our estimation, and we drank to the health of the rifleman.[53]

Sir John Moore began to disembark his troops at Maciera Bay on 26 August. He took command of the British forces in Portugal once Dalrymple and Burrard had left for Britain. The army moved southwards towards Lisbon and by the end of September the 5th Battalion's headquarters was at Queluz, nine miles from the capital.[54] The return of 1 October, the

52 Landmann, *Military Life*, Vol.II, p.281.

53 Landmann, *Military Life*, Vol.II, p.288.

54 Rigaud, *Celer et Audax*, p.57.

first since landing in Portugal, lists the battalion's strength as 55 sergeants, 22 buglers, and 883 rank and file. Corporal Schwalbach was still with Brigadier General Fane. Lieutenant du Chastelet, one sergeant, one corporal and six men were with the battalion's baggage at Belem. Half the battalion was detached and serving with Lieutenant General Sir John Hope's division, and Davy noted that 'no communication has been received from them since 24th September'. Thirty-one men had come back from being prisoners of war, 39 were listed as missing, and 26 killed 'in the several actions'. One man had been discharged and noted as being 'not recommended'. Two men had died and 24 had deserted. Lieutenants Charles Koch and Lewis Ritter were still in hospital after being wounded, 35 men were also in the general hospital and 18 sick in their quarters.[55]

Privates Marchefsky and Lemke were still awaiting execution pending the confirmation of their sentences for the murder in August, but on 4 September the assistant judge advocate wrote to the judge advocate general's office back in London:

> Sir, I have the Honour of Transmitting herewith the proceedings of a General Court Martial which assembled at Lavos on the 8th of August 1808. Lieutenant General Sir Arthur Wellesley has been induced to Pardon Francis Manschefsky and Christopher Lenky in consequence of the General good conduct of the Corps to which they belong particularly on the 17 and 21 of August. The whole of the Prisoners have been released and have joined their Regiment.[56]

Lemke returned to the 5th Battalion but was sent to serve in the 2/60th the following March. However, Wellesley ordered Marchefsky to be discharged and sent to serve in the fleet.[57]

On October 12th Brigadier General de Rottenburg wrote to Davy:

> You may easily conceive how highly I have been gratified on reading in the papers of your distinguished conduct in the field. The Duke of York spoke to me in high terms of the battalion, and I most sincerely congratulate you on the honour and glory you have acquired. I always told you that you might depend upon the bravery of my disciples, but I have been concerned to learn that three rascals deserted, were retaken, and have not been shot – ill-judged mercy to the guilty is injustice to the faithful soldier.
>
> My compliments to Majors Woodgate, Galiffe, and all our gentlemen.[58]

The 5th Battalion had acquitted themselves very well in their first major campaign, proving de Rottenburg's methods and training against an experienced enemy. They had taken a large role in all three skirmishes and battles with the French, and won praise from Wellesley each time. Unfortunately in their next campaign, when Sir John Moore led the British Army into Spain, a minority of the men would bring dishonour and shame upon themselves, and their battalion.

55 October 1808 Return, TNA, WO 17/179.

56 Jarvis to Rider, Judge Advocate General's Office, 4 September 1808, TNA, WO 1/228.

57 September 1808 Pay List, TNA, WO 12/7073.

58 De Rottenbur to Davy, 8 October 1808, quoted Rigaud, *Celer et Audax*, p.2, with an additional extract at the end from the same letter quoted on p.5.

13

Desertion and Recruitment

In September 1808 Major Davy received a reply to a request he had made, via Sir Arthur Wellesley, to Sir Hew Dalrymple:

> I am desired by the Commander of the Forces to acknowledge your letter of yesterday's date, with an inclosure from Major Davy commanding the 5th Battalion of the 60th regiment desiring permission to enlist deserters, and I am to acquaint you that his Excellency does not approve of deserters from the enemy being enlisted in a corps destined to do the duty of advanced posts; nor does he think it expedient, at this moment, to allow Hanoverians to be enlisted by any other corps than those composing the infantry of the German Legion, for the recruiting of which instructions have been received from home.[1]

The French army, then awaiting transport back to France, contained one Hanoverian battalion and two Swiss.[2] In August, in a letter, Brigadier General de Rottenburg had suggested to Davy that German units in French service could be a good source of recruits.[3] Dalrymple obviously thought differently but he was soon recalled to Britain and either Sir Henry Burrard or Sir John Moore, his subsequent successors, must have given permission for some recruiting as in September 1809 Davy wrote:

> I last year brought at some hazard from Oporto with me 200 fine Swiss recruits, who had served as Voltigeurs in the French army, and were particularly calculated for our arm, but have been much disappointed to find that they have, since, all been given to the 2nd battalion 60th foot destined for the West Indies.[4]

Soldiers of the 4e Régiment Suisse had deserted from French ranks during the Battle of Roliça and some were seemingly unwilling to return to France with the rest of Junot's army.[5]

1 Clinton to Wellesley, 16 September 1808, quoted in Rigaud, *Celer et Audax,* p.62.
2 Oman, *Peninsular War*, Vol. I, p.243.
3 Rigaud, *Celer et Audax*, p.63.
4 Davy to Bathurst, 13 September 1809, quoted in Rigaud, *Celer et Audax*, p.69.
5 Oman, *Peninsular War,* Vol. I, p.238.

Such recruits were not faced with a choice of British service or the prison hulks, as they were due to be shipped back to France. They may have been opting to serve the British for nobler motives than those recruited into the 5th Battalion in the autumn of 1806 from the prison camps on the south coast and the captured convoy. Of these men, approximately 12 percent had deserted or attempted to by the end of 1808.[6]

In 1808, just before the start of the Peninsular campaign, the number of foreign troops in British service stood at 31, 891 and rose to a peak of 52,416 in 1813,[7] growing from approximately one seventh to one fifth of the British Army's strength. In 1812 the then Secretary at War, Lord Palmerston, stated in Parliament:

> If any man would look at the map of Europe, and see what a proportion of its population the enemy had forced into hostility against this country, if he were also to consider the limited population of these two islands, and the extensive colonies we had to defend, and the navy we had to support, it appeared to him hardly possible that such a man could now adhere to the idea of not employing foreigners in our service.[8]

As the demand for men reached its peak in 1812 and 1813 even British and Irish regiments began to recruit foreigners into their ranks.[9]

The British Army's regimental system was generally meant to consist of regiments of two battalions each, with the first battalions serving overseas and the second battalions serving at home. The second battalions would recruit and then train the men before transferring them as needed to the first battalions. Whilst that was how the system was supposed to operate there were significant variations with some regiments having only one battalion, and a few three or four. Also, as the demands for manpower in the Peninsula and other theatres exceeded supply, more and more second battalions had to serve overseas.

With six battalions by 1799 and eight by 1813 the 60th was the largest regiment in the Army and operated very differently. All the battalions were usually posted overseas with only occasional and brief periods on the Isle of Wight or the Channel Islands. The 5th Battalion's stay in Britain and Ireland from 1806 to 1808 was very much the exception to the rule. Recruitment and basic induction for the 60th was undertaken by the Foreign Depot for much of the period that the 5th Battalion existed. The regiment shared the depot with the other foreign-recruited units that came under the jurisdiction of the Foreign Department of the War Office. Officers and NCOs from the various battalions of the 60th were seconded to the depot, and some were then sent to the continent to recruit. The depot was initially based at East Cowes on the Isle of Wight, was subsumed into the Army Depot there during the brief Peace of Amiens, but then re-established at Lymington on the British mainland after the resumption of the war. In September 1806 the deputy inspector general of foreign

6 An estimate calculated from tracking the recruits listed on the December 1806 pay list in WO 12/7072 through the subsequent years.

7 A. Bamford, *Sickness, Suffering and the Sword* (Norman: University of Oklahoma Press, 2013), pp.41-3.

8 Quoted in R. Knight, *Britain Against Napoleon* (London: Penguin, 2013), p.440.

9 Bamford, *Sickness, Suffering*, p.167.

troops in charge of the depot, Colonel Howard, said in a letter to Lieutenant Colonel de Rottenburg:

> On the 16th Ult. I received an order from the Adjutant General to post such recruits from time to time, to the 5th Battn. 60th Regt. as I should think particularly qualified for a Rifle Corps. Any recruits therefore that arrive here, who have served in Rifle Corps, I pass to your Battn. unless from any excuse they appear to me unfit for it.[10]

The Foreign Depot was usually where any French prisoners of war who volunteered for British service would be sent. Some of the foreign corps also maintained small recruiting parties at the major ports, and government alien agents who oversaw foreigners arriving in Britain could also send recruits to the depot, and receive a bounty in return. The depot had its own staff made up of the commandant, a staff captain, three subalterns, an adjutant, a paymaster, a storekeeper, a clerk, a sergeant major, quarter master sergeant, and 12 staff sergeants.[11] It had its own hospital at Lymington staffed by a surgeon and two hospital mates and another for invalids at Eling, near Southampton.[12]

Recruits were issued with their uniform and other basic equipment whilst at the depot. As well has handling some recruiting and training tasks for the foreign corps, the Foreign Depot also processed invalids and those soldiers being discharged. It arranged their passages back to the continent, including any wives and children. If a foreign corps was disbanded then those soldiers wanting to continue in British service could await reassignment to another unit at the depot. The number of recruits at the depot varied, as drafts came and went, but as an example on 21 September 1810 there were 21 officers, 1,613 other ranks, 57 women, and 53 children.[13]

The initial establishment of the 5th Battalion allowed for two recruiting companies but it is not evident from the surviving records if, or to what extent, these were ever formed, and they were in any case discontinued in 1801.[14] The two NCOs of the 5th Battalion listed in the muster books as 'recruiting in Germany' in early 1798, Sergeant Andreas Schneider and Corporal Michael Lesser, had both deserted by September of that year.[15] Captain Francis Gomer is then noted as being in Germany recruiting from 1799 to 1803 when Captain Charles Kenzinger took over.[16] Kenzinger was later assisted by Lieutenant Henry Hoffman and a sergeant.

The foreign department established a foreign recruiting depot at Stralsund in Pomerania, a Swedish territory on the German Baltic coast, and also had staff at Husum, in Schleswig-Holstein. The Stralsund depot was at one time commanded by Lieutenant Colonel von Mosheim, late of the 5th Battalion. Officers on recruiting duty would divide their time between Stralsund and Husum, but also travel to other German cities such as Hamburg.

10 Howard to de Rottenburg 7 September 1806, TNA, WO 7/77, p.15.

11 Establishment of the Staff of the Foreign Depot, TNA WO 7/81 p.190, which also includes a breakdown of their duties.

12 T. Keate, *Observations on the 5th Report of the Commissioners of Military Enquiry* (London: Hatchard, 1808), p.60.

13 Gomer to Viesturme, strength of the Depot, 21 September 1810, TNA WO 7/82, p.224.

14 Yorke to Fauquier, 31 August 1801, TNA, WO 7/32 p.250.

15 September 1798 Pay List TNA, WO 12/7066.

16 5/60th Pay Lists, TNA, WO 12/7066-70.

Recruits could approach them directly or via agents who would bring in parties of recruits and receive a bounty. The recruiting depot would carry out an initial assessment of the recruits and reject those that did not measure up. Recruits were then issued with slop clothing and greatcoats, and lodged in inns or private houses. They would then be shipped from ports like Cuxhaven or Husum, often in Royal Navy ships or troop transports. Wives and children could also accompany them. When the recruits arrived at British ports, such as Sheerness or Harwich, there would be an officer and NCOs to meet them and escort them to the Foreign Depot.[17]

The motivations of the recruits choosing to serve the British rather than their own state's armies are often unclear. The pay and food were better in the British Army, but not to the extent that there was any risk of the recruits making their fortune. However, when the 7th Battalion of the 60th was formed for service in North America during the War of 1812 recruits were offered land in Canada in return for their service. The British recruiting agents and officers were not the only ones seeking recruits, of course. Prussia and Austria also recruited from other German states as well as their own territories. Many German rulers would try and impede British recruiting, or even to kidnap the recruits. Factors that possibly limited the willingness of potential recruits to consider British service were a deeply-held aversion to sea travel that was common in many of the land-locked areas of Europe, the probability of service in the disease-ridden West Indies, and the very real prospect of never seeing their homes and family again.[18]

As the Napoleonic Wars progressed, the success of the French in defeating, occupying, or otherwise subduing the German states became the largest impediment to British recruiting in the area. Occupation of Hannover from 1803 led to the creation of the KGL from the former Hanoverian army, but later limited British recruitment from the area. The occupation of Stralsund by the French in 1807 forced the Foreign Recruiting Depot to move across the Baltic to Gothenburg in Sweden.[19] In February 1807 Colonel Howard wrote to de Rottenburg:

> In answer to your letter of the 6th Instant, I have the honor to acquaint you that by a letter I received from the Adjutant General of the 12th of last December I was directed not to post any more Recruits from this Depot at present to the Battalion under your Command. Indeed as the recruiting from Stralsund, is for the present suspended, we are now only receiving recruits raised from Prisoners of War & they have not been of that description, that in my opinion, would have suited your battalion.[20]

It was only in 1813 when the allies began to drive the French out of northern Germany that some limited recruiting activity on the continent could recommence.

Officers detached on recruiting duty often had to handle large amounts of cash and most of the surviving records deal with payments of various allowances and bounties. There was

17 Muster lists of the Foreign Recruiting Depot, TNA, WO 2/54 & WO 12/12012.

18 Wishon, *German Forces*, pp.152-156.

19 Muster lists of the Foreign Recruiting Depot, TNA, WO 12/12012.

20 Howard to de Rottenburg , 8 February 1807, TNA, WO 7/77, p.372.

obvious potential for officers to line their own pockets. In 1811 Captain Charles Kenzinger appeared in front of a general court martial at the Royal Hospital in Chelsea charged with embezzlement. Kenzinger had relocated to the island of Heligoland, in the North Sea off the German coast, following the closure of the depot at Straslund. The charges contained a long list of payments that he had allegedly pocketed, amounting to well over £2,000. Kenzinger was acquitted of all charges and so his only crime was perhaps one of poor accounting. He retired from the Army in 1814.[21]

On the June 1809 pay list there appears, for no obvious reason, information on the origin and former occupation of some of the men, seemingly at random. Of the 152 with such information 121 were previously labourers; a catch-all term for any unskilled manual worker. Three had been masons, eight tailors, nine shoemakers, one carpenter, one miller, one farrier, three weavers, two butchers, and three musicians. Of the three musicians two were, unsurprisingly, in the battalion band. The vast majority came from the various German states, with the remainder hailing from Hungary, Poland, the Low Countries and Switzerland.[22]

With recruitment struggling, greater emphasis was given to retaining existing recruits in the foreign corps when their limited time of service expired. Bounties of up to 10 guineas were offered for those willing to enlist for life.[23] The other way for the foreign corps to keep their numbers up was to recruit from the ever-increasing pool of French prisoners of war which, as the war progressed, became an ever more important source.

Accounts from prisoners of war who opted for British service are rare and none of the many who served with the 5th Battalion seemed to have written any record of their time with the British Army. However, Johann Christian Maempel, who eventually joined one of the rifle companies of the KGL, did leave a memoir; *Adventures of a Young Rifleman in the French and English Armies*, which was published in the 1820s. Maempel was born in the Electorate of Mainz. The son of a clergyman, he saw at first-hand the aftermath of a battle between the Prussians and the French, but nonetheless was persuaded to join the French army by an officer promising the usual quick path to glory and an easy life. His regiment was part of the forces raised by Napoleon from the newly created client-state of Westphalia. Maempel was sent to Spain and marched into Madrid in the early spring of 1808. He comments that his regiment received many recruits from Germans in Spanish service, in regiments such as the Walloon Guards, who deserted in the hope that a French unit would eventually lead them closer to home. Maempel fought against the Spanish, was spoken to by Napoleon during a review, and pursued the British army under Sir John Moore to Corunna in early 1809. Suffering sickness and wounds, and serving in several battles against the allied army during 1810 he was eventually captured retreating from Almeida in the spring of 1811:

> We were brought to Villa Formosa, where the English head-quarters were established under, Lord Wellington. He came with a number of other generals to see us,

21 C. James, *A Collection of the Charges, Opinions and Sentences of General Courts Martial* (London: Egerton, 1820), pp.380-1.

22 June 1809 Pay List, TNA, WO 12/7073.

23 Calvert to Bowyer, 10 November 1803, TNA, WO 3/35, p.353.

> and all reproached us, particularly those who were Germans by birth, for having so long served the usurper (for so they denominated the Emperor Napoleon). One general above all others, he was probably a German, abused us most unmercifully: this cruel treatment, as we were already unhappy enough, made a very unfavourable impression upon us.[24]

Generally well-fed and well-treated by the British, he was marched through Portugal and then shipped to Lisbon where, either by error or by design, they were starved for three days after which, on the fourth morning, recruiters from the British foreign corps arrived and found a very receptive audience. Maempel and 400 others volunteered. They sailed for Britain and landed at Yarmouth, on the Isle of Wight, where they were allowed to recover from the rigours of campaigning and helped locals bring in their harvest.

> At last in October the government considered that we were sufficiently restored and fit for service. We took the oaths, made an agreement to serve for seven years or until six months after the signing of a treaty of peace and received four guineas bounty. Shortly afterwards we received a complete English equipment and orders to join the regiment.[25]

Maempel arrived at Bexhill where he served in the rifle company of the 7th Line Battalion of the KGL. His unit left for Malta at the end of 1811 and he then found himself briefly back in Spain before sailing for Sicily and Naples. In 1816 he was discharged and he returned to his home town after an absence of nearly 10 years. Reading Maempel's memoir one gets the impression that he was as content in British service as he was in French, and that the soldier's typical priorities of food, drink, and a dry bed were more important to him than the flag he served under.

French deserters, or prisoners of war, from the Peninsula who volunteered for British service were sent back to the Foreign Depot and distributed to foreign corps serving in other theatres rather than Spain and Portugal, to reduce the temptation to desert back to their former comrades. When this policy was relaxed in 1811 and 1812 desertion did increase and it was reinstated.[26] The KGL and the 60th seem to have been slightly more discriminating in the prisoners that they recruited than some of the other foreign corps, such as the Chasseurs Britannique or Brunswick regiments, who suffered higher rates of desertion and poorer reputations. The Duke of Wellington had to order that the Chasseurs Britannique, who recruited from any nationality including French, not be employed on some outpost and picket duties to reduce the incidence of desertion.[27]

Sir Arthur Wellesley, or the Duke of Wellington as he became, had mixed feelings about recruiting French deserters and prisoners of war. He worried that desertions of foreign

24 J.C. Maempel, *Adventures of a Young Rifleman in the French and English Armies* (London: Henry Colburn, 1826), p.205.

25 Maempel, *Adventures*, pp.240.

26 D.S. Gray, 'Prisoners, Wanderers, and Deserters: Recruiting for the King's German Legion, 1803-1815', *Journal of the Society of Army Historical Research,* Vol. LII, p.155.

27 A. Nichols, *Wellington's Mongrel Regiment* (Staplehurst: Spellmount, 2005), pp.71-2.

troops set a bad example for British and Irish troops that they might emulate,[28] but at other times he was often willing to encourage French troops to desert. In April 1810 he wrote to the governor of Almeida:

> I request you to pay Señior Echcvarria all the expenses which he has incurred for the encouragement of desertion from the French army, and for the support of deserters, and to tell him that I request him to encourage desertion by the following measures. Let him send trusty persons to assure soldiers in the French army, induced to desert, that they shall be received here and treated in every respect as British soldiers; that their arms and horses, if they should bring them, shall be bought from them and paid for; that they shall have their option of enlisting into the British service or not; that if they choose to enlist they shall receive a bounty and shall have the choice of enlisting into any of the Foreign Corps with this army, or in England; and that, if they do not choose to enlist, measures shall be taken to send them out of the Peninsula, and to facilitate their return to their own country.[29]

Yet a year later he was not so willing to accept more foreigners into his army's ranks. He wrote to the secretary at war in September 1811:

> Major General Cooke has written to request that some arrangement may be made for the disposal of the battalion of foreign detachments doing duty at Cadiz. This battalion consists of some men belonging to the Chasseurs Britanniques, and of some recruits enlisted for general service, either at Gibraltar or on the eastern coast of the Peninsula, and not yet allotted to any regiment, and therefore but ill provided with clothing and appointments. Major General Cooke states that he has understood that these men are dissatisfied with the uncertainty of their situation, and he expresses an anxiety that they should be disposed of in regiments.
>
> I am not at all anxious to have any of them with this army. The number of foreigners with this army is a serious inconvenience, as they not only convey intelligence to the enemy, which they could acquire in no other manner, but they have nearly put a stop to desertion from the enemy's ranks by their accounts, unfounded or exaggerated, of the manner in which deserters are treated and disposed of in the British service.
>
> Those men who do desert now, therefore prefer to take their chance with the Spanish levies to coming to us; and they earnestly intreat that they may not be sent to us, as they have been informed by the deserters from our army that the deserters from the enemy are sent to the West India Islands, and have no chance of ever returning to Europe.
>
> I would beg to recommend, therefore, that those men of the battalion of foreign detachments at Cadiz, not belonging to the Chasseurs Britanniques, should be formed into a battalion of the German Legion, or of the 60th regiment, and that

28 Nichols, *Mongrel Regiment*, p.154.

29 Wellington to Cox, 1 April 1810, quoted in Gurwood, *Dispatches* Vol. VI, p.1.

> Officers should be sent to take charge of them, and that they should be clothed in the usual manner.[30]

The battalion of foreign detachments eventually formed the nucleus of the 8th Battalion of the 60th, and moved from Cadiz to Gibraltar.

Foreign recruiting had its political critics as well. In 1810 the radical politician and pamphleteer William Cobbett, a former sergeant major in the army, was convicted of libel for publishing a pamphlet that sought to spread discontent within the Army. The attorney general, prosecuting, 'dwelt with considerable severity on that part of it which more particularly traduced the German Legion, asserting on behalf of that gallant body of men, that the reproaches which this foul libel cast upon them were as false as they were wicked.'[31]

In 1812 an article in the *Royal Military Chronicle* began by lamenting the recruitment of foreigners into British regiments and the promotion of foreign officers to general commands and stated: '...I am convinced the voice of the country is completely against it, as well as that of the army, which must indeed consider itself as far sunk in the estimation of government which resorts to foreigners for that protection the sons of Albion can no longer afford.'[32] The article went on to say that it was unwise to recruit from prisoners of war and then entrust them with outpost duty, but the writer then advocated that the 60th be expanded and all foreign recruits be sent to the West Indies in place of British regiments. However, 'into no other British regiment ought any foreigner, not educated in England, to be introduced.' He also stated:

> The 5th Battalion of the 60th is now serving in Portugal with distinguished reputation, and if increased and kept efficient by drafts from the German Legion of both men and officers as they are required, that corps, the German Legion, might be gradually reduced to a proper establishment; at present, the only resource for filling up its ranks, and the men cannot be sent out of Europe, according to the agreement entered into on their leaving Hannover, is by receiving deserters from the enemy.

The article is signed 'The Soldiers Friend' which was the title of one William Cobbett's early pamphlets.

Another letter, published in *The Royal Military Panorama or Officer's Companion* in 1814, also lamented the increase in the foreign recruitment and the poor behaviour of some troops in America during the War of 1812. The correspondent also suggested the best place for them to serve was the West Indies, before stating:

> I must, before I conclude, pay that tribute of applause to the German Legion which their services in the Peninsula have so justly merited. Finer regiments do not, I believe, grace any service. But they are entirely German, and are composed of men who love liberty, and are enemies to the great subverters of it, the French. My observations apply only to corps formed indiscriminately of people of all countries, and

30 Wellington to Liverpool, 18 September 1811, quoted in Gurwood. *Dispatches*, Vol. VIII, p.292.

31 *The Edinburgh Annual Register for 1810*, Vol. Third, Part. Second, p.107.

32 *Royal Military Chronicle,* June 1812, p.127.

> these cannot be employed with advantage, but in common garrison duty; and as they are formed chiefly of men taken prisoners in the French service, they would never hesitate between continuing prisoners and serving in the 60th, or Grand Colonial Garrison Corps. We have of late had so many instances of the bad conduct of these made up corps, when they could be tampered with by the enemy, that I am surprised government have not before now determined to employ them only in the capacity I have already mentioned.[33]

However contentious the recruitment of French deserters or prisoners of war was, the demands for more men for the Army was unrelenting and the policy continued throughout the war. In June 1810 General Merck, a German formerly in French service himself, volunteered to go to Spain and recruit Germans from the French deserters and prisoners held there. During that year and the next he managed to recruit hundreds of men. However, judging by the surnames of the recruits, many were not German, but French or Italian.[34] In September 1811 Mosheim, at the Foreign Depot, had to complain that 350 out of a shipment of 575 recruits from Gibraltar were actually French, and not from those countries that he thought produced the best recruits for British service.[35]

From 1811 deserters from the French army were allowed to retain their ranks if they volunteered to enter British service. In June Mosheim, who had taken over from Howard at the Foreign Depot, wrote to Lieutenant Colonel Williams, who was then commanding the 5th Battalion:

> I have the honor of acquainting you that the three men viz Andreas Gross, Stephen Patrick, Machim Tablosska, have entered the British from French Service as Sergeants and have been posted as such to the 5th Batt. 60th Regt. Barth. Fisher is Corporal, and so is Theodore Ponlufsky who left the Foreign Depot on the 21st of Last February. All the Foreign Regiments have had a proportion of such non commissioned Officers Diserters from the enemy, allotted to them by order of the Commander in Chief, but I have queried as much as possible against overburthening your Battalion with them. They are to be born as supernumeraries in the first instance.[36]

Williams was obviously uncomfortable with the idea of recruits having previously served in the French army. In February of the same year Mosheim had told him:

> The men posted to the 5th Batt. 60th Regt. I beg to assure you are very carefully selected by me, for you aught to have lusty Men but if none from the Germans who have deserted from the Enemy are to be posted to the Battn. under your Command, you cannot expect to receive any Recruits from this depot at present.[37]

33 *The Royal Military Panorama, or Officers Companion*, January 1814, pp.360-1.
34 Various Returns of Recruits, TNA, WO 1/413.
35 Mosheim to Torrens, 4 September 1811, TNA, WO 1/648, p.61.
36 Mosheim to Williams, 27 July 1811, TNA, WO 7/84, p.26.
37 Mosheim to Williams, 27 February 1811, TNA, WO 7/83, pp.206-7.

Mosheim, a former officer of the 5th Battalion, seems to have gone out of his way to support the battalion with the best from the available pool of recruits. In 1812 he wrote to Williams:

> I have real satisfaction in acquainting you that the Detachment of Recruits for your Battalion now at the Foreign Depot & amounting to 159 men is a most select body, of lusty young men, all Germans, who I have carefully chosen, and they will no doubt give you every satisfaction.
>
> Your proposing to send an Officer to the Fgn. Depot, acquainted with the present System of the 5th Battn. 60th Regt. for the purpose of Drill by instruction; is what meets my full concurrence; I was going to make an application to Head Quarters to that effect, and request you will leave no time in sending me such an Officer. Be assured that I am very careful in procuring eligible men for your Corps and being myself a Rifle Officer by early services with that arm and by predilection. I would take it upon myself to drill and instruct your men, did my Official Avocations permit it...
>
> I will never loose sight of procuring you good officers, they are so truly essential with your battalion.[38]

The German troops with the army in the Peninsula, including the 5th Battalion, generally had a very good reputation amongst the men they served beside. Captain John Patterson of the 1/50th, which was brigaded with companies of the 5th Battalion at various times, wrote:

> The German troops are superior to any I ever met with for strict attention to duty. They are determined, brave, and cool in the hour of battle; and, should they be entrusted with the out-posts, the camp may sleep in safety and in full assurance of being vigilantly watched. – Hardy and inflexible, they conform under any state of things to their commanders, at whose will they move with the regularity of a piece of mechanism.[39]

Harry Ross-Lewin of the 32nd Foot highlighted the beneficial effect of the German troops on the British infantry and their differences in attitude in his memoirs:

> Our German sharpshooters improved them considerably in the several duties of light troops; still they never attained to such a degree of perfection as might have been expected from a consideration of their natural qualifications. Our men, particularly in the beginning of the war, entertained very generally the absurd notion that the taking advantage of any sort of cover which lay in their way, when skirmishing, was an act of cowardice, and some of our commanders, strangely as the assertion may sound, seemed desirous to encourage them in this way of thinking. When we consider our soldiers, as such, we cannot approve of their yielding to this sense of

38 Mosheim to Williams, 28 January 1812, TNA WO 7/86, p.213.

39 J. Paterson, *The Adventures of Captain John Patterson* (London: T & W Boone, 1837), p.356.

> shame; but we cannot fail to admire them, as men, for preferring danger to what they considered dishonour. How differently the old Germans thought! They were always to be seen dodging from tree to tree, or ensconcing themselves between rocks and fences, with admirable method and steadiness, while the British skirmisher would step out sturdily on the open space, and make a target of himself for the enemy.[40]

The foreign corps are often criticised for having higher desertion rates than the British units, but one statistical analysis of all soldiers of the cavalry and infantry between 1803 and 1812 found that the rate of desertion was slightly higher amongst British troops. It found the rate for foreign and colonial troops to be 93.21 per thousand men, whereas for British troops it was 103.7. The author suggested that since more of the foreign troops served abroad there were fewer opportunities for desertion. Most desertions took place within units based in the United Kingdom.[41]

For most of the almost six years they spent in Portugal, Spain, and on into France the 5th Battalion suffered less from desertion and indiscipline than some of the other foreign corps, but during the late autumn of 1808 they did suffer from a spate of desertions that temporarily blighted the reputation of the battalion.

Lieutenant General Sir John Moore took command of the British forces in Portugal on 8 October 1808, following the departures of Dalrymple and Burrard to face a board of enquiry investigating the Convention of Cintra.[42] The strategic and political situation had changed greatly in the three months since the British had landed at Mondego Bay. Portugal had been liberated, several Spanish armies were in the field opposing the French, and most of the rest of Spain was in open revolt against French rule. The Spanish had finally agreed to accept direct British military help and 12,000 British reinforcements under Lieutenant General Sir David Baird had arrived at the northern Spanish port of Corunna on 13 October.[43]

However, the expulsion of the French from Portugal and several defeats at the hands of the Spanish had attracted the attention of Napoleon himself, who had marched into Spain with reinforcements to take personal command of the French armies. Moore planned to unite his own and Baird's force at the Spanish city of Salamanca and then come to the aid of the Spanish armies. Moore's army was widely dispersed and this, to some extent, dictated the roads he used to enter Spain. He planned to use three routes, but was wrongly informed that two of them were impassable for artillery and not recommended for cavalry, so he sent the bulk of his guns, his two cavalry regiments, and four battalions of infantry, under Lieutenant General Sir John Hope, by a much more circuitous fourth route which cost him valuable time and meant that by the time Hope reached Salamanca the French had inflicted several defeats on the Spanish. The situation had changed and there was little Moore could do to positively influence the campaign. Baird had also been delayed by the initial refusal of the Spanish to let him land his troops. In-fighting between the various Spanish generals and

40 H. Ross-Lewin, *With the Thirty-Second* (Dublin: Hodges, Figgis & Co., 1904), pp 305-6.

41 W.B. Hodge, 'On the Mortality Arising from Military Operations', *Journal of the Statistical Society of London*, Vol. XIX p.239.

42 General Order 8 October 1808, National Army Museum (NAM), 1978-11-153.

43 Oman, *Peninsular*, Vol. I, pp.491-2.

juntas severely limited the level of co-operation that Moore could get from his allies and left his own army at risk of facing numerically superior French forces.

The 5th Battalion had been divided in two wings even before Moore had taken command, and would remain divided until March 1809. Major Davy commanded the wing with Moore's main force around Lisbon consisting of Galiffe's, McMahon's (commanded by Lieutenant Koch) Schoedde's, Salaberry's (commanded by Lieutenant MacKenzie), and Blassiere's companies. Major Woodgate commanded the wing with Sir John Hope's Division at Elvas near the Spanish border, which consisted of Andrews', Hames', de Wend's, Wolff's and Prevost's companies, the latter being commanded by Lieutenant Zühleke.[44] Davy's wing marched north with Major General Lord William Bentinck's brigade through Portugal to Castelo Branco and then to Ciudad Rodrigo until they reached Salamanca. Woodgate's wing marched with Hope's division that crossed the border to Badajoz, and then up towards Madrid, before turning westwards back to Salamanca.[45]

On 25 October Moore wrote, in a general order, to his troops:

> The Commander of the Forces trusts that the Troops on their entry into Spain will feel with him how much it is for their honor and advantage, to maintain the high opinion, and cherish the good will, which that high spirited and brave people entertain towards the British Nation. The troops upon their march will generally be quartered upon the Inhabitants: The Spaniards are a grave and orderly People – extremely sober, but generous and warm in their temper, and easily offended by any insult or disrespect that is offered them: They are grateful to the English and will receive their Troops with kindness and cordiality: This the General hopes will be met with equal kindness on the part of the Soldiers, and that they will endeavour to accommodate themselves to their manners, be orderly in the their Quarters, and not shock by their intemperance a People worthy of the attachment, and whose efforts they come to support in the most glorious of causes – to free them from French bondage, and to establish their National liberty and independence. Upon entering Spain, the Army will wear the Red Cockade in addition to their own, as a compliment to the Spanish Nation.[46]

The march was a hard one, whichever route was taken. The roads were poor and the autumn rains heavy. On 9 November Davy wrote an order to be read to the companies under his command:

> The Major, as yet, has had much reason to be satisfied with the behaviour of the men on the march, and only regrets that the misconduct of a few individuals should have reflected on the character of the whole; he strongly recommends a continuance of that meritorious conduct which has procured them the good wishes of the inhabitants of the towns in Portugal through which they have passed, and doubts not that they will, together with himself, see the necessity of more particularly

44 October to December 1808 Returns, TNA, WO 17/179.

45 P. Haythornthwaite, *Corunna 1809* (Oxford: Osprey, 2001), pp.20 & 23.

46 General Order 25 October 1808, NAM, 1978-11-153.

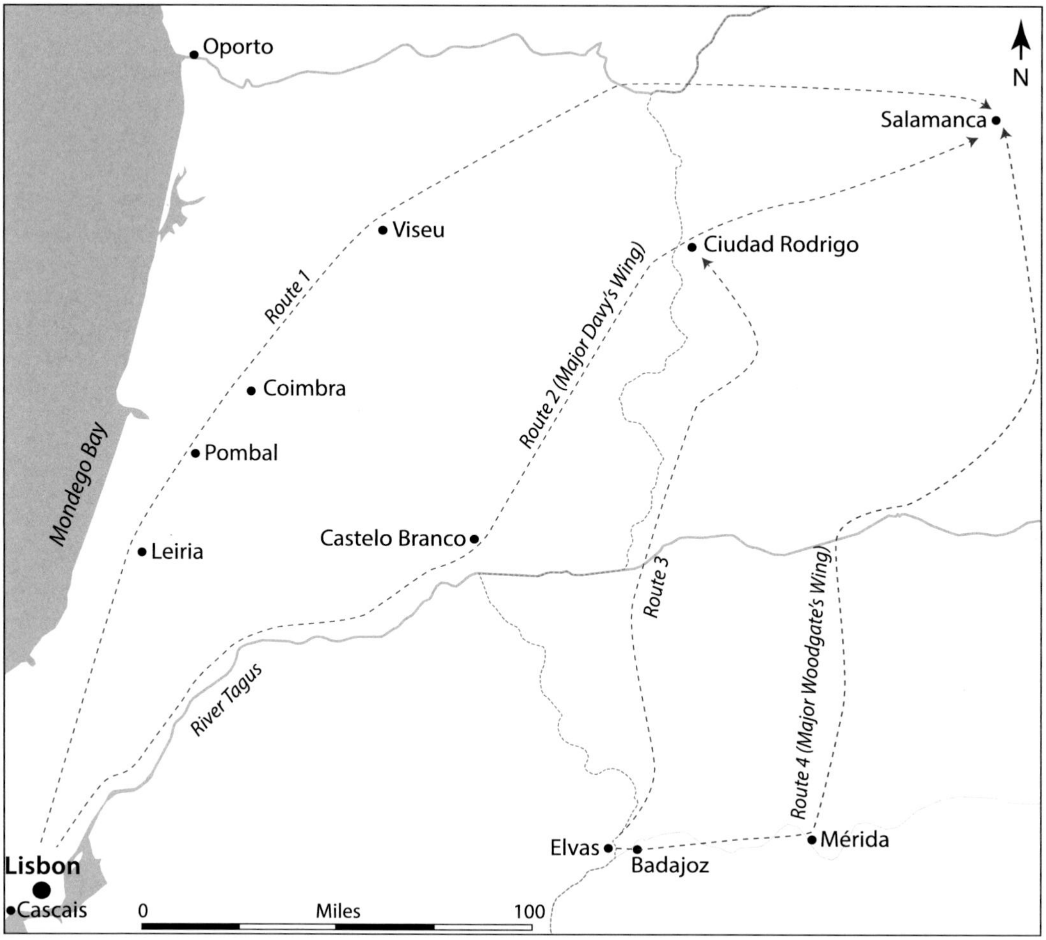

Moore's Advance into Spain, October to December 1808.

> conciliating the good-will of the Spanish nation, into whose territory the battalion is about to march.[47]

On 13th November, at Villa de Pedro Alonzo, he issued another order:

> It is with deep concern that the Major discharges a most painful part of his duty, that of announcing to the battalion that in consequence of the misbehaviour of the five companies detached they have been sent back to Lisbon; under these distressing circumstances the Major calls upon every individual of the regiment to use his utmost efforts to vindicate and maintain the well-merited reputation

47 Quoted in Rigaud, *Celer et Audax*, p.58.

> which the battalion has acquired in the field; and doubts not that with the cordial co-operation of the whole they will be able to do away that disgrace which must otherwise for ever reflect upon the character of the battalion.[48]

Davy added a note that the order be read in German to the men, to ensure it was understood.

By 16 November Davy's companies had reached Salamanca but he ordered that the men be ready to move. However, they were not to go onwards deeper into Spain but had been ordered back to Portugal as well. Captain John McMahon caught up with the battalion and joined on 27 November, and Lieutenant Ignace Franchini joined a day later.[49] Both officers had come from the 3/60th. Franchini had served as a volunteer with the Minorca Regiment in Egypt in 1801, before being commissioned in the 60th in 1802.[50] In 1806, whilst acting as adjutant, he had been stabbed by a prisoner whilst reading out the sentence of a regimental court martial.[51]

The battalion was used to escort the baggage and the sick back to Portugal via Ciudad Rodrigo.[52] Davy wrote his last order from Salamanca on 29 November, and later that same day Assistant Commissary Schaumann had the following encounter:

> Meanwhile a small detachment of the 60th Jägers marched through, escorting a convoy of baggage, women and children. My billet was the last house in the village, and the yard was full of chickens. In a moment there was a wild outcry. The 60th, all Germans, had killed some of the fowls, and taken them away with them. My hosts and some of the muleteers wanted to attack one of the soldiers. With cold-blooded phlegm, however, this man dropped on one knee and raised his musket to his shoulder, whereupon at least twenty of the Spaniards fled for their lives.[53]

In the March 1809 pay lists 14 men from Davy's wing have the comment '14 days no provisions on the march from Salamanca'[54] so in such circumstances plundering might have been somewhat justified but the detachment Schaumann saw would have just left the rest of the army and presumably still had their own rations.

The separation of the two wings of the 5th Battalion and the lack of administrative communication between them makes the pay lists and returns for the six months between October 1808 and March 1809 difficult to interpret with any degree of certainty. The pay lists especially are full of corrections and additional notations. However, what is evident is the very large numbers of desertions during this period.

48 Quoted in Rigaud, *Celer et Audax*, p.59.

49 1 December 1808 Return, TNA, WO 17/179.

50 J.A. Hall, *The Biographical Dictionary of British Officers Killed & Wounded, 1808-1814* (London: Greenhill, 1998), p.212. The Minorca Regiment later became the 97th (The Queen's German) Regiment.

51 Hall, *Biographical Dictionary*, p.213.

52 Oman, *Peninsular*, Vol. I, p.527.

53 A. Schauman, *On the Road with Wellington*, (London: Greenhill, 1999), p.75.

54 March 1809 Pay List, TNA, WO 12/7073.

Table 4: Major Davy's Wing Desertions October–December 1808, by company

	Galiffe's	Salaberry's	McMahon's	Schoedde's	Blassiere's	Total
1/10		2	1	2		5
2/10			2			2
15/10					1	1
18/10			1			1
19/10			1			1
20/10			2	1	2	5
10/11	1					1
12/11			1			1
5/12	1					1
10/12				1		1
13/12				4	2	6
24/12			1			1
Total	2	2	9	8	5	26
Returned	2	0	8	7	2	19

Source: TNA WO 12/7073 24 September to 24 December Pay Lists.

Table 5: Major Woodgate's Wing Desertions October–December 1808, by company

	Hames'	Andrews	Wendt's	Wolff's	Prevost's	Totals
6/10					1	1
15/10	1	2				3
16/10		2	2		1	5
17/10	2				2	4
18/10	5			3		8
19/10		1	1	3	2	7
20/10			1			1
22/10	1	1				2
28/10				1		1
29/10	3		8		7	18
30/10	5	2	3	7	8	25
31/10	8			5	1	14
2/11					2	2
3/11		2			1	3
11/11				1		1
30/11		1				1
7/12	1					1
16/12	1					1
Total	27	11	15	20	25	98
Returned	9	5	2	6	1	23

Source: TNA WO 12/7073 24 September to 24 December Pay Lists.

Tables 4 and 5 break down the desertions in Davy's and Woodgate's wings of the battalion respectively, for the period of October to December 1808. The two tables show a remarkably different pattern and extent of desertions. Table 4 shows a fairly random distribution of desertions with typically one or two men deserting from any company on any given day, with the exception of Captain Schoedde's company on 13 December. The table also shows that all but seven of the 26 eventually returned to the company, either by their own choice or by being apprehended.

Table 5 illustrates a far greater degree of desertion, but also more incidences of mass desertions with a large concentration at the end of October. The figures are even more disturbing when one considers that company strengths averaged around 75, implying that the worst-affected companies lost a quarter, or even a third, of their strength to desertion. The table also shows a smaller proportion of returnees. The desertions decrease dramatically from the start of November and this possibly marks the point that Hope sent them back to Portugal in disgrace, and presumably under greater supervision. Indeed, a return for Woodgate's wing dated 1 November states their location as 'on the road to Cascaes', which is on the coast near Lisbon and where they were to remain for much of the winter. The return lists a total of 324 rank and file, 18 women, six children, five horses and 11 mules. Two men had died, 111 deserted, and four re-joined.[55]

Many more of the deserters from Woodgate's wing returned to the battalion at the start of 1809 as the 25 March 1809 return, the first after communication was re-established between the two wings, shows a total of 118 desertions from Woodgate's companies for the entire period the wings were separated and 109 men returning.[56] This indicates perhaps that either the army was very efficient in capturing deserters, or more likely the deserters did not intend to absent themselves permanently from the battalion but became separated, straggled, or left the column in search of food or plunder, and then got caught up with other units before finding their way back.

Three deserters from the 5th Battalion were captured by a patrol of French dragoons. Their divisional commander, *Général de Division* Armand Lebrun de la Houssaye, informed Napoleon's headquarters:

> Monseigneur, I have the honour to report to your Most Serene Highness that one of my patrols met today on the road to Guadarrama three deserters from the British army who were brought to me and whom I questioned. These deserters, one of whom is a corporal, are French; they had been captured by the English in the battle of Trafalgar, and left the English army on the 13th of this month at Sotrico, the frontier of Portugal. It follows from their report that General Moore occupies Salamanca with 16,000 men, including two squadrons of cavalry. The first posts of the Spanish army are, they say, in Alva, where they saw 300 insurgents. The English army was still making no provision for its retirement to Portugal. The battalion of which these deserters were part, which is the 5th of the 60th regiment of infantry of line, is composed largely of Germans who seize every day the opportunity to pass

55 November 1808 Return, TNA, WO 17/2464.
56 March 1809 Return, TNA, WO 17/179.

> into our ranks. I will conduct these three deserters tomorrow to your Highness' headquarters.[57]

The three were brought before Napoleon on 19 December and gave him vital intelligence on the whereabouts of Moore's army, for which the Emperor rewarded them.[58] Unfortunately, from details given, it is not possible to narrow down who the men were but it is likely that they deserted near Ciudad Rodrigo from Major Davy's wing of the battalion.[59] The only corporal to desert during November and December had been with the battalion since 1799. Seven men deserted on 13 December but of those four re-joined the battalion. Of the remaining three, two were prisoners of war who had joined in late 1806, and the third had joined in April 1806.[60] The men may have embellished their stories to gain better treatment, or the story may have been changed in the retelling. Deserters giving intelligence to the enemy was always a serious risk.

The deserters information, though, was slightly out of date; by the end of November Sir John Moore had learned of the defeats the Spanish had suffered and had decided to retreat, and by 11 December had left Salamanca to march North and meet Baird's force before falling back on Corunna, closely pursued by the French along poor roads and in appalling weather.

Moore was frequently concerned with the behaviour and discipline of the army, even before the rigours of the long retreat. On 11 November he had informed them that a prisoner under sentence of death after a court martial for plunder or robbery would not be pardoned, and no mercy would be shown to others committing similar crimes.[61] In his diary on 14 November Moore wrote:

> I saw the 6th Regiment, as it is one of those to move on with me. Their conduct has been bad, and their officers have been shame-fully negligent. I spoke to them with great severity, and told them I should not take them into Spain; they were unworthy of it. One man had been sentenced to death by a general court-martial, and I ordered him to be executed.[62]

Moore also singled out the 1/6th as being the only exception to the good behaviour of the troops in a letter to Lord Castlereagh dated 24 November.[63] Hope's column reached Salamanca on 3 December but Moore must have already been as aware of the problems in Woodgate's wing of the battalion as Davy was. Discipline across the army began to decline as supply problems led to a lack of rations. On 7 December Moore issued another warning to his troops:

57 D. Balagny, *Campaign de l'Empereur Napoléon en Espagne 1808-1809* (Paris: Berger-Levraut, 1903) Vol. III, p.392.

58 J.W. Fortescue, *A History of the British Army (*London: Macmillan & Co,1906), Vol. VI, p.342.

59 S.G.P. Ward, 'Some Fresh Light on the Corunna Campaign', *Journal of the Society of Army Historical Research*, Vol. XVIII, pp.123.

60 April and December 1806 Pay Lists, TNA, WO 12/7073.

61 General Order, 11 November 1808, NAM, 1978-11-153.

62 Maurice, *Diary of Sir John Moore*, Vol. II, p.278

63 Moore to Castlereagh, 24 November 1808, TNA, WO 1/236 pp.81-2.

> The Commander of the Forces has observed with concern, the extreme bad conduct of the troops of late, at a moment when they are about to enter into contact with the enemy, and when the greatest regularity and the best conduct are most requisite.[64]

He issued similar warnings and admonitions on 30 December and 6 January, long after the 5th Battalion had marched in ignominy for Portugal. Davy and the officers of the companies he directly commanded wrote an appeal to Moore and received the following reply from the adjutant general:

> I have had the honour to lay your letter of 12th instant, and the memorial of the officers of the detachment of 5th Battalion 60th regiment under your command, enclosed therein, before the Commander of the Forces, and I am directed to desire that you will inform them, that his Excellency's motives for sending the detachment back arose from the inexpediency of keeping the battalion divided, and not from any idea of the nature which they apprehend.
>
> While his Excellency laments that circumstances have rendered it necessary to remove the detachment from the present scene of action, he desires that you will observe to the officers, that their station in Portugal is by no means uninteresting, and that their exertions there may be most usefully directed.[65]

On 9 December Brigadier General Henry Clinton, Moore's adjutant general, wrote to Lieutenant General Sir John Craddock, commanding at Lisbon, to inform him of the 5th Battalion's return to Portugal:

> I am directed by Lieut. Genl. Sir John Moore to inform you that 5 Companies of the 5th Battalion 60th Regt. under Major Davy have been ordered to return to Lisbon. The whole Battalion was included by his Royal Highness the Commander in Chief in that part of the Army which was ordered to march into Spain; 5 Companies under Major Woodgate were attached to Lt. Genl. Hope's Division, the remaining Companies marched with Major Genl. Beresford; the Detachment under Major Woodgate deserted so frequently upon approaching the Spanish frontier that upon a report from the Com[andin]g officer representing that he would not be responsible for the Soldiers, many of which had been inlisted out of French Prisons, Lt. Genl. Hope recommended their being ordered back, and Major Woodgate was ordered to return to Lisbon accordingly. Major Davy has lately made a similar representation viz. that there are a considerable proportion of his Men who are only watching an opportunity to desert, and that he does not think the Corps can be depended on near the Enemy. The commander of the Forces has therefore judged it expedient to order them away, and I have no doubt that you will be glad to avail yourself of the first opportunity of getting rid of them.

64 General Order, 7 December 1808, NAM, 1978-11-153.

65 Clinton to Davy, 19 December 1808, quoted in Rigaud, *Celer et Audax*, pp.60-1.

> As Sir John Moore is desirous of drawing to him every Soldier which can be spared, he has authorised Brig. Genl Anstruther who is commanding at Almeyda, or in his absence the Commanding Officer to detain this Detachment of the 60th Regt. in order that the 6th Regt. now in Garrison at Almeyda, may be liberated from that duty and sent forward to the army.
>
> The Adjt. Genl. of the Forces has received a report of the return of the first 5 companies of the 60th Regt., and you will possibly in consequence receive particular instruction in regard to the destination of that Battn.[66]

The 1/6th may have received a reprieve from the ignominy of being left in Portugal but the very existence of the 5th Battalion hung in the balance. In a letter to Craddock dated 10 December Moore referred to the 5 companies at Almeida being relieved by the 97th so they could return to Lisbon and said: 'They would desert if they had stayed here, and are of so bad a Composition that if not disbanded they should be sent to the Colonies'.[67]

The 5th Battalion may have missed Moore's campaign in Spain and the privations of the march to Corunna but the 2/60th was present in the Spanish port. They arrived on the *Leda* transport just after the bulk of Baird's force. With a strength of only 326 men they were assigned to garrison duties in and around Corunna.[68] Assistant Commissary Schaumann saw a detachment of the 2/60th on 11 January 1809 at Betanzos near Corunna, after marching for weeks in harsh conditions and few rations:

> There was also a detachment of the 60th Regiment established here, which all this time had been acting as a bodyguard over the stores. God! How well fed and smart the fellows looked beside us.[69]

Moore's army fought and won the Battle of Corunna on 16 January, but Moore was fatally wounded. The last troops were evacuated by the Royal Navy on the 18th.

The 5th Battalion, still divided into the two wings, spent the winter escorting supplies, the sick and invalids. In January the battalion was under orders to proceed to Cadiz but it is probable that Moore's defeat at Corunna and the continuing threat of French invasion meant that every unit was needed, no matter how untrustworthy, and so the battalion stayed in Portugal.[70]

Davy's wing moved from Lamego in central Portugal, west to Oporto, and then south to Pombal. The January and February returns list several officers leading detachments of men on escort duty down to Lisbon but some may also have gone north to Moore's army.[71] On 2 January Schaumann was at Villafranca del Bierzo in Spain, 150 miles north of Lamego in Portugal where Davy compiled the 5th Battalion's 1 January return. Schaumann and a KGL

66 Clinton to Craddock, 9 December 1808, TNA WO 1/232 pp.89-90.

67 Moore to Craddock, 10 December 1808, TNA, WO 1/232 pp.89-90.

68 2/60th November 1808 Return TNA, WO 17/179.

69 Schaumann, *On the Road*, p.132.

70 General View of the State of the British Forces in Portugal, January 20, 1809, TNA WO 1/232.

71 1 January, 1 February and 24 February 1809 Returns, TNA, WO 17/179.

Hussar officer were quartered in a room above what he describes as 'thirty Jägers of the 60th Regiment':

> But when I awoke one morning it was to find that some of the Jägers who were lodged below, and who had marched before dawn that day, had crept up to our room before leaving, and while I was asleep, had not only robbed me of one of my pistols, but had also taken the sausage, a bottle of rum, my biscuits and my gloves, together with the provisions and many other things belonging to the officer of the 3rd Hussars who shared the room with me – a discovery which upset us both very much.[72]

Schaumann's narrative is sometimes less than reliable and it is possible that he misidentified or misremembered the jägers' unit. However, he had served with the army for some time and was very familiar with the units of the KGL, the only other German troops in the Peninsula at the time, apart from the 2/60th at Corunna. Most of the 60th wore the standard red coats of the line infantry, but the light companies wore green jackets with white breeches, instead of the blue pantaloons of the 5th Battalion, and so might have been thought of as jägers by Schaumann if they had been escorting supplies from the port to the army.

Woodgate's wing remained at Cascais on the coast near Lisbon, with 97 returned deserters confined as prisoners on board the *Rosina* transport.[73] On 6 March the two wings of the battalion came together at Belem, and Davy could finally begin to address its problems.

On 7 March Davy reported to Brigadier General Sontag, commandant of Lisbon:

> I have the honour to acquaint you that the five companies of the 5th Battalion 60th regiment, under the command of Major Woodgate, have yesterday joined the other five companies here. It is my duty to state to you that from immediately after the action of Roleia on the 17th of August last the battalion has been divided into detachments which were attached to the several brigades of the army, and have thus gone through the arduous service of riflemen during the campaign, and since that period the battalion has never been united.
>
> The arms, accoutrements, appointments, clothing, &c. have suffered materially by the nature of the service peculiar to light troops; and the interior economy has necessarily been deranged by so many detachments.
>
> To establish that regularity without which no regiment can serve with credit, and to supply those deficiencies which have taken place. I think it necessary to request that some time may be allowed before the battalion is sent on actual service. I shall not lose a moment to effect these objects, but I think one month, or at least three weeks, will be required.[74]

72 Schaumann, *On the Road*, p.112.

73 February and March 1809 Returns, TNA, WO 17/2462.

74 Davy to Sontag, 7 March 1809, quoted in Rigaud, *Celer et Audax*, pp.65.

The Duke of York had been informed of the disgrace of the battalion and had issued the following order to Lieutenant General Sir John Craddock, commander of the forces in Portugal, on 7 December:

> I have it in command from the Commander-in-Chief to desire that you will be pleased to cause such men of the 5th Battalion of the 60th regiment as may have been taken from prison-ships, and are considered unfit to be trusted, to be selected and sent to England by the earliest opportunity in order to their being placed in the rifle companies of the same regiment serving on other stations; and you will be pleased to cause an accurate description return of such men to be sent with them.[75]

Craddock's military secretary, Lieutenant Colonel Thomas Reynell, passed the orders on to Davy:

> The Commander of the Forces has directed me to transmit, for your information and guidance, the enclosed copy of a letter from the secretary to his Royal Highness the Commander-in-Chief directing a selection to be immediately made from the battalion under your orders of such men as were taken from French prison-ships, and whom you may consider as subjects not to be confided in, in order that they may be sent to England to be disposed of in the rifle companies of the 60th regiment serving in other stations.
>
> You will be pleased to take the earliest practicable measures to obey the instructions of H. R. H., and as soon as you have selected the men that come under the description specified you will immediately transmit to Sir John Craddock a descriptive list of them conformably to the latter paragraph of Lieut.-Colonel Gordon's letter; when his Excellency will furnish you with orders respecting the mode in which they are to be conveyed to England.[76]

On 20 March Davy reported back to Reynell:

> I have the honour to acquaint you that agreeably to the commands of the 7th Dec. 1808 of H. R.H. the Commander-in-Chief, communicated to me through you by letter bearing date 8th January 1809, forty-four men of suspected character have been selected, and sent on board ships to be conveyed to England.
>
> The number of deserters, prisoners on board ships, amounts to 110, amongst which by Major Woodgate's report (ninety-three of them belonging to the companies detached under his command on 21st Sept. 1808) there are some he has reason to believe of good character, who may have been misled by the bad conduct of others; but in order to hold forth to the battalion a striking example (at this moment so particularly necessary) of the consequences attendant upon desertion,

75 Gordon to Craddock, 7 December 1808, quoted in Rigaud, *Celer et Audax*, pp.64-5.

76 Reynell to Davy, 8 January 1809, quoted in, Rigaud, *Celer et Audax*, pp.63-4.

> I have refrained from making any application to his Excellency to have them given up to the regiment.[77]

The March return stated the numbers of men being sent back to Britain as 56 invalids and 44 'suspected men' and 110 deserters, including eight men who had been court martialled for desertion in January at Lisbon and who had variously been sentenced to flogging, transportation as felons, or to be shot, but who had been pardoned.[78] The deserters were drawn mainly from Woodgate's wing of the battalion whilst the 'suspected men' were more evenly distributed, but with slightly more coming from Davy's wing, perhaps because the untrustworthy men in Woodgate's wing had already deserted. The March to June 1809 pay lists notes 142 men as 'Sent to England' with an additional notation 'to 2nd Battn. 25th March' indicating that the deserters and suspected men were transferred to the 2/60th. Forty-five men have the remark 'sent to England and invalided' next to their names. Six other men, including three sergeants, were also marked as being sent to England, perhaps as part of the escort under Lieutenant Charles Sawatsky and Ensign John Sprecher de Bernegg.[79]

Lewis Butler in *The Annals of the King's Royal Rifle Corps* assumes that the former prisoners of war that deserted had been enlisted from Junot's army in Portugal.[80] However, there is no evidence in the returns or the pay lists of any recruits joining the battalion between the landing at Mondego Bay and the following spring. The prisoners of war referred to and selected as 'suspected men' instead joined the battalion in late 1806, and possibly via the Foreign Depot also. Davy's own letter confirms that the men he tried to recruit from the Swiss regiments went instead to the 2/60th.[81] Not all the men who deserted can be positively identified in the surviving records as former prisoners of war. Some had served with the battalion for many years, for example Daniel Bickardy who deserted on 19 October had joined the Lowenstein Chasseurs in 1795 and was one of the original members of the battalion, as was Jakob Krach. Epphrain Furbmann had joined the battalion in 1802 as had John Jacob. Several more had joined from the Walloon Guards in 1799.[82] Not all former prisoners of war were weeded out from the battalion as many had already proved themselves worthy of trust and been promoted, and many would go on to serve in the battalion for many more years.

Over 500 men of the battalion deserted during the entirety of the Peninsular campaign,[83] however many of those would have soon returned to the ranks, one way or another. The desertion rate was usually just one or two per month but there were three other periods of high levels; during the retreats of 1812; when the army entered the Pyrenees; and after the peace in 1814. These are all periods when the army as a whole suffered peaks in desertion

77 Davy to Reynell, 20 March 1809, quoted in Rigaud, *Celer et Audax*, pp.66-7.

78 March 1809 Return, TNA, WO 17/179; Register of General Courts Martial Abroad, WO 90/1, p.68.

79 March to June 1809 Pay Lists, TNA, WO 12/7073.

80 Butler, *Annals*, Vol. II, p.65.

81 Rigaud, *Celer et Audax*, p.69.

82 Periods of Service 5/60th, June 1806, TNA, WO 25/1008.

83 Based on the regimental returns for the 5th Battalion July 1808 to June 1814, TNA, WO 17/178-80, WO 17/264, & WO 17/279,

rates but the rates in the 5th Battalion, and other foreign units, peaked more than in British and Irish units.

Many of the men who deserted got away with it; Geoffrey Uhl, captured aboard the *Armide* frigate on his way to the West Indies deserted in 1811, returned to the 26e Ligne, and in 1814 joined the elite grenadier company.[84] However, there was always the risk of being taken prisoner by the allies again. In June 1809 a court martial was convened at Coimbra to try Private Dietrich Gerlach who deserted on 31 January 1809 on the road from Lamego to Oporto. He entered French service but was captured 17 May. He was found guilty and executed by firing squad in front of the whole 5th Battalion and a company of each other regiment present in Coimbra.[85] Private Christian Nunkerchen was similarly tried for desertion and shot in July 1811,[86] and Michael Perlie and Samuel Leydell in October of the same year.[87] In January 1812, when the fortress of Ciudad Rodrigo was taken, 18 deserters were recaptured; three from the 95th, one from the Royal Horse Artillery, four from the 52nd, two from the 88th, one from the 23rd, one from the 43rd, one from the KGL, one from the 7th, as well as Privates Joseph Lambrecht, John Engle, and Conrad Eylich from the 5th Battalion of the 60th. All were tried, found guilty and ordered to be shot.[88] William Grattan of the 88th was present as the regiments gathered for the execution of all the men, including Curtis and Mangin of his own battalion:

> At eight o'clock the division was under arms, and formed in a hollow square of small dimensions; in the centre of it was the Provost-Marshal, accompanied by his followers, with pick-axes, spades, shovels, and all the necessary etceteras for marking out and forming the graves into which the unfortunate delinquents were to be deposited as soon as they received the last and most imposing of military honours that of being shot to death! In a few moments afterwards the rolling of muffled drums the usual accompaniment of the death-march was heard, and the soldiers who guarded the prisoners were soon in sight. The division observed a death-like silence as the prisoners defiled round the inside of the square; every eye was turned towards them; but Mangin, from his well-known good character, was an object of general solicitude. The solitary sound of the muffled drums at last died away into silence; the guard drew up in the centre of the square, and the prisoners had, for the last time, a view of their companions from whom they had deserted, and of their colours which they had forsaken; but if their countenances were a just index of their minds, they seemed to repent greatly the act they had committed! The three men of the 60th were in their shirts, as was also Mangin of the 88th, but Curtis wore the 'old red rag,' most likely from necessity, having, in all human probability, *no shirt to die in* – a circumstance by no means rare with the soldiers of the Peninsular army.

84 26e régiment d'infanterie de ligne. An XII-1815. SHD/GR 21 YC 239 26e régiment d'infanterie de ligne, 16 germinal an XII [6 avril 1804]-19 janvier 1806 (matricules 1 à 3 096), at http://www.memoiredeshommes.sga.defense.gouv.fr, (accessed 7 September 2018).

85 Duke of Wellington, *General Orders Spain & Portugal*, (London: Egerton, 1811-13} Vol. I, p.49.

86 Wellington, *General Orders*, Vol. III, p.138.

87 Wellington, *General Orders*, Vol. III, p.220.

88 Wellington, *General Orders*, Vol. IV, p.31.

> The necessary preliminaries, such as reading the crime and finding the sentence, had finished, when the Adjutant-General announced the pardon granted to Mangin, who was immediately conducted away, and placed at a short distance in rear of the division; the rest staggered onward to the spot where their graves had been dug, and having been placed on their knees, their legs hanging over the edge of the grave, a bandage was tied over their eyes. The Provost-Marshal then, with a party of twenty musketeers, their firelocks cocked, and at the recover, silently moved in front of the prisoners until he reached to within five paces of them, and then giving two motions of his hand the one to present, the other to fire the four men fell into the pit prepared to receive them. The three Germans were dead indeed they were nearly so before they were fired at! and if the state of their nerves was a criterion to go by, a moderate-sized popgun would have been sufficiently destructive to have finished their earthly career; but Curtis sprang up, and, with one of his jaws shattered and hanging down upon his breast, presented a horrid spectacle. Every one seemed to be electrified, the Provost-Marshal excepted; he, I suppose, was well accustomed to such sights, for, without any ceremony, he walked up to Curtis, and with the most perfect composure levelled a huge instrument (in size between a horse-pistol and blunderbuss) at his head, which blew it nearly off his shoulders, and he fell upon the bodies of the Germans without moving a muscle.[89]

The whole parade then marched past the grave and were given the command 'eyes right' so they could see the consequences of desertion.

The weeding out of the deserters and the suspected men in March 1809 severely reduced the strength of the 5th Battalion. The return of 24 April, completed at Pombal in northern Portugal, gives the battalion's strength as 49 sergeants, 47 corporals 15 buglers and 571 privates – a total of 682 excluding officers and staff, and 322 less than had landed at Mondego Bay the previous summer. Nineteen men had died during the winter. One sergeant and three men were still with the baggage at Belem. One sergeant was attached to Paymaster Gilbert and one private with Adjutant de Gilse. Gilbert was noted as 'being suspended from the functions of his office'. In April Davy wrote to Horse Guards that Gilbert was 'little qualified for his situation as paymaster'.[90] Captain Andrews, and then Captain Schoedde, acted as paymasters until Henry Biggs was appointed in 1812.[91] Fifty-seven officers and men were sick. Six officers were variously employed with the staff, including Lieutenant Hoffman who was then employed as a draftsman in the department of the quartermaster general in England. Lieutenant William Linstow was doing duty with the Loyal Lusitanian Legion, a volunteer corps made up mainly of Portuguese emigres and formed in Britain in July 1808. Seven officers were still on leave.[92]

Early in 1809 the Spanish suffered several defeats at the hands of the French and the evacuation of Moore's army had left *Marechal* Soult able to invade Portugal. By the end of March Oporto was back in French hands. Craddock's small force could not defend the entire

89 W. Grattan, *Adventures with the Connaught Rangers* (London: Edward Arnold, 1902), pp.172-4.
90 Entry in index to out-letters, 5/60th, TNA, WO 2/13, pp.289.
91 Willoughby Wallace, *Regimental Chronicle*, p.171.
92 March 1809 Return, TNA, WO 17/179.

country; on 1 January he only had 8,475 rank and file present and fit for duty.[93] Lieutenant General William Carr Beresford was placed in command of the Portuguese army and given the rank of *Marechal.* He began to organise and train fresh Portuguese units, many under British officers. During the spring British reinforcements began to arrive, raising the army's strength to 13,947 rank and file present and fit for duty by 1 April.[94] The 5th Battalion was divided again into two halves, one with Major General Cotton's brigade and one with Major General Mackenzie's.[95] Craddock felt confident enough to advance on the French but Sir Arthur Wellesley returned to take command and immediately began to make his own plans to drive the enemy out of Portugal again. In the coming campaign the 5th Battalion would be afforded every opportunity to repair the damage to their reputation.

93 January 1809 Return, TNA, WO 17/2464.

94 April 1809 Return, TNA, WO 17/2464.

95 List of brigades and stations dated 19 March 1809, TNA, WO 17/2464.

14

Oporto

Prior to taking up command again in Portugal Wellesley had submitted a memorandum to the British government arguing that just the presence a British Army in Portugal would aid Spanish resistance against the French. He also said that the Portuguese army could be rebuilt and retrained to effectively assist British forces, and that the defence of Portugal should be reorganised against any future French attempt at invasion.[1] These would be his long term aims but in the short term he had to choose which of two French *marechaux* to tackle first; Victor or Soult.

The French had 275,000 troops in Spain and Portugal: of these approximately 70,000 were sick and 35,000 were protecting French supply lines from Spanish guerrillas. The rest were mostly grouped into corps of around 15,000 to 22,000 men operating against the much smaller Spanish armies around the country. The two corps that concerned Wellesley were *Marechal* Soult's II Corps in Oporto, numbering around 20,000 men, and *Marechal* Victor's I Corps, of around 22,000 men, which was in the Tagus valley in Spain but threatening to invade southern Portugal.[2] Although he was vastly outnumbered, Wellesley believed that the French could not concentrate their strength against his army without surrendering control of large areas of Spain, and that he could achieve local superiority against the scattered French forces. Wellesley was tempted to link up with the Spanish army under *Capitán General* Cuesta and attack Victor but such coordination would have taken time. Soult's occupation of Oporto was the more immediate threat to Lisbon and dislodging him before attacking Victor made greater political sense for Wellesley, who had to ensure the support of his Portuguese ally.

Sir John Craddock had already marched the majority of the allied army as far Leiria, 90 miles north of Lisbon and towards Oporto, when he learned that Wellesley was replacing him on 24 April. Some of the more recently arrived reinforcements were still at Lisbon. Only five of the British infantry battalions in Portugal had fought with Wellesley at Vimeiro and the majority of the rest were inexperienced and understrength second battalions unexpectedly ordered for overseas service, containing many men who had recently transferred from the Militia. The army was also very short of cavalry with only four regiments, plus a

1 Esdaile, *Peninsular*, p.193.
2 A.W. Field, *Talavera* (Barnsley: Pen & Sword, 2006), p.5.

few smaller detachments. Scattered remnants of Sir John Moore's army who had been left behind, or who had been recovering in hospital, were grouped together in two battalions of detachments, one of which included a small company of riflemen from the 95th.[3]

Before handing over to Wellesley, Sir John Craddock had reorganised his army into a larger number of smaller brigades and the 5th Battalion was briefly united in Major General Hill's brigade. However, in a general order on 4 May, Wellesley made some adjustments to Craddock's organisation; integrating Portuguese battalions into the brigades, detaching five companies of the 5th Battalion into brigades that had no riflemen, and transferring the 1/3rd Foot to Hill to compensate. Wellesley also specified that:

> The light infantry companies belonging to, and the riflemen attached to each brigade of infantry, are to be formed together, on the left of the brigade, under the command of a Field-officer or Captain of light infantry of the brigade, to be fixed upon by the officer who commands it. Upon all occasions in which the brigade may be formed in line, or in column, when the brigade will be formed for the purpose of opposing an enemy, the light infantry companies and riflemen will be of course be in the front, flanks, or rear, according to the circumstances of the ground, and the nature of the operation to be performed. On all other occasions, the light infantry companies are to be considered as attached to their battalions, with which they are to be quartered or encamped, and solely under the command of the Commanding Officer of the battalion to which they belong.[4]

Wellesley was ensuring that each brigade had a large and flexible force of skirmishers at the disposal of the brigade commander.

In another general order on 6 May, Wellesley also wrote:

> The Commander of the Forces recommends the companies of the 5th Battalion of the 60th regiment to the particular care and attention of the general officers commanding the brigades of infantry to which they are attached; they will find them to be most useful, active, and brave troops in the field, and that they will add essentially to the strength of their brigades.
>
> Major Davy will continue to superintend the economy and discipline of the whole battalion, and for this purpose will remain with that part of the army which will be most convenient to him, with a view to that object.[5]

The battalion headquarters and five companies were to be attached to Major General Tilson's brigade but Davy had ensured that he obtained Wellesley's permission for him to attach himself to wherever he felt he was most needed.

The form used to record the battalion's pay changed in June. Instead of each company being recorded separately, all the men of each rank were listed together, with a number beside their names indicating 'No. of the Companies in which paid or borne'. In his history

3 Oman, *Peninsular War*, Vol.II, pp.313-4.

4 General Order, 4 May 1809, quoted in, Wellington, *Supplementary Despatches*, Vol. VI. p.251.

5 General Order, 5 May 1809, quoted in, Wellington, *Supplementary Despatches*, Vol. VI. p.253.

of the 5th Battalion, *Celer et Audax*, Gibbes Rigaud states the companies of the battalion were numbered as follows:

Galiffe's	1
McMahon's	2
Andrews'	3
Blassiere's	4
de Wend's	5
Hames'	6
Prevost's	7
Wolff's	8
Schoedde's	9
de Salaberry's	10[6]

However, the pay list for June makes it clear that they were numbered as follows:

Galiffe's	1
Salaberry's	2
Andrews'	3
McMahon's	4
Hames'	5
de Wend's	6
Schoedde's	7
Blassiere's	8
Wolff's	9
Prevost's	10[7]

The numbering in the pay list matches the seniority of the captains of the battalion.[8] Lewis Butler in volume II of *The Annals of the KRRC* repeats Rigaud's numbering and often refers to the companies by number from that point.[9] In a note he does add that the numbering changed during the campaign, but whilst many of the captains of the companies changed the numbering seems to have remained the same. The pay lists continue to show the same pattern of numbering but the numbers are not used in other documents, such as the casualty lists, where the companies continue to be referred to by the name of their captain, even if that captain was not present with the battalion at the time. Over the course of the Peninsular War there was a significant turnover of officers in the battalion and rather than refer to the companies by their captain referring to them by number will ensure greater brevity and clarity. When appropriate, whenever a member of the battalion is referred to, the number of their company will be indicated in parentheses.

The organisation of the infantry brigades that Wellesley formed was:

6 Rigaud, *Celer et Audax*, p.106.

7 Duplicate Certificates of Officers, June 1809 Pay List, TNA, WO 12/7073.

8 Willoughby Wallace, *Regimental Chronicle*, pp.58-9.

9 Butler, *Annals*, Vol II, p.103.

Guards Brigade – Brigadier General H. Campbell
1/Coldstream Guards, 1/3rd Guards & No. 5 company 5/60th.
1st Brigade – Major General Hill
1/3rd, 2/48th, 2/66th, & No. 6 company 5/60th.
2nd Brigade – Major General Mackenzie
2/24th, 2/31st, 3/27th, 1/45th.
3rd Brigade – Major General Tilson
2/87th 1/88th, & Nos. 1, 2, 3, 7, and 8 companies 5/60th.
4th Brigade – Brigadier General Sontag
97th, 2nd Battalion of Detachments, 2/16th Portuguese, & No. 10 company 5/60th.
5th Brigade – Brigadier General A. Campbell
2/7th, 2/53rd, 1/10th Portuguese, & No. 4 company 5/60th.
6th Brigade – Brigadier General Stewart
29th, 1st Battalion of Detachments, 1/16th Portuguese.
7th Brigade – Brigadier General Cameron
2/9th, 2/83rd, 2/10th Portuguese, & No. 9 company 5/60th.
KGL – Major General Murray
1st KGL, 2nd KGL, 5th KGL, 7th KGL.[10]

Major Woodgate would oversee the five companies in Tilson's brigade. Many of the company commanders were still absent; de Salaberry and Prevost were still serving with de Rottenburg's and Sir George Prevost's staffs respectively, and Captain McMahon had snapped his Achilles tendon mounting his horse on 15 April and was in Lisbon recovering.[11]

After the difficulties that the battalion had faced being divided under Sir John Moore's command Davy was at pains to ensure similar problems did not reoccur and issued a string of orders:

Regimental Orders.

Coimbra, May 5th, 1809.

1. The detachment under command of Major Woodgate, and the officers commanding companies attached to the several brigades, will send all returns and reports to their respective brigadiers. Duplicates of the weekly states, and monthly returns, together with the muster rolls, to be sent in sufficient time to the commanding officer to enable him to. make out the general returns at the stated periods, addressed to 'The Adjutant-General's Office at Head-quarters,' by those companies which have immediate communication with the commanding officer.

   The daily states of those companies within the reach of the commanding officer will be sent to him as usual.

10 Rigaud, *Celer et Audax*, pp.80-1, C. Oman, *Wellington's Army* (London: Edward Arnold, 1913) p.342.
11 Rigaud, *Celer et Audax*, p.81.

2. All standing, or such orders as may be given during the division of the battalion, must be strictly and rigidly executed, as the commanding officer will frequently visit the companies attached to the several brigades, and expects to find no deviation from them.
3. All requisitions must be made through the respective brigades, and reported by the first opportunity, as well as all extraordinaries, to the commanding officer,
4. The Major trusts that every officer of the battalion will use his best endeavours, in conjunction with himself, to keep up the interior economy and discipline of the battalion under circumstances in which he is well aware there are great difficulties to be encountered; but he trusts their zeal and attention will surmount them.
5. Ensign Fürst will act as adjutant to Major Woodgate's detail.
6. Lance-Serjeant Schwalbach to be attached to Captain de Wend's company.[12]

Corporal Schwalbach (No. 2) had returned to the battalion after doing duty as Brigadier General Fane's orderly, and then being in the general hospital. Davy had appointed him an acting, or lance, sergeant. The 5th Battalion also had three men of 2/60th attached who had been left behind in Portugal when their battalion was evacuated from Corunna.[13]

On 5 May Davy wrote to Major Woodgate:

> As the head-quarters of the battalion for the present is attached to one of the companies brigaded with the army, you will be pleased to consider yourself as commanding officer of the detachment of the five companies of the battalion now with you and act accordingly.
>
> You will of course send in the regular returns, as required by general orders, at the stated periods to your brigadier, and duplicates of the same to me, addressed to the 'Adjutant-General's Office,' in sufficient time to enable me to make out the general states, &c. of the regiment.
>
> You will of course also comply with His Majesty's regulations concerning the mustering of the companies; or, if divided, enjoin the several officers commanding companies to do the same, the muster rolls to be of course transmitted to me.
>
> I have not been able, with every representation to Sir A. Wellesley himself, to procure more than a certain proportion of pay upon the estimates of the current month, of which Captain Andrews will be the bearer, and distribute it agreeably to my directions.
>
> Ensign Fürst will also accompany Captain Andrews, and will, for the present, do the duty of adjutant to the detachment (Lieutenant Franchini's presence being absolutely required with his company). It will also be necessary for you to appoint an officer to act as quarter-master should you deem it requisite. Mr. Kemmeter will do duty as adjutant with me.

12 Rigaud, *Celer et Audax*, pp.81-2.

13 'Statement of Sums Added in annexed General State…', June 1809 Pay List, TNA, WO 12/7073.

> You will be pleased to use your utmost endeavours to keep the clothing as much in repair as its condition will admit, and see the men as much as possible provided with necessaries. I am aware that you will have, as well as myself, considerable difficulties to encounter in the situation in which the battalion has been placed since its landing in Portugal, almost unprecedented in the army; but I doubt not that you will, as well as myself, use your utmost endeavours for the best of the battalion and the service.
>
> Referring to the authority already given by the adjutant-general, I conceive you to be entitled to draw the allowances for the acting adjutant and quarter-master of your detachment should you deem it necessary to have officers in those situations.[14]

Wellesley decided to advance quickly on Oporto, whilst sending Beresford with a mixed British and Portuguese force of 5,800 men to cross the River Douro at Lamego, to cut off Soult's line of retreat.[15] The five companies of the 5th Battalion in Tilson's brigade marched with Beresford on 6 May. Beresford's column had reached Lamego by the 10th after joining up with further Portuguese troops. Some of Beresford's Portuguese units fought a small action with a French force under Loison on 10 May and then continued to drive the French rearguard back until by 12 May Beresford was at Amarante, on Soult's line of retreat.

Meanwhile, the rest of Wellesley's army marched from Coimbra towards Oporto on 7 May. In their way was a small French cavalry division commanded by *Général de Brigade* Franceschi, supported by one infantry regiment and some artillery. Wellesley sent Hill's and Cameron's brigades to turn Franceschi's flank by crossing a wide lagoon, which was part of a river estuary. Boats had been gathered at Aveiro and were to sail to Ovar, around 15 miles further north and far behind Franceschi's position. One French regiment, the 31e Légère was stationed near to Ovar, and an infantry division lay not far behind Franceschi's cavalry at Grijó.

Hill's orders from Wellesley were as follows:

> You will receive from the Quarter-Master-General a paper fully explanatory to you of all that it is intended you should perform; to which I have only to add – first, that you will find the boats ready for you at Aveiro, and will have to get boatmen only, in which Douglas, whom I send to you, will assist you; secondly, that I mean you should bring to to-morrow night in such a place as that the enemy cannot discover you, in that part of the river or lake of which the banks are swampy; thirdly, that you should land your light infantry below the town, where it is certain the enemy never is, in order to secure the unmolested disembarkation of the remainder of your corps at Ovar, where it is possible the enemy may have a small patrole.
>
> I recommend you to cook a day's provisions at Aveiro, for your men for the 10th, and to refresh your men at Ovar, while you will wait there to learn the progress of General Cotton, with his cavalry.

14 Davy to Woodgate 5 May 1809, quoted in Rigaud, *Celer et Audax*, pp.82-4.

15 Oman, *Peninsular War*, Vol. II, p.318. Details of the advance to Oporto are also taken from Oman.

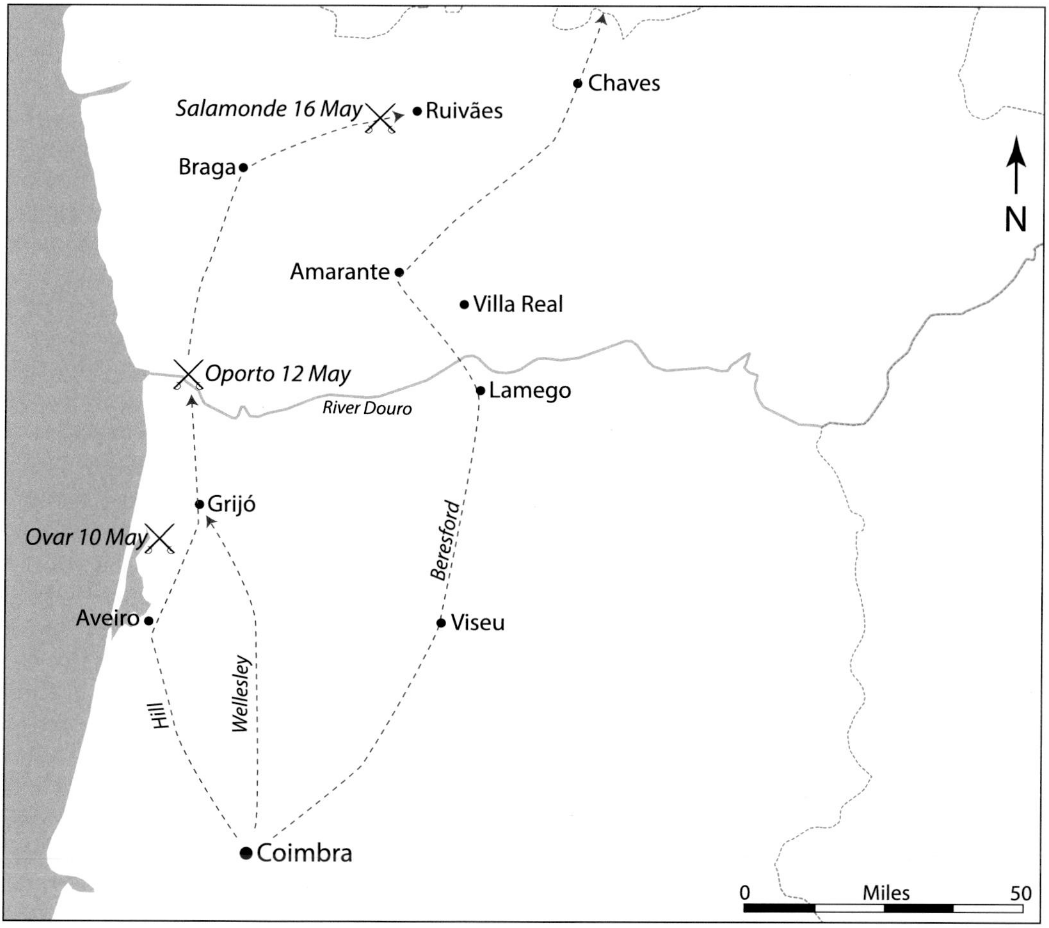

The Oporto Campaign May 1809.

> Having communicated with that General, you will then move from Ovar by the road which leads from Ovar to Feira, till that road meets the great road from Coimbra to Oporto. You will halt there till you will be joined by the cavalry. My intention is to push the enemy as far as I can on the 10th, even into Oporto, if possible.[16]

On the morning of 10 May the British cavalry advance guard, after a confused night march, made contact with Franceschi's pickets and then were brought to a halt by the rest of his division, drawn up and prepared for battle. Outnumbered, the British cavalry waited for infantry and artillery support. The delays allowed the French cavalry to retreat, after some small skirmishes, to Grijó.

16 Wellesley to Hill 8 May 1809, quoted in Sidney, *Lord Hill*, pp.92-3.

Sufficient boats were at Aveiro to ferry 1,500 men of Hill's brigade, including No. 6 company commanded by Captain de Wend, up to Ovar where they landed early on the morning of the 10th. Learning that Franceschi's division had not been driven back as early as had been planned, and that French infantry were nearby Hill stayed at Ovar, sending the boats back for Cameron's brigade. At midday Hill's pickets were driven in as three battalions of the French 31e Légère advanced towards him. Three companies of French *voltigeurs* skirmished with the British during the afternoon until Hill learned that Franceschi's division was retreating, pursued by the British cavalry, and he ordered an advance from Ovar. The French infantry retreated in good order back to Grijó.[17] No. 6 company lost Private Christian Kalck, killed in action, on 10 May. Kalck, a former Walloon Guard, had joined the battalion at Surinam in August 1799.[18]

On 11 May Wellesley's force advanced on the French at Grijó. He judged the French position to be a strong one and, after a brief skirmish, decided to outflank the French rather than commit to a frontal attack. Brigades were sent around to the right and left. Hill also advanced from Ovar on the left. The French had little option but to retreat, closely – and somewhat recklessly – pursued by the British cavalry. After several small rearguard actions the French crossed a bridge of boats over the River Douro into the city of Oporto. As soon as they were across, the bridge was blown up leaving the British on the other side of the wide and fast flowing river. Soult had already ordered that all barges and boats were safely moored on the far bank so the British could not cross. The French commander felt secure behind the natural defences of the river. He knew Beresford was threatening his flank but he thought that he could hold the city for several days, whilst he arranged his retreat back into Spain.

Wellesley's troops spent the night of 11 May in the fields, orchards and vineyards around Villa Nova. In the morning Wellesley looked across the 300 yard wide river at Oporto from a rocky outcrop called the Serra, which was on a bend in the river. On the opposite bank was a large building known as the seminary. It stood alone on another rocky hill and was surrounded by a high wall. Wellesley could see French troops in the town to his left but the area to his right and around the seminary appeared quiet. News had already reached Wellesley that a ferry that the French had sunk four miles upstream had been repaired and he had sent Major General Murray with a small force to cross there. One of Wellesley's intelligence officers, Colonel Waters, met a barber who told him of a small boat that had been missed by the French and with the help of some locals had managed to cross the river and bring back several large wine barges.

Wellesley immediately ordered troops from Hill's brigade to cross and secure the seminary and placed guns on the Serra to cover them. Two companies of the 1/3rd Foot were amongst the first to cross,[19] but it is likely that de Wend's No. 6 company also crossed in the first few boats. The troops got to the far side without being spotted, landed safely and then made their way up a path to the seminary. They occupied the building and closed its large iron gate. The boats then began to ferry the rest of the 1/3rd across.

17 Oman, *Peninsular War*, Vol. II, p.327.

18 June 1809 Pay List, TNA, WO 12/7073; Periods of Service 5/60th, June 1806, WO 25/1008.

19 T. Bunbury, *Reminiscences of a Veteran* (Uckfield: The Naval & Military Press Ltd., 2009), Vol.I, p.30.

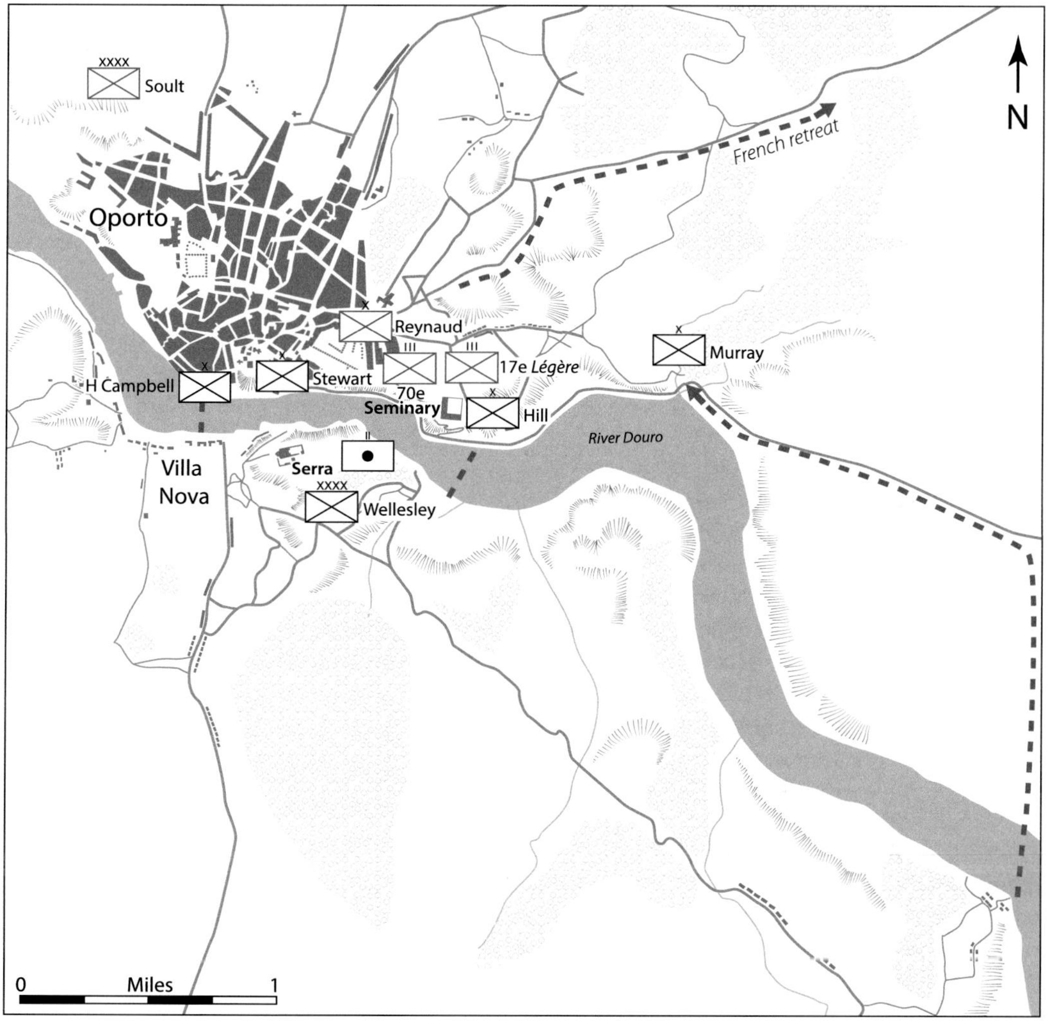

The Battle of Oporto, 12 May 1809. Sources: Lipscombe, *Atlas* & Wyld, *Maps & Plans*.

Ensign Thomas Bunbury of the 1/3rd's light company had time to refresh himself with wine and cake, before the closest French unit, the 17e Légère, responded to the British presence:

> The advancing French made a great noise when marching – every small party having a drummer thumping away with all his might, and against these poor devils of drummers our fire was principally directed. We shot several, and our opponents did not seem to get on well without them, and as they were driven before us, our officers armed themselves with the French muskets. All this was well enough, as long as we were going ahead, and we had very few of our party hurt – but at length we were brought to a stand still by a party of the enemy taking post behind the

> walls of an enclosure, to oppose our further progress. In our advance we had been reinforced and had now about twelve or thirteen men; amongst them was a most singular character; a German rifleman, who could not or would not understand a word of English. The fellow was a dead shot, but he would not waste his ammunition on trifles, and we could not get him to fire unless his victim was in a situation to allow of his going out to plunder him. The men were in the meantime anxious to blaze away, in order to give our opponents an idea that the party was more numerous, but our friend , when remonstrated with, would cooly turn his quid of tobacco and look on, shaking his stupid head. His conduct was very provoking, and we were almost tempted to lay violent hands upon him.
>
> With some loss we reached a cottage, the garden of which was walled round. The door was barred in such a manner as to prevent our admission, and we were, therefore obliged to dispense with this citadel, and confine ourselves to defending the garden wall. For a time we continued to beat back every attacking force that came against it. At length it became evident that our party, from its advanced and isolated position, was attracting considerable attention from the enemy, who, to the number of sixty men, accompanied by a large Newfoundland dog, seemed determined to drive us from the garden. We inflicted a heavy loss on our assailants during their advance, but a fine young fellow who led them succeeded in reaching the wall. On getting up it he waved his sword as a signal to his men to follow.
>
> Our friend the rifleman was all this time busily examining the contents of a pack he had brought in, but observing the officer on the wall, with some of the enemy already over it, he took a very deliberate aim, and tumbled the gallant fellow over. This so discouraged the rest that they got back again, and to our great delight, the whole ran away as fast as their legs could carry them.[20]

The officer, a young German, was severely wounded and later cared for by Bunbury and his men who carried him to the hospital. The rest of Hill's brigade, the 2/48th and 2/66th, continued to cross and the British batteries on the southern bank opened fire on the French columns marching towards the seminary. With many of the approaches to the building covered by British guns the French, crossing open ground on the far side of the building, took heavy casualties from the British troops firing from windows and behind the walls. The French 70e Ligne was sent to reinforce the 17e Légère and made a concerted attack but the British, now over 1,000 strong, would not be dislodged. Soult ordered Reynaud's brigade up that had been guarding the quays, and as soon as they left the townspeople took the boats across to the British bank and the Guards Brigade, with No. 5 company, and Stewart's brigade began to cross and attack the French troops advancing on the seminary in the flank. The Guards Brigade soon joined Stewart's and Soult ordered his forces to retreat. The French fled; the defenders of the seminary poured into the streets and, with the other brigades, drove them out of the town in confusion. The city's population, after suffering a brutal occupation, began to kill the French wounded until they were prevented from doing so by British troops.[21]

20 Bunbury, *Reminiscences*, Vol. I, pp.32-4.

21 Oman, *Peninsular War*, Vol. II, pp.333-9.

Passage of the Douro, by Henri Leveque (Anne S.K. Brown Military Collection)

Hill's brigade in the seminary had suffered only 77 killed or wounded in three hours of fighting.[22] The pay list of the 5th Battalion records no soldiers killed in action, or wounded. However, in his discharge papers George Koester (No. 6), did later state that he had been wounded in the foot at Oporto.[23] In total the British casualties were 23 killed, 98 wounded and two missing. The French lost around 300 killed or wounded and a similar number of prisoners taken, plus 1,500 sick or wounded captured in hospitals.[24]

Most of the contemporary accounts, and subsequent histories, mention only the 1/3rd as being the first to cross the Douro. One of the adjutant general's staff later wrote that three companies of the 3rd were involved in the initial crossing,[25] whereas Bunbury only mentions two, so it is possible that de Wend's company was the third. Bunbury's account does confirm that they were present at the seminary. On 13 May Hill thanked his brigade for their actions at Oporto:

> Major-General Hill is happy to embrace the earliest opportunity of acknowledging the highly distinguished Conduct of the brigade under his command in the action of yesterday. Their cool and determined Behaviour in passage of the Douro, their subsequent advance to take up and occupy a post of the high Grounds above that

22 Oman, *Peninsular War*, Vol. II, p.339.

23 Discharge Papers of George Koester, TNA, WO 97/734/56.

24 Oman, *Peninsular War*, Vol. II, pp.341-2.

25 G. Fitzclarence, *An Account of the British Campaign in 1809* (London: Colburn & Bentley, 1831), p.31.

> river, and their ready and gallant Conduct in receiving and repelling the attack of the Enemy, taking their Guns, and afterwards completely driving them, altho' much superior in number, of all the town and suburbs of Oporto before any reinforcement arrived, were never surpassed on any occasion.
>
> The Major-General therefore feels the highest satisfaction in returning his best thanks to Lieut. Colonel Drummond, and the Buffs, Lieut. Colonel Duckworth and the 48th, Major Murray, and the 66th, and to Captain de Wend, and the company of the 60th attached to his brigade, and begs that the same will be conveyed to the officers and men of these gallant corps accordingly.[26]

De Wend also received the following in a reply to a letter to Major Davy:

> It is with real satisfaction that I acknowledge the receipt of your letter of the 29th Ultimo, together with its enclosures. I have always had, as I trust you are well aware, the fullest confidence in the brave and gallant fellows, that compose the 5th Battn, 60th Foot, and can only regret that an opportunity was not offered to the whole Battalion, of participating in that honor which your Company has so deservedly acquired. I have directed Major Woodgate to insert the Brigade order transmitted in the Regt. orderly book as an honorable testimony of the Gallantry of the parties concerned, and request you will make my sentiments on this occasion known to your company.[27]

In 1819, when asked to write an account of Michael de Wend's services, John Galiffe also particularly emphasised his having distinguished himself at the passage of the Douro and the Battle of Oporto.[28]

The British cavalry pursued and attacked the retreating French on the afternoon of 12 May. Soult learned of Beresford's successful taking of the bridge at Amarante and the cutting off of the direct route into Spain in the early hours of the 13th. He realised that his army was at risk of being caught between Wellesley advancing from Oporto and Beresford from Amarante. His only option was a desperate march northwards over the mountains. He ordered his men to leave behind anything they could not carry. The guns were destroyed and the baggage abandoned. The men began their march into the hills as it began to rain heavily. The downpour continued for several days.

Wellesley had to wait for the rest of his men, guns and baggage to be ferried across the Douro and then allow his men some rest before giving chase to the French. He sent some of the KGL and cavalry after Soult on the 13th before following with the rest of his army on the 14th.

26 The Trial of Captain de Wend, TNA, WO 71/229. After leaving the 5th Battalion de Wend was court martialed following an altercation with other officers of 4/60th and used the letter and Hill's thanks to testify to his good character. He was found not guilty of most of the charges and only reprimanded on one more minor charge. The text of Hill's thanks used in Rigaud, *Celer et Audaux*, pp.90-1, was edited to include only the 3rd and the 60th.

27 The trial of Captain de Wend, TNA WO 71/229.

28 Copy of Certificate of Military Service of Michael de Wend, Sheffield City Archives, LD 755.

Beresford was ordered to head for Chaves to intercept the French, but he had already started his force marching in that direction, anticipating the order. The weather was appalling and the roads worse. With Beresford was Tilson's brigade. Major Hugh Gough, commanding 2/87th, wrote an account of the march from Amarante over the mountains:

> Orders to proceed to Chaves by forced Marches. Within a League of the town we had to ford the Tarmagar [Tamega], a small river in dry weather. It was the turn of the 87th, unfortunately, to be the Rear Regt. of the Column this day. The 60th crossed with the loss of one Man. The 88th took so long a time to ford it, that when the 87th Grenadiers came to cross, the River presented a most formidable Appearance. In short, the River rose so fast, from the dreadful rain of the preceding evening, and that Morning, that the Men were above their middles in a flooded Mountain River, in which the current was wonderfully rapid. One officer and 14 Privates were carried down by the Stream, but were providentially saved by the Exertions of the Mounted Officers. Two Companies were unable to pass. Here the misfortunes of the Brigade commenced.[29]

The only casualty listed in the 5th Battalion's pay list for 15 May was Private Francis Roer of No. 3 company, who is listed has having died but this was later corrected to deserted.[30] So it is possible, if the man swept away was Roer, that he survived. Gough went on to relate how both the men's bread rations and ammunition were ruined by the immersion in the river and the incessant rain. The villages they passed through were too small to offer anything in the way of food or shelter. The paths were so narrow they had to proceed in single file and men frequently fell down hillsides as Beresford forced his men to march late into the nights. The soldiers' boots fell apart as they climbed up into the mountains and the rain did not stop. On the third day, after many men had fallen by the wayside with hunger and fatigue, they came across a cart with rations for a Portuguese division which they requisitioned. They reached Chaves at midnight on the 16th and, learning that Soult's army was close, set off again at 3:00 p.m. and crossed into Spain where they finally caught up with the French cavalry rearguard, but the mounted men retreated faster than the exhausted British infantry could follow and Beresford abandoned the pursuit. Gough stated that the brigade was nearly annihilated by the march. They rested a day and then headed back to Chaves, picking up the stragglers and the sick as they went.[31]

The same day that Beresford originally reached Chaves, Wellesley's main force had caught up with Soult at Salamonde. The French had been slowed by several river crossings and encounters with Portuguese militia. Campbell's Guards Brigade at the head of Wellesley's infantry had caught up with the French rearguard which was well positioned behind a deep ravine, which the road crossed. The French right flank was secured by a river and the left by rocky ridge. Two British 3-pounders began to fire at the French centre while the light companies of the two Guards battalions and No. 5 company were sent to outflank the

29 R. Rait, *The Life and Campaigns of Hugh, First Viscount Gough, Field-Marshal* (Westminster: A Constable & Co. Ltd.,1903), Vol.I, p.33.

30 June 1809 Pay List, TNA, WO 12/7073.

31 Rait, *First Viscount Gough*, Vol.I, p.35.

French on some cliffs to the south. As the skirmishers opened fire the main body of the guards charged the French, who broke and fled. The Guards Brigade pursued closely and the French began to panic as they crossed a bridge, pushing each other over the side into the gorge. The British guns opened fire again adding to the confusion but as night fell the pursuit was halted. The next morning the men of the Guards Brigade advanced and found the chaos the French had left behind:

> Men and horses, sumpter animals and baggage, had been precipitated into the river, and literally choked the course of the stream. Here, with these fatal accompaniments of death and dismay, was disgorged the last of the plunder of Oporto, and the other cities north of the Douro. All kinds of valuable goods were left on the road, while above 300 horses, sunk in the water, and mules laden with property, fell into the hands of the grenadier and light companies of the guards. These active fingered gentry soon found that fishing for boxes and bodies out of the stream produced pieces of plate, and purses and belts full of gold and silver; and, amidst scenes of death and destruction, arose shouts of the most noisy merriment.[32]

The French continued their flight into Spain but Wellesley halted his column at Ruivães and only sent on some cavalry and Silveira's Portuguese brigade to follow the French.

Wellesley had achieved his aim of expelling Soult from Portugal quickly and with relatively few casualties; approximately 300 men were killed or wounded in the battles and skirmishes and a further 200 fell sick or straggled on the arduous marches. The French had been forced to abandon their baggage and their guns, and had lost around 4,000 men.[33] However, Soult's II Corps was only the first of two threats to Portugal and Wellesley began to move his army south to face *Marechal* Victor's I Corps. Beresford and most of the Portuguese regiments were left to defend Portugal and cover Wellesley's flank as he sought to move into Spain.

32 Fitzclarence, *British Campaign in 1809*, p.40.
33 Oman, *Peninsular War*, Vol. II, p.364.

15

Talavera

Wellesley's army concentrated around Abrantes in central-southern Portugal in early June. He could not advance immediately into Spain as the army needed time to recover from the forced marches of May, and reinforcements were due to arrive from Lisbon. Any action in Spain would also require the cooperation from the Spanish, which would take time to secure.

On 14 June Colonel Rufane Donkin replaced Tilson as commander of the brigade containing the five companies of the 5th Battalion.[1] Donkin's brigade was at Castello Branco, nearer the Spanish border, but the other brigades containing companies of the battalion were widely distributed around central Portugal.[2]

On 16 June Wellesley wrote to Donkin complaining that he had reports of disorders committed by the men of 2/87th and 1/88th in his brigade, and of the high numbers of stragglers on the march. Wellesley ordered that that corrective measures be taken to ensure the good behaviour of the battalions.[3] The fact that the 60th had not been included in the admonishment must have been a source of satisfaction for Major Davy after the events of the previous autumn, indeed Donkin was evidently impressed with the riflemen under his command as on 23 June Wellesley wrote to him: 'I have received your letter of the 21st. I am delighted with your account of the 5th Battalion 60th regiment. Indeed every thing that I have seen and known of that excellent corps has borne the same stamp'.[4]

The 5th Battalion's return of 25 June showed a strength of 48 sergeants, 15 buglers and 622 rank and file. Ten men were sick in their quarters and 49 were in hospital. The majority of the sick were from those companies that had endured Beresford's march over the mountains to Chaves. Three men had joined the battalion, including two from those left behind sick when the battalion sailed from Cork in 1808. Seven officers were still absent on staff duties, four were sick. Two officers were on leave, including Lieutenant MacKenzie who had been promoted into the 81st Foot.[5]

1 General Order 14 June 1809, Wellington, *General Orders*, Vol. I, p.64.
2 Wellington, *Supplementary Despatches*, Vol. XIII, p.327.
3 Wellesley to Donkin, 16 June 1809, Hartley Library, Southampton University, MS 61 Wellington Papers 1/265/66.
4 Wellesley to Donkin, 23 June 1809, quoted in Gurwood, *Wellington's Dispatches*, Vol. IV, p.459.
5 June 1809 Return, TNA, WO 17/179.

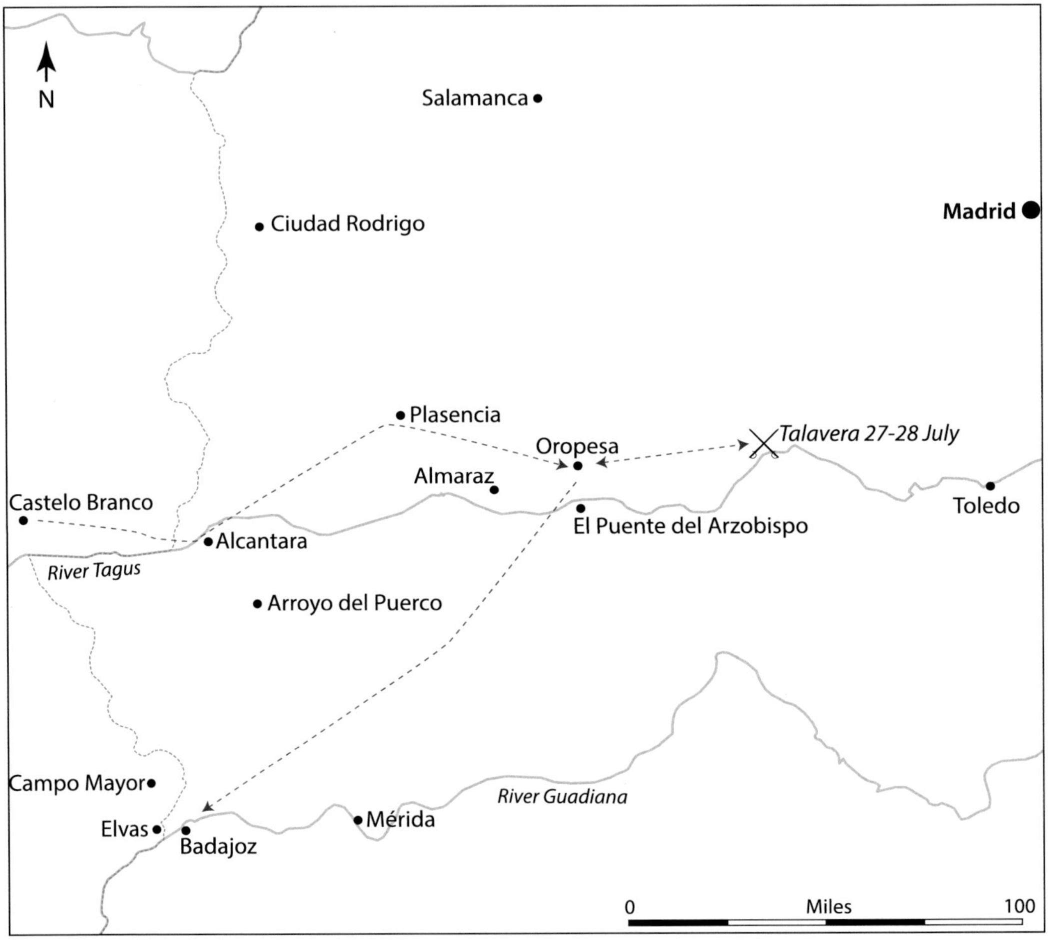

The Talavera Campaign May to August 1809.

Surgeon Parker had died on 4 June and was replaced in July by William McGillivray, assistant surgeon with the 14th Light Dragoons. McGillivray, who had no medical qualifications, had entered the Army in 1796 and had served with the 33rd Foot when it was commanded by Wellesley in India. In 1805 he was assistant surgeon with the 79th Highlanders but had to leave his post due to a 'mental disarrangement'. In October 1808 he had recovered enough to be appointed assistant surgeon with the 14th Light Dragoons. He was the longest-serving assistant surgeon in Portugal and Wellesley had recommended him for promotion.[6] McGillivray almost immediately exchanged into the 31st Foot but remained doing duty with the 5th Battalion until his death at Campo Mayor on 11 October. McGillivray was replaced by Assistant Surgeon Von Millenger of the 97th, who then promptly left to take up

6 Asst. Surgeon McGillivray memorial, TNA, WO 31/280.

the vacant position in the 31st. Assistant Surgeon Moore, from 82nd Foot was then promoted to surgeon of the 5th Battalion but never joined, whilst Assistant Surgeon Dumoulin left to be the surgeon of the 97th. Hospital Mate David Pearston took up Dumoulin's post.[7]

Johann Schwalbach, who managed to rise from rifleman to general, engraving circa 1840 by Joseph James Forrester. (Biblioteca Nacional de Portugal)

The return also showed that one man had been discharged on the orders of Sir Arthur Wellesley. This man was Lance Sergeant Johann Schwalbach who was to be commissioned in the Portuguese army. Whether he owed his promotion to his proficiency at obtaining wine, assisting to capture a French gun at Vimeiro, or general good conduct and aptitude is not recorded. Schwalbach, born at Trier in 1774, was commissioned into the 6th Caçadores, a light infantry regiment, and fought at the battles of Bussaco, Fuentes de Oñoro, Vittoria and the Pyrenees, where he was severely wounded. He stayed in Portuguese service after the war and by 1839 he was a *Marechal de Campo* (the equivalent of a major general). He was later given the title of Visconde de Setabal and promoted to *General*. He died in 1847.[8]

Whilst at Abrantes Wellesley undertook a major change to the organisation of his army. He grouped the various brigades into divisions. The divisional structure would make it easier for him to control the army as he could give a divisional commander an objective and not concern himself with which brigades were employed. Also each division was to have its own staff and so could operate independently. Over time artillery batteries, engineers, ambulance wagons, surgeons, and provost marshals were added to the divisions. The units incorporated into each division, including the various companies of the 5th Battalion, rarely moved and so each division developed its own reputation and *esprit de corps*. Wellesley was short of the required number of senior officers so initially some divisions were commanded by commanders of brigades. The distribution of the companies of the 5th Battalion stayed largely the same with the exception of Brevet Major Galiffe's and Captain McMahon's which swapped brigades, possibly due to Captain McMahon's continued absence. Major Woodgate continued to command the five companies in Donkin's Brigade.[9]

The Portuguese battalions were separated and placed under Beresford to defend Portugal. The organisation of the British infantry divisions was:

7 Wellington, *General Orders*, Vol. I, pp.186, 242, 243 & 246.
8 Butler, *Annals*, Vol. II, pp.79-80.
9 June 1809 return, TNA, WO 17/179.

1st Division – Lieutenant General Sherbrooke
Brigadier General H. Campbell
1/Coldstream Guards, 1/3rd Guards & No. 5 company 5/60th.
Brigadier General Cameron
1/40th 1/61st, 2/83rd, & No. 9 company 5/60th.
Brigadier General Langworth
1st KGL, 5th KGL.
Brigadier General Lowe
2nd KGL, 7th KGL, Detachment of 1st & 2nd Light battalions KGL.

2nd Division – Major General Hill
Brigadier General Stewart
29th, 1/48th, 1st Battalion of Detachments.
Major General Tilson
1/3rd, 2/48th, 2/66th, & No. 6 company 5/60th.

3rd Division – Major General Mackenzie
Major General Mackenzie
2/24th, 2/31st, 1/45th.
Colonel Donkin's Brigade
2/87th 1/88th, & Nos. 2, 3, 4, 7 & 8 companies 5/60th.

4th Division – Brigadier General A. Campbell
Brigadier General A. Campbell
2/7th, 2/53rd, & Brevet No. 1 company 5/60th.
Brigadier General Sontag (replaced by Colonel Kemmis 16 July)
2nd Battalion of Detachments, 97th & No. 10 company 5/60th.[10]

George Fitzclarence, ADC to the Brigadier General Charles Stewart, the adjutant general, commented upon the creation of the divisions:

> The light companies of the regiments composing them were formed into a battalion, which under some intelligent officer, ever marched at the head, and to which was added a company or more of the deadly riflemen of the foreign corps, the 60th.[11]

Wellesley consulted with the *Capitán General* Cuesta on various plans to attack *Marechal* Victor. Negotiations were slow as both men had a tendency to be stubborn and prideful. Eventually agreements were reached and plans finalised, just as news came of Victor's movements that radically changed the situation. Instead of heading for Badajoz, as originally planned, on 27 June the British troops began to advance towards Plasencia and Almaraz further north in Spain. The five companies of the 5th Battalion with Donkin's Brigade

10 Butler, *Annals*, Vol. II, pp.87-90; June 1809 Return, TNA, WO 17/179.
11 Fitzclarence, *British Campaign*, p.49.

formed part of the advance guard of the army.[12] They left early in the morning and marched once more in the heat of an Iberian summer.

At Castello Branco on 2 July, Davy told his men:

> The commanding officer in expressing his satisfaction to the officers and men of the detachment under the command of Major Woodgate on the favourable report be has received of the good behaviour of that part of the regiment corresponding with what he witnessed on the march to Guico, and return to Guarda, is happy at the same time to communicate to them that the companies attached to the several brigades of the army have been equally distinguished by the regularity of their conduct; and in participating with them the satisfaction he feels upon this occasion, doubts not that they will use every exertion to uphold the good name which the battalion has so justly acquired.[13]

The next day the advance guard crossed the border into Spain. On 8 July the first units of the army reached Plasencia, where they paused while Wellesley went to confer with Cuesta.

The allies had good intelligence of the position of French troops thanks to Spanish guerrillas. Those same guerrillas also restricted the French commanders' ability to know where the British and Spanish armies were. Victor's I Corps of around 20,000 lay across the Alberche River, which flowed into the Tagus to the east of Talavera de la Reina, *Général de Division* Sébastiani's IV Corps was at Madridejos with a similar number, although the allies thought he had substantially fewer men. King Joseph was in Madrid with a further 12,000 troops. Joseph was theoretically in charge of all French forces in Spain but in practice many of his commanders received orders directly from his brother, Napoleon. Joseph had little military experience and his ambitious subordinates had little respect for him. Thankfully for the allies there was little chance of other French forces further north coming south but Wellesley and Cuesta took the precaution of placing some Spanish and Portuguese troops on their northern flank.[14]

The plan was for *Teniente General* Venegas' 23,000 strong Spanish Army of La Mancha to advance to fix Sébastiani in place whilst Cuesta and Wellesley also advanced to Madrid with their combined force of 56,000, comfortably outnumbering Victor and King Joseph. However, the alliance between Wellesley and Cuesta was still not an easy one. Plundering by British troops as they moved into Spain did nothing to improve relations. The British perception was that Spanish army was poorly led, equipped, and disciplined. Cuesta himself was old and recovering from serious wounds. The Juntas and generals also spent far too much energy intriguing against each other, rather than co-ordinating their attacks on the French.

Wellesley's army began its march towards Madrid on 17 July and reached Oropesa on the 20th, where Cuesta's army was to join them. On 22 July the Spanish advance guard met Victor's cavalry, giving the French their first news of how close the allied army was to Madrid. The main body of the British army advanced on the French left flank and the

12 Order of March, June 1809, Wellington, *Supplementary Despatches*, Vol. XIII, pp 319-20.

13 Rigaud, *Celer et Audax*, pp.100-101

14 Field, *Talavera*, p.64.

cavalry advance guard helped to persuade the French to withdraw from Talavera. Victor's new position three miles to the east of the town across the Alberche River was sound, but the allies outnumbered the French. Wellesley proposed that they attack on the 23rd, and made the necessary preparations. Cuesta said he would consider the idea, but as the British moved into position for the attack during the night the Spanish troops stayed where they were and Victor retreated unmolested.

The allies moved forward and occupied Talavera de la Reina. Cuesta then decided that Victor's withdrawal was the ideal opportunity to advance to Madrid but Wellesley disagreed and only offered limited support, advancing his 1st and 3rd Divisions to the Alberche River. Wellesley's men were already on half rations as the area had been picked clean by the French and he did not want to extend his supply lines further. The Spanish advanced on their own and discovered, to Cuesta's chagrin, that Venegas had failed to stop Sébastiani uniting with Victor and Joseph, and that they were severely outnumbered. Cuesta withdrew back to the Alberche but only after Wellesley begged him did he agree join the British on the western side of the river, closer to Talavera.

On the morning of 27 July the British 1st and 3rd Divisions covered the Spanish army as it crossed the bridge across the Alberche to Wellesley's main position near Talavera. The companies of the 5th Battalion with Donkin's Brigade began the day positioned at the village of Cazalegas. When the first French cavalry were spotted at around noon the British troops fell back across the river. As they left they set fire to some huts the French troops had built the last time they had occupied the area. Sherbrooke led the 1st Division back towards Talavera whilst Mackenzie's 3rd Division (which included Donkin's and Mackenzie's own brigades, with Brigadier General Anson's light cavalry brigade) acted as a rearguard.[15] However, the terrain was heavily wooded and not suitable for cavalry so Anson's men were sent back.

Captain Andrews, the senior officer present with the five companies of the 5th Battalion in Donkin's Brigade, had been ordered by Mackenzie to proceed to the upper ford of the Alberche. There were four fords on the river and the one furthest up the river was on the extreme left of the British forces, approximately three miles from the ford closest to the bulk of the British troops on the river. They arrived at around 5:00 p.m. and Andrews sent Lieutenant Koch with a company to cover the right flank and Lieutenant Steitz to cover the left.[16]

General de Division Lapisse's French infantry division arrived at the Alberche unseen by the British troops, possibly due to the smoke from the burning huts, and three battalions of the 16e Légère proceeded across the river via a ford below where the five companies were stationed. They succeed in surprising the rest of Donkin's Brigade, the 2/87th and 1/88th, and the 2/31st of Mackenzie's Brigade, attacking them even before they could form up. Wellesley was himself at a ruined house, Casa Salinas, in the vicinity of the attack and barely escaped capture. The riflemen, outflanked by the attack, fell back through the woods and were able to fire on the French troops. Lieutenant Steitz recalled:

15 The general course of the action on 27 July are taken from Field, *Talavera*, pp.70-72

16 Details of the 5 companies' movements come from the later trial of Lieutenant Steitz, TNA, WO 71/219.

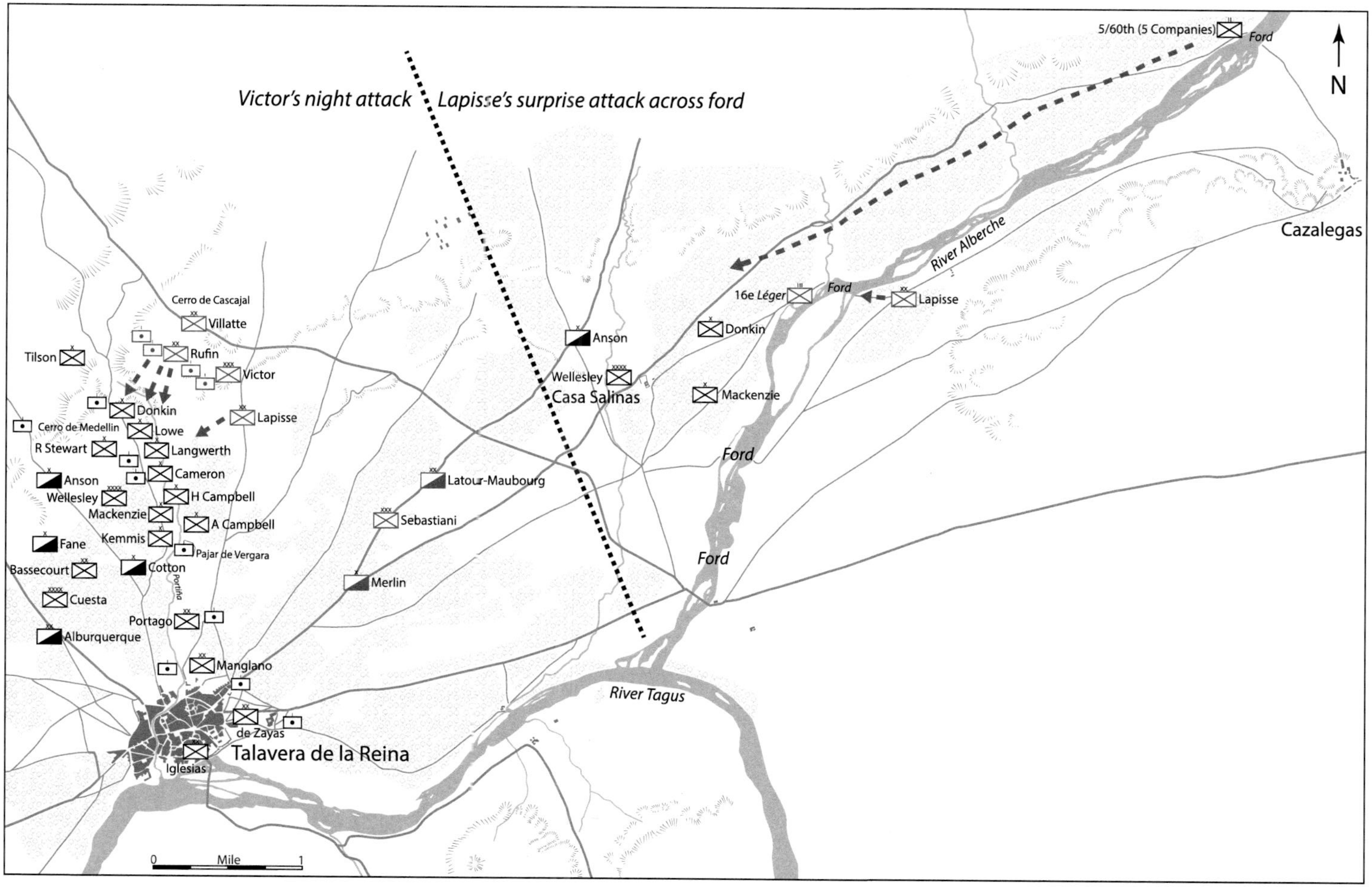

The Battle of Talavera, 27 July 1809.
Sources: Lipscombe, *Atlas* & Wyld, *Maps & Plans*.

> The enemy who threatened to attack our position near Casar Legas on other side of the Albreche on the 27th obliged the Advanced Corps under Command of the late General McKenzie to fall back behind that River, which retreat was however, unavoidably conducted with a great deal of Fatigue to the Troops, and in particular to the 5th Battalion 60th Regiment, attached to his Division. The Enemy unexpectedly crossing the River and with superior Force, obliged the Advanced Corps, after some resistance to retreat from the Alberche through the woods rather precipitately and as far as relates to the riflemen in a very dispersed state, arising from the nature of the ground, as well as from their dispersed way of fighting.[17]

At some point another British battalion mistakenly fired on some of the 5th Battalion.[18] The 2/87th, 1/88th and 2/31st fell back in disarray but the 1/45th held their ground. The volleys of the 1/45th and the steady fire of the riflemen advancing from the flank slowed the French advance, allowing Wellesley and other officers to rally the retreating troops before a more orderly fighting withdrawal commenced. The infantry were assisted by the light cavalry who had returned. Many of the riflemen, including Lieutenant Steitz, became cut off or lost in the woods as dusk came on and the light faded. Steitz, suffering from badly blistered feet and a leg ulcer, ended up going back to Oropesa, 20 miles to the rear, where the battalion baggage was. Total British losses were over 300 killed or wounded, and 90 taken prisoner. The 2/87th lost the most with around 200 casualties.[19]

On 29 July Wellesley praised the performance of the 5th Battalion in this action:

> Upon this occasion, the steadiness and discipline of the 45th regiment, and the 5th Battalion 60th regiment, were conspicuous, and I had particular reason for being satisfied with the manner in which Major General Mackenzie withdrew this advanced guard.[20]

Captain Andrews was awarded the gold medal, usually awarded only to commanding officers of regiments following a victory, as senior officer of the battalion present during this action.[21]

It was now almost dark, and Wellesley's and Cuesta's forces were spread in a long line anchored on the town of Talavera, which lay on the banks of the river Tagus. The town was walled, with olive groves, orchards and enclosures just to the north also offering good cover. Wellesley had asked Cuesta to deploy his 30,000 Spanish troops in and around the town in three lines, in the hope that the strength of their defensive position and depth of their lines could compensate for their perceived lack of quality and steadiness in the British commander's eyes.[22]

17 Trial of Lieutenant Steitz, TNA, WO 71/219.
18 Trial of Lieutenant Steitz, TNA, WO 71/219.
19 Field, *Talavera*, p.72.
20 Wellesley to Castlereagh 29 June 1809, quoted in Gurwood, *Wellington's Dispatches*, Vol. IV, p.506.
21 Butler, *Annals*, Vol. II, p.99.
22 Details of the allied position and subsequent actions are taken from; Field, *Talavera*, pp.70-122, Oman, *Peninsular War*, Vol.II, pp.507-58, Butler, *Annals*, pp.93-9, and N. Lipscome, *The Peninsular War Atlas* (Oxford: Osprey, 2014) pp.132-7.

The allied lines continued north, roughly following the line of a small stream called the Portiña. At the end of the flat area that the Spanish occupied was the Pajar de Vergara, a very low hill, beyond it was another relatively flat area of olive groves and tall grass. Then the ground rose increasingly steeply to the Cerro de Medellin, a much more substantial and prominent hill, with a lower ridge beside it that stretched eastwards towards another hill, the Cerro de Cascajal.

The British line began at the Pajar de Vergara, which had been improved with some earthworks and on which was placed a battery of 3-pounders. North of the battery was Alexander Campbell's 4th Division, including Nos. 1 and 10 companies. In the centre of the British position was the 1st Division, which included Nos. 5 and 9 companies. Behind the 1st Division would ultimately be Mackenzie's 3rd Division, with Nos. 2, 3, 4, 7 and 8 companies in Donkin's Brigade, but they were still withdrawing from the Alberche. Hill's 2nd Division, with No. 6 company, was to occupy the Cerro de Medellin but they too were not yet in their assigned position as night fell. Gun batteries were placed between the divisions. All along the British front the various companies of the 5th Battalion would have been placed forward in a skirmishing screen, along with the redcoat battalions' light companies, the rifle armed KGL light troops, and the few men of the 95th from the 1st Battalion of Detachments.

As Mackenzie's division took their place in the line Donkin's Brigade took post on the lower slopes of the Cerro de Medellin, behind the KGL brigades. Victor's corps arrived and took up positions on the opposite side of the line of the stream. French guns began a bombardment of the British lines whilst French cavalry covered the Spanish position around the town. As French cavalry patrols appeared in the olive groves to their front, four Spanish battalions fired a volley and then fled. As the darkness became complete the artillery fell silent, but the quiet was to be short-lived.

As Victor's troops occupied the Cerro de Cascajal he saw a chance to snatch the Cerro de Medellin from the British. Hill's division had not occupied the summit in strength, and Hill himself had dined in Talavera and had only arrived back at his division later in the evening and ordered it into its correct position. By then it was too late. Victor had already sent *Général de Division* Ruffin's division forward to take the summit, with Lapisse's division making a diversionary attack against the British centre. Ruffin's men advanced in three columns, one of which quickly dislodged Lowe's KGL brigade at the base of the hill before climbing past Donkin's brigade, who managed to fire at least one volley at the nearest French column.

Hill was moving his division up to the summit of the Medellin, but without sufficient haste. Bunbury of the 1/3rd recalled his battalion being delayed by one of Hill's ADCs telling them to form up in the proper order, and that in all the confusion of the surprise attack a German unit in British service was fired upon by mistake.[23] Hill went forward to the summit, arriving as the French reached the crest. He was nearly captured and one of his staff was killed. The 1st Battalion of Detachments were the first British troops to the top and they took heavy casualties before they were joined by the 29th. The French began to be forced back down the hill. Victor's gamble had almost worked but after heavy

23 Bunbury, *Reminiscences*, Vol.I, pp.40-1.

casualties on both sides the British remained in possession of a key position in their line. Stewart's Brigade occupied the summit with Tilson's Brigade, including No. 6 company, a little further south near the KGL.

The 5th Battalion's losses for the day are not broken down between the retreat from the Alberche and Victor's night attack on the Medellin. The pay list has 19 men listed as missing in action on the 27th, including the armourer sergeant, Thomas Miller. Miller was later listed as a prisoner of war, as are two others from the missing. Three men are listed as being known to have been taken prisoner rather than being missing. The battalion lost three killed: Corporal John Singer and Private Michael Muller from No. 9 company, and Private Francis Seland from No. 3. Both Seland and Muller were former prisoners of war who had joined the battalion in the autumn of 1806. Singer had enlisted at Portsmouth in July 1807.[24] Captain Wolff and four privates were wounded.[25] Captain Schoedde was sent back to Oropesa with a fever on the evening of the 27th.[26]

No. 9 company were probably amongst the forward pickets of the 1st Division when Lapisse made his diversionary attack, or it is possible that the casualties were inflicted later in the night when a false alarm led the division to fire on a non-existent French attack and kill and wound some of their own pickets.[27] It was not the only incident during the night. Fire was exchanged between the pickets, several alarms given, and all the time the British troops could hear the French getting into position for an attack in the morning. Private John Cooper of the 2/7th Fusiliers in A. Campbell's Brigade of the 4th Division recalled being sent forward at sunset with No. 1 company into a vineyard where they were told to lie down amongst the vines. The night was cold but they were not allowed to put on their greatcoats.[28]

Victor had launched his attacks without consulting his colleagues or his nominal superior, King Joseph. Victor's corps was still placed on the left of the British line opposite the Medellin. Sébastiani had brought his corps opposite the right of the British line and the Spanish, but Cuesta's men were only lightly covered by some light infantry and cavalry. The bulk of the French army lay poised to attack the British, including far more cannon than Wellesley had at his disposal. The reserve under King Joseph lay further back. At dawn Victor sent word to Joseph that he planned to attack again and asked for the support of the other corps. Joseph was cautious and only agreed to commit other troops if Victor's initial attack went well. Victor's plan was essentially a repeat of the night attack. Ruffin's division would attack the heights of the Medellin whilst Lapisse's division supported by cavalry would make a diversionary attack on the hill's lower slopes to the south.

At 5:00 a.m. a signal gun fired, 50 French cannon opened fire and began to inflict casualties on the British as the French marched forward in battalion-sized columns. Most of the British troops were told to lie down to minimise casualties from incoming howitzer shells and round shot.

24 December 1806 and July 1807 Pay Lists TNA, WO 12/7072; September 1809 Pay List, WO 12/7073.

25 Casualties 27 July, TNA, WO 1/238, pp.301-3.

26 Trial of Lieutenant Steitz, TNA, WO 71/219.

27 Field, *Talavera*, p.86.

28 J.S. Cooper, *Rough Notes of Seven Campaigns* (London: John Russel Smith, 1869), p.20. Cooper remembered the German riflemen as being from the Brunswick Light Infantry, but they had not joined the army yet.

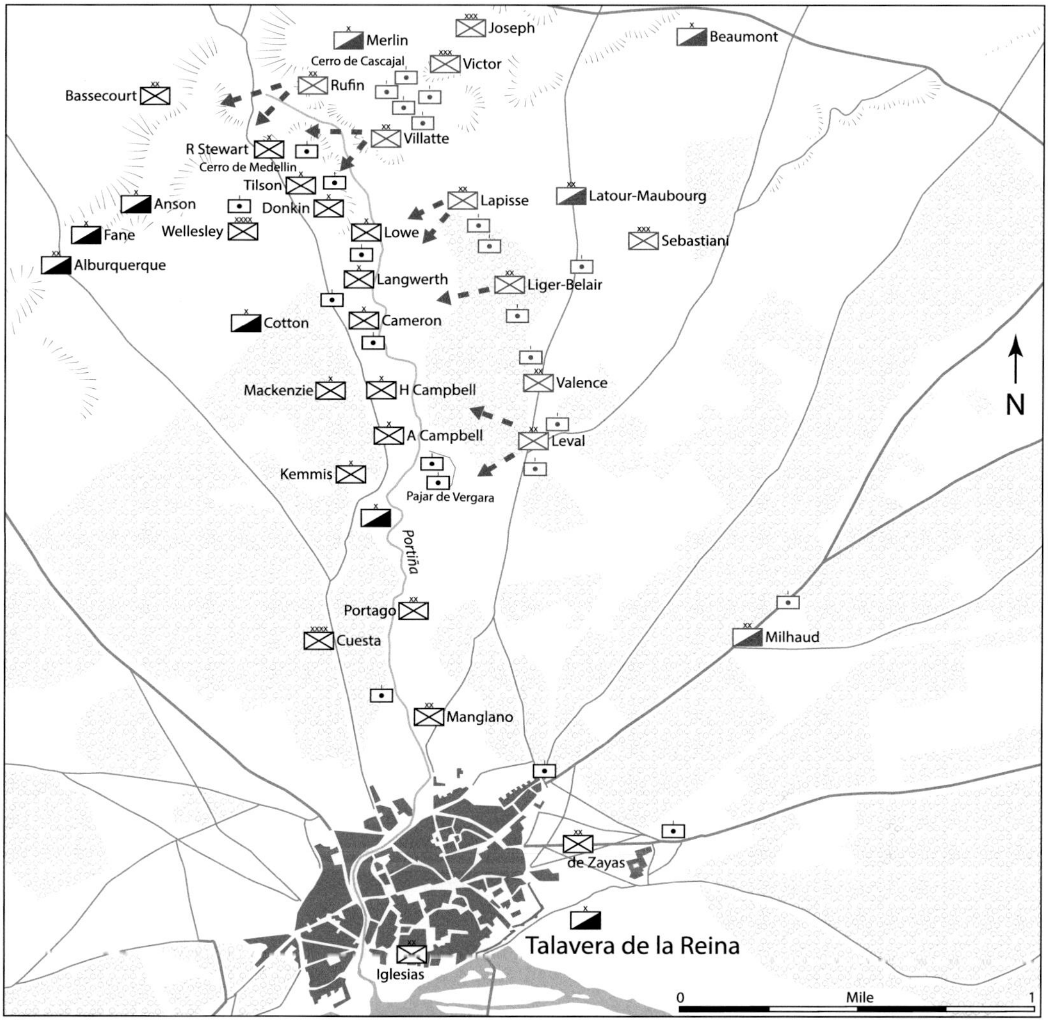

The Battle of Talavera, 28 July 1809. Sources: Lipscombe, *Atlas* & Wyld, *Maps & Plans*.

The British skirmish line, including elements of the 5th Battalion, succeeded in slowing the French light infantry as they fell back towards the summit. As the French guns ceased firing and the smoke drifted away Hill, commanding the 2nd Division on the top of the Medellin, saw the French columns approaching. His skirmishers were still keeping to their firing and retiring drills, working in pairs with one firing and then retreating a set number of steps, reloading as he walked whilst his file partner covered him. However, Hill wanted the skirmishers out of the way and ordered them to hurry, saying 'Damn their filing, let them come in anyhow'.[29]

29 Oman, *Peninsular War*, Vol. II, p.523.

He ordered the rest of his men to stand and advance so they were looking down the steep slope at the approaching enemy. The first volley from all six of Hill's battalions halted the French as the front ranks fell. Subsequent volleys increased the slaughter and began to drive the French back, their cohesion lost. Lapisse had not yet begun his attack and so some of the KGL troops on the lower slopes were able to wheel and fire upon the flanks of Ruffin's columns. Hill's division charged down from the summit and the French broke. The momentum of their charge took some of Hill's men across the stream and up the opposite slope to the waiting French guns and fresh troops, before they hurried back.

French losses were around 1,300 and British about 750, including Hill who was wounded and had to hand over command to Tilson.[30] The French troops retired to have their breakfast, much to the chagrin of the British troops who had little to eat. The sun was well up and the day was getting hot. Men from both sides began to get water from the meagre stream and an informal truce allowed each side to recover some of the wounded.

Whilst the troops had some respite the French commanders bickered between themselves as to what should happen next. Victor wanted to attack whilst Sébastiani favoured defence. Joseph was not sure what to do but a despatch from *Marechal* Soult stated that he was not ready to move and threaten Wellesley's lines of communication back to Portugal and another message warned that Venegas' Spanish troops were all too close to Madrid. Joseph's only option was to defeat Wellesley and Cuesta before turning to defend his capital. He ordered Victor to attack the Medellin again, but this time with a less direct approach around the British left flank. Sébastiani would launch his two divisions against the centre and right.

Wellesley had reinforced the Medellin by posting Donkin's Brigade closer to the summit, although the five companies of the 5th Battalion and the light companies remained on the lower slopes. Wellesley could also see the French preparations and sent some guns and cavalry to counter any flanking move by Victor on the left and requested reinforcements from Cuesta, who sent a battery of heavy 12-pounder guns to the British centre, and his reserve division to further secure the left flank.

The French guns opened fire along almost the entire British front at around 2:00 p.m. *General de Division* Leval's division of Sébastiani's corps was the first to attack. Advancing through olive groves they could neither see their enemy very well nor deploy into any of their usual attack formations, but they did have some initial success. The French skirmishers managed to surprise the British pickets in the close country, some by calling out that they were Spanish, and then drive back the rest of the British light infantry. Nos. 1 and 10 companies with the 4th Division would have had to face this attack and both took casualties. Some of Leval's men came from German or Dutch units and their green or white uniforms caused some confusion amongst British troops expecting to see the usual French blue coats. Once through the olive trees the French broke out into open country, but had no time to reform before facing the British battalion volleys and the fire from the reinforced battery on the Pajar de Vergara.

A portion of Leval's men did succeed in pushing back some of the British battalions, but when they did they were fired on in the flanks by others, and the fire of the central battery, including the Spanish 12-pounders, was instrumental in stopping the French charge.

30 Field, *Talavera*, p.96.

Campbell ordered the 4th Division forward and Leval's men retreated but the olive groves broke the momentum of Campbell's counter-charge and he stopped his men before they became fragmented and uncontrollable.

As Leval attacked the 4th Division, Sherbrooke's 1st Division suffered an hour-long bombardment from the French artillery. One officer later remembered that there was, however, a brief diversion:

> It is a circumstance worth mention, because it proves the coolness and intrepidity of the troops, that, during the action of the 28th, and at the time the enemy's guns were playing on the left of the British line with great effect, a solitary hare was started on the plain and valley on the left of the height, by a shell accidentally bursting near the cover of the affrighted animal, who, being discovered by the divisions on the height, and in the valley, a halloo was set up by the men, much to the annoyance of the general officers, who, however, could not prevent them enjoying the chase in fancy, until the timid creature, unable to extricate itself, (the artillery playing from every direction in which it attempted to retreat) was shot with a bullet by a soldier of the rifle battalion of the 60th Regiment.[31]

Eventually Lapisse and Liger-Belair, commanding another of Sébastiani's divisions, started their attack. The French advanced in two lines of battalion columns, the second line would act as the reserve.

The men of Nos. 5 and 9 companies and the other British light infantry were overwhelmed and forced back. Sherbrooke waited until the French were only 50 yards away before ordering his men to fire a crushing volley and then charge. H. Campbell's Guards Brigade though, chose to march forwards with fixed bayonets and only fired once the French were already fleeing. The effect of the volley and charge on the French columns was devastating and those not cut down turned and ran, hotly pursued by the redcoats. Only Cameron kept control of his men and stopped them from running to the waiting French second line. The KGL and Guards Brigade were now very vulnerable, their cohesion lost and their flanks unprotected. They began to withdraw in small groups around officers desperately trying to restore order and discipline.

The French drove them back over the stream and even Cameron's formed battalions had to perform a fighting withdrawal or risk being outflanked. It was far from clear, at this point in the battle, which side was getting the upper hand and casualties were mounting for both the French and British. Those men going to the rear of the British lines, either because of injury or simply abandoning the fight, began to tell those that they met that the battle was not going well. Assistant Commissary Schaumman, on the road from Oropesa to Talavera, recalled meeting a member the 5th Battalion:

> A German sharpshooter of the 5th Battalion of the 60th Regiment, looking quite black in the face from the sun, the dust, the gunpowder and perspiration, ran from the raging battle and flung himself on the ground in an exhausted condition,

31 Anon., *A History of the Campaigns in Spain & Portugal*, Vol. IV, pp.490-1.

> assuring me that he had fired off sixty charges. His tongue was cleaving to his palate with thirst; he was unable to fight any longer, and hardly ten of his company were still alive.[32]

The rifleman, or Schaumman, exaggerated the level of casualties but not, perhaps, the severity of the fighting and the sheer fatigue of fighting so long under the baking sun. Quartermaster Kemmeter had also met two wounded riflemen earlier in the morning who told him of the action the night before and how dispersed the companies in Donkin's brigade were, how they had been fired on by both sides and that 'all was lost'.[33]

The three battalions of Mackenzie's Brigade from the 3rd Division, that had been in the British second line, let the ragged remnants of the 1st Division through and then stood in line to halt the onslaught from six French battalions. A terrible exchange of volleys began which lasted half an hour, and in which more than a quarter of Mackenzie's men fell, including the general himself. The reformed Guards battalions joined the line and the disciplined fire of the redcoats began to win the day, but victory only came when British cavalry threatened the French flank and they were forced to retreat.

The 1/48th of Stewart's Brigade did a similar job for the broken KGL battalions as Mackenzie's Brigade did for the Guards; they stood firm and allowed the Germans to rally. Lapisse was hit and the French division fell back. The cost in French officers was particularly high; all four regimental commanders and seven out of 12 battalion commanders, plus 70 other officers in Liger-Belair's division became casualties.[34]

Leval had heard the heavy fighting to his right decided to relieve some of the pressure on Liger-Belair with a new attack of his own. At 4:00 p.m. his men advanced but were again disordered by the olive groves and failed to press home their attack when faced with volleys from the British and the battery of guns on Pajar de Vergara. A charge from Spanish cavalry routed them.

All through the afternoon, whilst the other British divisions had been locked in a series of desperate combats, the 2nd Division and Donkin's Brigade on the Medellin had to endure an almost constant French bombardment. Donkin's men, the most exposed, suffered around 195 casualties.[35]

Ruffin's attack on the Medellin was the last of the day. His troops were trying a new approach to the hill but came under fire from batteries Wellesley had placed specifically to harry such a flanking attack. Also, at the end of the long shallow valley that the French had to cross, were the British and KGL cavalry of Anson's Brigade. Anson's men charged but came across an unseen ditch which killed their momentum and caused some casualties. The survivors pressed home their attack but could do little against the French squares and were finally driven off by French cavalry. Having received news of the defeat of the other attacks, and still taking fire from allied cannon, the French withdrew without making their assault on the hill.

32 Schaumann, *On the Road*, p.187.
33 Trial of Lieutenant Steitz, TNA, WO 71/219.
34 Field, *Talavera*, p.113.
35 Oman, *Peninsular War*, Vol. II, p.544.

The Battle of Talavera, by Henri Leveque. (Anne S.K. Brown Military Collection)

Each army was back where it had begun at the start of the day. As a final trial for the exhausted troops the dry grasses of the battlefield caught fire and many of the wounded were burned, along with the bodies of those already dead. Joseph ordered the French army to fall back. Victor, frustrated, finally withdrew his men in the middle of the night.

British losses on the 28th were severe: 670 men killed, 3,406 wounded, and 445 missing, whereas the French lost, over both days, 761 killed, 6,301 wounded and 205 missing.[36] Spanish losses were very small as few of their troops saw action. Given that the French had more men engaged during the actual fighting their losses were proportionately lower than the British, who lost around one quarter of their strength, but the scale of losses did vary between the divisions. The British 4th Division had relatively few casualties but the 1st Division had lost two fifths of its strength, the 2nd lost one quarter, and the 3rd had lost one third of its men.[37] Two British generals, Mackenzie and Langwerth, had been killed.

The losses of the 5th Battalion were far lighter than many of the other British battalions. Seven men were killed in action: Bugler Jacob Kneist (No. 5) had joined the battalion in July 1806; Privates Jacob Muschel and Michael Biegel were both from No. 1 company, Beigel had been in British service since 1800 when he had joined the Lowenstein Jägers; Private Jacob Freys (No. 4) was another former French prisoner of war who had joined the battalion in the autumn of 1806. Three men were killed in No. 10 company: Private Charles Krug had joined from the Foreign Depot in 1806; Private Andreus Jansser had been with the French 66e Ligne before being captured in the convoy going to the West Indies and opting to enter British service; Private John Lerow was initially listed as missing in action but his entry in the pay list is corrected to having been killed on the 28th. Seventeen men are listed in the pay list dated 24 September as still missing from 28 July, of whom five were later identified as having been taken prisoner by the French.[38]

36 Field, *Talavera*, pp.173-6.
37 Oman, *Peninsular War*, Vol. II, p.560.
38 September 1809 Pay List, TNA, WO 12/7073.

Brevet Major Galiffe and Captain Andrews were slightly wounded. Lieutenants Zühleke, Ritter, Mitchell, and Ensign Altenstein were all more severely wounded. One sergeant and 24 privates also sustained wounds.[39] Some of the officers were injured when a French cannon-ball hit a tumbril – a hand cart used to transport ammunition – which then exploded.[40]

After the battle the men of the British army remained where they had fought; hot, tired, hungry and thirsty. Rations were issued, but only one half of what they normally had, and water was equally scarce. On 29 July rations were reduced to one third.[41] As the French moved off the men were allowed to return to their camps in the rear but many were occupied gathering the wounded and taking them to Talavera. The ground was too hard to bury the dead so they were gathered into piles and burned or thrown into ditches and dry streams and barely covered with the dusty earth.

Wellesley could not move his army to pursue the French, who stayed close until the 31st. His troops were too tired and he had too few rations. Many had begun to leave the camp in search of food and Wellesley had to order the roll to be called every two hours.[42] The arrival of a brigade of reinforcements on 29 July under Brigadier General Robert Crauford, including the 1/95th, gave him some fresh troops but also more mouths to feed.

At least one of the men of the 5th Battalion posted as missing managed to return to the ranks quickly. On 31 July Wellesley wrote to Cuesta's chief of staff:

> I have just received intelligence from a man of the 60th regiment, who was taken prisoner on the 28th, that the enemy are in the villages on the other side of the Alberche, and I think it would be desirable to adopt, at an early period, some mode of ascertaining this point, by the observation of officers or peasants or others, from this side of the Alberche, and from the other side the Tagus.[43]

Wellesley went on to say how concerned he was about the French manoeuvres to the north. Initially he had been inclined to advance with Cuesta on Madrid, but as he waited for his army to recover it became clear that Vanegas had failed to tie down any of the French army and that Joseph was free to gather more men and outnumber the allies. Cuesta's priority was still Madrid but Wellesley's was the defence of Portugal, and to avoid his army starving. Thinking that he still had the strength to confront Soult he began to move the army towards Plasencia on 3 August, but had only reached Oropesa when he learned that Soult's corps was twice as strong as he had thought. Wellesley had no choice but to return to Portugal and on 4 August ordered all the baggage to head for the closest bridge over the river Tagus at El Puente del Arzobispo. Soult's advance guard was only 15 miles from Oropesa.[44]

On 5 August, whilst the rest of the army proceeded to El Puente del Arzobispo Wellesley sent Crauford with his own brigade, and Donkin's including the five companies of the 5th Battalion, to secure another crossing over the Tagus near Almaraz, further west, so that the

39 Casualties 28 July, TNA, WO 1/238, pp.306, 310-1.

40 Anon., *Campaigns in Spain & Portugal*, Vol.IV, p.492.

41 Field, *Talavera*, p.126.

42 Fitzclarence, *British Campaign*, p.106.

43 Wellesley to O'Donoju 31 July 1809, quoted in, Gurwood, *Wellington's Dispatches*, Vol. IV, p.517.

44 Fitzclarence, *British Campaign*, p.109.

French could not cross there. After a march of 15 hours, across narrow mountain paths, they reached the river on the 6th and prepared defences around the broken bridge and ford.

Meanwhile, Cuesta, alarmed at the advance of Soult, had retreated from his position on the Alberche. The hospitals at Talavera were full of the sick and wounded, numbering around 4,000 men. The Spanish only provided a handful of ox-carts and mules for the evacuation, and the British managed to gather 40 other vehicles, but it was far too few. Those sick and injured that could walk had to do so. Around 2,000 managed to rejoin the army, 500 died on the march, and 1,500 of those too ill to move, not expected to survive, or who could not fit into the carts, were left behind and taken prisoners by the French.[45] The 5th Battalion had left 23 men in the hospital at Talavera. Of these 12 became prisoners of war and two managed to return to the battalion. The fate of the other nine is not recorded but they could have died at the hospital or during the evacuation, or opted for French service rather than the prisons. Captain Wolff, Lieutenants Zühleke, Freiss, and Mitchell, and Ensign Altenstein were also taken prisoner.[46] The surgeons who stayed with their patients were allowed to go free by the French, due to the care they had given to the French wounded.

Lieutenant Zühleke wrote to Major Davy in December from Madrid.

> I had the honour of addressing two letters to you from Talavera. The first, Mrs. Zühleke writes me, came to hand, and I hope the second, in answer to your favour of the 26th Sept., has reached you likewise; it was inclosed in a pack forwarded by an officer of the Coldstream Guards under the address of Mrs. Z., with the annotation, 'to be transmitted to you in case Mrs. Z. had left Portugal'. The pack also contained a letter for Captain Andrews.
>
> Since about the 1st of November I left Talavera. Most of the officers and men have been sent to France. Of the regiment under your command nobody but Captain Wolf and me are here now; and in the whole of the British only eighteen officers – five captains and thirteen subalterns.
>
> Captain Wolf desires to be most respectfully remembered to you; he is recovering, one of his wounds healed up, but has lost his martial attitude. My wounds have a good appearance, but there are still rags or bones in them which retard the healing.
>
> We inhabit the cells of the convent 'St. Francis' converted into a hospital, are well treated, and might live comfortable if the monthly supplies of money with which his Lordship the Commander of the Forces hitherto favoured us will not be withheld. For we have no opportunity here of drawing any bills, and shall not I apprehend receive any allowance in cash as *prisoners* till we arrive in France.
>
> I take the liberty of enclosing a letter for Mrs. Zühleke. She gave me hopes of being soon exchanged: may they not be disappointed, Lord Wellington's kind endeavours not fail, and I soon in person have the honour to testify my respects to you.[47]

45 Oman, *Peninsular War*, Vol. II, p.581.

46 September 1809 Pay List, TNA, WO 12/7073.

47 Rigaud, *Celer et Audax*, pp.113-4.

Zühleke had married whilst the battalion was stationed at Nova Scotia and his wife must have accompanied him to the Peninsula. Mitchell, Freiss, and Altenstein all reached Verdun in northern France by January 1810; Wolff joined them in August.[48] Verdun was where most British officer prisoners of war were held, Zühleke though, never made it there. He managed to escape in April 1810 and made his way to Lisbon.

Zühleke had written to Wellesley in July asking for his patronage to help secure a promotion to captain. He pointed out his long service, having been with the battalion since 1798, and also the fact that due to the many officer absences he had commanded a company almost constantly since 1802. Davy praised him in his covering letter and Wellesley included his own recommendation when he forwarded the letter to Horse Guards. Whilst Zühleke was still a prisoner Captain Farrer of the 3/60th had died at Martinique 'in the hospital in which he was confined as a Lunatic'. Zühleke was promoted, without purchase, to the vacancy.[49] However, on his return from captivity instead of leaving Portugal to join his new battalion in the West Indies he requested to be transferred to Portuguese service. He was appointed *Major* in the 2nd Caçadores and served with them for the remainder of the Peninsular campaign and many of the major battles, rising to *Tenente Coronel* and commanding the battalion.[50]

More British wounded and sick were captured at Plansencia on 1 August as French forces closed on the allies from the north. A total of 334 men were taken,[51] including one bugler and five privates of the 5th Battalion.[52] The pay list has one man as missing in action on 5 August, six on 7 August and two on 8 August. One account of the campaign does mention French cavalry firing on British advance posts around this time,[53] and *Marechal* Ney arrived at the crossing near Almaraz on 7 August,[54] so it is possible that patrols or pickets of each army clashed and that some of the men of the battalion were cut off, or were captured.

Once Wellesley got his army across the Tagus he felt safer, especially as the French became inactive due to Joseph's innate caution. However, the supply situation continued to deteriorate and on 20 August he fell back towards Portugal and occupied the more fertile region around Badajoz. In September Sir Arthur Wellesley learned that the government had given him the title of Viscount Wellington in recognition of his victory at Talavera.

The 5th Battalion's return for 25 August, completed at a camp near Arroyo del Puerco, listed a strength of 49 sergeants, 14 buglers and 611 rank and file. The return shows 10 men as having died since 25 July, which tallies with those killed in action at Talavera and indicates that none had died due to the privations of marching on short rations, but nine men are listed as 'missing on the road'. The battalion was far from healthy though, with 97 men sick, but that figure does include those left in the hospital at Talavera. One man had deserted. The return also notes that one sergeant had been left in charge of the sick at

48 T.J. Walker, *The Depot for Prisoners of War at Norman Cross Huntingdonshire, 1796 to 1816* (London: Constable & Co., 1913), pp.336-41.
49 Lt. Zuhlke Memorial, TNA, WO 31/291.
50 Rigaud, *Celer et Audax*, pp.114-5.
51 Oman, *Peninsular*, Vol. II, p.576.
52 September 1809 Return, TNA, WO 17/179.
53 Fitzclarence, *British Campaign*, p.110.
54 Oman, *Peninsular War*, Vol. II, p.587.

Talavera and four privates had also been left behind to look after the wounded officers, since taken prisoner. With those losses, and three officers sick, the battalion was desperately short of officers with No. 10 company being commanded by Ensign Barbaz.[55]

The British army remained around Badajoz and the Guadiana River until nearly the end of the year. Supplies became more plentiful and the men slowly began to recover from the privations of six months of hard campaigning. The battalion's return for 25 September shows the headquarters still at Arroyo del Puerco and with five companies still detached to the various brigades. The battalion's strength had increased, for a change, by two privates.[56] Private Michel Toth, a Hungarian, returned from missing in action on 27 July. Private Jacob Wolff also returned from missing in action, but in his case he had gone missing at the Battle of Rolica.[57] Where he had been from 15 August 1808 to 5 September 1809 is, unfortunately, not recorded.

The fertility of the Guadiana valley came at a high price. As the rains came in the autumn the troops began to suffer from a deadly fever. The army as a whole lost around 3,500 men dead over the four months from 25 October 1809 to 25 January 1810. Some battalions suffered over two hundred deaths and sickness rates as high as 60 percent. However, the 5th Battalion came through the epidemic relatively unscathed with the sickness rate peaking in October at just over 14 percent and a total of 19 deaths to the end of the year.[58] The actual sickness rate of the troops present would have been lower as the returns still included the sick and wounded left behind and captured by the French. Six men died in October, seven in November, and six in December.[59] At least one of those deaths though, was not due to disease; Bugler Joseph Thomy shot himself in November.[60]

The battalion also began to solve its chronic shortage of officers. Lieutenant Charles Koch was promoted to captain in October and the six vacancies for lieutenants were filled by promoting six ensigns; Mathew Fürst, William Wynne, John Joyce, Julius von Boeck, J. Louis Barbaz, & John Sprecher de Bernegg. The latter had recently returned to the battalion, along with Lieutenant Sawatsky, after escorting the deserters, suspected men, and invalids back to Britain. The headquarters of the battalion moved to Campo Mayor in Portugal in October, then Santa Olla in November.[61] In early December Davy wrote:

> 3rd December, 1809. The battalion by the detached companies, &c. commenced its march to Montemor-o-Novo.
>
> 4th December. Major Woodgate's detachment of five companies marched to Estremoz. I directed Major Woodgate, upon his arrival at Montemor on the 7th, to send the quarter-master to Lisbon for the clothing.

55 August 1809 Return, TNA, WO 17/179.
56 September 1809 Return, TNA, WO 17/179.
57 September 1809 Pay List, TNA, WO 12/7073.
58 A. Bamford, 'The Guadiana Fever Epidemic', http://www.napoleon-series.org/military/battles/1809/Peninsula/c_Guadiana1.html (Accessed 7 September 2018).
59 December 1809 Return, TNA, WO 17/179.
60 December 1809 Pay List, TNA, WO 12/7073.
61 October to December 1809 Returns, TNA, WO 17/179; December 1809 Pay List, WO 12/7073.

> 10th December. The battalion was this day united at Montemor-o-Novo, having been separated in detachments since 4th May.[62]

At least one of the brigade commanders was sad to see their company of the battalion leave. Brigadier General Alan Cameron wrote:

> My little company of the 60th, under your command, marched from hence yesterday morning agreeable to route. I was sorry to part with it, as consisting of the best behaved men I ever had attached to me in any military situation. There has been no instance of a complaint against any one of them since under my command. And should a similar distribution take place upon any future occasion I hope you will favour me with the same company back again. My interpreter Paylin came to me yesterday to know whether any allowance was made for interpreters under his circumstances. To which I replied in the negative. At least, that I did not know of any, but that you would be able to find out for him. He wishes to join his company and I send this by him. I believe he is a very steady honest man; and I hope you will promote him.[63]

No. 9 company had been attached to Cameron's brigade and was possibly commanded by Ensign Fürst, following the wounding and capture of Captain Wolff and Lieutenant Freiss. Private John Pohling, the closest match to 'Paylin' in No. 9 company was promoted to corporal in February 1810.[64]

The battalion may have been together again but as far as the officers are concerned it seems to have been far from united. Signs of discontent dated back to the summer. In July Wellesley, as he was then, wrote to Sir David Dundas, who had recently replaced the Duke of York as commander-in-chief of the army:

> I have the honor to enclose a letter which I have received this day from Colonel Donkin, who commands the brigade of infantry in which the 5th Battalion 60th regiment is serving, to which Lieut. Steitz, to whom these papers relate, belongs. In addition to the complaints contained in these papers of the conduct of Lieut. Steitz, I have to mention, that that officer waited on me last night with a letter from the Adjutant General, authorising him to serve with the Portuguese troops; and he desired that I would permit him to join them. I declined doing so, as I wished to wait for an answer to the letter which I had addressed to you on the 7th June, before I should allow any other officer to join and do duty with the Portuguese troops; and Lieut. Steitz then told me that he was very sorry that he could not do duty with his regiment, as he was unwell.
>
> I beg to recommend that officers, particularly belonging to regiments doing duty in Portugal, should not be permitted to serve with the Portuguese troops, unless

62 Rigaud, *Celer et Audax*, p.105.

63 Rigaud, *Celer et Audax*, p.108.

64 March 1810 Pay List, TNA, WO 12/7074.

> they should be recommended by the officers commanding the regiments to which they belong.[65]

On 23 October two companies, under the command of Lieutenant Frederick Steitz and Lieutenant Baron Franz de Eberstein, were performing a field exercise. As the companies were practising their retiring Steitz, the senior of the two, said that the files were not sufficiently extended, but de Eberstein claimed that they were at their proper distance. The two officers then argued, and after the exercise was completed de Eberstein again spoke disrespectfully in the street to Steitz, who went to complain to Major Woodgate about de Eberstein's behaviour. Woodgate then sent for de Eberstein and concluded that Steitz was owed an apology and told de Eberstein to go and see Steitz.[66]

Captain Andrews accompanied de Eberstein to Steitz's lodging. The apology was made and Andrews left. De Eberstein then warned Steitz to take care as to how he dealt with him in the future as 'a very heavy cloud was hanging over his head which was not forgotten', alluding to Steitz's absence during the Battle of Talavera. Steitz then hit de Eberstein on the temple, causing a cut and bruising. Steitz was subsequently placed under arrest.

On 15 November a court martial was convened at Badajoz. Major General the Honourable Galbraith Lowry Cole was president, and the members of the court were drawn from various regiments, but none from 60th. The charges were:

> For Scandalous and Infamous Conduct highly unbecoming the Character of an Officer and a Gentleman, in striking Lieutenant De Eberstein of the same Corps, on 23rd October 1809.
>
> For absenting himself without leave from his Regiment during the whole of the action of the 28th July 1809.

Major Davy was the prosecutor and he explained that he had already held a court of enquiry, at Steitz's request, into the absence but felt the first charge depended on the accusation in the second so he needed to prefer both charges. Woodgate and Andrews testified to the events relating to the first charge. Then Adjutant de Gilse gave evidence relating to the second charge. He related how the five companies of Donkin's Brigade had been attacked at the ford across the Alberche, and that Steitz on the left flank became separated. De Gilse then saw Steitz next on the 29th who told him that he had been unable to find the rest of his company and had gone to the rear because he was suffering from a leg ulcer and badly blistered feet.

Captain Schoedde, who was in Oropesa sick, Quartermaster Kemmeter, and Sergeant Francis Shilling all gave evidence that they saw Steitz in the rear and to the apparent condition of his feet. Lieutenant Ignace Franchini testified that he heard Steitz reporting his return to Davy on the 29th but did not hear mention of his feet. Franchini also said that Steitz's absence had been talked about as being unusual.

In his defence Steitz did not confirm or deny striking de Eberstein but concentrated on the second charge. He said he had been suffering with his legs since April, having missed the

65 Wellesley to Davy 1 July 1809, quoted in Gurwood, *Wellington's Dispatches,* Vol. IV, pp.456 & Hartley Library, University of Southampton, MS61 Wellington Papers 1/269/9.

66 The details of the original altercation and subsequent trial come from Trial of Lt. Frederick Steitz, TNA,WO 71/219.

Oporto campaign and only re-joined the battalion in June, not quite recovered. After being cut off from the rest of the companies during the action at the Alberche he had made efforts to find his way back but had been forced to abandon those attempts as he could hardly walk and he only got back to Oropesa by having a lift on a cart and then a mule.

Steitz also outlined his 18 years of military service, in both foreign and British service, and the fact that he had been wounded at Roliça but immediately returned to his company. His servant, Private Gabriel Albert, was the first witness who had to give evidence via translator, and he confirmed Steitz's account of the confrontation with de Eberstein and said he did not see any blow. Sergeant Raab and Private John Eisel, also via translation, confirmed elements of Steitz's account of the evening of the 27th. Adjutant de Gilse and Brevet Major Galiffe testified to Steitz's character.

The court acquitted Steitz of both charges. The first because of the extreme provocation he had received from de Eberstein, and the second because he was deemed to have given sufficient reason for his absence from the battle of the 28th.

However, the court martial did little to clear the air in the mess. In December Wellington wrote to Davy:

> I have perused your letter of the 10th instant to Colonel Bathurst, relative to the charge exhibited by Lieut. Steitz against Captain Andrews; and I am glad to find, that although the Captain did return Francis Bentze as Paymaster's clerk from October, 1808, to March, 1809, and drew an allowance for him in that capacity, but neither employed him nor paid him as such, he did so with the knowledge and permission of his commanding officer, Major Woodgate, and that he paid the sum which he received in the name of Bentze to Serjeant Lerche, who did the duty of Paymaster's clerk.
>
> Captain Andrews has therefore entirely cleared himself from any corrupt or improper motives in this transaction; and I shall certainly not gratify the malicious spirit by which Lieut. Steitz appears to be actuated in bringing forward this charge, by submitting the conduct of Captain Andrews to any further inquiry.
>
> I beg, however, to draw your attention, and that of Captain Andrews and Major Woodgate, to the impropriety of the whole of this transaction, and to a reflection on the risk which every officer incurs who allows himself to be involved in such. It affects the foundation of every military return, and exposes His Majesty and the public to frauds of every description; and such a transaction must positively never be repeated.
>
> If it were necessary to employ and pay one man for the performance of the duties usually allotted to two, under the regulations of the Service, application should have been made to the Commander of the Forces, at the time, for permission so to do, but on no account ought his pay to have been drawn in the name of another.
>
> I have also read your letter to the Adjutant General of the 10th instant, and I desire that you will direct the Paymaster of the 5th batt. 60th regiment to pay out of the subsistence of Lieut. Steitz, to Captain Schoedde, for the twelve pairs of shoes, the price of which has been awarded to him by the Court of Inquiry, of which Captain Andrews was President, held on the 9th November, Lieut. Steitz receiving the shoes, and disposing of them as he may think proper.

> I desire, also, that you will inform Lieut. Steitz that I will not order a Court Martial to be assembled for the trial of Lieut. De Eberstein on the 10th instant; the subject of that charge having already been incidentally before the General Court Martial.
>
> I desire, however, that you will put Lieut. Steitz in arrest, 'for unmilitary and unofficerlike conduct, in disturbing the peace and harmony which ought to subsist among the officers of the 5th batt. 60th regiment, contrary to the orders and warning given to him by the Commander of the Forces'.
>
> You will keep Lieut. Steitz in arrest with the regiment, as I know enough of the character and past conduct of that officer to be suspicious that his late conduct is to be attributed to a desire to leave his regiment during the time it may be actively employed.[67]

The return of April 1810 shows Steitz under arrest and by June he was recorded as being on leave and ordered to report to the Foreign Depot on Wellington's orders.[68] It seems unlikely that many of the officers of the battalion were unhappy to see him go. Steitz later wrote to the secretary at war to complain about his treatment. Lieutenant Colonel Torrens then asked Wellington to look into the complaints. Wellington replied with a very testy response in which he made clear his low opinion of Steitz, which began when he tried to remain away from the battalion on frivolous pretences. Wellington detailed the various enquiries and trials that Steitz had been involved with, including making complaints against Captain Andrews and Lieutenant de Eberstein immediately following the court martial. Wellington concluded his letter with:

> The Commander in Chief will be best able to judge from a perusal of these papers, whether there is any ground for further inquiry. If there is, I would submit that the inquiry ought to begin with myself, as my conduct and former decision upon the same point must be the basis of any inquiry into the complaint by Lieut. Steitz. If, however, the Commander in Chief should be of opinion that there ought to be no further inquiry into these complaints by Lieut. Steitz, I would submit that that officer ought to be tried by a General Court Martial, on a charge for forwarding direct to the Secretary at War a complaint of his superior officer, not transmitting it through the commanding officer of his regiment, according to His Majesty's Regulations.[69]

Steitz joined the 1/60th at the Cape of Good Hope, where the taint of his absence from Talavera followed him, probably with the aid of several other officers from the 5th Battalion who transferred at around the same time. In November 1811 he was court martialled 'For the wilful Murder of Lieutenant Thomas Sowerby of the 1st Battalion of the 60th Regiment

67 Wellington to Davy 13 December 1809, quoted in Gruwwod, *Wellington's Dispatches*, Vol. V pp.367 & Hartley Library, University of Southampton, MS61 Wellington Papers, 1/290/7.

68 June 1810 Return, TNA, WO 17/180.

69 Wellington to Torrens 19 October 1810, quoted in Gurwood, *Wellington's Dispatches*, Vol. VI, pp.524-5, & Hartley Library, University of Southampton, MS61 Wellington Papers, 1/318/19.

of Foot, on or about the 21st Day of November 1811, by shooting him in a Duel'.[70] Sowerby had accused Steitz of cowardice. As was usual in cases of duelling very little evidence was presented; the prosecution concentrated on the finding of the body and not the duel itself. Steitz offered no defence but was still found not guilty. However, Steitz was again court martialled in 1813, this time on seven charges of fraud and embezzlement.[71] He was found guilty of all charges and cashiered from the Army.

With the 5th Battalion nearly 350 men under establishment Davy also wanted to take the opportunity of the winter months to bring it up to strength. In September he wrote to Colonel Bathurst, military secretary to Wellington:

> Feeling exceedingly anxious to get the 5th Battalion 60th foot, now so much reduced, completed to its establishment, I take the liberty of requesting you to propose to his Excellency to write to England for that purpose. An opportunity is now offered of obtaining some most excellent recruits from among the prisoners taken at Flushing, but I am aware, that, unless the strongest instances are made to the contrary, we shall be filled up with a class of men who might again put the reputation of the battalion to hazard. I beg leave to mention that this was one of the objects which dictated my application to his Excellency for leave, in order that I might have it in my power to select men fit for the service, and therefore request he will mention that the Austrian-Hungarians, together with all Germans north of the Rhine, particularly Hessians, are those upon which we can place the most dependence.[72]

Davy went on to mention the 200 Swiss that he had tried to recruit in 1808. However, the battalion was not quite as understrength as Davy supposed. A letter from the regiment's agents informing him of a reduction in its establishment at the end of 1808, from 1,000 men to 800, had failed to reach him.[73] The new establishment reduced the number of sergeants as well as rank and file. Davy immediately appealed this decision, and wrote to the secretary at war:

> Having this day only received a duplicate of a letter dated the 29th March 1809 (original never came to hand) from Messrs. Greenwood and Cox acquainting me that a reduction of the 5th Battalion 60th foot had taken place from the 25th Dec. last to the establishment of 1 S.M. [sergeant major], 1 Q.M.S. [quartermaster sergeant], 1 O.S. [orderly sergeant]. 1 P.M.S. [paymaster sergeant], 40S. [sergeants], 40C. [corporals], 18 D. [drummers], 2 F. [fifers], 750 P. [privates], I beg leave to submit to your consideration some reasons respecting the same as relative to a Rifle Corps, in the situation and of the composition of the 5th Battalion 60th foot, such as I trust will justify me in requesting that the number of N.C.O'.s, may be kept up to its present strength.

70 Trial of Lt. Steitz, 27 November 1811, TNA, WO 71/224.

71 Trial of Lt. Steitz, TNA, WO 71/229.

72 Davy to Bathurst, 13 September 1809, quoted in Rigaud, *Celer et Audax*, pp.68-9.

73 Regimental Records, 5/60th, reduction in establishment, TNA, WO 380/1, pp.167.

I beg leave to mention that the battalion embarked from Ireland for foreign service with not less than 18 or 20 officers, including vacant commissions, short of its establishment, and the consequent injury to the service so deeply felt, and conspicuously instanced in this corps, may in some measure be attributed to this cause.

It is evident that a Rifle Corps acting as this has done (having constantly been employed during both the campaigns in Spain and Portugal by detachments not only of companies, but of subalterns' and serjeants' parties, and covering an extended chain of outposts – one I recollect of more than 10 miles – as well as performing the duties of light troops) cannot fairly admit of a parallel with the situation of regiments of the Line, nor of an application of those regulations which are more particularly referable to the latter: and, if this in a general point of view may be thought to merit consideration, I cannot but conceive that it bears with still greater force when applied to a regiment of foreigners, acting in a foreign country in whose service many of the subjects composing the corps have received pay, and against an enemy from whose armies a no less proportion have also deserted, and obviously demonstrates the necessity of having (independently of other considerations) a greater number of officers, and N.C.O'.s to preserve that control which is requisite, and restrain the dispersion (inherent to light troops, particularly Tirailleurs) which in the field after the firing of the first shot I should otherwise apprehend would take place.

The service of these corps has been so imperfectly understood in England (I trust I may be pardoned the observation) that they have, generally speaking, been modelled upon the system of regiments of the Line, which is as generally inapplicable to them; and manifold inconveniences and difficulties have resulted from hence.

And here I beg leave to remark that, though by the creation of a serjeant a regiment of the Line loses a musket, a Rifle Corps suffers no diminution in this respect in its strength; on the contrary, the serjeants are considered as the best marksmen, and by their example and instructions to others may make themselves conspicuously useful. I should willingly give up ten buglemen for a similar augmentation of this class of N.C.O., the former being comparatively unnecessarily numerous and of little service, and the latter by far too few for the important duties they have to discharge.

It was a maxim of the late Sir John Moore, and which he several times repeated to me, that 'one rifle-man should be deemed an equivalent, when posted, to three sentries of the Line, and that the parties must in all cases be commanded either by an officer or N.C.O.'

It would be impossible to adhere to it unless an adequate proportion of the latter is admitted, and so many economical and interior duties have the N.C.O'.s of this corps (by an ill-judged interference with them) to discharge in conjunction with the Line, that we really sometimes experience much difficulty in executing them.

Many observations might be added upon these heads, but I fear I have rendered an apology necessary for trespassing on your time with those already stated. I have the honour to subjoin a return of the present strength, and beg leave to conclude with remarking that though, for a considerable time, I did not fill up vacancies

> from a wish to select the men best qualified for the situation, yet after the action of Talavera (the necessity of rewarding those who had, by their conduct, entitled themselves to it, and the diminution of the officers by wounds, and sickness, and capture, one of the companies being now commanded by an ensign, and many having no more than one officer actually present) I felt it my duty to meet these circumstances by appointing N.C.O.s to the full establishment, having received no directions to the contrary, and trust they will be allowed to continue in their respective situations.
>
> I shall however fill up no vacancies that may hereafter occur until I have the honour to receive your orders.[74]

Davy's appeal worked and the battalion was allowed to keep its former establishment of NCOs. Davy had led the battalion through some difficult times and hard campaigns. He had, he felt, earned a promotion to lieutenant colonel and had written a memorial to state his case in June, which Wellesley had forwarded to Horse Guards with his endorsement:

> I enclose a memorial which has been given into my hands by Major Davy, which I beg you to lay before the Commander in Chief. I believe that his Royal Highness the late Commander in Chief had intended to promote all the Majors commanding battalions in the late service in Portugal; and certainly, if the services of any battalion could give to their commanding officer a claim to promotion, the conduct and services of the 5th Battalion 60th foot entitled their commanding officer to this advantage. I have had every reason to be satisfied with their conduct again upon this occasion, and I shall be very much obliged to you if you will recommend Major Davy to the favorable consideration of the Commander in Chief.[75]

In December, Davy requested leave to return to Britain which Wellington granted. Whilst Davy was handing over his command to Woodgate he received the news that his promotion to lieutenant colonel had come through, but it would mean that he would have to leave the battalion permanently. He was given the command of the 7th Garrison Battalion and left Portugal early in 1810.[76] However, before he could take up his new position his battalion was disbanded and he went on half-pay. His health had suffered after the arduous campaigns and he did not seek active employment again. His financial situation became difficult and he entered into a long and acrimonious correspondence in the 1820s with Lord Palmerston, then secretary at war, with regards to grievances over the level of his half-pay and he eventually published a pamphlet on the subject.[77]

74 Davy to Castlereagh 17 October 1809, quoted in Rigaurd, *Celer et Audax*, pp.69-72.

75 Wellesley to Gordon 17 June 1809, quoted in *Wellington's Dispatches*, Vol. IV, p.401.

76 Rigaud, *Celer et Audax*, p.07.

77 W.G. Davy, *The Substance of a Correspondence on a Matter Connected with the Distribution of Half Pay to the Reduced Officers of His Majesty's Army* (London: Privately printed, 1828).

Davy lived at Tracey Park, near Bath. He married in 1814 and then for a second time in 1840, aged 60, after the death of his first wife.[78] Being on half-pay and effectively retired did not stop senior officers, such as Davy, slowly making their way up through the ranks by seniority; something that did not happen for more junior ranks. By 1830 he was a major general and in 1842 he was appointed colonel commandant of the 1st Battalion of the 60th. He died in 1856, aged 76.[79]

The campaigns of 1809 had begun well for Wellington and his army. The retaking of Oporto and expulsion of Soult from Portugal had been achieved through hard marching, bold action and skilful manoeuvring. However, the foray into Spain had not gone so well. The Battle of Talavera had been won, but at high cost and none of the strategic aims of the campaign had been achieved. Wellington had learned, once again, that his men could stand and win against superior numbers of the French, but he had also confirmed his view that he could not rely on the Spanish for supplies, for steady troops, or for generals that cared more for defeating the French than with squabbling with each other.

There were faults to be found with the British army as well though. They had stood firm but the British infantry had been found lacking in vigilance on two occasions on 27 July, and the uncontrolled charges on the 28th had almost led to disaster.

For the 5th Battalion 1809 had also been a difficult year with many forced marches in difficult conditions, and long periods with inadequate rations. However, for almost all of the year they had been the army's main body of riflemen and had been at the vanguard in many of the actions and marches, acquitting themselves with distinction and garnering praise. Their casualties had also been relatively light compared to many other battalions. Their colonel commandant, Sir George Prevost, was more than satisfied with their conduct and wrote to Davy:

> I received a few days ago your letter from Abrantes of the 25th June, and at the same time the newspapers announced the great and glorious victory of Talavera. From the report of Sir Arthur Wellesley, I have the satisfaction to learn the 5th Battalion of the 60th regiment did its duty, and in consequence, the apprehensions respecting the bravery and loyalty of the corps are replaced by confidence and admiration. Experience has taught me to ascribe, with few exceptions, to the commanding officer of a regiment its perfections and imperfections. On the present occasion you have my congratulations, and the battalion has my thanks for having rendered itself worthy of being considered a British regiment.
>
> I shall have much satisfaction in receiving your particulars of a battle, which appears to have afforded the general a noble opportunity of displaying his science.
>
> I hope Major Galiffe and Captains Wolf and Andrews, and the subalterns who were wounded on that glorious occasion have recovered.[80]

78 England Marriages, 1538–1973, (via https://familysearch.org , accessed 7 September 2018/), William Gabriel Davy and Mary Ann Carruthers, 20 June 1814

79 Butler, *Annals*, Vol. II, p.104.

80 G. Prevost to Davy, 16 October 1809, quoted in Rigaud, *Celer et Audax*, pp.101-2.

If the French had been better led and their various corps better coordinated, things could have gone much worse for the allies. As the year closed the French did manage to inflict some serious defeats on the Spanish armies. Three fresh divisions marched over the Pyrenees to reinforce King Joseph's forces, including a force of mounted police raised to counter the guerrillas. Wellington was convinced they would try and invade Portugal again, and he was right. For the 5th Battalion 1810 would bring a new commanding officer and more hard fighting.

16

Bussaco

At the start of 1810 the 5th Battalion was still in winter quarters at Montemore o Nova. The return of 25 January, the last that Davy would sign, stated the strength of the battalion as 52 sergeants, 12 buglers, and 588 rank and file. However, Captain Andrews, one sergeant, one corporal, and one private were in Lisbon in charge of the baggage and superintending the long-delayed arrival of the clothing. Andrews was also addressing some issues with the battalion's pay. Another private was on duty at the general hospital at Elvas as an orderly. Five officers, three sergeants, two buglers, and 72 rank and file were either missing or prisoners of war. The number of men sick, including men left at Talavera, meant that only 46 sergeants, nine buglers and 481 rank and file were actually present. One man had died, one deserted, and one deserter had returned since the December return.[1]

The January to March pay list shows four of the sick listed as 'sick unknown where' which implies that the battalion had lost track of the men or perhaps that they had died but the news had gone astray. Newly appointed Ensigns Larbusch and Kruger are listed as being with a detachment at Hilsea Barracks, back in Britain. Two men of the 2/60th are still listed, but the deserters and suspected men sent to that battalion at the start of 1809 are finally crossed off the list. Private John Klasgy, who had been Sir George Prevost's servant, was discharged after providing a substitute, John Ecksteyl, in his stead.[2]

Davy's promotion and the promotion of most of the ensigns to lieutenants had created a number of vacancies. Brevet Major Galiffe lost no time in making his case to Wellington for the vacant majority in a memorial:

> The Memorial of Brevet Major John Galiffe of the 5th Battn. 60th Regiment of Foot.
>
> Humbly sheweth
> That your Memorialist has served as Captain in the late York Rangers from the 13th October 1796, as Captain in the 5th Battn. 60th Regiment Since 30th December 1797 and as Brevet Major Since 25th April 1808.

1 January 1810 Return, TNA, WO 17/180.
2 March 1810 Pay List, TNA, WO 12/7074.

> That in the course of nearly fourteen years service as captain he has never been absent from his Regiment. That he has been present at all the actions fought under your Lordships command in Spain and Portugal; has been slightly wounded at the Battle of Talavera and most humbly solicits your lordship may be pleased to recommend Your Memorialist for a Majority being the Senior Captain of all the Battns. of the 60th Regiment.[3]

Wellington forwarded the memorial to Horse Guards with his endorsement, and Galiffe was promoted to major, without purchase, on 15 March after nearly a decade of waiting.[4]

Wellington also recommended Charles Joseph de Franciosci, then serving as an officer of the Loyal Lusitanian Legion, for an ensigncy in 60th, who then joined the battalion in October 1810.[5] The musical chairs amongst the battalion's medical staff continued as Surgeon Beattie, who had never joined the battalion, was replaced. The Surgeon General, Thomas Keate wrote to Horse Guards in February:

> Sir, In consequence of an application from Surgeon Drumgold of the 2nd Battn. 79th Regiment to be appointed to a Corps which will give him a greater chance of Service in a Warmer Climate, I beg leave to recommend that he may be removed to the 5th Battn. 60th Regt. In Exchange with Surgeon George Beattie who is desirous of an appointment in a North British Corps.[6]

Active service in the Peninsula may not have been the sort of warmer climate that Drumgold was seeking and he did not remain with the battalion long, being replaced by Surgeon Dumoulin, formerly an assistant surgeon with the battalion, who returned in September.[7]

Prominent Swiss émigré Sir Francis d'Ivernois, a friend of Galiffe, noticed the promotions of the ensigns of the battalion and wrote to Horse Guards chasing a long-promised commission for an acquaintance of his, Andrew Visseux. Visseux was given an ensigncy and was with the battalion by June.[8]

Not all memorials were successful though, even with the backing of a powerful patron. His Royal Highness the Duke of Kent applied for a lieutenancy in the 60th for Anthony van den Borgh (sometimes known as de Borgh or de Burgh). Van den Borgh had formerly served with the Prussian army, and then the Hompesch Hussars. The Duke thought him 'Particularly qualified for the rifle battn. As he possesses great activity of body & mind and he has taken a great deal of pains to study and make himself master of his profession'.[9] Instead of the lieutenancy in the 5th Battalion that he sought, Van den Borgh was given an

3 Galiffe to Wellington 1 February 1810, TNA, WO 31/296, Memorial of Brevet Major Galiffe.
4 March 1810 Pay List, TNA, WO 12/7074.
5 Memorial of Ensign Franciosci, TNA, WO 31/295; October 1810 Return, WO 17/180.
6 Keate to Merry 20 February, TNA, WO 31/295, Memorial of Surgeon Drumgold.
7 September 1810 Return, TNA, WO 17/180.
8 D'Ivernois to Torrens 14 March 1810, TNA, WO 31/296, Memorial of Visseux; June 1810 Return, WO 17/180, June 1810 return.
9 Kent to Taylor 5 February, TNA, WO 31/295, Memorial of van de Borgh.

ensigncy in one of the other battalions, but was promoted to lieutenant in 1811 before transferring to Portuguese service as a captain with the 11th Caçadores.[10]

The reduction of the Prussian army following the Treaties of Tilsit had led to many Prussian officers seeking employment in British service. His Royal Highness the Duke of Cambridge, colonel-in-chief of the King's German Legion, unable to find room for Lewis de Ingersleben in the legion, recommended him for a commission in the 60th. Ingersleben, who had been a lieutenant in Prussian service, accepted an ensigncy and joined the 5th Battalion in July 1810.[11]

The most significant officer to join the battalion in 1810 was its new commander, Lieutenant Colonel William Williams. Born in 1776 and commissioned into the 40th Foot in 1792 he had served in campaigns in the Low Countries, the West Indies, during the Irish rebellion, and in Egypt. He had been a major with 2/81st at Corunna and had been wounded there.[12] Williams brought his servant, Private James Cullmare, with him from the 81st.[13] A good description of Williams is included in the memoirs of Major General Le Marchant, one of Williams' friends, written by Le Marchant's son:

> He was of that small, slight, but well-proportioned figure, in which strength is usually combined with activity, and his disposition, wary and collected, yet ready, resolute, and decisive, admirably qualified him for a light infantry officer. He had served in this war from its commencement with distinguished reputation. The three great generals of those days, Abercromby, Moore, and Wellington, had each in their turn borne public and private testimony to his merit. Picton loved him as his son. Yet with all these unequivocal proofs of talent, so little was apparent in the intercourse of social life of the abilities that had marked his career as a soldier, that he gained very inadequate credit for them out of his own profession, and, in fact, bore no higher character than that of a worthy, obliging, kind-hearted man.[14]

Williams would join the battalion in the spring and in the meantime Major Woodgate took command following Davy's departure.

In February the battalion moved to Villa Nova and was then was once more spilt into detached companies and distributed between the various brigades of the army. The battalion would not be reunited again until May 1814. Woodgate wrote to Davy in early March:

> I received your letter from Lisbon at Alcontri, but as I thought you would have sailed the next day I did not answer it from thence. 'Thus far into the bowels of the land have we marched without impediment,' and, until the last two days, without rain, but now it pours down in torrents. Galiffe and I dined yesterday with General Fane. His brigade of cavalry is stationed here. He begs me to send his remembrances

10 Hall, *Biographical Dictionary*, p.66.

11 KGL Office to Torrens 25 November 1809, TNA, WO 31/289, Memorial of Lewis di Ingersleben; July 1810 Return, WO 17/180.

12 Butler, *Annals*, Vol. II, p.113; *The Royal Military Calendar*, Vol. IV, p.271

13 June 1810 Pay List, TNA, WO 12/7074.

14 D. Le Marchant, *Memoirs of the Late Major General Le Marchant* (London: Bentley, 1841), pp.260-1.

to you when I write. I extract the general orders of the 22nd ult., as I know they will please you. 'No. 4. A company of the 5th Battalion 60th regiment is to be attached to each of the brigades of the army according to the plan directed in the orders of the 4th May 1809'.

'The Commanding Officer 5th Battalion 60th regiment will detach three companies to Lieut.-General Hill's division as soon as he will receive this order and a route from the Quartermaster-General for the purpose. And as the general officers commanding brigades have invariably expressed the highest satisfaction at the uniform good conduct of this invaluable body of men, which has always continued effective under many trying circumstances, the Commander of the Forces desires that, as far as possible, the same companies may be detached to the same brigades as formerly'.

You see, my dear Sir, His Lordship will not desert us, and although he has divided us more than last year, I trust we shall again be conspicuous if an opportunity offers. The orders go on to state –

'Two companies will be attached to Sir J. Sherbrooke's division – one for the brigade of Guards, and one for Brigd.-General Cameron's brigade. Two companies to the 4th division; being one for Major-General Cole's and one for Brigd.-General Campbell's brigade; and three companies with the head-quarters of the regiment to the 3rd division'.

The third division is commanded by your friend General Picton, and contains our old brigade of Colonel McKinnon, and another of General Lightburne; Crawfurd has a division called 'the light division,' and is out of our way. I have complied with his Lordship's directions about sending the same companies, although against my wish, but after the compliment the general have made, I could not do otherwise. I much wished to keep Wend with me for many reasons, but as General Hill also asked for him, I sent him there again. I send Schoedde to the Guards, and keep Hames at head-quarters; and, as he now has become one of the committee of paymastership, his presence with us will be necessary when Andrews is away. I keep Andrews', Hames', and Salaberry's companies with me.

I sent Wend's, McMahon's, and Blassiere's companies to Portalegre, where General Hill is, from Rio Maior. The other seven companies march with me tomorrow to Viseu, where I shall crave admittance to his Lordship and thank him for his kindness, &c., &c. This place is very full. Your old patron very kindly received me.

I have promoted those you wished, and filled up other vacancies, I believe according to merit, at least I hope so.

You may tell General de Rottenburg I am not very much obliged to him for sending out Colonel Williams, but I trust we shall have a bloody fight before he comes.[15]

At some stage Woodgate's intention to keep Hames with him and send Schoedde to the Guards must have been changed, or over-ruled, as Hames returned to the Guards Brigade

15 Woodgate to Davy 10 March 1810, quoted in Rigaud, *Celer et Audax*, pp.115-7.

with whom his company had served in 1809, and Schoedde remained with Woodgate in the 3rd Division.[16]

As spring approached Wellington began to distribute his army to defend Portugal from the invasion he felt sure would come. The two primary routes from Spain into Portugal were guarded by pairs of fortresses, one on the Portuguese side and one on the Spanish. In the south Elvas and Badajoz were both strong and well situated fortifications. Further north Almeida and Ciudad Rodrigo were weaker, which was one of the factors that led Wellington to believe that this more northerly route was the more likely. The southern route would also see the French having to cross the Tagus before approaching the capital. Wellington moved his headquarters and the 1st Division to Viseu in central Portugal, with the 3rd at Trancoso and the 4th at Guarda further to the east. The Light Division was placed on the frontier around Almeida, and the 2nd Division was kept further south in case the French came by that route.

Napoleon's defeat of Austria the previous summer freed up men and resources that the emperor hoped would put an end to the long running campaign in the Peninsula. Realising that the British troops were likely to be outnumbered by any attacking French army Wellington continued to reform, re-equip. and enlarge the Portuguese army commanded by Beresford. The Portuguese troops were taught British drill, armed with Brown Bess muskets, and drilled by British sergeants. Older and ineffective Portuguese officers were removed and British officers were recruited and integrated into the Portuguese units. British officers automatically advanced one rank on joining the Portuguese army so it was a tempting way to advance their careers.

The existing Portuguese light infantry units, the Caçadores, were expanded by 50 percent and by August 1810 two out of the six companies in each Caçadore battalion were armed with rifles.[17] Officers of the 5th Battalion who transferred to Portuguese service were often employed in the Caçadores, as we have seen with Schwalbach and Zühleke. Lieutenant Linstow also served with them after the Loyal Lusitanian Legion was disbanded to create more battalions of Caçadores. Ensign de Brunning joined the 3rd Caçadores. Another officer, Captain Gustavus Braun, who had left the 5th Battalion for the 6/60th in 1801 entered Portuguese service as a *major* in the 9th Caçadores. Braun was born in Arneburg in 1775. He served in the army of Saxony before joining British service as a lieutenant in Lowenstein's Chasseurs in August 1795 at the age of only 19.[18] In Portuguese service he rose to *tenente-coronel* and command of his battalion. He was wounded at the Battle of the Nive in 1813. In 1815 he was knighted as a Companion of the Bath. He returned to Portuguese service in the 1820s with the rank of *marechal de campo*. He then served in Brazil at the same rank and commanded troops during a conflict with Argentina. He died in 1859 aged 84.[19]

The Portuguese regulars developed into a capable and dependable part of Wellington's army. The Portuguese militia were less reliable but more numerous, and were used to garrison fortifications or were posted in areas where the allies needed a presence but were

16 March 1810 Return TNA, WO 17/180.

17 R. Chartrand, *Bussaco 1810* (Oxford: Osprey, 2001), p.27.

18 Foreign Corps Officer List, TNA, WO 65/167 p.60.

19 Butler, *Annals*, Vol. II, pp.159, 112, 211.

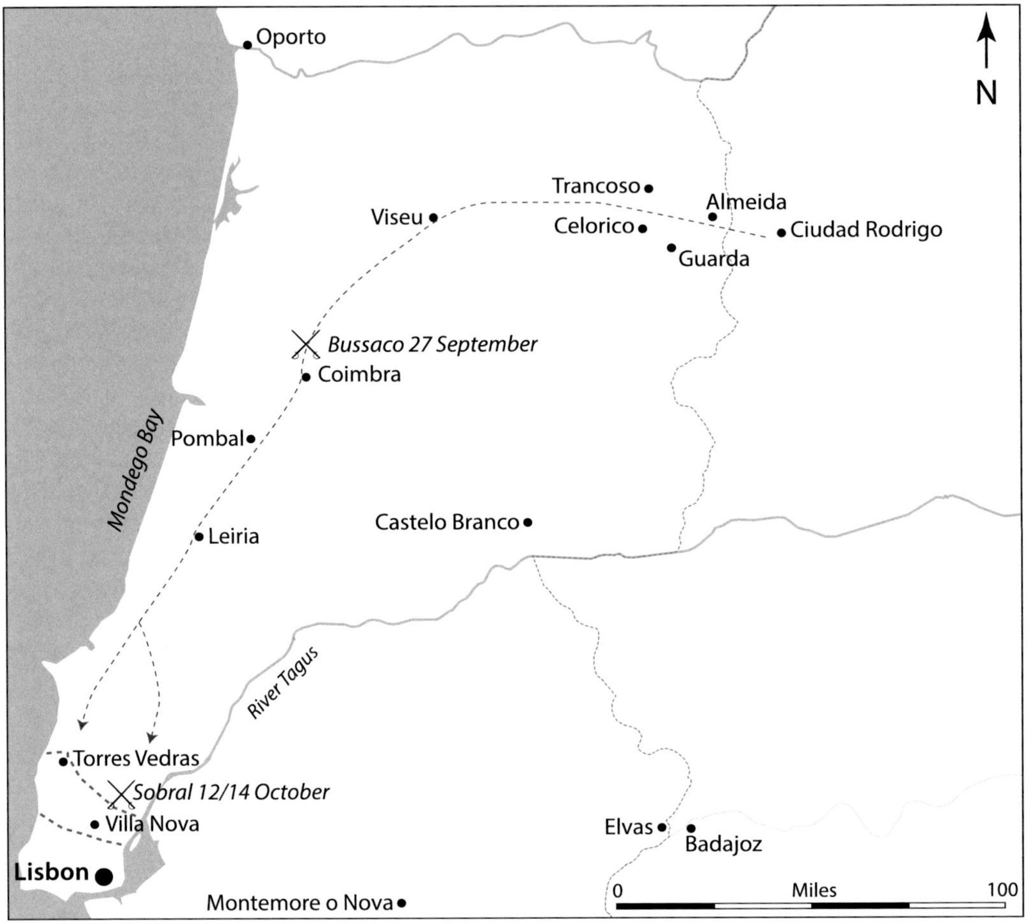

Massena's Invasion of Portugal, July to October 1810.

unlikely to be attacked. The last level of Portuguese forces was the *Ordenanças*, a local levy that was poorly trained and equipped, but adequate for garrisons and also useful in providing a guerrilla force to hamper French communications and to harass their supply convoys.

Wellington fortified the likely invasion routes into Portugal with a series of entrenchments and redoubts on the major roads at points where he thought he might have to fight the French. The topography of Portugal favoured defence, one reason it had managed to retain its independence from its bigger neighbour. The roads towards Spain were mostly very poor and few in number. There were plentiful stretches of rough, hilly terrain and the rivers often ran in deep gorges with few crossing points. Large swathes of the countryside were also sparsely populated with very little in the way of crops or livestock by which any invading force could hope to sustain themselves with. To exacerbate this Wellington laid plans to evacuate the population as the French advanced, and to destroy any food that could not be taken back towards Lisbon.

Officer of the 5th Battalion 1797, from a sketch of Lieutenant John Anthony Wolff. Reproduced from the original artwork for *The Annals of the King's Royal Rifle Corps, Appendix dealing with Uniform, Armament & Equipment.* (The Royal Green Jackets (Rifles) Museum)

Privates of the 5th Battalion, 1797 (left), and the rifle company of the 6th Battalion, 1799 (right). Reproduced from *The Annals of the King's Royal Rifle Corps, Appendix dealing with Uniform, Armament & Equipment.* (The Royal Green Jackets (Rifles) Museum)

Private of the 5th Battalion, 1812. Reproduced from the original artwork for *The Annals of the King's Royal Rifle Corps, Appendix dealing with Uniform, Armament & Equipment*. (The Royal Green Jackets (Rifles) Museum)

Officer of the 5th Battalion, 1812. Reproduced from the original artwork for *The Annals of the King's Royal Rifle Corps, Appendix dealing with Uniform, Armament & Equipment*. (The Royal Green Jackets (Rifles) Museum)

The medals and awards of Lieutenant Colonel John Galiffe. From the left: The Most Honourable Order of the Bath, C.B. (Military) Companion's breast badge; Army Gold Cross, for Vittoria, Nivelle, Orthez, and Toulouse; Field Officer's Gold Medal, for Vittoria, with clasp for Nivelle; Military General Service 1793-1814, with 11 clasps, Roliça, Vimiero, Talavera, Bussaco, Fuentes D'Onor, Albuera, Ciudad Rodrigo, Badajoz, Salamanca, Pyrenees, and Nive. Also his Order of the Bath chapel stall plate (top). (Dix Noonan Webb Ltd.)

Nos. 2, 3, & 7 companies 5/60th leading the way across the Rivellas stream at the storming of Badajoz. 'Point of No Return' © Christa Hook.

Miniature of Major William Gabriel Davy, who commanded the 5th Battalion in the opening years of the Peninsular War. Probably painted late 1808 or early 1809 as it shows his Field Officer's Gold Medal for Roliça and Vimeiro, without the clasp for Talavera. (The Royal Green Jackets (Rifles) Museum)

An original 5th Battalion officer's jacket. (The Royal Green Jackets (Rifles) Museum)

Illustration showing, from the left, a rifleman at ease, and then at attention with order arms, shoulder arms and support arms. (The Royal Green Jackets (Rifles) Museum)

'Major John Galiffe and Private Daniel Lochstadt, Albuera, 16th May 1811', © Christa Hook.

'60th rifles waiting to embark', c. 1820, unsigned. (Anne S.K. Brown Military Collection)

If the French managed to defeat, or out-manoeuvre his army, and find enough to eat on the march to the capital, Wellington planned one last line of defences that spanned the peninsula on which Lisbon lay. Stretching from the Atlantic to the River Tagus two lines of redoubts, batteries and forts had been begun in the autumn of 1809 by Portuguese labourers under the command of Wellington's senior engineer, Lieutenant Colonel Richard Fletcher. These defences would become known as the Lines of Torres Vedras, after one of the towns in the area.

In April Napoleon appointed *Marechal* Andre Massena to command his Army of Portugal, which was to consist of around 50,000 men from *Général de Division* Reynier's II Corps, *Marechal* Ney's VI Corps, and *Général de Division* Junot's VIII Corps. Massena was one of Napoleon's most experienced commanders but was perhaps past his prime, having become a little too attached the luxuries his position brought. His orders were to besiege Ciudad Rodrigo and then Almeida and not to invade Portugal until September, after the hottest weather.[20] Such a prolonged timetable suited Massena who traveled to Spain with a large staff, and his much younger mistress. He arrived at Salamanca in late May. Had the French chosen to bypass the two fortresses and advance directly into Portugal Wellington would have been far less prepared to receive them.

In April Major Galiffe, who had not yet heard of his promotion, wrote to Davy and updated him with news of the battalion's movements:

> You left us so abruptly that I had not even time to take leave of you, and really I expected that, as you had always been kind to me, you would have told me your resolution to leave us without saying anything. However I hope your friendship for me is not altered, and that you will still remember your friends of this battalion; and really situated as I am you can be of very great service to me, in assisting my getting the majority vacant by your promotion. Lord Wellington has been pleased to second it, and yet there is no answer made to my memorial.
>
> I don't know if there has been any obstacle thrown in my way; and nobody could better know what it is than you, as you are at head-quarters.
>
> I would beg you, dear Colonel, when you see Colonel Torrens to ask him if he has been kind enough to answer the memorial and what I am to expect. I am sure at the same time that your own recommendation will have great weight with him; and I have no doubt but what everything will succeed to my satisfaction if you will have the goodness to assist me.
>
> Since you sailed we have been separated again, but, instead of five, seven companies are detached. McMahon, Wend, and Blassiere are with General Hill at Portalegre; Wolf with General Cameron at Mengualda; Hames with the Guards at Viseu; Prevost's and mine, both under my command, with General Cole at Guarda and neighbourhood; and Andrews, Schoedde, and Salaberry's, with the staff, are attached to General Picton's division at Trancoso.
>
> Major Woodgate is very unwell, he has a kind of rheumatism in the head; his face is much swelled, and I believe he will be under the necessity of going to Lisbon for some time.

20 Oman, *Peninsular War*, Vol. III, p.227.

On our march from Coimbra to Viseu, Banes of my company, who belonged to the band, deserted in the night at Malliada during a most terrible storm, and he was supposed to have been drowned in the same place where last year (if you recollect) we lost two Swiss in coming from Oporto; but lately one of our serjeants passing by Coimbra found him in a gentleman's dress walking snugly through the streets; he is now at head-quarters, where he will have a severe punishment.

The men in general behaved very well, and they are the spoiled children of the division, in fact we are much more liked than the 95th.

The head-quarters are going to be removed from Viseu to Cea, half way to Coimbra on the road from Guarda to this place. Everybody here says that we are to retire; in a little time we will be under the necessity of doing so, even without an enemy before us, for we begin to feel the scarcity of provisions, and already there is almost no forage for our horses.

The French have retired also to Salamanca and Astorga; Ney has left that army to go to Paris, and they say that as there is to be war with Russia no reinforcements will come from France, and for that reason they are going to concentrate their forces near Madrid, and will act upon the defensive; and as we are in the same situation we may remain so the whole of the campaign.[21]

In May the battalion prepared for the coming campaign. Orders were given for the battalion's band to send their instruments to the quarter-master and the servants were to report to their companies.[22] Captain Andrews wrote to Davy from Pinhel, near Almeida:

Shortly after the date of my former we moved up here to protect the front, from Almeida, on the right to Ciudad Rodrigo on the left. General Crawfurd's left connects with us, extending his right to Gallegos and the villages perpendicular to Guarda.

About the 28th ult. the enemy moved a column from Salamanca to near Ciudad Rodrigo, which caused our second line to close up upon the first, when head-quarters removed at an hour's notice from Viseu to Celerico; but tranquillity soon prevailed again, and the advanced posts of both armies are on speaking terms, and only separated in one place by a small river.

All the late accounts induce a belief that the enemy will not be in a condition to make a forward movement till very considerable reinforcements arrive which are not yet on the road; this promises a lingering existence to us.

Within these last few days past we have had five recruits join us: Colonel Williams, Doctor Drumgold, and Ensigns Kruger, Larbusch, and Burghaagen, of whom I shall remark in rotation.

Colonel Williams is a short man; looking in profile at a short distance like Dumoulin (assistant-surgeon), but on nearer inspection in front much resembles Captain White, late lieutenant in this battalion. His manner is quick, peremptory,

21 Galiffe to Davy 2 April 1810, quoted in Riguad, *Celer et Audax*, pp.117-9.

22 Riguad, *Celer et Audax*, p.120.

> and at the same time courteous; he speaks with rather a studied tone of voice, something between the agreeable and the commanding; he bows like a statesman entering into office, and from all I have observed doubt not that General De Rottenburg has intrusted him with the talisman so essential to command this corps.
>
> Our Doctor is a promotion from the 2nd West India regiment to the 79th regiment, from which he was exchanged to us. He is a being with a circular head fixed on between his shoulders, without any neck. The deficiency is so well recompensed by the rotundity and size of his body that without any violation of language we may apply the old adage, 'Things are as broad as they are long'. 'Caledonia gave him birth'.
>
> With respect to the three Ensigns, I fear more interesting matter will deprive me of noticing them at present.
>
> De Bree is still in Lisbon, very unwell; I believe he is to be sent home to recruit.
>
> Schoedde has been confined for three weeks with fever; an application has been this day made to send him to Lisbon; his constitution will not stand this kind of life any longer.
>
> I most kindly thank you for the manner in which you mention the military object of my wishes. When you have seen General de Rottenburg possibly you may be able to let me know his opinion; from which, and your own, I shall make up my mind how to act.
>
> Major Woodgate is recovering fast; he presents his kindest regards, as does Schoedde, Galiffe, and Fürst.[23]

Andrews' enquiry about his future related to the possible paths of promotion to major. Captain Schoedde had returned to the battalion by September, after being prescribed 'the best of living, and at least two bottles of Madeira per diem' by his Portuguese doctor.[24]

The French began the siege of Ciudad Rodrigo in late May, but it progressed slowly due to problems finding enough supplies and transport in the region. Only on 25 June did French artillery begin a serious attempt at creating a breach in the walls. By 9 July, after the exploding of 800 pounds of gunpowder in a mine, a practical breach was created and the French troops stormed the fortress. The Spanish promptly surrendered without a fight.

Wellington's Light Division under Brigadier General Robert Craufurd was based around the fortress of Almeida, just 25 miles away from Ciudad Rodrigo. The division consisted of the 1/43rd, 1/52nd and 1/95th, and the 1st and 3rd Caçadores. Craufurd was a capable officer but could be stubborn and ill-tempered. As the French advanced the Light Division fell back towards the River Coa. Wellington knew he could not afford to confront the French on the plains around the fortress as the French had the advantage in numbers, and especially in cavalry, but his defensive strategy was not popular with some of his officers and elements of the Portuguese government.

Craufurd had orders withdraw across the river if pressed too hard by the French. However, he was too slow falling back and ended up fighting a fierce but unnecessary action on 24 July

23 Andrews to Davy 19 May 1810, quoted in Riguad, *Celer et Audax*, pp.126-8.

24 Riguad, *Celer et Audax*, p.130.

as he tried to get his troops across the one narrow bridge, in which the Light Division was only saved from disaster by the bravery and determination of its soldiers. With the Light Division out of their way the French began the process of besieging Almeida, bringing up supplies, creating batteries of heavy guns, and digging trenches.

It had been the Light Division that had been at the forefront of Wellington's army during the summer, engaging in small skirmishes and outpost actions with the French. The rest of the army, the companies of the 5th Battalion amongst them, did little apart from occasional changes of location based on the latest intelligence of French movements. One such precaution was the moving of the general hospital from Elvas, near the frontier, back to Lisbon. Private Frederick Wagner of the 5th Battalion died on the march when the sick were transported to the new location.[25]

The returns of the battalion place the headquarters at Pinhel, a day's march west of Almeida, from April to July. Captain Hames exchanged with Captain Howard of the 2/60th and left. Howard arrived to replace him in October. Sergeant Major Peter Broetz was promoted to Ensign, and Ensigns Burghaagen and Ingersleben joined the battalion, as did Lieutenant Sylvester O'Hehir. Captain James Prevost also re-joined his company after being an aide to his uncle, Sir George Prevost, at Halifax, Nova Scotia. James had become enamoured with a local girl and his uncle, knowing his young and extravagant nephew only had his Army pay for an income, thought it best that he returned to the battalion before he took things too far.[26]

The July return also noted that one prisoner of war returned to the battalion after escaping, stating that the man in question had been missing since 20 August 1808.[27] The pay list, though, has two prisoners of war coming back to the battalion around that time; Privates Joseph Deserteur and Balthasar Gulthals, but they went missing at Talavera on 27 and 28 July 1809 respectively. The only member of the battalion to go absent on 20 August 1808 was Private William Erhard, who was listed as having deserted. He does appear back on the pay list for June to September but there is no comment next to his entry. British prisoners of war were marched back to France and the columns were often attacked by Spanish guerrillas, freeing some of the men. Eventually some of these would make their way back to their units. However, with foreign troops, it is perhaps possible that the returnees had joined French ranks for a while, in order to gain an opportunity to desert back to the British. The June to September pay list also has two privates being sent back to Britain as 'suspected' men to be transferred to another battalion of the 60th.[28]

The French started work on trenches and batteries around Almeida on 14 August, and began their bombardment on the 26th. The next day a lucky shot landed in the courtyard of the old castle that was being used as a powder magazine. Over 150,000 pounds of gun powder and a million musket cartridges exploded, obliterating the castle and large portions of the town, killing around 1,300 of the soldiers and inhabitants.[29] Not surprisingly on the 28th the British commander, Colonel Cox, surrendered. Massena was free to advance further

25 August 1810 Casualty Return, TNA, WO 25/1923.

26 D. E. Graves, *Fix Bayonets!*, p.135.

27 April to July 1810 Returns, TNA, WO 17/180.

28 September 1810 Pay List TNA, WO 12/7074; September 1808 Pay List WO 12/7073.

29 D. Buttery, *Wellington Against Massena* (Barnsley: Pen & Sword, 2007) p.85.

in to Portugal but he was hampered by logistical issues, including his supply convoys being attacked by Spanish guerrillas.

During the siege the French advance guard was moved forward to Pinhel and Wellington concentrated his whole army on a line from Guarda to Celorico, covering the two possible routes that Massena could use to Lisbon. The southern route had good roads along the Mondego valley, whereas the more northern one had far worse roads. On 12 September Captain Andrews wrote to Davy again:

> About the 29th of July the army moved to the rear of Celorico, except the light brigade and cavalry. Our station was in a village half way up the Sierra de Estella, where, although the climate was uncommonly fine, we got more sickly than ever I knew, as out of our three companies we had near fifty in hospital; and I believe, even bad as this appears, we were more fortunate than the rest of the army.
>
> The sick of the whole army are immediately sent off to Coimbra and Lisbon, and everything kept in a state to facilitate a movement in that direction.
>
> Our head-quarters at present is at Gavio, a considerable town at the foot of the Estrella, four leagues behind Celorico. Cavalry at the latter place, light brigade at Minho, Cole's division at Pincenços, Picton's at Galines, La Rosa, etc.; and the first division at the Ponte de Marcell, about four leagues from Coimbra; we are all in houses of some sort.
>
> Our corps has been going on in the old way for a long time; the only change is that Prevost has arrived from America and now commands his company.
>
> Schoedde has rejoined, quite well; we have only had one officer-recruit for some time, a Lieutenant O'Heir from Brunswick, a genteel-looking man, an Austrian of Irish parents.[30]

Massena chose the harder more northerly route, possibly due to poor maps or lack of knowledge of the roads. As the French advanced Wellington pulled his army back, but as they went they burnt down houses, emptied storehouses, drove off livestock, and forced the population to abandon their homes. The French army, used to living off the land, found very little left. Scavenging parties were often attacked by the *Ordenanças*. Massena's army advanced very slowly, often having to rebuild the roads to make them passable. The French arrived at Viseu, finding it almost empty, on 19 September. The advanced guard pressed on the next day but the main army did not move again until the 24th, when the French clashed with the British rearguard from the Light Division. By taking the northern roads Massena had bypassed some of the prepared redoubts on the southern route but Wellington knew the ground and had already chosen the long Bussaco ridge, to the north east of Coimbra, as somewhere he could stand and fight.

The ridge was an excellent natural defensive position. About nine miles long and up to 1,800 feet high it stretched from the Mondego River on the right to the hills of the Serra de Alcoba on the left. The eastern side, from which the French would approach, was very steep with occasional rocky outcrops. The slopes were partially wooded but mostly covered

30 Andrews to Davy 12 September 1810, quoted in Rigaud, *Celer et Audax*, pp.128-9.

with gorse and scrub. Several ravines ran down the ridge, effectively dividing the potential battlefield. Two roads crossed the ridge, the larger was paved and twisted around a spur near the village of Sula before crossing the summit near a convent. The convent was surrounded by a ten foot high wall and Wellington used it as his headquarters. The smaller track led from Santo Antonio de Cantaro to Palheiros, and there were two further small footpaths that made their way up the slopes. These tracks and paths marked the most likely points the French would attack. The top of the ridge was often wide enough to allow easy movement of troops along it, and even for small numbers of cavalry to operate. The incline of the ridge was steep enough that any manoeuvres below would be seen but troops at the foot would not be able to see much of the disposition of the defenders. The only weakness of the ridge was that there was a mountain track that outflanked it to the north. Wellington placed a small force of Portuguese militia there in case the French discovered it.[31]

The allied army was brigaded and the companies of the 5th Battalion distributed as follows:

1st Division – Lieutenant General Spencer
Colonel Stopford
  1/Coldstream Guards, 1/3rd Guards, & No. 5 company 5/60th.
Lieutenant Colonel Lord Blantyre
  2/24th, 2/42nd, 1/61st, & No. 9 company 5/60th.
Major General Löwe
  1st KGL, 2nd KGL, 5th KGL, 7th KGL, & Detachments Light battalions KGL.
Colonel Pakenham
  1/7th & 1/79th.

2nd Division – Lieutenant General Hill
Major General W. Stewart
  1/3rd, 2/31st, 2/48th, 2/66th & No. 6 company 5/60th.
Brevet Colonel Inglis
  29th, 1/48th, 1/57th & No. 8 company 5/60th.
Lieutenant Colonel Wilson
  2/28th, 2/34th, 2/39th & No. 4 company 5/60th.

Major General Hamilton's Portuguese Division (attached to 2nd Division)
Coronel Archibald Campbell
  4th (2 battalions) & 10th (2 battalions).
Brigadeiro Fonseca
  2nd (2 battalions) & 14th (2 battalions).

3rd Division – Major General Picton
Colonel Mackinnon
  1/45th, 1/74th, & 1/88th.

31 Oman, *Peninsular War*, Vol. III, pp.359-64.

Major General Lightburne

2/5th, 2/83rd, & Nos. 2, 3, & 7 companies 5/60th with Lt. Col. Williams & Maj. Woodgate.

Coronel Champalimaud (Portuguese)

9th (2 battalions), & 21st (1 battalion).

4th Division – Major General Cole

Major General Alexander Campbell

2/7th, 1/11th, 2/53rd & No. 1 company 5/60th.

Colonel Kemmis

3/27th, 1/40th, 97th & No. 10 company 5/60th.

Coronel Collins (Portuguese)

11th (2 battalions), & 23rd (2 battalions).

5th Division – Major General Leith

Lieutenant Colonel Barnes

3/1st, 1/9th & 2/38th.

Brigadeiro Spry (Portuguese)

3rd (2 battalions), 15th (2 battalions) & Tomar Militia.

Coronel Eben (Portuguese)

Lusitanian Legion (3 battalions) & 8th (2 battalions).

Light Division – Brigadier General Craufurd

Lieutenant Colonel Beckwith

1/43rd, 1/95th (4 coys) & 3rd Caçadores.

Lieutenant Colonel Barclay

1/52rd, 1/95th (4 coys) & 1st Caçadores.

Independent Portuguese Brigades

Brigadeiro Pack

1st (2 battalions), 16th (2 battalions) & 4th Caçadores.

Brigadeiro A. Campbell

6th (2 battalions), 18th (2 battalions) & 6th Caçadores.

Brigadeiro Coleman

7th (2 battalions), 19th (2 battalions) & 2nd Caçadores.[32]

The total strength of the allied army at Bussaco was 26,843 British and 25,429 Portuguese troops[33], nearly 10,000 less than the French army that they faced which numbered 62,538. The terrain still gave Wellington the advantage though. His troops had been arriving for several days and he had plenty of time to deploy them along the ridge as the French slowly approached. At the northern end, the left of Wellington's position, was the 4th Division. The

32 Oman, *Peninsular War*, Vol. III, pp.544-7; September 1810 Return, TNA, WO 17/180.

33 Oman, *Peninsular War*, Vol. III, pp.543 & 547.

Light Division held the road through the village of Sula, with Pack's Portuguese brigade in support, with two more, A. Campbell's and Coleman's, nearby. Löwe's KGL were held in reserve near the convent. The 1st, 3rd, and recently-formed 5th Divisions were spaced along the ridge, with the 2nd Division on the heights on the right. Lastly, holding the right flank where the ridge met the Mondego River, was a battalion of the Lusitanian Legion.[34]

The ridge was so long that there were gaps and areas where it was lightly held. On the night of 26 September, in order to keep Massena guessing as to the strength and position of his men, Wellington ordered them to light no campfires. The men on the ridge though, were all too aware of the numerous French fires spread out on the slopes on the opposite side of the valley. For many of the men, especially the untested Portuguese units, the battle to come would be their first. The men lay wrapped in their greatcoats on the stony ground, exposed to a cold mountain wind.

The riflemen of the 5th Battalion though, were not on the top of the ridge. Along with the other light troops most were placed forward, down the slope, in a thick line of pickets ready to be the first to engage the French when morning came. During the night the light company of the 1/88th was driven back from its position at the base of the ridge and the pickets of the 4th Caçadores and 1/95th were both engaged but did not retreat.

Massena had examined Wellington's position on the afternoon of the 26th and made his plans. Reynier's II Corps was to attack what Massena thought was Wellington's right flank but was actually close to his centre and was the area held by Picton's 3rd Division. Once Reynier gained the top of the ridge he would turn right and roll up Wellington's line while Ney's VI Corps advanced up the road through Sula towards the convent.

The allied army was under arms two hours before daybreak on 27 September. Just as dawn came the men heard the first shots as the line of pickets were engaged. The base of the ridge was covered in a thick mist that hid the first movements of the French. Reynier's II Corps advanced towards the low point of the ridge held by Picton's 3rd Division. A thick screen of skirmishers preceded two large columns. The 11 battalions of Heudelet's division, 8,000 strong, marched up the left track, and the 11 battalions of Merle's division of 6,500 men on the right. The French artillery opened fire but could make little impression on the positions at the top of the ridge.[35]

Lieutenant Colonel Williams commanded the light companies of the 1/45th, 74th, and 1/88th in addition to his own three companies. The 74th and 1/88th light companies were to the north of the track near the hamlet of Santo António de Cântaro and the 1/45th light company and the three companies of the 5th Battalion, with Major Woodgate and Lieutenant Colonel Williams, were to the south near a ravine. The previous night some of the battalion's outposts had been attacked. Captain Lemonnier-Delafosse of the French 31e Légère described the British position prior to the battle:

> In front of these line black specs at equal intervals indicated the sharp-shooter outposts driven in on the evening of the 26th – Riflemen – whose short rifles were

34 Lipscombe, *Peninsular War Atlas*, pp.170-1.

35 The description of the battle is taken from: Rigaud, *Celer et Audax*, pp.132-5; Butler, *Annals*, Vol. II, pp.116-20; Buttery, *Massena*, pp.94-104; G.L. Chambers, *Bussaco* (London: Swan Sonnenschein,1910) pp.40-120; Chartrand, *Bussaco 1810*, pp.65-83; Lipscombe, *Peninsular War Atlas*, pp.170-5; Oman, *Peninsular War*. Vol. III, pp.359-89.

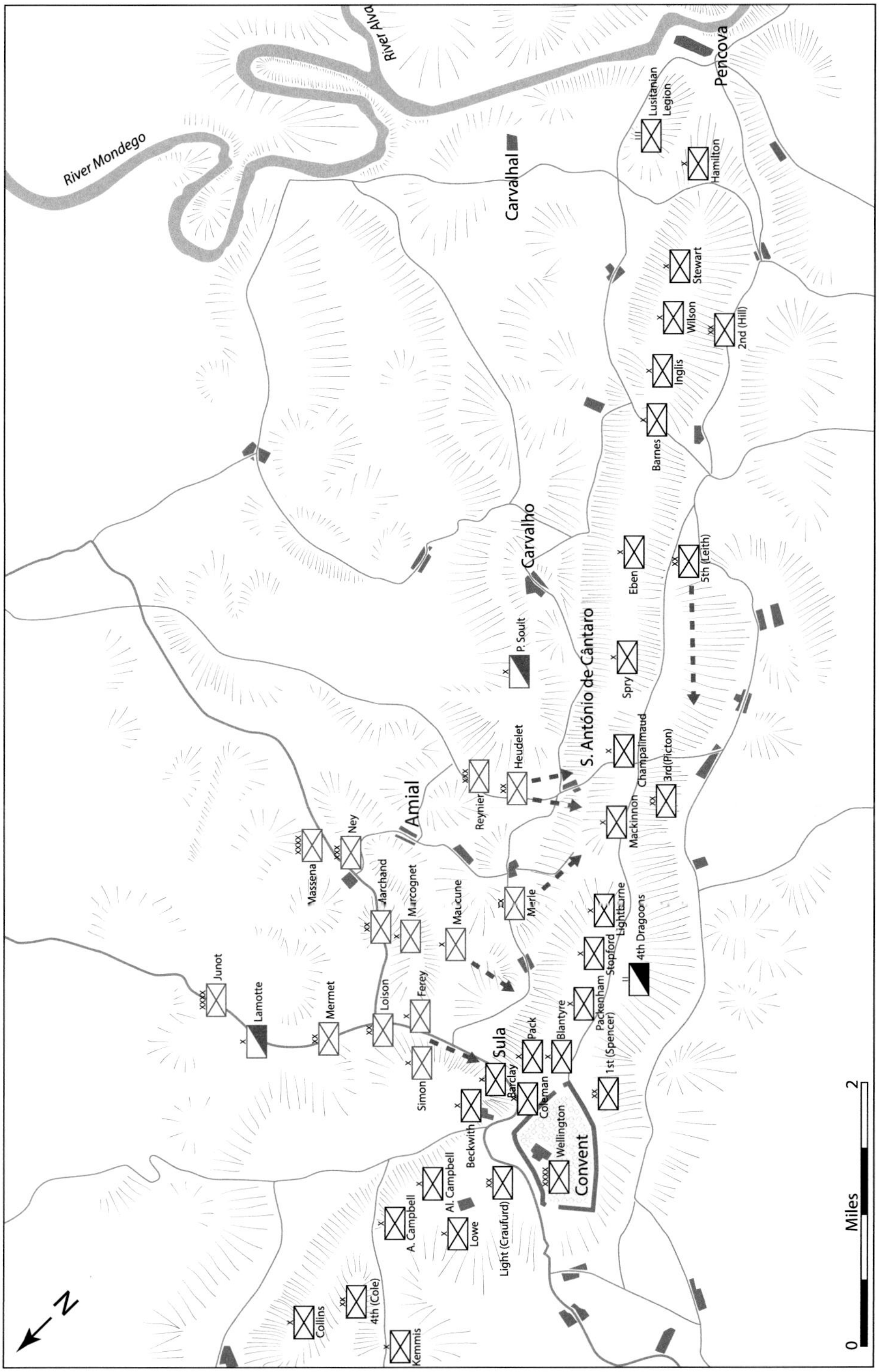

The Battle of Bussaco, 27 September 1810.
Sources: Lipscombe, *Atlas* & Oman, *History of the Peninsular War*.

> so murderous. Their bugle horns, a kind of short cornet lined with brass, could be heard emitting a sound so discordant and piercing that one might suppose they were sounding the call to awaken the dead at the Judgement Day.[36]

Severely outnumbered by the French skirmishers the British light troops began to withdraw as the columns approached. Williams turned his extended line and redeployed on the flank of Heudelet's column, which was headed by the 31e Légère, and continued to fire as the French marched towards the crest of the ridge. Portuguese artillery opened fire as the French came into range. The steep slope and incessant cannon and rifle fire began to disorder the French formation. When it neared the top it was met by disciplined volleys from the British 74th and Portuguese 21st, which prevented the French from deploying into line. The 31e Légère held their ground for some time but their formation began to collapse. When they retreated Williams turned his line again and followed them back down the slope to the position his men had held the previous night.

The attack of Merle's column drove back the light companies of the 1/45th and 1/88th but was met at the crest by the line companies 1/88th, half of the 1/45th, and the Portuguese 8th Regiment. After a series of volleys the 45th and 88th formed line together and bayonet charged the French. There was a vicious close quarter battle on the rocky slope before the French, fatigued by the climb, retreated with heavy losses and were pursued by the redcoats to the bottom of the hill. Reynier, seeing his first two attacks fail, sent in Foy's brigade who managed to gain a footing on the crest, but were eventually driven back by reinforcements from Leith's 5th Division.

Once Ney saw Reynier's columns reach the crest he launched his own attack around the road through Sula. His columns were met by sustained fire from the Caçadores and the 1/95th of the Light Division. The French skirmishers had to be reinforced to make progress. They took the village and then pressed on to attack the British guns at the top of the ridge. However, Craufurd had concealed the 1/43rd and 1/52nd in a ravine. As the French were about to charge the guns the two battalions stood up and fired volleys into the column. The Caçadores and the 1/95th supported the redcoats and then Craufurd ordered a charge which broke the French and forced them back down the hill. Another French column attacked Pack's Portuguese Brigade, driving back the 4th Caçadores before being halted by volleys from the rest of the brigade. Ney saw that he too had failed and ordered a retreat. It was still only 8:00 a.m.

Ney sent his light infantry forward again to engage the British light troops and a series of small skirmishes carried on for the rest of the morning, but the battle was effectively over with Massena seeing that it was pointless to attack again. Total allied casualties were 1,252 killed, wounded or missing, split evenly between British and Portuguese units. Total French losses were 4,498.[37]

French casualties were again particularly heavy in officers. A German, then in French service and who would later join the KGL, Johann Maempel, took part in the attack on Sula

36 Quoted in Butler, *Annals*, Vol. II, p.118.
37 Oman, *Peninsular War*, Vol. III, pp.384-5.

against the Light Division and remembered what it was like to be on the receiving end of accurate rifle fire:

> Our troops attacked with their usual impetuosity, but were so warmly received by the riflemen of the German legion, and of the 60th and 95th regiments, that they fell in all directions; every shot told and our regiment alone had seven officers killed, besides the wounded: in my company there were forty-eight killed and wounded; the captain was shot through the body, and was carried to the hospital at Coimbra. General Simon, who commanded our brigade, was also wounded and made prisoner. We attacked the heights at the point of the bayonet; but before we had reached half-way, we were driven back with great loss.[38]

The 5th Battalion lost three men killed in action: Private John Witting (No. 3), a labourer from Hannover, had joined the battalion in March 1806; Private John Kowalsky (No. 7), a shoemaker from Galicia, had joined from the Foreign Depot in September 1807. Both were in the companies with Lieutenant Colonel Williams. The other fatality was Private Jacob Stephan, from Lugar in Hungary who had been in British service since 1795 and had been with the battalion since formation. Stephan was is listed in the casualty return as No. 10 company, which was on the extreme left flank of the allied position in Colonel Kemmis' brigade of the 4th Division, but according to the pay list he was in No. 5 company. No. 5 company, with the Guards Brigade, were involved in a long firefight with French light infantry. The 4th Division was not engaged and seem to have suffered no other casualties so it is more likely Stephan was killed with No. 5 company.[39]

George Napier, of the 1/52nd, recalled that after the battle both sides began to attend to the wounded:

> When we got to the bottom, where a small stream ran between us and the enemy's position, by general consent we all mingled together searching for the wounded. During this cessation of fighting we spoke to each other as though we were the greatest friends and without the least animosity or angry feeling! One poor German officer in the French army came to make inquiries respecting his brother, who was in our service in the 60th Regiment, which was at that time composed principally of foreigners, and upon looking about he found him dead, the poor fellow having been killed.[40]

If the anecdote is true then the most likely candidate for the fallen brother is John Witting, being the only of the three killed from a German state. However the term German was often loosely used to encompass a wide swathe of northern and eastern Europe. The officer in

38 Maempel, *Adventures of a Young Rifleman*, p.193.

39 October 1810 Casualty Return, TNA, WO 25/1923; Periods of Service 5/60th, June 1806, WO 25/1008; September 1807 pay list, WO 12/7073; December 1810 pay list, WO 12/7074 , & Oman, *Peninsular War*, Vol. III, p.550.

40 W.C.E. Napier, *Passages in the Early Military Life of General Sir George T. Napier, K.C.B.* (London: Murray, 1884), p.145.

The Battle of Bussaco, by Henri Leveque. (Anne S.K. Brown Military Collection)

question may have been with the French Légion Hanovrienne, as Maempel was, or possibly the Régiment de Prusse.

Lieutenant Colonel Williams was wounded twice, but not severely. Captain Andrews and Lieutenants Joyce and Franchini were also slightly wounded, but Lieutenant de Eberstein was badly wounded. Sixteen riflemen were also wounded.[41] Corporal William Karth (No. 7), a saddler from Berlin, died from his wounds on road to Coimbra on 30 September.[42] All the officers who were wounded, with the exception of Joyce, were with Williams in the 3rd Division. Joyce commanded No. 5 company with the Guards in the 1st Division whose light troops were in positions amongst rocky outcrops on the slopes and who duelled with French voltigeurs for much of the morning.[43] Private John Keller, of the same company, died of wounds on 1 October.[44] Lieutenant Baron Franz Botho de Eberstein went to Lisbon and then back to Britain to recover his from his wound. He never served with the battalion again. He transferred to the 13th Royal Veteran Battalion in 1813, before returning home to Leipzig at the end of the war to find that his family home, Schloss Schönefeld, had been burned down during the Battle of Leipzig.[45]

Four men, all from the 3rd Division companies, were listed as missing in action on the 27th in the October casualty return, where there are also six men listed as having deserted

41 Butler, *Annals*, Vol.II, p.119.
42 October 1810 Return, TNA, WO 25/1923.
43 Chambers, *Bussaco*, p.15.
44 November 1810 Return, TNA, WO 25/1923.
45 Hall, *Biographical Dictionary*, p.186 & http://leipzig-days.blogspot.co.uk/2015/07/schloss-schonefeld.html (accessed 7 September 2018).

on the 26th and six on the 27th.[46] This is unusually high for this period in the battalion's history. These men are also listed as having deserted in the pay list for the period, but are not included in the figures in the regimental return. All but one deserted from the company commanded by Major Galiffe in the 4th Division. Three men are listed in the pay list as becoming prisoners of war on 27 September, all from No. 2 company with the 3rd Division.[47]

Wellington's dispatch after the battle failed to mention the 5th Battalion and their part in defeating Reynier's attack. Later in the year Major Woodgate wrote to Lieutenant Colonel Davy to explain why:

> Since my last to you we have had much to do, although by the papers and the mangled accounts of the affair of Busaco you might fairly conclude we had nothing to do in that business.
>
> The omission of our regiment among the number of those which distinguished themselves was owing to General Picton not making a written report of the conduct of his division. The fact is Lord Wellington was present during the whole affair, and on its termination thanked General Picton and said, 'You need not make any report to me, I have seen the whole myself, and shall mention your division particularly'.
>
> You may suppose we were much astonished, on the arrival of the despatch, to find that the efforts of the 'Americans' had escaped his Lordship's notice. Colonel Williams, who was in the thickest of the fight, and was twice wounded, was of course particularly annoyed, as he had a very fine command of light infantry who were engaged the whole day; and consisted of our three companies, the 45th, 88th, 74th, and 94th [the 94th were not present]. He applied to General Picton, who of course expressed his sorrow for the omission, and wrote to him the letter which I shall transcribe on the other part of this paper.
>
> I trouble you on this subject as I trust you still feel an interest for some of those who are still in the battalion, and that this unusual omission of the 60th may be accounted for.

Woodgate included a copy of General Picton's letter to Colonel Williams:

> On reading over the Gazette account of the action of the 27th ult. at Busaco I was much disappointed and concerned not to find your name among those of the commanding officers of corps in the third division who were particularly noticed on that occasion. You cannot have any doubt of my sentiments, as they were expressed in the Division Orders of that day; yet I fear that I must take the blame to myself for the omission, having neglected to make a written report of the circumstances of the day to his Excellency the Commander of the Forces, who, being present on a commanding situation, and immediately contiguous to that part of the position defended by the third division, I conceived to be fully acquainted with the merits and services of each particular corps; but, on reflection, I find the

46 October 1810 Casualty Return, TNA, WO 25/1923.
47 December 1810 Pay List, TNA, WO 12/7074.

> post you defended (with the light corps of the division) with so much gallantry, for so many hours; was situated so low in the ravine of St. Antonio d' Alcantara, that he would not probably have seen your situation, or witnessed your exertions; but you may be assured that I will take an early opportunity of mentioning to his Lordship that no commanding officer of any corps had more claim to public notice on that occasion than yourself.[48]

The confusion over the part the battalion played in the battle meant that it took nearly 70 years for the battle honour 'Bussaco' to be awarded to the regiment, and Williams was never given the medal clasp that he was entitled to.[49]

The day after the battle Massena received confirmation that there was a route that bypassed the ridge and on the afternoon of 28 September the French army began to march whilst their skirmishers kept the allied outposts busy. Wellington gave orders for his army to fall back on Coimbra and thence to Lisbon. He had achieved his aim in delaying the French and was confident that they would not succeed in taking Lisbon.

As the allied army fell back they rigorously, and sometimes forcefully, imposed the policy of destroying or taking any stores that could be useful to the French. An ever increasing number of refugees left their homes and walked south with the British and Portuguese troops. The city of Coimbra was largely deserted when the French entered on 1 October, but still the French troops ransacked the town and found anything left behind or hidden. Compensation was eventually paid by the British to those ordered to destroy or abandon their property. All the empty buildings were also tempting to those of the allied army seeking a little plunder. On 8 October Private Henry Wilke (No. 1) was 'assassinated by Portuguese peasants' but further details are not given in the casualty report.[50]

On the retreat back to Lisbon there were several clashes between the allied rear guard and the advance guard of the French. The 5th Battalion lost two men to the French as prisoners on 10 October and two more and two missing on 14 October. Private Frederick Goetz (No. 9), captured on 14 October, escaped and was back with the battalion by February 1811. Sergeant Adam Kranckel (No. 9) was not so lucky, he was killed in action on the 14th.[51] Kranckel was a labourer from Bamberg in Bavaria, who had joined the battalion from the Lowenstein Jägers in 1802.[52] All these casualties came from the two companies with Spencer's 1st Division.

On 12 October the advance guard of Junot's VIII Corps attacked and drove the 1st Division pickets out the village of Sobral. The 1/71st Highland Light Infantry placed a barricade across the road after the village to stop any further advance by the enemy. On the 14th the French attacked again, but the 1/71st and the pickets who had been driven out of the village, including men of the 5th Battalion, counterattacked and drove the French back to the edge of Sobral. Massena arrived in time to see the end of the skirmish. He saw for the first time the scale of the preparations Wellington had made and the strength of the

48 Woodgate to Davy 14 December 1810, quoted in Rigaud, *Celer et Audax*, pp.139-40.

49 Butler, *Annals*, Vol. II, p.122.

50 October 1810 Return, TNA, WO 25/1923.

51 October 1810 Return, TNA, WO 25/1923.

52 Periods of Service 5/60th, June 1806, TNA, WO 25/1008.

redoubts and batteries.[53] He rode down the lines and realised he had very little chance of taking them by force.

On 13 October Sergeant Peter Lind was sent by Quarter Master Sergeant Recknoy to protect 'money and other valuable articles contained in a portmanteau, to a very considerable amount' in the possession of Recknoy's wife. Instead of protecting the valuables Lind stole them and then deserted. He was caught in December and tried by court martial in February. He was found guilty and sentenced to be hanged. The sentence was carried out on the morning of 1 May 1811.[54] Lind, originally a glazier from Landau in Alsace, had been with the battalion since 1802 having joined from Lowenstein's Jägers.[55]

The Lines of Torres Vedras were manned mostly by Portuguese militia. The British and regular Portuguese troops were stationed to the rear in order to reinforce any point that was attacked. The allied troops were kept fed thanks to the supplies coming into the port at Lisbon. The city itself was overflowing with refugees, who quickly began to suffer from hunger and deprivation. For the French army it was even worse. With long supply lines constantly interrupted by Portuguese *Ordenanças* and Spanish guerrillas, and very little food to find in the region before the lines, sickness and hunger began to take their toll on the French. Massena made no attempt to breach the lines. Instead, most of the French army's attention was given to ever longer pillaging expeditions looking for any food that they could find. Hundreds of men deserted to the allies. In mid-November Massena withdrew his army to Santarém on the Tagus, a few days march from the lines, in the hope of finding more food and that Wellington might follow him and give battle on the plains.

Wellington did follow, but cautiously until he could fathom Massena's intentions. The leading elements of the allied army were soon in contact with the French at Santarém. Wellington did contemplate attacking but when it became obvious that Massena was planning to remain where he was for the winter Wellington decided to let hunger and the weather thin the French ranks for him. He drew most of his army back into winter quarters.

The companies of 5th Battalion remained with their various brigades. The October, November and December returns put the headquarters with the 3rd Division at Cardozes, Torres Vedras and Alcoentre respectively.[56] In October Ensigns Andrew Franciosci and Anthony de Brunning joined the battalion, but Ensigns Burghaagen and Larbusch were sent to the Foreign Depot on Wellington's orders, despite only having arrived in Portugal during the summer. Larbusch had been sick in Lisbon but the medical board reported 'that he has no complaint whatever that will prevent his doing his duty'.[57] Ensign Franciosci was appointed to be General A. Campbell's interpreter. Ensign Frederick Kruger and Captain Thomas Howard joined in November. In October a Drum Major was added to the battalion's establishment and Sergeant Charles Forgman was appointed, although he would have probably have been referred to as Bugle Major due to the lack of drummers in the unit. Private Andreas Talbo, missing in action at Talavera, returned in December having escaped French captivity.[58]

53 Oman, *Peninsular War*, Vol. III. p.444.

54 Wellington, *General Orders*, Vol. III, pp.78-80.

55 Periods of Service 5/60th, June 1806, TNA WO 25/1008; May 1811 casualty return, WO 25/1923.

56 October to December returns TNA, WO 17/180.

57 Wellington, *General Orders*, Vol. II, p.206.

58 December 1810 Return, TNA WO 17/180; September 1809 & December 1810 Pay Lists, WO 12/7074.

Reinforcements of nine battalions arrived in Lisbon during the autumn and early winter, including the Brunswick-Oels Jägers. Raised from German volunteers the Brunswickers included four rifle-armed companies, who wore a green jacket with red facings similar to the 5th Battalion. Three of these companies were distributed around the brigades to ensure as many as possible had riflemen. The musket-armed companies of the Brunswickers wore black with a distinctive death's head skull badge.

On 12 November Wellington wrote in a general order:

> 4. The Commander of the Forces refers the General officers commanding divisions and brigades to his orders on the formation and use of light infantry battalions in each brigade, and he desires that they may be strictly adhered to: he again recommends the detached companies of the 5th Battalion 60th regt., and those now detached from the Brunswick light infantry, to their care and attention, and desires that these companies, when not in battalions with the light infantry companies of the regiments, in the manner and at the time pointed out in the General Orders, may be kept at the head quarters of the brigade.[59]

Captain James Prevost's brother Harry, a lieutenant with 2/7th Fusiliers, was also in Portugal and the two had the good fortune to both be in the 4th Division. In November Harry wrote to their older brother Augustine, who would also soon to be in the Peninsula:

> Owing to the many difficulties of writing and constantly marching since we have been in this Country I have not been able to write to you before we arrived here in July & have been with the exception of a few days always on the move. On the 26th of Sept Lord Wellington took up a position on the heights of Busaco about 2 leagues from Coimbra the whole extent of which was eight miles & we could overlook the whole of the enemy's movements of force. On the 27th they made an attack both on our right & left. The glorious result of which you will see by the dispatches
>
> Our Regt. Unfortunately were not much engaged though we lost more than many Regt., poor Mair was wounded but is doing well. We have now fallen back to our fortified lines & the French are very near; looking at us but afraid to attempt anything. The wet season will now soon set in therefore to remain as we are is impossible We are all in villages & they send Canvas. In fact we are in the highest health & spirits we have a fine British Army and in the Portuguese we put highest confidence, should Massena attack us it will be a glorious Day for Old England; He is now only 6 leagues from Lisbon & the inhabitants are as quiet & carrying on in the same way they did five years ago. You know that both Battalions of the Fusiliers are here so I think I have a pretty good chance of a Company. Colonel Packenham commands our Brigade – I have not heard from America since I left Halifax & I am not able to write from want of conveyance & the difficulty there Is in allowing letters to pass to Foreign Countries as all letters are opened before they leave this Country. James' Company is attached to our division so we often meet – you may

59 General order 12 November 1810, quoted in Wellington, *Supplementary Despatches*, Vol.VI. p.640.

> imagine how great was our regret in leaving Halifax one of the best Quarters in the World Nothing would please me more than after this business is over to be ordered back. You must not find fault at my not often writing. I assure you it is impossible this bit of paper has been wet through at least a dozen times since I left Lisbon I have walked at least 200 leagues & the only Officer in the Regt. who has done the same.[60]

Harry also wrote to his father and sisters, back home in New York State, in December:

> James & myself by great good luck are in the same Division of the Army so we see each other every day he is coming to eat a bit of ration beef & biscuit with me today about the same hour that most eat what is called dinner. We have been here five months in this Country & think we have a prospect of being here for at least twelve more only the consolation of expecting promotion & that this country is better adapted to my circumstances and I know not what I should do.

Harry continued:

> I am generally marching 4 & 5 long leagues every day and at night perhaps am a guard on Piquet within a couple of hundred yards of some very unsociable Frenchmen Tell Frederic that for four months I have been working much harder than him. The greater part of which since I have laid on the ground with no other covering than a blanket & always without taking off my clothes if he could send me half a bushel of Potatoes they would be the greatest present he could send me. This Village is about 6 leagues from Lisbon you will trace it on the Map up the River Tagus had I a good opportunity I would send you a map of the Country, as you have not the small towns on a general one or I could put you in a way of the march of the Army up the Country you see I have made the most of that my last sheet of paper.[61]

The 25 December return stated the strength of the 5th Battalion as 53 sergeants, 15 buglers, and 533 rank and file; 51 fewer men than in January. If those sent home, absent sick, missing, and prisoners of war are removed from the figures then 50 sergeants, 13 buglers, and 457 rank and file were actually present with their companies. Doubtless brothers James and Harry would have done their best to see each other on Christmas Day. Sadly, it would be the last that either ever saw.

60 H. Prevost to A. Prevost 17 November 1810, AI, The Prevost Papers, CR549/II/3y.
61 H. Prevost to A. Prevost 8 December 1810, AI, The Prevost Papers, CR549/II/3z.

17

Fuentes de Oñoro

The French army spent the wet and cold winter months around Santarém waiting for the allies to attack. The French position was strong, enhanced by entrenchments around the town and protected by the Mayor River. Wellington did not oblige. He was content to let starvation thin the French ranks and force them to retreat. The 2nd Division occupied the eastern bank of the Tagus in case *Marechal* Massena tried to cross and head for southern Spain, or in case French reinforcements came from that direction. The rest of the Wellington's army was spread out south and west of Santarém, reaching across to the coast and down to the Lines of Torres Vedras.

View towards the Lines of Torres Vedras from the French position at Santarém, from *Views in Spain & Portugal, taken during the Campaigns of His Grace the Duke of Wellington*, by G. Cumberland.

Two extra divisions from Spain had joined Massena's army in December but these 6,000 men were not enough to alter the balance of forces in favour of the French, and were extra mouths to feed. The French foraging parties had to journey ever further to find food and were constantly harassed by *Ordenanças*. Portuguese Militia and other units operating in northern and central Portugal effectively cut the French off from communication with Spain and the Emperor. Discipline began to break down and desertions increased.

The 5th Battalion remained dispersed all winter. The headquarters and three companies were with the 3rd Division at Alcoentre, the other companies were with their respective divisions across southern Portugal. In January a much needed draft of new recruits arrived at the Belem depot, and in February three sergeants and 62 rank and file joined the battalion. The draft raised the numbers present with the battalion to 53 sergeants, 12 buglers, and 516 rank and file. Twenty-seven officers and five administrative or medical staff were also present. Five officers were employed on various staff duties and two were doing duty with other units. Seven officers were absent with leave and five absent without leave; in two cases their leave had expired, and in three they had not joined since being appointed. A total of 75 officers, NCOs and privates were prisoners of war and eight were missing. Nine men were sick or on furlough, three were on recruiting service and two had been invalided. In the first two months of the year two men re-joined from being prisoners of war, two had deserted and five had died.[1] Sergeants Andreas Gross, Stephen Patrick, and Martin Fablossky, and Corporals Bartholomew Fisher and Theodore Potossky who came with the draft from the Foreign Depot had all volunteered from prisoners of war and had retained their previous ranks from French service.[2] In a general order of 5 March Wellington formed the 7th Division from some of the recently arrived battalions and moved the headquarters and Nos. 2, 3 & 7 companies of the battalion to Colonel Mackinnon's brigade, still in Picton's 3rd Division.[3]

By the end of February, Massena, with food running out and discipline worsening, began to make preparations for a retreat. Wellington too was on the move. With fresh battalions arriving in Lisbon he thought he would soon have the numbers to defeat the French. He was also beginning to doubt if his policy of starving the French was working as they had managed to sustain themselves longer than he had expected. Wellington began to move up his rearmost divisions in preparation for an advance but the French began to withdraw on 4 March. They left straw-filled dummies in place of sentries and abandoned their baggage, managing to gain a day's head start on the allies. Wellington entered Santarém on 6 March and found it ransacked, filthy, and empty. Hundreds of sick trudged northwards with the French columns. As the hungry and frustrated soldiers passed through villages and towns they looted and burned houses, murdering or raping many of the inhabitants.[4]

The allied army pursued the French as it marched towards Coimbra. *Marechal* Ney was in charge of the French rearguard and made a brief stand at Pombal on 11 March. On 12 March Ney chose to force another action. He took a position on a plateau between two rivers near the town of Redhina. The terrain was hilly and forested. The British cavalry informed

1 January & February 1811 Returns, TNA, WO 17/180.

2 Mosheim to Williams 27 May 1811, TNA, WO 7/84, p.26.

3 General order 5 March 1811, quoted in Wellington, *General Orders*. Vol.III, p.49.

4 Buttery, *Massena*, pp.126-7.

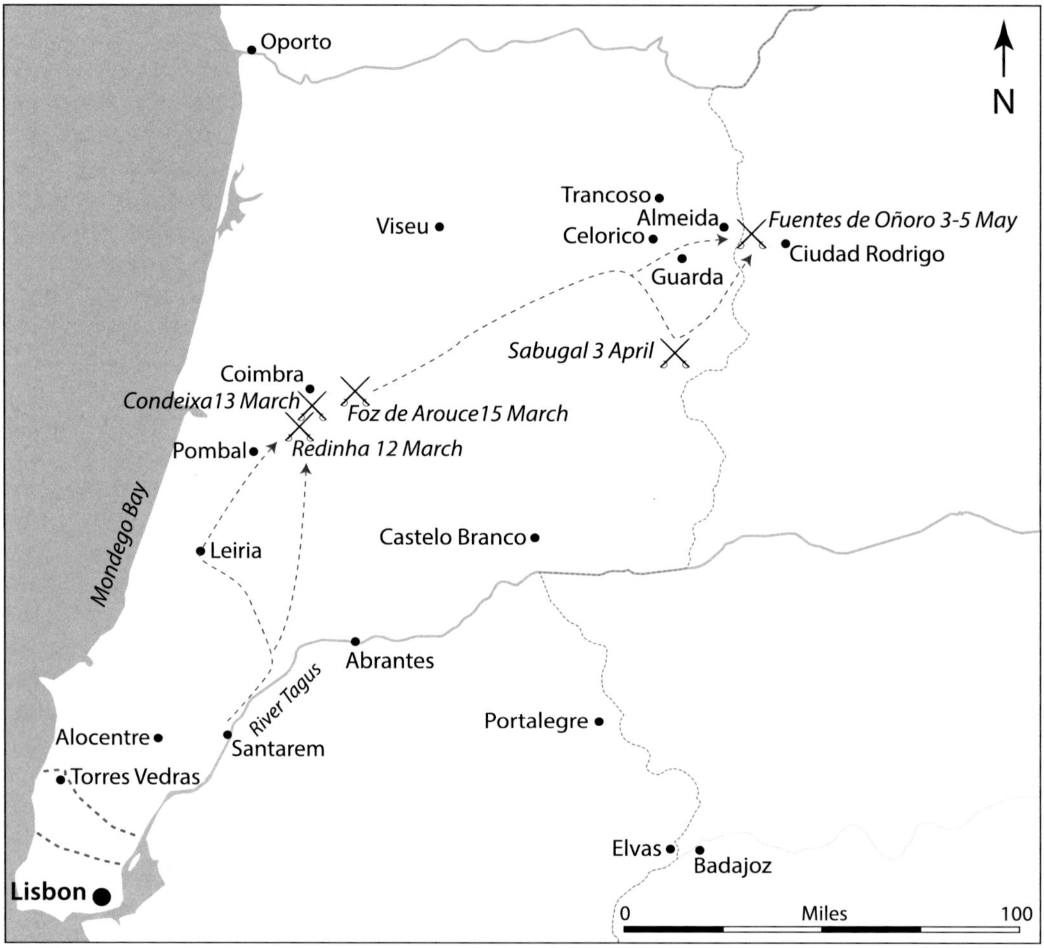

Massena's Retreat, March to May 1811.

Wellington that there were as many as 30,000 French in the area so he moved cautiously.[5] His three leading columns consisted of the Light Division on the left, Pack's Portuguese brigade in the centre, and Picton's 3rd Division on the right. Wellington waited until the 4th Division reinforced Pack in the centre and the 5th Division was nearby before sending the 3rd and Light Divisions to turn Ney's flanks early in the afternoon.

Lieutenant Colonel Williams commanded the 3rd Division light troops, including his three companies, on one flank. The infantry of the Light Division advanced on the other. The terrain was rough and heavily wooded. After twenty minutes of intense skirmishing the French were forced to draw back across a bridge to a second position on a ridge two miles

5 The details of the action on 12 March are taken from Oman, *Peninsular War*, Vol.IV, pp.142-3, Buttery, *Massena*, p.128, and Butler, *Annals*, Vol.II, pp 124-5.

further back. The men of the 3rd and Light Divisions chased the French over the bridge and redeployed on the flanks again while Pack and the 5th Division held the centre. As soon as his flanks were threatened Ney once more retired in good order.[6]

Ten men of the battalion were wounded and four reported missing in action on 12 March.[7] The missing men were all taken prisoner by the French. One of the men, Corporal Fischer (No. 7), had just joined the battalion with the draft and another, Private Kohler (No. 2), managed to escape quickly and was soon back in the ranks.[8]

The French had reached Condexia, the last point where Massena could choose between advancing northwards to Coimbra, which was held by Portuguese troops, or abandoning any hope of remaining in Portugal and turning east towards the Spanish frontier. With his hungry and exhausted army suffering from the rigours of the march, outnumbered by the allied army pursuing him, and with Ney and others eager to return to Spain he had little choice. He went east towards Celorico. Ney was ordered to hold Condexia for as long as possible but Wellington sent the 3rd and 6th Divisions around the flanks and Ney withdrew quickly to avoid getting cut off. Ney's rapid retreat put Massena himself in danger. Massena's staff and escort were discovered whilst they were eating under a tree by a patrol of German Hussars and were nearly captured. Massena and his aides had to flee towards the safety of a nearby division. Williams and the light troops of the 3rd Division caught up with them and engaged them as night fell but Massena managed to evade capture for a second time.[9]

There was further skirmishing on the 14th as the Light Division, mishandled by its temporary commander Major General James Erskine, was advancing through thick fog and became heavily engaged at Casal Novo with a much stronger French rearguard. The riflemen of the 5th Battalion extended the Light Division's line on the right, while rest the 3rd Division turned the French flank.[10] Williams and his light battalion were amongst the units and officers singled out for praise by Wellington in his dispatch.[11] Pressed hard, Massena ordered the burning of any unnecessary baggage and the disabling of unfit horses or mules by cutting their hamstrings and leaving them to suffer. Fog delayed the allied pursuit on 15 March and late in the day the 3rd and Light Divisions spotted Ney's rearguard in position along a line of hills, with a river to the rear, near the village of Foz de Arouce.[12]

The two allied divisions had begun to set up camp and send out pickets for the night when Wellington arrived just before sunset. Seeing that the French also seemed to have assumed no attack would come that day, as some of the French troops were already lighting their fires, he ordered an immediate attack. The 3rd Division attacked the French left and the Light Division their right. With surprise on their side the skirmishers of the two divisions made good progress and some French units began to flee across a bridge over the river, which quickly became packed with men. Some panicked, tried to wade across the fast flowing river and were swept away. Ney had to lead a battalion in a counter-attack to drive some of the

6 Oman, *Peninsular War*, Vol.IV, pp.142-3.
7 Butler, *Annals*, Vol.II, p.125.
8 March 1811 Pay List, TNA, WO 12/7074.
9 Butler, *Annals*, Vol.II, p.125; Oman, *Peninsular War*, Vol.IV, p.147.
10 Oman, *Peninsular War*, Vol.IV, pp.151 & Butler, *Annals*, Vol.II, p.126.
11 Wellington to Liverpool 14 March 1811, quoted in Gurwood, *Wellington's Dispatches*, Vol.VII, p.347.
12 Details of the action on 15 March from Oman, *Peninsular War*, Vol.IV, pp.156-8 & Buttery, *Massena*, pp.132-3.

allied units back in order to give other units time to cross. As night fell the fighting became more confused, limiting the advance of the allies, and most of the French escaped.

Lieutenant Wynne and three privates were wounded in the skirmishing on 13 March. On 14 March Private Joseph Deserteur (No. 7) was reported missing and was subsequently found to be a prisoner of war. Deserteur, from Switzerland, had also been taken prisoner at Talavera and had escaped to return to the battalion in the summer of 1810. At Foz de Arouce on 15 March eight of the battalion were wounded, and one lieutenant and three privates were killed: Francis Eger (No. 3) was a labourer from Tillingen in Germany and had been with the battalion since 1802; John Kraemer (No. 7) was a weaver from Grosswenden in Prussia; and John Gold (No. 2) was a labourer from Oldenburg who had joined with the recent draft. Lieutenant Charles Sawatsky had been a sergeant when the companies of the Hompesch chasseurs on the Isle of Wight joined the 5th Battalion. He rose to sergeant major and was then commissioned as an ensign in 1803. He was the first officer of the battalion to be killed in the campaign. On the casualty return it is noted that he was single, and that the 'Amount of the produce of the Officers Effects as per the annexed Inventory' was £94 14s 6d, which was willed to Surgeon Dumoulin and Lieutenant de Gilse.[13]

The day after the action at Foz de Arouce Wellington paused his pursuit of the French to allow time for his supply train to catch up with the army. He also received news that the French had taken the Spanish fortress of Badajoz. Fearing that the Portuguese stronghold of Elvas might have been next, he sent Beresford south with the 4th Division and a cavalry brigade to reinforce the 2nd Division. On 17 March Wellington's army was on the move again, following the French towards the frontier. Some of the allied divisions still had to slow their advance to allow their supplies to catch up and the French could have slipped away across the border. Instead, on 22 March, Massena issued orders for his army to head south-east, with the aim of threatening central Portugal again, despite the fact that his army was exhausted and starving. The region he was heading towards was practically barren, and Ney objected so strongly he was removed from his command. Five days later *Généraux de Division* Junot and Reynier wrote their own protests to Massena, and he reluctantly abandoned his plan and began to move the army back towards Almeida and Ciudad Rodrigo.

On 29 March the allied army drove the French from Guarda and by 1 April they had reached the River Coa near Sabugal where the three divisions of Reynier's II Corps were isolated from the other French units. Wellington gathered his army together, determined to bring the French to battle. The Light, 3rd, and the 6th Divisions were already in the vicinity and he waited for the 1st, 5th, and 7th to arrive before attacking on 3 April. Wellington's plan was for the 3rd Division to cross the Coa at a ford just south of Sabugal, whilst the 5th Division attacked the bridge leading to the town. The Light Division were to cross the river further south and take the French in the flank. The 1st and 7th Divisions were to provide support if required.

13 Butler, *Annals*, Vol.II, pp.126; March Casualty Return & Lt. Sawatsky casualty report, TNA, WO 25/1923; Periods of Service 5/60th, June 1806, WO 25/1008; & March 1811 Pay List, WO 12/7074. In the *Annals of the KRRC*, Vol.II, p.127, Butler proposes that Sawatsky was killed by the French memoirist de Marbot on 14 March. However, the entry on the casualty report places his death at Foz de Arouce on 15 March. Also Marbot describes his assailant as young and English. Sawatsky was 37, and he was definitely not English.

Unfortunately, the morning of 3 April was very foggy. Major Generals Thomas Picton and James Dunlop, commanding the 3rd and 5th Divisions, asked for confirmation that the assault was to proceed but Erskine ordered the Light Division to carry on regardless and cross the river. In the fog they missed their planned ford and crossed deeper water closer to the French. The French pickets opened fire on the men whilst they were still in the river but were quickly driven off. However, their fire had alerted the nearest French divisional commander, *Général de Division* Merle, who quickly marched the closest battalions towards the firing. The Light Division made some progress, fighting in torrential rain, but soon came up against the rest of Merle's division, and then further French reinforcements arrived and a long and hard firefight ensued. As the fog lifted Wellington and Reynier both saw they had troops in danger. Reynier had moved troops from his centre to combat the threat from the Light Division and now could see the other allied divisions ready to cross the river and attack. Wellington realised that the Light Division was outnumbered and that their flank had been turned. The light battalion of the 3rd Division, commanded by Williams and supported by Colville's Brigade, crossed the river to support the Light Division, hitting their French attackers in the flank.[14]

Captain Kincaid of the 95th saw Williams' men cross the river:

> While standing in our last position, awaiting the attack in our front, I was much amused in observing, on the opposite height, the approach of our 3d division, unnoticed by the enemy a French column occupied the top of what seemed to be almost a precipice overlooking the river; but I observed some of the 60th rifles clambering up the face of it on all fours, and, to see their astonishment, when they poked their heads over the brink, to find themselves within a couple of yards of a French column! They, of course, immediately concealed themselves under the bank; but it was curious to observe that they were unseen by the enemy, who were imprudent enough either to consider themselves secure on that side, or to give all their attention to the fight going on between their comrades and us; but certain it is they allowed the riflemen to gather there in formidable numbers.[15]

Kincaid did not see what happened next but later came across many French dead and wounded after they had been fired on from the flank by the 3rd Division troops. The French began to rapidly fall back and the 5th Division was able to cross into the town unopposed. The 3rd Division pursued the French but was ordered to halt by Wellington when the rain became even heavier.

The 5th Battalion lost two men killed in action at Sabugal: Private Conrad Pert (No. 7) was a tailor from Gravenhausen in the German state of Hesse and had joined with the draft at the beginning of the year; Private Frederick Meddel (No. 2) was a Prussian from Berlin.[16] Commissary George Head, came across one of these two men after the battle:

14 Wellington to Liverpool 9 April 1811, quoted in Gurwood, *Wellington's Dispatches*, Vol.VII, p.432.

15 J. Kincaid, *Random Shots from a Rifleman* (London: Boone, 1847), pp.170-1.

16 April 1811 Casualty Return, TNA, WO 25/1923.

> I particularly observed a fine fellow, a German rifleman, sitting, as it were reflectively, upon a fragment of rock, looking apparently with earnestness towards the ground, his right hand resting on his knee, his head reclining on his bosom. He was stupified and insensible, supported merely by a strong-built muscular form, and his glassy eyes were sightless and fixed. Though he sat up right, life had almost fled; for a musquet ball had perforated the skull, and the cold shadows of death enveloped his brow. Kind nature had applied her styptic, but in vain; the congealed blood, in form like an icicle lengthened to several inches, incessantly distilled from the wound, fast dripping in a red pool below; drops which, rather than moments, for time with him had ceased to be, served to measure the close of his existence.[17]

None of the KGL or the Brunswick-Oels units were engaged or suffered any casualties at Sabugal and so the rifleman must have belonged to the 5th Battalion.[18]

One sergeant and one private were wounded.[19] One man was listed as missing in action and three men died of wounds in early April; Corporals Frederick Steding (No. 3) and Michael Gross (No. 7), and Private John Vantusen (No. 7) – but it is not recorded where or when they were wounded. Private Lewis Mensing shot himself at the general hospital at Elvas on 7 April, but it is not evident when and why he was admitted.[20]

On 23 April Major Woodgate wrote to Lieutenant Colonel Davy to update him with news of the battalion.

> I can date this letter from no particular place, as I am not aware that the few houses we occupy are sufficient to create a village, or be called by any name; but we are between Almeida and Ciudad Rodrigo, near Alamadilla, having followed the enemy thus far 'without impediment.' I shall not attempt to give you a history of their retreat and our pursuit, as the despatches will tell you all, and with more accuracy than I can. I shall only say that your friend General Picton's division (and of them entirely the light companies, and our three companies, brigaded as before under Williams), together with the light division, were almost the only part of the infantry of the army engaged. We lost a few men and Sawatsky, whom, as an attentive and useful officer, I much lament.
>
> There are about 1500 men in Almeida who are destined, by our arrangements, to fall into our hands, not by besieging that place, but we purpose starving them out, and for that purpose have surrounded the fortress; but the opinion is that the French, after getting themselves a little refreshed, will march a considerable force to their relief, which may, if we choose to stand, bring on what has been so long postponed, something like a general engagement.
>
> On the retreat we never could bring them to stand. Their rear-guard, and that of great strength, 20,000 strong, under Reynier, was the only part of their army we could engage with, and they only fought because they were overtaken.

17 G. Head, *Memoirs of an Assistant Commissary-General* (London: John Murray, 1837), p.249.
18 Oman, *Peninsular War*, Vol.IV, p.616.
19 Rigaud, *Celer et Audax*, p.160.
20 April 1811 Casualty Return, TNA, WO 25/1923.

Every town on the road, Leiria, Pombal, Condeixa, &c., &c., has been burnt to the ground, and the road strewed with dead bodies of all ages, horses, mules, and baggage of every description.

We had two fine views of the enemy. We saw about 30,000 men march out from Condeixa, and at Guarda about 16,000 marched out, while our division was within 600 paces of them. The whole army was intended to have met there, and, cooperating, to have attacked them; but it so occurred that we, who had marched over the mountains, were the only people who arrived at the appointed time, and the enemy retiring on our first appearance, we had a fine opportunity of seeing them move off: as our force consisted of not more than 4000, we could do no more than quietly to march into the town when they marched out of it, which we did that evening.

Lord Wellington has left us for a week to go to the Alemtejo, to the camp there, and will probably attempt to retake Badajos, which you know has surrendered in the true Spanish way. General Hill's late division and General Cole's are on that side, with numerous Portuguese, under Marshal Beresford's command, who has been thought slow and dilatory. I think however we shall hear something good from that quarter soon.

You must have seen Andrews' promotion. He leaves us in a few days, having just come up to settle his pay-mastership accounts to March.

De Bree has not left England yet to join us, as Andrews hears from him last mail. He has most officiously (as usual) been sending out recruits to us without the least authority or leave from Colonel Williams; we received 64 of his selection lately, the greater part of whom were taken six months ago in this country. This is not giving the men or the regiment a fair chance. You will see him in London, as I am sure he will endeavour to find you out, on his way to join, when you can arrange the business about the stores.

I trust your plan of getting employed will succeed; I mean in the Guards, because I well know many lieut.-colonels on full pay would be glad to exchange with you, but I think with you the Guards more eligible. Thinking of you the other day, it struck me that if you wished something immediately, while your other engagements are going on, that it would suit to be on this staff as assistant adjutant-general, which I have no doubt you could procure with much ease.

You will doubtless see Austin in London; tell him I received his friendly letter from Martinique, and now I know he is in England I shall write to him. We are going on much the same, only I am heartily tired of this concern, and I must at all events come over for a few months before winter.

After our last skirmish near Sabugal, I found the French 'Ordre du jour' of the 1st April, which stated that a 'feu de joie'[21] would be fired on the following day, in consequence of the Empress of France having been delivered of a son, the King of Rome, on the 20th of March. It was the first news we heard of it, which we find confirmed by the papers; and I only mention it to show the expedition with which the intelligence reached the French army. I understand they have telegraphs from the Pyrenees to Madrid.

21 A *feu de joie* is a rolling volley with each soldier firing in turn, used as a salute or celebration.

> Steitz has been removed to the 1st battalion, and Gilse has resigned the adjutancy, and Broetz is appointed.[22]

Lieutenant Charles de Bree was doing duty at the Foreign Depot in Lymington.[23] Letters later in the year from the commandant, Mosheim, to Williams indicate that attempts were being made to select the recruits for the battalion with some care.[24]

During the spring the newly promoted Major Andrews, who had been doing duty in Lisbon as acting provost marshal, left for the 1/60th. Andrews was later promoted to lieutenant colonel and commanded the battalion. He died in 1823 in Jamaica. Lieutenants Steitz and Bock, and Ensigns Larbusch and Burghagen went with Andrews. Captains Edward Purdon and Charles Schaw transferred from the 1st Battalion and Captain Alexander Livingstone from the 3rd. Ensigns Kruger and Ingersleben were both promoted to lieutenant, without purchase. Ingersleben had been recommended by Williams for the vacancy created by Charles Sawatsky's death. Wellington had sent on Williams' recommendation to Horse Guards along with his own that Sergeant Major James Kent from the 1/43rd was given the ensigncy vacated by Ingersleben. The battalion's long-serving adjutant, Baron Frederick de Gilse, resigned the appointment and Ensign Peter Broetz replaced him.

Two officers who had been with the battalion since the beginning also made their departures; Captains de Wend and Koch.[25] Michael de Wend was ill and went on leave. When he was recovered he transferred to the 4/60th where he became a brevet major in 1814. He died in May 1816 on Barbados from apoplexy, just after his battalion had been involved in the suppression of a major slave rebellion. His wife, Sarah, was with him on the island, and they had had three further children during their time in the Caribbean; in 1812, 1814, and 1815. After Michael's death Sarah returned to her family in Scotland. Two of their children died in the same month in 1817 and a third in 1823, leaving Sarah with just her eldest, James. Michael de Wend had served for 21 years, joining the Lowenstein Chasseurs in 1795 aged 20. He had been present at the capture of four islands in the West Indies, the expedition to Puerto Rico, the capture of Surinam, and the Battles of Roliça, Vimeiro, Oporto, and Talavera.[26] Charles Koch, long since appointed to the 2/60th finally left to join his proper battalion, taking with him the last remaining private from that battalion who had been left behind after Corunna. Captain Thomas Howard also left to join the 70th Foot, and Ensign Visseux was promoted into the Sicilian Regiment.[27]

Following the defeat at Sabugal, Massena withdrew the bulk of his army across the Coa and into Spain. He left the French garrison in place at the fortress of Almeida, the defences of which had been repaired since the great explosion, and two divisions to keep an eye on the allies. The rest of his force was based around Salamanca, further into Spain. The allied army advanced and surrounded Almeida but did not have heavy enough guns to attempt to breach the walls. Wellington knew that Massena's troops were in a poor state but was at

22 Woodgate to Davy 23 April 1811, quoted in Rigaud, *Celer et Audax*, pp.161-3.

23 April 1811 Return, TNA, WO 17/180.

24 Mosheim to Williams 26 July 1811, WO 7/83, pp.206-7.

25 April to June 1811 returns, TNA, WO 17/180; Memorial of Ensign Ingersleben, WO 31/321.

26 Sheffield City Archives, LD 751-4, & de Wend-Fenton family records courtesy of Michael Cayley.

27 March to June 1811 Returns TNA, WO 17/180.

the end of his own supply lines and could not risk advancing into the Spanish plains whilst the French had such a large superiority in cavalry. Massena's invasion of Portugal had been finally defeated but the allies were not yet strong enough to advance into Spain.

The Light Division was pushed forward towards Ciudad Rodrigo and kept contact with the French divisions left to cover the allies. The other divisions were spread around villages and towns in the area to recover after a month of hard marching and fighting. Wellington felt sure enough that Massena's army would be in no condition to be a threat for some time that he rode south to oversee Beresford's operations around Badajoz for a few days. However, Massena was not about to let the campaign end so ignominiously for him. He received reinforcements of cavalry and artillery and began to advance back towards Almeida at the end of April with a force of over 48,000 men.[28]

Wellington received word of Massena's movements and hurried back from the south, arriving on 29 April. The allied army totalled 37,504.[29] The organisation of the infantry and the disposition of the companies of the 5th Battalion were as follows:

1st Division – Lieutenant General Spencer
Brigadier General Stopford
    1/Coldstream Guards, 1/3rd Guards, & No. 5 company 5/60th.
Major General Nightingall
    2/24th, 2/42nd, 1/79th, & No. 9 company 5/60th.
Major General Löwe
    1st KGL, 2nd KGL, 5th KGL, 7th KGL, & Detachments Light battalions KGL.
Major General Howard
    1/50th, 1/71st, 1/92nd, 1 company 3/95th.

3rd Division – Major General Picton
Brigadier General Mackinnon
    1/45th, 74th, & 1/88th & Nos. 2, 3, & 7 companies 5/60th, with Lt. Col. Williams & Maj. Woodgate.
Major General Colville
    2/5th, 2/83rd, 2/88th, 94th.
Coronel Power (Portuguese)
    9th (2 battalions), & 21st (2 battalions).

5th Division – Major General Erskine
Brigadier General Hay
    3/1st, 1/9th & 2/38th, & 1 company Brunswick Oels.
Brigadier General Dunlop
    1/4th, 2/30th & 2/44th, & 1 company Brunswick Oels.
Brigadeiro Spry (Portuguese)
    3rd (2 battalions), 15th (2 battalions) & 8th Caçadores.

28 Oman, *Peninsular War*, Vol.IV, p.628.
29 Oman, *Peninsular War*. Vol.IV, p.621.

6th Division – Major General Alexander Campbell
Colonel Hulse
1/11th, 2/53rd & 1/61st, & No. 1 company 5/60th.
Brigadier General Burne
2nd & 1/36th.
Brigadeiro Eben (Portuguese)
8th (2 battalions) & 12th (2 battalions).

7th Division – Major General Houston
Major General Sontag
51st, 85th, Chasseurs Britanniques, & Brunswick Oels (8 companies).
Brigadeiro Doyle (Portuguese)
7th (2 battalions), 19th (2 battalions) & 2nd Caçadores.

Light Division – Major General Craufurd
Lieutenant Colonel Beckwith
1/43rd, 1/95th (4 coys), 1 company 2/95th & 3rd Caçadores.
Colonel Drummond
1/52nd, 2/52nd, 1/95th (4 coys) & 1st Caçadores.

Independent Portuguese Brigade
Coronel Ashworth
6th (2 battalions), 18th (2 battalions) & 6th Caçadores.[30]

Wellington was outnumbered, especially in cavalry, and the ground on which he had to fight did not offer the defensive advantages of a position such as Bussaço, but he chose his ground as well as he could and gathered his divisions along the line of the Dos Casas stream, which ran parallel to the River Turones two miles further west. The allied left was anchored on the ruined Fort Concepcion in the north, and the right on the village of Fuentes de Oñoro in the south. The Dos Casas was not a deep river but at the northern end of the line it flowed in a deep ravine, which made it a considerable obstacle. At Fuentes de Oñoro the banks became much shallower. The landscape was mainly meadows and arable land but around two miles south of Fuentes de Oñoro there were woods and marshy ground around the village of Poço Velho. The five miles between Fort Concepcion and Fuentes de Oñoro were well protected by the ravine but the two miles to Poço Velho were much more open. Fuentes de Oñoro itself rose steeply upwards from the stream to a rocky, partially wooded, hill on which stood the village church. The streets were narrow and the stone-built cottages surrounded by walled gardens and courtyards. Six miles behind the allied position was the River Coa, with only one good bridge for wheeled transport and guns, but numerous fords for infantry and cavalry. If the allied army was defeated and pushed back retreat would have been awkward, but not impossible.[31]

30 Oman, *Peninsular War*, Vol.IV, pp.618-21; Butler, *Annals*, pp.122-3, April 1811 Return, TNA, WO 17/180.
31 Details of the position and subsequent battle are from Oman, *Peninsular War*, Vol.IV, pp.307-40, Buttery, pp.146-67, *Massena* and Lipscombe, *Peninsular War Atlas*, pp.206-11.

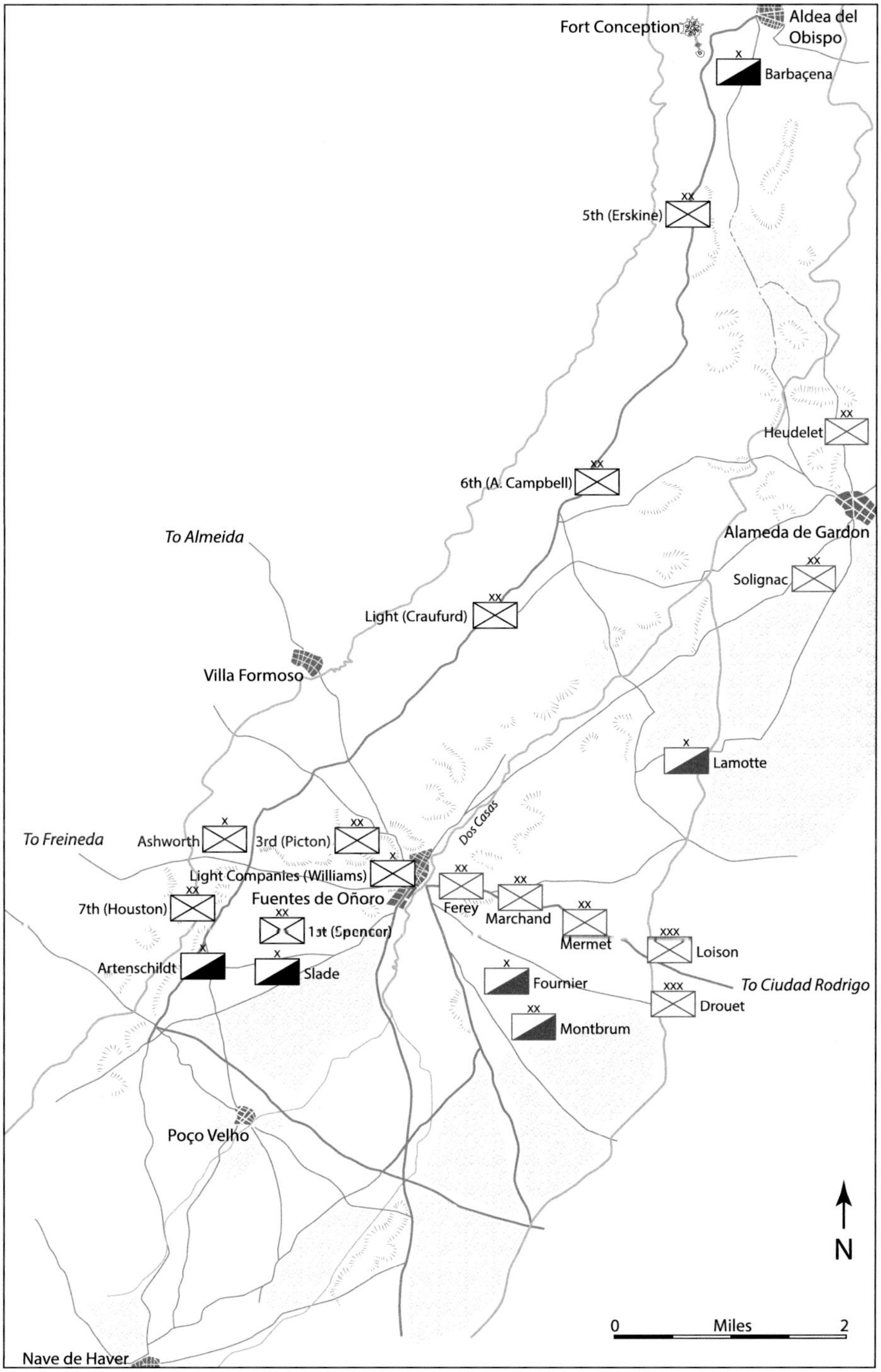

The Battle of Fuentes de Oñoro, 3 May 1811.
Source: Lipscombe, *Atlas* & Wyld, *Maps & Plans*.

Wellington deployed the 5th and 6th Divisions along the line of the ravine from the fort to the village. Behind Fuentes de Oñoro was the 3rd Division and Ashworth's Portuguese Brigade. To the south the 1st and 7th Divisions, along with the bulk of the allied cavalry, covered the more open flank. A Portuguese cavalry unit was placed north of the fort. When the Light Division fell back they were to take a position just to the north of the village. Fuentes de Oñoro itself was garrisoned by the light companies of Nightingall's, Howard's, and Löwe's brigades of the 1st Division (including elements of the KGL, the company of the 3/95th and No. 9 company of the 5th Battalion), and the light companies of Mackinnon's, Colville's, and Power's brigades of the 3rd Division (including Nos. 2, 3, and 7 companies) with the 2/83rd in support. The senior officer in Fuentes de Oñoro was Lieutenant Colonel Williams, with approximately 1,800 men in the 28 light and rifle companies plus 460 men of the 2/83rd under his command.

The French army left Ciudad Rodrigo on 2 May, driving the Light Division and allied cavalry steadily back. The French halted for the night around 5 miles from the main allied position. In the morning the advance continued and the Light Division fell back and took up their position to act as Wellington's reserve. French cavalry approached the banks of the Dos Casas:

> On the day of the battle of Fuentes de Onoro, Colonel Schaumann tells us, a Scottish Line Battalion was deployed in order in the gardens of the village when the enemy cavalry advanced.
>
> The Scots, scorning every cover, stood upright as in line. One of the wiser ones had moved behind a wall to get a better shot. No sooner did his comrades notice this than when they said: 'Cannot you damned fellow show your enemies that you can face them!' They rushed at him, berated him, and applied to him a sound thrashing on a sensitive part of his body.
>
> The battalion was replaced by a battalion of Jägers of the 60th Regiment, who better understood light duties and the appropriate use of cover; they also rapidly thinned the saddles of the French, who had ventured too boldly, without suffering any loss.[32]

The riflemen inflicted some casualties and drove the rest of the French cavalry back.[33]

Massena and his army arrived on the banks of the Dos Casas. After a quick survey of the allied position in the early afternoon, Massena ordered a frontal assault on Fuentes de Oñoro, and a small diversion to tie down the 5th Division to the north. The attack on the 5th Division commenced first and caused Wellington to send the Light Division to support them, but the action did not develop beyond prolonged skirmishing across the ravine.

Around the village though, it was very different. *Général de Division* Ferey's division of ten battalions, totalling over 4,000 men made a frontal assault across the stream.[34]

32 H. Dehnel, *Erinnerungen Deutscher Officiere in Britischen Diensten aus den Kriegsjahren 1805 bis 1816* (Hannover: Rümpler, 1864) p.345.

33 M. Combermere, *Memoirs & Correspondence of Field-Marshal Viscount Combermere* (London: Hurst & Blackett, 1866), p.196.

34 Oman, *Peninsular*, Vol.IV, p.626.

The light companies fired from the windows, doorways and walls of the village as the French approached. The defenders blockaded the narrow streets and the fighting soon became hand-to-hand with bayonets and musket – or rifle – butts. Each garden, house, or street corner was fiercely contested. The streets began to fill with dead and wounded. The light troops fought hard but the sheer weight of numbers against them began to push them back up the hill towards the church and some stone-walled enclosures just outside of the village.

Williams rallied his men around the church and the rocky outcrops of the hill, gathered his reserves, and drove the French back down through village streets all the way down to the stream, only to be driven back again by French reinforcements. Williams was severely wounded at around this point. During the afternoon the red-coated French Légion Hanovrienne were mistaken for a British unit first by the allies as they came through the village, the mistake only being realised when they opened fire, and then by the French who fired on them when they were driven back across the stream. In the confused fighting in the village small pockets of men of either side became isolated in individual houses and had to wait for the tide of the battle to flow back in their side's favour before emerging.

Joseph Donaldson of the 94th's light company later recalled:

> In particular places of the village, where a stand had been made, or the shot brought to bear, the slaughter had been immense, which was the case near the river, and at the small chapel on our side of the town; among the rest lay one poor fellow of the 88th light company, who had been severely wounded, and seemed to suffer excruciating agony, for he begged of those who passed him to put him out of torture. Although from the nature of his wound there was no possibility of his surviving, yet none felt inclined to comply with his request, until a German of the 60th rifle battalion, after hesitating a few moments, raised his rifle, and putting the muzzle of it to his head fired the contents of it through it. Whether this deed deserved praise or blame, I leave others to determine.[35]

The defenders were once again driven to the edges of the village by fresh waves of French infantry and even cavalry who charged up the winding alleys and lanes. Wellington sent two Highland regiments, the 1/71st and 1/79th, and the 2/24th to support the light troops. Lieutenant Colonel Cameron of the 79th took over command in the village from Williams, with Major Woodgate assuming command of the 3rd Division's light troops. The Highlanders bayonet-charged the French. After a bloody fight they pushed them across the Dos Casas, and up the far bank before being driven back themselves by French cavalry. More French battalions were sent from another division but the reinforcements and the light companies held the village.

At 6:00 p.m. orders were given for a chain of pickets to be established along the length of the Dos Casas, and for the 7th Division to put strong pickets into the woods around Poço

35 J. Donaldson, *Recollections of the Eventful Life of a Soldier* (Philadelphia: Zieber & Co.,1845), pp.126-7.

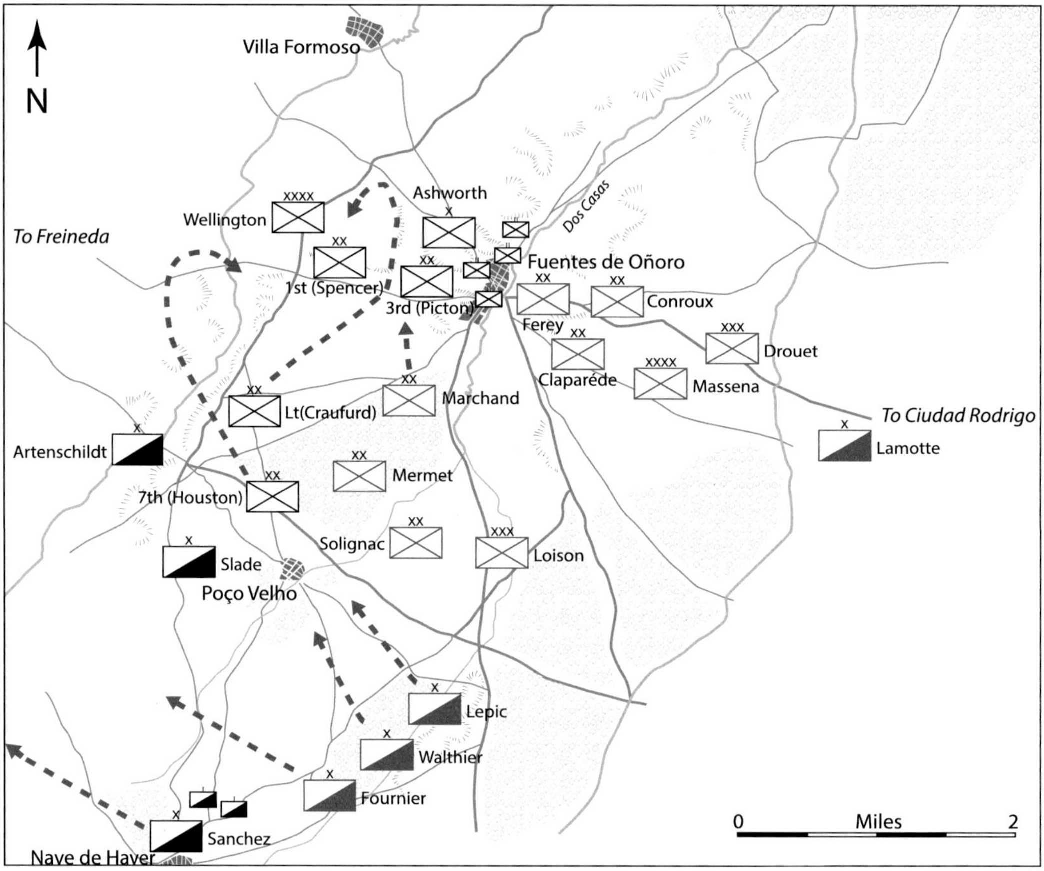

The Battle of Fuentes de Oñoro, 5 May 1811.
Sources: Lipscombe, *Atlas* & Wyld, *Maps & Plans*.

Velho.[36] The troops settled down for an uneasy night as sporadic firing continued around Fuentes de Oñoro. The French attackers had taken 652 casualties, whilst the advantage of good cover meant that those of the defenders had been much lighter at 259.[37]

The allied army was under arms half an hour before dawn on 4 May. As the sun rose the troops holding the village exchanged fire with the French but the fighting stopped at 10:00 a.m. as a truce was called to gather in the wounded. French and allied soldiers mixed freely, helping each other with the often gruesome tasks. French bands began to play across the stream as the men of both armies cooked meals and rested.[38] Massena was not idle though. He sent cavalry to probe the allied position around Poço Velho. The reports came back that

36 Instructions issued after the repulse of the French attack, 3 May 1811, quoted in Wellington, *Supplementary Despatches*, Vol.XIII, p.629.

37 Oman, *Peninsular War*, Vol.IV, p.314.

38 Anonymous, *Journal of a Soldier of the 71st* (Edinburgh: Tait, 1819), p.135.

the ground was more open and that Wellington's flank could be turned. Massena decided to attack there the following day, with his cavalry and three infantry division, whilst a demonstration was again made against the 5th Division and another frontal assault on Fuentes de Oñoro attempted.

Massena tried to mask his moves during the night but a combination of information from deserters and allied cavalry patrols meant that Wellington had an idea of what he intended and moved some cavalry out beyond his flank and the 7th Division, his least experienced, marched to Poço Velho. The weary and depleted light companies were pulled back but remained in positions to support the 1/71st, 1/79th, and 2/24th in the village.

The French flanking attack began early in the morning on 5 May, driving in the British cavalry outposts and some Spanish guerrillas before surprising elements of the 7th Division, many of whom had not seen combat before. The French attack was stronger than Wellington had envisaged. The French cavalry and supporting infantry vastly outnumbered the allied units and began to push them back. Wellington sent the Light Division, once more commanded by Craufurd, to support the withdrawal of the 7th Division. Wellington realigned his front along the road that ran from Fuentes de Oñoro to Freineda, moving the 1st and 3rd Divisions to a line that started at the rocky hills at the rear of Fuentes de Oñoro. The 7th and Light Divisions marched slowly across the open ground, often in square, fighting off repeated French cavalry attacks and under artillery fire. They were bravely defended by the few allied cavalry. If the two divisions had collapsed the French could have cut Wellington off from the bridge across the Coa.

With his flank attack gaining ground Massena ordered the attack on Fuentes de Oñoro to start and once again the French dashed across the stream and began to drive the defenders back up the streets to the church. The defenders rallied and pushed the French back down the hill, only to be pushed back again when the French sent 18 companies of grenadiers to support the attack. Lieutenant Colonel Cameron was mortally wounded and Cadogan of the 1/71st became the third officer to lead the defence of the village. The French captured almost all of the buildings but could not advance further because of the combined fire of the light companies and the ejected defenders. Both sides poured in reinforcements and after the 1/88th made a bayonet charge into the village, supported by the 74th, the allies began to drive the French back down the hill and across the stream once more.

The 7th and Light Divisions conducted their withdrawal to the new line with admirable coolness and bravery, largely keeping their formations and minimising their losses. As they approached, pursued by the French, the skirmishing line of the Guards Brigade, including No. 5 company, was in extended order along the foot of the slope in front of the new position and had to form square and fight off a French cavalry attack. Lieutenant Colonel Hill of the 1/3rd Guards, commanding the skirmishers, then ordered his men back into extended order without realising another French cavalry unit was close by. The French charged the three companies in the flank killing or wounding 68 and capturing 21.[39] The survivors, gathered into small knots of men with bayonets facing outwards, were rescued by British cavalry.

With the failure of the attack on Fuentes de Oñoro, Massena knew that any general attack on the allied line would likely fail. In the early afternoon the fighting died down to

39 Oman, *Peninsular*, Vol.IV, p.328.

Battle of Fuentes D'Onor, taken from the right of the position occupied by the 1st, 3rd and 7th Divisions on the 5th May, 1811, by Thomas Staunton St. Clair. (Anne S.K. Brown Military Collection)

occasional skirmishing, which ended at dusk. Wellington ordered entrenchments dug to strengthen the allied position, just in case the French renewed their attacks. On the 6th the armies again saw to their wounded and by the 8th Massena began to withdraw back towards Ciudad Rodrigo. On 10 May laxness by some of the troops blockading Almeida allowed the French garrison to slip away in the night.

Allied losses on 3 May were 36 killed, 201 wounded, and 22 missing or taken prisoner. French losses were 76 killed, 409 wounded, and 167 missing or taken. On 5 May the allies lost 205 killed, 1,046 wounded, and 294 missing or taken and the French 267 killed, 1,878 wounded, and 47 missing or prisoners.[40]

Losses for the 5th Battalion on the 3rd and 4th were three privates killed, nine wounded, and eight missing. Lieutenant Colonel Williams and Lieutenant du Chastelet were also wounded. Williams would not be back with the battalion until July. On the 5th Major Woodgate, Lieutenant Wynne, one sergeant and 11 privates were wounded and one man was reported missing.[41]

All the casualties on 3 May, unsurprisingly, came from the companies defending the village: Corporal Christian Wentz (No. 2) was a butcher from Wurthenberg, Germany, and had only been promoted from private a week before the battle; Corporal Henry Milleke (No. 9), from Brunswick, was killed on the 4th, presumably during the night or during the initial skirmishing before the morning truce – he had been with the battalion since formation; Private Matthew Corn (No. 9) came from Kirchberg, in the Duchy of Luxembourg. Private

40 Oman, *Peninsular*, Vol.IV, p.622-30.

41 Rigaud, *Celer et Audax*, p.169.

Niclaus Bidinger (No. 5), with the Guards Brigade attacked by French cavalry, was one of the wounded on 5 May and he died of his wounds on the 6th.[42]

The wounded were taken to a hospital established at the nearby village of Vilar Formoso. On 6 May William Grattan of the 1/88th visited the hospital:

> Near the gate an assistant-surgeon was taking off the leg of an old German sergeant of the 60th. The doctor was evidently a young practitioner, and Bell, our staff-surgeon, took much trouble in instructing him. It is a tolerably general received opinion, that when the saw passes through the marrow the patient suffers most pain; but such is not the case. The first cut and taking up the arteries is the worst. While the old German was undergoing the operation, he seemed insensible of pain when the saw was at work; now and then he would exclaim in broken English, as if wearied 'Oh! mine Got, is she off still?' but he, as well as all those I noticed, felt much when the knife was first introduced, and all thought that red-hot iron was applied to them when the arteries were taken up. The young doctor seemed much pleased when he had the sergeant fairly out of his hands, and it would be difficult to decide whether he or his patient was most happy; but, from everything I could observe, I was of opinion that the doctor made his debut on the old German's stump. I offered up a few words prayers they could not be called that, if ever it fell to my lot to lose any of my members, the young fellow who essayed on the sergeant should not be the person to operate on me.[43]

It is not clear from the surviving records who the sergeant was, as no sergeant is listed as being invalided out of the service in 1811, as one would expect of an amputee, nor as being in the general hospital. One sergeant did die of wounds on 16 May but he is listed as being from one of the companies attached to Beresford's army in the south. Private Frederick Radka, discharged in April 1812, did lose a limb on 3 May, but his discharge papers do not specify if it was an arm or leg.[44] It is possible that Grattan misremembered the rank or the unit of the unfortunate patient.

Williams was praised in Wellington's dispatch and Major Woodgate was recommended for a brevet promotion to lieutenant colonel for his service during the campaign.[45] With Massena's army defeated Wellington turned his attention southwards. The 3rd and 7th Divisions marched toward Beresford's force on 13 and 14 May, but some troops were sent ahead immediately after the battle including Major Galiffe and a detachment of the 5th Battalion who accompanied a party of the Royal Artillery.[46] Galiffe and his men would arrive in time for yet another battle.

42 May Casualty Return TNA, WO 25/1923 & Periods of Service 5/60th, June 1806, WO 25/1008.

43 Grattan, *Connaught Rangers*, pp.77.

44 Certificate of Service Frederick Radka, TNA, WO 121/118/251.

45 Wellington to Liverpool 8 May 1811, & Wellington to commander in chief 14 May 1811, quoted in Gurwood, *Wellington's Dispatches*, Vol.VII, pp.515 & 543.

46 Butler, *Annals*, Vol, II, p.138.

18

Albuera

A French force of 20,000 men under *Marechal* Soult had advanced into the Spanish province of Extremadura at the start of January 1811 with orders to support *Marechal* Massena in Portugal.[1] The French took several towns, defeated local Spanish forces, and had taken the provincial capital and fortress of Badajoz by 11 March, after a short siege.

Once it became evident that Soult had little desire, or resources, to advance beyond Badajoz Wellington started to make plans to retake the Spanish fortress. Major General Hill had been in command of the forces in southern Portugal, and was Wellington's usual choice for an independent command, but he had returned to Britain on sick leave. So Wellington chose *Marechal* William Carr Beresford instead. Beresford, head of the Portuguese army, was a thorough and competent officer who had gained Wellington's trust and respect. A large character in almost every way he was physically strong, blind in one eye, and was usually described as being somewhere between unkempt and looking like a ruffian. His manners were poor and his temper worse. He was popular with his soldiers, but not all of his officers. Wellington gave Beresford orders to attempt to retake Badajoz, and in early March sent him the 4th Division and a cavalry brigade to add to the 2nd Division, the Portuguese Division, an independent Portuguese brigade, and four brigades of British and Portuguese cavalry that he already commanded. The distribution of the 5th Battalion's companies in the 2nd and 4th Divisions was as follows:

2nd Division – Major General Stewart
Lieutenant Colonel Colborne
  1/3rd, 2/31st, 2/48th, 2/66th & No. 4 company 5/60th.
Major General Lumley
  2/28th, 2/34th, 2/39th & No. 8 company 5/60th.
Major General Hoghton
  29th, 1/48th, 1/57th & No. 6 company 5/60th.

1 G. Dempsey, *Albuera 1811* (Barnsley: Frontline Books, 2008), p.35.

4th Division – Major General Cole
Brigadier General Kemmis
3/27th, 1/40th, 97th & No. 10 company 5/60th.
Colonel Pakenham
1/7th, 2/7th, 1/23rd & 1 Company Brunswick Oels.
Coronel Collins (Portuguese)
11th (2 battalions), 23rd (2 battalions) 7th Cacadores.[2]

The campaign got off to a slow start, partly due to the fact that the 4th Division arrived with their shoes falling apart after marching 110 miles on rough mountain roads in six days, on top of all the miles following Massena's retreat. An initially successful cavalry operation against the French around Campo Mayor was marred by errors in communications between the cavalry commander and Beresford. Further delays occurred when the allies had to build a bridge to cross the Guadiana River. In early April Cole's 4th Division was tasked with re-capturing the fortified town of Olivenza. The French garrison was small but Cole chose to wait for heavy guns from Elvas. Once the batteries were built and the bombardment started, the French commander surrendered within a few hours. In his dispatch to Beresford, Cole credited the suppressing fire from men of No. 10 company, the Brunswickers, and other light companies with keeping casualties low.[3]

After Wellington's visit to the south in April Beresford was left with a detailed series of instructions for besieging Badajoz. Wellington also called on the Spanish forces in the area to closely co-operate with Beresford, which they did to a greater extent than in previous years. Beresford spent time manoeuvring to push the French out of the province before he felt he could safely invest Badajoz.

The town of Badajoz lay on the southern bank of the Guadiana River, protected on one side by the river which was 300-500 yards wide. The walls that surrounded the town were over 20 feet high with numerous bastions rising to 30 feet, and several outer redoubts. In the north-east of the town was a hill, topped by an old castle. Across the river was a similar hill, San Cristobal, on which a fort had been built to stop attackers overlooking the town. A 600-yard long bridge to the town crossed the river a little way down from San Cristobal.[4]

Wellington's chief engineer, Lieutenant Colonel Fletcher, had come up with a plan to first take Fort San Cristobal and then erect batteries in and around it to fire down on the town and create a breach in the walls. Diversionary works were to be made on the other detached defences to the south east of the town. Trenches would be dug and batteries built to bombard the walls of the fort. Tools were brought from Olivenza to cut the wood that would be needed and dig the trenches. A bridge was built upstream from the town to enable Beresford's troops to cross more easily. Additional stores, ammunition and 32 heavy calibre guns were taken from Elvas.[5]

2 Dempsey, *Albuera*, Appendix A, pp.261-3; Oman, *Wellington's*, p.351; Butler, *Annals*, Vol.II, pp.122-3; March & April 1811 Returns, TNA, WO 17/180. Which companies were in which brigades is difficult to be certain of, due to the subsequent changes that the 2nd Division went through.

3 Cole to Beresford 16 April 1811, Wellington, *Supplementary Despatches*, Vol.XIII, pp.614-5

4 J. T. Jones, *Journals of Sieges Carried on by the Army under the Duke of Wellington* (London: John Weale, 844), Vol.I, pp.11-2.

5 Jones, *Sieges*, Vol.I, pp.16-8.

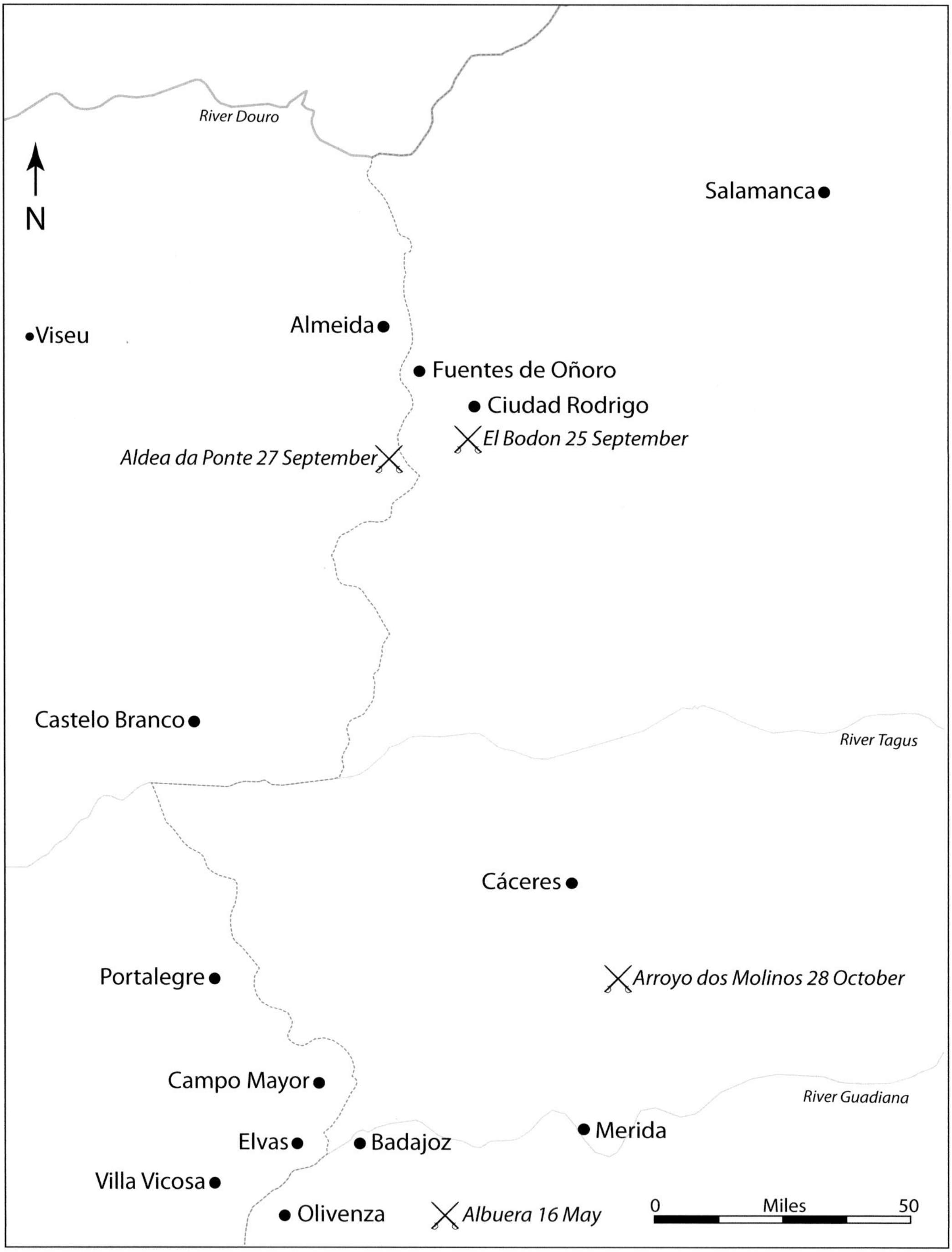

Beresford's Campaign in the South & Operations of Autumn 1811.

On 30 April Colborne's brigade of the 2nd Division, including No. 4 company, and with a squadron each of Portuguese and Spanish cavalry, undertook a wide sweep south-east into the Sierra Morena mountains to force the French forces there back away from the siege. After clearing many towns and achieving their mission the brigade had arrived back in the vicinity of the rest of the allied army by 11 May.[6]

Meanwhile, on 4 May, the rest of 2nd Division marched from Talavera la Real at midnight and took up positions on the south bank of the Guadiana at Badajoz in the morning. The north bank was occupied by the allies in the early hours of 8th when Major General Lumley, with Kemmis' Brigade of the 4th Division and the Portuguese 17th Regiment, was ordered to take up positions opposite the fort. As Lumley approached with the light companies of the brigade, including No. 10 company, a force of French cavalry and infantry attacked them, but were driven back after a charge from the grenadiers of the 17th.[7] The intrenching tools, sand-bags, gabions, and timber needed were then placed ready, and officers and men drawn from the besieging divisions to assist the engineers.[8]

As night fell on 8 May work began on the trenches and batteries in front of the fort, and at the locations of the other diversionary attacks. The work was carried out at night to minimise casualties as the garrison in the town would attempt to disrupt the work by cannon and musket fire. However, the ground near the fort was found to be very hard and rocky and little progress was made. At daylight there was little cover for the troops. The French kept up an incessant barrage, killing or wounding many men in the working parties. Not much more was achieved during the day or the next night.

During the initial operations around Badajoz the battalion suffered two fatal casualties: Private George Lewis Jahn (No. 6), from Dinhiem in Germany was killed in action on 6 May; Private Bartholomew Lefever (No. 10) was killed on 9 May. Lefever, serving in Kemmis' brigade, had joined the Hompesch Light Infantry in 1795 and had transferred to the 2/60th when they were disbanded at the end of 1797, before moving to the 5th Battalion in 1803.[9]

At 7:00 a.m. on 10 May 1,200 French infantry and two field-guns made a sortie from the town, and crossed the bridge near San Christobal.[10] Captain James Prevost was in command of the men guarding the siege-works. Later in the year his brother Augustine included an account of what happened in a letter to their father:

> Now as to James he has obtained much credit and what seldom falls to the job of a Captain of a Company, I send you a copy of the thanks he received from the Honorable General Lumley (sent to him by the General) for his conduct before Badajos at the sortie of the French it was here James got a shot through one arm and a shell touched his left but he is quite recovered and acting Aide de Camp to General Cole who was also wounded as well as his Brigade Major & Aide de Camp this situation will give James some repose, and better living, with less fatigue. General

6 Oman, *Peninsular War*, Vol.IV, p.284.

7 Beresford to Wellington 16 May 1811, quoted in Wellington, *Supplementary Despatches*, Vol.XIII, p.644.

8 Jones, *Sieges*, Vol.I, pp.19-22; Oman, *Peninsular War*, Vol.IV, p.284.

9 May 1811 Casualty Return TNA, WO 25/1923; Periods of Service 5/60th, June 1806, WO 25/1008.

10 Beresford to Wellington 16 May 1811, quoted in Wellington, *Supplementary Despatches*, Vol.XIII, pp.644-5.

> Lumleys order is as follows 'Captain Provost 60th Reg at this time in Command of about 100 Lt Infantry & Riflemen and in charge of the batteries wisely foreseeing with his great inferiority of force that the risk of suffering his flanks to be turned was of more importance than the temporary loss of the Battery fell back some paces, this had the desired affect in some degree of shaking the Enemys flank movements, the Battery was however, in possession of their centre for a few seconds at this moment
>
> Lt Col Harcourt the Field Officer of the Trenches came up with the reserve. The whole including the detachments of the Infantry and the Riflemen and Captain Provost again advanced the Enemy tho still greatly superior in numbers were driven down the slope with the rapidity of a Torrent &c &c
>
> To Captain Provost whose conduct was as conspicuous as the post in which he was placed was important I feel the greatest obligations, signed W Lumley M. G.'[11]

Unfortunately the pursuit was carried too far and the allied troops, encouraged by their officers, chased the French into the range of the guns and muskets of the fort. They took 400 casualties.[12] James Prevost was sent to the hospital at Elvas but was back with his company by the end of June.[13]

The battery was completed the next night and opened fire at dawn on 11 May, but accurate counter-battery fire from the fort disabled some of the guns and more had to be brought up. Work continued on the siege-works, but only briefly. News had reached Beresford that Soult was marching to relieve Badajoz. On 12 May Beresford sent a letter to the commander of the French garrison, *Général de Brigade* Phillipon, asking for his surrender in a last minute bluff. Phillipon refused the offer and Beresford raised the siege, ordering all the guns and stores out of the batteries and back to Elvas. The gabions and timber were burned. The first allied units left Badajoz on 13 May and the last two days later.

During April Soult had tried to learn what he could of Beresford's operation but he had had no word from Badajoz; Colborne's sweep had driven his forward forces back and he was unsure where the Spanish troops in the region were. However, he knew he had to do something to support Badajoz and so gathered together around 23,000 men from various corps.[14] In the vain hope of keeping news of his departure from the enemy Soult marched from Seville in the middle of the night of 9-10 May. Usually it would have taken an army 10 days to get to Badajoz but he pushed his men hard, at twice the normal speed.

Kept informed by Spanish guerrillas, spies and exploring officers of Soult's moves Beresford met with *Capitán General* Castaños and *Teniente General* Blake to discuss whether to give battle to the French or to retreat. Blake convinced Beresford to fight and preparations were made to unite the Anglo-Portuguese and Spanish forces at a position chosen in advance by Wellington. The allies would make their stand at the largely abandoned village of La Albuera, 16 miles south-east of Badajoz on the road from Seville. The village lay in a valley created by three small rivers or streams, none of which were very deep and over, or through,

11 A. Prevost to A. Prevost, undated, AI, Prevost Papers, CR 544/II/4a
12 Oman, *Peninsular War*, Vol.IV, p.285.
13 May & June 1811 Returns, TNA, WO 17/180.
14 Dempsey, *Albuera*, p.74.

which there were bridges and fords. The lines of the streams were lightly wooded and to the west the land rose slowly to a ridge of open meadow, with two slightly higher hillocks along the line of the ridge; the first a mile south-west of the village and the second 500 yards further south. On the eastern side of the valley was level ground backed by woodland.[15]

The allied cavalry posted towards Seville fell back but kept in touch with Soult's advance guard as the French approached. On 15 May the allied army began to take up their positions. The British cavalry, which had been shadowing the French as they advanced, arrived in the afternoon, closely followed by their French counterparts. The Spanish divisions under Blake arrived during the night and, after some confusion in the dark, were in their positions soon after dawn. Beresford expected Soult to attack the village from the east, and had deployed his forces accordingly.

On the right of the allied line, south-west of the village, were the Spanish divisions of *Teniente General* Ballesteros and *Mariscal de Campo* Lardizabal. Behind them in a second line were a brigade commanded by *Brigadier* de España, and *Mariscal de Campo* Zayas' division. The Spanish cavalry protected the allies' southern flank, but the two hillocks on the ridge were not occupied. Alten's Brigade, consisting of the 1st and 2nd KGL Light Battalions, occupied the village of La Albuera. Behind the village was Stewart's 2nd Division, and then on the left of the allied line was Hamilton's Portuguese Division. Cole's 4th Division was still arriving and was in reserve at the rear. However, Kemmis' Brigade had been forced to march by a different route from Badajoz because a rise in the river had prevented them from fording where they planned to. They missed the battle, with the exception of the three light companies who were present. Beresford's total strength was 10,603 British, 10,201 Portuguese and 14,552 Spanish troops, a total of over 35,000 which far outnumbered the French.[16]

Soult did not think that Blake or Cole's troops had arrived and believed that he had the advantage of numbers. Seeing the strength of the allies around the village and the more open and less defended ground to the south he decided to make a flanking attack. A diversionary assault on the village would occupy the allies while the bulk of the French army, which had marched overnight, got into position. Four regiments of French cavalry with a battery of horse artillery approached the village and drove in the allied skirmishers. To make the diversion convincing Soult then sent in the rest of his cavalry and two brigades of infantry.[17]

British cavalry drove some of the French horsemen back after prolonged skirmishing. French *Général de Division* Godinot's infantry brigade marched on the village where the KGL were in good cover amongst the houses and walled gardens. The KGL's rifle companies concentrated their fire on the French officers and the French did not advance very far, or very quickly. However, the attack did have the result that Soult required in that Beresford began to move some of his forces towards the village and the centre of the allied line.

Meanwhile the bulk of Soult's V Corps, commanded by *Général de Division* Girard, made their way through the woods to the south, unseen by the allies. The first officer to spot them was Lieutenant Colonel von Schepeler, on the Spanish staff, who saw the French as

15 Dempsey, *Albuera*, pp.79-80.

16 Dempsey, *Albuera*, pp.93-4.

17 Details of the battle are taken from Dempsey, *Albuera*, pp.91-198, Lipscombe, *The Peninsular War Atlas*, pp.216-20, and Oman, *Peninsular War*, Vol.IV, pp.372-95.

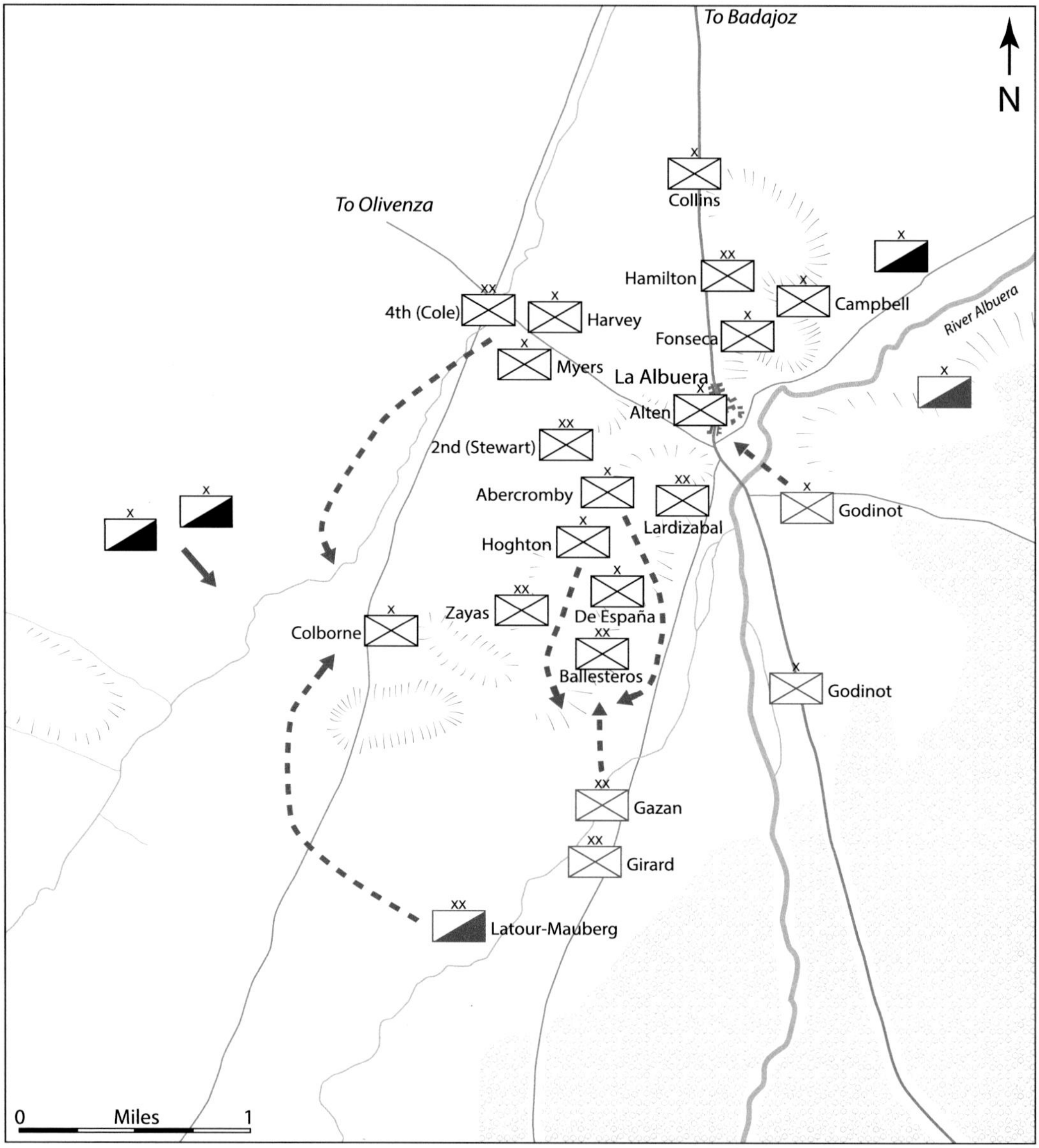

Battle of Albuera, 16 May 1811.
Sources: Lipscombe, *Atlas* & Oman, *History of the Peninsular War.*

they crested some high ground and descended to cross the stream. The French light cavalry and *volitgeurs* crossed first and deployed on the allied bank. As soon as word reached him Beresford acted quickly to meet the new threat. He asked Blake to redeploy some of his troops at right angles across the ridge and moved the 2nd Division to support the Spanish and the 4th Division to cover the Valverde road in open ground west of the ridge. Portuguese units were repositioned to support the KGL in the village.

It took the French time to get all their troops across the stream and back into their formations on the crest of the ridge, and the allies should have had plenty of time to redeploy, but Blake had dithered and refused to reposition his troops, unconvinced the flank attack was the enemy's main effort. By the time it became obvious that it was the main threat Beresford's staff officers had bypassed Blake and the Spanish divisional commanders had complied willingly and in time. The new line ran from the northernmost of the two hillocks westwards across the ridge. The southern hillock was occupied by some Spanish light companies. The commencement of the French flank attack was further delayed by a sudden downpour of rain and hail accompanied by strong winds, but at around 11:00 a.m. the French veterans approached the Spanish, whom they had beaten many times before.

The Spanish light companies defended the southern hillock against the French *volitgeurs* but fell back in the face of the line infantry. The French columns marched on towards the Spanish line and were met with disciplined volley fire supported by cannon. The Spaniards stopped the French columns and Girard, belatedly and disastrously, tried to redeploy his men into line and took heavy casualties, especially amongst officers. Meanwhile Colborne's Brigade of the 2nd Division deployed in line on the left flank of the French columns and added to the slaughter with their own volleys and then bayonet charges, but some of the French turned to face them and the fighting became ferocious and confused. The British brigade had their flank open to the enemy, a mistake the French were quick to exploit.

A mass of French cavalry, led by a regiment of Polish lancers, slammed into the unprotected side and rear of the British infantry, butchering three of the four battalions. The redcoats who were not immediately killed or wounded ran, surrendered, or gathered together in clumps, bayonets outwards, in the hope of fending off sabres or the deadly eight-foot long lances. Five of the six colours of the three hard-hit battalions were captured, despite heroic efforts by the defenders. The French cavalry rode on to attack a battery of KGL artillery.

Four squadrons of British and Spanish cavalry were sent to stop the French charge with only limited success. The final battalion of Colborne's Brigade, the 2/31st, were still marching in column when the French cavalry charge hit and were able to form a hurried square which ably resisted the lancers, who were by then disordered with the momentum of their attack spent. Beresford and his staff were attacked and the allied commander had to defend himself by grasping a Pole around the neck and unhorsing him.

With the first French attack defeated both sides relieved their battered front line units. The Spanish retired through the line of the 2nd Division and the British brigades marched forward. At the same time the leading French division fell back to be replaced by fresher troops from the rear. The two new formations marched towards each other on the former line of the Spanish around the northern-most height on the ridge.

Hoghton's Brigade was first to open fire on the French columns but as the French returned fire Hoghton was hit. Normally, after one or two volleys the redcoats would charge but they did not on this occasion. It may have been the wounded and dead strewn on the ground in front of them, the fact that the battalions had been widely spaced to allow the Spanish through, or the death of their brigade commander that made them just stand and exchange volleys with the French. With cannon adding to the weight of fire from each side casualties were murderously heavy, but the British line stubbornly held as further squalls of rain obscured the combatants from each other. The 1/57th earned themselves the nickname 'Die Hards' during the prolonged firefight. Abercromby's Brigade joined the line to the left of

Hoghton's brigade and faced the combined grenadier companies of the French division. The exchange of volleys lasted about an hour, the rate of fire probably slowed by the rain and sheer fatigue. The smoke of the battle could be seen from Elvas, 16 miles away.

With the French and British battalions fighting themselves to a bloody stalemate it was the enemy's turn to lose a commander as *Général de Brigade* Maransin, commander of the French troops attacking the 2nd Division's line, was hit in the stomach and taken to the rear. Beresford tried and failed to get Spanish and then Portuguese units to attack the flank of the French column. The Spanish commanders would not move without orders from their own chain of command and the Portuguese were not where they were supposed to be. Beresford galloped off to find the Portuguese, leaving the allied army without a commander at a crucial point. The ranks of Hoghton's Brigade were rapidly thinning and a fresh push forward by the French could have tipped the balance.

Fortunately, one of Beresford's staff, Captain Hardinge, took the initiative and rode to Cole and urged him to attack with the 4th Division. Cole had orders not to move without word from Beresford, but chose to disobey them and moved his division forward, protecting his flanks with the light companies of the division, including those of Kemmis' Brigade, on one side and the 7th Cacadores (formerly the Loyal Lusitanian Legion) on the other. French cavalry charged the Portuguese brigade but were repulsed by steady volleys. The Fusilier Brigade, consisting of two battalions of the 7th and one of the 23rd, marched towards a French column attempting to pass through the units shattered by the volleys from the 2nd Division. The fusiliers held their fire until only 20 yards from the French, who were trying to deploy into line. The redcoats fired a volley and then charged. The French infantry began to fall back, and not even another charge by the lancers could halt the allied advance. Abercromby's Brigade, again at the urging of Hardinge, moved forward and attacked the troops on French right flank, which also began to fall back in what became a general French retreat.

A rout was only avoided by the quick thinking of a French artillery commander who deployed his guns against the oncoming allies and gave the retreating units the time and the spirit to reform in an orderly fashion. The last act of the battle was performed by the KGL who had been withdrawn from the village. A French regiment had occupied it but the Germans charged back in and drove the French over the bridge. The allies had won the day but it was a victory of British and Iberian tenacity and steadfastness rather than good generalship. Beresford was widely condemned for his conduct of the battle and the initial positions of his forces, not all of the criticism was earned but much of the mud stuck. The Spaniards also came in for undeserved denigration but it was very much an allied victory as troops from all the nations present on the allied side had proven to be steady in difficult circumstances.

Casualties at Albuera were horrendous. The British lost 883 killed, 2,753 wounded, and 563 missing or taken prisoner: a total casualty rate of 39 percent of those present. The Spanish and Portuguese suffered less at 9.5 percent and 4 percent respectively. The French lost 886 killed, 4,154 wounded, and 896 missing or prisoners, or 26 percent of those present.[18]

However, the aggregate figures disguise great variation between units. The 1/3rd, which bore the brunt of the lancers' attack, lost 85 percent of their strength, and the 2/48th 76

18 Dempsey, *Albuera*, p.285.

percent, with another six British battalions loosing over 50 percent. The losses were so severe that the two battalions of the 48th were merged and the rest of Colborne's and Hoghton's Brigades placed into one provisional battalion. The 5th Battalion lost 14 percent, amongst the lowest rates of the British units engaged.[19]

Two riflemen were killed in action: Sergeant Balthasar Kessler (No. 4), from Reiden in Hesse, and Private Peter Landgraff (No. 6) from Nieder-Saulheim, also in Hesse. Both had joined the battalion in 1802 from the Lowenstein Jägers, and both were in companies attached the 2nd Division. Two men were listed as missing. Sergeant Christian Pritz (No. 4) died of his wounds on the day of the battle. Lieutenant Ingersleben, two sergeants and 16 rank and file were wounded. Ingersleben was severely wounded and, after initial treatment at Elvas, returned to Britain on leave until August 1812.[20]

It is not clear from the surviving accounts, or subsequent histories, what part the companies of the battalion played in the battle as they are not mentioned specifically. Mentions of any light troops or skirmishers on the allied side are few. It is evident from the casualties that the three companies with the 2nd Division were engaged and were probably fulfilling their role in providing an initial skirmishing screen and then subsequently working on the flanks. Perhaps the high number of officer casualties amongst the French is, partly, evidence of their accurate rifle fire.[21]

The whereabouts of No. 10 company, attached to Kemmis' Brigade on 16 May, is even more uncertain. The rising of the river at Badajoz had prevented Kemmis' Brigade from fording the river there and forced a march via Elvas to the pontoon bridge at Juromenha. Riguad in *Celer et Audax* and Butler in *The Annals of the KRRC*, both state the company was not present but both statements seem to be based on the absence of Kemmis' Brigade as a whole and no source is referenced.[22] Dempsey in *Albeura 1811* makes it clear that the light companies of Kemmis' brigade were present at the battle and saw action when the 4th Division moved forward but he cites Butler as his source to say that No. 10 company was not present.[23] Contemporary sources mention 'the light companies of the 4th division'[24] or 'detachments' from Kemmis' Brigade,[25] without specifically mentioning which companies are being referred to. It would seem odd if the divisional light battalion had been assembled and the light companies of the line regiments in Kemmis' Brigade detached, that the rifle company was left with the brigade. However, with Prevost injured Lieutenant Francis Holmes was the only other officer of the battalion with the 4th Division at the time and he does not seem to have been present at the battle.[26] Also none of the casualties are listed as coming from No. 10 company. When the 4th Division withdrew from Badajoz some pickets were inadvertently left behind. The officer responsible for them only remembered them

19 Dempsey, *Albuera*, pp.272-4.

20 May 1811 Casualty Return, TNA, WO 25/1923; Periods of Service 5/60th, June 1806, WO 25/1008; January; August 1812 Returns, WO 17/180, & Butler, *Annals*, Vol.II, p.138.

21 Dempsey, *Albuera*, p.158.

22 Rigaud, *Celer et Audax*, p.173 &; Butler, *Annals*, Vol.II, p.139.

23 Dempsey, *Albuera*, pp.185, including footnote 30.

24 C.B. Vere, Marches, *Movements & Operations of the 4th Division* (Ipswich: Dece, 1841), p.15

25 Cooper, *Rough Notes*, p.60.

26 April & May 1811 Returns, TNA, WO 17/180; Butler, *Annals*, Vol.II, p.252.

when the division was nearly at Albuera. Cole ordered him back to get them, it is possible that No. 10 company were part of the picket.[27]

More certain is the location of Major John Galiffe and the detachment who had marched south soon after the battle of Fuentes de Oñoro. They did arrive in time for the battle and Galiffe commanded the 2nd Division's light troops.[28] Galiffe and Private Daniel Lochstadt later claimed medal clasps for both battles.[29] Lochstadt was on the roll of No. 6 company and there is no record of why he had been detached.

Amongst the dead was Captain Harry Prevost of the 7th Fusiliers, James' brother, who had been mortally wounded.[30] In the same letter in which he told their father of James' wound, Augustine also wrote:

> Poor James is recovering fast, he has been labouring under the greatest dissatisfaction of spirits on account of his finances & the consequent fears of having offended all his friends by his imprudence. The death of his dear Companion & Brother had nearly overcome him. I say all I can to ease his mind & I hope my dear father like myself, has now got over the shock he must have felt at the melancholy news contained in my last letter, every voice bears testimony to the gallantry of your brave son Henry to the feelings of a father how consoling it must be to hear such praises 'Tell my dear father says James, that poor Henry behaved nobly at the head of his Company in front of his Regiment when advancing to the charge within twenty paces of the Enemy, here he nobly fell' Lt. Colonel Blakeney, his Commanding Officer speaks thus 'Henry poor fellow received his wound nobly doing his duty on the memorable 16th May and bore his sufferings with equal manfulness, indeed the Surgeon declared him as a strong instance of what we mortals can bare when dire and fearful necessity required it.'[31]

The sheer volume of wounded after the battle presented problems for both the French and allied armies. Those that could not walk to get themselves to a surgeon lay on the battlefield for at least one night, drenched by the rain, before getting any help. There were too many wounded and too few survivors to assist them, although some still had the energy to plunder the wounded and the dead. The rest of Kemmis' Brigade arrived on the morning of 17 May after marching all night and were horrified by what they saw. Both armies began transporting the wounded to hospitals in the rear but lacked sufficient carts to meet demand, especially in the allied camp. The dead were put in mass graves hundreds of yards long. Soult marched his army away on the 18th, leaving behind the wounded he could not take with him.

As the French left Beresford dispatched troops to renew the siege at Badajoz. Wellington arrived at Elvas on 19 May with the 3rd and 7th Divisions a few days behind him. The allied commander had felt the need to put a positive spin on Beresford's post-battle dispatch, due

27 Dempsey, *Albuera*, p.99.

28 Dempsey, *Albuera*, p.262.

29 Burnham & McGuigan, *The British Army*, p.313; Butler, *Annals*, Vol.II, pp.138-9.

30 Graves, *Fix Bayonets!*, p.260.

31 A. Prevost to A. Prevost undated, AI, Prevost Papers, CR 549/II/4a

to the large loss of life and the fact that questions were already circulating amongst the army regarding Beresford's conduct. Beresford was sent back to Lisbon to administer the Portuguese army and did not have a major independent command again, but he still played an important part in the eventual victory in the Peninsula. He was much affected by the criticism he received, especially the extreme losses under his command, and was unwell for some months after the battle.

Wellington kept to the same plan for the second siege of Badajoz, and had the same problems of lack of supplies, poor quality guns, and hard ground. The 7th Division made two attempts to storm the fortress, on 6 and 9 June, but both failed. On 10 June Wellington learnt that *Marechal* Marmont, who had replaced Massena, may have been bringing his army south to unite with Soult. The allied army was moved to Albuera again but once it was confirmed that the two French armies were working together Wellington withdrew his army, including the recently arrived, 1st, 6th, and Light Divisions, back into Portugal and abandoned the siege. Soult and Marmont, unwilling to risk attacking Wellington's army again on ground of his choosing, opted not to advance into Portugal.

In July the allied divisions were dispersed to avoid the fever-ridden Caya and Guadiana river valleys. The June return shows the headquarters companies of the 5th Battalion with the 3rd Division at Campo Mayor and by the July return they were further north at Castello Branco, along with the company attached to the 6th Division.[32] The other companies were with 1st Division at Portalegre, the 2nd at Villa Vicosa, and the 4th at Pedrogão. A draft of 1 corporal and 37 privates left Lymington in early June, arriving with the battalion later in June and in July. The recruits had left the Foreign Depot before their arms and accoutrements had arrived. One fell sick at Lisbon and died before joining.[33]

In August a detached company of the 3/95th was removed from Major General Howard's brigade, which had transferred from the 1st to the 2nd Division to reinforce that division after the losses at Albuera. A company of the 5th Battalion was moved from Colborne's brigade to replace the men of the 95th.[34] This was probably Captain Blassiere's No. 8 company.

In August Wellington moved the bulk of his army back to the north, leaving the recently returned Hill in command of the 2nd Division, Hamilton's Portuguese Division, and four brigades of cavalry to cover the southern frontier of Portugal. The French forces were positioned so that they could respond to move against either Badajoz or Ciudad Rodrigo, but had to be widely dispersed in order to find enough food to feed the troops. French reinforcements were expected but largely failed to arrive over the summer, whereas Wellington received fresh units from Britain and drafts that more than made up for the losses of the spring. One of the reinforcements that had arrived was a proper siege train of heavy cannon, which had been sorely lacking in operations against Badajoz. This, coupled with the disposition of French forces, led Wellington to plan a very tentative move against Ciudad Rodrigo.

By mid-August the Light and 3rd Divisions had surrounded the fortress, but kept their distance. Wellington's aim was to cut the French garrison's supply and communication routes but not to begin a full siege until the siege train arrived. The rest of the divisions were positioned, quite widely scattered, either to watch possible approaches for the French

32 June 1811 return, TNA, WO 17/180.

33 Mosheim to Williams 3 June 1811, TNA, WO 7/84, pp.57-8; August 1811 Return, WO 17/2468.

34 Wellington to Hill 23 August 1811, quoted in Gurwood, *Wellington's Dispatches*, Vol.VIII, p.218.

or to be ready to support the divisions investing Ciudad Rodrigo. Marmont took until mid-September to respond and managed to bring together 58,000 men, outnumbering the allies' 46,000.[35] Wellington guessed that Marmont's aim was to simply resupply the beleaguered fortress, and not to seek battle, and so he was slow to concentrate his own troops, or to fall back to more favourable ground than the plains around Ciudad Rodrigo. However, once he found that the allied army was still dispersed Marmont sought to take advantage of Wellington's complacency.

On the morning of 25 September two strong columns of French cavalry supported by infantry probed forwards from Ciudad Rodrigo, driving back the allied cavalry screen around Carpio. One column approached the 6th Division. The light companies of Hulse's Brigade, with No. 1 company, were sent to the edge of a wood to support the 14th and 16th Light Dragoons who were falling back as the French advanced.[36] The light companies and riflemen fired a volley, surprising the French cavalry, who were then charged by the light dragoons. The French broke and were driven back.

The other French cavalry column of 2,500 men pushed forward, through the allied cavalry screen, and rode towards the 3rd Division, which was in the process of concentrating. Lieutenant Colonel Williams commanded the advance guard of the 3rd Division, consisting Nos. 2, 3 and 7 companies and the 74th, on high ground near the village of Pastores.[37] Two other battalions were nearby at El Bodon and the other brigades of the division were similarly divided. Wellington, realising the threat to the 3rd Division ordered elements of Colville's Brigade, cavalry, and Portuguese artillery to stand firm to allow the troops at Pastores and El Bodon to withdraw. After some sharp fighting the French cavalry were driven back. The troops at Pastores, cut-off, had to take a long route back to safety, fording the River Agueda and reaching the 4th Division at sunset. At one point they had encountered a French cavalry patrol which they captured, but during the day five riflemen had to be left behind, sick, during the forced march and were taken prisoner.[38] The covering force of Colville's Brigade retreated, constantly harried by French cavalry and horse artillery, but maintained good order and the infantry's squares beat off the French charges.

Marmont started to bring up his infantry, some of which continued to march through the night, whilst Wellington tried to unite his scattered divisions into a prepared entrenched position at Fuente Guinaldo. The gathering of forces continued on 26 September but Marmont was unwilling to force a battle too quickly, given what had happened at Bussaco and Fuentes de Oñoro when assaults were made with proper preparation and planning.[39] This hesitation allowed Wellington the time to concentrate his forces and slip away during the night to a position at Alfayates, and enabled the allied army to escape from a potentially perilous situation.

On 27 September French cavalry, probing forwards again, were stopped, near Wellington's position, at the village of Aldea da Ponte by the pickets of the 4th Division and allied cavalry.

35 Oman, *Peninsular War*, Vol.IV, p.560.

36 Oman, *Peninsular War*, Vol.IV, pp.563-4.

37 Butler, *Annals*, Vol.II, p.141.

38 October 1811 Return, TNA, WO 17/180, December 1811 Pay List, WO 12/7074, & C.W. Vane, *Narrative of the Peninsular War, 1808 to 1813* (London: Henry Colburn,1828), p.602.

39 Oman, *Peninsular*, Vol.IV, p.574.

The village straddled several important road junctions. French infantry arrived on the scene and the senior officer, *Général de Division* Thiebault, sent forward three battalions to drive the light companies of the fusilier brigade out of the village. Wellington then ordered the whole of the Fusilier Brigade to take back the village, which they did after a brisk fight, supported by the rest of the 4th Division and Pack's Portuguese Brigade.[40] The French were driven back but received reinforcements and managed to retake the village at sunset, before being driven back again by the 4th Division.

The 5th battalion's casualties on 27 September were one private missing in action from No. 7 company, subsequently found to be a prisoner of war, and one officer wounded.[41] During the action at Aldea da Ponte Captain James Prevost acted as an aide to Brigadier General Edward Pakenham, who was leading the Fusilier Brigade. Unfortunately his brother's reassurances to their father that service as an aide would offer James an easier life than leading a rifle company proved sadly incorrect as James was again wounded. Pakenham wrote to James' brother Augustine:

> My task is severe, I have to acquaint you of your Brothers continued indisposition of the utmost danger from a wound which he received on the 27th Sept in the advance of the enemy from Ciudad Rodrigo to Adda de Ponte. The shot passed as near as possible in a direct line through his body & Although time has shown that it miraculously has made that traverse without destroying the intestines, the necessary loss of blood to prevent inflammation has reduced him to the lowest span. Captain Mair of the Fusileers and Surgeon Mahony (a young man of the most allowed talent) remains with him at Sabugal to which place he was removed & a very excellent woman as his nurse. Attentions from the people a good constitution and the help of providence may bring him through & there my friend are the only hopes of which you are to admit toward the preservations of this most amiable & gallant Young Man. The first in advance the rear in Retreat. His conduct whilst with the Army has been equally conspicuous in the field, as it has ever has been marked by modesty in society.
>
> My friend I will write no more but I think I may have often to write on this subject of a Young Man for whom I have such an affection I shall omit no opportunity till his *fate is decided*.[42]

Another surgeon who treated James was George Guthrie, who later included James' case in one of a series of articles for the medical journal *The Lancet*, which were then subsequently published in a book:

> Captain Prevost, aid-de-camp to Sir E. Packenham, was wounded by a musket-ball, on the 27th September, 1811, on the heights of Saca Parte. It penetrated the chest from behind, splintering the ninth and tenth ribs of the left side, and made its exit a little below and to the right of the xiphoid cartilage. A good deal of blood was lost

40 Vane, *Narrative*, p.606.

41 Oman, *Peninsular*, Vol.IV, p.648; October 1811 Casualty Return, TNA, WO 25/1923.

42 E. Pakenham to A. Prevost, October 9th, AI, CR549/II/4e.

> from the posterior wound, but he did not spit up any. He was carried to Alfaiates, and there he threw up a small quantity of bloody matter by vomiting. The posterior wound was enlarged and continued to discharge some blood, the intercostal artery being in all probability wounded. Sixteen ounces of blood were taken from the arm, giving great relief, and the bowels were opened by the sulphate of magnesia.
>
> Sept. 29th.-Bleeding to eighteen ounces; on the 30th he was bled again to thirty-two ounces, from which great relief was obtained; he fainted, however, on making a trifling exertion to relieve his bowels.
>
> Oct. 1st.- Accession of symptoms as yesterday, relieved by bleeding in a similar manner; bowels open.
>
> 3d.- The inflammatory symptoms recurred this morning, and were again removed by the abstraction of sixteen ounces of blood. Beef-tea.
>
> 5th.- Passed a sleepless night, and was evidently suffering from considerable internal mischief; wandered occasionally; pulse quick, 120, and small; felt very weak and desponding. A little light, red wine given, with beef-tea and bread; opium night and morning.
>
> 6th and 7th.-Much the same; pulse always quick, with much general irritability.
>
> 15th.- The wounds discharged considerably, particularly the posterior one; has a little cough; pulse continues very quick; spasms of the diaphragm troubled him for the first time, and caused great pain and uneasiness; they were relieved by opium in large and repeated doses.
>
> On the 18th the spasmodic affection of the diaphragm and the pain returned with great violence, so as to threaten his dissolution, which took place on the 20th.
>
> On examination, I found that the ball had passed through the under part of the inferior lobe of the left lung, and through the pericardium under the heart, through the tendinous part of the diaphragm, and into the liver, before it made its exit. The wound in the lung was suppurating; the matter and fluid from the cavity of the chest had a free discharge by the shot-hole; the edges of the wound in the diaphragm were smooth as if cicatrized, leaving between them an elliptical opening an inch long. The injury to the liver was through the substance of the anterior part of its right lobe; the matter having a free discharge, and generally slightly yellow, as if tinged with bile in small quantity. The skin did not show a yellowish tinge, neither were the conjunctive discolored.[43]

James died on 20 October. His treatment illustrates the limits of medical science at the time. With no antibiotics there was little that could have been done to fight the inevitable infection following such a severe trauma, and one does not have to be a medical expert to suspect that having over four pints of blood removed did little to help. Augustine, who had returned to Britain, wrote to his father in early 1812, enclosing Pakenham's letter quoted above:

> Since my arrival I wrote to inform you of my return to this country. I also mentioned the situation of our dear James supposing that you were informed of his having

43 G.J. Guthrie, *Commentaries on the Surgery of War* (Philadelphia: J P Lippincott & Co., 1862), pp.458-9.

> been wounded at the last affair of the British Army which was communicated to me by General Pakenham, his noble and worthy friend, a copy of whose letter I now enclose that you may be properly informed of the high estimation your brave son holds in the army, his over anxiety to distinguish himself having laid him open to much risque and danger. I also wished to prepare you for the worst that may happen, such a wound being at all times precarious & I have received another letter yesterday from the officer who has always attended James, with so favourable changes, it therefore becomes my duty to state this to you, that you may be prepared to bear so severe a loss. I have long been bringing my own mind to sustain with firmness the melancholy event that may be expected. I am conscious my dear father your feelings when you read this letter but I also know the strength of your mind which will enable you to bear up under this great calamity.
>
> Both your Sons Harry & James have displayed virtues that have endeared them to all that know them, General Pakenham feels like a Brother for them. General Cole has acted like a father & Lord Wellington has expressed his high opinion of them. Can we then my dear Father quit this transient scene with greater hopes of future awards & happiness than these Young Men have enjoyed. No indeed, we must ever reflect upon them as having done their duty in this World, to their Country they sacrificed much as Sons none could be more attached to their parent, as Brothers they were all we could expect. This must be real religion, & most estimable in the sight of their Creator. General Barton told me to tell you, that awful as your loss must be, his misery will never cease having two only sons a disgrace to themselves & to their family & if they could have been called from this world with honours on their heads such as your two noble sons have earned, he should have been happy indeed.
>
> I shall take the earliest opportunity of seeing you.[44]

Augustine Prevost senior, himself a former officer in the 60th, had lost two of his sons in the same year. As Americans, neither had been fighting to defend their own country but each had been continuing a family tradition of service in the British Army that predated the War of Independence.

With the allied army once more in a strong defensive position Marmont again declined to attack and instead withdrew back towards Salamanca, distributing his army into winter quarters. With the threat removed Wellington too dispersed his divisions, with Light, 3rd, and 4th Divisions re-establishing a blockade around Ciudad Rodrigo.

In the south, Hill with 16,000 Anglo-Portuguese troops faced a roughly equal number French.[45] The two forces shadowed each other over the summer months, each waiting for the other to make a move. In September Marmont's drawing off of troops to support the relief of Ciudad Rodrigo meant that one French division moved northward to fill the gap. Hill, seeing that the division, commanded by *Général de Division* Girard, was beyond the reach of immediate support from the rest of the French forces in the area applied to Wellington

44 A. Prevost to A. Prevost, March 1812, AI, CR549/I/5L.
45 Oman, *Peninsular War*, Vol.IV. p.595.

for permission to take the offensive. Wellington agreed. Girard advanced to Caçeres to drive off a small Spanish force that kept mounting small raids. Hill gathered approximately half of his troops and had the support of 2,600 more Spanish infantry and cavalry.[46] Hill's force gathered at Portalegre and on 23 October marched 30 miles over mountains to Albuquerque. Hill had to strike at Girard quickly because if the French knew he was coming then they could either withdraw or send for support. Hill took two of the brigades the 2nd Division with him, including Nos. 4 and 8 companies commanded by Captains McMahon and Blassiere, respectively.[47]

The Spanish joined Hill on the 24th. On the 25th Portuguese cavalry encountered the French outposts. Hill made a night march to Malpartida, only a few miles from Caçares, but Girard had already left. The allies pursued him in another forced march of 28 miles in bad weather over more mountains. On the night of the 27th the leading brigades of Hill's column were 5 miles from the French camp at Arroyo dos Molinos, a small town at the foot of a high ridge. The weather was cold and wet. Hill ordered that no fires be lit in case they were seen by the French and the troops spent and uncomfortable night in the open. The light companies were sent into the surrounding villages to prevent the locals alerting the French.

Captain Peter Blassiere left the allied lines and made a close reconnaissance of the French position. Having successfully infiltrated the French camp he returned to give Hill his report. Blassiere may have been previously employed on intelligence duties and apparently knew the area well.[48] Captain John Patterson of the 1/50th served in the same brigade with Blassiere and wrote a detailed description of him in his memoir:

> There was a company of the 60th rifles attached to our Brigade, who were all Germans, They were commanded by Captain Philip [sic] Blassiere, a singularly active and zealous officer. Throughout the whole period of our warfare he never was absent from his station. With unwearied perseverance he braved the hardest weather and the roughest service; his athletic frame and iron constitution enabling him to withstand it all, holding out with stubborn tenacity while hundreds gave way around him. Undergoing all hardships in common with his men, he walked by their side, partook of the same fare, and shared not only with them the dangerous trade of fighting, but all the miseries of cold and famine with their attendant train of horrors. He was foremost on all occasions, where shot and shell abounded, and was at the rendezvous before a man of the brigade was assembled; and long before the march commenced, there was Blassiere ready with his Germans for any thing that might be wanted.
>
> The external appearance of this man was well calculated to excite surprise, and corresponded with his character for self-denial. His wardrobe was of the most scanty nature; the jacket and other parts of his attire, the original colour of which could not be distinguished by the most microscopic eye, were worn out, patched, and threadbare, and were pierced in various places; and the whole of his costume seemed at least for the last seven years to have retained its original situation on

46 Oman, *Peninsular War*, Vol.IV. p.600.

47 October 1811 Return, TNA, WO 17/180.

48 E. Fraser, *The Soldiers Whom Wellington Led* (London: Methuen, 1913) pp.195-6.

> the person of its owner. Thus accoutred he trudged along, indifferent about the elements; as fast as he got wet, he got dry again, for he never changed his clothes. His muscular neck was enclosed by a hard leather stock and brass clasp to match, and all his trappings were of the same coarse materials as those worn by his men. The haversack, manufactured of rough canvass, sometimes proved a treacherous friend, for through many rents and breaches, made by the hand of time, the mouldy and crumbling biscuit found its way, leaving but the fragments of his bare allowance. The blue canteen, well clasped with iron hoops, afforded him a source of comfort; its contents being to him a certain panacea for all evils.
>
> With habits somewhat eccentric, he was never known to indulge in any thing beyond the rations; and having no desire for the society of others, he discussed his frugal meal in solitude, avoiding even the luxury of a tent. His good humoured though weatherbeaten countenance was the index of his mind, which was cheerful and contented.[49]

Armed with Blassiere's intelligence Hill's men advanced silently towards the French at 2:30 a.m., their movement covered by pouring rain.[50] No French outposts were encountered. Hill halted his men just half a mile from the town. Wilson's Brigade, with No. 4 company of the 5th Battalion and three Portuguese battalions, were sent southwards to block the Truxillo road, all the cavalry were sent to stop any escape down the roads to Merida and Medellin, and the rest of the infantry were to attack from their current position. Howard's Brigade led the attack and came upon the first French pickets just outside of the town. Most were captured but some raised the alarm. Part of the French army had already left so Girard had only 4,000 men to face the allies' 10,000.

Whilst the light companies of Howards' Brigade moved to block the exits from the town, the 1/71st, followed by the 1/50th and 1/92nd, burst into the town while the French were still forming up, capturing the French baggage. Girard ordered a hasty retreat, but seeing the cavalry blocking his escape sent his own horsemen to occupy them whilst he led the infantry to the Truxillo road. The French cavalry, outnumbered, were soon beaten and broken up, with the survivors fleeing in small groups.

Wilson's column was also racing for the Truxillo road. As the rain stopped Girard saw them and the French infantry broke into a run. Wilson's light companies were ahead of the main body, moving swiftly over the rough ground. When they were 100 yards from the French on the road the light companies opened fire. Girard ordered his men to leave the road and run into up into the hills. The light companies, bayonets fixed, then charged into the French column, despite being vastly outnumbered. The leading French companies and Girard got clear by scrambling up near vertical cliffs but over a thousand lay down their weapons and were taken prisoner as the rest of the allied troops came up. The light companies carried on the pursuit of Girard but he, and around 500 men, escaped. British

49 Paterson, *Adventures*, pp.357-9.

50 Details of the action are taken from Oman, *Peninsular War*, Vol.IV, pp.602-5; Paterson, *Adventures, pp.172-6;* R. Blakeney, *A Boy in the Peninsular War* (London: John Murray, 1839), pp.224-31; E. Sidney, *The Life of Lord Hill.*, pp.167-71.

losses were seven killed, and 64 wounded.[51] The 5th Battalion had no casualties. In his dispatch, after praising other officers, Hill wrote: 'I cannot in justice omit Captain Blaquiere [sic] of the 60th regiment, who went into the town of Arroyo Molinos, in the night of the 27th, and brought me the most correct information of the enemy's situation'.[52] His objective completed, Hill returned with his troops to Portalegre and took up the defence of the Portuguese frontier again for the rest of the year.

The returns and pay lists for the last three months of the year show the usual comings and goings in the battalion. Lieutenant Francis Holmes was promoted to captain in the 3/60th, but did not leave until February 1813. Lieutenant Lewis Ritter was promoted into the 100th Foot, and left in January 1812. Ensigns Franciosci and Broetz were both made lieutenants, Gentleman Cadet Cuthbert Forneret, from the Royal Military College, was appointed an ensign in the battalion but would not join until he had completed his studies. The November returns shows eight men died in between 25 October and 25 November, an unusually high number. However, two of those were Privates Michael Bierle (No. 7) and Jammel Leidel (No. 2) who deserted on 5 October, were retaken on the 13th, and executed on the 29th. In December the prisoners of war and missing, a total of 96 men, were taken off the battalion's strength. The December return showed 53 sergeants, 12 buglers, and 515 rank and file.[53]

The year had been largely one of stalemate. The French could no longer concentrate enough men to invade Portugal and drive out the British. Wellington's army had received significant reinforcements but still did not have sufficient numbers to take and hold ground in Spain. In 1812, with Napoleon drawing off troops from Spain for his invasion of Russia, the balance would tip in favour of the allies and Wellington could at last take the offensive. It would be the bloodiest year yet for the 5th Battalion.

51 Oman, *Peninsular War*, Vol.IV. pp.604-5.

52 Hill to Wellington 30 October 1811, quoted in Gurwood, *Wellington's Dispatches*, Vol.VIII, p.388.

53 December 1811 Pay List TNA, WO 12/7074; October to December 1811 Returns, WO 17/180; October to December 1811 Returns, WO 17/2468.

19

Life on Campaign

For the riflemen of the 5th Battalion life on campaign was brutally hard. They had to cope with cold winters, hot summers, and heavy rain. They carried heavy loads over rough terrain for days at a time. The commissariat struggled to keep them fed adequately, and frequently failed to feed them at all. At night they would often have to sleep without any shelter, whatever the weather. When they became ill, as they repeatedly did, the surgeons attached to the army, and indeed medical science at the time, had no effective treatments for the range of bacterial and viral infections that beset them.

The daily ration allowance for soldiers in a garrison was 1½ lbs flour or bread, 1 lb beef (or ½ of pork), ¼ pint of pease, one ounce butter or cheese, one ounce rice, and five pints of beer.[1] Various substitutions were allowed if any of the elements were unavailable. The allowance was often more than the soldiers would have had in civilian life and probably just adequate in calorific, if not nutritional, value by today's standards.

On campaign in Portugal and Spain the troops got far less to eat. The typical ration was just 1½ lbs of bread or 1 lb of hard biscuit, 1 lb of beef or mutton, and a pint of wine or one third of a pint of rum.[2] This daily diet was deficient in many essential vitamins, minerals, and even protein. It would have contributed to ill health amongst the soldiers.[3] However, there were many times when the supply system failed to deliver sufficient food to the army and the men were reduced to half, quarter, or no rations at all for days at a time. Such failings often occurred during rapid advances or retreats, when the men needed sustenance the most. If food was scarce the men were issued whatever could be procured, even it was un-milled wheat or barley meant for horses.

The men of the 5th Battalion, though, had a reputation of making the most of the food that they were given. James Campbell, who served in the 3rd Division with companies of the 5th Battalion, contrasted the behaviour of the German troops with the British:

1 Burnham & McGuigan, *The British Army*, pp.195-6.

2 Cooper, *Rough Notes*, p.147.

3 Bamford, *Sickness, Suffering*, pp.238-9, summarising research by E. Coss, *All for the King's Shilling: The British Soldier Under Wellington, 1808-1814* (Norman: University of Oklahoma Press, 2010).

> The comfort in which the men of the 5th battalion 60th regiment (who were chiefly Germans,) lived upon service was very striking, when compared with the wretched diet of the generality of British soldiers…
>
> …It seemed to be settled amongst themselves, that every man of the mess of the 5th Battalion 60th, had to carry something, that is say – highly-spiced meats, such as sausages, cheese, onions, garlic, lard, pepper, salt, vinegar, mustard, sugar, coffee, &c.; in short, whatever could add to or make their meals more palatable, nourishing, or conducive to health. As soon as the daily allowance of beef was issued, they set to work and soon produced a first-rate dinner or supper, which were often improved by certain wild herbs which they knew where to look for, whereas, in attempting this, I have known instances of our men poisoning themselves; and what a contrast to this were the ways of our too often thoughtless beings who rarely had any of the above articles – day after day they boiled their beef, just killed, in the lump, in water, which they seldom contrived to make deserving the name of soup or broth. This and their bread or biscuit was what they usually lived upon.[4]

When food was scarce soldiers, naturally, tried to forage for what they needed. On 9 August 1809, during the retreat following the Battle of Talavera Wellington issued an order that since the men had not received regular rations since 22 July the rate of stoppages for their food would be reduced from 6d to 3d. The same order outlined measures to stop the men mobbing the convoys coming into the camps and taking the food before it was properly issued, and also to prevent the men leaving camp to find food for themselves and in particular to stop them taking root vegetables from the fields.[5]

The prevalence of the plundering of food from the countryside is evident by the number of orders Wellington had to issue to try and prevent it. For example, an order of 16 August 1809 prohibited the plundering of beehives, but then on 7 September Wellington had to write:

> Notwithstanding the repeated orders given out upon the subject, the soldiers of the 4th division of infantry plundered bee hives, in the neighbourhood of Badajoz, on the day before the division marched from that place: it is impossible these outrages can be committed daily, and that this last outrage, in particular, could have been committed, without the Officers obtaining some knowledge of it. The Officers with the army do not appear to be aware how much they suffer in the disgraceful and unmilitary practices of the soldiers, in marauding and plundering everything they lay their hands upon. The consequence is, the people of the country fly their habitations, no market is opened, and the Officers, as well as the soldiers, suffer in the privation of every comfort and every necessary, excepting their rations, from the neglect of the former and the criminal misconduct of the latter. The Commander of the Forces has done, and will continue to do, every thing in his power to put an end to these disgraceful practices; but it is obvious that all his efforts must be fruitless,

4 J. Campbell, *A British Army As It Was, – Is, – and Ought to Be* (London: T & W Boone, 1840), pp.105-6.

5 General Order 9 August 1809, quoted in Wellington, *General Orders*, Vol.I, pp.122-3.

> unless the Officers of the army, generally and individually, exert themselves for the same object.[6]

The 4th Division repeated the offence a few days later, and was forced to remain on parade all day until the culprits were caught, which they were two days later. In desperate times the men would find and eat what they could. On the retreat from Burgos in November 1812 many even resorted to eating acorns.[7]

The French army relied on plundering to feed itself, this caused natural antipathy amongst the Spanish and Portuguese populations and helped fuel resentment, rebellion, and recruitment for the guerrillas. As the leader of an allied army of liberation Wellington had to try and prevent his men from taking from the population they were mean to be helping. Rations were bought from the locals with receipts that could be redeemed in Lisbon. Such a system relied on the goodwill of the population and this was put in jeopardy by looting and plundering. Harsh punishments were given out to those found plundering, and especially for abusing the local population. On 11 November 1811 Private Charles Flack of the 5th Battalion was court martialled for ill-treating a Portuguese man, to the extent that the man died. He was found guilty of the ill-treatment, but not of causing the man's death, and sentenced to 500 lashes.[8] Whenever the army was encamped officers had to take roll-call and visit their men regularly during the day to ensure that none had gone out of the camp without permission, and after episodes of excessive plundering the rolls were called hourly.

As the war continued large swathes of Portugal and Spain became deserted as the armies marched over the same ground year after year. Many farms and houses were abandoned. Crops left in fields and orchards heavy with unpicked fruit must have seemed like fair game to a hungry soldier, and if no one was around it may have been easy to assume a field was abandoned even if it was not, tempting even the best behaved soldiers – an epithet not always applicable to the riflemen of the 5th Battalion.

After entering France in 1814 Surgeon Walter Henry was quartered in a farmhouse and the farmer's wife was cooking a goose for him whilst he went on duty, later he returned with a fellow officer:

> As we approached the house, we heard sounds indicative of something wrong about the establishment; cocks and hens were screaming and cackling, dogs were barking, pigs grunting, with other similar noises, ominous of evil, that made us hasten our steps to find out what was the matter. When we entered, O sight of horror! the first object we beheld was a half-drunken German soldier of the 60th Regiment bearing away the spit and innocent goose, streaming with its rich juices, in his unhallowed clutch. The frightened farmer had shut himself up in the barn, but the gallant dame contended bravely, although fruitlessly, against the Philistines. When we entered, she brightened up wonderfully, and just found breath enough to say, 'Il y a un autre voleur dans la cave, la cave, la cave,'[9] The goose-robber bolted out of the back door,

6 General Order 7 September 1809, quoted in Wellington, *General Orders*, Vol.I, pp.153-4.
7 Haythornthwaite, *Wellington's Armies*, p.63.
8 General Order 14 December 1811 quoted in, Wellington, *General Orders*, Vol.III, pp.275-7.
9 Translation: 'There is another thief in the cellar, the cellar, the cellar'.

> spit and all, the instant he descried us, but I soon caught him, whilst my companion dived into the cellar, and found the other in the very act of suction at a wine-cock. The disturbed bird was then remanded to its roasting evolutions before the fire, whilst we conducted our prisoners to the Provost Marshal, took the farmer with us, and had the satisfaction of seeing them receive fifty lashes each. Farther and more severe measures had been in contemplation, but we requested that this might be the maximum of punishment, considering the cruel disappointment of the rogues, and that they had got their goose the wrong way.[10]

Also in 1814, Bugler Krulg and Private Jorgens were sentenced 800 lashes each for leaving the ranks while their company of the battalion was on the march and expecting to engage the enemy, and for plundering the inhabitants of the French town of Tarbes.[11]

Alcohol of any and every kind was often a favourite item of plunder, and care even had to be taken to moderate the wine or rum issued so that several days' rations were not given out at once. Given the harshness of the life, many soldiers took any chance they could to overindulge.

Water was essential in the heat of the heat of the summer but finding sufficient potable water sources for an army of tens of thousands could be problematic, as was the case at Talavera in 1809 when many soldiers fought through the heat of the day with nothing to drink. Water was also required for cooking, especially if salted meat had been issued. Three heavy iron camp kettles were issued per company, and were carried by mules. In 1813 these were replaced by lighter tin ones issued one for every six men and carried in turn.[12]

Water sources were also often used for bathing, but probably more to give respite to the heat than any attempt at cleanliness. A soldier of the 71st recalled an occasion when the men's ablutions in the river Tagus were rudely interrupted:

> One day, while a number of men were bathing in the river, a party of French cavalry came in sight. This naturally caused every one to make the best of his way towards the shore, with the exception of a droll fellow, who stood for some time slapping a nameless part in derision of the Frenchmen. On seeing this some of them unloosed their carbines and fired a shot or two at our hero, who then thought proper to fly. Some of the 60th Riflemen turned out from their quarters on hearing the noise; and by discharging a few shot, soon made the horsemen scamper out of sight.[13]

Even if food and water were in good supply the troops might not have been able to find enough firewood to cook. Once several thousand men camped in a given area it would not have taken long for every available combustible branch, bush, or tree to be chopped down. One of the advantages of the lighter tin kettles was that they took much less wood to boil than the iron ones. The night before some battles fires were banned to prevent the enemy

10 W. Henry, *Events of a Military Life* (London: William Pickering, 1843), pp.184-5.

11 List of General Courts Martial, HRO, 170A12W/D/1183.

12 General Order 1 March 1813, quoted in J. Gurwood, *The General Orders of Field Marshal The Duke of Wellington K.G. in Spain, Portugal & France* (London: Egerton, 1837), p.42.

13 Anonymous, *Vicissitudes in the Life of a Scottish Soldier* (London; Colburn, 1827) pp.225-6.

Troops bivouacked near the village of Villa Velha, on the evening of the 19th of May, 1811, by Thomas Staunton St. Clair. (Anne S.K. Brown Military Collection)

learning the location and number of allied forces, meaning that the men might begin an action not having had a decent meal. Wellington issued orders to prohibit his men from taking wood from local buildings.

On 26 November 1812 at the village of Calvarrasa de Arriba, near Salamanca, a wood party of the 5th Battalion, under the command of Ensign James Lawless, was on the roof of a house pulling off tiles so they could get to the beams. Acting Assistant Provost Marshal of the 3rd Division Sergeant Charles Button, of the 45th Foot, saw them and struck one of them with his whip, ordering them to stop. The men said they had been ordered to take the wood from the house by their officer, Ensign Lawless. Button then informed Lawless that removing wood from houses was contrary to orders. Lawless marched his party away but Button saw them taking wood from another house later the same night and reported the incident to his superiors.

On 20 January 1813 Lawless was court martialled for disobeying a general order and persisting after being warned it was against orders.[14] Button gave his evidence first and then Sergeant Oswald Doller, who was the sergeant with the wood party. Doller began testifying in English but then had to have an interpreter as he could not understand the questions posed to him. He stated that the party had been pulling down the roof of the house when Button stopped them but that the second house was a ruin. He also said that parties from

14 Trial of Ensign Lawless, TNA, WO 71/229.

other regiments were doing the same. There was no other source of wood in the area and the division had arrived after dark. Ensign Lawless had told him that the party could only take wood that he pointed out and Doller had relayed that to the men in German, but that some being Poles and Russians would not have understood the order. Lawless had also ordered the men from the roof just prior to Button arriving.

Lawless' defence was that he was only recently commissioned and had just arrived with the army, and had not been informed of previous general orders. He also called witnesses from the 88th Foot to try and establish that obtaining wood from ruined houses was common practice when no other wood could be found, a claim that was refuted by the prosecution. Lawless was found guilty and sentenced to six months suspension from rank and pay.

After food and drink, not necessarily in that order, the next priority for the men was shelter. Wellington's army landed with tents in 1808 but they were soon sent back to the rear as there was not the logistical capacity to transport them. Instead, in the early years of the campaign, the soldiers would build simple shelters out of brushwood and branches, if sufficient materials could be found. It became necessary to dissuade the troops from using olive and fruit trees unless absolutely necessary. Parties would be formed for cutting branches with bill-hooks, dragging the branches to camp and then building the huts.[15] Makeshift tents could also be made from the soldiers' blankets or greatcoats stretched over cut branches.

If the enemy were close, there were no materials to hand, or there had been no time to construct a proper camp, then the soldiers would simply wrap themselves in their greatcoats or blankets, pull their forage caps over their ears, and use their knapsack as a pillow. Constant exposure to the elements, with wool clothing that could become saturated and take a long time to dry out, were contributing factors to much of the sickness in the army. It was something that commanders did their best to minimise by aiming to get the best shelter they could for their men in the circumstances.

Officers were able to draw tents from the stores from 1809; one for each field officer (majors and above), one per company, and one for the staff.[16] Officers usually formed a mess to pool their food and would purchase better and more varied provisions from the local inhabitants. They could have soldier servants and the more senior would hire their own servants as well. The January to March 1811 pay list shows that Lieutenant Colonel Williams, Major Woodgate, and Paymaster Gilbert all had hired servants.[17] The life of an officer, though, was not luxurious, and they shared many of the privations of campaigning with their men, especially when the baggage had been sent to the rear. Officers had a slightly higher chance of getting wounded and of being killed in battle or dying of wounds than their soldiers, but their men were far more likely to die from disease or accident.[18]

Thirteen mules were allocated to each battalion; one per company to carry the camp kettles, one for the surgeon's instruments, one for the paymaster's books and one for entrenching tools.[19] When the iron camp kettles were exchanged for tin ones in 1813 the mules that had been carrying the kettles became available and so tents were able to be issued

15 Gurwood, *General Orders*, pp.xxxvi & 198 (five General Orders).
16 General Order 24 May 1809, quoted in Gurwood, *General Orders*, p.289.
17 March 1811 Pay List, TNA, WO 12/7074.
18 Burnham & McGuigan, *The British Army*, p.213.
19 General Order 19 June 1809, quoted in Gurwood, *General Orders*, p.217.

without putting extra strain on the logistics of the army. Every company was issued three tents, each able to accommodate 20 men. Wellington also then ordered that the men's great-coats should be put into store for the campaign, so that they had less to carry.[20]

Most officers had horses, often more than one. In August 1813 two officers of the 5th Battalion came to blows over a disagreement about the stabling their horses. Lieutenant Ingersleben had found an abandoned building not far from his billet and placed his horse inside. Unbeknownst to Ingersleben, Lieutenant Wynne, his senior, had also been using the same building as a stable. When Wynne's bâtman told him that Ingersleben's horse was there Wynne asked Ingersleben to move it elsewhere. Ingerseleben refused, saying there was plenty of room. Wynne said then he would move the horses by force, calling Ingersleben 'a German Bugger and a Rascal' before using language that was not repeatable in the subsequent court martial. Ingersleben punched Wynne, pushed him against a wall, picked up a stick and threatened him with it until Lieutenant Hamilton came between them. Ingersleben said that he was sorry he did not have his sword with him as would run Wynne through with it. He called him 'a blackguard, coward and Irish Rascal'. Wynne told Ingersleben to consider himself under arrest. Ingersleben replied that he did not give a damn. Wynne got the guard to remove Ingersleben's horse.

A court martial was convened on 10 September 1813 at Oiartzun in Spain.[21] The president was Major General Stopford, the brigade commander, who had tried to get the two officers to reconcile and apologise to each other. The charges against Ingersleben were: disobedience to orders in refusing to withdraw his animals from the stables after being ordered to do so; scandalous and infamous conduct unbecoming the character of an officer and a gentlemen in openly resisting the authority of his superior officer; using opprobrious and disgraceful language, and striking Wynne. He pleaded not guilty.

The various witnesses outlined what had occurred, with the three bâtmen, two of Wynne's and the one for the company, giving evidence in German, Polish, and Hungarian. Ingersleben's defence was that neither he nor Wynne were billeted on the house where the horses were stabled; that there was room for six horses; and that Wynne had struck him first. Ingersleben was found guilty of all charges and sentenced to be cashiered from the Army. Stopford wrote to Wellington asking for mercy, and seven members of court bore witness to Ingersleben's character and good conduct, especially at the Battle of Albuera. Wellington replied and asked the court to revise their sentence, saying that it had been a private quarrel; that Wynne was himself guilty of a breach of good order; and that neither had the right to the stable. The court reconsidered their verdict but thought wording of charge and of the article of war gave them no choice, but they too asked Wellington for clemency and Ingersleben was allowed to retain his post.

Whereas the officers had the benefit of their horses a large portion of a soldier's day during a campaign would be spent marching on foot. The roads in Spain and Portugal were notoriously bad and often little more than rough paths. The mountainous terrain, the high temperatures of the summer, and the wet autumn and winters often made marches very arduous. Edward Costello of the 95th estimated the weight of uniform, equipment, weapons

20 General Orders 1 March & 25 April 1813, quoted in Gurwood, *General Orders*, pp.290 & 173.

21 Trial of Lieutenant Ingersleben TNA, WO 71/235.

Crossing of the Tagus at Villa Velha, near Badajoz 1812. (From *Views in Spain & Portugal, taken during the Campaigns of His Grace the Duke of Wellington*, by G. Cumberland)

and ammunition that a rifleman had to carry in the peninsular to be 80 lbs, which was possibly a slightly high estimate. John Cooper of the 7th Fusiliers listed his own equipment as 61 lbs and itemised the weights.[22] Riflemen sometimes carried more ammunition, and the sword-bayonet was heavier than the redcoats' bayonet, but the extra weight probably was not 19 lbs. William Surtees, a quartermaster in the 95th, estimated a rifleman carried a load of around 40 or 50 lbs.[23] As a campaign progressed many items, such as spare shoes, would wear out, or be discarded despite the penalties for doing so.

As well as their personal kit the soldiers would take turns carrying a bill-hook, an axe, and later the tin canteen. Whatever the weight carried successive days of marches of around 15 miles per day could begin to take their toll and soldiers would start to straggle, fall down from exhaustion or even die, especially in the heat of summer or the depths of winter. When the men halted for the day they still had to prepare their camp, gather wood, light fires, collect their rations, cook their food, and mount pickets.

Some of the challenges facing officers commanding detachments on the march are illustrated by the case of Lieutenant Augustine Evans, who was ordered to march a party of recruits from Lisbon to the 5th Battalion in the autumn of 1812. Word of problems during the journey had obviously reached Wellington as the adjutant general's office issued a long

22 Burnham & McGuigan, *The British Army*, pp.198-9.

23 W. Surtees, *Twenty-Five Years in the Rifle Brigade* (London: Greenhill, 1996), p.228.

order demanding that Lieutenant Evans answer whether he had given permission for four other officers to march separately from the column, if he had inspected the men's necessaries every day, and, if he had done, whether he had punished any of the 52 out of 60 soldiers who had sold their blankets. The order was distributed amongst the army so that Evans would learn of it and then send his answers back to headquarters.[24]

Wellington was obviously not satisfied with Evans' report as the unfortunate lieutenant was put on trial for unmilitary conduct, disobedience of orders, and neglect of duty on 29 January 1813.[25] The charges included allowing his men to straggle, in addition to those outlined in the order. Two riflemen of the detachment testified, in English. Corporal Julius Keine, the only NCO with the party, stated that the detachment had marched in good order until just outside Santarém when some recruits fell out ill. Evans ordered Keine to stay with the sick men and bring them along at a slower pace. He also said that Evans had inspected the men's equipment each day, barring one night when they arrived at their quarters in the dark, and that he had rapidly discovered that most of the men had sold their blankets to Portuguese peasants and that this had been reported to senior officers in Santarém. Two of the soldiers had been court martialled and one punished with 150 lashes when the column reached Abrantes. Private Joseph Fleury confirmed Keine's evidence.

Evans' defence was brief, given that the prosecution's witnesses had already largely exonerated him. He said that the recruits had only just arrived in Portugal after being on board ship and the roads were very bad. This had contributed to their fatigue on the march. He claimed to have taken steps to deal with every problem as they occurred. As far as the other four officers were concerned he had not insisted that they march with the rest of the party as their animals were heavily loaded with baggage, and more importantly there was little point in their accompanying the recruits as they could not speak German and so could not give them orders.

Evans also said that he could not offer any character witnesses from his superiors in the battalion as it was 'so much divided'. He briefly asked members of the court, some of whom were obviously in command at some of the places where the column had halted, if he had reported the issues to them and they agreed that he had. He was acquitted of all charges.

Evans was 23 years old, from Ireland, and had been in the Army for five years. He transferred to the 5th Battalion from the 2/60th, arriving in Lisbon shortly before he took command of the recruits.[26] His claim that the other officers could not give orders to the recruits because they did not speak German obviously implies that Evans could. It is likely that the longer-serving soldiers of the battalion did pick up some English. Certainly, as evidenced by the two riflemen who testified in the case, some did speak the language well. In many of the anecdotes from memoirists in other regiments the riflemen do so too, even if the accent is emphasised in the text for comic effect. However, it is also clear from the trial of Ensign Lawless that some of the NCOs had only a basic grasp of English, and that some of the men spoke no German. Language must have been another issue that the battalion had to cope with that most other units did not. Colonel Mosheim at the Foreign Depot was clear that he thought that officers of the battalion needed to be able to speak German:

24 Adjudant General's Office 7 October 1812, quoted in Wellington, *General Orders*, Vol.IV, pp.190-1.

25 Trial of Lt. Evans TNA, WO 71/229.

26 November 1812 Return, TNA, WO 17/180; inspection of Blassiere's company October 1813, WO 27/122.

> Much depends on one in my opinion most essential circumstance viz to have Officers who can speak the German Language and who treat those men as much as possible in the manners they have been accustomed to, and then you can depend on their proper and faithful conduct.[27]

There were occasions when the battalion was praised for its discipline on the march. In March 1813 Major General Colville, commanding the 3rd Division, commented in an order:

> A detachment of the 5th battalion 60th, has arrived at head-quarters under the command of Captain Kelly, and which having left Lisbon consisting of fifty men, has brought up all but one man who was left sick at Coimbra, and no prisoners.
>
> This is so unlike the report of any detachment of the British part of the division that has arrived at quarters since the Major-General's taking the command of it, that he cannot help mentioning the mortifying distinction, in the hopes that there may be yet left among the good men of the division regard enough for their own honours to keep a check upon the conduct of those of an opposite character.[28]

One thing that German troops were known for amongst Wellington's army was their singing on the march, which often cheered both themselves and the less musical British troops. John Westcott, bandmaster of 1/26th, recalled an arduous march in late November when the 1st Division were ordered towards Ciudad Rodrigo after word came that the French were going to attempt to resupply it:

> The First Division received the route and marched towards Ratoeira, the Brigade of Guards assembled at Sobral da Serra, at two o'clock in the afternoon, the 26th Regiment and the rifle company of the 60th Regiment, marched at seven o'clock at night... the night was very cold the regiment marched very fast in order to keep themselves warm, the moon being up it assisted us very much in marching over the rough ground we were amused on our march through the night by the rifle company of the 60th Regiment singing their national German songs, that Battalion of the 60th were all Germans, to do them justice they certainly sing better, at least together they sing more musical in parts [i.e. in rounds or in canon] than any of the British soldiers, indeed they appear to be more fond of music than any of the British soldiers, singing and smoking is the German soldiers chief amusement. We arrived about twelve o'clock at night to the village of Sobral da Serra, where we remained that night.[29]

Two factors that would have made life on campaign slightly more arduous for the 5th Battalion than many other soldiers of the allied army were their role as light infantry, and the fact that most of the companies were detached from the battalion headquarters. As

27 Mosheim to Keane 29 April 1813, TNA WO 7/89, pp.410-2

28 Campbell, *A British Army*, pp.105-6.

29 John Westcott, 'Journal of the Campaign in Portugal by John Westcott Late Master of the Band 1st Battalion 26th Cameronian Regiment'. BL, Add.MS. 32468

light infantry they would have been called on to provide the advance or rear guards for any march, which would have often meant progressing over rough country alongside the roads, rather than on them. They would also have been used more for outpost and patrol duty. They would have often had to travel lighter, further ahead of the baggage and rough camp more often. Conversely, such isolated duties away from the column could also have presented more opportunities for plunder.

The logistical system of the army was very much based around the battalion structure for the infantry. The quartermaster, quartermaster sergeant, armourer sergeant, paymaster, paymaster sergeant, surgeon and his assistants, together formed the battalion headquarters along with the commanding officer and the adjutant. Between them they oversaw all the administrative, supply, pay, and medical needs of the unit. The regimental returns make it clear that the staff of the 5th Battalion largely remained with the companies in the 3rd Division. It does not even appear that the assistant surgeons were sent to do duty with the companies in the other divisions on a regular basis. There were sometimes hundreds of miles between the divisions and so the company officers and their NCOs must have taken on some of the duties usually carried out centrally and the companies must have relied on the resources of the brigades they were attached to. However, no records or orders have survived to explain how the logistical challenges were tackled.

The efficiency of the companies does not seem to have been effected by their isolation. Colonel John Byng's half yearly report on No. 6 company with his brigade of the 2nd Division in May 1812 was very positive:

> Officer – Lt. Franchini is the only officer that has been with the Company, during the last six months. He is an intelligent officer, has paid proper attention and is qualified to command it.
>
> Sergeants & Corporals – The Non Commissioned are steady well behaved men, and understand their duty.
>
> Privates – The privates are but few in number, most of them old soldiers. Steady well behaved men. During the Half Year, I have not had to find fault with any one man belonging to the company. Their accounts have been regularly stated, & of them has no complaint.
>
> Clothing – The Clothing in wear is still good. That for this year has not been received.
>
> Arms & Accoutrements – The Arms & Accoutrements are serviceable and in good order.
>
> Fusil Movement & Exercise – The whole company have been properly trained to the service of Light Troops and are conversant with their duty.[30]

The report stated the numbers present and under arms as one lieutenant, five sergeants, four corporals, one bugler and 27 privates. Three men had 18 to 20 years of service, seven 14 to 17 years and further eight between seven and 13 years. Over half of the men had enlisted for unlimited service. Two men were 55 years old or over, and a further 10 were 45 to 54. Only

30 Inspection of Dundas' company May 1812, TNA, WO 27/107.

two men were younger than 25. The only item of clothing or equipment marked as 'bad' were the sergeants' sashes.

Major General Howard's report on Captain Blassiere's No. 8 company in the same year was less detailed but similarly complimentary, stating that the company was 'in a perfect state of discipline', he praised the NCOs, said that the men were 'sober and orderly', but again noted that many were 'old soldiers'. The numbers present were one captain, five sergeants, and 48 rank and file. The report concludes with: 'In short it is a very efficient company which conducts itself in an orderly fashion on a march and in quarters'.[31]

The surviving 1813 reports show some changes in Nos. 6 and 8 companies, and contain reports on others not included in the previous year.[32] No. 6 company's strength in October had risen slightly to one lieutenant, one ensign, five sergeants, three corporals, and 39 privates but no bugler. Just less than a fifth of the accoutrements, sword belts, pouches, belts and rifle slings, were noted as being 'bad' and the clothing for that year had not reached the company. There were no soldiers over 55 and with a greater proportion of the men in their twenties and having served for shorter periods. The report noted that Captain Erskine had been wounded on 25 July and that since then Lieutenants Paisley and Eccles had been in command and continued;

> I cannot report so favourably of the Company, as I have before done. I have had frequent irregularities to notice. An amendment has however taken place since I spoke them on the subject, but I do not think the present officer in command (Lt. Eccles) fit to superintend a company detached from its Regiment. Captain Erskine, and Lt. Paisley were active and attentive officers.
>
> The Sergeants of the Company are good. The Privates are stout healthy men. The old soldiers well behaved, but among those joined within the year some much the worse.

The numbers present with No. 8 company in October 1813 had gone up slightly to six sergeants, one bugler and 55 rank and file, with a lieutenant and ensign as well as Captain Blassiere. Approximately a third of the accoutrements were noted as being 'bad' and the clothing for that year had also not reached the company. Major General Walker's report noted that 'Blassiere's subalterns back yesterday, appear to be intelligent & to have been instructed'. The NCOs were similarly intelligent and 'attentive to their duty' and the bugler was 'correct in his soundings'. The private men were 'a very good body of men, extremely healthy & as clean as their bad state of Clothing will allow'. Some of the men were noted as being 'not sufficiently active for their particular duty' but they were all 'Generally sober & well behaved'. It was also noted that their field exercises were not as quick as the nature of their duty required. Walker also praised the perfect knowledge that Blassiere had of his men and their conduct.

31 Inspection of Blassiere's company May 1812, TNA, WO 27/107.

32 October & November 1813 inspections 5/60th, TNA, WO 27/122.

In November 1813 Captain McMahon's No. 4 company had two lieutenants, four sergeants, four corporals, one bugler, and 48 privates present and under arms. One bugle is marked as 'wanting' so presumably the bugler could not perform his duties.

The report on No. 4 company of Major General Pringle's brigade of the 2nd Division dated 22 November 1813 was also favourable. It noted that Lieutenant Evans had been in command of the company since August and the sole officer, barring a few days. The privates were 'a tolerably good body of men, with a general appearance of health & cleanliness'. The clothing was in good condition but that year's had not been issued. The strength of No. 1 company attached to Major General Pack's brigade of the 6th Division shows one lieutenant, one ensign, five sergeants and 38 rank and file present, but 22 absent sick, including the sole bugler. The report concludes: 'Lieutenant Müller has been the commanding officer. He has taken much pains with it, and its state in every respect is excellent, and does him a great deal of credit'.

One vital part of the battalion that has left very little evidence of its presence in the surviving accounts and records are the women and children. Sixty wives and 50 children sailed from Cork with the battalion in 1808 but very little mention is made of them after that.[33] When Sergeant Major Caspar Schreiber was killed in action in 1812 the £5 and 12s pay he was owed was given to his wife, and there are other similar cases in the records. In July 1811 Private Christian Neunkirchen was executed for desertion and the casualty return notes that £1 11s 6d was paid to his widow, which raises the question of whether he had run from his wife as well as the army.[34] The wife of Captain George Zühleke, Crithiana, accompanied him to the Peninsula and apparently survived the ordeal as the couple had a child in June 1815.[35] The wife of Quartermaster Sergeant Recknoy is mentioned as being the victim of a theft by Sergeant Peter Lind in a court martial.[36]

Some of the men met their wives while on campaign. George Koester, who rose from private to colour sergeant during the six years of the Peninsular campaign, met his wife whilst in Spain, possibly when the army entered Madrid in 1812. Antonia Tolosa Ruiz was ten years his junior and probably accompanied the battalion back to Ireland with her husband in 1814 as the two remained together for the remaining years of his service, and subsequent settling in Canada. Koester was lucky as most of the Spanish and Portuguese women were forced to return to their original homes. In April 1814 the adjutant-general of the army Major General Pakenham wrote in a letter to the divisional commanders:

> Although the Field Marshal foresees the necessity of leaving the greater part of the foreign women behind, who with reasonable provision may accompany the Portuguese troops to the rear; yet I am to observe there will be no objection to a few of those, who have proved themselves useful and regular, accompanying the soldiers to whom they are attached, with a view to their being ultimately married:

33 Rigaud, *Celer et Audax*, p.284.

34 General Order 9 July 1811, quoted in Wellington, *General Orders*, Vol.III, pp.138-9; July 1811 & January 1812 Returns, TNA, WO 17/180.

35 Statement of Services of Captain Charles William Zühleke, TNA, WO 25/779/40.

36 General Order 30 April 1811, quoted in Wellington, *General Orders* Vol.III, pp.78-80.

> it will appear evident to you, however, that from the unsettled life and habits of followers of the army, such selection should be made with the greatest caution.[37]

The women accompanying the army did occasionally create problems. In the summer of 1809 they had to be prevented buying up the bread that was being baked in the villages near the army's encampments, and in the autumn of that year measures had to be taken to prevent women traveling on the carts bringing up the regiments' clothing from Lisbon.[38] Wives were entitled to half a soldier's ration, and children a quarter.[39] The 1813 inspection reports note one legally married wife with No. 8 company, and two male children over ten and one younger. No. 6 company had three wives and no children.

Given the paucity of the soldiers' rations and the harsh conditions it must have been difficult to survive and feed growing children on so little. The women necessarily became expert foragers and plunderers. They also helped with the laundry, cooking, and care of the wounded. If a husband was killed or died, then his wife would often rapidly remarry to remain with the unit, although allowances were paid to widows and orphans if they did wish to leave the country. When the battalion was in the West Indies in 1799 a letter to the regimental agents, Cox and Greenwood, requested them 'to procure a passage to Germany for Johanna Ellers, the wife of a soldier in this Regt. & Charge the expense against her Husband'. They were also asked to pay her maintenance during the passage. The reason for the journey is not stated.[40]

Whenever it was perceived that the army, or a particular division, was going to be based in an area for a long period they were generally put into cantonments. This usually happened in the winter but also at other times of relative inactivity. The troops were normally quartered in towns with each unit being allocated streets or areas of the town. The officers would be billeted in the same streets and regularly visit their men to ensure their quarters were being kept clean, that bedding straw was changed, blankets aired, the streets swept, and that the inhabitants did not have any complaints of their enforced guests. Where insufficient housing was available then huts and tented camps were used.[41]

Whilst the troops were in cantonments the heavy baggage could be brought up. The bands would retrieve their instruments and entertain the officers while they dined, and play at dances or concerts. The officers would hunt, gamble, put on plays, race horses, and hold balls. The men however, were kept busy to maintain discipline; undertaking drill, training, fatigues, and other duties. Life was easier in the cantonments though, and offered some respite from the rigours of active campaigning. However, with so many men packed into every usable space, and the inevitable large quantities of human and animal waste that an army generated, there were often outbreaks of typhoid, typhus, and other diseases. Even so, whenever troops were in longer term quarters and not subject to the hardships of campaigning the sickness rates did decrease.[42]

37 Adjutant General's Office 26 April 1814, quoted Gurwood, *General Orders*, pp.323-4.

38 General Orders 23 August 1809 & 1 October 1809, quoted in Gurwood, *General Orders*, pp.321-2.

39 Haythorntwaite, *Armies*, p.61.

40 Regimental Records, Index to Out-Letters, 5/60th, TNA, WO 2/3, p.121.

41 Various General Orders, quoted in Gurwood, *General Orders*, pp.43-6.

42 Bamford, *Sickness, Suffering*, p.232.

The biggest killer in the Peninsula was disease, not enemy action. In the years from 1812 to 1814 5,706 men were killed in action[43]. A further 2,699 men who had been admitted to regimental and general hospitals subsequently died of their wounds. In the same years 10,999 succumbed to the top three diseases; dysentery, continued fever, and typhus.[44] Dysentery was caused by bacterial, viral, or parasitic infections and spread through infected water or food, and by touch. Continued fever was a catch-all phrase for anything from the common cold, to influenza and typhoid. Typhus was spread amongst the troops by body lice. Fatigue and poor diet made soldiers more susceptible to any disease. The mortality rate of foreign and colonial troops was around 20 percent lower than for British troops. In a study of the army between 1803 and 1812 the death rate amongst the British troops was 53.23 per thousand, whereas the rate amongst foreign troops was 42.15, despite the fact that the foreign and colonial troops were more likely to be posted to disease-ridden areas like the West Indies.[45]

At the start of the Peninsular campaign medical care in the army was poorly organised and under-resourced. The battalion surgeon and his assistants were the first level of medical care. Their level of training and skills varied greatly but most performed as well as they could within the confines of medical knowledge at the time. With no idea of the causes of most diseases and infections treatments often did little to help; bleeding and purgatives were favourites. Many of the medicines used at the time, such as antimony and various forms of mercury, were poisonous. Surgeons would have had a supply of stretchers, bedding, instruments, and medicines to treat both wounds and diseases. The detached companies of the battalion would have had to rely on either the staff surgeons with brigades and divisions, or the surgeons of other regiments for their immediate medical care. The 1813 inspection of No. 4 company noted under the heading of Regimental Hospital 'None. The sick in charge of the Senior Regt. of the Brigade'.[46] The August 1812 return shows that one man died while in the regimental hospital of the 71st.[47]

A lack of transport for medical equipment, and a preference for centralised medical care over that provided by the regiments, meant that many of the wounded and the sick had to make long journeys to a general hospital if they needed longer term treatment, often under the hot sun and over rough roads in un-sprung carts. From October 1810 three sprung wagons were allocated to each division for the transport of sick and wounded. These would have had a capacity of between six and 24 men depending if they were able to sit or had to lie.[48] Each division could have several thousand men so the number of wagons was far below what was needed. Later in the war greater resources were allocated to the regimental, brigade, and divisional hospitals and prefabricated hospitals accompanied the army, which meant the men got the treatment they needed sooner and could return to duty more quickly.

43 Burnham & McGuigan, *The British Army*, pp.214.

44 M. Howard, *Wellington's Doctors* (Staplehurst: Spellmount, 2002) p.237.

45 W.B. Hodge, 'On the Mortality arising from Military Operations', *Journal of the Statistical Society of London*, Vol.XIX p.238.

46 Inspection of McMahon's company November 1813, TNA, WO 27/122.

47 August 1812 Return, TNA, WO 17/180.

48 Howard, *Doctors*, p.74.

General hospitals were established at places like Lisbon, Abrantes, Elvas, and Oporto, and many more temporary locations as the army advanced and retreated.[49] A hospital would have a small staff of surgeons, physicians, apothecaries, and hospital mates. A ward-master and six orderlies, drawn from the regiments, looked after up to 100 men in each ward. From June 1811 the pay lists of the 5th Battalion begin to have the comment 'Warthmaster in General Hospital' with various non-overlapping dates ranges after sergeants' names.[50] The battalion's returns also often show the surgeon or assistant surgeons doing duty at one of the hospitals and men acting as orderlies.

The hospitals were often overcrowded and the conditions poor. Significant improvements were made during the campaign with hospitals becoming better organised, cleaner and healthier places. Between December 1812 and December 1813 35 men of the 5th Battalion died in hospital.[51]

Some hospitals were set up for specific purposes. Receiving hospitals triaged and delivered first aid to soldiers before they moved on to nearby general hospitals. Passing hospitals were set up along the routes from the army to the general hospitals to deliver some care to those traveling in sick convoys. Convalescent hospitals, such as the one at Belem, enabled men to fully recover before returning to duty. Sometimes men took the opportunity to remain away from their units for as long as possible, and given the conditions on campaign it was hardly surprising that some extended their stays to the point of malingering. With such a wide network of hospitals it is understandable that the pay lists of the battalion sometimes seem uncertain where a sick or wounded soldier was. During 1812 men from the battalion spent a total of 3,142 days in 11 different hospitals.[52]

The soldiers' mental health was not addressed in any way. The intense stress of combat must have had similar impacts as it did in later wars, and still does, but the only indication we have of the mental state of the men of the battalion are perhaps the suicides which occurred with some regularity. Those that occurred while men were in hospital could either be an indication of severe wounds they felt they could not live with, or mental distress.

Sick or wounded officers could not use the hospitals and were quartered in private houses. They even had to pay for their care in the early part of the war. Surgeons would visit them where they lodged, taking them away from their other duties. Officers could then convalesce at Lisbon, or elsewhere. Lieutenant Colonel Williams recovered from one of his many wounds in Oporto in the spring of 1812.[53] Convalescent officers had to attend medical boards to judge their fitness for duty. In October 1810 Lieutenant de Bernegg was one of several officers warned that they would be ordered to return to duty if they did not attend.[54]

Those men of the battalion too wounded or ill to return to active duty were sent to the Foreign Depot invalid hospital at Eling for assessment and possible discharge. Surviving records of soldiers examined at the hospital during 1812 and 1813 give an idea of the toll

49 Howard, *Doctors*, p.95.

50 June, September & December 1811 Pay Lists, TNA, WO 12/7074.

51 Deaths in Hospital in the Peninsula, January 1814, Wellington, *Supplementary Despatches*, Vol.VIII, p.474.

52 December 1812 Pay List, TNA, WO 12/7074.

53 J. Collville, *The Portrait of a General* (Salisbury: Michael Russell, 1980), p.102.

54 General Order 17 October 1810, quoted in Wellington, *General Orders*, Vol.II, pp.186-7.

that campaigning took on the men of the battalion.[55] Michael Kramer, 40, from Baden, had served for 15 years. He was lame and could only walk with crutches after several musket ball wounds to the legs at the Battle of Salamanca. He was discharged from the Army. Peter Tumbert, 28 years old and from Bamberg, must have joined the Army at a young age as he had served two years with one of the Lowenstein regiments and then 12 with the 5th Battalion. He was 'Ruptured by an effort on the right side at the retreat of Talavera in Spain'. Today a rupture would be called a torn or strained muscle. Tumbert was also discharged. Invalided soldiers were frequently sent from the depot back to the continent via the port of Harwich and across the North Sea to Heligoland.

As well as being discharged the men could also be assessed as being unfit for active service but fit for garrison duty, and would then be assigned to one of the Garrison or Royal Veteran Battalions. The soldiers would then still be paid and perform a useful function until their time of service expired. Hungarian Paul Fielas was 58 and had been in the Army for 16 years. He was found to be 'Worn out by age & service & having received a wound by a sword at the abdomen', but was still deemed able to serve in a garrison. Private Humbach, 42, from Bielefeld, was lame from a musket ball wound, in his case to the right leg and sustained at Badajoz, but again was judged fit for garrison duty. So were George Cottschy, 40, from Hungary, who had a rupture on the right side, and Henry Kasey, 27, from Nassau, who was lame from a musket ball wound in the thigh at Talavera. John Alles, 30, had poor eyesight and could hardly see in the dark but was still considered able enough to be employed in a garrison.

55 Return of Foreign Invalids, TNA, WO 25/668, pp.179-184

20

Ciudad Rodrigo and Badajoz

Despite withdrawing around 25,000 men from Spain for his Russian campaign,[1] Napoleon still expected his local commanders to take the offensive against the allied armies and continued to dictate strategy in the Peninsula from a distance, often acting on outdated information. *Marechal* Marmont received orders to send troops to support operations against some of the Spanish armies in other provinces to the east. Marmont did not protest the orders and sent the men. It was winter and he expected the cautious Wellington to wait for better weather before making any move. However, when Wellington heard of the weakening of Marmont's army he realised he had an opportunity and decided to take it. His infantry, both British and Portuguese, were more numerous and more experienced than ever before, he had double the cavalry he had had at the start of 1811, and he had, at last, a proper siege train ready at Almeida. If he was going to take the offensive in Spain he needed first to secure the fortresses of Ciudad Rodrigo and Badajoz.

Ciudad Rodrigo would be his first target. His army was spread along the Portuguese border with the Light Division close to the fortress. At the start of January 1812 Wellington gave orders for the 1st, 3rd, and 4th Divisions to concentrate at the Agueda River. They were in place by 5 January after marching through heavy snow and sleet. The army had to wait for the siege train to struggle along the muddy roads but had invested Ciudad Rodrigo by 8 January.

Ciudad Rodrigo sits on a low hill on the northern bank of the Agueda. A Roman bridge crosses the river, and the entrance to the town is protected by an old Moorish castle. The Moorish and Medieval town walls had been modernised and were around 30 feet high, with a ditch and a glacis – an earth bank – in front of them for much of the circumference. A hill, the Greater Teson, overlooked the town, and more importantly the walls, 600 yards to the north-east. A smaller hill, the Lesser Teson, lay 300 yards closer to the town. The fortified convent of Santa Cruz stood to the east of the town and that of San Francisco and some suburbs to the north and north-west respectively. The garrison was just under 2,000 men.[2] Redoubt Renaud, a small fort that the French had built to defend the Greater Teson,

1 Esdaile, *Peninsular*, p.370.

2 Oman, *Peninsular War*, Vol.V, p.163.

The Siege of Ciudad Rodrigo, 8-12 January 1812.
Sources: Lipscombe, *Atlas* & Wyld, *Maps & Plans*.

was taken by the Light Division on the evening the allies arrived. Trenches were started immediately.

The weather remained harsh, with sharp frosts and cold winds. There were few villages near the fortress and most troops were camped in the open, huddling around large fires when they could. Men going to the trenches had to ford the icy river, often up to their chests, and so were cold and wet before their work began. The four divisions took shifts of 24 hours; digging the trenches and protecting them. The 1st Division still had two companies of the 5th battalion, the 3rd Division three, and the 4th Division one so only when the Light Division took their turn were there no riflemen of the 5th Battalion at the front.

The headquarters and Nos. 2, 3 and 7 companies were in Major General Mackinnon's Brigade of the 3rd Division. In his journal for 11 and 12 January he wrote:

> We had to march about eleven miles to the trenches. We marched this day at seven o'clock in the morning – were relieved the following day at one o'clock by the light division. My brigade lost this day 2 killed, 17 wounded, and 2 of the 60th deserted to the enemy. The fatigue of the march, and the severity of the work (being one half of the fore in the trenches), will be more severely felt than the loss by the enemy's cannon. The loss the whole division was 53; of whom about 5 were killed. As there is only one house in the neighbourhood, which is reserved for the wounded, we were all obliged to sleep out, and the cold was intense.[3]

The two deserters were Privates Joseph Lambrecht and Frederick Schoen, both from No. 2 company. Lambrecht had been with the battalion since 1799, so one has to wonder what made him run after serving for so long.[4]

Despite well-aimed enemy cannon fire, construction of the trenches and three batteries progressed rapidly. Casualties increased as the French gunners used both round shot and shells to try and disrupt the work. A second parallel trench, further down the slope of the Greater Teson and closer to the fortress, was started on the 13th. The fortified convent of Santa Cruz was close to the site of the new parallel and Wellington ordered that it be taken. The 1st Division was at the front and the attack was made by 300 men of the KGL and a company of the 5th Battalion. Nos. 5 and 9 companies were still with the 1st Division and it is not clear which was involved. The assault party, commanded by Captain la Roche de Stackenfels of the 1st Line Battalion KGL, came under heavy fire as it approached the convent. KGL skirmishers broke through the palisades surrounding the convent and the garrison fled. The KGL lost three killed and 34 wounded.[5] There were no casualties in the 5th Battalion.

The next morning, during the shift change between the 1st and 4th Divisions, the French made a sortie with 500 men and retook the convent. They briefly entered the trenches before withdrawing as British reinforcements arrived. Later that day the 27 guns in the three batteries opened fire and began to batter the walls.[6] On the night of the 14th

3 H. MacKinnon, *A Journal of the Campaign in Portugal & Spain* (Bath: Charles Duffiled, 1812), pp.99-100.
4 March 1812 Pay List, TNA, WO 12/7074; Periods of Service 5/60th, June 1806,WO 25/1008.
5 N.L. Beamish, *History of the King's German Legion* (London: Thomas & William Boone, 1837), Vol.II, p.31.
6 Oman, *Peninsular War*, Vol.V, p.173.

The storming of Ciudad Rodrigo, by the Light Division on the night of the 19th of January 1812. (Anne S.K. Brown Military Collection)

the 4th Division took the convent of San Francisco and the French withdrew from the surrounding outposts. The work on the trenches continued and the batteries carried on firing at the walls and the earth bank in front of them. With the allied guns concentrating on breaching the walls rather than counter-battery fire, work in the trenches, and especially the second parallel, became even more hazardous as the French kept up an incessant and accurate fire upon them. Nevertheless, the second parallel was completed by the 18th and a battery of two guns installed on the Lesser Teson, just 180 yards from the walls. Pits were dug just in front of the trench and picked riflemen kept up steady suppressing fire on the enemy's gunners.[7] The riflemen of the 5th Battalion's companies would have taken their turn in the pits on the days when their divisions were at the front. The battalion had two men wounded on the 18th.[8]

By 19 January the new battery had brought down a tower and the breaches were judged practicable for an assault. The main breach was to be attacked by the 3rd Division. Mackinnon's Brigade, with Nos. 2, 3, and 7 companies, was to attack directly from the second parallel. Campbell's Brigade was to attack from the convent of Santa Cruz with the 2/83rd providing covering fire. The Light Division was to assault the smaller breach. The 2nd Caçadores and a company of the 2/83rd were to attack across the Roman bridge to take two

7 Oman, *Peninsular War*, Vol.V, p.176.

8 Rigaud, *Celer et Audax*, p.185.

French guns that threatened the flank of the assault, and Pack's Portuguese Brigade was to make a diversionary attack on the eastern end of the town.

As darkness fell the troops made their way to their starting positions. At 7:00 p.m. the assaults began. Mackinnon's Brigade was headed by 300 volunteers from all the battalions. The men climbed over the parapet of the trenches and ran towards the walls, instantly coming under heavy fire from the French. Sappers with hay bags threw them into the ditch to soften the landings of the men jumping down.

Campbell's Brigade had reached the breach slightly before the storming party of Mackinnon's Brigade and they all began to climb up the rubble of the walls together, still under very heavy fire. At the top two French 24-pounders decimated the attackers with caseshot from either side, while bags of powder exploded on the slopes throwing those still climbing up into the air. The first ranks of the attackers were almost completely wiped out.

There was a pause before the attackers again managed to reach the crest and were again swept away by grape shot. In front of the few survivors was a 16-foot drop into the town, but it was covered with obstacles, including *chevaux de frise*; wooden beams studded with sword blades. The French set off a large mine at the top of the breach which killed Mackinnon and many more, but the attackers continued to climb up the breach, struggling over the bodies of those that had fallen. Unable to go any further forward the men of the 74th and 1/88th attacked the French positions on either side of the breach with just their bayonets, dropping their muskets to clamber over the stones and run across planks left by the French.

The defenders, hearing the Light Division entering the town from the smaller breach, began to fall back to the Plaza Mayor and lay down their weapons. The Portuguese attacks had also succeeded and allied troops poured into the town. Some of them took the opportunity to plunder and many became drunk, robbing and assaulting the inhabitants. After a few hours officers began to restore order and the garrison was led away as prisoners. Total allied casualties in the storming were 560.[9] The 5th Battalion lost one sergeant killed, and Captain Livingstone and three men wounded.[10] Lieutenant Colonel Williams was reported to have said of the assault: 'The carnage was terrible until we attained the summit, and were near enough to close on them with the bayonet; we then made short work of it, and the place was virtually won'.[11]

The sergeant listed as killed was Sergeant Major Caspar Schriebor, from Hesse Cassel. He had been with the battalion since 1798, and was a corporal when the companies formed on the Isle of Wight. Jacob Remler, from Brussels, serving with No. 10 company with the 4th Division, was also killed on the 19th but not in the assault. Private Christian Lamm (No. 5) died of his wounds at the end of January. He had been with the Guards Brigade of the 1st Division during the siege.[12]

Captain Alexander Livingstone had joined the battalion in May 1811. He had begun his career as a cornet in the 12th Light Dragoons, with whom he served in the Egyptian campaign of 1801. He was promoted lieutenant into the 1st Regiment of Life Guards in 1803

9 Oman, *Peninsular War*, Vol.V, p.588.

10 Rigaud, *Celer et Audax*, p.185.

11 Le Marchant, *Memoirs*, pp.193.

12 January 1812 Casualty Return TNA, WO 25/1923, Periods of Service 5/60th, June 1806, WO 25/1008; March 1812 Pay List, WO 12/7074.

View of Badajoz from the north side of the Guadiana near Fort Christobal.
(From Cumberland, *Views in Spain & Portugal*)

and then to captain in the 3/60th in 1805, serving in the West Indies before transferring to the 5th Battalion. It would have been slightly unusual for an officer to transfer from a fashionable cavalry regiment into less popular regiments like the 60th that spent long periods in the Caribbean. Livingstone was so severely wounded that he had to return to England in April to recover and subsequently transferred to a garrison battalion a year later.[13]

The capture of Ciudad Rodrigo had been achieved more quickly than Wellington had anticipated, but with Marmont still close he could not have afforded a lengthy siege. With the northern route into Portugal secure he began to move his forces southwards towards Elvas and his next objective; the more formidable fortress of Badajoz.

The returns for the first three months of the year show a large number of new arrivals joining the 5th Battalion. A draft of 40 men had left the Foreign Depot in early October to board the *Eliza Tupper* transport, but were delayed by contrary winds until late November.[14] Another 60 men sailed aboard the *Osbourne* transport in early December.[15] Thirty-two men from the first draft joined the battalion in January, with a further three, plus 53 from the second draft, in February. The remainder joined later. The strength of the battalion on 25 January was 54 sergeants, 12 buglers, and 532 rank and file.[16]

13 1805 Army List, TNA, WO 65/55; pp.57, 1803 Army List, WO 65/53 pp.57; May 1811 Return, WO 17/180; July Return WO 17/264 & Hall, *Biographical Dictionary*, p.349.

14 Mosheim to Williams 4 October 1811, TNA, WO 7/85, pp.151-2.

15 Mosheim to Williams 1 December 1811, TNA, WO 7/85, p.570.

16 January & February 1812 Returns, TNA, WO 17/264.

Lieutenant de Bree had returned from the depot in England and, with a sergeant and two privates, was on duty at Belem overseeing the new arrivals. The officers on recruiting and staff duty remained unchanged. Sixteen officers were on leave including Captains Livingstone and Purdon, and Lieutenants Fürst, de Eberstein, and Ingersleben, who were all recovering from wounds or illness. February saw Ensign John William von Dalman joining from the Chasseurs Britannique. He had been commissioned in February 1811 and joined the Chasseurs in the Peninsular in June.[17] In March Lieutenant Stern arrived from the 3/60th after being ill in Lisbon from January. Brevet Lieutenant Colonel William Woodgate left on 18 March to join the 4/60th, which he commanded from 1814 but he left the regiment in 1817 when his battalion was reduced. He died in Paris in 1861, aged 80.[18] Sergeant Gottlieb Lerche replaced Schriebor as sergeant major, but he was not in the rank for long. In April he was promoted to ensign, a jump that previous sergeant majors had only achieved after some time in the job. Sergeant Joseph Wolff became sergeant major when Lerche was commissioned.[19]

Woodgate's replacement was Brevet Lieutenant Colonel John Forster Fitzgerald. Fitzgerald had been commissioned as an ensign in the 79th Highlanders in 1793, whilst still less than 10 years old. He was a captain a year later, and was on the rolls of the 46th Foot and New Brunswick Fencible Infantry for brief periods before becoming a major in the 60th in 1809, and brevet lieutenant colonel in 1810. When he joined the 5th Battalion he was still less than 30 years old.[20]

Wellington began to move his divisions southwards on 19 February. To disguise his intentions he, and his headquarters, remained near Ciudad Rodrigo until early March. The heavy guns of the siege train travelled to Elvas on a circuitous road, river, and sea route via Oporto. By early March almost the whole of Wellington's army was near, or nearing, Elvas. With approximately 60,000 men he had enough troops to both invest Badajoz and position strong screening forces in case the French marched to relieve the fortress.[21] Just as with Ciudad Rodrigo Wellington was aware that he had only a limited time before the French managed to gather enough forces to challenge him and try to break the siege. On 16 March the 3rd, 4th, and Light Divisions crossed the Guadiana River on a pontoon bridge and surrounded Badajoz.

At the same time, Hill's 2nd Division with Hamilton's Portuguese Division, plus cavalry, headed towards Merida, whilst the 1st, 6th, and 7th Divisions, again with cavalry, under Lieutenant General Sir Thomas Graham, marched for Villafranca. Their orders were to push back the closest French divisions, which they did without major engagements. Six out of the ten companies of the battalion marched with these two columns.

The defences of Badajoz had been significantly improved after the two aborted sieges of 1811. Fort San Cristobal had been improved and a redoubt built on the location where the allies had previously sited their batteries. More guns had been placed in the castle and the previous breeches repaired and strengthened. The Rivellas stream that flowed around

17 Nichols, *Mongrel Regiment*, p.188.

18 March 1812 Return, TNA, WO 17/264; Butler, *Annals*, Vol.II, p.157.

19 June 1812 Pay List, TNA, WO 12/7074.

20 Butler, *Annals*, Vol.II, pp.157 & 356; *The Royal Military Calendar*, Vol.IV, pp.290-1.

21 Oman, *Peninsular War*, Vol.V, p.227.

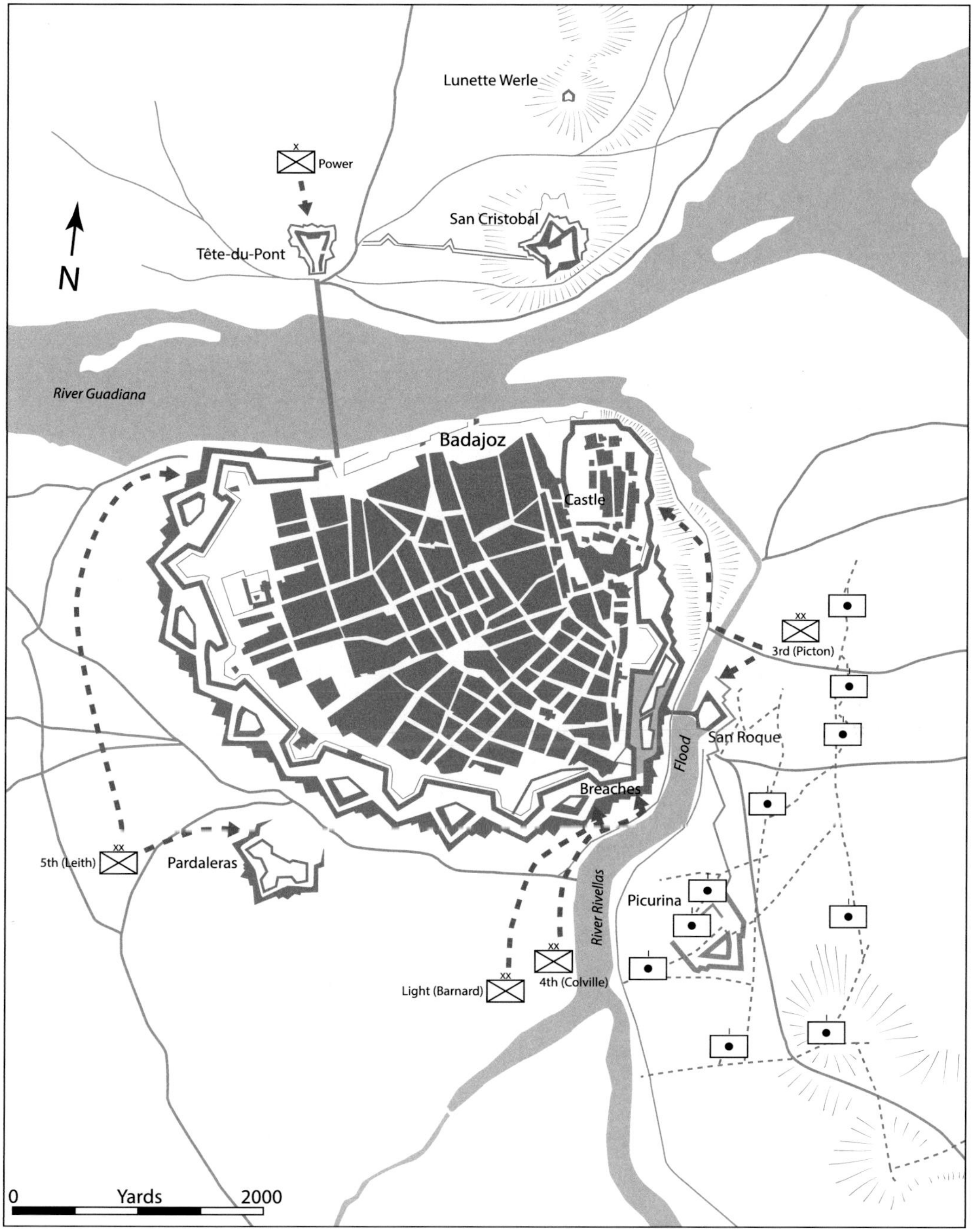

The Siege of Badajoz, 16 March to 6 April 1812.
Sources: Lipscombe, *Atlas* & Wyld, *Maps & Plans*.

the north east of the fortress had been dammed to make it harder for troops to approach from that direction. Some of the outer-works were now connected to the town by protected trenches, many of the bastions had been improved, and mines had been placed at likely approaches to the walls. The garrison, largely the same men who had successfully defeated the two previous attempts to take the town, numbered around 4,700.[22] Their commander, *Général de Division* Phillipon, was confident he could hold out until help arrived.

The sieges of 1811 had concentrated on the northern side of the fortress where Fort San Cristobal and the castle were. This time Wellington, and his senior engineer Lieutenant Colonel Richard Fletcher, decided to attack the south-eastern section around the bastions of Santa Maria and La Trinidad. Fort Picurina stood where the allies would have to site their breaching batteries and needed to be captured first. On the night of 17 March 1,800 men dug the first parallel trench around 160 yards from the fort, along with a long communication trench to the rear. The night was stormy and dark and the howling of the wind covered the sounds of digging.[23]

The heavy rain continued to make excavating the trenches even more fatiguing over the next few days. Wet soil would slide back into the trenches rather than form protective banks around them. However, the rain cut visibility so much that it became difficult for the French to accurately target the trenches. Work carried on through the 18th and two batteries were dug for the guns that would breach the walls of the fort. The speed of progress worried Phillipon and on 19 March he sent out a sortie of around 1,500 men, including cavalry, to take and destroy the trenches.[24]

The French infantry ran up the hill and drove off the working parties, capturing entrenching tools, but they did not have the time to do much damage before the allied guards and trenching parties formed up and drove them off in a short and sharp struggle. The French cavalry got as far as the engineers' park and sabred some of the sappers. British losses were 150 and the French twice as many.[25] Fletcher was badly wounded but continued to direct the siege from his tent while he recovered. Corporal Martin Kauffman (No. 7), from Neustadt in the Palatinate, and Privates John Basil (No. 3), and Sebastian Ritsch (No. 3), both from Alsace, were all killed in action on the 19th. No. 3 and 7 companies were attached to the 3rd Division. Private Henry Petersen (No. 10) was killed on 21 March. He was from Antwerp and had joined at Stapleton prisoner of war camp in 1806.[26] No. 10 company was with the 4th Division. It is possible that Petersen was killed when the French brought forward cannon to enfilade the parallel and a party of riflemen were detailed to fire on the gunners, which led to the guns being withdrawn.[27]

Over the next few days the rain got even heavier, causing the pontoon bridge to wash away, flooding the trenches, and threatening to bring the siege-work to a halt. By the 24th though, the weather had improved enough for the guns to be emplaced in the batteries and on the 25th they opened fire on Fort Picurina and the main walls of the fortress. The guns

22 Oman, *Peninsular*, War Vol.V, p.235.
23 I. Fletcher, *Badajoz 1812* (Oxford: Osprey, 1999) p.53.
24 Fletcher, *Badajoz*, p.53.
25 Oman, *Peninsular War*, Vol.V, p.238; Jones, *Sieges*, Vol.I, p.174.
26 March 1812 Casualty Return, TNA, WO 25/1923; December 1806 Pay List, WO 12/7072.
27 Jones, *Sieges*, Vol.I, p.179. The regiment of the riflemen is not specified.

The Siege of Badajoz, by Henri Leveque. (Anne S.K. Brown Military Collection)

of the fort were soon silenced and Wellington ordered that it was to be stormed that night. Major General Kempt with 500 men of the 3rd and Light Divisions attacked at 10:00 p.m. Almost a fifth of the men were brought down by heavy musket fire from the fort before they reached the ditch. Finding the defences stronger than expected the attackers struggled to find a way in but eventually took the fort by laying ladders across the ditch and by breaking through the damaged walls. The garrison continued to offer stiff resistance but eventually surrendered, with a few escaping. Casualties amongst Kempt's men were over 50 percent.[28]

By the end of March the guns were positioned in all the batteries; including those built at Fort Picurina, which had been completed under heavy fire. The long hard work of battering the walls began. The allied gunners were often under fire from French marksmen on the ramparts, and riflemen were placed in the trenches to provide suppressing fire, which they did to good effect.[29] By 4 April the damage to the walls could be clearly seen, as could the reception the French were preparing in the way of obstacles and defences within the walls. The besiegers continued to take heavy losses from French cannon fire, although the garrison was starting to run short of ammunition. Private Peter Mores (No. 2), from Berlin, was killed on 31 March and several men wounded in this final period of preparations.[30]

By 5 April the two breaches were practicable, but Wellington ordered a third one made between the Santa Maria and Trinidad batteries, which was achieved the next day. The attack was planned for that night. The 3rd Division was to cross the Rivellas and attempt to scale the castle walls with ladders. The 4th Division was to storm the breach in the Trinidad Bastion, as well as the breach in the wall next to it, and the Light Division was to take the Santa Maria breach. Firing parties were to try and keep the defenders' heads down while the storming parties advanced. Each assault was headed by the optimistically named 'Forlorn Hope', comprised of volunteers. These men carried hay bags to throw into the ditch and

28 Oman, *Peninsular War*, Vol.V, p.240.

29 Jones, *Sieges*, Vol.I, pp.199 & 208.

30 March & April 1812 Casualty Returns, TNA, WO 25/1923; Butler, *Annals*, Vol.II, p.153.

The storming of Badajoz, by J.A. Atkinson. (Anne S.K. Brown Military Collection)

were to be the first into the breaches, and probably the first to die. Survivors, if any, would receive promotion and glory.

The 5th Division was to make a diversionary attack on Fort Pardaleras, and if possible scale the walls of the San Vincente Bastion. Other diversions were to be made at San Cristobal and San Roque. The attacks were to be started at 7:00 p.m. but preparations and positioning of the attacking formations were not completed in time and it was put back to 10:00 p.m. This gave the French valuable extra time to prepare their defences, including mines, *chevaux-de-frises*, and spiked planks. The assault was going to be very costly.[31]

The 4th and Light Divisions approached their target breaches unseen by the enemy. Only when they were entering the ditch between the glacis and the walls were they spotted. The French began firing at the attackers with artillery and muskets, illuminating the attackers by throwing fireballs down into their midst, quickly followed by grenades. The leading men of the 4th Division jumped down into the water-filled ditch, not realising how deep it was, and drowned. The following men moved left and descended where the ditch was drier. The Light Division also poured down into the ditch in front of their target, the Santa Maria Bastion. The forlorn hopes were quickly slaughtered by the weight of fire being brought to bear upon them. Once the ditch was full enough of struggling redcoats and riflemen the French engineers fired a series of mines and powder barrels that wiped out almost all of the 500 men leading each division, including the engineer officers sent to guide them. Firing parties, including most likely the riflemen of No. 10 company with the 4th Division, had been ordered to remain on the glacis to target the defenders but the heavy fire of the French and the slow progress of the assaults prevented the plan being carried out.

31 The details of the storming of Badajoz are taken from Oman. *Peninsular War*, Vol.V, pp.243-58, Rigaud, *Celer et Audax*, pp.188-90, Butler, *Annals*, pp.150-4, Fletcher, *Badajoz 1812*, pp.61-79, & Jones, *Sieges* Vol.I pp.213-27.

As the main columns of the two divisions arrived at the ditch they became mixed together. Men jumped down into the now burning ditch and in the confusion headed mainly for the two outside breaches which the French had had the time to properly defend rather than the easier central breach. Flashes from explosions illuminated the scene for brief moments, creating momentary tableaus of the dead and dying, of those still hoping to reach the top of the breach, and those that hoped they had found somewhere safe to lie until it was all over. The few men who did make it to the top of the breaches were stopped by the *chevaux-de-frises*, shot, bayonetted, or blasted apart by grape-shot. Attack after attack was attempted and brutally defeated. After two hours Wellington admitted defeat and ordered their withdrawal. The shattered divisions left the ditch and the breaches carpeted with dead and wounded. Wellington's main attack against Badajoz had utterly failed.

Fortunately, the men of the 3rd Division were having more success. Lieutenant General Picton had petitioned Wellington to be allowed to attack the castle, reasoning that it was such a strong position that it might be lightly garrisoned. Wellington agreed and the 3rd Division were to form up in the first parallel and move down towards the flood caused by the damming of the Rivellas Stream. The seven light companies of the division and Nos. 2, 3 and 7 companies of the 5th Battalion, all under the command of Lieutenant Colonel Williams, would lead the way and would then deploy to cover the assault.

The French saw Williams' men as they approached the Rivellas and opened fire from the whole of eastern section of the walls. The riflemen of the 5th Battalion, under the immediate command of Brevet Lieutenant Colonel Fitzgerald, were the first to cross the water via a mill-dam, wading knee deep in single file and taking heavy fire. Once across they, and the light companies, began to fire at the French above them on the ramparts. The storming parties broke down a palisade on the other side of the stream and struggled up the steep slope at the base of the walls but found that their ladders were too short. They tried standing on each other shoulders at the tops but could still not reach the parapet, or were bayonetted or shot in the attempt. The defenders threw fireballs, stones, and anything else they could find down onto the seething mass of men below. The first assault failed and Picton was wounded, but as the other brigades crossed the water around 4,000 men were soon spread along 200 yards of wall.

Two officers of the 5th Foot found a section of wall which was lower and managed to reach the top. Slowly the sheer weight of numbers began to tell and the attackers began to pour into the castle, but the garrison continued to resist. All the exits from the castle except one had been bricked up. Phillipon, hearing that the castle had fallen, sent his reserve to retake it but the 3rd Division beat them back and by midnight they were entering the town.

However, it was the attack by the 5th Division that really sealed the fate of Badajoz. Starting later than planned, they arrived at the San Vincente Bastion after some of the defenders had been drawn away to defend the main breaches. Under heavy fire they managed to find a section of wall low enough for their ladders and streamed up onto the ramparts. In desperate fighting they managed to drive their way towards the main breaches before being driven back and then regaining their ground with a counter-attack. They swept along the bastions and down into the streets. When the weary and bloodied 4th and Light Divisions rallied for one last attempt at the main breaches they found them nearly uncontested as the defenders were already surrendering. Phillipon escaped across the river to San Cristobal and capitulated the next morning.

The allied losses in the assault were appalling: 806 were killed and 2,855 wounded.[32] Six of the 5th Battalion were among the dead. Lieutenant John Stern had arrived at the battalion on 24 March. Two weeks later he was dead. He had begun his army career as an ensign with the 8th West India Regiment before being promoted into the 60th in 1810, joining the 3rd Battalion at Martinique and then transferring to the 5th. Stern was serving with the 3rd Division. Also killed in the attack on the castle were: Privates Francis Reiber (No. 2), from Magdeburg; Michael Toth (No. 2), from Ulm in Austria; and Francis Zobel (No. 7), a farrier from Ratibor in Silesia with over ten years of service in the battalion. There were also two fatalities from No. 10 company in the 4th Division: Corporal Charles Grundman, from Gera in Saxony, who had joined the battalion in 1800; and Private Francis Schwindok, a Pole, who had joined in 1803.[33] Lieutenant Colonels Williams and Fitzgerald, Lieutenants de Gilse and Broetz, two sergeants, and 24 riflemen were wounded. Lieutenant Peter Broetz, adjutant of the battalion, had to have a leg amputated and later left Spain for England where he joined the 1st Royal Veteran Battalion.[34] Williams and Fitzgerald were amongst those officers singled out for praise in Picton's dispatch.[35]

The victors streamed into Badajoz, traumatised but exultant that they had survived, and searched for drink, plunder, and women. By the conventions of the time a town that failed to surrender after the walls had been breached could be sacked, and after the severity of the assault the allied troops were not going to be denied. For three days they rampaged through the town, drinking themselves insensible, burning down houses, stealing what they could find, and even resorting to rape and murder.

An officer of the 88th recalled an incident just after the taking of the castle, while the French were laying down their arms and being taken prisoner:

> Among others, I happened to capture and save the life of the Colonel commanding the artillery in the citadel, at the very moment our men pursued him at the point of the bayonet. He threw himself upon me, and finding I understood French, entreated that I would save him from our infuriated soldiers, which I found it extremely difficult to do, as each successive party, on perceiving his large gold epaulettes and orders, evinced a strong anxiety to make further acquaintance with him; and upon one occasion I was obliged to use my sword to protect him from a few of the 60th, who advanced upon him in rather a suspicious and business-like manner.[36]

Attempts were made to stop the violence from 7 April, Wellington having decided that the men had sufficiently indulged themselves, but incidents continued and many troops remained out of control. Eventually the debauchery faded as the men exhausted themselves, and the town's supply of drink. They gradually returned to their camps. One last 5th Battalion casualty of the assault was perhaps Private Joseph Schultz (No. 2) who is recorded

32 Oman, *Peninsular War*, Vol.V, pp.594-5.

33 April 1812 Casualty Return ,WO 25/1923, March & April 1812 Returns, WO 17/180, June 1812 Pay List, WO 12/7074, 1809 Army List; WO 65/59, p.337; 1810 Army List, WO 65/60 p.243.

34 Hall, *Biographical Dictionary*, p.75.

35 Butler, *Annals*, Vol.II, p.153.

36 W.H. Maxwell, *Peninsular Sketches* (London: Henry Colburn, 1845), Vol.I, p.301.

as having shot himself on 7 April. Whether it was trauma, guilt, drunkenness, being severely wounded, or sheer melancholy that drove him to suicide is not recorded.

With Williams once again wounded Fitzgerald took command of the battalion and signed the April return, with Williams resuming command for the May return. In May 154 men joined the battalion having sailed from Britain on the *Mermaid* transport, raising the strength of the battalion to 54 sergeants, 11 buglers, and 732 rank and file. With the recruits came Lieutenant Roepel, Ensigns Lawless, Hamilton, and Currie, and Assistant Surgeon Berger. Govert Roepel had been a cornet in the 1st KGL Dragoons. James Lawless had briefly been with the 6th Battalion, John Currie transferred from the 3rd Battalion and John Hamilton from the 2nd. Colonel Mosheim at the depot particularly recommended Hamilton to Williams as a fine young man and a promising officer. He also pointed out to Williams that Sergeant Frederick Seidel had been an officer in French service and wished to be recommended to his new commander. One of the corporals that sailed on the *Mermaid* was not a recruit; Corporal Christian Schmaltz had been taken prisoner at Talavera, escaped from France, and had made his way to the Foreign Depot to re-join the battalion. Also noted on the June return was the death of Paymaster George Gilbert, who had been suspended from his duties for over three years and had been living in Lisbon. Mosheim and Williams had been working together to try and recruit more buglers for the battalion. Mosheim tried to recruit boys at first but then requested a 'worn out bugler' from Williams to train some recruits. Three of these men came with the May draft, paid as privates but with their own bugles, and were subsequently appointed as buglers.[37]

Lieutenant Matthew Fürst, who had been on sick leave in Britain, was posted to the 4/60th and appointed a staff subaltern at the Foreign Depot in June. Fürst, who had been promoted from the ranks, was still a lieutenant with the 60th in 1830 and took an offer of promotion to captain to retire on half-pay. He had served for 30 years.[38]

While Wellington had besieged Badajoz, *Marechal* Marmont had marched, on Napoleon's orders, into Portugal. Ciudad Rodrigo was surrounded but could not be attacked as the French siege train had been there when it was taken by the allies. Leaving a covering force around the fortresses the French marched towards Sabugal. Marmont thought that Wellington would be occupied at Badajoz for some time and was surprised when in middle of April news reached him that the town had been taken and that the allied army was free to move north and confront him and cut off his line of retreat. Wellington knew far more about Marmont's movements than Marmont knew about his, and had begun to march seven of his divisions north on 11 April. Enough to crush Marmont, if he could be caught.

Lieutenant General Hill with the 2nd Division, two Portuguese brigades, and cavalry were left behind to cover the French forces in the south. Nos. 4, 6, & 8 companies of the 5th Battalion were still with the 2nd Division, nominally attached to Wilson's, Byng's, and Howard's Brigades respectively but often operating along with the light companies as the divisional light battalion. Dispatches captured from the French informed Wellington how important the French commanders thought the bridge over the Tagus at Almaraz was,

37 June 1812 Return, TNA, WO 17/180; Mosheim to Williams, 7 October 1811 WO 7/85, Mosheim to Williams 22 January 1812, 28 January 1812, & 18 April 1812, WO 7/86, pp.191, 213-4 & 541.

38 June 1812 Return, TNA, WO 17/180; *London Gazette*, Issue 18688, 8 June 1830, p.1127.

and that there was only one French division two days march away from it.[39] If the bridge was destroyed it would severely hamper the ability of Soult and Marmont to reinforce one another.

Wellington ordered Hill to strike at Almaraz on 7 May. Hill took Howard's and Wilson's Brigades, Ashworth's Portuguese Brigade, British and Portuguese cavalry. The column reached Merida on the 12th, was delayed by the repair of a bridge, and then reached Truxillo on 15 May after some hard marching. The baggage was left there and the troops began to cross the three mountain ranges that lay between Truxillo and their target on the Tagus. After a night march on the night of 16/17 May they reached the pass at Miravete. Hill had planned to take the French fort there but it proved to be too well-sited and almost impregnable. As well as the old tower that had been improved, the French had fortified a house near the road. The way forward for Hill's guns was effectively blocked.

The pontoon-bridge at Almaraz was protected by a fort on each bank. Fort Napoleon on the southern bank was the stronger one with a good ditch, palisades, and a tower. Fort Ragusa on the northern bank was smaller. Further defences stood at both ends of the bridge. The garrison at the bridge was around 700, with a further 300 in the fort at Miravete five miles away.[40]

On 18 May Hill decided to make a diversionary attack with Wilson's Brigade and the artillery against the fort at Miravete whilst Howard's Brigade, including both No. 8 company and No. 4 company from Wilson's Brigade, and the 6th Portuguese Regiment would make an arduous trek through the hills over goat tracks, carrying scaling ladders, and attack Fort Napoleon. The troops marched through night and were a mile from their target at dawn. They advanced through thickets to within 300 yards of the fort whilst the sounds of the attack at Miravete attracted the attention of the garrison.

The night march over rough country, often in single-file, caused many of the troops to be well behind those at the front and rather than wait Hill decided to attack with the 900 men he had available. The 1/50th and half of the 1/71st ran toward the fort in three columns. The French opened fire as they approached, with cannon and musketry, but the storming parties soon managed to gain the ramparts and the garrison either fled or surrendered. Those that ran headed for the bridge and with the redcoats close on their heels the detachments there could not fire without hitting their comrades. The southern end of the bridge was taken quickly but some of the pontoons had sunk and the bridge could not be crossed.

Fort Ragusa opened fire but the captured guns of Fort Napoleon, served by a detachment of the Royal Artillery, returned fire and the garrison of Fort Ragusa soon fled too. Boats were found and used to repair the bridge, enabling the occupation of the northern bank. Total allied casualties were 189, whilst the French lost around 400 men.[41] The bridge was burned, the stores destroyed and the forts blown up, and Hill retired back to Truxillo with his mission accomplished. The two companies of the 5th Battalion, Nos. 4 and 8, were held in reserve during the attack with the 6th Portuguese Regiment.[42] Neither of the companies took any casualties.

39 Oman, *Peninsular War*, Vol.V, p.319.

40 Oman, *Peninsular War*, Vol.V, p.324.

41 Oman, *Peninsular War*, Vol.V, p.328.

42 Rigaud, *Celer et Audax*, pp.193-4.

While Hill protected the southern flank Wellington, with the rest of the army, moved north towards Marmont's forces as rapidly as he could. His divisions were delayed by having to cross the Tagus over a single bridge at Villa Velha, and by heavy rains, but by 22 April the allied troops were soon within striking distance of the French near Ciudad Rodrigo. Marmont was unaware how close Wellington was and fortuitously ordered a retreat back towards Salamanca, due to of a shortage of supplies rather than any knowledge of the allied army's movements.[43] After 10 days of forced marches Wellington ordered his men to halt on 24 April. Marmont had escaped, for the moment, but Wellington had the numbers on his side and the successes of the early part of the year secured him greater co-operation from the Spanish generals who became more active and tied down some of the troops that may have reinforced Marmont. Raids by the Royal Navy in northern Spain also helped to keep other French commanders occupied.

On 13 June Wellington's army of 48,000 men began to advance again.[44] They began to encounter the French outposts on the 16th, just six miles from Salamanca. Marmont had only managed to gather 40,000 men and was desperately waiting for more men to join him from other commands.[45] Both generals knew that a battle had to be fought but neither wanted to force the issue before they felt sure they could win. For Marmont that meant stalling until he received more men, and for Wellington it meant trying to manoeuvre Marmont into attacking him on ground of his choosing.

43 Oman, *Peninsular War*, Vol.V, p.294.
44 Oman, *Peninsular War*, Vol.V, p.335.
45 Oman, *Peninsular War*, Vol.V, p.355.

21

Salamanca

The allied army encircled Salamanca unopposed on 17 June. Wellington led the 6th Division, with the 14th Light Dragoons, into the city. The allied troops were cheered and welcomed by the population. However, the French had not entirely left the city and 800 men garrisoned three fortified convents.[1] Wellington ordered the 6th Division to commence siege operations against them. Major Galiffe and No. 1 company were still attached to Hulse's Brigade of the 6th Division.

The three convents occupied high ground in the south-west corner of the city, on the banks of the River Tormes. The largest, Fort San Vincente, was divided from the others, Fort La Merced and Fort San Cayetano, by a steep valley. The forts covered the approaches to each other. Houses had been demolished around them to establish fields of fire, and the convents had been well fortified. If Wellington had brought with him the siege train that had been used at Ciudad Rodrigo and Badajoz the heavy guns would have made short work of the improvised forts, but as it was the siege was carried out with inadequate resources and inexperienced troops.

Work on the first battery began straightaway, and a mine was commenced towards the walls. Fire from the forts hampered progress and a light battalion of the KGL was required to give suppressing fire. By the 19th the first battery was finished and opened fire. It soon opened a small, but not practicable, breach. A second battery came under heavy French fire and failed to make a second break in the defences. Shortage of ammunition and troops being withdrawn to counter moves by *Marechal* Marmont slowed down the siege. On 23 June an assault was attempted on Fort San Cayetano by the light companies of Hulse's and Bowes' Brigades, but without much hope of success. Losses were heavy as the stormers came under fire from San Vincente as well as their target. Major General Bowes was killed, and the attack failed.[2] Three days later new supplies of ammunition had been received for the guns and their battering began to have an effect, especially when heated shot was used to start fires within the convents. A practicable breach was achieved at San Cayetano on 27 June and the troops were about to assault it when the French raised a white flag. Negotiations failed and the assault went ahead but met nearly no opposition. The commander of San

1 R. Muir, *Salamanca 1812* (New Haven: Yale, 2001), p.6.
2 Oman, *Peninsular War*, Vol V, p.371; Jones, *Sieges*, pp.280-1.

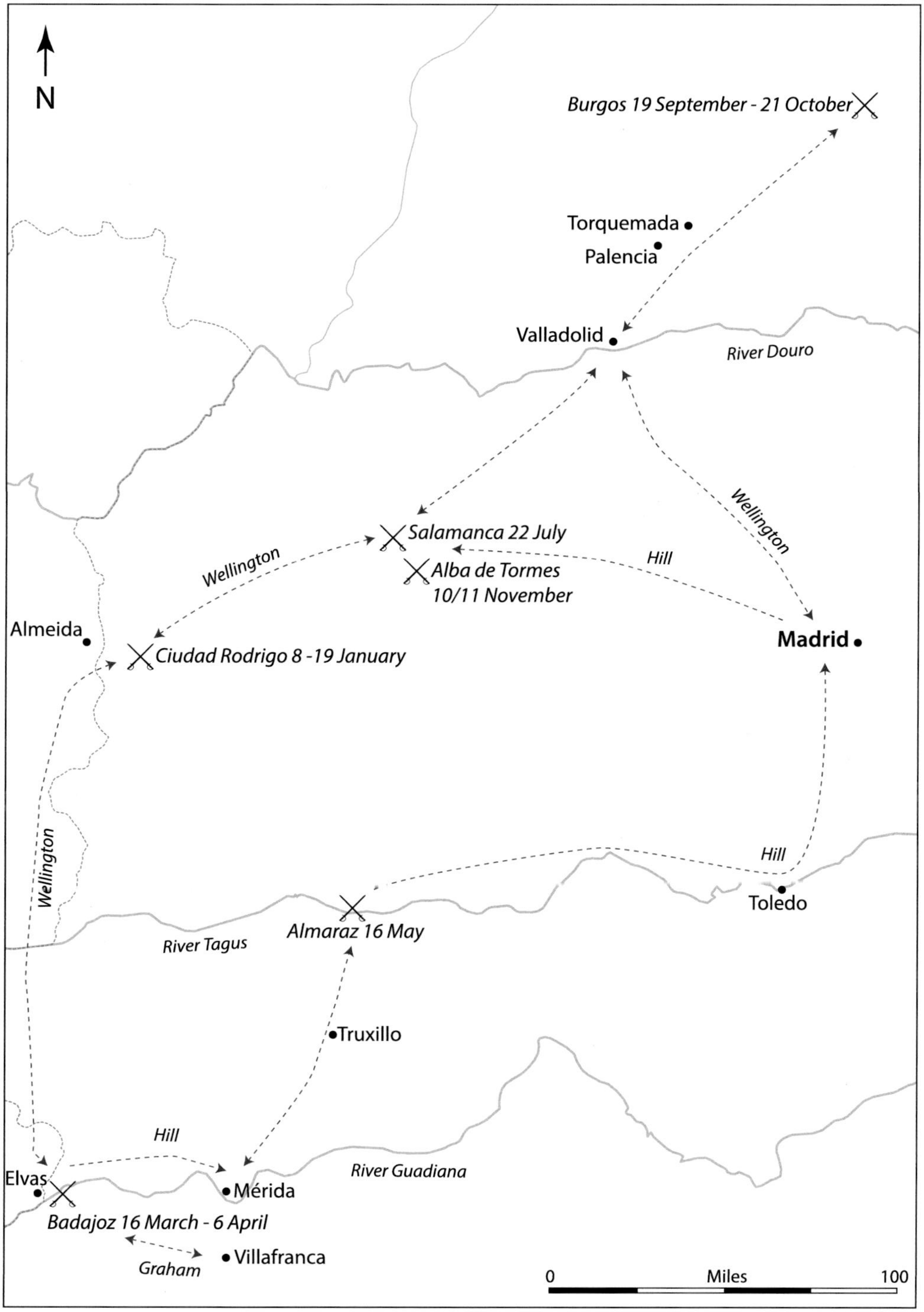

Fortresses, Advances & Retreats, January to November 1812.

Vincente then tried to surrender but would not agree to Wellington's terms, but when the 9th Caçadores attacked they too met little resistance.

The 5th Battalion had one man killed and two wounded during the period of the sieges.[3] Private Joseph Ruthmeyer (No. 1), who had joined with the May draft and came from Regensburg, was killed 23 June, presumably during the failed attempt to storm Fort San Cayetano.[4]

Whilst the sieges of the convents had been carried out the rest of Wellington's and Marmont's armies had manoeuvred in front of each other like two boxers waiting for the other to throw the first punch. Marmont advanced towards Salamanca to relieve the forts on 19 June and Wellington occupied a typically good defensive position on the heights of San Cristobal. The French approached on the 20th and there were some skirmishes and a determined French attack on a village held by the 68th Light Infantry. Marmont, outnumbered, was taking a large risk in coming so near the allied position and Wellington planned to fight the next morning, but instead of going down the slope to attack Marmont he hoped that Marmont would come to him. Marmont was persuaded not to attack by his subordinates, who all too well remembered previous occasions when the allied army had been attacked in strong positions. Wellington made some small opening moves hoping to provoke a major action but the French did not take the bait and fell back.

The manoeuvring continued over the next few days with Marmont skilfully marching his army across the River Tormes and back, waiting for Wellington to make a mistake. Wellington countered each move successfully. More skirmishing took place on 23 June but again a major battle was prevented by the French falling back when pressed. The capture of the convents removed the need for Marmont to attack Wellington before receiving reinforcements and he instead fell back to a defensive position across the River Douro, 40 miles north of Salamanca.

The two armies enjoyed a break from all the marches for two weeks as they faced each other across the river. For once food was plentiful, as was wine, and the soldiers mixed and bathed together in the waters. Wellington reconnoitred the various fords and crossing and on 3 July he ordered Lieutenant Colonel Williams with some of the 5th Battalion riflemen from the 3rd Division to ford the river at Pollos, but the river was too deep for the rest of the Division to cross.[5] The companies with the 3rd Division had two men taken prisoner on 4 July and one on the 5th.[6]

Marmont received some of his long-anticipated reinforcements on 7 July which brought the two armies up to almost equal numbers. Wellington was getting reports of more French troops on the way whilst waiting to hear if a planned attack on the Spanish east coast was going to go ahead using troops from Sicily. Marmont worried that either Spanish troops or Hill's 2nd Division might arrive to tip the balance back in Wellington's favour. Both generals were getting anxious that their chances to win a convincing victory were fading.

During the period of manoeuvring the 5th Battalion suffered ten desertions. One man deserted on 19 June, two on the 21st, seven on the 22nd and one on the 24th. Some, like

3 Rigaud, *Celer et Audax*, p.194.
4 July 1812 Casualty Return, TNA, WO 25/1923; June & September 1812 Pay Lists WO 12/7074.
5 Butler, *Annals*, Vol II, p.159 ; Le Marchant, *Memoirs of the Late Major General Le Marchant*, p.259.
6 September 1812 Pay List, TNA, WO 12/7074; July 1812 Casualty Return, WO 25/1923.

Private Anton Valenton, had arrived with the battalion recently, but others had much longer service, such as Sergeant John Raab. Valenton was retaken but then deserted again in August. Raab had been with the battalion since 1802. Most of the men who ran were serving with No. 2 company in the 3rd Division.[7]

There was also some discontent amongst the officers of Wellington's army, with many frustrated that Wellington had not been bolder. Major Galiffe wrote to a friend on 13 July:

> I have been wanting to write to you for a long time now, but Lord W does not spare us an instant. We have marched all over Portugal at least two or three times and then, after the capture of Badajoz, we had marched without stopping until we reached Salamanca, which my Division took with the loss of some officers because we saw it fit to assault its walls without so much as inspecting its forts first, which were much better fortified than we had thought. The following day, we marched with the rest of the army to follow the French and we have been going back and forth from Toro to Medina, all the while threatening to cross the Douro at this point or at that point that Marmont just does not know where to focus his attention. Our army is about 35,000 men strong excluding Silveria and his 5,000 Portuguese at Zamora, of which 1,300 are cavalry, and Abaila with 7,000 Spaniards from Castanos' Army, actually at Astorga having come up from Zamora and the former having been besieged by the rest of that army's 27,000 men. Caffarelly's Division joined up with Soult yesterday and Joseph himself arrived a few days ago with 5,000 men. We believe that Marmont might now have between 45 and 50,000 men. However, he is forced to remain on the defensive and has abandoned provinces where the local population have armed themselves to cause him mischief on his retreat. In this province alone, we have been able to raise 30,000 men all of whom are former soldiers from the Duke del Parque's old army. I fear that we actually do not have sufficient weapons to arm all of them. Soult is looking at beating Sir Rowland Hill, who remains close to Badajoz, and it is said that he had beaten him yesterday (something I do not personally believe) but is it so, the Army of Andalusia will be destroyed and Suchet will be forced to retreat to Navarre. It is also rumoured that 10,000 British, having come over from Sicily, will land in Catalonia.
>
> That is where we actually find ourselves, so you can see how busy we have been lately and why it has taken me so long to write to you.[8]

On 10 July the French began to repair a bridge across the Douro at Toro and Marmont moved his troops towards the crossing. On 16 July two divisions crossed the bridge. Wellington heard of the move that evening and issued orders for his divisions to march to a position to intercept the French. However, during the night the French turned around, crossed back over the river, blowing up the bridge behind them, and crossed the river well to the east. By the 17th the French were across and Wellington's 4th and Light Divisions were isolated and threatened.

7 June 1812 Pay List, TNA, WO 12/7074.
8 Galiffe to Sir Francis D'Ivernois, 13 July 1812, BG, ms fr 2752d pl61 f0001-2 (translated).

Wellington had to secure the safe withdrawal of the two divisions and moved the 5th Division to cover their southern flank. Allied cavalry patrols had started skirmishing with the French early in the morning and both sides brought up artillery and commenced firing. Wellington and his staff had to defend themselves from a French cavalry charge. The allied troops began a slow withdrawal, constantly pressured by the French with men who straggled from heat exhaustion having to be left behind. The light companies of the 4th Division, including No. 10 company, and the divisional artillery screened the division when the French moved a battery to fire on the column. The divisions reached the Guarena River safely though, and Wellington's army was united again in a reasonable defensive position. Marmont halted for the day but one of his subordinates, *Général de Division* Clausel, crossed the Guarena with two divisions.

The French were met first by allied cavalry and then by Anson's Brigade of the 4th Division, which included No. 10 company, supported by two Portuguese regiments. The allied troops bayonet-charged the approaching French and succeeded in driving them back. Allied casualties on 18 July were 542.[9] The 5th Battalion had one man wounded and two went missing, but these men probably returned quickly as they are not listed in the battalion's casualty return.[10]

On 19 July, after letting his men rest for most of the day, Marmont marched his army southwards towards Salamanca across open plains, along the line of the Guarena. Wellington's army kept pace with the French and the parallel marches of nearly 80,000 men continued on the 20th. The armies drew closer together until they were barely a mile apart. Both marched ready for battle. All that needed to be done was for one army to turn towards the other, but neither did. The allied army halted near the heights of San Cristobal. The French marched on and secured a crossing over the Tormes, which threatened Wellington's southern flank.

The 5th Battalion had seven men taken prisoner on 20 July, mostly from companies with the 3rd Division who marched as the reserve further from the French. Six are listed as 'missing on the road' implying they fell behind and were taken by the French. Two more men are listed as deserting.[11]

On 21 July the bulk of the French army crossed the Tormes, and Wellington followed leaving the 3rd Division and some cavalry at San Cristobal to protect Salamanca from the one French division still north of the river. As night fell a heavy thunderstorm drenched the troops, but despite the soaking their spirits remained high. Many on the allied side were still frustrated that they had not engaged the French and hoped the next day would see battle joined.

The brigading of Wellington's infantry, and the distribution of the companies of the 5th battalion, on 21 July was as follows.

1st Division – Major General H. Campbell
Colonel Fermor
    1/Coldstream Guards, 1/3rd Guards, & No. 5 company 5/60th.
Major General Wheatley
    2/24th, 1/42nd, 2/58th, 1/79th, & No. 9 company 5/60th.

9 Muir, *Salamanca*, p.15.

10 Rigaud, *Celer et Audax*, p.195; July 1812 Casualty Return, TNA, WO 25/1923.

11 September 1812 Pay List, TNA, WO 12/7074; July 1812 Casualty Return WO 25/1923.

Major General Löwe
    1st KGL, 2nd KGL, & 5th KGL.

3rd Division – Major General Pakenham
Lieutenant Colonel Wallace
    1/45th, 74th, & 1/88th & Nos. 2, 3, & 7 companies 5/60th, with Lt. Col. Williams.
Lieutenant Colonel J. Campbell
    1/5th, 2/5th, 2/83rd, & 94th.
Coronel Power (Portuguese)
    9th (2 battalions), 21st (2 battalions) & 12th Caçadores.

4th Division – Major General Cole
Major General Anson
    3/27th, 1/40th, & No. 10 company 5/60th.
Lieutenant Colonel Ellis
    1/7th, 1/23rd, 1/48th & 1 Company Brunswick Oels.
Coronel Stubbs (Portuguese)
    11th (2 battalions), 23rd (2 battalions) & 7th Caçadores.

5th Division – Lieutenant General Leith
Lieutenant Colonel Greville
    3/1st, 1/9th & 1/38th, 2/38th & 1 company Brunswick Oels.
Major General Pringle
    1/4th, 2/4th, 2/30th, 2/44th, & 1 company Brunswick Oels.
Brigadeiro Spry (Portuguese)
    3rd (2 battalions), 15th (2 battalions) & 8th Caçadores.

6th Division – Major General Clinton
Major General Hulse
    1/11th, 2/53rd & 1/61st, & No. 1 company 5/60th.
Colonel Hinde
    2nd, 1/32nd & 1/36th.
Brigadeiro Rezende (Portuguese)
    8th (2 battalions) & 12th (2 battalions) & 9th Caçadores.

7th Division – Major General J. Hope
Colonel Halkett
    1st KGL Light, 2nd KGL Light, & 9 companies Brunswick Oels.
Major General De Bernewitz
    51st, 68th, & Chasseurs Britanniques.
Coronel Collins (Portuguese)
    7th (2 battalions), 19th (2 battalions) & 2nd Caçadores.

Light Division – Major General Alten
Lieutenant Colonel Barnard

1/43rd, detachments 2/95th & 3/95th, & 1st Caçadores.
Major General Vandeleur
1/52nd, 1/95th (8 coys) & 3rd Caçadores.

Independent Portuguese Brigades
Brigadeiro Pack
1st (2 battalions), 16th (2 battalions) & 4th Caçadores.
Brigadeiro Bradford
13th (2 battalions), 24th (2 battalions) & 5th Caçadores.

Spanish Division – *Mariscal de Campo* de España
2nd Princesa, Tiradores de Castilla, 2nd Jaen & 3/1st Seville.[12]

The storm had gone by morning and 22 July dawned bright and clear. The allied army had been under arms an hour before first light, as was normal in the presence of the enemy, but they were soon dismissed to their duties. Marmont planned to continue to manoeuvre, forcing Wellington to retreat and abandon Salamanca. Wellington was reluctantly resigned to falling back and gave orders for the baggage to begin the move to Ciudad Rodrigo. The bulk of each army was hidden from the other by the undulating landscape.[13]

Général de Division Foy sent patrols from his division to learn where the allied army was positioned. French *voltigeurs* probed forward to the Calvarrasa de Arriba ridge and soon met the pickets of the Brunswick Oels Light Infantry from the 7th Division. A skirmish started and both sides sent additional units. The fighting spread sporadically along the line of a stream to include elements of the KGL. The skirmishing lasted into the afternoon but, whilst protracted, the fighting was not fierce.

The landscape to the south of Salamanca was largely open and gently rolling. Two rocky hills rose above the surrounding ground. The Lesser Arapile, a small but significant hill, was occupied by Anson's Brigade of the 4th Division. Wellington rode there as Marmont moved his army south and when he arrived he realised that the Greater Arapile, a larger ridge several hundred yards long with steep sides and rocky outcrops, overlooked Anson's position. Both sides quickly sent troops to occupy the Greater Arapile but *Général de Division* Bonnet's men were there first. Marmont began to shift his army behind the ridge whilst Wellington drew his divisions together around the Lesser Arapile. Wellington ordered the 1st Division forward to the village of Los Arapiles with the aim of attacking the French on the Greater Arapile, but then aborted the plan and withdrew the division. The light companies of the Fermor's Guards Brigade, with No. 5 company, were left behind to support the light companies of the Fusilier Brigade of the 4th Division, along with their rifle company of the Brunswick Oels, and hold the village.

The French forces began to pivot around their position on the Greater Arapile to cut off the allies' line of retreat. Marmont wanted to force Wellington to withdraw, and to perhaps attack the allied rearguard. He did not want a full-scale battle. He was looking for a small

12 Muir, *Salamanca*, Appendix II; June 1812 Return, TNA WO 17/180.

13 The following details of the battle are taken from Muir, *Salamanca*, pp.47-207, Oman, *Peninsular War*, Vol.I, pp.418-468, & Butler, *Annals*, pp.160-4.

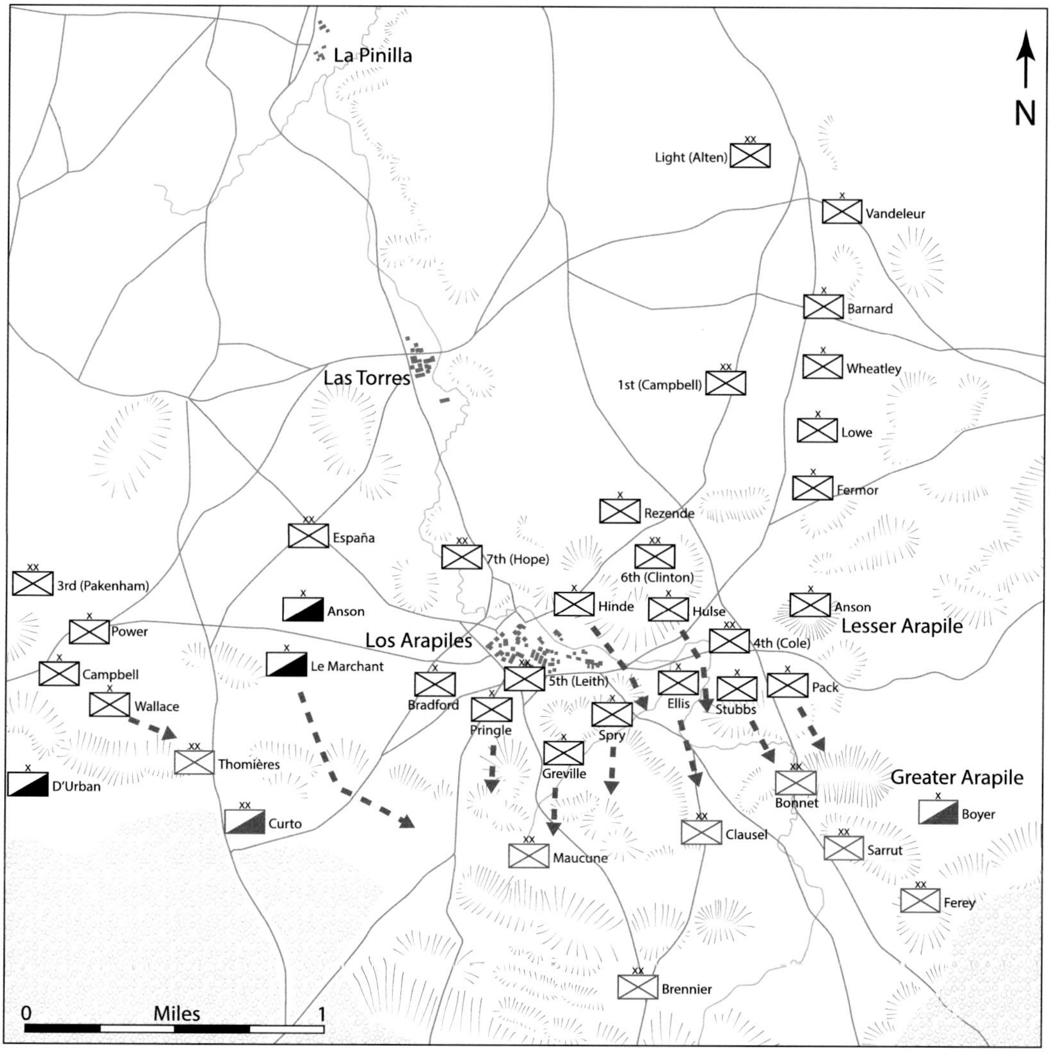

The Battle of Salamanca, 22 July 1812.
Sources: Lipscombe, *Atlas* & Wyld, *Maps & Plans*.

victory with little risk. Wellington was still intending to fall back, but was also looking for an opportunity to attack, if the French gave him an opening.

A company of French *voltigeurs,* from *Général de Division* Maucune's division, approached the allied light troops deployed in extended order in front of the village of Los Arapiles. The skirmishers opened fire and the French brought forward reinforcements and artillery, pressing the light companies back into the village. British guns opened fire, stopping the French advance. The light companies charged out of the village and drove the French off. The French renewed the attack with more troops, once more advancing to the village before allied reinforcements arrived to hold it. The fighting dissolved into skirmishing again until the French abandoned the attack. No. 5 company had two men taken prisoner on the 22nd.[14]

Wellington thought that the attack on the village might have been the start of a general attack and brought up the 5th Division to Los Arapiles, which allowed the 4th Division to shorten its line. The 6th and 7th Divisions moved behind the 4th and 5th Divisions respectively to act as reserves. French guns started a prolonged and heavy bombardment of the allied positions. Two French divisions, *Général de Brigade* Thomière's and Clausel's, emerged from wooded ground behind the Greater Arapile and began to move west. A gap opened up between Thomière's and Maucune's divisions as the former kept on moving west. The French line had become dangerously extended and perilously thin. Wellington took his chance.

The Light Division was ordered to hold the left flank, and the 1st remained in reserve. The 4th and 5th Divisions, with Pack's Portuguese Brigade, were to assault Maucune's, Clausel's and Bonnet's divisions in the main portion of the French line stretching from the Greater Arapile westwards. The 6th and 7th Divisions were to provide support for this attack. Wellington then rode to the 3rd Division, which had crossed the Tormes River that morning and expected to be used as a rearguard for the retreat. The troops were in the process of cooking a meal when Wellington arrived and ordered the divisional commander, his brother-in-law Edward Pakenham, to advance from his position at Aldea Tejada and turn the French left flank. Wellington deployed cavalry and other units to support 3rd Division's move. It was now 4:00 p.m. At about this time Marmont was seriously wounded and Bonnet assumed command until Clausel, the senior *général de division,* could be located. A little later Bonnet was himself wounded and Clausel took over. For a crucial period of the battle the French leadership was in a state of flux.

The 3rd Division advanced in three brigade columns, with the light companies, the 12th Caçadores, and the three companies of the 5th Battalion, led by Williams, on the left flank.[15] The division marched along the line of a small country road, out of sight of the French. The columns turned and climbed a slope, appearing before the leading French battalion. The allied division outnumbered the French considerably. Thomières was surprised by the appearance of the 3rd Division so close to his column but rapidly redeployed his battalions and opened fire with his artillery. The 3rd Division's artillery replied. The heat of the day had dried the ground after the rains of the night before, so any movement of troops raised large clouds of dust. Combined with the powder smoke this made the battleground a confused and almost claustrophobic place to be with the men of each unit unable to see much beyond their immediate surroundings. Portuguese cavalry charged one of the French battalions just prior to the 3rd Division's attack, adding to the confusion in the French ranks.

French skirmishers advanced down the hill and engaged their allied opponents. Wallace's Brigade (that formerly commanded by Mackinnon) was in the lead and advanced steadily up the hill. As they neared the crest of the hill French cavalry charged the brigade's right flank, one officer recalled:

14 September 1812 Pay List, TNA, WO 12/7074; July 1812 Casualty Return, WO 25/1923.

15 Campbell, *A British Army*, pp.223-8.

> The ridge of heights up which we were about to advance, was of considerable altitude, yet not steep, and we proceeded without obstacle or obstruction, till within about 50 yards of the summit, when a body of German riflemen, belonging to a battalion of the 60th, who had been advanced to the front, and had already crowned the height, came running back at full speed, exclaiming, 'Der Deivel, dere are de French horse coming!'.[16]

The 45th wheeled three companies to meet the charge and fired on the French cavalry, who went on to inflict heavy casualties on the 5th Foot in the following brigade before retreating after a counter-charge by allied heavy cavalry.

When Wallace's Brigade reached the top it was met by the bulk of Thomières' division, who marched forward and fired a volley. Wallace's line, which stretched in a crescent onto the flanks of the French, staggered but did not break and continued upwards to close with the enemy. The French fired a second, more sporadic volley. When the redcoats cheered and charged the French infantry broke. Thomières was killed and his division decimated. The allied light troops and artillery advanced with the cavalry to ensure the pressure was kept up on the retreating French. Lieutenant Colonel Williams was once again wounded.

By the middle of the afternoon the 5th Division was drawn up in two lines near Los Arapiles, with the light companies, 9th Caçadores, and two companies of Brunswickers deployed in a skirmish line to the front. They had been taking casualties from the French bombardment but had to wait for the 3rd Division's attack to begin before marching forward to engage Maucune's division. The skirmishers pushed their French counterparts back as the division crossed the valley and headed steadily up the far slope. As the line of redcoats neared the French, the 5th Division light troops cleared to the flanks mingling with the 3rd Division light troops as they continued to press forward. The leading brigade of the 5th Division closed with the enemy, fired a volley, cheered, and then charged. The French battalions did not stand. Already disrupted by a cavalry charge on their flank their formations began to disintegrate as men turned to run to the rear. The same British heavy cavalry that had charged in support of the 3rd Division against Thomières' division now added to the destruction of Maucune's. Two French eagles were captured in this portion of the battle.

The French left flank may have collapsed but the fighting in the centre was harder and less successful for the allies. Cole's 4th Division and Pack's Portuguese Brigade were supported by the 6th Division, with the 1st in reserve. Anson's Brigade was still posted on the Lesser Arapile and so Cole only had one British and one Portuguese brigade available for his attack on the French centre. Pack's Portuguese Brigade was to attempt to assault the Greater Arapile and advanced on the left of the 4th Division, but they failed to make any progress and fell back with heavy casualties, leaving the flank of the 4th Division unprotected.

The two brigades of the 4th Division advanced across a valley towards the French. When they reached the top of the hill the French were waiting for them and the two lines exchanged volleys. Cole was badly wounded and both sides were shaken, but it was the French that fell back. However, they did so in good order. Another brigade of the French was waiting nearby

16 Spencer Moggridge, 'Letters from the Peninsula', in *Blackwood's Edinburgh Magazine*, May 1828, p.546 However, Moggridge was a *nom de plume* for Captain Thomas Hamilton who was not at Salamanca but who was writing a history of the Peninsular campaign. See, Muir, *Salamanca*, p.81.

The Battle of Salamanca, July 22, 1812 by J.A. Atkinson. (Anne S.K. Brown Military Collection)

and counter-attacked. The allied troops fired loose volleys but the French kept coming and the British and Portuguese battalions broke, running back down the hill.

French cavalry charged into the flank of the broken 4th Division, who hastily formed squares or retired to the protection of the 6th Division advancing to their aid. The 6th Division was marching in two lines of battalion columns. Hinde's Brigade was on the right, Hulse's on the left with Rezende's Portuguese Brigade behind them. Major Galiffe, with No. 1 company, was with or near the 2/53rd on the far left of the division, a little apart from the rest of Hulse's Brigade. The 2/53rd was very understrength and it is possible the rifle company had been assigned to it to bolster its numbers, or simply that they were covering that flank of the brigade. The French dragoons which had harassed the 4th Division slammed into the isolated battalion and cut it to pieces. Major Galiffe was severely wounded and three of his company taken prisoner.[17]

French infantry followed their cavalry but were beaten back by the rest of Hulse's Brigade and the 1/40th from Anson's Brigade, who had come forward. The fusiliers of the 4th Division had also recovered their cohesion and covered the left flank of the 6th Division. The French counter attack had been defeated. As the remains of the 4th and 6th Divisions advanced they pushed the French further back. *Général de Division* Ferey's division, which had not yet seen action, was deployed on a low ridge in front of wooded ground to delay the

17 September 1812 Pay List, WO 12/7074; July 1812 Casualty Return, WO 25/1923.

allied troops and allow time for their comrades to retreat. They made a spirited defence, firing volleys into the redcoats, with artillery on the flanks firing canister. The fusiliers and the 6th Division took more heavy losses as they closed with them and drove them off the ridge, but the French troops achieved their aim of giving the rest of their army time to withdraw. The Light Division, with the 1st in support, pursued the French as darkness fell but did not engage heavily as most of the French managed to escape into the woods and then across the Tormes River at Alba de Tormes, south-east of Salamanca.

In another letter to his friend, Sir Francis d'Ivernois, Major Galiffe gave an account of the battle. The letter was dated 25 July and Galiffe can be forgiven for getting the date of the battle wrong, given the severity of his wounds:

> I am rushed to tell you the good news: We engaged and beat the French on the 23rd instant. We had followed them almost to the other side of the Douro when Marmont, having assembled all that he could, chanced to attack us himself or rather to try and force us to accept a decisive battle. His plan was to manoeuvre so as to force us to cross the Tormes and abandon Salamanca, that he had promised to take back in a few days, which almost happened in a way as he narrowly escaped being taken back to the city as a prisoner.
>
> On the 22nd, the French crossed the Tormes which we then crossed ourselves during the night. On the morning of the 23rd, we took up a position near to the town whilst our cavalry skirmished with the enemy. Towards midday, Lord Wellington, having spotted that the French were extending themselves too much, decided to approach them to get a better look. The two armies remained in such a manner for almost two hours, until Lord Wellington spotted the French cavalry completely turning our right and cut us off the road to Ciudad Rodrigo, with their divisions so extended that they couldn't support each other. He then decided to launch General Leith's 5th Division in an attack, along with the 3rd and 4th, so as to knock out the enemy's left that had overtaken us, with the 6th in support.
>
> The French held on for a long time: the ground was favourable to them and their artillery vastly outnumbered ours. Despite this advantage, we pushed them back on all sides but since they wanted to concentrate their principal forces on this side, our division (the 6th) found itself not in the supporting role intended but in the front line. We chased the enemy off almost all the heights but, as we pushed on, their divisions became more and more concentrated in such a manner that the 4th and 6th eventually found themselves before a corps of more than 15,000 men and 3 batteries that raked us in the front and flank. We were forced, for the moment, to retire. Their cavalry chased the 53rd Regiment (which I was with) and since this battalion was very weak and unsupported, they charged us the moment that we had gained higher ground. The fight was short and, for an instant, cut the regiment in two but they were forced back, which cost us a lot of men. But the enemy's fire was so lively on this side that our ranks melted before our eyes. The French charged us again but this time, we completely threw them back and chased them from the heights into the plain, without giving them the opportunity to reform and the battle was won with the loss of 3,000 men on our side, but the French lost 8,000 dead, wounded and prisoners. Lord Wellington pursued them the next day,

> harassing them relentlessly and having separated three of their divisions from the main body, sent in the German cavalry. The Germans attacked them on heights that were so steep that it was said that only infantry could hope to climb them, but nothing could stop them. The cavalry charged through their divisions three times, killing nearly 2,000 men and making 1,500 prisoners. Over these two days, we had taken 25 artillery guns. At every moment, we were bringing back prisoners in bands of 500 and we have calculated that Marmont's army has been reduced to half its strength. Furthermore, they no longer have any order, discipline or fight left and flee as fast as they can, casting aside their arms and wishing to be captured by the English. Their officers only manage to keep them in their ranks by telling them that we have promised the Spaniards to hand all our prisoners to them. I was not able to follow Lord Wellington in these victories because, during the French cavalry charge I have previously spoken about, I was wounded by three sabre cuts to the head and two sabre thrusts to the chest.
>
> Roverea says that without my 'Swiss head', I would have been killed but thanks to my thick skull, I am doing much better and I have even dined with General Cole today, who was also badly wounded, but not dangerously.
>
> Regarding our generals, we had General Le Marchand killed, Marshal Beresford, as well as Lt-Generals Sir Stapleton Cotton, Leith and Cole, have all been wounded. My brigade, which started out with 1,100 men, now only has 150 fit for service and the 11th, 53rd and 61st, with the company from the 60th, can only form a small battalion. The 4th division has likewise suffered badly. It is these two divisions that have bore the brunt of losses, followed by the 3rd and the 5th, but such a victory would never have been possible without losses.
>
> This victory is as complete as can be possible and its consequences will be felt throughout Spain. Soult and Suchet will be forced to abandon Cadiz and Valencia in order to fall back on Madrid, but we will receive General Hill, the army at Cadiz, and Ballasteros' as reinforcements, and 10,000 men that await in Sicily and that will land in Catalonia.
>
> My head, whilst being Swiss, can no longer think of what to write. Therefore, I will stop and ask that you give me some of your news.
>
> It is said that Marmont has died from the wounds he has sustained during the battle. Bonnet and Clausel, as well as another general, were also severely wounded.[18]

Marmont did not die but French losses were heavy, amounting to around 12,500.[19] The allies lost 694 killed, 4,270 wounded, and 256 missing.[20] Salamanca was one of Wellington's finest victories. He had started the day resigned to ignominious retreat, but nonetheless positioned his forces well enough that they could exploit any mistake made by the French. When an opportunity arose he boldly and expertly took it. The French had long known that Wellington's army could stand and fight if attacked. They now knew that they were as

18 Galiffe to Sir Francis D'Ivernois, 25 July 1812, BG, ms fr 2752d pl61 f0003-6, (translated). Roverea probably refers to Captain Alexendre de Roverea, Cole's ADC, and a fellow Swiss emigre.

19 Muir, *Salamanca*, p.208.

20 Muir, *Salamanca*, p.209.

formidable in offence as they were in defence. The confidence of the French commanders and troops was shaken. The confidence of Wellington's own troops, and those of his allies, was boosted.

The official return of casualties made the day after the battle lists the recently promoted Ensign Lerche as being amongst the wounded, as well as Lieutenant Colonel Williams and Major Galiffe. It also states that the 5th Battalion lost six men killed in action, and that one sergeant and 23 rank and file were wounded. Three rank and file were also returned as missing.[21] However, the regimental return made on 25 July lists only three dead in the entire month from 25 June: one was killed in action on 23 June and was not included in the June return; one died in the general hospital at Coimbra on 3 July; only one rank and file is listed as being killed in action on 22 July at Salamanca.[22]

The battalion's casualty return from 25 June to 24 July confuses things still further by not listing anyone killed in action on 22 July, but Corporal Joseph Reith (No. 7) is listed as dying from his wounds on 23 July. Six men are listed as being taken prisoner on the 22nd.[23] The pay list, completed much later in September, confirms Reith's death from wounds and also has no one listed as being killed in action on 22 July. Five men are listed as being taken prisoner on the day of the battle.[24] It would seem likely that the one man listed as being killed in action on the regimental return was Reith, and that the six men listed as being killed on the post-battle casualty return were subsequently found to have been taken prisoner, wounded, or simply turned up a day or so after the battle.

The 5th Battalion's casualties were light compared to some of the line battalions, for example the three battalions in Hulse's Brigade, which had the heaviest losses, suffered casualty rates of 66 percent, 42 percent and 67 percent .[25] Only five of the seven companies of the 5th Battalion present appeared to have been significantly engaged during the day. If the after-battle casualty return is incorrect, as seems to be the case, it is surprising that the battalion managed to avoid more than one fatality, but, by the nature of their role, light troops had more opportunities to take cover, or simply get out of the way of trouble, than the line infantry. The companies of the battalion were present at several key junctures of the battle and played their part in the action, but appear to have been very lucky not to have paid a higher price. It is likely that many of the wounded came from No. 1 company in Hulse's Brigade but no breakdown of the wounded has survived. The June return notes Ensign Lerche's promotion but does not list him as assigned to any one of the divisions and by the July return he is listed amongst the absent officers, but when he returned to duty in August he was assigned to No. 1 company and so it is possible that he was also with them at the battle. Major Galiffe returned to duty in November.[26]

Lieutenant Colonel Williams left the battalion on 27 July, never to return. Wounded in action six times he had exchanged into the 13th Foot, then stationed in the West Indies. Perhaps he was seeking a quieter posting and thinking his own luck could not last much

21 Casualty Return 23 July 1812, TNA, WO 1/255.

22 July 1812 Return, TNA, WO 17/180.

23 July 1812 Casualty Return, TNA, WO 25/1923.

24 September 1812 Pay List, TNA, WO 12/7074.

25 Muir, *Salamanca*, Appendix II.

26 November 1812 Return, TNA, WO 17/180.

Marching the French prisoners into Salamanca after the Battle of 1812, by J.H. Clark and M. Dubourg after Captain Wilmot, Royal Horse Artillery. (Anne S.K. Brown Military Collection)

longer. Unfortunately for him the United States had declared war on Britain a little over a month before he left the battalion and the 13th were sent to Quebec in 1813. Williams was present at two more battles and again distinguished himself. He was knighted in 1815 and died in 1832 with the rank of major general.[27] Brevet Lieutenant Colonel Fitzgerald took command of the battalion until the officer Williams had exchanged with, Brevet Colonel Keane, arrived from the 13th.

British and KGL cavalry caught up with the French rearguard at Garcia Hernandez on 23 July and inflicted a heavy defeat on them in one of the most successful cavalry charges of the war. The French continued to retreat in a series of long and gruelling marches, keeping ahead of their allied pursuers. On the 25th Wellington gave up the chase. His men were weary after weeks of manoeuvre and combat. The French marched on to Valladolid, and after allowing his men some rest Wellington followed. The French abandoned the town, but, rather than carrying on to pursue the broken remains of Marmont's army, Wellington left some cavalry to keep up the pressure, and placed the 6th Division to cover any move southwards, whilst he lead the rest of his army to Madrid.

King Joseph had marched with as many men as he could gather to go to Marmont's aid, but on hearing of the defeat at Salamanca he had hurriedly returned to Madrid. With the approach of the main allied army Joseph did not have enough men to mount a defence of his capital and so he made preparations to leave. French cavalry checked the allied advance guard on 11 August but Wellington and his men entered Madrid unopposed on the 12th.

27 Butler, *Annals*, Vol II, p.325.

They were greeted jubilantly by the Madrileños. Crowds began to line the roads five miles from the city. The troops marched with colours unfurled and their bands playing. The men were showered with gifts of flowers, fruit, bread, and wine. They were embraced and kissed. The city's church bells were rung and so many people thronged onto the streets it was difficult for the battalions to make progress. Three days of intensive celebrations started.

Not all the troops could join the party though. A French garrison of over 2,000 had been left at some makeshift fortifications in the centre of Madrid but after a barely opposed initial assault on 13 August they surrendered on the 14th.[28] Wellington and his men had taken the Spanish capital for very little loss, and only had to suffer the effusive attentions of a grateful populace. The officers attended rounds of dances and soirées, the men relished the local wines and the local women. The troops were well fed, and well housed in barracks and other large buildings in Madrid, and at Escorial nearby.

The August and September returns for the 5th Battalion were completed at Madrid. The August strength was 54 sergeants, 13 buglers, and 687 rank and file. Seven men returned to the battalion after being prisoners of war over the two months. The rigours of eight months of almost constant campaigning were evident from the large numbers of men sick. A total of 154 sergeants, buglers, and rank and file were sick in August, over 20 percent of the battalion's strength. Assistant Surgeon Berger was still at Salamanca tending to the wounded from the battle.[29]

Lieutenant General Hill, with the 2nd Division including three companies of the 5th Battalion, had spent the summer keeping Soult occupied in the provinces of Estremadura and Andalusia. In early August the long awaited expedition from Sicily landed at Alicante, tying down more French troops. Soult was forced to undertake a withdrawal to eastern Spain, which allowed Hill to move north to Madrid. This in turn allowed Wellington to turn his attention northwards again. French dispatches were frequently intercepted and deciphered. Wellington often knew more about the situation of the various French armies than the other French commanders did. King Joseph had been made commander-in-chief but his orders were often ignored or openly disobeyed by Soult and others. This continued lack of co-ordination helped the allied cause enormously.

Wellington left the 3rd, 4th, and Light Divisions in and around Madrid and on 1 September the 1st, 5th, and 7th Divisions marched north through the Sierra de Guadarrama to link back up with the 6th Division and other forces around Valladolid. Wellington's four divisions, plus cavalry and Portuguese brigades, amounted to around 28,000 men.[30] Castaños's Spanish divisions were also expected to join the allied forces. Wellington's objective was the strategically important town of Burgos, which sat astride a vital junction on the road to France and was an important army depot. Clausel still commanded the battered army that had been defeated at Salamanca and could field around 25,000 men.[31]

News reached the army that Wellington had been granted the title of marquis on 4 September, the same day that he and his troops reached Valladolid. The French had already withdrawn and marched north. Over the next two weeks Wellington cautiously advanced

28 Oman, *Peninsular War*, Vol.V, pp 507-516.

29 August & September 1812 Returns, TNA, WO 17/180.

30 C. Divall, *Wellington's Worst Scrape* (Barnsley: Pen & Sword, 2012), p.25.

31 Oman, *Peninsular War*, Vol.VI, p.8.

and tried to bring the French to battle, but each time they slipped away. The weather for the march to Burgos began fair and clement. The troops were travelling through wine country and helped themselves to the ripening grapes. However, the autumn rains soon began and dampened the men's spirits. On 16 September the Spanish troops joined and on the 19th the allied troops arrived at Burgos. Clausel had withdrawn most of his troops on the 18th but he left behind a garrison of 2,000 men in the old castle that dominated the town and covered the bridges across the Arlanzon River.

The castle stood on a steep sided and rocky hill: parts of it dated back to the medieval period but its defences had been much improved by the French, with a battery being constructed in the keep. To the north of the keep, at a distance of around 275 yards, was the outwork of San Miguel. A deep ravine split the outwork from the keep. The old fortifications were surrounded by three lines of walls, ditches, and palisades. Each line would have to be breached in turn by the allies if the castle was to be taken.[32] In many ways Wellington repeated the same mistakes that he had made with the siege of the convents in Salamanca. He had again underestimated the strength of the position, had not brought his siege train north with him, and he assigned less experienced troops to the siege. The army was also suffering from a lack of engineers as so many had been killed or wounded at Ciudad Rodrigo and Badajoz.

The 1st Division and Pack's Portuguese Brigade were the troops chosen to carry out the siege, with the 6th Division and some Spanish troops holding the southern bank of the river. The rest of the forces were positioned to the northwest of the town to cover any attempt to relieve the castle. As the allied troops moved into position they drove back the advanced posts of the garrison in prolonged skirmishes. After reconnoitring the defences Wellington ordered an attack on the outwork that night.

The 300 men of 42nd Highlanders were to provide covering fire for 200 men of Pack's Brigade and a storming party, also from the 42nd, who would escalade the two demi-bastions. The light companies of Stirling's Brigade, including No. 9 company, were to mount a diversionary attack on the outwork from the rear.

It was a bright, moonlit night and the firing party from the 42nd came under fire as they approached, taking heavy casualties. The two storming parties both failed to gain entry, as they were thwarted by the staunch defence of the garrison. The 140 men of the light companies, led by Major Cocks of the 1/79th, also came under heavy fire as they approached. They made their way into the ravine between the keep and the outwork, then successfully cut through, or climbed over, the palisade. They converted their diversionary attack into an actual assault. Cocks led one party forward onto the parapets and left another guarding the exit. The attackers bayoneted, shot, or captured 198 of the garrison of 500 men. The remainder overwhelmed the guards at the gate and ran for the safety of the keep. The assaulting troops on the 19th suffered 421 casualties.[33]

No 9. company's share of the losses were one sergeant and three privates killed, plus one officer and seven men wounded. The fatalities were: Sergeant John Pohling, from Savoy, who had been with the battalion since 1799, when he joined from the Walloon Guards in Surinam;[34] Private Michael Kolodinsky, from Warsaw, who had joined in 1801; Francis Madolesky, a

32 Divall, *Worst Scrape*, p.39.

33 Divall, *Worst Scrape*, pp.41-43; Oman, *Peninsular War*, Vol VI, pp.27-8.

34 Pohling was formerly the translator for Brigadier General Cameron, see page 226.

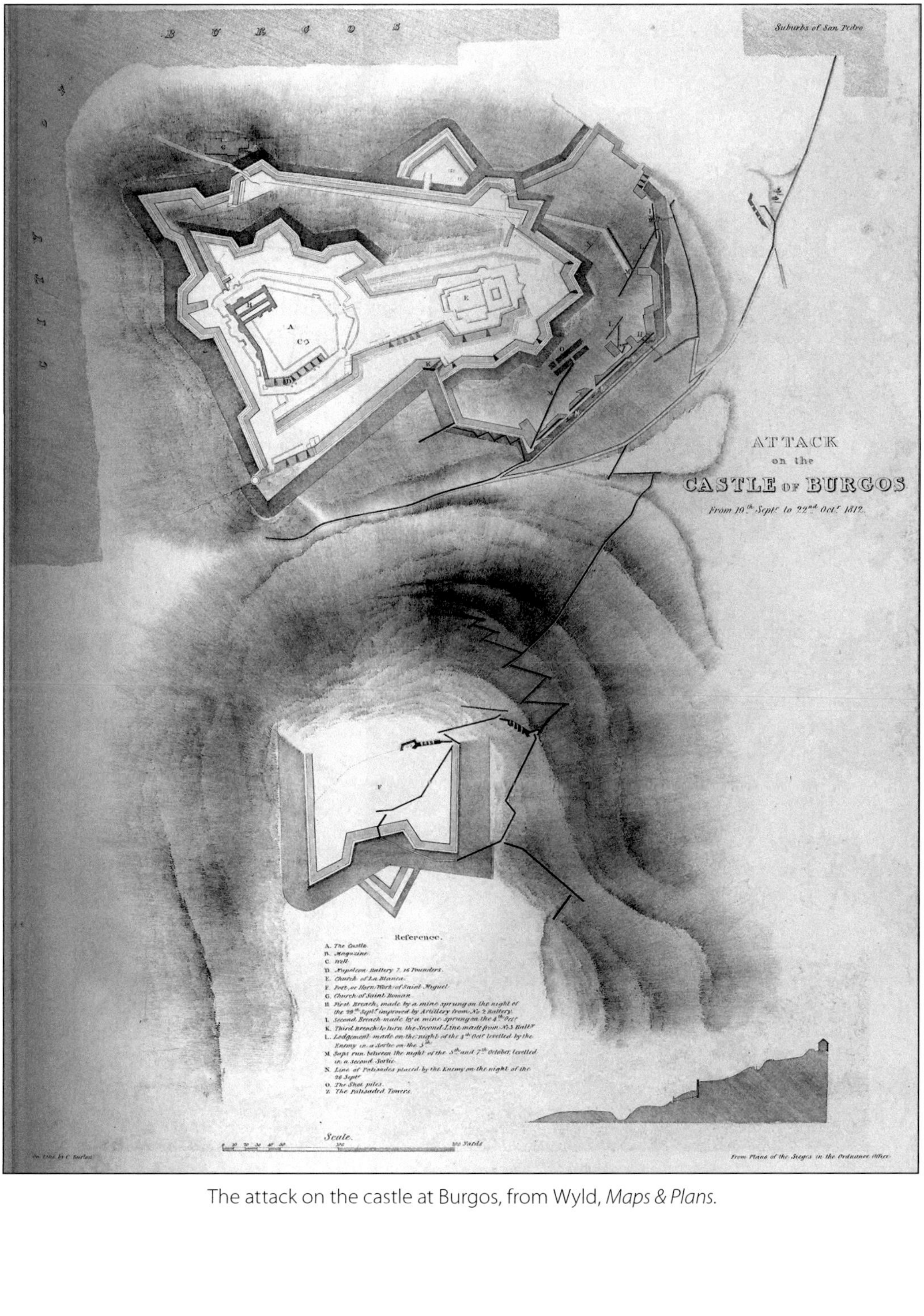

The attack on the castle at Burgos, from Wyld, *Maps & Plans*.

tailor from St. Petersburg, who had been one of the men who had briefly deserted during the winter of 1808 to 1809; Joseph Ruska who had been with the Hompesch Light Infantry in 1797 when it was incorporated into the 2/60th, and had transferred to the 5th Battalion in 1803. Lieutenant Sylvester O'Hehir, who was leading the company, was listed as severely wounded but does not seem to have been absent from his company for long as he was present on the next return.[35]

As soon as the outwork was taken the besiegers came under heavy fire from the battery in the keep. Over the next few days and nights trenches and batteries were dug, with the working parties continuing to take losses from French artillery and musket fire. On 22 September some of the guards protecting the working parties were placed in the trenches to provide suppressing fire. Given the 200-yard range these men were probably riflemen from No. 5 company, as on that day Private Joseph Mosar, from Hungary, of that company was killed in action. He had also joined from the Walloon Guards in Surinam.[36]

On the 21st the rains had returned, slowing progress further. The guns available were inadequate, ammunition became scarce and the defenders continued to put up a dogged and effective resistance. Wellington decided to try another escalade on the 23rd, this time on the outer ring of defences. A party of 400 men of the 1st Division were to make the main assault, whilst the 9th Caçadores would make a diversion on the opposite side of the defences. The caçadores were commanded by Lieutenant Colonel Gustavus Braun, formerly of the 5th and 6th Battalions of the 60th. The main assault was mismanaged and failed to gain a footing on the walls, and the diversionary attack was repulsed by the weight of fire from the defenders.

With the available guns not powerful enough to efficiently create breaches it was decided to attempt to drive a mine under the walls, and then explode a charge of powder to bring them down. The tools available were not suitable for mining and the men had little experience in digging underground so progress was slow. Work in the trenches and batteries continued to be harassed by enemy fire, and the rain carried on coming down in torrents that flooded the trenches and soaked the working parties. It is likely that the riflemen of the two companies with the 1st Division would have taken their turns in the working parties, amongst the guards, and amongst those providing suppressing fire. Sergeant Bartholomew Zawitsky (No. 1) with the 6th Division, from Bohemia and also another former Walloon Guard, was killed on the 26th, and one rifleman was wounded during this stage of the siege.[37]

On the night of 29/30 September the first mine was exploded and a small advance party found a practicable breach. However, the main storming party got lost and returned to report that there was no breach. Meanwhile the handful of men in the advance party had been driven off by the French, who had soon recovered from the surprise of the detonation. By this time two batteries were active, but were suffering from accurate counter-fire from

35 Rigaud, *Celer et Audax*, p.203; September 1812 Casualty Return, TNA, WO 25/1923; September 1812 Pay List, WO 12/7074; Periods of Service 5/60th, June 1806, WO 25/1008; March 1809 Pay List, WO 12/7066.

36 Jones, *Sieges*, Vol I, p.305; September 1812 casualty return TNA, WO 25/1923; Periods of Service 5/60th, June 1806, WO 25/1008.

37 Rigaud, *Celer et Audax*, p.203; October 1812 Casualty Return, TNA, WO 25/1923; Periods of Service 5/60th, June 1806, WO 25/1008.

the French and making little impression on the defences. A second mine was commenced. Morale amongst the allied troops was very low due the worsening weather and the continual arduous work under incessant enemy fire. They had also not been paid for months.

On 4 October the second mine was exploded and the breach stormed successfully, as was a smaller breach formed by the batteries. The first line of defences had been crossed, but two more remained. On the 5th the French made a sortie, taking back one of the breaches for a short time before being driven back, leaving 150 of the besiegers dead or wounded behind them.[38] The French then made another sortie on the 8th, again inflicting heavy casualties. The siege work trudged on for another ten days until on the 18th Wellington judged breaches in the second line practicable and an assault was attempted by elements of the Guards Brigade, KGL, and 9th Caçadores. After initially taking the breaches the attackers were driven back by the French with heavy loss. The Guards Brigade left the siege the next day and other troops followed until four days later the siege was raised. *Général de Brigade* Dubreton, the French commander, had conducted a masterful defence, whereas Wellington had begun the siege with little hope of success and uncharacteristically squandered the lives of his men in an operation that was inadequately resourced and poorly led.

During the later stages of the siege the 5th Battalion lost another three men killed in action: Privates Michael Bombeck (No. 9), from Flanders; Michael Kaminsky (No. 5), a Pole and yet another former Walloon Guard; and Joseph Lehman (No. 5) from Saxony. Five rank and file were wounded, and one man died of his wounds.[39] The total allied losses during the siege were 509 killed, 1,511 wounded, and 44 missing or prisoners.[40]

Wellington's decision to abandon the siege was made partly because of increased French activity to the north, but mostly because of developments in the south. Soult and Joseph had finally stopped bickering and had begun to advance on Hill's forces around Madrid, hoping to catch him in a pincer movement. On 25 October French cavalry fought a brief skirmish with Hill's cavalry screen at Ocaña. Hill withdrew across the Tagus and then moved closer to Madrid. On 27 October Howard's Brigade of the 2nd Division was at Fuentidueña de Tajo when a French cavalry patrol approached the river to discover the condition of the bridge. Captain Blassiere's No. 8 company lined the banks of the river and engaged the horsemen. The range was too long for many of the shots to hit their target but the sustained rifle fire dissuaded the French from coming any closer and they withdrew.[41]

Wellington had ordered Hill to fall back rather than risk being cut-off by the French. The divisions in and around Madrid were brought forward but by the end of October Hill had withdrawn his forces north of the Sierra de Guadarrama and was close to uniting with the rest of the allied army.

The French in the north had received reinforcements and a new commander, *Général de Division* Souham. With the numbers now in his favour he began to advance towards Burgos, coming into contact with the outposts of the 7th Division on 18 October. Wellington drew

38 Divall, *Worst Scrape*, p.59.

39 Rigaud, *Celer et Audax*, pp.203; October 1812 Casualty Return, TNA, WO 25/1923; December 1812 Pay List, WO 12/7074; Periods of Service 5/60th, June 1806, WO 25/1008. There is also one other possible private killed in action, Jacob Kerspe, but the records are contradictory and he may have died of wounds in August.

40 Oman, *Peninsular*, Vol VI, p.49.

41 J. Hope, *The Military Memoirs of an Infantry Officer 1809-1816* (Edinburgh: Anderson & Bryce, 1833), p.194.

up his covering force ready to give battle but Souham knew that events in the south would force the allies to withdraw and so merely probed the allied positions. Two French divisions, plus cavalry, advanced to Quintana where the Chasseurs Britanniques made a gallant stand, and the attacking divisions were almost caught in the flank by the 1st and 5th Divisions.

The allied withdrawal began on 21 October. The divisions of the covering force quietly marched southwards, leaving their camp fires burning to deceive the French. The remaining troops covering the castle at Burgos were also withdrawn. The army, split into two columns, headed back to Valladolid. The allies managed to steal a march on the enemy but the French cavalry of their advance guard was soon in contact with the allied rear guard cavalry and a long series of skirmishes began. To keep ahead of the French Wellington's men had to march for many hours each day, sometimes covering over 25 miles. The speed of the march was not helped by the men of the 1st and 6th Divisions breaking into the wine vaults of Torquemada on the 23rd and the majority of them drinking themselves insensible, with some actually drowning in the wine.[42]

Fortunately the French commanders had the same problem keeping their troops away from the wine vaults whilst the hungover 1st and 6th Divisions carried on marching south. It is perhaps not coincidental that the 24th saw the first men of the 5th Battalion taken prisoner by the French. Nine men are marked on the pay list as being captured that day, all from the companies with the 1st and 6th Divisions. It is possible that they had not sobered up enough to begin the march or, suffering the after effects, straggled and were taken up by the French.[43]

By the 25th Wellington had drawn up all his divisions on the River Carrion around Palencia and had ordered all the bridges in the area to be prepared for demolition. However, the French captured the bridge at Palencia intact, and other French forces forded the river and had to be driven back by the 5th Division. The allies were forced to continue the retreat to Valladolid. Here Wellington again arranged his divisions on the far side of a river, this time the Pisuerga, a tributary of the nearby Douro, with the 7th Division holding Valladolid. French pressure forced a withdrawal across the Douro on the 29th. All but one of bridges over the Pisuerga and Douro been destroyed and so, for a few days, there was a pause while the French repaired them and Souham considered his next move. Wellington had positioned his troops on a fortified line near the one intact bridge at Tordesillas, ready to fight if needed. However, events in northern Spain drew off 10,000 of Souham's men and he no longer had such an advantage in numbers that he could threaten the allied army in front of him.[44]

While Wellington had been retreating south, Hill had abandoned Madrid and was withdrawing north. The two armies were, by the end of October, within a few days march of one another. Hill's march had been a hard one though, with rain falling for days on end. Many men straggled and were taken by the French, whilst some chose to desert. Seven companies of the 5th Battalion were with Hill and in the first ten days of November 18 men were taken prisoner, many being listed as 'missing on the road' at first, and 12 men deserted.[45]

42 Divall, *Worst Scrape*, p.107.

43 December 1812 Pay List, TNA, WO 12/7074.

44 Oman, *Peninsular War*, Vol VI, pp.85-6.

45 December 1812 Pay List, TNA, WO 12/7074; November 1812 Casualty Return, WO 25/1923.

Soult's cavalry had begun to harass Hill's rearguard on 4 November but Joseph had left the pursuit to reclaim his capital. However, as the junction of Wellington and Hill's forces became more likely Soult's army would have been outnumbered, and so Joseph was forced to leave Madrid to reinforce him. Madrid was promptly re-liberated by Spanish guerrillas. Hill's troops – tired, wet, and hungry – reached the town of Alba de Tormes on 7 October. By the next day most of his men were across the river. Howard's Brigade of the 2nd Division, including No. 8 company, were left holding a small bridgehead in the town on the far bank, and the bridge was prepared for demolition. Hamilton's Portuguese Division remained on the other side of the river as a reserve and a small Spanish garrison held the castle. The 3rd, 4th and Light Divisions marched to join Wellington.

By this time Wellington was back at Salamanca. He had been uncertain of the strength Souham still fielded and unsure of the security of his own position on the Douro. So, he opted for the stronger defensive positions he knew so well from the summer. Souham did not pursue Wellington but the French did not need to act to thin the allied ranks as the long months of campaigning and cold wet weather were already causing a rapid increase of the sick lists. The French needed time to unite their three separate armies and bring up their baggage and so there was another brief pause.

On 10 November Soult was ready to test Wellington's resolve to hold his position. The allied cavalry screen around Alba de Tormes had already been driven in and by mid-afternoon French artillery had been sited on the hills overlooking the town and started to bombard Howard's Brigade. Twelve companies of voltigeurs formed up into columns and went forward. Shells and shot from the French guns smashed into the town while the defenders manned the town's walls and barricaded the streets. The voltigeurs attacked three times and were beaten back each time. As night fell two Portuguese battalions reinforced the defenders. At daybreak the attacks and the bombardments started again until Soult gave up as neither the artillery, nor the voltigeurs, were making much impression on the defenders. The town was held, without further attack until the 14th when the garrison was outflanked and forced to blow up the bridge. Allied losses were 21 killed and 92 wounded. Those of No. 8 company were eight men wounded.[46]

The French forded the Tormes well south of Alba de Tormes on 14 November and on the 15th Wellington deployed his divisions along the Arapiles and the heights of Calvarisa de Arriba, where the battle had been fought in July. Wellington, cautious as ever, gave orders for the baggage to begin to move back towards Ciudad Rodrigo. The French advanced but did not attack as they were all too familiar with the strength of the allied position. By the middle of the afternoon Wellington decided that the risk of a flanking move by the French to cut off his line of retreat was too great and ordered a careful withdrawal. As the army marched the rain turned from a light drizzle to torrents, and the roads became quagmires.

The French let the allies go. The heavy rain limited the French commander's view, made movement difficult and would have caused problems for the muskets of the infantry. King Joseph occupied Salamanca with 40,000 men leaving Soult with 50,000 to harry Wellington's retreat.[47] There were three roads from Salamanca to Ciudad Rodrigo and the allied divisions

46 Divall, *Worst Scrape*, p.149; Riguad, *Celer et Audax*, p.205; Gurwood, *Wellington's Dispatches*, Vol IX, pp.558-9.
47 Oman, *Peninsular War*, Vol VI, p.141.

were formed into columns along each. Unfortunately the commissary sent the men's rations by an entirely different, more northerly, route. That night, when the weary troops bivouacked there was no food, no shelter, and the fires were hard to light in the pouring rain.

The march continued for four more days, as did the rain. The tracks were so narrow that the troops often had to march in single file. The terrain was mountainous and mostly forested, with few settlements. With no rations to speak of the men foraged in the woods. Herds of pigs were discovered, feeding on acorns. The men hunted the pigs, but also resorted to eating the acorns. Discipline collapsed and there was much plundering, straggling, and desertion. Many of the officers were suffering just as much as the men. Boots wore out, clothing became sodden, ague and dysentery took hold. Men were left to die on the side of the tracks. There were several skirmishes between the rearguards and the French but the pursuit was not pressed very hard. Conditions for the pursuing French were no better and Soult ordered his infantry to halt on the 17th and the cavalry soon after. The weather turned colder, with heavy frosts in the morning but by the 19th the ragged allied army reached the Agueda River near Ciudad Rodrigo, where rations awaited them. The troops went gratefully into their winter quarters. Wellington, meanwhile, wrote a stinging rebuke to his divisional and brigade commanders for the losses and ill-discipline during the retreat.

The pay list and casualty return shows that 5th Battalion suffered significant losses during the march. Three men were taken prisoner on 14 November, seven on the 15th, 21 on the 16th, 25 on the 17th, 31 on the 18th, and finally two on the 19th. A grand total of 89 men were taken prisoner, four of whom subsequently escaped. Six men deserted during the march, including Sergeant Vincent Shefsky, who had only been promoted from corporal the month before. Among the prisoners of war was Sergeant Frederick Seidel, the former French officer, who was taken on the 17th. Several men are listed as being wounded and left on the road. Several more died during November but are marked as dying in hospitals, therefore they were unlikely to have been victims of the retreat. Private Frederick Muller, who had joined the battalion that summer, shot himself in one of the general hospitals on 10 October.[48]

The October regimental return showed that two buglers and 192 rank and file had arrived at Belem from the Foreign Depot, which meant that the battalion was briefly very close to its establishment, wanting just one paymaster and five buglers to complete. However, by November the battalion learned that its establishment had been raised to 65 sergeants, 22 buglers and 1,010 rank and file. Accounting for the increased establishment and the losses of the retreat, including the 113 riflemen listed as missing, they were seven sergeants, five buglers and 170 rank and file short on the November return. The lack of a paymaster had been solved by the appointment of Henry Biggs. The sick list remained high with 116 in October, 183 in November, and 165 in December. Eight men joined from desertion or from being prisoners of war during the last three months of the year and there was evidently some reassessment of whether men had deserted, gone missing or been taken prisoner, as the numbers in the returns do differ slightly from the pay lists. The December strength of the battalion was 60 sergeants, 15 buglers, and 699 rank and file. However only 48 sergeants, 13 buglers and 510 rank and file were present and fit for duty.[49]

48 December 1812 Pay List, TNA, WO 12/7074; November 1812 Casualty Return , WO 25/1923.

49 October to December 1812 Returns; TNA, WO 17/180.

The returns also state that Captain James Stopford joined in October from the 99th Foot; he was given command of Captain Prevost's old company, No. 10, in the 4th Division. Ensign Alan Cairnes joined in September from the 3/60th and was promoted to lieutenant by the end of the year. Captain John Harrison arrived in November and was briefly placed in command of No. 1 company in the 6th Division, before moving to No.9 in the 1st in the new year.[50] Harrison had been serving with the 2/67th in the campaign on the eastern coast of Spain, fighting at the Siege of Cadiz and the Battle of Barossa. He had also served briefly in the Royal Navy between 1800 and 1802, and been present at the battle of Algeciras Bay.[51]

Ensigns James Kent and John Hamilton were promoted to lieutenants. Lieutenant William Rafter joined from the 2/60th and Ensign Christopher Martin from the 6/60th. Lieutenant Augustine Evans arrived in November, with a party of recruits, and was noted as being under sentence of his court martial.[52] Lieutenant Ingersleben had been in command of the draft from the depot and sailed with them on the *Rolla* transport from England on 31 August. He had been on leave recovering from the wound he received at Albuera and was possibly re-joining the battalion reluctantly as he had applied to Colonel Mosheim for a position at Harwich.[53] During his absence he had been treated at a Laverstock House near Salisbury, by a Dr William Finch. He had left there 'whilst in a state of derangement' without his paying his bill.[54] Laverstock House was an insane asylum catering for the wealthier classes. Finch was a pioneer of enlightened and compassionate treatment for the mentally ill. An 1830 prospectus stated:

> The situation of Laverstock House is peculiarly eligible. Surrounded by large Gardens and Pleasure Grounds in the midst of a fine and extended Country, it is at once retired and cheerful, and affords the most ample means for indulgence in those exercises which are so essential to the happiness and health of the Patients.[55]

Brevet Colonel John Keane also arrived in the peninsular in October. An Irishman from an aristocratic family he was 31 years old and had purchased his way up through the ranks. First commissioned aged 13, he had served as a captain in the 44th Foot during the 1801 expedition to Egypt, then on the staff in Malta. He purchased a majority in the 60th in 1802 and bought his lieutenant colonelcy in the 13th a year later, aged 22. He served with the 13th in Gibraltar, Britain, Ireland, and then the West Indies. As the year had taken its toll on the officers of the 3rd Division, Keane was appointed to temporary command of the brigade containing the headquarters companies, with Fitzgerald retaining command of the battalion.[56]

50 October 1812 to January 1813 returns; TNA, WO 17/180.

51 Lionel S Challis's 'Peninsula Roll Call' http://www.napoleon-series.org/research/biographies/GreatBritain/Challis/Images351-400/355.pdf (accessed 7 September 2018).

52 See page 303.

53 Mosheim to Keane 29 & 31 August 1812, TNA, WO 7/86, pp.30 & 38.

54 Mosheim to Keane 14 July 1813, WO 7/90 pp.92-3.

55 Quoted in Margaret Moles, *Pauper and Private: Early Mental Health Care in Wiltshire*: http://www.wshc.eu/blog/item/early-mental-health-care.html Accessed 7 September 2018.

56 R. Burnham & R. McGuigan, *Wellington's Brigade Commanders, Peninsula & Waterloo* (Barnsley: Pen & Sword, 2017), pp.153-4.

Towards the end of the year some reorganisation took place within and between divisions. In the 1st Division a new 1st Guards Brigade was formed from the newly arrived 1/1st Guards from Britain and the 3/1st Guards from Cadiz and No. 5 Company of the 5th Battalion moved to the new brigade from what became the 2nd Guards Brigade. Wheatley's old brigade was transferred to the 6th Division but No. 9 Company remained with the 1st Division, moving to No. 5 Company's place in the 2nd Guards Brigade.[57]

The year 1812 had seen significant drafts arrive for the battalion, but also had seen significant losses. The campaigns had started early and well but the failure at Burgos and the arduous and costly retreat marred the victories at Ciudad Rodrigo, Badajoz and Salamanca. However, even though the army ended the year where it had started on the Portuguese border, the balance of power in the Peninsula had shifted and the French had been permanently ejected from southern Spain. During 1813 they would at last be forced out of the rest of the country and by the end of the year Wellington's army would enter France and be on the cusp of victory.

57 Oman, *Wellington's Army* p.361, placing of companies derived from subsequent regimental returns and inspections, 1812 returns, TNA, WO 17/180; WO 1813 returns WO 17/279; 1814 Inspections, WO 27/127.

2nd Division – Lieutenant General William Stewart
Colonel Cadogan
1/50th, 1/71st, 1/92nd & No. 8 company 5/60th.
Major General Byng
1/3rd, 1/57th, 1st Provisional Battn. & No. 6 company 5/60th.
Colonel O'Callaghan
1/28th, 2/34th, 1/39th & No. 4 company 5/60th.
Brigadeiro Ashworth (Portuguese)
6th (2 battalions), 18th (2 battalions) & 6th Caçadores.

3rd Division – Lieutenant General Picton
Major General Brisbane
1/45th, 74th, & 1/88th & Nos. 2, 3, & 7 companies 5/60th, with Col. Keane.
Major General Colville
1/5th, 2/83rd, 2/87th, & 94th.
Marechal de Campo Power (Portuguese)
9th (2 battalions), 21st (2 battalions) & 11th Caçadores.

4th Division – Lieutenant General Lowry Cole
Major General Anson
3/27th, 1/40th, 1/48th, 2nd Provisional Battn. & No. 10 company 5/60th.
Major General Skerrett
1/7th, 20th, 1/23rd, & 1 Company Brunswick Oels.
Coronel Stubbs (Portuguese)
11th (2 battalions), 23rd (2 battalions) & 7th Caçadores.

5th Division – Major General Oswald
Major General Hay
3/1st, 1/9th & 1/38th, & 1 company Brunswick Oels.
Major General Robinson
1/4th, 2/47th, 2/59th & 1 company Brunswick Oels.
Brigadeiro Spry (Portuguese)
3rd (2 battalions), 15th (2 battalions) & 8th Caçadores.

6th Division – Major General Pakenham
Major General Stirling
1/42nd, 1/79th & 1/91st, & No. 1 company 5/60th.
Colonel Hinde
1/11th, 1/32nd, 1/36th & 1/61st.
Marechal de Campo Madden (Portuguese)
8th (2 battalions) & 12th (2 battalions) & 9th Caçadores.

7th Division – Lieutenant General Lord Dalhousie
Major General Barnes
1/6th, 3rd Provisional Battn. & 9 companies Brunswick Oels.

Colonel Grant
51st, 68th, 1/82nd & Chasseurs Britanniques.
Marechal de Campo Le Cor (Portuguese)
7th (2 battalions), 19th (2 battalions) & 2nd Caçadores.

Light Division – Major General Alten
Major General Kempt
1/43rd, 1/95th, 3/95th & 1st Caçadores
Major General Vandeleur
1/52nd, 2/95th, 17th Portuguese (2 battalions) & 3rd Caçadores.[13]

There was also one Portuguese Division, two independent Portuguese brigades and two Spanish divisions. In total Wellington had around 75,000 men on hand to attack the French, while Joseph could only field around 57,000.[14]

The city of Vittoria was in a valley, roughly six miles wide by 12 long, through which ran both the main road to France and the Zadorra River. To the south lay the high ground of Allaras de Puebla, while the Sierra de Morillas were to the west and further high ground to the north. The ground was undulating, with the city on rising ground at the northern end. The valley floor was dotted with villages, crossed by multiple roads with many bridges and fords across the river. It was not a naturally strong defensive position and the French forces were spread thinly.[15]

View of the city of Vittoria, from Cumberland, *Views in Spain & Portugal.*

13 Oman, *Peninsular War*, Vol.VI, pp.751-2; May 1813 Return, TNA WO 17/264; Army in Spain & Portugal by Brigades & Divisions WO 17/2473,.

14 Oman, *Peninsular War*, Vol.VI, p.388.

15 The details of the battle on 21 June are taken from Oman, *Peninsular*, Vol.IV, pp384-450, Butler, *Annals*, Vol.II, pp.185-90 and Ian Fletcher, *Vittoria 1813* (Oxford: Osprey, 1998) pp.35-72.

Joseph assumed that Wellington would come from the west. *Général de Division* Gazan's Army of the South covered the south-west entrance to the valley, with *Général de Division* d'Erlon's Army of the Centre behind forming a second line. *Général de Division* Reille's Army of Portugal was placed behind Vittoria, with other cavalry and infantry units covering other likely approaches.

Wellington divided his army into four columns. On the right Hill, with the 2nd Division, Morillo's Spanish and Silveira's Portuguese divisions, plus cavalry, would attack Gazan's troops on the Allaras de Puebla and try to turn the French left flank. The 4th and Light Divisions plus cavalry would cross the river at Nanclares and attack the French centre. The 3rd and 7th Divisions would ascend the Sierra de Morillas by mountain tracks and then drive southwards into the rear of Gazan's line. Graham with the 1st and 5th Divisions, plus Portuguese and Spanish units, and cavalry, were already marching even further north in an attempt to cut off the French line of retreat.

The allied attack began at around 8:00 a.m. on 21 June. The rain and mists of the previous few days soon cleared after day break and it turned into a bright and fine day. Cadogan's Brigade of the 2nd Division crossed the river first and headed up the main road towards Vittoria. Morillo's Spanish division was tasked to press forward and clear the French from the high ground on the right. The Spaniards had to climb the almost vertical rocky slopes but drove the French from the first summit. French reinforcements stiffened their resistance and the Spanish were beaten back from the second peak. Hill ordered Cadogan forward with the 1/71st and the light companies of his own and Byng's brigades under Fitzgerald, which included No. 6 and No. 8 companies of the 5th Battalion.

The pipers of the 71st played while the highlanders, riflemen, and light infantry scrambled up the hill. The heights were thick with brush and small trees that made progress difficult. As they hurried to support the Spanish the men could see the rest of the armies spread out across the valley beneath them. The Spaniards had finally managed to take the second peak but the French counter-attacked and began to drive them back again before the reinforcements arrived to steady the line.

Hill sent the rest of Cadogan's Brigade to assist and the French were forced to retreat. The allies continued forward on the heights while O'Callaghan's Brigade advanced along the lower slopes and attacked the village of Subjiana de Alava, supported by Byng's Brigade and Ashworth's Portuguese. They took the village after a prolonged and difficult fight but more French reinforcements prevented any further movement.

While the French were counter-attacking Hill and hence weakening their centre, Wellington, with the 4th and Light Divisions concealed in dead ground, waited for the flanking attacks from the north to commence. The French forces facing Graham's northern column fell back. Graham sent the 5th Division and a Spanish brigade to take the villages of Gamarra Mayor and Minor to the east. The Spanish took Gamarra Minor and then tried to take the village of Durana, which lay on the road to France and was a key position. It was fiercely defended by Spanish troops in French service and only taken late in the afternoon. The 5th Division too had a long and hard struggle to capture Gamarra Mayor and after doing so could advance no further. The 1st Division and Portuguese brigades advanced towards Abechuco but Graham held them there while the other attacks developed.

At around noon Wellington learned that the bridge at Tres Puentes over the river was not defended and sent Kempt's Brigade of the Light Division, with cavalry, to cross the

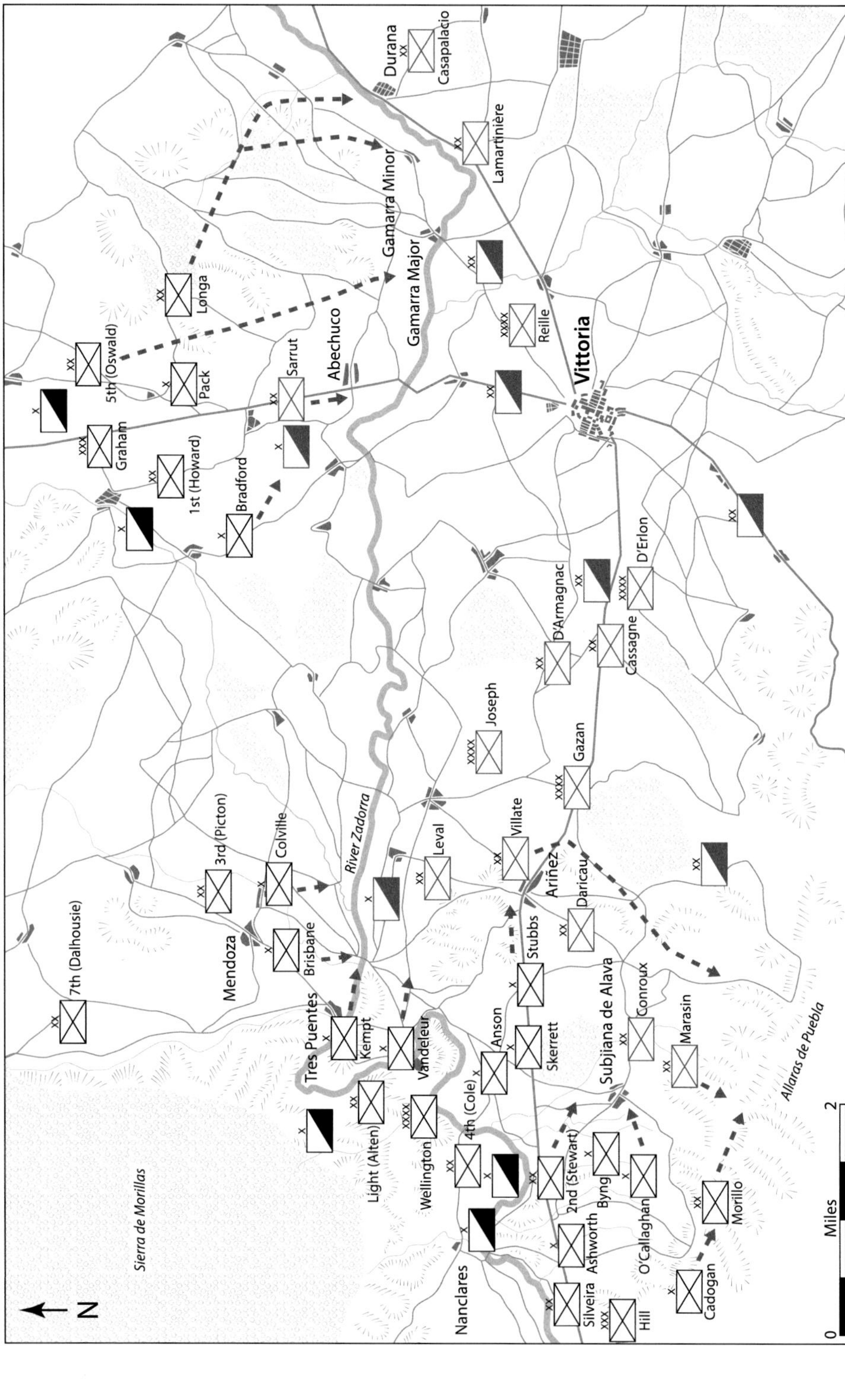

The Battle of Vittoria, 21 June 1813.
Sources: Lipscombe, *Atlas* & Wyld, *Maps & Plans.*

river. Meanwhile the 7th Division had been delayed marching through the mountains and Picton, commanding the 3rd Division, decided to attack rather than wait for Dalhousie and the 7th. Towards mid-afternoon Brisbane's Brigade, with the headquarter companies of the 5th Battalion, advanced quickly towards the bridge to the south of Mendoza, with Colville's brigade heading for a nearby ford. James Campbell, on the staff of the 3rd Division recalled:

> I went on with the advance, consisting of our Light Infantry companies, and the 5th Battalion 60th German riflemen, all experienced troops, and well acquainted with and accustomed to their work. To my surprise, and I believe that of SirThomas Brisbane, and many others, we met with no opposition in passing the Zadorra.[16]

Kempt's Brigade had supported the 3rd Division's crossing, with riflemen of the 95th driving off a French horse artillery battery before they could engage Brisbane's men crossing the bridge. The rest of the Light, 3rd, 4th and the leading elements of the 7th Divisions crossed the river and moved east. This forced the French to withdraw towards Vittoria, where they reformed along a line around a hill and village at Ariñez.

Some companies of the 95th had attacked and entered Ariñez before being ejected by the French. Brisbane's Brigade then marched forward with Power's Portuguese on their left and the rest of Kempt's Brigade in support. The 1/88th went to the right of the village and engaged a French regiment there, while three companies of the 74th and the three companies of the 5th Battalion dashed into the village and drove out the French. The three brigades then continued forward, driving a wedge into the French centre.

Hill continued to force the French back along the heights on their left flank. His men had been fighting for several hours and were tired and slightly disordered, but they pressed forward eager to keep the pressure on the enemy. However, French reinforcements were coming up and succeeded in taking the 1/71st and light companies in the flank, resulting in heavy losses and some prisoners being taken. Fortunately the rest of the brigade, now command by Cameron of the 1/92nd after Cadogan had been fatally wounded, arrived and counter attacked. The allies continued forward and turned the French left flank. The 7th and Light Divisions did the same on the right and the French were forced to withdraw and redeploy further east.

At around 4:00 p.m. Wellington drew up his men in a long line opposite the French. Brisbane's, Byng's and O'Callaghan's Brigades were included, with their five companies of the 5th Battalion probably forming a skirmish line with the light companies. A sixth company, No. 10, was with Anson's Brigade in the second line made up of 4th and Light Divisions. The mass of allied infantry moved forward under heavy French artillery fire but the allied guns were brought up and began the largest artillery duel of the Peninsular campaign.

Cadogan's Brigade came down from the heights into the French left and a gap between French units along the main road was exploited by the allied skirmishers, and then by the main bodies of the 2nd and 4th Divisions. Graham could have made things much worse for the French by advancing in their rear but chose to be cautious and much of 1st Division was barely engaged all day. Only in the closing hours of the battle did they take Abechuco and

16 Campbell, *A British Army*, p.238.

The Battle of Vittoria, 1813, by Adam Neale. (Anne S.K. Brown Military Collection)

cross the river. The cutting of the route back to France by the Spanish at Durana began to spread panic in the French ranks. Gazan, fearing being outflanked and cut off, ordered a further retreat eastwards, enhancing the jeopardy of d'Erlon's divisions. D'Erlon's men kept on fighting and inflicted heavy casualties on the 3rd Division, but they were soon outflanked on both sides. At 5:30 p.m. d'Erlon received an order from Joseph for a general retreat to the east, along the narrow road to Pamplona.

Reille's forces held out for long enough on the French right to allow the other two French armies to flee eastwards. With Morillo's Spanish and Cadogan's Brigade coming down from the high ground on the left, the French retreat soon became a panicked rout. The fleeing infantry and cavalry became held up and mixed in with the immense and slow moving baggage train of hundreds of carts, carriages, and mules of the thousands of camp followers, and administrators. The streets of Vittoria became blocked by the weight of traffic and had to be bypassed on minor tracks. Many of the French troops fled across fields and open country, hotly pursued by the allied infantry and by some of the allied cavalry.

Individual French units, or ad-hoc groups of soldiers, would pause at every defensible position to try and slow the allied pursuit but eventually discipline broke down and the French began to drop their weapons in their haste to escape. Joseph himself was almost captured by British hussars, leaping out of one side of his carriage as they opened the door on the other. The few roads out of the valley became blocked by over-turned or broken carts and carriages. The vast convoy contained all the regiments' baggage, and that of the French generals and staff, including all of King Joseph's personal belongings. Large numbers of Spanish collaborators were trying to escape retribution, carrying all they could with them.

French camp followers and soldiers began to plunder the convoy, pausing briefly to fill their packs with coin, jewels, fancy clothes and anything else they could carry. Many allied soldiers soon joined them, despite the entreaties of their officers. For years the French rulers had systematically robbed Spain of its riches. That wealth was now rapidly redistributed. Money chests lay spilled on the ground along with every manner of luxury furnishings, church plate, wine and fine foods. All but one of the 152 French guns were taken, along with 415 artillery caissons, and 100 artillery wagons. Five million Francs had recently arrived from France to pay the army and very little of it ended up being officially captured. Five hundred prostitutes and officers' mistresses were also found in the convoy and provided further distraction for the victors.[17]

The allied units that maintained order and marched on in pursuit of the French gave up the chase as darkness fell. Despite their tiredness many then slipped away in the night to claim their share of the booty, which most of them then proceeded to fritter away on drink and women. Some officers could also not resist the temptation and many British regimental messes were to feature King Joseph's possessions for years to come. *Marechal* Jourdan's baton was later presented to the Prince Regent.

The French losses during the battle and immediate retreat were 756 killed, 4,414 wounded, and 2,824 missing or prisoners. The allied losses were 840 killed, 4,040 wounded and 266 missing.[18] Most of the allied casualties were sustained by the 2nd and 3rd Divisions.

The 5th Battalion lost two men killed, both from No. 8 company in the 2nd Division. Corporal Julius Kayne came from Brunswick and Private John Eisel from Nassau. Seven men were reported missing, five of whom became prisoners of war. Four of the missing were with the 3rd Division and three with the 2nd. Captain Franchini and Lieutenant Joyce, serving with the 3rd and 2nd Divisions respectively, were both slightly wounded, as were four sergeants and 43 rank and file.[19]

Amongst the French prisoners was Sergeant Frederick Seidel, the former French officer who had joined the 5th Battalion from the Foreign Depot the previous year and had been reported taken prisoner during the retreat in November. He was captured wearing the uniform of a French sergeant, and so was tried for desertion, found guilty, and executed by firing squad on 22 August.[20]

The allied army halted for the night several miles beyond Vittoria whilst the retreating French marched on through the darkness until they were forced to stop by exhaustion. Units were still very disordered and the 22nd dawned wet, with thunderstorms, which made the march towards Pamplona even more taxing. Fortunately for the French, the allied cavalry began the pursuit long after dawn and failed to catch up with the weary and defeated soldiers. The allied infantry, many of whom had spent the night plundering, marched north even later, leaving many men behind, still drunk among the debris of the convoy.

The 5th Division was left to guard Vittoria, with the 6th, who were marching from the rear. The two Spanish divisions were sent along the Bayonne road whilst Wellington took the rest of the army towards Pamplona in pursuit of the French. That evening Graham was ordered to take the 1st Division, two Portuguese brigades, and cavalry across the hills towards Villafranca in order to attempt to cut off other retreating French forces. Wellington

17 Esdaile, *Peninsular*, p.450.

18 Oman, *Peninsular War*, Vol.VI, p.760-1.

19 June 1813 Casualty Return, TNA WO 25/1923; June Pay List, WO 12/7075; Return of Casualties 21 June 1813, WO 1/258.

20 General Order 20 August 1813, HRO, 170A12W/D/1183.

Victory of Vittoria, by John Massey Wright, illustrating the aftermath of the battle. (Anne S.K. Brown Military Collection)

continued after the main French army, which was still retreating swiftly. The British advance guard skirmished with the French rearguard on 24 June.

Most of the French army bypassed Pamplona and carried on towards France. Clausel, with the French Army of the North, was still in the area but Wellington was unsure exactly where. He broke off the pursuit of Joseph's army in the hope of finding Clausel, who managed to elude him by marching south-west before looping north, back to France. Graham's column engaged French forces at Villafranca on the 24th and again at Tolosa on the 26th, the fighting becoming intense on both occasions. However, with his men exhausted Graham did not press the pursuit any further and the French retired over the River Bidassoa into France.

Meanwhile, on 27 June Wellington had ordered Lieutenant General Hill to send Major General Byng, with his brigade of the 2nd Division, a Portuguese brigade, and Morillo's Spanish Division to follow Joseph's army from Pamplona to the pass at Roncesvalles and the French frontier. Their objective was to confirm the French retreat across the border and prevent any return. Byng was authorised to cross the frontier and urged to send officers to explore the area.[21] No. 6 company, commanded by Captain Erskine, was with Byng's brigade.

Byng's column soon reached Roncesvalles, just a few miles south of the border. Captain George L'Estrange who commanded the light company of the 2/31st, which was part of the 1st Provisional Battalion recalled:

21 Wellington, *Supplementary Despatches*, Vol.XIV, pp.242-3.

> The next day our light companies were informed that they would be required to make a sort of secret movement, in as light marching order as possible. This was to a place about three miles to the front, on the road to St. Jean Pied de Port. Our commandant, I believe, had sealed orders, not to be opened till after our arrival at [a] Quinta [farmhouse]... The country was in all the gorgeous beauty of midsummer, the trees many of them fruit-bearing: cherry-trees were plentiful, with quantities of fruit ripe and delicious they were in the sultry heat. Things altogether seemed very much altered for the better; we had, in fact, passed the frontier into France, which had not been ravaged by war like unhappy Spain and Portugal, and we were the first of the 'enemies' troops, over the French frontier. We had thus the satisfaction of being the first to enter the territory of La Belle France and the Grande Empire. We took up our quarters for the night in and about the Quinta; but kept a sharp look out, as we were on rather dangerous ground. The rear-guard of the French Army was, as before said, halted in a small village a mile or two in our front, and the sealed orders were that early in the morning we were to make a dash at the village, rush through it without firing a shot, and make prisoners of this small rear-guard if possible. We should probably have succeeded had it not been for a German soldier of the single company of the 60th Rifles attached to our little light brigade. He could not resist the opportunity of firing a shot into the village before we had reached it. The report, of course, alarmed the little garrison, who were instantly on the move, and, with the rapidity of French soldiers, the greater part of them escaped.[22]

From this evidence it would seem that riflemen of the 5th Battalion were amongst the first troops to enter France, indeed given the long standing practice of including rifles in the advance guard they may well have been the first, and it seems at least one rifleman let his eagerness get the better of him.

At the start of July, with most of the French across the border, Wellington had several very good reasons not to cross in force into France after them. The rapid march had taken him beyond his own communication lines and supplies had not yet reached the army from the northern Spanish port of Santander. The long marches had exhausted the army and many stragglers had yet to re-join the ranks. However, the main reason for Wellington to pause was the armistice that had been signed on the central European front, which had the possibility of taking the Prussians and Russians out of the war and freeing up French divisions to counter-attack any incursion into their homeland.

Instead of entering France Wellington decided to besiege the fortress at San Sebastian, blockade the city of Pamplona, and to consolidate his army along the Bidassoa River. The 2nd, 7th, Light, and Portuguese Divisions marched north in early July while the 3rd, 4th and 6th Divisions remained at Pamplona until relieved by Spanish troops in the middle of the month.

On 4 July Hill's 2nd Division, minus Byng's Brigade which was still detached, reached the highest point of the Belate Pass. The advance guard, made up of Cadogan's old brigade

22 G.B. L'Estrange, *Recollections of Sir George B. L'Estrange* (London: Sampson Low, Marston & Searle, 1874), pp.96-8.

which was still commanded by Cameron of the 1/92nd, met French light troops and pushed them back as far as the village of Ziga but soon came up against their parent division. Hill pulled his troops back to a better defensive line on a ravine and brought up his other brigades. The French soon had two full divisions in their line, outnumbering Hill. The two sides skirmished for the rest of the day, while they waited for their full strengths to deploy. Wellington arrived on the 5th, along with a Portuguese brigade, and took over from Hill. He sent Cameron's Brigade around the French flank while other troops crossed the ravine towards the French centre.[23]

The French commander, Gazan, unaware that he had the advantage in numbers and fearing that other allied forces were advancing to his rear, fell back to the Maya Pass. The two forces remained facing each other on the 6th, during which time Wellington ordered the 7th Division to manoeuvre behind Gazan's position. On 7 July Wellington attacked Gazan's front with the 2nd Division and got him to commit his reserves but thick fog caused the 7th Division to get lost and so the decisive blow was not delivered. However, Gazan simply withdrew the next day, allowing the 2nd Division to occupy the pass. The 7th and Light Divisions and Portuguese brigades occupied other important passes through the mountains.

Wellington, satisfied that the main French force was contained for the moment behind the border, turned his attention to the siege of San Sebastian, which the 5th Division and a Portuguese brigade were undertaking. The position of the fortress on a high rock at the end of an isthmus was formidable but the full siege train of the army was available. Outer-works were soon taken and a breach created in the walls of the town. An assault was attempted on 25 July but defeated, partly by a tenacious defence but also partly due to poor planning. On the 26th the siege had to be raised as news came that the French had attacked the passes in the Pyrenees.

Marechal Soult had taken command of the forces facing Wellington. He had reorganised the various armies into one optimistically named Army of Spain, with Reille, d'Erlon and Clausel each commanding a corps of three divisions plus a reserve under Villatte. The full force totalled just over 55,000 men.[24] Once the army was re-organised, re-equipped, and in place he went on the offensive. Soult would lead Reille and Clausel's corps through the pass at Roncesvalles and d'Erlon would advance through the pass at Maya. The attacks commenced at dawn on 25 July.

Byng's Brigade and Morillo's Spanish division at Roncesvalles had been reinforced by Cole's 4th Division a few days before. Cole's men were camped lower down the mountain slopes. Behind Byng's forward pickets, which had been attacked during the night, were the three light companies of his brigade, with No. 6 company, a Spanish battalion, and three Spanish light companies. They were placed either side of the road in good cover amongst rocks on a mountainside. Two diversionary attacks were met and effectively countered by nearby Portuguese and Spanish troops but did have the desired effect of getting the attention of the allied commanders. At around 6:00 a.m. French *tiraileurs* from the leading French brigade attacked the seven light companies and the Spanish battalion. The allies comfortably held off the attack and inflicted heavy casualties.

23 Oman, *Peninsular War*, Vol.VI, pp.537.

24 I.C. Robertson, *Wellington Invades France* (London: Greenhill, 2003), p.57.

The French took cover amongst the scrub and a prolonged exchange of fire lasted well into the morning until the commander of the French was threatened with being cashiered if he did not get the attack moving again. Two further assaults were repulsed and the light companies and Spanish only fell back after their ammunition was running low, more French guns were brought up and the French began to make moves on their flank. They retreated to Byng's formidable main position two miles further up the pass and the French did not press their pursuit. A second French attack on a different part of the pass was fought to a standstill by the 4th Division, which had come forward during the morning. As evening fell so did the cloud level and the fighting ceased as the visibility was reduced by thick fog. Byng and Morillo's 6,000 men, most of whom were not engaged, had held off 17,000 French for 11 hours, taking only 120 casualties.[25] The French reported 160 casualties with a high proportion of officers.[26] This may have been the result of riflemen in good cover having plenty of opportunity to choose their targets.

At Maya the other two British brigades of the 2nd Division held the pass, with Portuguese brigades in neighbouring ones. The main position was on a wide grassy saddle between two slopes. The surrounding terrain was crossed by ravines, dotted with jagged rock outcrops, and surrounded by almost vertical slopes. Even in mid-summer patches of snow survived in clefts and hollows. The main road through the pass was covered by Cameron's Brigade. The battalions' camps were just behind the crest on each side of the road. A Portuguese battery covered the position from a nearby rise. Pringle's Brigade, formerly O'Callaghan's, was cantoned just over two miles to the south in the village of Maya. Pringle had positioned a small picket of 80 men to cover a small track on the eastern side of the pass. Reports of French movement at first light led Pringle to reinforce the picket with his four light companies, including No. 4 company.

Late in the morning the French advanced unseen to within a mile of the picket. Then eight light companies of the French division, 700 men, ran forward, supported by a light infantry regiment, and enveloped the knoll that the picket occupied. The picket, numbering around 400 men, were fired on from all sides. They withdrew to the rocky outcrops at the summit and beat off several attacks in desperate fighting lasting three quarters of an hour. They inflicted heavy casualties on the French before being overrun; 140 were captured and many of the other 260 were killed or wounded, although some did manage to escape. One of the captured officers, Captain Sherer of the 34th who had commanded the original picket, was presented to d'Erlon and the French general complimented him on the heroic defence of the knoll.[27]

Rushing up mountain tracks the battalions of Pringle's brigade arrived one at a time and out of breath, too late to save the picket and the light companies. Each did their best to stop the French but they were vastly outnumbered. Cameron sent the 1/50th and part of the 1/92nd to support Pringle by attacking the French flank but they too could do little to throw back the enemy. Pringle reorganised his shattered battalions into a deep defensive line, constricted by the narrow spine of the hill to a front of just 20 men. The redcoats and the French exchanged volleys at close range. Pringle's battalions took further heavy casualties and were forced back to Maya village, pursued by the French.

25 Robertson, *Wellington Invades*, p.69.
26 Oman, *Peninsular War*, Vol.VI, p 616.
27 Robertson, *Wellington Invades*, p.62.

Cameron's already depleted battalions attempted to rally and hold back the French but they too were outnumbered and threatened with envelopment. Lieutenant General Stewart, commander of the division, arrived and pulled his men back to into a two rank line. Each rank fired and then retired, marching back through the battalions' camps. The French troops promptly paused to plunder the tents but then continued driving forward. By late afternoon a battalion of the 7th Division had arrived to support the beleaguered 2nd. Another French attack pushed the British troops back again to yet another position. Two more battalions of the 7th Division came up and finally managed to stop the French advance and drive them back to the top of the pass. D'Erlon, fearing that the entire 7th Division had come forward, called off his attack. During the night the battered and exhausted allied units withdrew from both the Maya and Roncesvalles Passes, opening the way for Soult to march back into Spain.

Cameron's brigade suffered 800 casualties out of 1,900 men present. Pringle lost 530. D'Erlon reported 2,100 casualties.[28] The three companies of the 5th Battalion with the 2nd Division lost Lieutenant John William von Dalman and eight rank and file killed in action, Lieutenants John Barbaz and John Joyce were wounded, as were 10 rank and file. The casualty return of 25 August lists 30 men missing or taken prisoner, but the pay list, completed 25 September, reduced that to 25 prisoners and one missing, so presumably four men returned to the battalion in the intervening period.[29]

It is not possible to say which officer was with which company on 25 July as the regimental return only lists the division they were attached to, not the individual brigades. Von Dalman had joined the battalion the previous year from the Chasseurs Brittanique. Barbaz and Joyce had served with the battalion since before the start of the Peninsular campaign. Both were severely wounded and taken prisoner, so it seems likely that they were with the light companies on the knoll. As Captain McMahon was on leave it is possible that Joyce was commanding the company. The French later reported that Barbaz died of his wounds and Joyce was mistakenly listed as killed in the British casualty report. He managed to escape from the French and was on leave in England by October.[30]

Captain Erskine's No. 6 company with Byng's Brigade lost two men killed: Private William Pierre was from Coblenz, and Private John Rollofs was a sailor from Sweden. The casualty return shows one sergeant, one corporal and six privates missing. Some of these men could have been wounded and left behind when the light companies withdrew from their initial position. The casualties amongst No. 4 company with Pringle's Brigade on the knoll were, unsurprisingly, the heaviest of the day with four men killed: Private Christoph Schulte came from Germany; Bugler Peter Dindas was a weaver from Braband who had joined the battalion in February 1812; Private Ludwig Fischer was from Holland and had been with the battalion since formation, joining with the Hompesch chasseurs on the Isle of Wight; Private John Mathes was a miller from Bohemia who had joined in 1802 with Lowenstein's Jägers.

28 Robertson, *Wellington Invades*, pp.64-5.

29 September 1813 Pay List, TNA, WO 12/7075; August 1813 Casualty Return TNA, WO 25/1923; Casualty Return, 25 July 1813 WO 1/259.

30 August, October & December 1813 Returns; TNA, WO 17/264; Butler, *Annals*, Vol.II, pp.247, 249 & 252.

Captain Blassiere's No. 8 company, with Cameron's Brigade, had two men killed in action: Private Joseph Thomaschofsky was another of the long serving former Walloon guardsmen and Private Anton Winter had only joined the battalion the previous summer. Two men of the company also died of their wounds on the 25th and nine were reported missing.[31]

On 26 July the allied divisions fell back towards Pamplona and Wellington had to reconfigure his line following the unexpected withdrawal from the passes. Fortunately for the allies the difficult terrain delayed the French advance. French cavalry patrols caught up with the rearguard of the 4th Division near the village of Espinal, and Clausel ordered infantry to pursue them as they continued to withdraw. Late in the afternoon the French engaged the light companies of Anson's Brigade, which included No. 10 company commanded by Captain Stopford. The companies were in the process of falling back on Anson's main position on high ground behind the Erro River at Linzoain. While the French infantry exchanged shots with the British, French cavalry charged their rear. Both attacks were successfully driven off and the light companies withdrew. Picton's 3rd Division joined the 4th and Soult made some tentative attacks but they were not pressed home and the allied units withdrew during the night. Anson's Brigade had suffered 164 casualties during the day.[32] One of those was Ensign Christopher Martin, with No. 10 company, who was severely wounded. At just 21 years of age he was deemed unfit for further military service and sent back to England. He was promoted to Lieutenant but went on half pay, eventually receiving a pension of £70 per year for his wounds. He settled in Ireland, married, and had children.[33] One rifleman was also wounded.[34]

On 27 July the 3rd and 4th Divisions formed a defensive position near the village of Sorauren, just to the north of Pamplona. Wellington arrived to take charge as the French troops neared. Soult probed the allied line but made no concerted attack as many of his units were still coming up. That evening there was a heavy thunderstorm that drenched both armies as they waited for the coming battle.[35]

The morning of 28 July was much brighter. Cole's 4th Division occupied a ridge near the village of Zabaldica. Late in the morning Pack's 6th Division moved into position on either side of the valley that ran from Oricain to Sorauren. Cole placed a strong line of skirmishers forward down the slope, including No. 10 company. The allied second line, further south, consisted of Picton's 3rd Division and O'Donnell's Spanish along the heights of San Cristobal and high ground near Huarte. The movements of the 6th Division caused Clausel on the French right to attack earlier than Soult had planned. The French division that marched forward was caught in a crossfire between Pack's brigades and forced to retire.

The main French attack centred on a spur at the left of Cole's position and the saddle of the ridge to the north-west. Campbell's Portuguese Brigade was pushed back on the saddle by one French column, before a counter attack by Ross' Fusilier Brigade drove the French back down the hill. A second French column was similarly defeated but a third did manage

31 August 1813 Casualty Return, TNA, WO 25/1923; September 1813 Pay List, WO 12/7075.

32 Oman, *Peninsular War*, Vol.VI, p.653.

33 Hall, *Biographical Dictionary*, p.397.

34 Casualty Return 27 July 1813, TNA WO 1/259.

35 The details of the first Battle of Sorauren are taken from Robertson, *Wellington Invades*, pp.74-86 and Oman, *Peninsular War*, Vol.VI, pp.654-80.

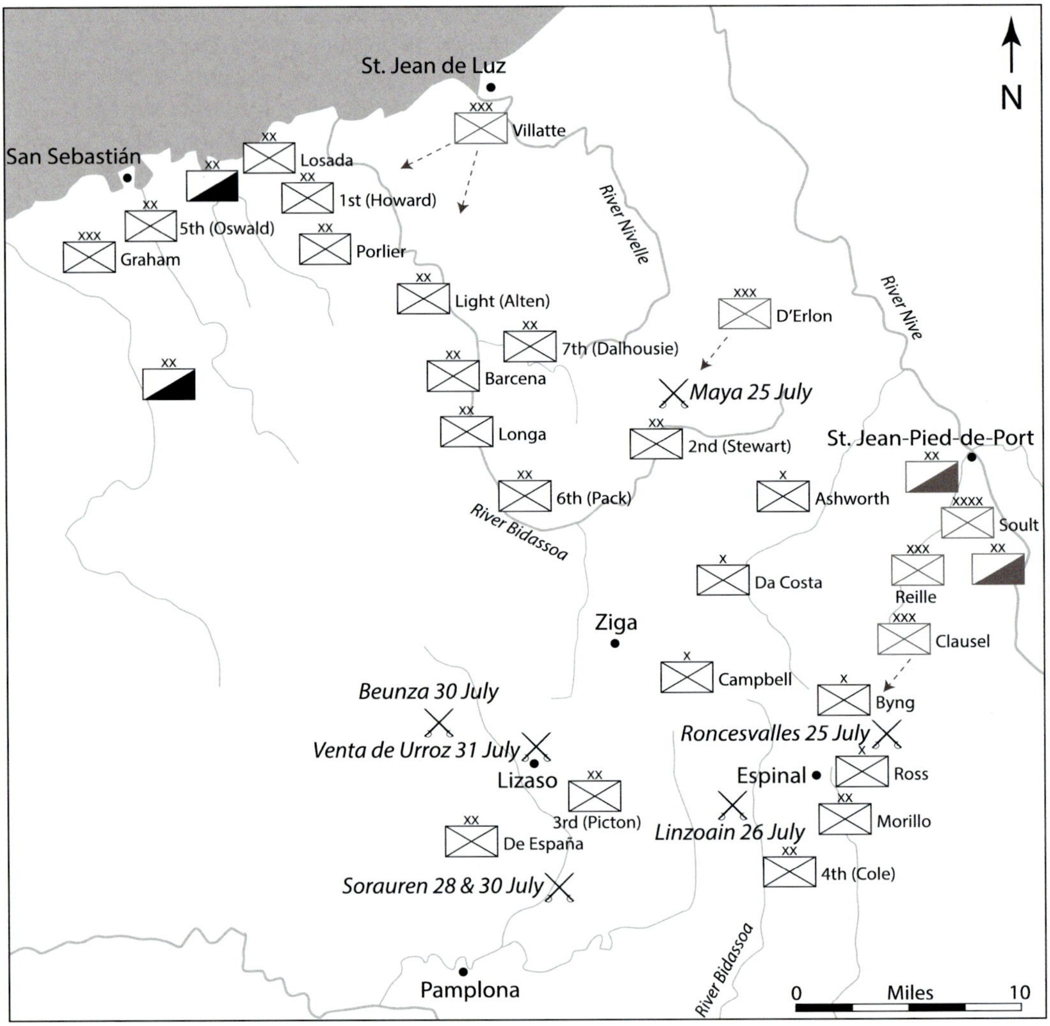

The Battle of the Pyrenees, 25 July to 1 August 1813.
Sources: Lipscombe, *Atlas* & Oman, *History of the Peninsular War.*

to get a toehold on the crest of the ridge, but they were held there and were subjected to repeated volleys from allied troops. A further French column was met by Anson's Brigade and after ten minutes was driven back with heavy losses. The French continued to press the allied position hard and Wellington ordered Byng's Brigade forward to support Ross' Brigade. Anson was ordered to advance on the flank of the French attacking on the saddle. Anson's men charged diagonally down the hill and shattered the French column.

Multiple attacks up the steeper slopes of the spur were similarly defeated by the volleys of the allied defenders. Pack, seeing the trouble the main French attack was in, attempted an advance on the village of Sorauren but was unable to break the French defence. The fighting petered out after Soult ordered his men back to their starting positions.

Allied losses were 360 killed, 2,141 wounded and 66 missing.[36] French losses were over 3,000.[37] The 5th Battalion's No. 1 company with Stirling's Brigade and No. 10 with Anson's were probably the only two to see action on the 28th. Private Anthony Siedler (No. 10) from the Rhine Palatinate, who had only joined in February, was killed in action, and four men were wounded.[38]

On 29 July the two armies saw to their dead and wounded. Both Soult and Wellington had fresh units coming up. The 7th Division arrived and took up positions behind and to the flank of the 6th Division before Sorauren, extending the allied line. Ross' and Campbell's battered brigades were drawn back and replaced with Byng's and Stubbs'. Soult decided on a risky plan to disengage and move north-west across Wellington's front so that he could advance into the gap between Wellington's and Graham's forces, with the hope that Graham would then have to raise the siege of San Sebastian. During the night of the 29th the French divisions began to march, leaving their campfires burning.

As dawn broke on 30 July allied artillery opened fire on the French divisions still present and moving across the front. The 6th Division advanced on Sorauren, with their skirmishers to the front, including No. 1 company. Byng's and Stubbs' Brigades moved forward in support. The allies managed to trap some of the French troops in the village. They fought hard for two hours, trying to break out, but eventually had to surrender; 1,700 prisoners were taken.[39] The 7th Division also moved forward to attack French troops massing around Ostiz and harassed them as they moved north. Picton's 3rd Division also advanced with the light companies, commanded by Keane, at the fore. They harried Foy's division up into the hills so hard that many of the French surrendered.[40] Under sustained and widespread allied pressure the French movements had turned into a disorderly retreat.

On the 27th Wellington had ordered Hill, with the 2nd Division and attached brigades, to cross the mountains and head for Lizaso. Hill's men were caught in the heavy thunderstorm of that evening while they were high up in the passes. Visibility dropped to zero and the men were almost blown off their feet. Many had to sit and wait for the rain to pass. Several guns were lost as they strayed off the narrow tracks and rolled down the steep slopes. At daylight the next day they continued on their arduous march down from the pass, reaching their goal in a bedraggled and fatigued state, where they paused briefly to recover. Lieutenant James Hope of the 1/92nd recalled:

> The officers of the first brigade were reclining under the cooling shade of a wide-spreading tree on the 29th of July, and cracking their jokes, as if each had received a fifty years renewal of his earthly existence, when an officer of the 50th regiment, who had been stationed at Lisbon, passed them in a very comfortable state of equipment. On his dismounting to report his arrival to the commanding-officer, — Colonel Fitzgerald of the 60th, then commanding the light companies of the second division, rose and cried, 'Come, is any one inclined for a bet ?' His query

36 Oman, *Peninsular War*, Vol.VI, p.770.

37 Oman, *Peninsular War*, Vol.VI, p.680.

38 August 1813 Casualty Return, TNA WO 25/1923; Oman, *Peninsular War*, Vol.VI, p.770.

39 Robertson, *Wellington Invades*, p.85.

40 Colville, *Portrait of a General*, p.134.

> being answered in the affirmative, — 'I will bet twenty dollars to one,' rejoined the Colonel, 'that the officer just arrived in our bivouac is either killed or a prisoner with the enemy in twenty-four hours'. The bet was taken, — the officer, horse and all, was in the hands of the French before the expiry of the period named by Fitzgerald, but the bet was never paid, for the latter was only a few hours later in following the other into the Gallic dominions.[41]

On the 30th Hill was in place on a wooded ridge near Beunza, in the path of d'Erlon's corps. Ashworth's Portuguese brigade was in the centre, a Spanish regiment on the right and the remains of Cameron's Brigade, which had suffered so heavily at Maya, was on the left. Fitzgerald was in command of the brigade, Cameron having been wounded. With Hill in over-all command and Stewart also wounded the 2nd Division was commanded by Pringle, with his brigade in reserve commanded by O'Callaghan. At the edge of the wood the light companies, including Nos. 4, 6, and 8 companies, and a caçadore battalion formed a heavy skirmish line.

The French outnumbered the allies by almost two to one.[42] D'Erlon sent one division to fix the allied centre while another went up into the hills to turn the left flank. The Portuguese held and defeated the centre attack. The flank attack missed its way and ended up charging the front of the 1/50th and 1/92nd instead, who also held firm and threw back their assailants. The French then finally managed to turn the flank but the 2/34th came forward from the reserve and gave the brigade time to retire, although 36 men were taken prisoners, including two officers.[43] It is probable one of the two was the subject of Fitzgerald's gallows-humour wager. The loss of the flank meant the centre had to retreat across a valley, pivoting on the right flank units which were able to maintain their position on high ground. Hill's men managed to repulse one final attack on the new line before the arrival of allied reinforcements at around 4:00 p.m. dissuaded d'Erlon from further action. Allied losses were just over 1,000 and French around 800.[44] The allies had managed to hold off the French for seven hours and with Soult's disastrous moves around Sorauren d'Erlon's tactical victory had little strategic significance.

Soult abandoned plans for any further advance. He would take his army back across the border, with d'Erlon's, the most intact of his three corps, acting as the rearguard. On 31 July the French headed for the mountain passes with Wellington ordering his various divisions to pursue or intercept them. The flank companies of Byng's Brigade captured a French food convoy at Elizondo but had to order the brandy casks smashed in case his men became drunk on their prize.

Hill pressed d'Erlon's corps hard. Towards the middle of the afternoon Fitzgerald's much depleted brigade numbering less than 1,000 was ordered by Stewart to attack a French division of 7,000 positioned on a steep, wooded hill known as the Venta de Urroz.[45] Fitzgerald led his men forward but they were far too few and were quickly pushed back. Fitzgerald was

41 Hope, *Military Memoirs*, p.330.
42 Oman, *Peninsular War*, Vol.VI, p.703.
43 Oman, *Peninsular War*, Vol.VI, p.703.
44 Oman, *Peninsular War*, Vol.VI, p.704.
45 Oman, *Peninsular War*, Vol.VI, p.711.

wounded and taken prisoner, amongst many other casualties. The irony of his bet may well have occurred to him as he was captured. A second assault by the survivors and Pringle's Brigade was also defeated but after a third attack the French withdrew. Low cloud prevented any further fighting.

On 6 August Fitzgerald wrote to Lieutenant General Stewart from captivity:

> I take the liberty of addressing these few lines to you in hopes you might have it in your powers to render me some assistance in my present situation. After you had given me the command of the advance & wishing to push the enemy as closely as possible I went myself with the leading section of the advance. Owing to the intricacy of the woods I found myself alone among the enemy. I was knocked down with the butt end of a musket & stabbed in two places by a bayonet, on recovering I found a French officer along with me but I was plundered of everything I had about me.
>
> I know not if it could be possible for me to be exchanged, but as I am without anything [I] shall esteem it the greatest favour to have my clothes sent to me.[46]

Fitzgerald also informed Stewart that two captured officers from the 1/50th, Lieutenants Power and Bartley, were with him.

On 1 August the French retreat and allied pursuit continued towards the Bidassoa and the frontier. Pressed from multiple directions Soult's retreat became increasingly desperate and disordered. Several small skirmishes hurried the French on their way. The pursuers, impeded by the detritus left by the French and marching over mountains on poor roads with few rations became increasingly exhausted. With many men lacking shoes and ammunition, and after having taken so many casualties, the 2nd Division was the first to be ordered to halt by Wellington on the 1st. He ordered the rest of his divisions to stop the pursuit on the 3rd and began to deploy them along the frontier.

Soult's losses during his excursion back into Spain had been heavy with 1,308 killed, 8,545 wounded, and 2,710 taken prisoner. The losses were particularly severe amongst officers; one third of his infantry officers had become casualties. Allied losses were around 7,400.[47]

In the actions from 30 July to 1 August the 5th Battalion lost one man killed in action, with Lieutenant James Kent, the battalion adjutant with the 3rd Division, being slightly wounded on the 30th. Two sergeants and 19 rank and file were also wounded and eight men went missing.[48] Private John Meyer (No. 1) was the fatality. He fell on 30 July, probably as the 6th Division attacked Sorauren. Meyer was a mason from Nassau who had joined the battalion in September 1807 from the Foreign Depot.[49] John Forster Fitzgerald recovered and spent the remainder of the war in captivity. The 1st Guards Brigade, including No. 5 company, re-joined the army in August after marching 268 miles from Oporto in the full heat of an Iberian summer in 22 days.[50]

46 Fitzgerald to Stewart 6 August 1813, Dorset History Centre D-MIC/X/53.

47 Robertson, *Wellington Invades*, p.96.

48 Casualty Return for 30 July 1813 and Supplementary Casualty Return for 30 July, TNA, WO 1/259.

49 August 1813 Casualty Return, TNA, WO 25/1923; September 1807 Pay List, WO 12/7073.

50 Robertson, *Wellington Invades*, p.264.

23

The Regiment

The 5th Battalion was part of the largest regiment in the British Army. At the beginning of the wars against France the 60th Regiment had four battalions and by the end there were eight. The standard regimental model of a first battalion serving abroad with a second serving at home, acting as a depot and a source of recruits and officers, did not apply to the 60th. All the battalions served overseas, with the Foreign Depot carrying out the role of a home second battalion. Whilst transfers of rank and file between the 5th Battalion and the others were rare, the wider regiment was by far the most common source of officers coming in to the battalion, and also the most common destination for those leaving. However, unless an officer moved from one battalion to another there seems to have been little other interaction between the battalions. When John Galiffe was asked in 1816 if he knew an officer in the 7th Battalion he replied, 'as our battalions are as strange to each other as two Regiments of different numbers can be and as I have never left the 5th; I am less than anyone to know the officers of the other battalions'.[1]

In the early part of the war the 60th largely remained within its intended area of operations in the Americas, the definition of which included the colonies which later formed Canada, the West Indies, and the colonies on the north coast of South America. Battalions were also stationed at the Cape of Good Hope on the southern tip of Africa after it was captured from the Dutch in 1806. The 5th Battalion was the only one to have an extended stay in Europe with the others often returning only briefly to the Channel Islands or the Isle of Wight to recruit and rebuild after suffering losses from disease. The wide geographic spread of the regiment often meant that when the 5th Battalion had a vacancy for an officer it would take many months to be filled as letters and orders criss-crossed the Atlantic before the officer began their long journey to the battalion. For example, in 1802 Lieutenant George Bent of the 6th Battalion was promoted to a vacant captaincy in the 5th. He purchased his passage from Jamaica to Halifax, sold off many of his possession, bought his provisions for the voyage, and was actually embarking on the ship when an orderly caught up with him and told him that his orders had been countermanded and he was to stay with the 6th Battalion in the West Indies. The sudden change of orders proved fatal as Bent died from a fever within a year.[2]

1 John Galiffe to James Galiffe, 26 March 1816, BG ms fr 2751c pl23 f026.

2 M. Bent, 'A Royal American', *Journal of the Society of Army Historical Research*, Vol.I, p.103 & 15.

Being part of such a large regiment meant that vacancies and promotions often arose, especially as the regiment was stationed in such unhealthy locations, but also that there were always plenty of officers to fill them.

In 1816 Captain Charles Leslie joined the 2nd Battalion and noted:

> Never in the annals of military records or arms was such a battalion seen. From the regiment having been raised to serve exclusively in America, they were termed the Royal Americans; and an act having been passed declaring the West Indian Islands in that continent, it became, from there being no chance of ever serving in England, to all intents and purposes a condemned corps. Hence there was no difficulty in anyone getting a commission in it. Young men of money or interest on getting a commission in the regiment, or obtaining promotion in it, were always certain that they could effect an exchange into some other more select corps which wished to get quietly rid of a black sheep. The number of battalions also increased the evil. When an officer committed a misdemeanour, he was permitted to try his luck by exchanging with an officer of another battalion, who, perhaps, was obliged to do so under similar circumstances.[3]

The removal of Lieutenant Frederick Steitz to the 1/60th in 1811 was one such case of a 'black sheep' being off-loaded to another battalion. However, there are also many cases of deserving officers moving between the battalions to gain a step up in rank.

When the 5th Battalion was formed it was exclusively made up of foreign recruits with foreign officers. When the 1/60th was inspected in May 1797 at Quebec it had a strength of 448 men, of which 197 were English, 55 Scottish, 97 Irish, and only 99 foreign. Most of the men had ten years or more of service behind them, with around a quarter having served more than 20 years and who would have been with the Army during the American War of Independence. There was also only one foreign officer, and he was the chaplain. When the 2/60th was inspected the same year out of 439 men 211 were English, 25 Scottish, 80 Irish, and 123 foreign, with a similar pattern of long service. Six officers were foreign.[4]

In 1797 the composition of the regiment began to change as it absorbed many of the foreign corps, although this process was not always smooth. In December of that year *The Hampshire Chronicle* reported that:

> The remaining detachments of Montalembert, De La Tour, Lowenstein and Waldstein, were a few days since landed at Guernsey, to be incorporated in the 60th regiment for West India service; but we find this was not effected so easily as was expected, as much refractory language was used by the soldiers, who insisted they had engaged to act under their own officers, and then for a limited time only. The latter conditions was assured them by the commanding officer, and they at last yielded their reluctance to enlist anew in an English regiment.[5]

3 Leslie, *Military Journal*, pp.283-4.

4 Inspections of 1/60th & 2/60th, TNA, WO 27/80.

5 *The Hampshire Chronicle*, Saturday 16 December 1797.

When the 1/60th was inspected in 1812 at the Cape of Good Hope the national make-up of the battalion was radically different: six English, one Scot, six Irish, and 1,060 foreign. There were also 20 black pioneers on the strength. Most of the men had two years or less service. Similarly, when the 2/60th was inspected in the same year the men were also over 90% foreign.[6] Inspections for the 3rd and 4th Battalions show a similar pattern of an increasing proportion of foreign soldiers over time. The reason for this shift is likely to be not only the absorption of many of the foreign corps but the increasing availability of prisoners of war as a source of recruits.

The 5th Battalion seems to have been unusual in being exclusively foreign recruited with almost no British or Irish riflemen. The 5th Battalion attempted to restrict itself to German recruits, even though that definition seems to have included most of northern and central Europe, but the other battalions included a wider spread of nationalities. One officer, sailing from the Isle of Wight for the West Indies in September 1800 to join the 2/60th noted that:

> The detachments of the six battalions of the sixtieth, were composed of Russians, Poles, Germans, Italians, French, &c.; we had one Cingalese. These men were enlisted from the foreign brigade, viz. the Duke de Castre's corps, York hussars, chasseurs Britannique, le regiment de Mortemarte, and Prince Charles of Levenstein's corps, &c…
>
> …I take this opportunity to correct a general error regarding the sixtieth regiment. The battalions were composed entirely of foreigners, enlisted for five years, and was the only regiment in the colonies that did not receive condemned men; but all the other regiments of the line received them in quotas.[7]

However, British and Irish prisoners and deserters from regiments serving in the British Isles were sent to the West Indies and incorporated into the 60th, at least in the years prior to 1800.[8] These were probably the source of the large numbers of English, Scottish, and Irish men in the ranks. Many Irish rebels were convicted and sentenced to service for life in the West Indies after 1798, and some joined the 60th. The inclusion of such men meant that they had to be transferred to another unit prior to a battalion embarking for Europe. In 1803 ridding itself of its condemned men reduced the 2nd Battalion to just 47 men.[9] The composition of the battalions seems to have changed as they left their British and Irish manpower in the West Indies with other battalions and they came back to Europe to replenish their ranks with prisoners of war and other foreign recruits. By 1807 some battalions were still a quarter British and Irish while others, like the 4th Battalion, which had more recently recruited were almost all foreign.[10]

Prisoners of war may have been a ready supply of men but recruiting them was not without problems. In 1796 the *Caroline* transport was taking 300 French prisoners to join the 2/60th

6 Inspections of 1/60th & 2/60th, TNA, WO 27/107.

7 T. Fernyhough, *Military Memoirs of Four Brothers* (London: William Sams, 1829), p.6.

8 Butler, *Annals*, Vol.I, p.229.

9 M. Durey, 'White Slaves: Irish Rebel Prisoners and the British Army in the West Indies 1799-1804', *Journal of the Society of Army Historical Research*, Vol.LXXX, p.310.

10 60th Regiment Inspections, TNA, WO 27/92.

in Quebec when they mutinied and tried to take the ship and sail for France. The captain foiled the attempt, erected a barricade with carronades pointing forwards, and forced the prisoners to work the sails until they arrived at their destination.[11]

The 5th Battalion was unique in the regiment for its prolonged and active service in the Peninsula, and also for being the only fully rifle armed battalion. However, officers coming into the battalion were not necessarily devoid of combat experience as all the battalions formed before 1814 did see some action. At the outbreak of war the 1st and 2nd Battalions had been based in Montreal and Quebec for many years, and the 3rd and 4th were based in the West Indies. The 4th Battalion took part in the capture of Tobago in April 1793 and then elements of that battalion and the 3rd took part in a failed attempt to take Martinique. The 3rd Battalion, decimated by disease, transferred many of its men to the 4th and sailed for the Channel Islands to recruit in 1794. The 4th Battalion then played a part in the second and successful attempt on Martinique, and the capture of St Lucia and Guadeloupe. The battalion was also praised for its part in defeating French supported uprisings on the islands in 1795. The 3rd Battalion returned to the West Indies in 1796 and it was then the 4th's turn to go to the Channel Islands to rebuild its numbers. The 3rd Battalion then took part in the campaigns on St. Vincent, Tobago, Trinidad and Puerto Rico.[12]

The 1st Battalion's men were drafted into the 2nd in 1797 and a cadre sailed home to recruit. Restocking its numbers with royalist French and Dutch soldiers the 1st Battalion was posted to Barbados in 1799. Lieutenant General Trigge, commander in chief of the Leeward Islands at the time, referred to them as 'the most efficient Corps under my command.'[13] Several companies of the 2nd Battalion were sent to the West Indies in 1798, with the rest sailing there in 1800.

The 1st-4th Battalions were all red-coated conventional line battalions with a grenadier company, a light company, and eight centre companies. However, following the raising of the 5th Battalion, rifle companies were gradually introduced to the other battalions. This may have been due to many of the foreign corps merged into the 60th already having had rifle companies. The first to include a rifle company seems to have been the 6th Battalion, which was officially raised in July 1799 but the rifle company had existed since February and had joined the Helder campaign in September whilst the rest of the battalion was still forming.[14] The battalion sailed for Jamaica in 1800 and stayed there, almost continually, until 1817.[15] Whilst it was probably formed with mostly foreign recruits in 1812 the 6th Battalion did have a significant proportion of men from the UK; out of 802 privates 32 were English, six Scottish, and 97 Irish.[16] It is likely that many of these men were condemned and had come from other battalions as they rotated back to Europe.

When he joined the 6/60th on the Isle of Wight in 1800, George Bent claimed: 'I never saw a finer battalion than the 6th (such flank companies!), and a noble band has been added – to please the Jamaica ladies.'[17] When the battalion arrived back in Jamaica he wrote that they:

11 S.W. Fullom, *The Life of General Sir Howard Douglas* (London: Murray, 1863), p.67.
12 Butler, *Annals*, Vol.I, pp.235-54.
13 Trigge to Dundas 19 March 1799, TNA, WO 1/87 p.95.
14 Butler, *Annals*, Vol.I, pp.254-8.
15 Willoughby Wallace, *Regimental Chronicle*, pp.24-5.
16 Inspection of 6/60th, TNA, WO 27/107.
17 Bent, 'A Royal American', p.16.

> ...marched in high style to Up Park camp, about a mile and a half from Kingston, where we now are – a very healthy station, the best in the island to season new comers. I had fancied that we should never find battalions here of more than two or three hundred rank and file, and yet the first and fourth battalions of our own regiment are each six hundred strong; and the three leading divisions of our own battalion, who have been here now nearly six weeks, have not lost a man.[18]

Rifle companies soon replaced light companies in the other battalions as well. The 2nd Battalion seems to have been the first, in September 1801, with the 3rd also having rifles by the summer of 1804. The companies do not seem to have always received the Baker designed infantry rifle though, despite the fact that the simplified West India model was probably intended for them. The 4th Battalion was still using old Dutch rifles in 1808 and did not get the newer model until the following year.[19] It also seems that the training of rifle companies did not always get the attention required. An inspection of the 1/60th in 1807 found that the men of the rifle company were poor shots, did not practice target firing regularly, and that their rifles were badly maintained.[20]

During 1801 and 1802 all six battalions were in the Caribbean region.[21] Once the war resumed in 1803 the battalions received fresh recruits from the garrisons of the French and Dutch colonies that surrendered. In 1806 the 3rd Battalion again had to return to the Channel Islands to recruit, returning the next year. The 2nd Battalion did the same in 1808 and hence were in Europe to serve their part in the Corunna campaign. Replenished with men of the French Swiss regiments recruited by Major Davy for the 5th Battalion, and the 'suspected men' sent back from Portugal, the 2nd returned to the West Indies in 1809. In 1806 the 4th Battalion was sent to the Cape of Good Hope but was back in the West Indies two years later. The 3rd and 4th Battalions took part in the capture of Martinique, again, in 1809 and elements of the 2nd and 4th in the taking of Guadeloupe in 1810. However, they did not always win praise. Sir George Beckwith, commander of the Guadeloupe expedition, wrote to the Secretary at War:

> I have no confidence in troops recently arrived from England in a motley mixture. The flank companies of the 2nd Battalion of the 60th, and the grenadiers of the 4th battalion behaved shamefully in the face of the enemy. I repeat my request that certain corps in this army be no longer loaded with men polluted by civil crimes, congregated with French prisoners and deserters.[22]

The 1st Battalion went to the Cape of Good Hope in 1811 and remained there for eight years. During the war of 1812 against the United States companies of the 2nd and 4th Battalions served as marines and fought several actions against American privateers. The 2nd, 3rd, and 4th Battalions continued to be stationed in the West Indies until well after Waterloo.[23]

18 Bent, 'A Royal American', p.20.
19 Bailey, *Flintlock Rifles*, pp.155-6.
20 Inspection of 1/60th, TNA, WO 27/92.
21 Willoughby Wallace, *Regimental Chronicle*, p.24.
22 Beckwith to Liverpool, no date given, quoted in Butler, *Annals*, Vol.I, p.274.
23 Butler, *Annals*, Vol.I, pp.279-84.

In September 1813 the 7th Battalion was raised in Guernsey, mostly from prisoners of war. However, when it was inspected in 1814 nearly a quarter of its sergeants came from the British Isles and there was one English drummer and two privates.[24] The new battalion wore green, like the 5th, but had a mix of 200 riflemen and 640 light infantry. The 7th Battalion was soon sent to Halifax and saw action during the war with the United States, fighting at the Battle of Hampden. The battalion contained many French and Italian prisoners of war, some of whom were the cause of discipline problems in the unit, and who found it difficult to adapt to the drill of the British Army.[25]

The 8th Battalion was formed in 1814 from a unit composed of French deserters that had been in Cadiz since 1810, and had been originally intended for the Chasseurs Brittanique.[26] It too wore green, and was meant to have two rifle companies with the rest being light infantry, but there is no evidence they were ever issued with rifles.[27] The battalion moved from Cadiz to Gibraltar and stayed there until 1816.

A letter in the *The Royal Military Panorama* complained that the officers for the new battalions were largely drawn from other regiments:

> …in the addition of two battalions to the 60th regiment, very recently; not one Major of that regiment out of twelve got a Lieutenant-Colonelcy, nor one Captain a Majority; they were conferred on officers from the Peninsula: this was certainly right in principle, but could it be fair to neglect entirely the officers of the 60th, who, although deprived of opportunities of brilliant service, had served long and steadily in a pestilential climate?[28]

Charles Leslie who had joined the battalion prior to its incorporation into the 60th wrote:

> On joining the provisional battalion at Cadiz, I instantly got command of a company of about 120 strong. The men were supposed to be all Germans, but many entered as such were French, Italian, or Poles. They were a remarkably well-conducted set of men, no drunkards or idlers. The generality of them were always employed, when off duty, in making fancy-work of all descriptions, carving in bone, plaiting hair-chains, &c., repairing watches, making busts. They had great power in acquiring languages. My servant, although a German, talked French, Spanish, and Italian, and English at last, remarkably well. He had been servant to a French General who was killed at Barossa.[29]

24 Inspection of 7/60th, TNA, WO 27/127.
25 Bamford, *Sickness, Suffering* , p.165.
26 Andrew Bamford, 'British Forces at Cadiz 1810-1814: Organisation, Strength, and Losses', <https://www.napoleon-series.org/military/organization/Britain/Strength/Cadiz/c_Cadiz1.html> (accessed 7 September 2018).
27 Bailey, *Flintlock Rifles*, pp.156-7.
28 *The Royal Military Panorama*, January 1814.
29 Leslie, *Military Journal*, pp.232-3.

In 1815 the 1st to 4th and the 6th battalions were designated as light infantry and exchanged their red coats for green. The 5th Battalion had introduced the role of a specialist light infantry battalion to the regiment. The laurels they had won in the Peninsula proved that the experiment had been successful, and the regiment would continue to evolve into a purely rifle corps in the years ahead.

24

The Nivelle and the Nive

The battalion received a draft of two corporals, three buglers, and 87 privates from the Foreign Depot in August 1813, and another of 52 men in October. Amongst them was Private Peter Louis who had managed to escape from French captivity and make his way back to the depot via the port of Bordeaux. He had been taken prisoner the previous November and was anxious to claim his back pay. The men were much needed as the companies of the 2nd Division had been whittled down to strengths of around 30 rank and file apiece by the fighting in the mountains. Ensigns Edward John Bruce, from the 4/60th, and Henry Shewbridge, from the 2/60th, sailed with the first draft, as did Lieutenant Cuthbert Forneret who had finished his studies at the Royal Military College.[1]

Colonel Mosheim wrote a separate letter recommending Forneret to Colonel Keane:

> I cannot suffer the Detachment of the 5th Batt 60th Regt which embarked today for the purpose of joining you in Spain to depart without recommending to your particular notice and attention Lieut. Forneret as a very well behaved and truly promising young Officer who has received his military education at the Royal Military College. I have no doubt he will justify, what I conceived my Duty on his account.
>
> I must also avail myself of this opportunity of mentioning the whole Detachment in terms most favourable to your notice. The men have been carefully selected, their conduct while under my command has been most exemplary and soldierlike; and they have all gone through a regular course of drill and instruction in the Rifle exercise and manoeuvres.[2]

The drafts were a welcome boost to the battalion's numbers as desertion had risen significantly, with 102 men deserting during the last six months of the year. However, the pay list only has half that number listed as having deserted with a much higher number of prisoners of war than the monthly returns.[3] This might indicate that many men thought to have deserted had in fact straggled or had been missing in action and were subsequently taken

1 Mosheim to Keane 19 July & 4 August 1813, TNA, WO 7/90 p.107, pp.144-5; May, July, August & October 1813 Returns, WO 17/264.

2 Mosheim to Keane 19 July 1813, TNA, WO 7/90, p.108.

3 July to December 1813 Returns, TNA WO 17/264; September & December 1813 Pay Lists, WO 12/7075.

prisoner, but the differences between the returns and the pay list make the true situation unclear. The increase in desertion was a problem across the army; however it was higher in foreign regiments.[4] On 27 July the Chasseurs Brittanique lost 148 men to desertion in a single day.[5]

The French were actively encouraging desertion and printed leaflets that were left in the path of the allied advance:

> Advice
> The soldiers of all Nations, French Italian, German, Polanders, English, Spaniards an Portuguese who are in English service are advised that the deserters coming to the French imperial Army are perfectly well received; they are paid for the arms and the horses they bring with; none of them is obliged to serve; pass-ports are delivered to them to return to their native country, if they chuse, or go to inner parts of France where they may freely exercise their professions; they are moreover treated with all sort of regard. They are warned that the whole French Nation is armed, and that in the case of the English, Spaniard and Portuguese army should treat his territory, they would not find any where but death and destruction.[6]

From June one sergeant from each company was selected for the newly created rank of colour sergeant. Of the ten sergeants selected in the 5th Battalion: Thomas Petry (No. 8), Henry Bresser (No. 9), and John Scheming (No. 10) had been with the battalion since its formation on Barbados; Anton Koenigschenck (No. 6) and Michael Schmidt (No. 5) had joined from the Walloon Guards in 1799; Dionius Reckeis (No. 7) had joined in 1802 from the Lowenstein Jägers; George Koester (No. 2) was one of the many recruits from the convoy captured in the autumn of 1806; Henry Vannesel (No. 1), George Borst (No. 3), and William Vanbergen (No. 4), had all joined the battalion in 1806 or 1807.[7]

In July Captain Schoedde was given a brevet majority. Lieutenant Hoffman, who had been on recruiting duty for many years, joined the 37th Foot. Ensign Hugh Dickson joined from the 3/60th and Ensign John Moore came from the 99th Foot. Moore, Dickson, and Ensign Lerche were all promoted to lieutenant. In September Lieutenant Maximilian du Chastelet left to join the newly formed 7/60th. At the end of the year Captain Erskine was appointed deputy assistant adjutant general to the expedition to Holland. Surgeon Dumoulin was appointed surgeon to the forces and was replaced by Assistant Surgeon Cassel from the Chasseurs Brittanique. Assistant Surgeon Wehsarg joined the Brunswick Light Infantry and was replaced by Hospital Mate William Stevenson. In October Lieutenant Ingersleben exchanged with Lieutenant Peter Van Dyke of the 2nd KGL Light Battalion.[8] Ingersleben went on to serve with his new regiment for the rest of the Peninsular campaign, in the Netherlands in 1814, and at Waterloo in 1815.[9]

4 Oman, *Peninsular War*, Vol.VII, p.3.
5 Nichols, *Mongrel Regiment*, p.142
6 Quoted in Robertson, *Wellington Invades*, p.161.
7 September 1813 Pay List, TNA, WO 12/7075; Periods of Service 5/60th, June 1806, WO 25/1008.
8 July to December 1813 Returns, TNA, WO 17/264.
9 Beamish, *King's German Legion*, Vol.II, p.569.

With Soult's forces back across the frontier, Wellington turned his attention again to San Sebastian. Extra guns were shipped from Britain and the bombardment of the walls had begun again by late August. New breaches were soon formed and on 30 August the 5th Division prepared to assault the fortress, supported by 750 volunteers from the 1st, 4th, and Light Divisions. On the 31st the storming parties went forward. After a hard fight the town was taken, and promptly sacked by the allied troops. The French withdrew into the citadel where they refused to surrender until 8 September despite having no hope of relief and suffering an intense bombardment.[10] Some men from the 5th Battalion may have been amongst the volunteers but if any riflemen did participate they suffered no casualties.

As San Sebastian was being stormed Soult was attempting to drive across the River Bidassoa and relieve the beleaguered garrison. His army had recovered, somewhat, from the battles of July and the subsequent retreat with new drafts and stragglers making their way back to their units. The steep banks of the river and the few available fords limited the number of places an attack was possible and Wellington, learning of Soult's intentions, repositioned his forces accordingly. The French forded the river in several places on 31 August but were readily and convincingly beaten back with heavy losses, largely by Spanish and Portuguese units and the Light Division.

News reached Wellington in early September that the war had recommenced in northern Europe and was not going well for France. The allied army in Spain had received reinforcements in the form of a fresh brigade from Britain plus the recovered 1st Guards Brigade from Oporto. With Soult unlikely to get any reinforcements of his own, the time seemed ripe for a move into France. The French commander, surprised that the allies had not already crossed the frontier, prepared a series of defensive lines. Soult expected the main attack to come from the mountain passes in the east and Wellington took measures to confirm this view, while planning a strike in the west, near the sea. The French considered the Bidassoa estuary impassable and the area was only light garrisoned.

Early on the morning of 7 October the 5th Division crossed fords near Fuenterabia and the 1st Division waded through the river a little further inland above Irun. The 5th Division had crossed to the other bank before they came under fire, and the Guards and KGL brigades of the 1st Division were halfway across before they were spotted. The French defenders were vastly outnumbered and fell back rapidly. The 1st Division's light companies, including Nos. 5 and 9 of the 5th Battalion, advanced along the French bank until they began to encounter stiff resistance at Behobia. Portuguese and Spanish units also crossed the river further upstream. With those French units that did stand rapidly outflanked and forced to withdraw the French were pushed back, surrendering the high ground near the river.

Further inland the Light Division, with Spanish support, had a harder fight for the Great Rhune hill and the area around Vera but still won the day. No. 1 Company with the 6th Division was involved in skirmishing against d'Erlon's corps but this was a demonstration to convince Soult that the main effort was due in the east and not a concerted attack. The 7th Division made a similar feint. By the end of the day the allied army had a firm toehold

10 Robertson, *Wellington Invades*, pp.99-111.

in French territory. Allied casualties were around 1,600 killed, wounded and missing.[11] The 5th Battalion had one man wounded, and two taken prisoner; all from No. 5 company.[12]

Wellington did not immediately follow up the crossing of the French frontier with further advances. Despite the weakness of the French forces he was still cautious in case Napoleon beat the allies in Germany and then turned his attention south. He was also concerned that if he led his Portuguese and Spanish troops into France they might seek to revenge themselves on the populace and provoke an insurrection. As the fate of the French on their northern frontier became clearer and Pamplona was finally starved into submission, freeing up the blockading troops, Wellington did eventually begin to plan his next move.

Winter had come and both armies endured cold winds, snow, and sleet, especially those high up in the mountains. The allied army may have had little to do but keep warm for the month following the river crossings but the French had not been idle. Soult had prepared 20 miles of redoubts, strong points, batteries, trenches, and forts along the line of the River Nivelle.[13] Each defensive position was covered by others and there were fall-back positions in second, and sometimes third, lines each taking every advantage of the rough terrain. Villages and towns had also been fortified. After the disaster of his Bidassoa defence he garrisoned the seaward end very heavily, at the expense of the longer landward stretch.

Wellington brought forward all the troops he could to attack the French positions, amassing around 82,000 infantry to Soult's 62,000.[14] Given the terrain, neither cavalry nor artillery could play a large role in the allied assault. The largest portion of the allied divisions would attack the centre of the French line, with more limited and diversionary attacks taking place at either end. The forces on the right, in the mountains, were the 2nd and 6th Divisions with a division each of Spanish and Portuguese under Hill. Beresford had the 3rd, 4th, 7th, and Light Divisions, with two Spanish divisions and a Portuguese brigade, in the centre. At the seaward end was the newly arrived Lieutenant General Sir John Hope with the 1st, 5th, and two Spanish divisions plus one British and one Portuguese independent brigade. The 5th Battalion had representation in each section of the front. Hill's men were up to their knees in snow and unable to move into position on time but by 10 November all the pieces were in place.

Hope's orders were to just demonstrate in his sector. The 5th Division drove in the French pickets opposite them but stopped short of the French line and continued to skirmish sporadically for the rest of the day. The 1st Division's KGL brigade pushed back the French line but then held position and Aylmer's independent British brigade took the village of Urrogne.

The Light Division, on the hill known as the Great Rhune, had the onerous task of crossing the deep ravines that separated it from the lower Lesser Rhune. They would be supported by Spanish units. The 4th Division were to assault the St. Barbe redoubt and the positions in front of the village of Sare. The 7th were to take another redoubt and then also advance to Sare. The 3rd Division would attack slightly later and its objectives were the fords of the Nivelle and the bridge at Amotz.

11 Oman, *Peninsular War*, Vol.VII, p.133.

12 Rigaud, *Celer et Audax*, p.230; December 1813 Pay List; TNA, WO 12/7075.

13 Oman, *Peninsular War*, Vol.VII, p.162.

14 Oman, *Peninsular War*, Vol.VII, p.168.

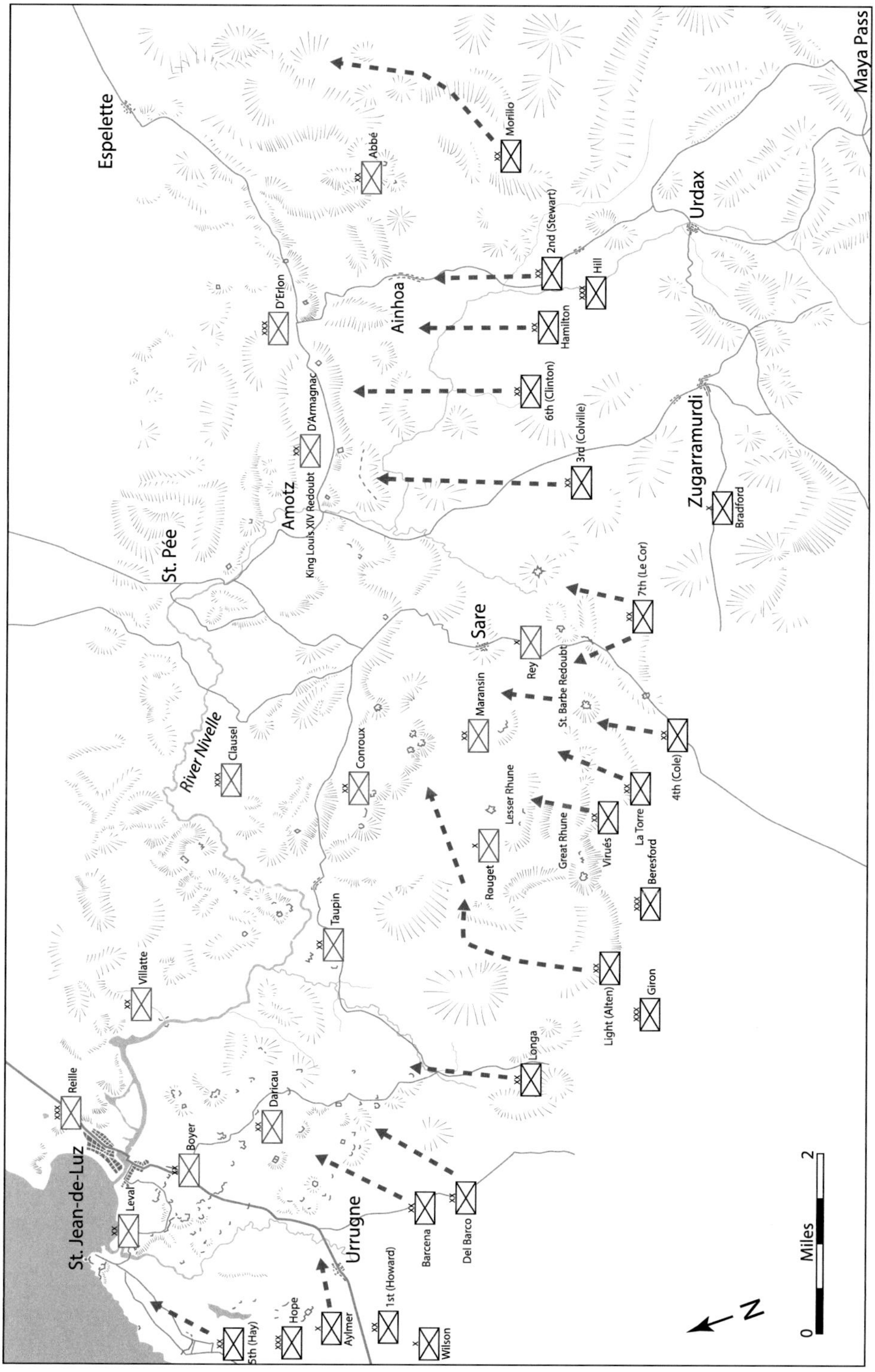

The Battle of the Nivelle, 10 November 1813.
Sources: Lipscombe, *Atlas & Wyld*, *Maps & Plans*.

The 3rd Division's move would be supported by the 6th taking the defences overlooking Amotz, with Hamilton's Portuguese Division on their right. The 2nd Division would advance towards Ainhoa and the redoubts nearby while Morrillo's Spanish division would move on the French flank. Colonel Keane was now commanding a brigade in the 3rd Division and with Fitzgerald a prisoner Major Galiffe took command of the battalion, and the light troops of the 3rd Division, while Brevet Major Schoedde led the headquarters companies.

At dawn on 10 November three guns fired from the top of a hill in the centre of the allied line to signal the advance. The day was cold, clear and bright. The Light Division were the first to attack. The Lesser Rhune's frontage was a series of small cliffs and its summit was covered by redoubts and other fortifications. The division stormed forward from positions close to the French and rushed the enemy. Some attacks were stalled but others overwhelmed the defenders and the division was able to push on into the second line as the French fell back. On the Light Division's left the 4th and 7th Divisions also overwhelmed the French, streaming between the fixed defences. Anson's Brigade, with No. 10 company, led the 4th Division's attack. Allied guns kept the French heads down while the infantry went forward and some of the French redoubts were abandoned with little or no fight.

On the right of the allied centre the 3rd Division went forward with the light troops, including Nos. 2, 3 and 7 companies, in the lead and Keane's Brigade following. They crossed a ravine and then came up against a mile-long abattis – A line of trees and branches laid with the sharpened points facing the enemy – with two redoubts behind. The vital bridge at Amotz, guarded by breastworks on both sides of the river, lay below the redoubts and formed the link between two French corps. It took three assaults to take the abattis, and then one battalion took the bridge at a run while the rest of Keane's Brigade took the redoubts on the heights after strong resistance from the French.

With the initial attacks successful Beresford paused to get his troops organised before pushing on. The divisions were formed up with light companies in front, a lead brigade and then two in support. At around 10:00 a.m. the allies advanced on the next line of French positions and the units that had rallied. The 3rd Division pressed forward from the area around the bridge making short work of the disheartened French in front of them. The troops around the King Louis XIV redoubt held on longer against the 4th and 7th Divisions, using case shot to fight off the first attacks. The Light Division made good inroads on their front, turning the flank of some French positions.

On the right of the British line Hill's divisions had much further to march to get into position and so did not begin their attacks until around 9:00 a.m. The 6th Division was the furthest left and advanced with a battalion of caçadores and the light companies of the lead brigade forward. Pack's Brigade, with No. 1 company, was further back in support. The division crossed the Nivelle using fords hidden by trees and waited for Hamilton's Portuguese Division, which crossed further up and with some opposition before advancing on the French positions. The two divisions skirmished up steep slopes to the main French trenches and redoubts but found the French already retreating as the 3rd Division had taken the bridge at Amotz and were threatening the rear of their line.

The 2nd Division advanced with the light companies of Byng's Brigade, including No. 6 company, skirmishing in front. Byng's Brigade attacked the Finodetta redoubt on the height whilst Ashworth's Portuguese Brigade tackled another on the left, supported by the light companies of O'Callaghan's Brigade including No. 4 company.[15] The French in the Finodetta redoubt put up a strong defence, and a battery of two large naval carronades loaded with double charges of grapeshot inflicted heavy casualties on the attackers. When all his men had reached the crest of the hill Byng formed his brigade into line and advanced on the French, who wavered and then broke. The battery was also then taken. Surgeon Walter Henry, serving with the 2nd Division wrote:

> We lost a good many people in storming this mountain. The Light Companies of the Division, who were up first, suffered severely – every officer was hit, and Major Ackland, 57th, who commanded them, was killed. The death of his pretty spaniel – that had during the action amused itself by barking at the dust the balls raised as they struck the ground – preceded its master's fall only by a few minutes.[16]

With the allies victorious all along the central and eastern sections and the French falling back it was the fading light of a short November day and the need to re-order formations that limited the allies' advance more than the enemy. The allied troops entered a French camp and set fire to the huts, the blaze lighting up the dusk. Beresford managed to advance some of his divisions as far as the French camp at Serres while others got as far as St. Pée. By dusk Wellington's men had been fighting for ten hours over very arduous terrain and were too exhausted to continue.

Allied losses in the battle were 404 killed, 2,048 wounded, and 73 missing. The French casualties were 451 killed, 2,637 wounded and 1,233 missing.[17] The 5th Battalion lost eight killed, had 61 wounded and two listed as missing, one of whom was taken prisoner. Lieutenant Thomas Eccles was amongst the dead. He had only been with the battalion for six months, having joined from the 34th Foot. The 2/34th was in O'Callaghan's Brigade of the 2nd Division and it seems likely that Eccles was serving with No. 4 company in that brigade as George Bell of the 34th recalled:

> On the evening of the 9th of November we bivouacked on the broadside of a heather brae (out of sight of the French out-posts not far away) to eat our supper off whatever might be found in the old haversack; little and good would have been acceptable, but it was generally less and bad. We lay in groups and talked of the morrow, and of a great battle sure to come off, for which the two game-cocks of England and France were long preparing.
>
> 'Now Tom Eccles,' I said, 'good night, and mind that if you run your jolly red nose into danger, as you always do at the first flash of fire, we will miss you to-morrow evening.' This was a most excitable, young, thoughtless Irish officer, who had fought through the whole way up to the present Lord Mayor's day. He had nearly lost one of the colours of the regiment in Albuera by running far in advance of the battalion while fighting in line; the staff of the flag was cut by a shot in his hand, while he was loudly cheering on the men. Nobody could hold him, he was always in the front of

15 Stewart to Hill, 11 November 1813, Wellington, *Supplementary Despatches*, Vol.VIII, pp.359-60.

16 Henry, *Military Life*, p.179.

17 Oman, *Peninsular War*, Vol.VII, p.544.

The Battle of Nivelle, 10 November 1813, by William Heath. (Bibliotheques de Toulouse)

> the battle. When the morning signal-gun fired for our advance, the whole army already being under arms, loaded and ready for action, we went forward by divisions, brigades, and regiments, according to the nature of the ground and previous arrangements. Skirmishers to the front. In ten minutes or so the dawn was lighted up by the flashing of great guns and small arms. The fusilade ran down the line like wildfire. Poor Eccles, always foremost, was riddled to death with French bullets.[18]

Three sergeants of the 5th Battalion were amongst the dead, all from No. 6 company in Byng's Brigade: John Hausman, from Bramstein, had been with the battalion since 1806 and had only recently been promoted; Frederick Meissner, a former bugler, had also only recently been made sergeant; Henry Graff had joined the battalion from the Lowenstein Jägers in 1802. The four privates all came from companies in the 3rd Division: Lucas Buschinsky (No. 3) was one of the few originals left and had been in British service since 1795; Michael Andreas (No. 7), from Poland, had joined the battalion in 1807; Lewis Ellassen (No. 3) had joined in September 1812; Balthasar Stotz had joined at the end of 1810.[19]

Eighteen year old Ensign Henry Shewbridge, with No. 1 company in the 6th Division, was also wounded, but he had only been slightly hurt. Captain James Stopford, commanding No. 10 company in the 4th Division, was severely wounded, as was Lieutenant John Passley,

18 G. Bell, *Rough Notes by an Old Soldier* (London: Day & Son, 1867), pp.121-2.

19 November 1813 casualty return, TNA WO 25/1923, Periods of Service 5/60th, June 1806, WO 25/1008; Butler, *Annals*, Vol.II, p.205.

who was with the headquarters companies in the 3rd Division. Stopford was back with his company in December but Passley returned to Britain to recover.[20] Three sergeants were amongst the wounded so the casualties amongst officers and NCOs were proportionately very high. Major Galiffe was singled out for praise by Major General Colville, who commanded the 3rd Division, for leading the advance.[21] Major General Byng put in his report that Lieutenant Lerche, who commanded No. 6 company in his brigade, 'conducted himself in a manner deserving of my notice.'[22]

The 5th Battalion's November return, the first completed in France, noted that Captain Purdon's company (No. 5) had joined the headquarters in the 3rd Division from the 1st Division. The company had been in the rear with the fever ridden 1st Brigade of Guards but no reason for the transfer is recorded and no other company replaced it.[23]

In the days following the defeat on the Nivelle, Soult withdrew the French army to a new line behind the River Nive, deeper into France. However, due to the topography of the area Soult did not feel that the line could be held and withdrew most of his army to the city and fortress of Bayonne. Wellington advanced his troops to a line from Bidart, on the coast, to Ustaritz on the Nive and then up the riverbank to Cambo. The allied army were able to enter cantonments in the various villages and towns, which provided some respite from the cold.

In December there was a break in the weather and Wellington set into motion a plan to cross the Nive. Hill with the 2nd Division, plus a Portuguese and a Spanish division, would cross via fords at Cambo, rebuild a bridge that the French had destroyed, and then advance down the river taking any French units in the flank. Meanwhile Beresford with the 3rd and 6th Divisions would use the ford at Ustaritz, build a pontoon bridge and then link up with Hill towards the main roads into Bayonne. Hope, with the 1st and 5th Divisions and attached brigades, would push along the coast towards Biarritz until they reached the main French line around Bayonne. The Light Division would support Hope's movement.

On the morning of 9 December the leading troops of the 2nd Division waded into the icy water and crossed to the opposite bank to either side of the broken bridge. Pringle's and Barnes' Brigades struggled through the deep river, coming under fire from French pickets, but the enemy quickly fell back as the 6th Division threatened to outflank them with their crossing at Ustaritz. The leading brigade of 6th Division, crossing to an island in the river via pontoons, soon forded the second channel, swept away the French pickets, and constructed a second pontoon span for rest of their division and the 3rd Division that followed on. The roads were thick with mud and progress towards Bayonne was slow. Hill ordered a Portuguese brigade to take the village of Villefranque, which they did, but the French counter-attacked and retook it. Hill sent the Portuguese back in, supported by Pringle's Brigade of the 2nd Division and the village exchanged hands again. Dusk was now falling and the allied advance halted. Soult, thinking Hill's force was stronger than it was, pulled his forces back and the following morning Hill's patrols were able to advance up to the outer defences of Bayonne.

20 Hall, *Biographical Dictionary*, pp.459 & 539; December 1813 Return, TNA, WO 17/264.

21 Colville to Beresford, undated, Wellington, *Supplementary Despatches*, Vol.VIII, p.369 Galiffe's name is mistakenly written as Griffiths.

22 Byng to Stewart 10 November 1813, Wellington, *Supplementary Despatches*, Vol.VIII, pp.360-1 Lerche's name was misspelled.

23 November 1813 Return, TNA, WO 17/264.

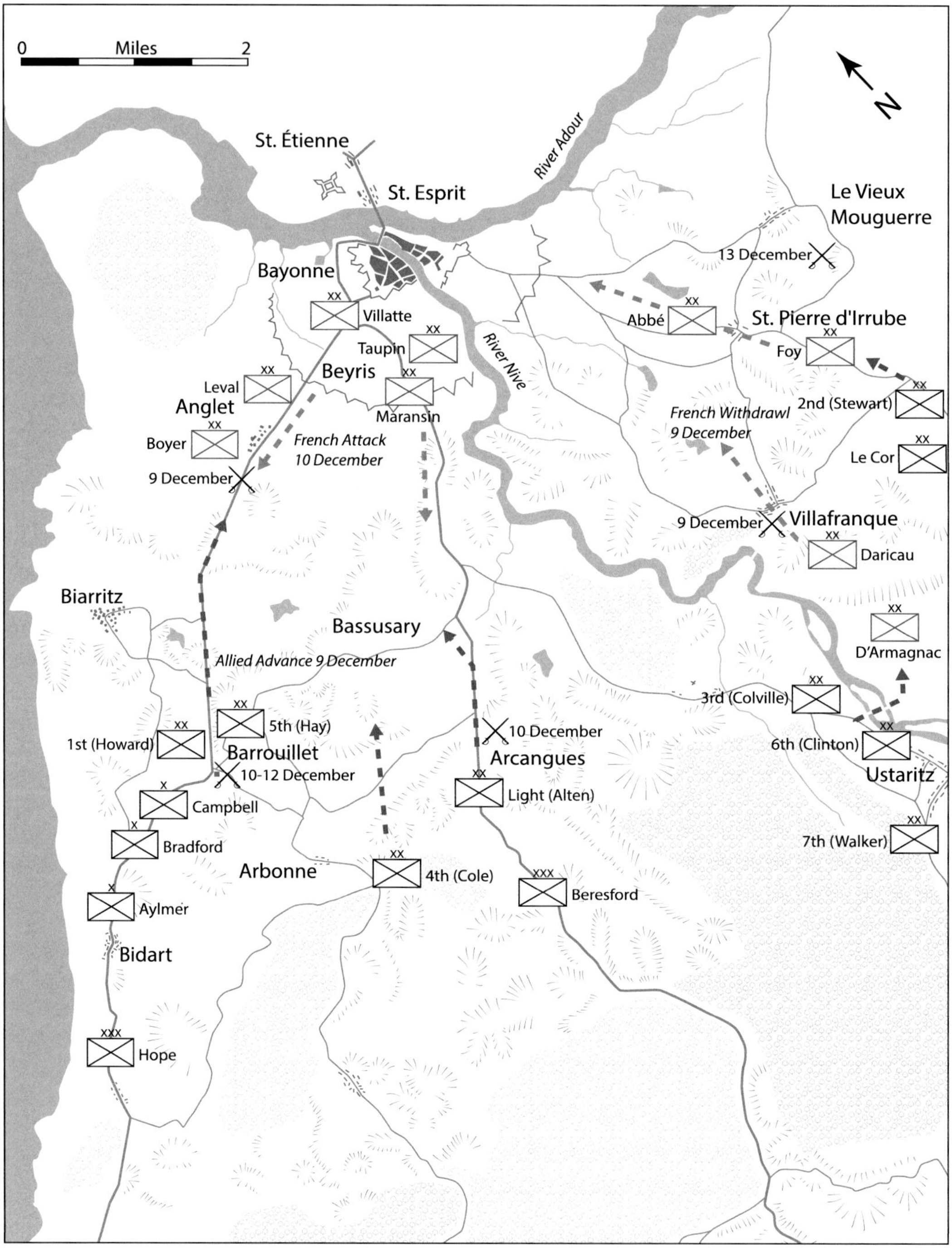

The Battles of the Nive, 9-13 December 1813.
Sources: Lipscombe, *Atlas* & Wyld, *Maps & Plans*.

At the same time as Hill's troops were fording the Nive, Sir John Hope's wing of the army had begun to advance over the difficult country nearer the coast. The terrain was a mix of a narrow plateau of varying width, and ravines, woods, and marshy ground that tended to restrict the scope of movement for both the allies and the French. The 5th Division marched closest to the sea while the two Guards brigades of the 1st Division took the main road with the KGL on their left. French outposts were driven in but Hope stopped when he reached the main French line at the fortified camp at Beyris. At dusk Hope sent the 1st and 5th Divisions to the rear and left two Portuguese brigades holding the front.

With Wellington's army now divided by the Nive, Soult saw an opportunity to strike. During the rainy night he pulled four divisions of weary men back from facing Hill and across the river to add to the five he had near the coast. It took until 9:00 a.m. on 10 December for all the troops to be in place. French light infantry began the attack by rushing the Light Division's pickets and either driving them in or taking them prisoner. As the French reached the main body of the division progress began to slow and then came to stop at Arcangues, which the Light Division stubbornly held until allied reinforcements came up and the French abandoned their attacks.

The French assault nearer the coast was pressed harder and the fighting became much fiercer than the attacks on the Light Division. Hope's line was thinly held with the bulk of his troops well in the rear. The British and Portuguese pickets were soon brushed aside by a surprise French attack. One of the Portuguese brigades fell back to a small chateau at Barrouillet, where the other Portuguese brigade and one from the 5th Division joined them. The fighting around the chateau was prolonged and hard. The French were on the brink of success when the lead elements of the 1st Division arrived and persuaded them to call a halt to the attacks. The fighting wound down to skirmishes in the woods.

During the night three German battalions marched over from the French lines. The commander of the 2nd Nassau Regiment had been contacted by the state's ruler and negotiations had taken place via an old friend in the KGL. The battalions were embarked for Germany and Soult took the precaution of disarming his other German regiments.

On the morning of 11 December Wellington pushed forward one brigade of the 5th Division to drive in some French outposts and later in the afternoon the French retaliated with a general attack on Hope's outposts, which were again caught by surprise. Hope was wounded rallying his men before the French attack fizzled out. The 1st moved up to take the place of the weary and battered 5th Division. The 12th passed tensely with an artillery duel but little skirmishing. During the night of 12-13 December Soult moved men over to Hill's side of the river, hoping to catch the allies unprepared there too but Wellington had taken the precaution of ordering another pontoon bridge built so that the 6th and 7th Divisions could cross to support Hill if needed.

Hill had cautiously moved his units forward towards Bayonne, occupying high ground, and creating defensive positions in chateaux and villages so that he had a good, defensible line three miles long anchored on the Nive and Adour Rivers at either end. Its only weakness was the two gullies that divided the line into three sectors that could not easily communicate, but any attacker would face the same issue. The 2nd Division's brigades held the front, with Pringle on the left, Barnes and Ashworth in the centre, and Byng on the right, with supporting units just to the rear.

The morning of the 13th was foggy and as the mists cleared French columns, advancing from St. Pierre d'Irrube towards the allied positions, became visible. At around 8:00 a.m. the first shots were fired. The ground narrowed the possible front so that the huge numeric advantage of the French with four divisions facing just one could not easily be brought to bear on the defenders. Much of the ground was suitable for skirmishers rather than dense columns of men. The first attack fell on the light troops of Ashworth's Brigade who began to fall back. Stewart, commanding the 2nd Division, sent the light companies of Barnes' Brigade, including Captain Blassiere's No. 8 company, forward in support, before following them up with other units of the brigade. The light companies of Byng's Brigade, including No. 6 company, were moved forward to support the 1/3rd. The French kept up the pressure and, although they fought hard, some of the allied units were pushed back. The light companies fired and retired, contesting every bit of cover. Some of the French reserves were committed but counterattacks by individual allied units succeeded in stopping any breakthrough. The 1/3rd was forced to retire from the heights at Le Vieux Mouguerre but the village was retaken and the enemy driven back by the light companies.[24]

The attack on Pringle's Brigade, stationed in a chateau, did not develop beyond a prolonged skirmish but by midday all the other brigades were being sorely tested after four hours of fighting. Reinforcements were coming up and Hill personally led a desperate counter-attack to try and buy some more time. Both in the centre and on the right tired allied soldiers made one last one effort against the equally fatigued French. The enemy gave way rather than fight. Soult ordered another brigade into the fray but they refused to advance.

With Wellington on the scene and the 3rd and 6th Division coming up Hill finished the battle off. Pringle sent his light companies, including No. 4 Company, in pursuit of the retreating French and then followed when his position was relieved by the 3rd Division. Byng advanced on the right flank and the French hardly resisted at first but stood firm at the summit of some high ground and Byng led his brigade forward to storm the position and the French then undertook a fighting withdrawal down to the Adour. Another French counter-attack was thwarted by a caçadore battalion from the 6th Division with artillery support. The battle ended at around 3:00 p.m. with the French back at their starting positions.

Total allied losses between 9 and 13 December were around 731 dead, 3,337 wounded and 593 missing. French casualties were just under 6,000 in total.[25] The 5th Battalion lost five men killed in action, or who were wounded and died soon after, during the period. The deaths do not seem to coincide with major actions for the divisions the men were serving in, so some may have died during skirmishes or clashes between outposts. Serving with No. 3 company in the 3rd Division Privates Frederick Oswald and Herman Siebrand, the former from Germany and the latter from Holland, were both fatally wounded and died 10 December. Both men had joined the battalion in 1811. Two men of No. 9 company in the 1st Division were killed: Private John Kierstman, from Mühlebach, fell on 12 December, and Private Joseph Schmidt was fatally wounded and died on 13 December. Both men had only joined the battalion at the end of the summer. Private Mathew Fischer (No. 4) died of wounds on 15 December. No. 6 company lost yet another sergeant on the 13th when Samuel

24 Stewart to Hill 14 December 1813, Wellington, *Supplementary Despatches*, Vol.VIII, p.439.

25 Oman, *Peninsular War*, Vol.VII pp.547 & 549.

Taubel was listed as missing; two men of the company were taken prisoner on the same day. Sergeant John Zeitler (No. 8) also went missing on 13 December.[26]

Lieutenant Hugh Dickson was wounded on 9 December and Lieutenant Gotlieb Lerche and Ensign William Rutledge were wounded on 13 December. All three were serving in the 2nd Division. Dickson and Lerche were both only slightly wounded but Rutledge, who had only recently volunteered from the North Devon Militia, died of his wounds five days later.[27] Lieutenant Peter Van Dyke's brief service with the battalion was cut short when he was taken prisoner on 13 December. He was also with the 2nd Division, and so with all the casualties the December return shows only two officers, Blassiere and Evans, present with these three companies. One sergeant and 12 rank and file were wounded on 9 December and two sergeants and 16 men on the 13th.[28]

Soult had had the advantage of numbers when he had attacked each half of the allied army, and yet still failed. His men had taken heavy casualties and morale was low. The French took up a new line on the River Adour and within Bayonne. The allied army fortified their positions and settled into winter quarters.

Soult was often eager to blame his subordinates for his failures but he also found time to complain about the enemy. On 1 September he had written to the Minister of War to complain about the high casualty rate amongst his officers:

> The loss in prominent and superior officers, sustained for some time past by the Army, is so disproportionate to that of the rank and file that I have been at pains to discover the reason; and have acquired the following information, which of course explains the case of so extraordinary a circumstance.
>
> There is in the English army a battalion of the 60th consisting of ten companies – the regiment is composed of six battalions, the other five being in America or the West Indies. This battalion is never concentrated, but has a Company attached to each Infantry Division. It is armed with a short rifle; the men are selected for their marksmanship; they perform the duties of scouts, and in action are expressly ordered to pick off the officers, especially Field and General Officers. Thus it has been observed that whenever a superior officer goes to the front during an action, either for the purposes of observation or to lead and encourage his men, he is usually hit.
>
> This mode of making war and of injuring the enemy is very detrimental to us; our casualties in officers are so great that after a couple actions the whole number are usually disabled. I saw yesterday battalions whose officers had been disabled in the ratio of one officer to eight men; I also saw battalions which were reduced to two or three officers, although less than one-sixth of their men had been disabled. You can imagine that if these casualties should recur, it would be very difficult to provide for the replacement of officers even though the nominations were made beforehand.[29]

26 December 1813 Casualty Return, TNA WO 25/1923; December 1813 Pay List, WO 12/7075.

27 Hall, *Biographical Dictionary*, pp.167, 343-4 & 503.

28 Butler, *Annals*, Vol.II, p.210; December 1813 Return, TNA WO 17/264.

29 Butler, *Annals*, Vol.II, pp.199-200, quoting from J B Dumas, *Neuf Mois de Campagnes à la suite du Maréchal Soult* (Paris: Henri Charles-La Vauzelle, 1907) pp.42-43.

With the 5th Battalion being so widely distributed, especially amongst the 2nd and 3rd Division brigades who bore much of the fighting in the Pyrenees, it is the case that in a large proportion of actions and battles the riflemen of the 60th would have been present and obviously carrying out their task of disrupting the French command and control very effectively. Another French officer put the number of officers killed by riflemen between 24 July and 31 August as 500, including eight generals. As far back as Vimeiro in 1808 one of Junot's staff had lamented the clear differences between soldiers' and officers' uniforms that made it possible for riflemen to pick their targets so easily.[30]

By the end of 1813 allied armies had crossed the northern frontiers of France. Defeat was becoming increasingly inevitable but Napoleon was not ready to give up and the new year would see more heavy fighting for the 5th Battalion. The December return showed a total strength of 738 sergeants, buglers, and rank and file. Five months later the May return would show only 493.[31]

30 Butler, Annals, Vol.II, pp.200-1; Dumas, *Neuf Mois,* p.43.

31 December 1813 Return, TNA, WO 17/264; May 1814 Return, WO 17/279.

25

Orthez and Toulouse

The winter of 1813 to 1814 was exceptionally cold. In London the Thames froze and a frost fair was held on the ice. Wellington's army had to endure long weeks of low temperatures and heavy rain. Units rotated between occupying the forward positions and thawing out in winter quarters further to the rear. During the deepest weeks of winter Wellington bided his time and made no further advances. The roads had turned to quagmires, preventing any major movements, and he was still waiting cautiously for the outcome of events on the northern border of France before committing his own forces. Meanwhile, the pickets and outposts of the two opposing army fraternised, traded, and generally tried to make life as tolerable as possible in the circumstances.

The regimental returns of the 5th Battalion for the first three months of 1814 show a marked drop in desertions, reducing to a handful per month. By the February return a total of 27 officers were absent on staff duty, serving with other corps, on leave, or recovering from wounds. The latest staff appointment was Lieutenant Roeppel, sent as an interpreter to the forces in Holland. He had spent all of 1813 on leave. Only 16 officers, including Major Galiffe who was still in command, were present with the companies. In March Captain Stopford purchased a majority in the 7/60th, Lieutenant Rafter was promoted to captain, and Ensign Stewart to lieutenant. Assistant Surgeon Berger died and 60 men lost in the general hospital system were struck off as presumed dead. No. 5 company, commanded by Captain Purdon, which had been in the 1st Division, remained with the 3rd so that four companies were present with the battalion headquarters.[1] On 1 January Wellington wrote to the Commissioners of Transports, who supervised the exchange system for prisoners of war, requesting that Brevet Lieutenant Colonel Fitzgerald be exchanged. However, the war would be over before he would return to the battalion.[2]

The brigading of the allied infantry at the start of the year was as follows:

1 January to March 1814 Returns, TNA, WO 17/279.

2 Wellington to the Commissioners of Transports 1 January 1814, quoted in Gurwood, *Wellington's Dispatches*, Vol.XI, p.411.

1st Division – Major General Howard
Colonel Maitland
    1/1st Guards, 3/1st Guards.
Major General Stopford
    1/Coldstream Guards, 1st Scots Guards, & No. 9 company 5/60th.
Major General Hinüber
    1st KGL, 2nd KGL, 5th KGL, 1st KGL Light & 2nd KGL Light.
Major General Aylmer (attached)
    2/62nd, 76th, 77th, 85th.

2nd Division – Lieutenant General William Stewart
Major General Barnes
    1/50th, 1/71st, 1/92nd & No. 8 company 5/60th.
Major General Byng
    1/3rd, 1/57th, 1st Provisional Battn. & No. 6 company 5/60th.
Major General Pringle
    1/28th, 2/34th, 1/39th & No. 4 company 5/60th.
Brigadeiro Ashworth (Portuguese)
    6th (2 battalions), 18th (2 battalions) & 6th Caçadores.

3rd Division – Lieutenant General Picton
Major General Brisbane
    1/45th, 74th, & 1/88th & Nos. 2, 3, 5 & 7 companies 5/60th.
Brevet Colonel Keane
    1/5th, 2/83rd, 2/87th, & 94th.
Marechal de Campo Power (Portuguese)
    9th (2 battalions), 21st (2 battalions) & 11th Caçadores.

4th Division – Lieutenant General Lowry Cole
Major General Anson
    3/27th, 1/40th, 1/48th, 2nd Provisional Battn. & No. 10 company 5/60th.
Major General Ross
    1/7th, 20th, 1/23rd & 1 Company Brunswick Oels.
Brigadeiro Vasconcellos (Portuguese)
    11th (2 battalions), 23rd (2 battalions) & 7th Caçadores.

5th Division – Major General Colville
Major General Hay
    3/1st, 1/9th & 1/38th, 2/47th & 1 company Brunswick Oels.
Major General Robinson
    1/4th, 2/59th, 2/84th & 1 company Brunswick Oels.
Coronel de Regoa (Portuguese)
    3rd (2 battalions), 15th (2 battalions) & 8th Caçadores.

6th Division – Lieutenant General Clinton
Major General Pack
1/42nd, 1/79th & 1/91st, & No. 1 company 5/60th.
Major General Lambert
1/11th, 1/32nd, 1/36th & 1/61st.
Coronel Douglas (Portuguese)
8th (2 battalions) & 12th (2 battalions) & 9th Caçadores.

7th Division – Major General Walker
Lieutenant Colonel Gardiner
1/6th, 3rd Provisional Battn. & 9 companies Brunswick Oels.
Major General Inglis
51st, 68th, 1/82nd & Chasseurs Britanniques.
Coronel Doyle (Portuguese)
7th (2 battalions), 19th (2 battalions) & 2nd Caçadores.

Light Division – Major General Alten
Major General Kempt
1/43rd, 2/95th, 3/95th & 1st Caçadores.
Colonel Colborne
1/52nd, 1/95th, 17th Portuguese & 3rd Caçadores.[3]

The winter was not an easy one for the French either. Demands from Napoleon for cadres of officers and NCOs for new battalions deprived Soult of useful veterans and, worse still, he had had to send off half his cavalry and 10,000 infantry to reinforce the armies in the north. His force was reduced to just over 60,000 whilst Wellington's Anglo-Portuguese divisions totalled 67,000, with Spanish troops available in addition.[4] On 3 January Clausel's corps attempted to drive back the allied right flank and succeeded in dislodging a Portuguese brigade. Wellington brought up the 3rd, 4th, 6th, and 7th Divisions but torrential rain prevented any counter attack until the 6th. The 3rd and 4th Divisions, with Portuguese support, pushed the French back to their previous positions.[5] The 5th Battalion lost five men taken prisoner from the companies with the 3rd Division.[6]

By early February the weather, and also the strategic situation, had become clear enough for Wellington to begin an offensive. He would attack Soult's left and drive the French eastwards away from the fortified city of Bayonne. Soult would be forced to draw men from the Bayonne garrison and then Wellington would cross the mouth of Adour and complete the investment of the city. The 1st and 5th Divisions, with cavalry, Spanish and Portuguese brigades, would be left around Bayonne while the majority of the rest of the army was involved in the advance. Hill would move around the French flank with the 2nd Division and Le Cor's

3 Army in Spain and Portugal, by Brigades and Divisions 25 January 1814, TNA WO 17/2475; Oman, *Wellington's Army*, pp.371-2.
4 Oman, *Peninsular War*, Vol.VII, p.309.
5 Oman, *Peninsular War*, Vol.VII, p.317.
6 March 1814 Pay List, TNA, WO 12/7075

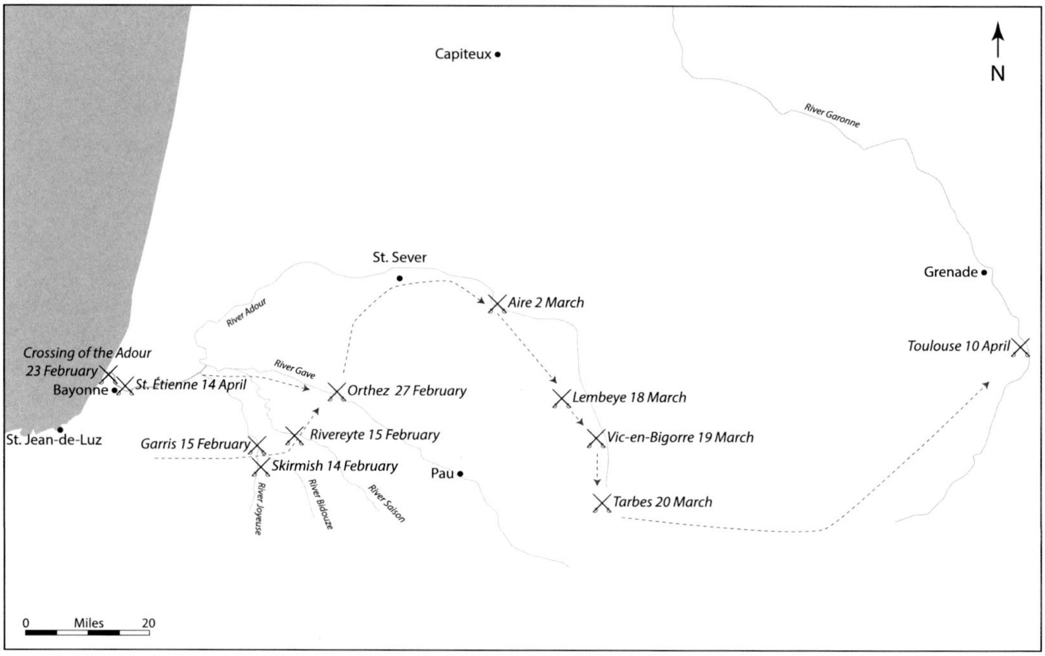

The Invasion of France, January to April 1814.

Portuguese Division, plus cavalry. Picton's 3rd Division would protect Hill's flank. The 4th, 6th, 7th, and Light Divisions, under Beresford, would constitute the main body of the allied movement. However, the French would have to be pushed back across several swollen rivers with few passable fords, and this would afford them multiple natural lines of defence.

On 14 February Hill began his advance in two columns from Urcarray. The French, severely outnumbered, fell back across the Joyeuse River after only a brief skirmish, during which three riflemen were wounded and Captain Peter Blassiere was severely wounded.[7] Blassiere had led No. 8 company for the whole of the Peninsular campaign, through dozens of battles, actions and skirmishes. He died of his wounds on the 22nd. Captain John Patterson of the 1/50th, who served in the same brigade as Blassiere, wrote: 'After buffeting all the storms, roughing it through thick and thin, and standing out in the pelting of many a shower of bullets, this gallant veteran fell at last in battle when the army entered France.'[8] When Victorian novelist James Grant wrote *The Romance Of War*, based on his own father's experiences fighting with the 1/92nd who were also in the same brigade, Blassiere featured as a character. Called Blacier in the book he is portrayed as something of a cliché with a thick German accent, a big meerschaum pipe always in his hand, and a predilection for eating sauerkraut. There is, however, no evidence he was German and, given his Francophone name, he may have been born in the Low Countries or Switzerland.

7 Butler, *Annals*, Vol.II, p.265; Hall, *Biographical Dictionary*, p.61.

8 Paterson, *Adventures*, p.357.

The withdrawal of some French units the previous day meant that on the 15th more units had to pull back or risk being outflanked. *Général de Division* Harispe's division reached Garris and decided to hold on a long hill behind a ravine known as the Motte de Garris. It was late in the day and the 2nd Division and Le Cor's Portuguese were slowly getting into position for an assault while harassing the French with cannon fire. As the French were outnumbered Hill expected them to withdraw so he was in no hurry to attack. However, Wellington arrived on the scene and ordered Pringle's Brigade to take the hill before nightfall. The brigade would be supported by Portuguese and Spanish units making flanking attacks.

The light companies of Pringle's Brigade, including No. 4 company, led the attack and descended down into the ravine, quickly driving back the French light troops whilst the allied guns opened fire on the French on the hill. The 1/39th followed the light companies with bayonets fixed in a close column. The slope on the other side of the ravine was very steep and the French kept up a murderous fire of musketry as the British troops struggled up the slope. Pringle, leading from the front, was severely wounded. Once at the top the 1/39th was charged twice by the French and the fighting became hand to hand. One witness recalled:

> Lieutenant Evans, the brave commander of the 60th Rifles, attached to the light companies of the brigade, personally grappled with a French captain, and they both fell to the ground together. Evans was a small man, and no match for his antagonist; but he kept up the unequal contest, till a grenadier of the 39th, stepping forward to his assistance, the Frenchman was made prisoner.[9]

The 1/28th joined the 1/39th on the crest and the French were driven back by the weight of fire from the two battalions' volleys. The rest of the 2nd Division was moving forward in support, the Portuguese were making headway with their assault, and the Spanish were moving around the French flank. The French began to withdraw but many units were in such close combat that they found it difficult to disengage and some were surrounded. The retreat became a rout. Those units that could fell back rapidly across a bridge at St. Palais and, blowing the bridge behind them, carried on for another 10 miles.[10]

All three companies of the 5th Battalion with the 2nd Division suffered losses at Garris. Four privates were killed: John Pieler (No. 8) was the longest serving having joined in 1802 from Lowenstein's Jägers; Brunswicker Private John Stocker (No. 8), blacksmith Private Henry Bolde (No. 4), and Private Francis Mezenberg (No. 6) had all joined in 1812 or 1813.[11] Eight rank and file were wounded, as was Lieutenant Gotleib Lerche who lost his left arm.[12] Lerche, promoted from the ranks, had served in the 1801 campaign in Egypt with Lowenstein's Jägers before joining the 5th Battalion while they were in Halifax. In April 1814 he went back to England on leave where he transferred to the Royal Waggon Train

9 'Garris', 'Take the Hill before Dark', *United Services Journal*, 1839, Part III, pp.168.

10 Oman, *Peninsular War*, Vol.VII, pp.323-4.

11 February 1814 CasualtyR, TNA, WO 25/1923, Periods of Service 5/60th, June 1806, WO 25/1008; also various Pay Lists, WO 12/7074, & WO 12/7075.

12 Butler, *Annals*, Vol.II, p.223.

and went on half-pay due to poor health, with a pension of £70 per year for his wound. He returned to Germany and got married in Brunswick in May 1815, had a child, and later settled in Salzgitter, Hannover.[13]

The drubbing of Harispe's division compromised Soult's plans to hold the line of the Bidouze River. On the 16th Hill's engineers quickly repaired the blown bridge and the 2nd Division were soon marching across it. Soult was forced to pull his forces back again, and to call up reinforcements from Bayonne. Both Beresford and Hill pushed their troops forward to keep pressure on the French.

The 2nd Division, tired after a long march, again confronted Harispe's division late in the afternoon of the 17th. The French held the far bank of the Saison River and there was a blocked and fortified bridge at Rivereyte. Two fords were quickly captured after brief fights and the French, outflanked, were once again forced to retreat. No. 8 company suffered another fatal casualty during the advance; Private Peter Friend, a watchmaker, had only been with the battalion since September 1813.[14] Three riflemen were wounded on the 16th and 17th.[15] Wellington paused his advance while the rear divisions caught up and he put into motion the second part of his plan.

The Royal Navy and the Royal Engineers had been gathering local coastal craft called *chasse-marées*, as well as pontoons, timber, and rope cables to construct a bridge across the mouth of the Adour. This was much lower down the river than the French expected any crossing to be attempted. However, a storm delayed the attempt and it was not until the 22nd that the weather became favourable. During the night leading into the 23rd Lieutenant General Sir John Hope ordered the 1st Division to march from Bidart and Biarritz towards the river. The paths led through a long pine forest and deep sand dunes. It proved difficult to drag the guns and carry the pontoons and supplies. By dawn Stopford's Brigade was in position, but there was no sign of the *chasse-marées*. The boats had been blown out to sea by the wind. After waiting most of the morning for them to appear Hope ordered the other brigades of the 1st Division to make diversionary attacks, and for allied guns to fire on a French corvette and gunboats close inshore. Congreve rockets were also used to good, if haphazard, effect. Hope decided to make the crossing with the resources he had to hand.

The roughly 50 men of No. 9 company, led by Captain Harrison and Lieutenant Hamilton, got into five small jolly boats and rowed across the river, towing a large cable behind them. The river was around 300 yards wide and the wind made the water choppy. They landed and surprised the guards of French battery, who promptly fled. The cable was secured and the riflemen took covering positions as the light companies of the Guards began to be ferried across on rafts. By 5:00 p.m. six companies of the Guards and a detachment of the rocket battery were across.[16]

Just as it was getting dark two French battalions advanced towards the 500 Guards, riflemen and rocketeers. They came into contact with the light companies' skirmish line

13 Hall, *Biographical Dictionary*, pp.343-4.

14 February 1814 Casualty Return, TNA, WO 25/1923, Periods of Service 5/60th, June 1806, WO 25/1008; December Pay List, WO 12/7075.

15 Butler, *Annals*, Vol.II, p.265

16 Butler, *Annals*, Vol.II, pp.224-5; Rigaud, *Celer et Audax*, p.243.

View of Bayonne, taken from the Sand Hills on the left of the Adour, when occupied by the British forces on the 12 of March, 1814, by George Grander Willis. (Anne S.K. Brown Military Collection)

that stretched from the river to the sea, using the dunes as cover. Lieutenant Gleig of the 85th was watching from the far bank:

> We saw one column of British troops form on the sands beside Boucaut. In front of it was body of German riflemen, who pressed leisurely forward in skirmishing order, till they reached a piquet of the French troops. Of the enemy, on the other hand, a heavy column showed itself upon the high ground, where it halted, and continued to send out numerous parties to support the outposts, between whom and the Germans a hot skirmish soon began. But it could not be said that any decided advantage was gained by either party during several hours.[17]

Eventually the French drove the light troops back and advanced in column, drums beating. The riflemen fired and retired and the Guards began volley fire. British howitzers lobbed shrapnel shells into the French ranks from across the river. Rockets burned through the darkening sky, hitting the column and terrifying the French. Congreve rockets came in various sizes and the most likely model used at the Adour was the 12-pounder, which could come with either an explosive or case-shot warhead attached to an eight-foot long stick, not unlike a modern firework. They were fired from a tripod.[18] One witness described their effect on the French column approaching the small British force:

17 G. Gleig, *The Subaltern* (London: Blackwood's Standard Novels, Undated) p.214.

18 W. Congreve, *A Treatise on the General Principles, Powers and Facility of Application of the Congreve Rocket System* (London: Longman, Rees, Orme, Brown, & Green, 1827), Plate 13.

> The rockets, alone saved them: the second that was let off, carried away the two legs of one man, set the knapsack of another on fire, and knocked about many more, throwing them into great confusion, and wounding several. An old serjeant whom we made prisoner, said, during all his service, he had not known what fear was before; but these machines were perfect devils, running up and down, and picking out and destroying particular victims, as it were, in one place, and then in another. The rockets were discharged at the time when they produced the greatest effect, in a battery ten abreast.[19]

After repeated attacks the French retreated and left the bridgehead unmolested for the night. The Guards lost eight wounded but No. 9 company had no casualties. French losses were estimated at around 300.[20]

The night was cold, clear and still, with a bright moon and a hard frost. At slack tide more troops were ferried across the river by the light of large bonfires on either bank. At dawn the *chasse-marées* arrived and began to be placed in position while the rest of the 1st Division was ferried across on the rafts. The bridge was finished by the afternoon of the 26th. The 1st Division, and other units, marched from the river to complete the encirclement of Bayonne.

On 27 February Hope ordered the taking of all the minor fortifications around the suburb of St. Étienne. These consisted of earthworks, barricades and fortified houses. The French were only evicted after some very costly street fighting. Captain John Harrison, commanding No.9 company in Stopford's 2nd Guards Brigade, was struck in the face by a musket ball. It cost him his sight, and his senses of smell and taste, so it probably passed across his face and injured his eyes and nose. He was given a pension of £200 for each eye and another for the loss of his two other senses.[21]

Wellington now planned to reinforce Hill and drive a wedge through a gap in the French lines and perform another outflanking manoeuvre while Beresford launched attacks to fix the French centre. On 24 February Hill's columns forded the Gave d'Oloron river on a wide front and in the face of little opposition from the French. Outflanked once again French forces retreated towards Orthez, where Soult concentrated his divisions and decided to make a stand. Wellington transferred divisions from Hill to Beresford so that the next turning movement would be on Soult's other flank. Hill reached Orthez on the 25th. The Light Division drove back the French pickets from the southern bank and skirmished with *voltigeurs* holding a well defended and virtually impassable bridge.

Beresford got his troops into position during the 26th, with British cavalry pushing back the French outposts. By dawn on the 27th five divisions and two cavalry brigades had crossed the Gave de Pau. The town of Orthez sat on the river. A high ridge ran north-west from the town, the slopes of which were open and exposed, towards the village of St. Boes. Marshy ground and ravines limited the approaches to the ridge. Soult arranged his 36,000 men and 48 guns on good defensive positions along the high ground with his line anchored on the town, with small forces guarding fords further upstream.[22]

19 T. Camden, *The History of the War in Spain & Portugal* (London: Stratford, 1813) p.673.

20 Butler, *Annals*, Vol.II, p.227.

21 Butler, *Annals*, Vol.II, p.229; Hall, *Biographical Dictionary*, p.263.

22 Oman, *Peninsular War*, Vol.VII, pp.353-5.

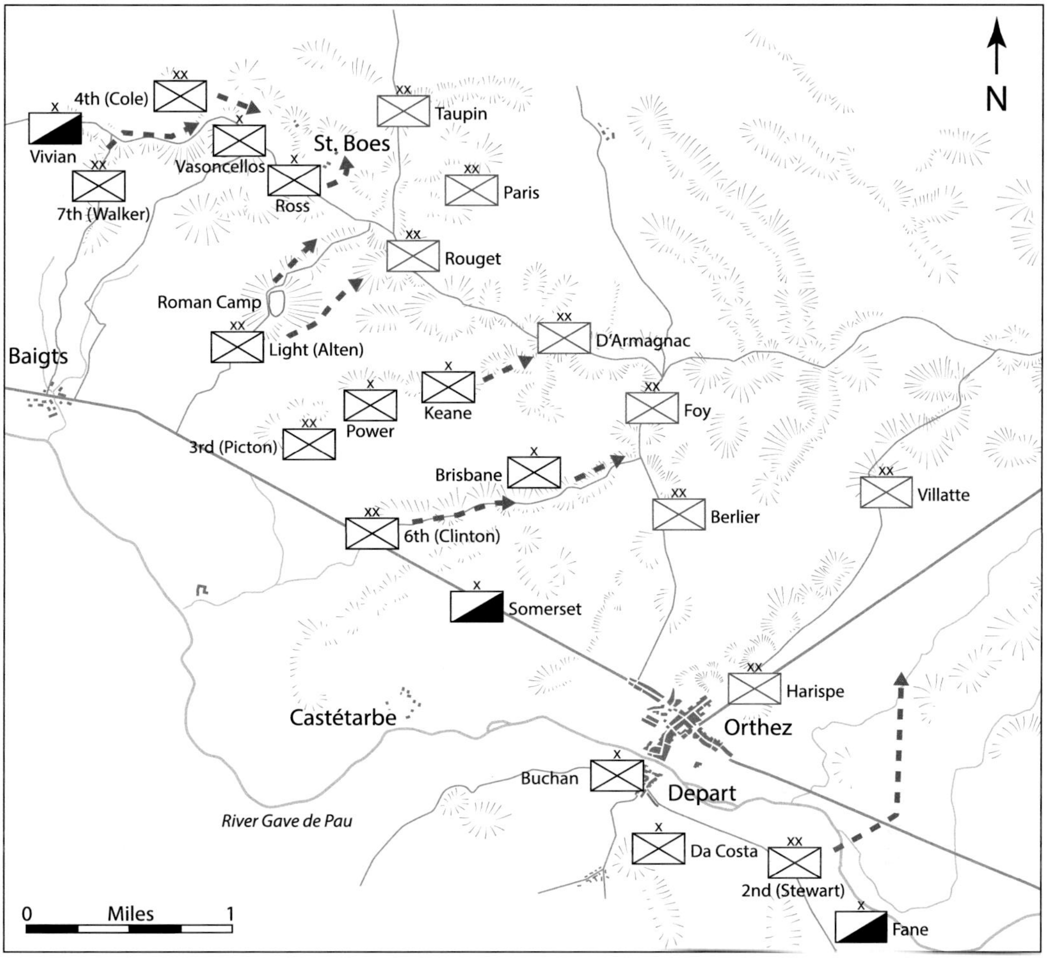

The Battle of Orthez, 27 February 1814.
Sources: Lipscombe, *Atlas* & Wyld, *Maps & Plans*.

Wellington was not certain that Soult intended to fight at Orthez until, on the morning of 27 February, he received a report from Beresford at first light that the French army had concentrated. He decided on a plan of attack that involved Beresford turning the French right flank round St. Boes while Hill crossed the fords above Orthez on the French left, and also made a diversionary attack on the town. Picton would occupy the troops in the French centre with another diversion. The divisions marched into position along muddy roads, screened from the French by hills. Wellington had 38,000 infantry, 3,300 cavalry, and 1,500 sappers and gunners. He outnumbered Soult by approximately 7,000 men.[23]

23 Oman, *Peninsular War*, Vol.VII, p.357.

The morning was clear and cold. At around 8:30 a.m. Ross's Brigade of the 4th Division started the attack by assaulting the church at St. Boes, which sat on a small hill and marked the end of the French lines. The church was taken but the resistance became stiffer as the redcoats and Brunswickers moved along the ridge to the village itself. Artillery and reinforcements were brought up but a second assault on the village also ground to a halt. A French counter-attack pushed the allied troops back. The attempt to turn the French right flank had failed.

Picton, attacking the centre, sent two columns forward, each up a spur of the ridge. Keane's Brigade headed one and Brisbane's Brigade with his four companies of the 5th Battalion led the other. Both columns were preceded by a screen of their light companies. The French skirmishes, deployed well forward down the slope, were easily pushed back. As the heads of the columns began to take losses from the French guns Picton ordered only the light troops to continue to the crest. There were seven light companies of the redcoat regiments, the four rifle companies of the 5th Battalion, and a regiment of caçadores, making a total of 15 companies.[24]

The light troops advanced to contact with the main French line but the enemy held their position. Behind them the columns continued to take casualties from cannon fire for two hours while the stalemate continued.

Keane described the opening of the battle in a letter to Major General Colville:

> The morning of the 27th set in fine, but very few thought the enemy would stand. The Lord [Wellington] had reconnoitred and each corps was in the place by nine o'clock and moved forwards as follows; 3rd on the right, Light in the centre and 4th on the left. The 6th supported the right, the 7th the left. The enemy's position was well chosen for defence, keeping also a good eye to retreat as each ridge they occupied was connected with the great Bordeaux road. Once in motion we were soon in fire and for two hours it was furious. The ground certainly was well contested. Crapaud [the French] truly fought to endeavour to restore his lost honour.[25]

At around 11:30 a.m. Wellington, seeing that the flank attack of the 4th Division had stalled, ordered a general, frontal assault on the French right and centre by the 3rd, 6th and elements of the Light Division. The 7th Division supported the 4th on the flank.

Brisbane's Brigade pushed forward again up the hill, driving the French back to the top of the ridge. French skirmishers continued to fire into the British column while Brisbane dithered, until ordered to send the 1/45th forward as additional skirmishers. After taking heavy losses the French were pushed back. Following a charge and then a counter-charge Brisbane's Brigade held their ground. Two brigades of the 6th Division took over the advance. The 3rd Division's guns were brought up and opened fire. French cavalry charged the battery but were checked by volleys from the 1/88th. *Général de Division* Foy, the French divisional commander, was wounded and his troops began to fall back pursued by Pack's Brigade of the 6th Division, which included No. 1 Company.

24 Oman, *Peninsular War*, Vol.VII, p.360, but Oman counts only three rifle companies when four were present.

25 Colville, *Portrait of a General*, pp.169-70.

The retreat of Foy's division left the troops in the town vulnerable and they too began a hurried withdrawal leaving the bridge over the river undefended. Keane's Brigade, supported by Power's Portuguese began to make progress on their spur and the retreating French divisions reformed on the next ridge line to the north-east. The allied guns, now along the main road, opened fire on the new French positions inflecting heavy losses on the already battered French troops. Wellington renewed the attack on Soult's right flank with all of the the 7th Division, Anson's Brigade of the 4th, and the Light Division. This time the attack worked and the village of St. Boes was taken. A charge by the 1/52nd almost cut-off the retreating French defenders. By this time Hill had crossed the river, easily driven off the vastly outnumbered French in front of his troops, and successfully turned the enemy left. The French tried to form and hold at various points but each time they were forced back.

Soult, seeing his line broken in several places and his flank turned, ordered a general retreat. His battalions retired in good order but came under continued fire from the allied guns and were pressed hard by the allied infantry. An orderly retreat soon became a confused rout. French losses were around 4,000. Allied casualties totalled 2,164. Wellington was amongst the wounded, his sword-hilt having been struck by a musket ball and driven against his thigh.[26]

The 5th Battalion lost six men killed in action, or who died of wounds on the day of the battle. Serving with Picton's 3rd Division were: Sergeant Frederick Fischer (No. 5), a Prussian who had been with Lowenstein's Jägers; Corporal John Schoeffter (No. 7), a cabinetmaker from Hamburg; and Private Frederick Heydoua (No. 2) who had joined with a draft in 1810. Colour Sergeant Henry Vannesel, a sailor from Flanders, and Private Frederick Steydel, who joined the battalion in 1812, were both with No. 1 company in the 6th Division and probably fell as their brigade took over the advance from the 3rd Division. Serving in the 2nd Division was Corporal Henry Schroeder (No. 8) who had also joined in 1812 and who must have been killed as Hill turned the enemy's left flank.[27]

Captain Ignace Franchini, with the 3rd Division, and Lieutenant John Currie with No. 1 Company in the 6th, were both wounded as were 35 riflemen.[28] For Franchini it was the third time he had been wounded. He was listed as slightly wounded but had been hit by musket balls in his right arm and right leg, both of which limbs were permanently impaired.[29] Despite this he returned to duty before the end of March.

Soult withdrew his army towards Toulouse to the east, away from the coast. Wellington followed as far as St. Sever and then kept his headquarters there for a week. The mayor of Bordeaux had contacted Wellington to say that the city was ready to rise up against Napoleon. Consequently Beresford was sent with the 4th and 7th Divisions, plus cavalry, to take France's third largest city. On 2 March the 2nd Division, probing forward along the Adour from St. Sever, came into contact with the French rearguard around Aire and fought a series of skirmishes and minor actions, including street fighting within the town itself, but the French resistance was patchy and the enemy quickly fell back. The battalion

26 Oman, *Peninsular War*, Vol.VII, pp.372-3.

27 March 1814 Casualty Return, TNA, WO 25/1923; March 1814 Pay List, WO 12/7075.

28 Butler, *Annals*, Vol.II, p.230.

29 Hall, *Biographical Dictionary*, pp.212-3.

The Battle of Orthez, 27 February 1814, by William Heath. (Anne S.K. Brown Military Collection)

suffered another six men wounded at Aire.[30] There followed a pause in the action as both commanders sought to reorganise and gather their forces.

Soult, ordered to go on the offensive by Napoleon and aware that two divisions had been sent to Bordeaux, advanced cautiously on 13 March towards the allied army. The French pushed aside some allied cavalry in minor skirmishes but did not advance far. Wellington called forward his divisions and set in progress a flanking move by the Light Division, which was to be joined by the 4th Division plus cavalry units under Beresford. The troops had to perform some long forced marches to get into position. Soult, nervous of the accumulation of force against him, began to fall back towards Tarbes to the south. Wellington advanced, hoping that he could trap the French between his main army and Beresford's force. On 18 March another six riflemen of the battalion were wounded near Lembeye.[31]

Early on the morning of 19 March British and KGL light cavalry skirmished with their French counterparts. The KGL succeeded in driving the French away from the important road junction at Vic-en-Bigorre. Soult had been planning to use the crossroads to get his army to Tarbes. He ordered d'Erlon to Vic-en-Bigorre with his two divisions. The leading French units were just getting into position above the village when Picton's 3rd Division arrived and attacked. The four companies of the 5th Battalion were at the forefront of

30 Butler, *Annals*, Vol.II, p.265.
31 Butler, *Annals*, Vol.II, p.265.

Picton's advance once again. The French were in good cover behind walls and hedges. The riflemen made slow progress and took heavy losses but succeeded in driving the enemy back. The arrival of the Light Division on his right flank made d'Erlon order his men to retreat to a second position, where the other French division also joined the line.

James Campbell, on the 3rd Division staff, recalled that once again the division had to add to its skirmishers to make progress against the French:

> But even in acting as skirmishers on a large scale, when Sir Thomas Picton's division had, at Vic Bigore, to contend with two French divisions, each at least equal in number to the 3rd, the same system of fighting was, as far as practicable, observed. Besides the 5th Battalion 60th, a battalion of Portuguese caçadores and our light infantry companies, whole regiments, (and here we felt the want of knowledge of light infantry movements in all corps), only retaining some companies in reserve and for support, were engaged as sharpshooters. They were, however, constantly pushed forward upon the French, and recommended not to throw away their fire in long shots, but rather, as much as possible, to endeavour to close with them; and if a halt was any where perceived in any part of the advancing skirmishers a staff officer was invariably sent to the point to ascertain the cause. The French, therefore, invariably gave way, and in their confused retreat they became exposed, in running from one enclosure to another, to the fire of our troops.[32]

Picton's men were soon supported by the 6th Division. With his flank still threatened d'Erlon retreated up the road to Tarbes as night fell.

Soult positioned one division in the town of Tarbes and two more on high ground nearby. Three other divisions were placed guarding one of the two remaining routes the French could take to Toulouse. Soult wanted to fight a series of delaying actions while the bulk of his army made their escape. The allied columns came into contact with the covering divisions late in the morning. Wellington began to deploy units to outflank the French positions. The Light Division was the first into action with all three battalions of the 95th advancing up a steep, wooded hill, and then being engaged closely by the French. The 6th Division were also sent on a flanking march further to the east and once the French found their rear threatened they fell back rapidly. Dusk was approaching and Wellington decided not to commit to a general attack. During the night the French made their escape.

On the 19th the four companies of the 5th Battalion lost three men killed and 26 wounded out of around 180 present. Two of the three dead were Sergeant John Schumbeck (No. 5), from Holland who had enlisted in 1807, and Private Simon Killy (No. 7), a shoemaker from Swabia who had been with the battalion since 1803. There is some disagreement between the pay list and the casualty return over who the other casualty might be. Private Anton Schub (No. 5) has the unusual comment on the pay list 'Killed in Action & Joined the Corps' but he was not a new recruit as he had served more than seven years. He may have been a very unlucky returning prisoner of war. He does not appear on the casualty return. Captain Robert Kelly was severely wounded leading No. 5 Company, and Lieutenant Cuthbert

32 Campbell, *A British Army*, p.252.

Forneret was slightly wounded. On the 20th Private Peter Fritz (No. 2) was killed in action, he had been with the battalion since 1810. The 3rd Division was not engaged around Tarbes but Fritz may have been with a picket or advance guard. Three riflemen were also wounded.[33]

Wellington followed Soult to Toulouse along poor and muddy roads but did not pursue closely. The French entered the city on the 24th while the nearest allied units were still two days march behind them. Toulouse was a major French army depot and Soult was able to reequip his forces, feed them properly, and also gather reinforcements from the garrison. However, the townspeople sent representatives to Wellington assuring him that once the French army was driven away the city, like Bordeaux, would declare itself for the returning king, Louis XVIII. However, the position of the city and its defences would make any assault a very difficult and costly affair.

The western approaches to Toulouse were guarded by the wide Garonne River. The closest bridge at St. Cyprien was fortified and well defended. The town walls were old but for most of their length, to the north and east, they were protected by the 100 yard wide Royal Canal. The topography was further complicated by the Ers, a tributary of the Garonne, and a ridge of high ground, Mont Rave, to the east that loomed over the city. The ridge and many other parts of the surrounding countryside had been well fortified since Soult arrived. The best direction to attack the city from was the south but this would mean that the allied army would have to first cross the Garonne.

On 27 March the 4th, 6th, and Light Divisions made a diversionary attack on the western defences which fooled Soult into thinking a crossing would be made below Toulouse but the spot that Wellington chose was above the city. Unfortunately the attempt that night failed as the pontoons available were not sufficient to span the swollen river. A second attempt to cross the Garonne was made three miles to the south, above where the Ariège tributary joined the river. Hill, with two divisions and attached brigades, did manage to cross but then found he could not cross the Ariège as all the pontoons had been used and there was no bridge close by. Wellington ordered him to return back over the Garonne. While the allies tried to cross the river Soult redoubled his efforts to fortify the city, mounting many large calibre guns in new batteries. On 4 April the pontoon bridge was successfully laid below Toulouse at La Capellette. The 3rd, 4th, and 6th Divisions, plus cavalry, crossed unopposed. Unfortunately the weather then turned and heavy rain made the river swell, breaking the bridge and leaving the troops on the far bank isolated. Not until the 8th was the bridge re-laid but on the 9th it was moved closer to the city as Wellington's forces advanced to the outer defences. The 10th, Easter Sunday, was the day set for the attack.

Wellington's plan was for Hill, with the 2nd Division, plus his Portuguese and Spanish units, to threaten the St. Cyprien bridgehead on the west bank of the Garonne and tie down the French forces there. The 3rd and Light Divisions were to make similar diversionary attacks on the western defences near the canal. The 4th and 6th Divisions would make the real assault on the eastern defences, with two Spanish divisions attacking from the north.

The battle started soon after 5:00 a.m. Hill sent O'Callaghan's Brigade to capture a mill on the river that marked the outmost part of the French defences. It was taken and then the

33 Butler, *Annals*, Vol.II, pp.233 & 265, March 1814 Casualty Return, TNA, WO 25/1923; Periods of Service 5/60th, June 1806, WO 25/1008; March Pay List, WO 12/7075.

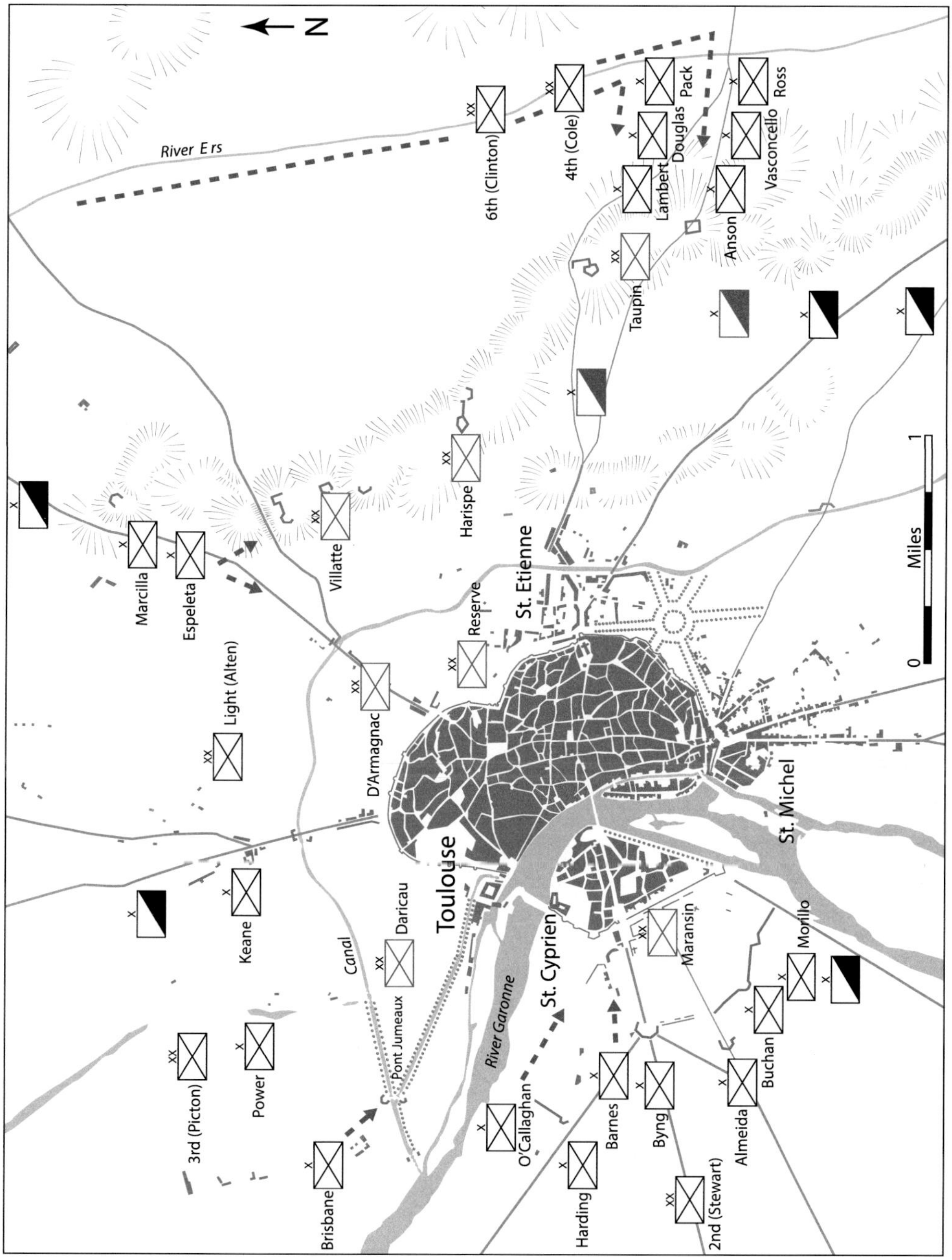

The Battle of Toulouse, 10 April 1814.
Sources: Lipscombe, *Atlas & Wyld, Maps & Plans.*

brigade worked their way down the rear of the first French line, making the French evacuate to their second and much stronger line of defence. Barnes' Brigade was sent forward in support and the two brigades faced the French behind their walls but held back from an assault. The light companies, including Nos. 4 and 8 companies, were then sent into the suburb of St. Cyprien. George Bell, fighting with the light company of the 2/34th recalled:

> It is always ugly, dangerous work fighting in a town; so many holes and corners, hiding-places and loop-holes, where one may be picked off by an unseen enemy. This was just our case, fighting from house to house and from street to street, our men having their bones cracked, and dropping off at every corner. As the enemy retired, or were driven back, they fired the houses they left, to arrest our progress, not sparing their own property. We found in many houses the furniture piled up in rooms, ready for the torch. The streets were barricaded, and cannon planted at every entrance, pounding away at the first blink of any red coat; but our men dashed on through fire and smoke, and carried on the work surely and gradually, for we lost nothing that we gained.[34]

The fighting in the town continued until nightfall. No 6. Company was held in reserve with the rest of Byng's Brigade and saw no action.

On the other side of the river Picton's division advanced towards the canal to make their demonstration to tie down the French forces there. Keane's Brigade and Power's Portuguese advanced, sent out their light companies, and drove back the French outposts but did no more.

Picton, often impetuous, could not resist pushing the bounds of his orders. Near the Pont Jumeaux bridge across the canal was a fortified farmhouse. Picton ordered Brisbane's Brigade to capture it. Brisbane formed his brigade and launched the assault soon after 7:00 a.m. Storming through orchards, over walls, and into outbuildings the brigade managed to take the farm but not without significant casualties. A soldier of the 1/45th, William Brown recalled in his memoirs that as the 3rd Division advanced three companies of the 1/45th, three of the 74th, and three of the 5th Battalion, were detailed to deal with a threat on the flank of the advance and it is possible he is recalling the attack on the farmhouse. He wrote that following their being detached:

> A smart encounter ensued, in which the enemy were worsted, and compelled to retire to the shelter of some houses, from which they were immediately driven in gallant style by our party. From these houses we kept up a brisk fire upon the enemy, who had taken possession of some of the neighbouring buildings.[35]

Picton then decided to take things further and to attempt to take the bridge itself, which was well protected by substantial palisades and the fortified buildings of the canal company. The four companies of the 5th Battalion, along with the light companies, charged from the

34 Bell, *Rough Notes*, p.165.

35 W. Brown, *The Autobiography, or Narrative of a Soldier* (Solihull: Helion & Company, 2017), p.159.

cover of the farm and surrounding buildings. They succeeded in taking some of the French-held houses and redoubts. Some even got as far as the canal but they were then driven back into the shelter of the houses by fire from the far bank and the main French positions. The fighting then degenerated into the same kind of bitter house to house fighting their colleagues in the 2nd Division were enduring. They made repeated charges towards the canal but were beaten back each time. Brown then recalled:

> On being repulsed in one of these charges, and when all that were able had returned to the house, a German, belonging to the 60th Rifles, remained on the beam, or lever of the canal lock, from which he fired several shots. The firing ceased on both sides, and for a few seconds the attention of friend and foe was riveted on the author of this 'deed of high daring'. He however, fell a victim of his temerity; he received a shot in the breast, and fell into the canal. This action I think was more strongly tinctured with frenzy than courage.[36]

Unfortunately the 5th Battalion suffered too many casualties that day for the rifleman in question to be identified.

Alten, commanding the Light Division, stuck to his orders and merely skirmished with the French. The Spanish pushed back the first line of French defences and, despite taking heavy fire from cannons and then muskets, did manage to approach the main French redoubts on Mont Rave. However, as the troops entered the shelter of a sunken road many were not inclined to climb up the other side back into danger. The attack stalled. The French counter-attacked from each end of the road and fired down into the massed troops, who then broke and fled back down the hill.

Beresford led the 4th and 6th Divisions, screened by cavalry, in a long march across wet ploughed fields to get into position. The divisions wheeled into line and advanced on the far right of the French trenches. The long march had given French reserves time to get into position behind the ridge. As three allied lines, one behind the other, marched up the hill two French columns charged down from the crest. At the same time the enemy infantry in the trenches and the guns in the batteries opened fire, and French cavalry rode in on the flank. Anson's Brigade, with No. 10 company, was at the front on the left flank. Pack's Brigade, with No. 1 company, was on the right at the rear.

As the French columns marched towards them the leading British battalions fired repeated volleys into the massed ranks, causing heavy casualties. The allied divisions kept advancing, making the French retreat in disarray. Congreve rockets added to the panic. The French fell back to their second line and fresh units were rushed forward to counter the expected allied assault down the slope of Mont Rave. Beresford though, had to call a halt. He deployed his men on the height, taking the redoubts, but did not want to advance without the cover of his artillery which was still coming up. As soon as they were in position, some two hours later, Beresford sent the 6th Division along the ridge behind those redoubts that the French still held, taking them in turn. Pack's Brigade was in the lead and French resistance was stiff. The 1/42nd and 1/79th began to take the French trenches but were then counter-attacked

36 Brown, *Autobiography*, p.161.

The Battle of Toulouse, 10 April 1814, by William Heath. (Anne S.K. Brown Military Collection.)

and driven back loosing some redoubts with heavy losses. The 1/91st, Pack's reserve, and the 12th Portuguese then advanced again, pushing the French back before being counter-attacked with the redoubts changing hands once more.

Finally Lambert's Brigade of the 6th Division managed to break the French, but not without heavy losses. The French still held the main redoubt. The second attempt by the Spanish to take it had failed. The light companies, Brunswickers, and No. 1 Company of the 6th Division used dead ground to get close to the rear of the redoubt and then sniped the artillery horses, so the guns could not be withdrawn, and also shot a considerable number of the gunners.[37] Around 5:00 p.m. the French withdrew, manhandling the guns down the hill. At about the same time the allied guns began to run out of ammunition. As darkness fell the skirmishing that had extended around most of the city began to die down. The troops slept where they had fought. On the 11th it took so long for Wellington to replenish the guns and reposition his divisions that by the time everything was ready it was too late to recommence the assault. That night the French marched out of the town and the following morning the allies were invited in by the jubilant inhabitants.

Total allied losses at Toulouse were 4,568 and the French casualties totalled 3,236.[38] The 5th Battalion lost 14 dead and 47 wounded, their heaviest loss in a single battle of the entire

37 Oman, *Peninsular War*, Vol.VII, p.488.
38 Oman, *Peninsular War*, Vol.VII, p.494.

war. Six men's lives were thrown away in Picton's pointless attacks on the canal: Colour Sergeant Michael Schmidt (No. 5), once a miller, was the last of many former Walloon Guards to fall; Sergeant Henry Scherge (No. 2), like so many of the fallen before him, had joined the Lowenstein Jägers 14 years before; Private Frederick Strauchmeyer (No. 3) had been a sergeant when the battalion landed in 1808 but was reduced to private soon after; Private Vincent Gistel (No. 2), a shoemaker, had also managed to survive all the way from the beach at Mondego Bay only to die in the last act; Private Henry Schmidt (No. 5) and Private Jacob Güster (No. 7), who was from Braband, were relative newcomers having joined in 1812. Captain Edward Purdon, commanding No. 5 Company in the 3rd Division received three severe wounds. Ensigns Henry Shewbridge and Edward Bruce were also both severely wounded whilst serving with the companies in the 3rd Division. In the fighting around St. Cyprien the companies of the 2nd Division also lost six: Privates John Meyer (No. 4) and George Lubkisch (No. 8) had been with the battalion since its formation on Barbados; Private Michael Gudry (No. 8) was also yet another former Lowenstein Jäger; Private Christian Rottenhuasen was an American-born Royal American, having joined while the battalion was in Nova Scotia; Privates John Beringer and Joseph Kramer, both from No. 4 Company, had joined in 1812 and 1813 respectively. Sergeant Andreus Lichtaller (No.1), from the Palatinate, was killed serving with Pack's Brigade of the 6th Division, he had joined the battalion in 1806. Private George Kretz (No. 10), listed as being French and who had joined in 1813, died with Anson's Brigade of the 4th Division.[39]

The campaign of 1814 was very costly for the 5th battalion. The battalion suffered over 200 casualties from a strength of around 550 at the start of the year.[40] While the allied army under Wellington had been inflicting defeat after defeat upon the French in the south, the allies had entered Paris. Napoleon abdicated on 4 April and renounced all claims on the throne on 6 April, four days before the Battle of Toulouse. Wellington learned of the victory of the allied coalition on the 12th and informed Soult on the 13th. The French *marechal* was initially incredulous but an armistice was signed on the 17th. On 21 April Wellington issued the following general order to his army:

1. The Commander of the Forces has the pleasure to inform the army that he has agreed upon the following convention, for the suspension of hostilities between the allied armies under his command and the French armies opposed to them, and hostilities are forthwith to be suspended accordingly.
2. Upon congratulating the army upon this prospect of an honorable termination of their labours, the Commander of the Forces avails himself of the opportunity of returning the General Officers, Officers, and troops, his best thanks for their uniform discipline and gallantry in the field, and for their conciliating conduct towards the inhabitants of the country, which, almost in an equal degree with their discipline and gallantry in the field, have produced the fortunate circumstances that now hold forth to the world the prospect of genuine and permanent peace.

39 April 1814 Casualty Return, TNA WO 25/1923, June pay list, WO 12/7075; Periods of Service 5/60th, June 1806, WO 25/1008, Butler, *Annals*, Vol.II, p.238, Hall, *Biographical Dictionary*, pp.481, 515-6 & 84.

40 Butler, *Annals*, Vol.II, p.265; January to April 1814 Returns, TNA, WO 17/279.

3. The Commander of the Forces trusts that they will continue the same good conduct while it may be necessary to detain them in this country, and that they will leave it with a lasting reputation, not less creditable to their gallantry in the field than to their regularity and good conduct in quarters and in camp.[41]

The war was over. Unfortunately, some French commanders took the news better than others.

The investment of Bayonne had continued without any major operations. Private Frederick Suvingedon (No. 9), from Braband, with the 1st Division had been killed on 1 March.[42] He had joined the battalion in 1806. The mood between the French and British pickets had been cordial and Hope had only carried on the siege works in a very leisurely fashion. News of Napoleon's defeat reached both the French and the allies around Bayonne on 10 April. *Général de Division* Thouvenot, the commander of the French garrison, either did not believe the news, did not want to, or perhaps was just overcome with anger at the defeat. On 14 April he gathered half his men for a large and completely pointless sortie.[43]

Three columns emerged from the city at around 3:00 a.m. The night was moonless and dark. The French headed for the suburb of St. Étienne. The pickets in the path of the French came from Stopford's Guards Brigade including No. 9 Company, Hay's Brigade of the 5th Division, and the KGL. Hay was general of the day in command and news had reached him from a French deserter that the sortie was planned but the scale of it took the allies by surprise. The initial French assault swept aside the pickets, many of them being captured. Hay was killed and his brigade took heavy casualties as they tried and failed to maintain their hold on the village. The fighting was fierce and confused. Hope charged forward to take personal command but was wounded and taken prisoner with his aides.

Hinüber of the KGL and Major General Howard of the 1st Division both gathered forces for a counter attack. The KGL swept the French back out of St. Étienne and Howard, with Maitland's Brigade and the remains of Stopford's, attacked the flank of the French column still fighting around a Jewish cemetery on the road to Bordeaux. The French fled back to the safety of the citadel and the city as fast as they had left, leaving almost 1,000 dead and wounded behind them. The allies lost around 600 killed or wounded and over 200 taken prisoner.[44] Thouvenot continued to refuse to surrender until he received orders to do so. On 26 April he received a copy of Soult's armistice with Wellington and finally capitulated.

Private John Schulz (No. 9) was either killed during the sortie or died of his wounds soon afterwards. Four other riflemen were wounded and five reported missing. Lieutenant Passley, who had only recently returned after recovering from his wound received on the Nivelle, was commanding the company and was wounded again. The other officer with the company, Lieutenant John Hamilton, was also badly wounded on the 14th and died the same day. He is buried with the Coldstream Guards he fought beside in Bayonne. Private

41 Wellington, *General Orders*, Vol.V, p.311.

42 March 1814 Casualty Return, TNA, WO 25/1923.

43 Oman, *Peninsular War*, Vol.II, p.508.

44 Oman, *Peninsular War*, Vol.VII, p.511.

Paul Fohrer (No. 9) died on 16 April and holds the very dubious honour of being the last riflemen of the battalion to be killed in action. He had joined the battalion in 1812.[45]

The return of 25 April shows the headquarters of the battalion at Grenade, a small town just north of Toulouse on banks of Garonne. The companies were still scattered among the divisions and only 10 officers were left fit and present for duty with the battalion, including Major Galiffe who had received word he had been given a brevet lieutenant colonelcy. By 25 May the companies of battalion were finally united again, for the first time since February 1810, at Capitieux, which was closer to the coast and south of Bordeaux. Three wounded officers had returned to duty and Captain William Wilkinson had arrived after exchanging from the 7th Fusiliers. Five staff were present. Only 46 sergeants, five buglers, and 291 privates were present and fit. During the preceding month one sergeant and three rank and file had died in hospital, and three buglers and 79 rank and file had deserted. With the war over the temptation to simply walk back home across France must have been very strong for many of the riflemen. Even senior men, such as Armourer Sergeant Charles Dilletter, succumbed.

Twenty men were sick in the regimental hospital or in their quarters, six were still at Belem near Lisbon, 22 were at Passages, 17 at St. Jean de Luz, and 63 just listed as 'in rear'. One sergeant and two rank and file were in charge of the baggage, and one sergeant and one private in charge of the clothing. Three rank and file were orderlies in hospitals and 15 were with absent officers. One sergeant, one bugler, and one rank and file were on recruiting service. Five invalids had been sent home.

Five sergeants, two buglers and 171 rank and file were prisoners of war as were Brevet Lieutenant Colonel Fitzgerald, Captain Wolff, Lieutenants Freiss, Mitchell, and Van Dyke, and Ensign Altenstein. One sergeant and three rank and file had joined from being prisoners. Brevet Colonel Keane was still commanding his brigade. Captain Kenzinger and Lieutenant Erdberg were still recruiting on Heligoland. Captain Erskine and Lieutenant Roeppel were on the staff of the army in Holland. Captain Sewell, who had come on the strength of the battalion in 1813 from the 16th Light Dragoons but never joined, was an ADC to Marshal Beresford. Lieutenant Linstow was still with Portuguese army, with whom he had served for almost the whole Peninsular campaign. Lieutenant de Gilse was on duty at the Foreign Depot. Lieutenant Franciosci was still an interpreter with the 6th Division. Six officers were absent without leave and four on leave with permission, all of whom were, or had been, sick or wounded. Nine officers had been appointed but had not joined.[46]

An inspection for No. 9 Company dated the 6 May, the only one for the period to have survived, shows Captain Wilkinson as the only officer with the company. His length of service is stated as 22 years, which implies he had been serving since the outbreak of the Revolutionary War in 1792. Major General Stopford noted that 'as yet he knows little of his company' which is not surprising. Stopford also lamented that the company had not had new clothing since the year before last but that the arms and accoutrements were in good order. There was only one woman officially attached to the company, and no children.[47]

45 Butler, *Annals*, Vol.II, p.241; April 1814 Casualty Report TNA, WO 25/1923.

46 April 1814 Return, TNA, WO 17/249; June 1814 Pay List, WO 12/7075.

47 Inspection of Captain Wilkinson's company 5/60th, TNA, WO 27/127.

One of the men that died in hospital in May was Private John Roth. He was under the treatment of Surgeon Guthrie, who wrote up his case:

> John Roth, of the 5th Battalion of the 60th Regiment, aged twenty-nine, had been wounded by two balls, one on the 10th of April, 1814, at the battle of Toulouse, which grazed the left temporal bone; the other had gone through the upper part of the right chest, in the Pyrenees, the autumn before. Both wounds had healed. He was seized on the 8th of May, after a little intemperance, with pains in his body and joints, pain in the chest, and cough, with bloody expectoration; skin hot, tongue foul, and bowels confined. On the 9th he was bled, and purged by calomel, antimony, and salts. On the 10th symptoms augmented, pulse 120, small, and wandering, but no pain in the head. Repeat the medicines. Head shaved and cold applied; bleeding to ten ounces. 11th. Every symptom increased; great pain on touching the chest; pulse 126; skin hot. On the 12th passed his urine and faeces involuntarily; and on the 13th he died, his body being covered by petechiae [spots caused by bleeding under the skin].
>
> The head, on examination, showed pus under the dura mater, at and behind the situation of the wound he had received. The right lung adhered to the walls of the chest where the ball had entered and passed out, the track made by it being very visible, indurated, and inflamed, from the last attack: the parts otherwise sound; no fluid in the cavity.[48]

From Capitieux the battalion marched to Blanquefort, just north of Bordeaux. The June return shows that another sergeant and five rank and file had died in hospital. Nine sergeants, one bugler, and 74 rank and file were discharged as their time of service had expired. One sergeant, one bugler, and 50 rank and file had taken matters into their own hands and deserted. The prisoners of war were beginning to return; Lieutenant Friess, taken at Talavera, returned to Britain and was promoted to captain, and one rank and file joined.[49]

Whilst the war with France might have been over the war with the United States of America was still going on. On 16th May Wellington issued orders for the 5th Battalion to be included with 17 other infantry battalions and one cavalry regiment to be sent across the Atlantic.[50] Many of these units, like the 5th Battalion, had fought for much of the Peninsular campaign. However, the discharges and desertions of the recent months had reduced the battalion's strength too severely and the plan to send the riflemen to fight another war was abandoned. Keane, promoted to major general, did serve in the American war. He arrived in November, and was wounded at New Orleans but recovered to serve at the capture of Fort Bowyer in February 1815.[51]

The battalion was eventually awarded sixteen battle honours for its long campaign in the Peninsula and into France. Fifteen were for battles: Roliça, Vimieiro, Talavera, Bussaco,

48 Guthrie, *Commentaries on the Surgery*, p.443.

49 June 1814 Return, TNA, WO 17/249.

50 R.N. Buckley, *The Napoleonic War Journal of Captain Thomas Henry Browne* (London: Army Records Society, 1987), p.276.

51 McGuigan & Burnham, *Brigade Commanders*, p.155.

Fuentes de Oñoro, Albuera, Ciudad Rodrigo, Badajoz, Salamanca, Vitoria, Pyrenees, Nivelle, Nive, Orthez, and Toulouse. The sixteenth was 'Peninsula' to cover the countless small actions and skirmishes that were the battalion's stock-in-trade. Not all of the battalion was at each battle, of course, but the companies that were present on each occasion played their role in the victories.

The soldiers who fought at Waterloo were given a medal, and credited with two years extra service and pay soon after the campaign. The soldiers who fought for six years through Portugal, Spain, and France received no medal until 1847 when they had to apply for the General Service Medal 1793-1815. They had to prove which of 29 battles or actions they were present at, for each of which they would receive a clasp on the medal's ribbon. Many of the men who fought with the 5th Battalion would have died by then, and many others would have returned to their German, Polish, Russian, Hungarian homes, and so only 30 medals were awarded to the battalion. Daniel Lochstadt was given 15 clasps, a total matched by only one other soldier. Twenty-four officers who served with the battalion were awarded the medal, with Major Schoedde receiving 14 clasps to his.[52]

Senior officers were given medals during the campaign. The Army Gold Medal was awarded to the commander of a unit, and some staff. Clasps for subsequent actions were then awarded and once an officer had a medal and two clasps he was awarded the Army Gold Cross for his fourth battle, and again clasps for subsequent ones. All the men who commanded the battalion during the war, Davy, Woodgate, Williams, Fitzgerald, Keane, and Galiffe received gold medals, with multiple clasps, and in most cases gold crosses. Alexander Andrews and James Schoedde received gold medals for leading portions of the battalion. In addition Major General Keane was created a Knight Commander of the Bath and Williams, Fitzgerald, and Galiffe were made Companions of the Bath.[53]

Prize money for the Peninsular veterans was awarded in 1816, with different amounts being payable for each of six sections of the campaign, and different ranks receiving different sums. Major Galiffe would have been eligible for all six payments, and at the second level reserved for field officers. In total he should have received £597 16s 3d, equivalent to an income of around £620,000 today. A captain, such as James Schoedde, who was present at all the relevant stages of the campaign and entitled to sums from the third level, would have received £103 16s 5½d, worth around £107,000 today. An ordinary soldier, such as Daniel Lochstadt, was entitled to the sixth and lowest level of payments but if he had been present in all the sections he would have received £4 8s 8½d, worth around £4,600 pounds today and equivalent to about four months' pay.[54] Average payments would of course have been lower as most recipients would not have been present at all six sections of the campaign.

In early July the battalion marched the 20 miles to Pauiliac on the Gironde River and 18 officers and staff, and 232 riflemen were ferried out to HMS *Clarence* for the voyage back to Ireland. They arrived in Cork on the 25th, the same city that the battalion had left almost six years previously with 33 officers and 1,007 riflemen in three transports.[55] Of the officers

52 Butler, *Annals*, Vol.II, pp.270-1.

53 Butler, *Annals*, Vol.II, pp.244 & 268-9.

54 *The Gazette*, 27 January 1816, pp.153-4; Wellington, *Supplementary Dispatches*, Vol.X, p.750. Modern values calculated at https://www.measuringworth.com/calculators/ppoweruk/ (accessed 7 September 2018).

55 Butler, *Annals*, Vol.II, p.273.

and staff only Brevet Lieutenant Colonel Galiffe, Major Schoedde, Lieutenant Muller, and Quartermaster Recknoy had been with the battalion when it landed at Mondego Bay. Recknoy had been the sergeant major then. It is likely that at least one third of the soldiers who returned to Cork had managed to survive the whole campaign.[56] After many years at war the riflemen of the 5th Battalion would now have to adjust to the mundanity of peacetime soldiering.

56 June 1814 Pay List, TNA WO 12/7075. Estimate based on proportion of men entitled to extra pay for 7 or 14 years of service. For 25 June 1814 pay list there were 198 men out of a total on the strength of 727 rank and file, and this figure does not include sergeants and buglers who were not paid extra for long service, and in the case of sergeants were more likely to be longer serving.

26

The End

For many of the foreign officers, peace in Europe must have offered them the first chance to visit homes and families for many years. Brevet Lieutenant Colonel Galiffe had not seen his home in Geneva for over two decades and was desperate for leave. He had made plans to travel via Bordeaux, Toulouse, and Lyon so that he could revisit friends he had made whilst campaigning in the area. However, with the 5th Battalion having been split into companies for so many years there was a lot of administration that needed his attention. Writing to his brother he said:

> ...I found myself the sole superior officer my presence was absolutely necessary to examine the accounts and sign lots of passports for men who were too old to continue to serve or who had been made invalids during the campaign; after 20 [years] service in this Battalion all these old sergeants & soldiers had become very dear to me particularly after a campaign so long & bloody; some new officers had succeeded and replaced [illegible] those under whom they had learned to fight and I found myself the only superior officer out of the small number of these last, it is not at all surprising that they repose much trust in me and as the accounts were very confused I had a great deal of work to do with the Paymaster to get them straight;[1]

It would not be until Brevet Lieutenant Colonel Fitzgerald, freed from French captivity but on leave, arrived to take command that Galiffe could get away.

Many of the men's terms of service had expired and they had to be discharged and passage arranged back to the continent via the Foreign Depot, which moved to Harwich in August 1814. Also, many men were unfit for further duty and had to be invalided out of the Army. Even at the end of the year there were still men recovering in hospitals in France.[2] For example; Corporal John Hamel was severely wounded at Bayonne on 20 February 1814 and his left leg had to be amputated at the thigh. He was discharged 14 December. Born in Aachen, Hamel had enlisted in October 1806 and was probably one of the French soldiers who had been on their way to the West Indies when their convoy was taken by the Royal

1 John Galiffe to James Galiffe 10 September 1814, BG, ms fr 2751c pl23 f005/6 (translated).
2 December 1814 Pay List, TNA, WO 12/7075.

Navy. It was noted on his discharge certificate that his character was 'highly commendable'.[3] Other soldiers, like Colour Sergeant George Koester who had enlisted at the same time, decided to reenlist rather than go back to their homes.[4]

Of the four officers who had been wounded at Talavera and captured when the French took the hospital, William Freiss was already back with the battalion and Lieutenant Baron Henry von Altenstein also returned following a period of leave. Captain John Wolff, 52 years old, asked to be placed on half-pay due to ill health. Examined by a medical board he was granted a pension of £100 per year, back-dated to 1811. He retired to Hamburg, never married, and lived off his pension and half-pay.[5] Lieutenant Robert Mitchell purchased a captaincy and joined one of the other battalions in 1815. He got married a year later.[6] Lieutenant Van Dyke, captured in 1813, came back to continue to serve with the battalion.

The regimental returns for the battalion are missing from July 1814 until the start of 1816 and so there is little evidence of what became of the other ranks held prisoner by the French. They appear on the pay lists until July 1814 but then are not there on subsequent ones. Very few are noted as re-joining and most were probably discharged on release.

In November diplomats gathered at the Congress of Vienna to settle the peace and decide Europe's new boundaries whilst Napoleon got used to his exile on the island of Elba. In December the Treaty of Ghent ended the American War, although the fighting would continue for a few more weeks until the news crossed the Atlantic. After not only financing their own armed forces but also subsidising their coalition partners, the British government faced debts of around £850,000,000. As soon as the guns fell silent they had begun to cancel contracts with suppliers and plan reductions to the armed forces. In 1815 approximately 350,000 men were discharged from the Army and Royal Navy, or roughly one in six of the men of fighting age in the country.[7] Foreign corps were a natural early target as discharging them would not add to the men seeking work in Britain and Ireland. The Chasseurs Brittanique were disbanded in October, with others units following rapidly.

The records of the 5th Battalion show numerous marches of small parties of men around the Cork area but offer no real insight into the battalion's activity during this period. Recruits were coming from the Foreign Depot but the inflow was being roughly matched by the outflow of continued discharges. Several boys were enlisted, who were quite probably the sons of men already in the battalion. There is no record as to how the men adjusted from the constant hardship and intermittent intense danger of war to the slower pace of peacetime soldiering. The adjustment for some may have been harder than for others. Colour Sergeant Frederick Auberl shot himself on 7 February 1815.[8] He had joined the battalion at the end of 1810 and served through the rest of the campaigns in Portugal, Spain and France, but there could have been many reasons for his decision to end his life and it may not have been related to his service.

3 Discharge Papers, John Hamel, TNA, WO 97/731/17.
4 December 1814 Pay List, TNA, WO 12/7075.
5 Return of Service, John Wolff, TNA, WO 25/778/149.
6 Return of Service, Robert Mitchell, TNA, WO 25/768/70.
7 J. Uglow, *In These Times* (London: Faber & Faber, 2014), p.631.
8 March 1815 Pay List, TNA, WO 12/7075.

Most of those who were discharged from the battalion had been in its ranks for a long time. Sergeant Philip Becker was discharged in June 1814. From Fürth, near Nuremburg, he had enlisted in British service in 1795 aged 22 and served for 24 years and 14 days, over seven of those in the West Indies. He was wounded seven times in the Peninsula, the first time at Roliça. Unsurprisingly he was unfit for further service.[9] Paymaster's Clerk Francis Schilling had joined Rohan's Hussars in 1794, moved to the York Hussars in 1796, and came to the 5th Battalion in 1803. He left in March 1815 for a commission as ensign in the 2nd West India Regiment.[10] Corporal John Angebrand, court martialed in 1806 for desertion and sentenced to 600 lashes, was discharged in April 1816. He was from Würzburg and had served 13 years and 258 days since joining the Lowenstein Jägers. He had been with the battalion throughout the Peninsular campaign, had been promoted from bugler, and been wounded. He was 36 years old and suffering from rheumatism.[11] Private Francis Gross was discharged from the 2/60th in 1818 due to 'mental imbecility' which was apparently caused by a head wound during time with the 5th Battalion in Portugal. Gross claimed he had enlisted in March 1809. The only Francis Gross that served with the 5th Battalion was a bugler who actually enlisted in 1801 but was sent back from Portugal in March 1809 as a 'suspected man' and transferred to the 2nd Battalion.[12]

With such an oversupply of officers following the war and the subsequent reductions of the Army, many Peninsular veterans suffered from very slow promotion over the subsequent years. However, some, such as James Stopford, could still progress quickly if they had the funds. Having purchased a majority in February 1814, Stopford paid for a lieutenant colonelcy in November 1815, jumping ahead of many more senior offices such as Galiffe and Fitzgerald who were both still only brevet lieutenant colonels. Captain McMahon returned to the battalion after a long leave of absence and was promoted to major in August 1815.[13] Long-serving former adjutant, Lieutenant Frederick de Gilse, chose to transfer to the Royal Wagon Train and to go on half-pay due to ill-health in March 1815. He settled in Römersberg, Hesse, married and started a family.[14]

Some of those riflemen who were discharged could claim a pension from the Royal Hospital Chelsea. The amounts were not large and had to be applied for rather than being given as right. The sums granted varied according rank and any disability. The hospital records show a total of 188 men stated that they had served in the 5th Battalion when they claimed their pension, and there were many more who put 60th Regiment without specifying a battalion. The longest serving was John Able who claimed his pension in 1811 after 26 years of service in the 15th Hanoverian Regiment, Lowenstein's, the 5th Battalion of the 60th, and the 97th Foot. Thomas Petry served for 23 years and claimed his pension in 1814. He had been with the battalion since formation on Barbados. Frederic Jacob and Phillip Wagner both had served 20 years when they claimed their pension in 1815, and both had been with the companies formed on the Isle of Wight in 1798. In total seven of the men

9 Discharge Papers, Philip Becker, TNA, WO 97/724/142.

10 Periods of Service 5/60th, June 1806, TNA, WO 25/1008; March 1815 Pay List, WO 12/7075.

11 Discharge papers, John Angebrand, TNA, WO 97/724/50.

12 Discharge Papers, Francis Gross, TNA, WO 97/730/80.

13 Army List 1814, TNA, WO 65/64, p.280; Army List 1815, WO 65/65, p.294.

14 Return of Service, Frederick de Gilse, TNA, WO 25/756/76.

claiming pensions had served 20 years or more, 34 between 15 and 20 years, and a further 21 men between 10 and 15 years.[15] Captain Augustine Evans became a Captain of Invalids at Chelsea from 1836 until his death in 1858 aged 69.[16]

John Galiffe was finally able to go on leave once Fitzgerald had arrived and taken command of the battalion. Unfortunately the first ship he embarked on began to take on water and had to be beached and the second was detained after it was found to be carrying contraband. He was forced to rearrange his leave and travel via England and across the shorter Channel crossings rather than via Bordeaux. In London he applied for, and got, a longer leave from the Duke of York. He also attended a medical board to receive £300 compensation for the wounds he suffered at Salamanca.[17]

At the end of February 1815 Napoleon slipped away from Elba. The news soon reached London. On 10 March Galiffe was writing to his brother that he was still planning to travel to Geneva and that he expected that Napoleon would not head for France but Italy, adding: 'See how he again attempts to sit in his blood-stained throne and if he succeeds we will have a new war to wage because with this man there can be no hope of peace.'[18] However, it would not be war that affected Galiffe's travel plans, but love, or at least marriage. Writing to his brother in January 1816 he explained:

> During my stay at Cork before our expedition to Portugal I received the attentions of a family to which I was very attached (the mother the sister of one of my comrades) on my return from France I was once again received as a child of the household and the elder of the girls, who had always shown me a most lively attachment although too young for it to have been of any consequence had grown up, become more attractive and proved to be very well brought up; our relationship recommenced and at my departure for Geneva she appeared so feeble and so cast down by our separation that I promised to marry her on my return from Switzerland. That consoled her only a little and my embarkation only augmented the illness. On my arrival in England I learnt that she was so ill that she had been advised to take a change of air and she arrived at Clifton; they despaired of saving her and she wrote to me to come and see her for the last time. As I had business to finish in Bristol I took advantage of this reason to visit her. I was struck by the ravages that the illness had wrought upon her, her situation appeared to me to be hopeless and I wished to give her proof of my affection by joining myself to her. I remained with her for three weeks and went back to London hardly believing that she would be still alive for any length of time. This was in January. I was to embark in May and was able in the interval to see her several times: her health was always the same and she returned to Ireland without having improved. She was on her arrival at Cork at the extremity [Illegible] for several weeks and certainly I had not the least idea that she would be drawn out of her illness. I awaited the arrival of every post to learn that she had

15 Royal Chelsea Hospital Admission Books, TNA, WO 23/135, Royal Chelsea Hospital pension records, WO 22/170; Periods of Service 5/60th, June 1806, WO 25/1008.

16 The Royal Hospital Chelsea, Secretary's Office to W.S. Coutts 6 April 1916, HRO, 170A12W/D/1183.

17 John Galiffe to James Galiffe 1 February 1815, BG, ms fr 2751c pl23 f007-8.

18 John Galiffe to James Galiffe 10 March 1815, BG, ms fr 2751c pl23 f009 (translated).

died and I had no thought of speaking of my marriage before being sure that I had, in truth, a wife. When I arrived in England I learned that she was a little better that she was [Illegible] in such a manner that when I believed I was once again free I had become the father of a little girl who had [almost] cost the life of her mother. She is seven months [Illegible] and mother and daughter are in such a state that when I arrived that one would believe it impossible that they could have escaped it. This nevertheless is what had happened and for some time she has been getting better and better, the little one has a wet-nurse...

He then went on to complain about his finances:

> ...she certainly had no money of her own and in consequence instead of finding myself in credit with the Paymaster I found myself on arriving here very much in debt by the expenses of doctors, wet-nurse &c and my account with the Paymaster had risen to £145 or thereabouts. I could not in consequence touch the money that that I had not paid to him and I counted upon my money prize money to help me as my salary is £298 from which it is necessary to deduct the expenses of the band and my mess bills and the rent of a house; you see therefore that it was necessary for me to live for six months under the strictest economy in order to recover my finances. I do not yet know how much this prize money will bring me & I doubt that the first payment will be above £200, on the contrary I believe that it will be much less.

He went on to admit:

> I believe, my good friend, that in marrying as I have done that I have hardly calculated the inconvenience and that now it is too late for me to repent of it, it is necessary that I make the best of it that I can, but I [Illegible] on me to divulge my marriage, I have no wish to speak of it and even less that people speak to me of it; I will correct myself that with time but at the moment it costs me much and a great deal more than I can say to you. All that I can add is that she loves me a great deal, that she is very interesting, well made, of a reasonably pretty appearance and all good.[19]

Galiffe married Catherine Mathis on 31 March 1815.[20] Their daughter Catherine-Anna Galiffe was born on 12th July 1815, suggesting perhaps another reason for his reticence in talking about his marriage.[21] Galiffe did still travel to Geneva, undertaking several errands for his friend and patron, the Duke of Kent, and was there during the 100 days of Napoleon's return. Galiffe was offered command of a Swiss regiment but declined.[22]

Napoleon, of course, did not head for Italy but returned to France. The 5th Battalion was still far too depleted to take any part in the campaign that culminated at the battle of

19 John Galiffe to James Galiffe, 7 January 1816, BG, ms fr 2751c pl23 f018-9 (translated).
20 *Oxford University & City Herald,* 8 April 1815.
21 Services of Lt. Col. Galiffe, HRO, 170A12W/D/0066/12, pp.9.
22 Kent to Galiffe, 7 February 1815, NAM, 1982-12-24.

Waterloo on 18 June. Captain the Honourable Esmé Stuart Erskine was on Wellington's staff as a deputy assistant adjutant general. On 17 June, during the retreat from Quatre Bras, he was severely wounded and captured by the French. He was taken to Napoleon and questioned by him, although the Emperor already seemed to have good information on the strength of the allied forces. He was then taken to a French surgeon who amputated his arm. He received a brevet majority as a reward for his services and he then transferred to the 2nd Ceylon Regiment, rising to lieutenant colonel before his death in 1817.[23]

By 1 July 1815 news of the allied victory at Waterloo had reached Cork. Captain Aubrey Carteret Bowers, one of the many new officers of the battalion, wrote to Major Green, the town major at Cork:

> I am requested by Major Schoedde commanding, to solicit permission for the Battn. to be allowed to fire a feu de joye on the Mall this evening at eight o'clock in honour of the recent victory, obtained by his Grace the Duke of Wellington, over the French army commanded by Bonaparte.[24]

The fact that the letter has been preserved does suggest that permission was granted for the battalion to fire the feu de joie, a continuous rolling salute with each soldier firing in turn.

In October Galiffe was in Paris, on his way back from Geneva, and was detained there much longer than he wished on battalion business. He had previously written about having to collect an award, probably his Companion of the Bath. He found Paris very expensive, the political atmosphere febrile, and he noted that Wellington was hated by both the French and the Prussians. He was told that the battalion would soon move to Flanders to recruit, where he was hopeful it could rebuild its numbers.[25]

With Napoleon finally defeated the reductions and disbandments in the British Army could continue, and the recession caused by the end of the wars deepened. In April 1815, whilst Europe prepared for the brief resumption of the war, the volcano of Tambora in Indonesia erupted and spewed huge clouds of ash into the atmosphere. Europe was plunged into a volcanic winter that caused crops to fail, widespread famine, and deep social unrest. 1816 became known as the year without summer.[26]

For the 5th Battalion the year began with a change of location. On 8 and 9 February the *Mariner*, *Bedford*, and *Ilfracomber* transports left Cork and arrived at Cowes, on the Isle of Wight on the 17th and 18th. The battalion was based at the barracks at Sandown, with detachments at Ryde, Brading, White Cliffs, and Grange Chine. The February return shows a strength of 33 sergeants, sixteen buglers, and 236 rank and file, still far below even its reduced establishment of 45 sergeants, 22 buglers, and 610 rank and file. However, 103 men, along with Major Schoedde, Lieutenant Muller, and a dozen NCOs, were at the Foreign Depot. In March 101 of those men would join the battalion and further 258 followed from the depot in April. Most of these were former soldiers of the KGL, which had been ordered

23 C. Dalton, *The Waterloo Roll Call* (London: Eyre & Spottiswoode, 1904), pp.31-2.

24 Bowers to Green 1 July 1815, HRO, 170A12W/D/0441.

25 John Galiffe to James Galiffe 2 October 1815, BG, ms fr 2751c pl23 f016/17.

26 Uglow, *Times*, pp.633-4.

to disband at the end of 1815,[27] and whilst most returned to Germany some opted to remain in British service. Many of the men had served at Waterloo. Others who came from the depot had been serving in the Royal Marines and when discharged, due to the laying up of much of the fleet, had opted to serve in the Army.[28] The battalion was also still recruiting in Heligoland but many of the recruits were being rejected, possibly because they had already endured long service in other armies.[29] The February return also notes that Lieutenant Hugh Dickson deserted on 21 January 1816 rather than face a court martial that had been ordered in Cork. He did not return to the battalion and no record of the charges, or any subsequent trial, can be found.[30]

In March Catherine Galiffe was still ill and her husband still desperately waiting for the prize money to arrive. He was also missing Geneva: 'I am in despair not being able to settle down in Geneva as I wished so hard, but I feel the impossibility to it for a long time certainly not before being a Major General, this will not happen as soon as I was entitled to hope;' and then saying 'it is a thorn in my heart that I can not tear out; nevertheless less I do not believe that I am a bad husband or that I let my wife feel that I am not happy'.[31] In April he wrote of his wife: 'she feels better but still is very weak; however the little girl is in excellent shape she is so joyful and never crying she is really an exceptional child particularly for me as I do not like their shrieks'.[32]

It was inevitable that the round of reductions and disbandments would eventually begin to effect the 60th, which was still the largest regiment in the British army, and whose ready supply of recruits from prisoners of war had long since gone back to their homes. The first battalion earmarked for disbanded was the 8th. Captain Charles Leslie was in command of the men returning to the depot at Harwich for discharge in December 1815:

> We did not reach Portsmouth until the 4th December. I there received a discretionary order to march the men for Harwich. I chose the route through Godalming and Guildford by London. The frost was so intense that water left in a tumbler over night was a lump of ice in the morning. The men having no arms or stores, I put their knapsacks into a waggon, so that they marched with perfect ease, and made long marches every day. On the 12th December we marched through London, to the surprise of the natives seeing so many men in green rifle uniform, not one of whom could speak a word of English. When the order was made known at Gibraltar, many of the men entitled to go wished to remain, and others who were anxious to return home paid them a handsome sum to allow them to take their places.[33]

The men left at Gibraltar would be transferred to the 5th Battalion, which was soon under orders to sail there. The men at the depot, and their families, would be given passage back to

27 Beamish, *King's German Legion*, Vol.II, p.388.
28 1816 Pay Lists, TNA, WO 12/7076.
29 Pay List Foreign Corps Depot Detachments, 5/60th 1816, TNA, WO 12/11623.
30 January to April 1816 Returns, TNA, WO 17/308.
31 John Galiffe to James Galiffe 17 March 1816, BG, ms fr 2751c pl23 f024 (translated).
32 John Galiffe to James Galiffe 11 April 1816, BG, ms fr 2751c pl23 f027 (translated).
33 Leslie, *Military Journal*, p.271.

the continent. In the summer of 1817 the Foreign Depot itself was closed and the remaining staff sent to the Army Depot at Chatham.[34]

The 5th Battalion embarked on the *Minerva* and *Isabella* transports in May 1816. There were 15 officers and staff, 491 riflemen, 37 women, and 26 children on board the two ships. They disembarked at Gibraltar at the end of the month. The *Duncombe* carried another 12 officers and Quartermaster Recknoy.[35] When the battalion arrived 24 sergeants, nine buglers, 20 corporals, and 280 privates from the 8th Battalion joined the 5th. Four officers and two staff were also attached, with the others going on half-pay.[36] The 8th Battalion had been at Cadiz, originally as the Battalion of Foreign Recruits, and then Gibraltar for the entirety of its short existence. In the opening of the confidential report in the final inspection of the battalion, Lieutenant General George Don wrote that the unit had been: 'commanded by Major Fitzgerald since its formation in Cadiz, in the year 1810, and the present state of the corps does great honor and credit to that officer'.[37] The 5th Battalion was now well over its establishment with a total strength of 1,094 men. Many sergeants and corporals had to resign to help solve the surplus of NCOs, and 62 recruits were rejected as being unfit. Desertion also increased.[38]

The 5th Battalion was inspected twice by Don in 1817. The May inspection still shows the battalion well over its establishment. There were three English riflemen; a sergeant, a corporal and a private. Most of the rank and file fell into the 25 to 30 age range, with most sergeants being between 30 and 35 years old. Only one rifleman was over 50, and 33 were over 40. One sergeant had served for between 21 and 25 years, and four sergeants and two privates had served for between 18 and 21 years; which implies it was still possible that some men had been with the battalion since formation. The NCOs and men were praised but 264 rifles were found to be unserviceable. The rest of the uniform and equipment was in good order. The list of courts martial showed a range of offences from petty theft and drunkenness to striking NCOs and using abusive language to an officer. Sentences varied from 100 lashes to periods of confinement, some of them solitary, of up to two months.[39]

Don's main criticism was for the atmosphere in the mess and amongst the officers. He claimed that the placing of Brevet Major Purdon under arrest by Brevet Lieutenant Colonel Fitzgerald had caused a great deal of disunity. A court martial had been convened on 19 July 1817 and Purdon was tried on seven charges of unofficer-like conduct, four of which related to his alleged reaction to being informed that he had to vacate his quarters whilst awaiting passage to England and the subsequent disagreements over the matter with Fitzgerald, with the other three charges relating to minor infringements of regimental rules that seem to have been added for good measure. Fitzgerald was the prosecutor and at one point Purdon asked the court: 'Do you conceive the Prosecutor as influenced by Zeal for the Service, or by Private Pique against Major Purdon?'[40] The transcript of the trial ran to over 250 pages.

34 Foreign Depot Out-Letters, TNA, WO 7/95.
35 Butler, *Annals*, Vol.II, pp.298-9.
36 June 1816 Return, TNA, WO 17/308
37 Inspection of 8/60th,TNA, WO 27/137.
38 July 1816 Return, TNA WO 17/308; June & September 1816 Pay Lists, WO 12/7076.
39 Inspection of 5/60th, TNA, WO 27/137.
40 Trial of Brevet Major Purdon, TNA, WO 71/246.

Most of the prosecution witnesses seemed to have been reluctant or forgetful and Purdon was found not guilty of five of the charges. He was found to be guilty of two charges but the court found extenuating circumstances and sentenced him to just be admonished by Lieutenant General Don. After the trial Purdon was ordered to England and later joined the 3/60th.[41] The atmosphere in the officers' mess must have been strained in the wake of the trial, although Captain Colin Campbell, who became Field Marshal Lord Clyde, remembered his time with the battalion as the happiest of his life.[42]

The November inspection showed a lower strength and that the defective rifles had been replaced. Don was, however, still not happy about the way Fitzgerald had handled the problem with Purdon. After praising Fitzgerald's attention to the battalions' field exercises he continued: 'Yet I feel it my duty to state that I cannot approve of the mode in which this officer as in general conducted the command of the battalion since the last Inspection'. Don stated that errors in Fitzgerald's judgement had exacerbated the disunity amongst the officers and implied that he had lost the respect of some of them. He also said that he had recommended a senior officer be assigned to take over command from Fitzgerald.[43] The reduction in strength noted in the inspections was due to continued discharges and men being invalided: for example 78 men were invalided in August alone.[44] Many of these invalids would have simply been worn out by their long years of service, others would have had their health broken by the periodic fevers that beset the garrison. The number of Peninsular and Waterloo veterans in the ranks would still have been high but was constantly shrinking. In March 1817 Sergeant Frederick Geiling shot himself, the final recorded suicide in the battalion. Geiling had served with the battalion from Mondego Bay all the way to France.[45]

In February John Galiffe told his brother:

> In general terms the climate is not at all bad. During nine months of the year the temperature is excellent and it is only during July, August and September that the heat is excessive and that the fever ravages us severely. The last year was very healthy but it is feared that this one will not be as good because we will have a very hot summer.[46]

He also said that he expected that the battalion would be sent to Upper Canada later in the year and complained that everything was expensive in Gibraltar, but that having a thrifty wife helped. Catherine was six months pregnant and in delicate health again.

In June 1817 the 7/60th was disbanded in Nova Scotia with 400 men going to the 3rd and 4th Battalions. In October the 6/60th was ordered back from Jamaica to Britain to be disbanded, which it was in February 1818 with some of the men being sent to the 3rd Battalion.[47] In May the Prussian ambassador wrote to the 5th Battalion requesting that

41 August 1817 Return, TNA, WO 17/320.
42 May, June & December 1816 Returns, TNA, WO 17/308; Butler, *Annals*, Vol.II, p.299.
43 Inspection of 5/60th, TNA, WO 27/142.
44 August 1817 Return, TNA, WO 17/320.
45 March 1817 Pay List, TNA, WO 12/7076.
46 John Galiffe to James Galiffe 24 February, BG, ms fr 2751c pl23 f032/33 (translated).
47 Butler, *Annals*, Vol.II, pp.293-4.

200 Prussians serving in the ranks be sent home, but there is no sign that the request was granted.[48]

At the end of October 1817 six officers were returning to, or joining, the battalion from Cowes when they were shipwrecked off the Spanish coast. One of them wrote a letter back to his family that got widely published in the press:

> The following is an extract of a letter from an officer on board the Ellice transport, lately wrecked on the coast of Spain, dated Ferol Nov. 6 1817
>
> With gratitude for my deliverance from shipwreck, I hasten to inform you of my safety, yet I hardly know how to relate the disastrous story of my misfortune. On the 24th ultimo we sailed from Cowes, having taken on board a detachment of troops. – The wind was very favourable, and on the 26th we took our departure for the Land's End. After leaving the Channel, the wind proved directly contrary, and the ship was driven into the Bay of Biscay, not by storms or tempests, but by what is termed in a sea phrase, lee-way, and we were laying-to for a more favourable wind till the day before our unfortunate wreck. The wind now sprung up in our favour, and we were going at a rate of seven or eight knots; making, as I understood, for Cape Finisterre. On the 1st instant, the day became extremely thick and foggy. At about half past three, an alarm was given of breakers a-head, and the dreadful coast of Spain was presented to us in all its horrors. We were immediately driven by the swell under a tremendous rock (perhaps 150 feet perpendicular), and so near to it, that in less than ten minutes the ship struck. All endeavours to get her off proved vain; and a scene of distressing confusion, of course, followed – every one rushing in a moment to the quarter-deck. There were 145 souls on board, many of them women, whose screams added to the terror that pervaded the crew. The vessel was now rolling from side to side on its keel, which, together with the flapping of the sails and rigging, threw us against each other from larboard to starboard at the mercy of every swell that came under her, which drove her still further on to the reef of rocks. At length the boats were got out with much difficulty, when another danger became probable, for as in such cases every body conceives they have a right to save their lives, an over loaded boat boat may happen to go down. No regularity could, however, be expected in so awful a moment; and although we had arranged that the females should be first put into the boat, the officers were obliged to fight with the soldiers in order to prevent their jumping in, in which scuffle, having let go my hold by a heave of the sea, I narrowly escaped being precipitated into it. After the boats had made the first landing they came back to our succour; but the swell was then running so strong, that they dared not approach the wreck. To behold them so near us, and at the same time unable to save us, was the most melancholy moment of our suffering: I thought of you at home, as if I was at the last moment of my life, and nobody to communicate to you my fate; for my friend Lieut. Wallace, in endeavouring to reach a boat, was struggling with the waves below the quarter of the vessel where I kept my hold.

48 60th Foot, 5th Battalion, TNA, WO 2/23.

He was drowned, though I threw him a rope, but he was not able to catch it. The scene was too distressing to dwell upon! Night at length, came on; I was standing on the quarter-deck, supported by the rudder-case, which went to pieces; on which the master, who had climbed the projection of the rock, called to me to follow him: I did so, by making across one of the masts which had gone over-board. Happily I reached the rock, and gained a standing place about 30 feet up, whence I was extricated by a rope from above about eleven o'clock that night; and by the same means all who had been able to resist the breakers during the night, were hauled up early the next morning. Some Spanish peasants, or rather fishermen, took me to a miserable hut; but which, being on terra firma, was quite comfortable to me, after the perils I had undergone. When I recovered strength enough to speak a few Spanish words of thanks, the whole village came about me, to know the particulars; I happened to be the only one who could make himself intelligible to them. On this account, I was the next day considered the fittest person to be dispatched to tell the dismal tidings to the Consul at this port, at whose residence I arrived after two days hard travelled, over a wild mountainous country, upon a little horse without a saddle, frequently in mud up to his belly or else over craggy paths, where it was dangerous for him to tread, and safest for me to dismount.

My escape, indeed, has been most providential. The scratches I received on my shoulders, knees, hands and feet, were nothing to the wounds which some of the poor women (wives of solders) experienced, who were literally dragged up the rock, in almost a lifeless state, with infants thus clinging to their breasts for protection! I am, it is true, now destitute of everything; but I still look back with horror to the moment when I would have given every thing to have been safely landed any where. To say, however, that I am not a little down-hearted, would seem too stoical to be natural. The sea had done its destructive work so effectually, that nothing of the vessel remained together when I was extricated from my resting-place; all was spars and cordage. In describing this melancholy event, I cannot omit to mention the very handsome reception and treatment which I experienced from the Vice-Consul, Don Fransisco Fernandez, at whose house I now am.[49]

Around 30 people died in the wreck, including Lieutenant Wallace of the 5th Battalion, and 10 men of the 75th Foot, who were en route to Corfu from Edinburgh.[50] The author of the above letter may have been Lieutenant Ridd who later made a complaint against the consul at Coruña, and claimed for lost baggage along with four other officers.[51]

On 15 December 1817 Sir Harry Calvert, the Adjutant General, wrote to Lieutenant General Robinson, who was still the colonel commandant of the 5th Battalion:

I have the Commander in Chief's Commands to notify, for your information, that arrangements have been made to relieve the 5th Battn. of the 60th Regiment at Gibraltar. His Royal Highness the Prince Regent having been pleased to direct

49 *London Courier & Evening Gazette*, 6 December 1817.

50 *Morning Post*, 26 December 1817 & *Public Ledger & Daily Advertiser*, 3 December 1817.

51 60th Foot, 5th Battalion, TNA, WO 2/23.

> that that Battalion should be brought to this country for the purpose of being disbanded.[52]

It was a brief and perfunctory note to inform the general of the loss of his role and the end of twenty years of service for the 5th Battalion.

On 25 April 1818 the 5th Battalion began to embark on to the transports *Borodino*, *Ocean*, and *Kennersley Castle* for the voyage back to the Isle of Wight. One man deserted while the ships were still in the bay. On 18 June they landed at Cowes and marched to Albany Barracks. The final regimental return is dated 24 July. Present were 15 officers, four staff, 35 sergeants, 20 buglers, 38 corporals, and 427 privates. Of the officers only Brevet Lieutenant Colonel Fitzgerald, Brevet Major Schoedde, Captains Kelly and Franchini, Lieutenants Muller, Evans, O'Hehir, and Stewart, Paymaster Biggs, Quartemaster Recknoy, and Assistant Surgeon Stevenson had served with the battalion in the Peninsula. Recknoy and O'Hehir soon left the regiment.[53] Another five of the peninsular veteran officers were on leave, and a party of 25 invalids were at Chatham. John Galiffe had narrowly missed serving with the battalion from formation to disbandment as he had been posted to the 1/60th in June.[54]

Whilst most of the riflemen were retained some were discharged, and many of the officers were placed on half pay after September.[55] On 6 August the *Sarah* and *Ann* transports took 400 men, under the command of Fitzgerald and Schoedde, to Quebec to be incorporated into the 2/60th. The *Sarah* arrived in Montreal on 9 September, the *Ann* twenty days later after dropping off settlers at Halifax.[56]

The 5th Battalion existed for 20 years and seven months. In total approximately 3,500 men served in the battalion during that time. The records are incomplete but more than 900 riflemen died, most from disease, with around 140 being killed in action, first in Ireland in 1798 and then in the Peninsular campaign.[57] In 1854, when Britain was once more in dire need of men for the Army, John Forster Fitzgerald, by then an MP, rose in the House of Commons to speak in support of a bill to allow the enlistment of foreigners again. In his speech he referenced his time with the 5th Battalion and his words form a suitable epitaph for the battalion:

> I myself have served during the last war for eleven years in a German rifle regiment, and for the chief part of that time in command of it, the late 5th battalion of the 60th Regiment. At the siege of Badajos, who formed the covering party to the troops employed in the trenches at the storming of Badajos? — Who went in front of the forlorn hope to escalade the castle?— the 5th battalion 60th Regiment. Can any one read the orders of the late Duke of Wellington, relating to the services of this battalion in the Peninsula, and not agree with me that most valuable assistance can be obtained by the enlistment of foreigners?[58]

52 Calvert to Robinson 15 December 1817, TNA, WO 3/67, p.306.

53 Army List 1818, TNA, WO 65/69.

54 June 1818 Return, TNA, WO 17/320; Butler, *Annals*, Vol.II, p.300.

55 60th Foot, 5th Battalion, TNA, WO 2/23.

56 *Morning Chronicle*, 8 August 1818 & *Montreal Gazette*, various dates September 1818.

57 Estimates based on regimental returns, casualty returns and pay lists.

58 Hansard, 19 December 1854, Enlistment of Foreigners Bill, 2nd reading https://api.parliament.uk/historic-hansard/commons/1854/dec/19/enlistment-of-foreigners-bill Accessed 7 September 2018.

27

Legacy

On 16 July 1818 the Prince Regent issued the following order: 'That in consequence of the 5th or Rifle Battalion being about to be disbanded, the 2nd Battalion of that Regiment be clothed, equipped, and trained as a Rifle Corps'.[1] The men of the 5th Battalion who sailed to Quebec were to remain riflemen. At the start of 1819 the 2nd Battalion had a strength of 634 men, the majority being former members of the 5th Battalion. A total of 15 officers and three staff had also transferred to the 2/60th from the 5th Battalion. The 4/60th was disbanded in 1819 and the 1/60th in 1820. At that point the 2nd Battalion was renumbered as the 1st, and the 3rd became the 2nd. The commander of the old 1st Battalion, Lieutenant Colonel Alexander Andrews, who had served with the 5th Battalion for the first half of the Peninsular campaign, took command of the new 1st Battalion.[2]

At Montreal in 1821 the 1st Battalion received a draft of 200 German recruits, but in 1823 at Ontario 150 Irish recruits joined, and further recruits came mainly from the British Ilses.[3] In June 1824 this change in the makeup of the battalion was formalised and it was ordered back to the United Kingdom to recruit and replace its foreign personnel. The 60th lost the title of The Royal American Regiment, the 2nd Battalion was converted to a rifle battalion, from light infantry, and the regiment became the Duke of York's Own Rifle Corps.

The remaining foreign riflemen in the 1st Battalion were offered the choice to transfer to the 2nd Battalion, or to take discharge in Canada and become settlers. Many of those who took the option to remain in Canada had served with the 5th Battalion. Private Niclas Volmer had joined in 1810 and served for 14 years. Amongst the causes listed for his discharge were an old gunshot wound to the right arm, varicose veins, and persistent ulcers.[4] Colour Sergeant George Koester was discharged in August at York, Upper Canada. He had gone from a 21-year-old French conscript, to prisoner of war, to rifleman in the space of a few short months in 1806. He then served throughout the Peninsular War and was wounded at Oporto.[5] Koester had married a Spanish girl and they settled in Montreal to run a tavern. Colour Sergeant George Lange, from Leipzig, who also joined in 1806, had

1 Butler, *Annals*, Vol.II, p.297.
2 Butler, *Annals*, Vol.II, pp.301-3.
3 Butler, Annals, Vol.II, pp.309-10.
4 Discharge papers, Niclas Volmer, TNA, WO 97/743/135.
5 Discharge papers, George Koester, TNA, WO 97/734/56.

been wounded in the head during the storming of the castle at Burgos in 1812. He had been discharged two years earlier in 1822.[6] Joseph Wolff, who had been sergeant major since 1812, was commissioned in 1821 as an ensign in the battalion and appointed adjutant.[7] Originally from Poland he had been in British service since 1801.[8] Along with the rest of the foreign officers he too was forced to leave the battalion.

The foreign officers were given the choice of going on half pay or selling their commissions. Unsurprisingly, they were not happy in being forced out. One officer protested to Horse Guards that his wife would no longer be entitled to a pension if he took the half-pay offer. The government relented and allowed the officers to be treated as if the battalion had been reduced, which would protect the rights of their wives and family. However, they were given a limited time to take the offer.[9] Captain Ignace Franchini put off the decision by transferring to the 2nd Battalion until he was forced out of that battalion too and took half-pay. His health was marred by the many wounds he had suffered, and the fevers he had caught whilst in the West Indies. He settled in France and died alone, in Paris, in 1832. Amongst his effects were numerous letters from his former comrades.[10]

James Schoedde, although of German descent, had been born into the regiment his father was serving with and was British. He was promoted to major in 1825 and went with the 1/60th when it was sent back to Portugal in 1826 to protect the country from Spanish aggression. In 1829 he was promoted to lieutenant colonel in the 48th Foot and then in 1833 took command of the 55th, later becoming a brevet colonel. He was made an aide de camp to Queen Victoria in 1841 and later that year saw action at the Battle of Chapu, in China, during the First Opium War, and again the following year when he commanded a brigade with the army rank of major general during the Battle of Chinkiang. He was subsequently knighted and then retired on half-pay in 1845 after 45 years of service. He died in 1861 having risen by seniority to the rank of lieutenant general.[11]

John Galiffe continued to serve in the 2/60th. In 1819 he was returning to his unit when he was shipwrecked off Sable Island in the Atlantic. His wife and three children were with him, the youngest less than six months old. Some of the women and children, including Galiffe's family, boarded the boats first and got to shore. The remaining passengers were rescued later.[12] Galiffe served as commandant in Halifax, Bermuda, and Berbice in British Guiana, before being promoted to full lieutenant colonel in 1825 and given command of the 2/60th. He retired six months later and sold his commission. He was never to get the rank of major general that he coveted but he did retire to his beloved Geneva. He died in 1847, just before the issuing of the General Service Medal. Queen Victoria ordered the medal to be issued anyway, and sent to his widow.[13]

Galiffe's obituary in the *Naval and Military Gazette* noted that:

6 Discharge papers, George Lange, TNA, WO 97/734/31.
7 Willoughby Wallace, *Regimental Chronicle,* p.196.
8 Periods of Service 5/60th, June 1806, TNA, WO 25/1008.
9 Correspondence relating to conversion of 2/60th to a British corps, TNA, WO 43/227.
10 Hall, *Biographical Dictionary*, pp.212-3 & *Gazette des Tribunaux*, 15 August 1850.
11 Rigaud, *Celer et Audax*, pp.273-7.
12 *Public Ledger & Daily Advertiser*, 10 July 1819
13 Services of Lt. Col. Galiffe, HRO, 170A12W/D/0066/12 p.8; Butler, *Annals*, Vol.II, p.319.

> His brilliant conduct in command of the Light Troops of the 3rd Picton's (the fighting) Brigade [sic] frequently called forth the applause of that Distinguished General, and the admiration of his brethren-in-arms, and obtained for him the *Order of the Bath*, and a *Cross* for the Battles of *Vittoria, Nivelle, Orthis* and *Toulouse*.
>
> The effects of long service in a Tropical Climate acting on a constitution impaired by seven severe wounds received in the Service, obliged him to retire by the sale of his Commission, after the War, and having invested the proceeds of his long and meritorious services in the Mexican Funds, he lost all and has left a wife and four children very scantily provided for, and who have a strong claim on the bountiful consideration of the country.[14]

John Forster Fitzgerald exchanged into the 20th Foot in 1824 and went to India. He became a major general in 1830 and lieutenant general in 1841. He served as an MP from 1852 to 1857, and was knighted in 1862. He retired to France where he died in his nineties with the rank of field marshal and was, by order of the French Minister of War, buried with the full military honours of a Marshal of France.[15]

Baron Francis de Rottenburg, who was so instrumental in shaping the 5th Battalion into the efficient rifle corps that it proved to be in the Peninsula, was promoted to major general and given various commands during the War of 1812. He returned to Britain in 1815 and was knighted in 1816, but then languished on half-pay, getting automatically promoted by seniority to lieutenant general in 1819. He died at Portsmouth in 1832.[16]

The story of the development of light infantry and rifle-armed troops in the British Army during the Revolutionary and Napoleonic Wars is dominated by Sir John Moore and the 95th Rifles, whilst both de Rottenburg and the 5th Battalion are often overlooked. De Rottenburg's *Regulations for the Exercise of Riflemen and Light Infantry and Instructions for their Conduct in the Field* remained the standard text on the subject throughout the period. His work built upon those that went before him, like von Ewald, and codified established practice in European armies, but his development of those ideas and their implementation with the first truly specialist light infantry and rifle battalion marked a turning point in the history of the British Army. Written in German sometime before 1798 and then translated and published in that summer, the manual was first put into practice in the companies of the battalion that formed on the Isle of Wight. It specified not only tactical formations, but also marksmanship training, and the importance of *esprit de corps* and individual initiative. Those light infantry proponents and innovators that came later built upon de Rottenburg's work in their turn. General François Jarry's *Instructions Concerning the Duties of Light Infantry in the Field*, published three years later, concentrated on aspects of *le petit guerre*, and did not address the basics of formations and training that de Rottenburg did.

When Colonels William Stewart and Coote Manningnham came to form the Experimental Corps of Riflemen, the unit that later became the 95th, they were, as David Gates wrote in *The British Light Infantry Arm*: 'Clearly influenced by the military thinking of Jarry and Rottenburg, the two officers sought to create a force of light infantry that was based on the

14 Quoted in *The Services of Lt Col Galiffe*, HRO, 170A12W/D/0066/12.

15 Butler, *Annals*, Vol.II, pp.310 & 327.

16 Rigaud, *Celer et Audax*, p.268.

models found within the writings of those theorists'.[17] Stewart and Manningham evolved the ideas contained in the existing texts and also added innovations of their own. Stewart was also a proponent of companies of riflemen being deployed with light infantry, as the 5th Battalion came to be used, rather than as entire battalions of rifles, as was often the case with the 95th in the Peninsula.[18]

When the 52nd Foot was selected to be converted to a specialist light infantry unit at Shorncliffe in 1803, Major General Sir John Moore selected Lieutenant Colonel Kenneth Mackenzie as its commander. It was Mackenzie, an experienced light infantry officer, who developed his own light infantry tactical system that diverged from de Rottenburg's manual. Moore was initially resistant but subsequently authorised its adoption by the 43rd and 95th also at Shorncliffe. The adoption of Mackenzie's system was limited to only those battalions, which would go on to form the core of the Light Division in the Peninsula.[19] The rest of the light infantry continued to use de Rottenburg's system. However, elements of de Rottenburg's manual were still used at Shorncliffe. In a letter to Mackenzie dated August 1805 Moore made it clear that the method of marksmanship training was to be based on de Rottenburg's work:

> I have spoken to Stewart about some Light practice for the 52nd. One Company is to practice firing ball at a target daily, and the Company to be instructed as Lt. Troops. At this I shall be present. What is wanted at first is a method; hitherto our practice has been too desultory, I mean therefore to make de Rottenburg the ground work, noting in the margin whatever changes we make from him, but on reading over his book attentively I perceive much good in it; it only requires to be properly applied; at this I shall endeavour, and you shall know our progress.[20]

The light infantry battalions at Shorncliffe were trained to fight both in the line and as skirmishers and it is perhaps for this development that Sir John Moore deserves the most credit. Soldiers that were adaptable, independent, but also capable of the conforming to the strictures of fighting in close order required better leadership and training from their officers, new methods of discipline and motivation, and marked a shift away from treating men as mere automatons. The genesis of Moore's thinking in this area can be seen in his instructions for the militia light infantry he commanded in Ireland in 1798 and 1799. The instructions mixed both line and a light infantry drill.[21] Under his command at the same time were two companies of the 5th Battalion of the 60th. The light infantry sections are very similar to de Rottenburg's manual published the same year, although de Rottenburg himself did not arrive in Ireland until July of 1798 and it is not clear exactly when Moore's instructions were written.

17 Gates, *Light Infantry*, p.106.
18 Gates, *Light Infantry*, p.107.
19 Gates, *Light Infantry*, pp.112 , 118-9, & 121.
20 Moore to MacKenzie, 30 August 1805 quoted in J.F.C. Fuller, 'Two Private Letters from Major-General Sir John Moore, K.B'., *Journal of the Society of Army Historical Research,* Vol.IX, p.165.
21 J.F.C. Fuller, 'Sir John Moore's Light Infantry Instructions of 1798-1799', *Journal of the Society of Army Historical Research,* Vol.XXX pp.68-75.

When the army field and drill regulations were updated in 1824 the new manual, *Field Exercises and Evolutions of the Army*, contained 40 pages on light infantry, and they were clearly closely based on de Rottenburg's work.[22] After leaving the 5th Battalion, de Rottenburg trained a brigade containing the 68th, 71st, and 85th as light infantry at Brabourne Lees, and led them and two companies of the 95th in the Walcheren Campaign. He also commanded a light infantry training camp in Ireland prior to the expedition leaving for the Peninsula in 1808.[23]

The 5th Battalion made up the bulk of the Light Brigade in Wellesley's 1808 campaign in Portugal, and their effectiveness led to their being dispersed amongst the brigades, and then divisions, when Wellesley resumed command in 1809. The fact that they operated alongside the light companies of so many line battalions for so long would have inevitably seen some of the riflemen's skills and tactics influencing their red-coated comrades. Similarly, the many officers that passed through the battalion would have taken that experience to the other battalions of the 60th, and to other regiments. For example, Lieutenant Colonel William Williams went to the 13th Foot and concentrated on improving the battalion's light infantry skills during the War of 1812. He commanded the 13th for seven years, leaving shortly before it officially converted to the light infantry role in 1822.[24]

The 5th Battalion clearly also had major influence on the development of the 60th as a whole. The change to being designated as light infantry and wearing green for the entire regiment came after the 5th Battalion had been proven such a success and had won so many laurels in the Peninsula. Much credit is also due to the Duke of York. As commander-in-chief he proposed and supported the many innovations in light infantry and rifle corps that occurred during the period. As colonel-in-chief of the 60th he was responsible for the raising of the 5th Battalion, the introduction of rifle companies, and its eventual evolution into the Duke of York's Own Rifle Corps. The Duke died in 1827 and following the accession of William IV in 1830 the 60th received a new title: The King's Royal Rifle Corps.

In 1881 the 60th, in common with the rest of the army, lost its number and became simply The King's Royal Rifle Corps. Having served in the many small wars during Victoria's reign the KRRC went on to fight with distinction in the First and Second World Wars. The regiment was merged with its old rivals, the Rifle Brigade, and the Oxfordshire and Buckinghamshire Light Infantry in 1966 to form the Royal Green Jackets. The Royal Green Jackets was then merged with the Devonshire and Dorset Light Infantry, Royal Gloucestershire, Berkshire and Wiltshire Light Infantry, and the Light Infantry to form The Rifles in 2007.

The two previous historians of the 5th Battalion, Lieutenant Colonel Lewis Butler and Major General Gibbes Rigaud, both served in the KRRC during the Victorian period and were both very clear about the importance of the 5th Battalion in the regiment's history and traditions. Butler mainlined that rather than the 2nd Battalion absorbing the 5th when the latter was disbanded it was more the other way around. He quotes a letter from Horse Guards dated 1825, after the 2nd became the 1st Battalion, that refers to the '1st, late 5th Battalion'.[25] He goes on to say:

22 H. Torrens, *Field Exercise & Evolutions of the Army* (London, William Clowes, 1824), pp.217-59.

23 Rigaud, *Celer et Audax*, p.267.

24 H. Popham, *The Somerset Light Infantry* (London: Hamilton, 1968), p.148.

25 Butler, *Annals*, Vol.II, p.302.

> The customs of the 5th Battalion were adopted by the 1st; amongst others that of carrying rifles with 'butts up' when marching at ease; a practice which although at the present common in the whole regiment was for many years confined to the 1st Battalion. For many years the members of the 1st Battalion were in the habit of designating it as the 5th.[26]

Rigaud, in 1879, wrote:

> For sixty years the 60th has been employed in all parts of the world, and, like Henry Lawrence, 'has tried to do its duty'. In the attempt it has been stimulated by its old traditions, and the necessity of maintaining the high reputation which it inherited from its predecessors, and it is partly with a view of recording the past that these pages have been compiled; but partly also in the hope of animating a future generation to emulate their deeds…[27]

One hundred and forty years later The Rifles still use the motto conferred on the 60th (Royal American) Regiment by Major General James Wolfe in 1759: 'Swift and Bold'.

26 Butler, *Annals*, Vol.II, p.303.
27 Rigaud, *Celer et Audax*, p.266.

Bibliography

Archival Sources

Bibliothèque de Genève (BG)
CH BGE Ms. fr. 1329-1335, Ms. fr. 2751-2860bis, Papiers de la famille Galiffe.

Hampshire Record Office (HRO)
49038 Wickham Family Papers.
A12170 The Royal Green Jackets Regimental Archive.

Hartley Library, University of Southampton
MS61 Wellington Papers.

Library & Archives Canada (LAC)
British Military and Naval records. C Series.
Francis de Rottenburg fonds MG 24 F 78, R4156-0-4-E, address to de Rottenburg.

National Army Museum (NAM)
1978-11-153, The bound manuscript order book of Sir John Moore.
1982-12-24, Collection of letters and papers relating to the service of Col. Jean Pierre Galiffe.

Sheffield City Archives
LD 710-886, Underbank Hall muniments, Certificates, and account of military service, of Major M. de Wend.

The Albany Institute of History & Art (AI)
Prevost Family Papers CR 549.

The British Library Additional Manuscripts (BL)
Add. MS. 32468 John Westcott.

The National Archives (TNA)
ADM 103, Registers of Prisoners of War.
ADM 98/233, Letters Relating to Prisoners of War, Norman Cross.
CO 318/20-1, West Indies Correspondence, Original – Secretary of State: Military despatches.

HO 100/73-7, Ireland: Home Office correspondence on military affairs.
WO 1/1100, War Department Miscellaneous In-letters 1797.
WO 1/255-9, British Army in Spain, Portugal and France (1808-1820). Wellington.
WO 1/413, General Merck's Mission (1810-1811).
WO 1/648, War Department In-Letters, Other Government Departments, Commander-in-Chief.
WO 1/87-9, War Department In-Letters, Windward and Leeward Islands. Commander-in-Chief, West Indies.
WO 1/900, War Department In-Letters, Foreign Troops on British Pay.
WO 1/903, War Department In-Letters, Conditions of service, numbers, and miscellaneous papers.
WO 12/12012, Musters and pay lists regarding HM Foreign Recruiting Depot.
WO 12/7065-76 & WO 12/11623, Muster Books and Pay Lists 5th Battalion 60th Foot.
WO 121/118, Certificates of Service.
WO 17, Monthly Returns to the Adjutant General, Returns for 60th Foot.
WO 17/1160, Office of the Commander in Chief: Monthly Returns to the Adjutant General, General Returns.
WO 17/2464-75, Monthly Returns to the Adjutant General, Spain & Portugal.
WO 17/2489-94, Monthly Returns to the Adjutant General, Windward & Leeward Islands.
WO 2/2-23, Indexes to Out-letters, General Administrative. Indexed under Regts.
WO 2/54, Indexes to Out-letters, Foreign Troops.
WO 22-3, Royal Hospital Chelsea Records.
WO 24/1112, Capitulation Book: record of establishment of foreign regiments in the British Army.
WO 24/608, War Office: papers concerning establishments.
WO 25, Returns of Officers' Services.
WO 25/1008, Statements of the Periods of service of all NCOs and Men, also of those who were liable to serve abroad on 24 June 1806.
WO 25/1923, Casualty Returns 60th Foot 4th & 5th Battalions.
WO 25/3213, Estimate for Foreign Corps.
WO 27, Office of the Commander-in-Chief and War Office: Adjutant General and Army Council: Inspection Returns.
WO 3, Office of the Commander-in-Chief: Out-letters.
WO 31, Office of the Commander-in-Chief: Memoranda and Papers.
WO 380/1, Regimental Records.
WO 4/170, Secretary-at-War, Out-letters.
WO 40/10-1, Secretary-at-War, In-letters and Reports.
WO 42/49, British Officers & their Families.
WO 43/227, The 2nd battalion of 60th Foot to be converted from a foreign to a British corps.
WO 6, Secretary of State for War and Secretary of State for War and the Colonies, Out-letters.
WO 65, Printed Annual Army Lists.
WO 7/31-2, Clothing Board Out Letters.
WO 7/77-95, Depot of Foreign Troops Out Letters.
WO 71, Courts Martial proceedings.
WO 97, Royal Hospital Chelsea: Soldiers Service Documents.

Warwickshire County Record Office (WCRO)

CR114A/332 Surinam papers. Secret orders and intelligence relating to the taking of Surinam under the command of Lord Hugh Seymour.

Published Sources

Abell, F., *Prisoners of War in Britain 1756 to 1815* (Oxford: Oxford University Press, 1914).

Anderson, J., *A Few Facts and Observations on the Yellow Fever of the West Indies* (Edinburgh: Mudie, 1798).

Arielli, N. & Collins, B. (ed.), *Transnational Soldiers – Foreign Military Enlistment in the Modern Era* (Basingstoke: Palgrave Macmillan, 2013).

Arvers, P., *Historique du 82éme Regiment D'Infanterie de Ligne* (Paris : Typographie Lahure, 1876).

Bailey, D.W., *British Military Flintlock Rifles 1740-1840* (Lincoln: Andrew Mowbary Inc., 2002).

Balagny, D., *Campaign de l'empereur Napoléon en Espagne (1808-1809)*, Vol.III (Paris: Berger-Levraut, 1903).

Bamford, A., *Sickness, Suffering and the Sword* (Norman: University of Oklahoma Press, 2013).

Beamish, N.L., *History of the King's German Legion*, 2 Vols. (London: Thomas & William Boone, 1837).

Beaufoy, H., *Scioppetaria* (London: Egerton, 1808).

Bell, G., *Rough Notes by an Old Soldier* (London: Day & Son, 1867).

Berkeley A.D. (ed.), *New Lights on the Peninsular War* (Almada: The British Historical Society of Portugal, 1991).

Blakeney, R., *A Boy in the Peninsular War* (London: John Murray, 1839).

Brown, W., *The Autobiography, or Narrative of a Soldier – The Peninsular War Memoirs of William Brown of the 45th Foot* (Solihull: Helion & Company, 2017).

Buckley, R.N., *The Napoleonic War Journal of Captain Thomas Henry Browne* (London: Army Records Society, 1987).

Bunbury, T., *Reminiscences of a Veteran* (Uckfield; The Naval & Military Press Ltd. 2009).

Burnham, R. & McGuigan, R., *The British Army against Napoleon, Facts, Lists, and Trivia 1805-1815* (Barnsley: Frontline Books, 2010).

Burnham, R. & McGuigan, R., *Wellington's Brigade Commanders, Peninsula & Waterloo* (Barnsley: Pen & Sword, 2017).

Butler, L., *The Annals of the King's Royal Rifle Corps*, Vol. I (London: Smith, Elder & Co., 1913).

Butler, L., *The Annals of the King's Royal Rifle Corps*, Vol. II (London: John Murray, 1923).

Buttery, D., *Wellington Against Junot* (Barnsley: Pen & Sword, 2011).

Buttery, D., *Wellington Against Massena* (Barnsley: Pen & Sword, 2007).

Byrne, M., *Memoirs of Miles Byrne*, Vol. I (Dublin: Maunsel & Co, 1907).

Calvert, H., *General Regulations and Orders for the Army* (London: W. Clowes, 1811).

Camden, T., *The History of the War in Spain & Portugal* (London: Stratford, 1813).

Campbell, J., *A British Army As It Was, – Is, – and Ought to Be* (London: T & W Boone, 1840).
Chambers, G.L., *Bussaco* (London: Swan Sonnenschein, 1910).
Chartrand, R., *Émigré and Foreign Troops in British Service (1)* (Oxford: Osprey, 1999).
Chartrand, R., *Vimeiro 1808* (Oxford: Osprey, 2001).
Chartrand, R., *Bussaco 1810* (Oxford: Osprey, 2001).
Colville, J., *The Portrait of a General* (Salisbury: Michael Russell, 1980).
Combermere, M., *Memoirs & Correspondence of Field-Marshal Viscount Combermere*, Vol. I (London: Hurst & Blackett, 1866).
Congreve, W., *A Treatise on the General Principles, Powers and Facility of Application of the Congreve Rocket System* (London: Longman, Rees, Orme, Brown, & Green, 1827).
Contamine, H., *La Vie Aventureuse d'un Émigré Lorrain: Guillaume de Lasalle de Louisenthal* (Metz: Académie Nationale de Metz, 1930).
Cooper, J.S., *Rough Notes of Seven Campaigns* (London: John Russel Smith, 1869).
Coupland, R., *The War Speeches of William Pitt the Younger* (Oxford: Clarendon Press, 1916).
Cumberland, G., *Views in Spain & Portugal, taken during the Campaigns of His Grace the Duke of Wellington* (London: William Nicol, 1823).
Cusick, R., *Wellington's Rifle* (Barnsley: Pen & Sword, 2013).
Dalton, C., *The Waterloo Roll Call* (London: Eyre & Spottiswoode, 1904).
Davy, W.G., *The Substance of a Correspondence on a Matter Connected with the Distribution of Half Pay to the Reduced Officers of His Majesty's Army* (London: privately published, 1828).
de Rottenburg, F., *Regulations for the Exercise of Riflemen and Light Infantry and Instructions for their Conduct in the Field* (London: Egerton, 1803).
Debrett, J., *The Peerage of the United Kingdom of Great Britain & Ireland* (London: Woodfall, 1820).
Dehnel, H., *Erinnerungen Deutscher Officiere in Britischen Diensten aus den Kriegsjahren 1805 bis 1816* (Hannover: Rümpler, 1864).
Demet, P., *We Are Accustomed to do Our Duty* (Warwick: Helion & Company, 2018).
Dempsey, G., *Albuera 1811* (Barnsley: Frontline Books, 2008).
Divall, C., *Inside the Regiment* (Barnsley: Pen & Sword, 2011).
Divall, C., *Wellington's Worst Scrape* (Barnsley: Pen & Sword, 2012).
Donaldson, J., *Recollections of the Eventful Life of a Soldier* (Philadelphia: G. B. Zieber & Co. 1845).
Dumas, J.B., *Neuf Mois de Campagnes à la suite du Maréchal Soult* (Paris : Henri Charles-La Vauzelle, 1907).
Durey, M., (ed.), *Andrew Bryson's Ordeal* (Cork: Cork University Press, 1998).
Elliot-Wright, P., *Rifleman* (London: Publishing News, 2000).
Esdaile, C., *The Peninsular War* (London: Allen Lane, 2002).
Fernyhough, T., *Military Memoirs of Four Brothers* (London: William Sams, 1829).
Field, A.W., *Talavera* (Barnsley: Pen & Sword, 2006).
Fitzclarence, G., *An Account of the British Campaign in 1809* (London: Colburn & Bentley, 1831).
Fletcher, I., *Badajoz 1812* (Oxford: Osprey, 1999).
Fletcher, I., *In Hell Before Daylight* (Tunbridge Wells: The Baton Press, 1984).

Fletcher, I., *Vittoria 1813* (Oxford: Osprey, 1998).
Fortescue, J.W., *A History of the British Army*, Vols. IV-X (London: Macmillan & Co, 1906).
Fosten, G., & Gibbs, G., *The British Infantry Shako 1800-1897* (Chelsea: The Military Historical Society, 2008).
Fraser, E., *The Soldiers Whom Wellington Led* (London: Methuen, 1913).
Fuller, J. F. C., *Sir John Moore's System of Training* (London: Hutchinson & Co, 1925).
Fullom, S.W., *The Life of General Sir Howard Douglas* (London: John Murray, 1863).
Gahan, D., *The People's Rising* (Dublin: Gill & Macmillan, 1995).
Gates, D., *The British Light Infantry Arm c. 1790-1815* (London: Batsford, 1987).
Gleig, G., *The Hussar*, Vol. I (London: Henry Colburn, 1837).
Gleig, G., *The Subaltern* (London: Blackwood, Undated).
Glover, R., *Peninsular Preparation: The Reform of the British Army* (Cambridge: Cambridge University Press, 1963).
Gordon, J., *History of the Rebellion in Ireland in the Year 1798* (London: Dewick, 1803).
Grant, J., *Romance of War* (London: Routledge, 1866).
Grattan, W., *Adventures with the Connaught Rangers* (London: Edward Arnold, 1902).
Graves, D.E., *Fix Bayonets!* (Stroud: Spellmount, 2007).
Green, J., *The Vicissitudes of a Soldier's Life* (Louth: Jackson, 1827).
Gronow, R.H., *Celebrities of London and Paris* (London: Smith, Elder & Co., 1865).
Grouvel, R., *Les Corps de Troupe L'Émigration Française (1789-1815)* (Paris : Les Édtions de la Sabretache, 1857).
Gurwood, J., *The Dispatches of Field Marshall the Duke of Wellington*, Vols. I – XIII (London: John Murray, 1835).
Gurwood, J., *The General Orders of Field Marshal The Duke of Wellington K. G. in Spain, Portugal & France* (London: Egerton, 1837).
Guthrie, G.J., *Commentaries on the Surgery of War in Portugal, Spain, France & the Netherlands* (Philadelphia: Lippincott & Co., 1862).
Hall, J.A., *The Biographical Dictionary of British Officers Killed & Wounded, 1808-1814* (London: Greenhill, 1998).
Hanger, G., *A Letter to Lord Castlereagh* (London: Ridgway, 1808).
Harris, B., *The Recollections of Rifleman Harris* (London: Century, 1985).
Haythornthwaite, P. J., *Weapons & Equipment of the Napoleonic Wars* (Poole: Blandford, 1979).
Haythornthwaite, P. J., *The Armies of Wellington* (London: Arms & Armour, 1994).
Haythornthwaite, , P. J., *British Rifleman 1797-1815* (Oxford: Osprey, 2002).
Haythornthwaite, , P. J., *British Light Infantry & Rifle Tactics of the Napoleonic Wars* (Oxford: Osprey, 2016).
Haythornthwaite, , P. J., *Corunna 1809* (Oxford: Osprey, 2001).
Head, G., *Memoirs of an Assistant Commissary-General* (London: Murray, 1837).
Henry, W., *Events of a Military Life* (London: Pickering, 1843).
Hope, J., *The Military Memoirs of an Infantry Officer 1809-1816* (Edinburgh: Anderson & Bryce, 1833).
Howard, M., *Death before Glory* (Barnsley: Pen & Sword, 2015).
Howard, M., *Wellington's Doctors* (Staplehurst: Spellmount, 2002).

Wyld, J., *Maps & Plans, Showing the Principal Movements, Battles & Sieges in which the British Army was Engaged During the War from 1808 to 1814 in the Spanish Peninsula and the South of France* (London: Wyld, 1841).
James, C., *A Collection of the Charges, Opinions and Sentences of General Courts Martial*, (London: Egerton, 1820).
Jarry, F., *Instructions Concerning the Duties of Light Infantry in the Field* (London: Dulau & Co. 1803).
Jones, E. H. S., *An Invasion that Failed* (Oxford: Blackwell, 1950).
Jones, J.T., *Journals of Sieges Carried on by the Army under the Duke of Wellington*, Vols. I-III (London: Weale, 1844).
Keate, T., *Observations on the 5th Report of the Commissioners of Military Enquiry* (London: Hatchard, 1808).
Kincaid, J., *Random Shots from a Rifleman* (London: Boone, 1847).
Knight, R., *Britain Against Napoleon: The Organisation of Victory 1793-1815* (London: Penguin, 2013).
L'Estrange, G. B., *Recollections of Sir George B. L'Estrange* (London: Sampson Low, Marston & Searle, 1874).
Landmann, G., *Recollections of my Military Life*, Vol. II (London: Hurst & Blackett, 1854).
Le Marchant, D., *Memoirs of the Late Major General Le Marchant* (London: Bentley, 1841).
Leach, J., *Rough Sketches of the Life of an Old Soldier* (London: Longman, Rees, Orme, Brown, & Green, 1831).
Leslie, C., *Military Journal of Colonel Leslie, K. H, of Balquhain* (Aberdeen: Aberdeen University Press, 1887).
Lipscome, N., *The Peninsular War Atlas* (Oxford: Osprey, 2014).
MacCarthy, J., *Recollections of the Storming of the Castle of Badajos* (Staplehurst: Spellmount, 2001).
MacKinnon, H., *A Journal of the Campaign in Portugal & Spain* (Bath: Charles Duffield, 1812).
Maempel, J.C., *Adventures of a Young Rifleman in the French and English Armies* (London: Colburn, 1826).
Maurice, J. F. (ed.), *The Diary of Sir John Moore*, Vol. I-II (London: Arnold, 1904).
Maxwell, W. H., *History of the Irish Rebellion in 1798* (London: Cruikshank, 1871).
Maxwell, W. H., *Peninsular Sketches*, Vol. I-II (London: Colburn, 1845).
McLaren, A., *A Minute Description of the Battles of Gorey, Arklow, and Vinegar-Hill*, (Place and publisher unknown, 1798) .
Milne, S., & Terry, A., *The Annals of the King's Royal Rifle Corps, Appendix Dealing with Uniform, Armament & Equipment* (London: Murray, 1913).
Muir, R., *Salamanca 1812* (New Haven: Yale, 2001).
Napier, W. C. E., *Passages in the Early Military Life of General Sir George T. Napier, K. C. B.* (London: John Murray, 1884).
Neale, A., *Letters from Portugal and Spain* (London: Richard Phillips, 1809).
Nichols, A., *Wellington's Mongrel Regiment* (Staplehurst: Spellmount, 2005).
Oman, C., *A History of the Peninsular War*, 7 Vols. (Oxford: Clarendon Press, 1902).
Oman, C., *Wellington's Army 1809-1814* (London: Arnold, 1913).

Pakenham, T., *The Year of Liberty: The Great Irish Rebellion of 1798* (New York: Times Books, 1998).
Paterson, J., *The Adventures of Captain John Patterson* (London: T & W Boone, 1837).
Philippart, J. (ed.), *The Royal Military Calendar*, 3rd. Edition, Vols. I -V (London: Egerton, 1820).
Plon, H., & Dumaine, J., *Correspondance de Napoléon 1er*, Vol. III (Paris: Imprimeur de l'Empereur, 1863).
Popham, H., *The Somerset Light Infantry* (London: Hamilton, 1968).
Rait, R., *The Life and Campaigns of Hugh, First Viscount Gough, Field-Marshal* (Westminster: Constable & Co., 1903).
Rigaud, G., *Celer et Audax* (Oxford: Hall & Stacy, 1879).
Robertson, I. C., *Wellington Invades France* (London: Greenhill, 2003).
Ross-Lewin, H., *With the Thirty-Second* (Dublin: Hodges, Figgis & Co., 1904).
Scharnorst, G., *Handbuch für Officiere, in den anwendbaren Theilen der Krieges-Wissenschaften: Von der Tactik: worin von den Waffen, der Stellung und den Bewegungen der Cavalerie und Infanterie, von dem Verhalten derselben in Actionen* (Hannover: Helwing, 1790).
Schaumann, A., *On the Road with Wellington* (London: Greenhill, 1999).
Schneid, F.C., *European Armies of the French Revolution 1789-1802* (Norman: University of Oklahoma Press, 2015).
Sherer, M., *Recollections of the Peninsula* (London: Longman, Rees, Orme, Brown, & Green, 1827).
Sidney, E., *The Life of Lord Hill* (London: John Murray, 1845).
Simmons, G., *A British Rifle Man* (London: A & C Black, 1899).
Sparrow, E., *Secret Service, British Agents in France 1792-1815* (Woodbridge: The Boydell Press, 1999).
Surtees, W., *Twenty-Five Years in the Rifle Brigade* (London: Greenhill, 1996).
Teeling, C.H., *Sequel to Personal Narrative of the Irish Rebellion of 1798* (Belfast: John Hodgson, 1830).
Torrens, H., *Field Exercise & Evolutions of the Army* (London: Cowes, 1824).
Tuckey, F. H., *The County & City Remembrancer* (Cork: Osborne, Savage & Son, 1837).
Uglow, J., *In These Times* (London: Faber & Faber, 2014).
Vane, C. W., *Narrative of the Peninsular War, 1808 to 1813* (London: Henry Colburn, 1828).
Vere, C. B., *Marches, Movements & Operations of the 4th Division* (Ipswich: Deck, 1841).
Verner, W., *The First British Rifle Corps* (London: Allen & Co, 1890).
Verner, W., *The History & Campaigns of the Rifle Brigade*, Vol. I (London: John Bale, 1912).
von Sack, A., *A Narrative of a Voyage to Surinam* (London: G & W Nicol, 1810).
Walker, T.J., *The Depot for Prisoners of War at Norman Cross Huntingdonshire, 1796 to 1816* (London: Constable & Co. 1913).
Weale, G., *An Interesting Memoir of George Weale* (Leamington: Weale, 1838).
Weddeburne, W., *Observations on the Exercise of Riflemen and on the Movements of Light Troops in General* (Norwich: Stevenson & Matchett, 1804).
Wellington, Duke of, *General Orders Spain & Portugal*, Vols. I-IV (London: Egerton, 1811-13).

Wellington, Duke of, (2nd), *Supplementary Despatches, Correspondence and Memoranda of Field Marshal Arthur Duke of Wellington, K. G.*, Vols. VI – XIV (London: Murray, 1860).

Wheeler, H. F. B. & Broadley, A. M., *The War in Wexford* (London: Lane, 1910).

Willoughby Wallace, N., *A Regimental Chronicle & List of Officers of the 60th, or the King's Royal Rifle Corps* (London: Harrison, 1879).

Wishon, M., *German Forces and the British Army; Interactions and Perceptions 1742-1815* (Basingstoke: Palgrave Macmillan, 2013).

Anon., *Journal of a Soldier of the 71st* (Edinburgh: W. & C. Tait, 1819).

Anon., *The 7th Report of the Commissioners of Military Enquiry* (London: The House of Commons, 1809).

Anon., *A History of the Campaigns of the British Forces in Spain & Portugal*, Vols. I-V (London: Goddard, 1812).

Anon., *The Report from the Secret Committee of the House of Commons* (Dublin: King, 1798).

Anon., *Vicissitudes in the Life of a Scottish Soldier* (London: Colburn, 1827).

Anon., *Essays on Theory & Practice of the Art of War* (London: Phillips, 1809).

Journal Articles

Arnold, J., 'A Reappraisal of Column versus Line in the Napoleonic Wars', *Journal of the Society of Army Historical Research*, Vol. LX, pp.196-208.

Atkinson, C. T., 'Foreign Regiments in the British Army 1793-1802 Part 1', *Journal of the Society of Army Historical Research*, Vol. XXI, pp.175-181.

Atkinson, C. T., 'Foreign Regiments in the British Army 1793-1802 Part 2', *Journal of the Society of Army Historical Research*, Vol. XXII, pp.2-14.

Atkinson, C. T. 'Foreign Regiments in the British Army 1793-1802 Part 4', *Journal of the Society of Army Historical Research*, Vol. XXII, pp.107-115.

Atkinson, C. T., 'Foreign Regiments in the British Army 1793-1802 Part 6', *Journal of the Society of Army Historical Research*, Vol. XXII, pp.234-250.

Bent, M., 'A Royal American', *Journal of the Society of Army Historical Research*, Vol. I, pp.15-20 & pp.98-104.

Carman, W.Y., 'Infantry Clothing Regulations, 1802', *Journal of the Society of Army Historical Research*, Vol. XIX, pp.200-235.

Durey, M., 'White Slaves: Irish Rebel Prisoners and the British Army in the West Indies 1799-1804', *Journal of the Society of Army Historical Research*, Vol. LXXX, pp.296-312.

Fuller, J. F. C., 'Two Private Letters from Major-General Sir John Moore, K. B.', *Journal of the Society of Army Historical Research*, Vol. IX, pp.162-167.

Fuller, J. F. C., 'Sir John Moore's Light Infantry Instructions of 1798-1799', *Journal of the Society of Army Historical Research*, Vol. XXX, pp.68-75.

Garris, 'Take the Hill before Dark', *United Services Journal*, 1839 pt. 3, pp.166-171.

Gray, D.S., 'Prisoners, Wanderers, and Deserters: Recruiting for the King's German Legion, 1803-1815', *Journal of the Society of Army Historical Research*, Vol. LII, pp.148-158.

Hamilton Smith, C., 'Experiments on the Comparative Effect of Rifle and Musketry Fire on Different Colours', *Aide-Mémoire to the Military Sciences*, 1853, pp.257-259.

Hodge, W.B. 'On the Mortality arising from Military Operations', *Journal of the Statistical Society of London*, Vol. XIX, pp.219-271.
Muir, R. & Reiter, J., 'A New Letter on the Battle of Salamanca', *Journal of the Society of Army Historical Research*, Vol. XCVI, pp.21-32.
Cathaoir, E. Ó., 'German Mercenaries in Ireland 1798-1807', *The Irish Sword*, Vol. XXII no. 90, pp.406-426.
Peaty, J., 'Architect of Victory: The Reforms of the Duke of York', *Journal of the Society of Army Historical Research*, Vol. LXXXIV, pp.339-348.
Vanguard, 'Distribution of Light Cavalry and Infantry in the Field', *United Services Journal*, 1831 Part II, pp.205-209.
Ward, S. G. P., 'Some Fresh Light on the Corunna Campaign', *Journal of the Society of Army Historical Research*, Vol. XXVIII, pp.107-126.

Index

From Reason to Revolution – Warfare 1721-1815

http://www.helion.co.uk/series/from-reason-to-revolution-1721-1815.php

The 'From Reason to Revolution' series covers the period of military history 1721–1815, an era in which fortress-based strategy and linear battles gave way to the nation-in-arms and the beginnings of total war.

This era saw the evolution and growth of light troops of all arms, and of increasingly flexible command systems to cope with the growing armies fielded by nations able to mobilise far greater proportions of their manpower than ever before. Many of these developments were fired by the great political upheavals of the era, with revolutions in America and France bringing about social change which in turn fed back into the military sphere as whole nations readied themselves for war. Only in the closing years of the period, as the reactionary powers began to regain the upper hand, did a military synthesis of the best of the old and the new become possible.

The series will examine the military and naval history of the period in a greater degree of detail than has hitherto been attempted, and has a very wide brief, with the intention of covering all aspects from the battles, campaigns, logistics, and tactics, to the personalities, armies, uniforms, and equipment.

Submissions

The publishers would be pleased to receive submissions for this series. Please contact series editor Andrew Bamford via email (andrewbamford18@gmail.com), or in writing to Helion & Company Limited, Unit 8 Amherst Business Centre, Budbrooke Road, Warwick, CV34 5WE

Titles

No 1 *Lobositz to Leuthen. Horace St Paul and the Campaigns of the Austrian Army in the Seven Years War 1756-57* Translated with additional materials by Neil Cogswell (ISBN 978-1-911096-67-2)

No 2 *Glories to Useless Heroism. The Seven Years War in North America from the French journals of Comte Maurés de Malartic, 1755-1760* William Raffle (ISBN 978-1-1911512-19-6) (paperback)

No 3 *Reminiscences 1808-1815 Under Wellington. The Peninsular and Waterloo Memoirs of William Hay* William Hay, with notes and commentary by Andrew Bamford (ISBN 978-1-1911512-32-5)

No 4 *Far Distant Ships. The Royal Navy and the Blockade of Brest 1793-1815* Quintin Barry (ISBN 978-1-1911512-14-1)

No 5 *Godoy's Army. Spanish Regiments and Uniforms from the Estado Militar of 1800* Charles Esdaile and Alan Perry (ISBN 978-1-911512-65-3) (paperback)

No 6 *On Gladsmuir Shall the Battle Be! The Battle of Prestonpans 1745* Arran Johnston (ISBN 978-1-911512-83-7)

No 7 *The French Army of the Orient 1798-1801. Napoleon's Beloved 'Egyptians'* Yves Martin (ISBN 978-1-911512-71-4)*

No 8 *The Autobiography, or Narrative of a Soldier. The Peninsular War Memoirs of William Brown of the 45th Foot* William Brown, with notes and commentary by Steve Brown (ISBN 978-1-911512-94-3) (paperback)

No 9 *Recollections from the Ranks. Three Russian Soldiers' Autobiographies from the Napoleonic Wars* Translated and annotated by Darrin Boland (ISBN 978-1-912174-18-8) (paperback)

No 10 *By Fire and Bayonet. Grey's West Indies Campaign of 1794* Steve Brown (ISBN 978-1-911512-60-8)

No 11 *Olmütz to Torgau. Horace St Paul and the Campaigns of the Austrian Army in the Seven Years War 1758-60* Translated with additional materials by Neil Cogswell (ISBN 978-1-911512-72-1)

No 12 *Murat's Army. The Army of the Kingdom of Naples 1806-1815* Digby Smith (ISBN 978-1-912390-09-0) (paperback)

No 13 *The Veteran or 40 Years' Service in the British Army. The Scurrilous Recollections of Paymaster John Harley 47th Foot – 1798-1838* John Harley, with notes and commentary by Gareth Glover (ISBN 978-1-912390-25-0) (paperback)

No 14 *Narrative of the Eventful Life of Thomas Jackson. Militiaman and Coldstream Sergeant, 1803-15* Thomas Jackson, with notes and commentary by Eamonn O'Keeffe (ISBN 978-1-912390-12-0) (paperback)

No 15 *For Orange and the States! The Army of the Dutch Republic 1713-1772. Part I: Infantry* Marc Geerdinck-Schaftenaar (ISBN 978-1-911512-15-8)*

No 16 *'Men who are Determined to be Free': The American Assault on Stony Point 15 July 1779* David Bonk (ISBN 978-1-912174-84-3)*

No 17 *Next to Wellington. General Sir George Murray. The Story of a Scottish Soldier and Statesman, Wellington's Quartermaster General* John Harding-Edgar (ISBN 978-1-912390-13-7)

No 18 *Between Scylla and Charibdys: The Army of Friedrich August II of Saxony, 1733-1763. Part I: Staff and Cavalry* Marco Pagan (ISBN 978-1-912174-89-8)*

No 19 *The Secret Expedition: The Anglo-Russian Invasion of Holland 1799* Geert van Uythoven (ISBN 978-1-912390-20-5)

No 20 *'We Are Accustomed to do our Duty' German Auxiliaries with the British Army 1793-95* Paul Demet (ISBN 978-1-912174-96-6)

No 21 *With the Guards in Flanders. The Diary of Captain Roger Morris 1793-95* Peter Harington (ISBN 978-1-911628-15-6) (paperback)

No 22 *The British Army in Egypt 1801. An Underrated Army Comes of Age* Carole Divall (ISBN 978-1-911628-17-0)*

No 23 *Better is the Proud Plaid. The Clothing, Weapons, and Accoutrements of the Jacobites in 1745* Jenn Scott (ISBN ISBN 978-1-911628-16-3)*

No 24 *The Lilies and the Thistle. French Troops in the Jacobite '45* Andrew Bamford (ISBN 978-1-911628-17-0)*

No 25 *A Light Infantryman With Wellington* *Gareth Glover* (ed.) (ISBN 978-1-911628-10-1) (paperback)

No 26 *Swiss Regiments in the Service of France 1798-1815. Uniforms, Organisation, Campaigns* Stephen Ede-Borrett (ISBN 978-1-911628-12-5)*

No 27 *For Orange and the States! The Army of the Dutch Republic 1713-1772. Part II: Cavalry and Specialist Troops* Marc Geerdinck-Schaftenaar (ISBN 978-1-911628-13-2)*

No 28 *Fashioning Regulation, Regulating Fashion. Uniforms and Dress of the British Army 1800-1815 Volume I* Ben Townsend (ISBN 978-1-911628-09-5)

No 29 *Riflemen. The History of the 5th Battalion 60th (Royal American) Regiment, 1797-1818* Robert Griffith (ISBN 978-1-911628-46-0)

No 30 *The Key to Lisbon: The Third French Invasion of Portugal, 1810-11* (Kenton White)

No 31 *Command and Leadership: Proceedings of the 2018 Helion & Company 'From Reason to Revolution' Conference* (Andrew Bamford (ed.))

No 32 *Waterloo After the Glory: Hospital Sketches and Reports on the Wounded After the Battle* (Michael Crumplin and Gareth Glover)

No 33 *Fluxes, Fevers, and Fighting Men: War and Disease in Ancien Regime Europe 1648-1789* (Pádraig Lenihan)

No 34 *'They Were Good Soldiers': African-Americans Serving in the Continental Army, 1775-1783* (John U. Rees)

No 35 *A Redcoat in America: The Diaries of Lieutenant William Bamford, 1757-1765 and 1776* (John B. Hattendorf (ed.))

No 36 *Between Scylla and Charybdis: The Army of Friedrich August II of Saxony, 1733-1763: Part II: Infantry and Artillery* (Marco Pagan)

No 37 *Québec Under Siege: French Eye-Witness Accounts from the Campaign of 1759* (Charles A. Mayhood (ed.))

No 38 *King George's Hangman: Henry Hawley and the Battle of Falkirk 1746* (Jonathan D. Oates)

No 39 *Zweybrücken in Command: The Reichsarmee in the Campaign of 1758* (Neil Cogswell)

No 40 *So Bloody a Day: The 16th Light Dragoons in the Waterloo Campaign* (David J. Blackmore)

No 41 *Northern Tars in Southern Waters: The Russian Fleet in the Mediterranean 1806-1810* (Vladimir Bogdanovich Bronevskiy / Darrin Boland)

No 42 *Royal Navy Officers of the Seven Years War: A Biographical Dictionary of Commissioned Officers 1748-1763* (Cy Harrison)

No 43 *All at Sea: Naval Support for the British Army During the American Revolutionary War* (John Dillon)

No 44 *Glory is Fleeting: New Scholarship on the Napoleonic Wars* (Andrew Bamford (ed.))

No 45 *Fashioning Regulation, Regulating Fashion: Uniforms and Dress of the British Army 1800-1815 Vol. II* (Ben Townsend)

No 46 *Revenge in the Name of Honour: The Royal Navy's Quest for Vengeance in the Single Ship Actions of the War of 1812* (Nicholas James Kaizer)

No 47 *They Fought With Extraordinary Bravery: The III German (Saxon) Army Corps in the Southern Netherlands 1814* (Geert van Uythoven)

No 48 *The Danish Army of the Napoleonic Wars 1801-1814, Organisation, Uniforms & Equipment: Volume 1: High Command, Line and Light Infantry* (David Wilson)

No 49 *Neither Up Nor Down: The British Army and the Flanders Campaign 1793-1895* (Phillip Ball)

No 50 *Guerra Fantástica: The Portuguese Army and the Seven Years War* (António Barrento)

No 51 *From Across the Sea: North Americans in Nelson's Navy* (Sean M. Heuvel and John A. Rodgaard)

No 52 *Rebellious Scots to Crush: The Military Response to the Jacobite '45* (Andrew Bamford (ed.))

No 53 *The Army of George II 1727-1760: The Soldiers who Forged an Empire* (Peter Brown)

No 54 *Wellington at Bay: The Battle of Villamuriel, 25 October 1812* (Garry David Wills)

No 55 *Life in the Red Coat: The British Soldier 1721-1815* (Andrew Bamford (ed.))

No 56 *Wellington's Favourite Engineer. John Burgoyne: Operations, Engineering, and the Making of a Field Marshal* (Mark S. Thompson)

No 57 *Scharnhorst: The Formative Years, 1755-1801* (Charles Edward White)

No 58 *At the Point of the Bayonet: The Peninsular War Battles of Arroyomolinos and Almaraz 1811-1812* (Robert Griffith)

No 59 *Sieges of the '45: Siege Warfare during the Jacobite Rebellion of 1745-1746* (Jonathan D. Oates)

No 60 *Austrian Cavalry of the Revolutionary and Napoleonic Wars, 1792–1815* (Enrico Acerbi, András K. Molnár)

No 61 *The Danish Army of the Napoleonic Wars 1801-1814, Organisation, Uniforms & Equipment: Volume 2: Cavalry and Artillery* (David Wilson)

No 62 *Napoleon's Stolen Army: How the Royal Navy Rescued a Spanish Army in the Baltic* (John Marsden)

No 63 *Crisis at the Chesapeake: The Royal Navy and the Struggle for America 1775-1783* (Quintin Barry)

No 64 *Bullocks, Grain, and Good Madeira: The Maratha and Jat Campaigns 1803-1806 and the emergence of an Indian Army* (Joshua Provan)

No 65 *Sir James McGrigor: The Adventurous Life of Wellington's Chief Medical Officer* (Tom Scotland)

No 66 *Fashioning Regulation, Regulating Fashion: Uniforms and Dress of the British Army 1800-1815 Volume I* (Ben Townsend) (paperback edition)

No 67 *Fashioning Regulation, Regulating Fashion: Uniforms and Dress of the British Army 1800-1815 Volume II* (Ben Townsend) (paperback edition)

No 68 *The Secret Expedition: The Anglo-Russian Invasion of Holland 1799* (Geert van Uythoven) (paperback edition)

No 69 *The Sea is My Element: The Eventful Life of Admiral Sir Pulteney Malcolm 1768-1838* (Paul Martinovich)

No 70 *The Sword and the Spirit: Proceedings of the first 'War & Peace in the Age of Napoleon' Conference* (Zack White (ed.))

No 71 *Lobositz to Leuthen: Horace St Paul and the Campaigns of the Austrian Army in the Seven Years War 1756-57* (Neil Cogswell) (paperback edition)

No 72 *For God and King. A History of the Damas Legion 1793-1798: A Case Study of the Military Emigration during the French Revolution* (Hughes de Bazouges and Alistair Nichols)

No 73 *'Their Infantry and Guns Will Astonish You': The Army of Hindustan and European Mercenaries in Maratha service 1780-1803* (Andy Copestake)

No 74 *Like A Brazen Wall: The Battle of Minden, 1759, and its Place in the Seven Years War* (Ewan Carmichael)

No 75 *Wellington and the Lines of Torres Vedras: The Defence of Lisbon during the Peninsular War* (Mark Thompson)

No 76 *French Light Infantry 1784-1815: From the Chasseurs of Louis XVI to Napoleon's Grande Armée* (Terry Crowdy)

No 77 *Riflemen: The History of the 5th Battalion 60th (Royal American) Regiment, 1797-1818* (Robert Griffith) (paperback edition)